D1809430

SERIES CONTENTS

READI
TRIAL AD
AND THE
SO

A Four

o

Series Ed

ROBE

Ohio Sta
College

A GAR

VOLUME

1

JURIES

Formation and Behavior

Edited with introductions by

ROBERT M. KRIVOSHEY

GARLAND PUBLISHING, Inc.
New York & London
1994

Library of Congress Cataloging-in-Publication Data

Juries : formation and behavior / edited with an introduction by
Robert M. Krivoshey.
    p.   cm. — (Readings in trial advocacy and the social
sciences ; v. 1)
   ISBN 0–8153–1419–1 (alk. paper)
   1. Jury—Social aspects. 2. Jury—Psychological aspects.
I. Krivoshey, Robert M. (Robert Martin), 1942–
II. Series.
K2292.J85   1994
306.2'5—dc20   93–31981
                                                CIP

Printed on acid-free, 250-year-life paper
Manufactured in the United States of America

To the Memory of My Father
Max Krivoshey

CONTENTS

SERIES INTRODUCTION

"... Therefore, a competent number of sensible and upright jurymen, chosen by lot from among those of the middle rank, will be found the best investigators of truth, and the surest guardians of public justice."

Blackstone, Commentaries on the Common Law

"In all criminal prosecutions, the accused shall enjoy the right to a speedy and public trial, by an impartial jury of the State and district wherein the crime shall have been committed, which district shall have been previously ascertained by law. ..."

Sixth Amendment to the United States Constitution

"In Suits at common law, where the value in controversy shall exceed twenty dollars, the right of trial by jury shall be preserved, and no fact tried by a jury, shall be otherwise re-examined in any Court of the United States, than according to the rules of the common law."

Seventh Amendment to the United States Constitution

The origin of the right to trial by jury is shrouded in the historical past. Some historians trace its origin to Saxon or Norman practice; others to early Scandinavian tribunals or even Germanic custom. Whatever its origin in England, however, the reception of the common law by the American colonists insured that it would become an essential feature of American views of their own liberties. The trial of John Peter Zenger for libel in 1734 demonstrated the power of colonial juries to defy what they considered the tyranny of the Crown and its Governors. Ultimately, the First Continental Congress in 1774 declared it "a great and inestimable privilege" and ended up condemning the King in the Declaration of Independence for depriving Americans of that benefit. In order to guarantee that trial by jury would be a bulwark against arbitrary governmental power, it was embedded in the Bill of Rights to the United States Constitution. Although its meaning and application have been the subject of countless cases since its adoption, there can hardly be any doubt that it will remain the primary vehicle for the settlement of disputes in the foreseeable future.

It is only recently, however, that jury trials have been the subject of systematic study. Within the past twenty-five years, psychologists, sociologists, and speech communication experts have applied the basic techniques of the social sciences to the study of jury trials and their outcomes. Some of these studies have cast doubt on many long-cherished notions of the practicing bar, while others have enhanced our knowledge and understanding of the most effective means of persuasion and communication. These studies have been published in a vast array of publications, ranging from the Journal of Applied Psychology to the Southern Speech Communication Journal, hence making access difficult for scholars, students, attorneys, and others interested in how the social sciences have modified our views of the jury trial process.

Recently, books for practicing attorneys or for sociology and criminal justice courses have synthesized new research, and called attention to its implications for the jury trial process. However, these books' citations do not meet the immediate needs of the scholar interested in examining the original study. This series offers sourcebooks containing over one hundred of the most significant articles from over fifty journals, to increase our understanding of courtroom dynamics.

The volumes in this series correspond to the phases of a jury trial. The first volume on the formation and behavior of juries, includes articles covering such issues as jury research, jury decision making, juror bias, jury selection, and extrinsic factors influencing jury verdicts. The second volume covers issues as diverse as nonverbal communication, the use of language, and the effects of the opening statement on mock juror verdicts. The third volume focuses on presentation of evidence and includes articles on the impact of the physical appearance of attorneys and witnesses, special issues involved in rape cases and the use of child witnesses, eyewitness identification, expert testimony, and the effects of different types of evidence. The final volume raises issues ranging from ability of jurors to understand judicial instructions to the ability of attorneys to predict the outcome of pending litigation.

The series was made possible through the help of many people, most notably Professor Philip Sorensen of the Socio-Legal Center of the Ohio State University College of Law and Joseph Murray, my research assistant. Professor David Goldberger, director of the clinical programs, was always generous with his time and Professor Barbara Snyder provided crucial encouragement. Professor Michael Saks of the University of Iowa made invaluable recommendations. Finally, Professor Goldie Shabad, my wife and the editor's editor, provided the one gift without which this could never have been completed; time.

INTRODUCTION

Trial lawyers have long believed that cases could be won were they to have the perfect social, economic, ethnic and/or religious composition of the jury panel. However, many of the beliefs regarding the "perfect" juror were based on nothing more than crude stereotypes supported solely by the attorney's intuition. Advice such as the following was regularly dispensed to law students in the early seventies when they were studying the most effective methods of trying cases to a jury:

1. "People whose name and appearance indicate an origin of a southern European country might be more likely to be plaintiff jurors. People of Oriental extraction or of other extremely small minorities exercise moderate influence on a jury. They are more apt to go along with the majority expression in order to avoid dissension."

2. "Men and women who have never married are more likely to be introverted, maladjusted, severe, or have an unhappy outlook on life and should be considered defendant jurors."

3. "Plump people, or if you prefer 'fat,' who are quick to smile, may lean toward the plaintiff. A thin person who has a grim, unsmiling demeanor and is not responsive can make a good defendant juror.[1]"

During the past twenty-five years there has been an extraordinary increase in the scholarly study of jury selection and jury behavior. These studies have come from university psychology, communication, speech and other departments. All have been concerned with deciphering the clues that lead to the most effective means of selecting jurors and predicting their behavior. Juror consultants have become ubiquitous and have attempted to assist trial counsel in voir dire; shadow juries have been employed in order that the attorney may get daily advice on the presentation of his case; and even institutes have been established designed to integrate the results of this research into the evidentiary presentation.

Coinciding with this explosion of research, attacks on the viability of the jury system itself have emerged. The apparent inability of jurors to understand jury instructions, their use of factors extrinsic to the evidence and the complexity of many current civil cases have challenged the fundamental bases of adjudication by jury trial. Indeed, for many behavioral scientists, juror impartiality is purely a convenient legal fiction without basis in fact. Thus, this entire body of research has assumed an importance far beyond the limited needs of the trial lawyer and has been used to aid and abet both sides in an ongoing dispute.

Unfortunately, only in extremely rare cases has a researcher been able to eavesdrop on a real jury when it deliberates. This has necessitated simulation studies with the attendant problem of external validity, i.e. can we generalize from a simulated trial to an actual trial or does the fact of simulation change the nature of the experience and distort the results? Or, more narrowly, ". . . if mock jurors are exposed to brief and unrealistic stimulus trials with impoverished evidentiary components, the weight of the biasing component in determining judgment would be atypically prominent while the weight of the evidentiary component would be atypically small."[2] The first articles in this volume discuss the theoretical problems inherent in this method of study, as well as outline the general development of jury research.

Assuming, however, that the intellectual objections to the simulation model have either been overcome or the limitations of the model have been recognized, social scientists have then considered the manner in which juries reach the decisions that they do. Those studying small group behavior and decision making have used various forms of empirical research, including but not limited to computer simulation and interviewing real jurors who have recently served on actual cases. They have used these models to both observe and reach conclusions as to the nature of deliberations and how individual jurors process the information presented during the course of the trial.

Of course, the deliberations and the processing of evidentiary information will to a very considerable extent be dependent upon the bias or prejudice that the individual juror brings with her to the courtroom. Therefore, this second section in the current volume discusses issues such as information processing and whether jurors in a carefully controlled environment can actually presume innocence. It concludes with a surprising study indicating that personal characteristics, such as occupation, sex and educational experience, do not correlate with juror bias as much as does the attitude of the juror toward the jury system itself. That is to say, those jurors most firmly convinced of the value of the jury system are the most likely to convict in criminal cases.

It would be foolish indeed to ignore other factors when choosing jurors. Numerous studies have concentrated on whether gender makes a difference, the importance of an authoritarian personality, the age, occupation and body language of the potential juror, as well as a myriad of other extra-legal factors that can be used to glean information. Much of this will be discussed here. A subsequent volume will consider and analyze the crucial variables involved in the presentation of evidence.

The last set of articles in this volume concentrates on jury selection and the ability of observers to decipher juror signals that would reveal bias. Included in this section are two articles that stress the importance of evidence, particularly physical evidence, to the outcome of jury deliberations. This ultimately significant variable may outweigh all others and its importance may be underestimated while one is busy scanning the available literature.

To aid the reader this volume has been organized in the following fashion:

1. Jury Research: Questions and Criticisms
   (4 articles)
2. Jury Decision Making
   A. Reaching a Verdict (4 articles)
   B. Juror Bias (3 articles)
   C. Juror Judgment and Sex-Role Differentiation (2 articles)
   D. Authoritarianism, Empathy and Autonomy
      (3 articles)
3. Other Effects on Jury Decision Making
   (2 articles)
4. Jury Selection
   A. The Effects of Evidence (2 articles)
   B. Voir Dire (6 articles)
   C. Factors Influencing Jury Verdicts
      (6 articles)

Robert M. Krivoshey

NOTES

1. Alan E. Morrill, *Trial Diplomacy*, 2nd ed. (1974), pp. 18–19.
2. Geoffrey P. Kramer and Norbert L. Kerr, "Laboratory Simulation and Bias in the Study of Jury Behavior: A Methodological Note," *Law and Human Behavior 13* (1989):90

Juries

THE LOGIC OF SIMULATION IN JURY RESEARCH

GORDON BERMANT, MARY McGUIRE,
WILLIAM McKINLEY and CHRIS SALO
Battelle Seattle Research Center and
University of Washington

For both substantive and methodological reasons, laboratory research into the functioning of mock jurors and juries may not be a useful foundation for the practical understanding of actual jury functioning. Data are provided to demonstrate that changes in the structural verisimilitude ("realism") of a simulated trial can produce systematic changes in juror response. However, the modal verdict in the most realistic simulation was not the verdict in the actual trial upon which the simulation was based. In general, we conclude that researchers should make all efforts to maximize the applicability of their findings by tailoring their methods and means of subject selection more closely to the realities of courtroom practice.

The paper proceeds in the following fashion: First, the concept of "simulation" is characterized in a relatively precise way, drawing on one of the uses of the work found in systems analysis and engineering. Second, the concept is applied to laboratory-based research into the functioning of jurors and juries; this application leads to a critical view of much of this research. Third, data are presented to support the conclusion

Authors' Note: *This is based on a paper presented by the first author to the First National Convention of the American Psychology-Law Society, San Francisco, April 29, 1974. Research was supported by the Battelle Institute Program in Behavioral and Social Sciences.*

Criminal Justice and Behavior, Vol. 1 No. 3, September 1974
© 1974 American Association of Correctional Psychologists

that, at the very least, results of most laboratory-based studies are of unknown and generally unknowable generality. Fourth, an attempt is made to account for why the data turned out the way they did.

To begin, then, with a word: simulation. What does it mean? Historically, to simulate means to pretend or to feign. Virtually all the nonscientific usages have a negative connotation—that is, that simulation is deceptive or misleading. However, modern scientific usage has no such negative ring.

A survey of a number of texts and reference works in the modern field of simulation reveals that experts do not agree on a precise definition of simulation. Discussions of definition and related descriptive issues for various fields using the concept of simulation may be found in Abelson (1968), Bellman and Smith (1973), Fodor (1968), Guetzkow et al. (1972), Inbar and Stoll (1972), Gordon (1969), McLeod (1968), Mihram (1972), and Turner (1971). Definitions range from the very broad, as in Abelson (1968), where the term seems to be used almost synonymously with "model," and in McLeod (1968: 6), where one commentator declares that simulation is "a frame of mind," to the quite specific, as indicated by the example below. It is beyond the intention of this brief paper to review the various arguments about the most useful definition of simulation; the purpose here is to make some distinctions that will hopefully shed some light on the nature of some kinds of psycholegal research.

Within systems theory, simulation is conceived as one form of model, in particular, that form of model in which the components do not have the physical characteristics of the object or system modeled, nor are the workings of the model completely specified by analytic mathematics or computing routines (Mihram, 1972: 7). In this sense, simulations are distinguished from replications and formalizations. Replications are models "that display a significant degree of physical similarity between the model and the modeled" (Mihram, 1972), while formalizations do not possess physical similarity, but their symbols are manipulated "by means of a well formed discipline such as mathematics or logic." Thus, examples of replications include things like model trains, wind tunnels with model planes, and so on. To introduce a phrase that will appear again later, replications possess a high degree of *structural verisimilitude* with respect to the object or system being modeled. Neither formalizations nor simulations possesses structural verisimilitude. Their success depends upon their *functional verisimilitude* —i.e., the useful equivalence of their conduct under specified conditions to the conduct of the object or system being modeled. However, formalizations (which we normally think of as "mathematical models") operate under completely specified rules of procedures, while simulations do not.[1]

The distinction between a simulation and a replication is particularly useful for present purposes because it leads immediately to an appreciation of a closely related distinction, which is between simulation and experimentation. In the physical sciences, experiments are typically performed on replications. That is to say, the object or system that is experimented upon within the laboratory bears a very close physical relationship (even the identity relationship) to the object or system which is of general scientific interest. Of course, one can also say that one is "doing the simulation" or simply "simulating." For purposes of this paper, the word "experiment" is reserved for use with replications, not with simulations.

How do these general considerations relate to the specific case of research apparently designed to give insight into the functioning of juries? Of particular concern is the "laboratory" research in which mock jurors are asked to render decisions about guilt, innocence, or appropriate compensation after they have been exposed to information about a particular case or issue. Particularly good examples of this research include Simon's (1967) *The Jury and the Defense of Insanity* and Jurow's (1971) work on death-qualified juries. Mention of this work should not be taken to mean that it typifies the work of which we are critical, for in fact they have gone the furthest to avoid the criticisms we offer. It is not intended here to review the relevant literature in detail; references to a good portion of it published before 1970 may be found in Erlanger (1970). Rather, our argument begins with the conclusion that, in all but a very few cases of this research, there has been little explicit attention paid to the problems of achieving structural and functional verisimilitude, and hence to the generalizability of the results of the studies to the conduct of the system being modeled—namely, real juries functioning in real trials.

The argument begins with a consideration of the dimensions of verisimilitude of a model. It helps in considering this to borrow some computer jargon, in particular the ideas of input, throughput, and output. In regard to models of jury behavior, input becomes the material presented to participants, throughput becomes the individual and joint activity of the participants during the research, and output becomes the record of participants' decisions and the relevant behavior. In addition to these dynamic features of the model, one can also specify the state variables of the model, which in the case under consideration become such characteristics of the participants as age, sex, race, prior jury experience, psychological characteristics (for example, authoritarianism, and the like), and social characteristics (for example, income, occupation, education, and so on). Generally speaking, research on models of juries has consisted of looking for differences or changes in throughput or output produced by differences or changes in input or state variables.

From this viewpoint, one can see that concern with *structural verisimilitude* is concern with input and state variables. Put most plainly, we ask the following two questions: First, "how realistic are the setting and circumstances wherein participants are asked to behave as jurors?" and second, "How similar are the participants in the research to persons likely to serve on real juries?" Our concern with *functional verisimilitude,* on the other hand, is concern with throughput and output. Put most plainly, the question here is "How well does this model mimic the behavior of actual juries behaving under conditions of similar input?"

5

An examination of the available literature suggests that most researchers have not expended much effort in attempting to produce reasonable degrees of structural verisimilitude. For example, participants in most of this research have been college students whose participation was part of classroom activity. A comparison of the social characteristics of courtroom juries with those of typical college students leads to the conclusion that there is in fact little overlap between these two populations.[2] Thus, the structural verisimilitude of the relevant state variables is minimal. Similarly, attempts to achieve structural verisimilitude of the input have not been very strenuous. The typical procedure has been to present participants with written material describing some case or synopses of testimony. In a few cases, audiotaped dramatizations or readings of testimony have been used, and in a still smaller number of cases visual input (videotape, moving pictures, still pictures) has also been provided.

It is a reasonable judgment of the structural verisimilitude found in the bulk of the studies of juror and jury behavior to say that at best the studies 'are simulations rather than replications of the system being modeled. Strictly speaking, then, they are not "experiments on jury behavior." Of course, this would count as no criticism at all if it can be shown that they are only intended as simulations and hence that they are to be evaluated on the basis of their functional verisimilitude. As with simulations generally, if the mock juries behave as real juries do, then their lack of similarity to real juries does not matter. What is required is to show that, under some specified conditions of normalcy (a baseline condition), the mock juries established under some simulation procedure are a good model of real juries. Unfortunately, however, this is, for jury research in particular as for other social psychological research, a very difficult criterion to meet. Some of the reasons for this difficulty are obvious; others, perhaps, are not.

The most obvious difficulty is that every real trial happens only once; it is a unique event. There is no way and little point in trying, from the scientific point of view, to simulate a *particular* trial functionally, for that would mean only that the simulated verdict was the same as the real verdict. Clearly, what is desired is to simulate classes of trials, or classes of events within trials, that may present features of social-psychological interest. In the attempt to do that, however, one runs the risk of abstracting out just the particularities which generated the results in the actual trials. Ideally, of course, from the scientific point of view, one would bypass this tedious problem by observing the activities of real juries at work. But this is illegal and may well remain so (Anonymous, 1974). This means that we can establish only indirectly what we want the throughput of an adequate simulation to look like. Thus, there is no empirical reason to believe, in regard to the great bulk of research published to date, that it generalizes to the conduct of real juries.

As a further illustration of the kinds of difficulties involved in this research area, we shall present the results of a methodological study intended to help us understand how to measure or estimate the degree of structural verisimilitude present in the input of a jury simulation. The plan of the study was to vary the structural verisimilitude of the input of a "jury trial" over a relatively wide range while making every attempt to hold the factual, legally relevant features of the input, and the nature of the state variables, as constant as possible. We were interested to determine if changes in the verisimilitude of the input mattered in terms of output. If they did not, and the output in all cases was the same as the verdict of the actual trial being simulated, then the concerns we have been expressing here would not be empirically supported.

The circumstances of the study were as follows: Each of four groups of undergraduate students received a different input simulation of a murder trial that actually took place in Detroit, Michigan, about a decade ago, and ended with a verdict of manslaughter. Operating on the assumption that increasing structural verisimilitude involves both the amount of information[3] in a single sensory modality as well as the number of sensory modalities engaged in the simulation, the following

7

simulations were used. In condition 1, the maximum degree of verisimilitude employed, participants observed a fifty-minute automated slide show which depicted persons in a courtroom acting the roles of judge, prosecutor, defense attorney, defendant, witnesses, courtroom audience, and court reporter. Slides changed on the screen once every ten seconds, on the average, during the entire presentation. The changes were triggered automatically in conjunction with an audiotaped dramatization of an edited version of the original trial transcript. At the end of the trial, individuals were asked for individual verdicts, then formed into juries for group decisions, then once again asked for individual verdicts.

Condition 2 involved the audiotape alone, without the visual input. In condition 3, participants were asked to read the thirty-page transcript on which the audiotape was based. And, finally, in condition 4, participants read a four-page summary of the evidence and the judge's instructions. No group decisions were requested in condition 4. Data analysis was based on the individual verdicts submitted before any group discussion had taken place.

Tables 1 and 2 present the data in different degrees of aggregation. Table 1 displays all the verdicts collected in each condition, while Table 2 collects all forms of guilty verdict together. The message is clear in both tables: the proportion of not guilty verdicts was directly related to the degree of input verisimilitude. When given the brief summary, 30% of the participants voted not guilty; given the transcript, 43% voted not guilty; given the audiotape, 67% voted not guilty; and given

TABLE 1
DISTRIBUTION OF VERDICTS BY STRUCTURAL
VERISIMILITUDE

	Not Guilty	Man-slaughter	Second Degree	First Degree	Σ
Summary	15	14	17	4	50
Transcript	9	9	2	1	21
Audiotape	16	5	2	1	24
Audiovisual	18	4	1	0	23

8

TABLE 2
NOT GUILTY VERSUS ALL FORMS OF GUILTY

	Not Guilty	Guilty	Σ
Summary	15	35	50
Transcript	9	12	21
Audiotape	16	8	24
Audiovisual	18	5	23
Σ	58	60	118

$$\chi^2 = 18.42, P < .001$$

the audiovisual presentation, 78% voted not guilty. Participants exposed to more complex, verisimilous simulations were more likely to provide a verdict of not guilty. The outcome of the simulation was dependent on the degree of verisimilitude of the input, with the variables held as constant as possible.

What can be learned from this finding? It is susceptible to several worthwhile interpretations, but for current purposes we offer the following one: changes in the structural verisimilitude of a model such as this can lead to major changes in the outcome, even when the fundamental factual features of the input are held constant. For the data under consideration, the change was systematic: greater structural verisimilitude produced larger proportions of not guilty verdicts. However, it must not be inferred from these findings that, in the real trial of which this one was a model, the jurors voted unanimously not guilty. For, as already mentioned, the verdict in the case was manslaughter. *If* the criterion for the success of the simulation is its functional versimilitude, and that is defined in terms of the proportion of manslaughter verdicts, *then* the presentation of the transcript was the best simulation input because it produced the largest proportion of manslaughter verdicts. If, alternatively, functional verisimilitude is defined as the proportion to guilty verdicts of any kind, then the presentation of the summary material was the best simulation.

To the extent that we are willing to accept actual trial outcome in this case as the proper outcome, then we would

9

have to conclude that increasing the structural verisimilitude of the input, given these participants and background conditions, decreased the functional verisimilitude of the output. But for the reasons suggested above, this definition of functional versimilitude is limited. For all one knows, the verdict of manslaughter in the actual case was in fact *incorrect,* and that the modal not guilty verdict in the more verisimilous simulations was the more accurate, just decision. In general, the actual verdict in a given trial is simply inadequate as the sole criterion of functional verisimilitude of the simulation.

No completely convincing theoretical accounting for these results is available, but there are some promising speculative lines to follow. In particular, when very little pretense at verisimilitude is offered (e.g., a brief trial synopsis is presented), participants appear to "fill in the gaps" by constructing their own images of the persons and events in the trial. When one increases the pretense of verisimilitude, however—for example, by using an audiovisual slideshow—participants begin to exercise critical analysis of the simulation as judged against standards of commercial entertainment. The set of the participants changes as a function of the degree of verisimilitude offered, thereby partially offsetting the apparent gain achieved by the work of presenting a more realistic input. As shown here, some of the effects of this changed set seem to be systematic.

NOTES

1. An example of a relevant formalization is Gelfand and Solomon's (1974) model of jury decision-making.

2. A survey of 76 jurors in videotaped trial presentations in Erie County, Ohio, revealed a median age of 47 years. Women reported primary activity as housewife or secretary; employed men were typically semi-skilled or unskilled. These characteristics appear in other reports of jury composition as well.

3. "Information" is used here only in its everyday sense.

REFERENCES

ABELSON, R. P. (1968) "Simulation of social behavior," pp. 274-356 in Volume 2 of G. Lindzey and E. Aronson (eds.) The Handbook of Social Psychology. Reading, Mass.: Addison-Wesley.

Anonymous (1974) "Jury eavesdropping: a scalpel in the hand of the 'recognized scholar.' " Northwestern Univ. Law Rev. 68-908-921.

BELLMAN, R. and C. P. SMITH (1973) Simulation in Human Systems. New York: Wiley-Interscience.

ERLANGER, H. S. (1970) "Jury research in America: its past and future." Law and Society Rev. 4: 345-370.

FODOR, J. A. (1968) Psychological Explanation: An Introduction to the Philosophy of Psychology. New York: Random House.

GELFAND, A. E. and H. SOLOMON (1974) "Modeling jury verdicts in the American legal system." J. of Amer. Stat. Assoc. 69: 32-37.

GORDON, G. (1969) System Simulation. Englewood Cliffs, N.J.: Prentice-Hall.

GUETZKOW, H., P. KOTLER, and R. T. SCHULTZ [eds.] (1972) Simulation in Social and Administrative Science. Englewood Cliffs, N.J.: Prentice-Hall.

INBAR, M. and C. S. STOLL [eds.] (1972) Simulation and Gaming in Social Science. New York: Free Press.

JUROW, G. L. (1971) "New data on the guilt determination process." Harvard Law Rev. 84: 567-611.

McLEOD, J. [ed.] (1968) Simulation. New York: McGraw-Hill.

MIHRAM, G. A. (1972) Simulation: Statistical Foundations and Methodology. New York: Academic.

SIMON, R. J. (1967) The Jury and the Defense of Insanity. Boston: Little, Brown.

TURNER, M. B. (1971) Realism and the Explanation of Behavior. New York: Appleton-Century-Crofts.

11

Psychological Bulletin
1977, Vol. 84, No. 2, 323–345

Justice Needs a New Blindfold: A Review of Mock Jury Research

Kathleen Carrese Gerbasi, Miron Zuckerman, and Harry T. Reis

University of Rochester

Studies on factors that may influence jurors' verdicts are reviewed. These factors include characteristics of the jurors, characteristics of the victim and defendant, judges' instructions regarding pretrial publicity and inadmissible evidence, number and severity of decision alternatives, jurors' conception of guilt, and size of the jury and its decision rule. Data have indicated that many extra-evidential factors contribute to mock jurors' verdicts. However, the applicability of these results is limited by the many methodological and sampling problems inherent in the studies. It is suggested that efforts to develop methods of minimizing biases would be most successful if undertaken conjointly by legal experts and social scientists.

It is beyond argument that a variety of extra-evidential factors influence jury decisions. Whether or not this should be so is a highly debated issue that is beyond the scope and purpose of this review (for discussions of the positions involved, see Brooks & Doob, 1975, and Kadish & Kadish, 1971). Reviewing judges' written reports of over 3,500 real criminal cases, Kalven and Zeisel (1966) found that judges and juries disagreed on the verdicts in approximately 20% of the cases, with most disagreements in the direction of jury leniency. The judges indicated that the reasons for the disagreements included characteristics of the defendant and victim, the type of crime prosecuted, and the jury's evaluation of that crime. Although it is possible that the judges' self-reports were somewhat biased, studies by Reed (1965) and Wolfgang and Reidel (1973) have reached conclusions similar to those of the judges.

Reed (1965) documented individual differences in juror's deliberation behavior via self-report questionnaires administered to a sample of Louisiana jurors. He found significant differences between guilty and not guilty votes, as a function of juror birthplace, previous jury duty, and socioeconomic status.

Requests for reprints should be sent to Kathleen C. Gerbasi, who is now at the Department of Psychology, State University of New York at Buffalo, 4230 Ridge Lea Road, Buffalo, New York 14226.

Experienced jurors and jurors born in Anglo-Saxon northern Louisiana gave more guilty verdicts than inexperienced jurors and those born in the French southern part of the state. Higher status jurors were also more likely to vote guilty than were lower status jurors (no data were reported on the relationship between juror status and birthplace). Finally, high status defendants were treated more leniently than low status defendants. However, Reed's conclusions are qualified by a sampling bias—Only 56% of the jurors contacted agreed to answer the questionnaires. Wolfgang and Reidel (1973) reported on racial differences in the imposition of the death penalty for rape, based on court records of selected southern states (at the time, rape was punishable by death only in southern states). It was found that blacks convicted of the rape of a white woman had an execution rate 18 times greater than any other racial combination of victim and defendant.

In short, there is a large and diverse body of factual data that documents the existence of various kinds of extra-evidential influences on real juries' decisions. The goal of this paper is to review and critically evaluate behavioral science research data that investigate these influences. These data come from the work of sociologists, psychologists, and lawyers, and the problems studied and the approaches employed vary widely from laboratory to laboratory. Because of this diversity, this review has been organized into the following content-based sections: early jury research, the jury as a group, the jurors as individuals, characteristics of the defendant and victim, applications and ethics, and research on legal issues. Unfortunately, little continuity or generalizability exists from one content area to another. (For a catalog-type review of the legal and sociological literature prior to 1970, see Erlanger, 1970.)

The reader should be forewarned of several problems that make comparison among studies and generalization of results problematic: Procedures differ widely from one study to another, some relying on individual verdicts and others employing group deliberation. Dependent measures taken from subjects vary greatly from study to study (e.g., length of sentence, severity of the crime, evaluation of the defendant) and are generally not the same responses requested of actual jurors. Finally, experimental subjects (usually college students) are rarely representative of the typical jury pool. Some of these notions will be cited in dealing with inconsistencies between experimental results. It must also be recognized that although the comparability of mock and real jurors' behaviors has recently become a topic for research (see Diamond & Zeisel, 1974, and Kerr, Nerenz, & Herrick, Note 1), the extent of comparability between responses of mock jurors, whose judgments have no real impact, and verdicts of real jurors is unknown. Although this question will be dealt with, as it is central to the external validity of these studies, the primary purpose of this paper will be to review mock jury research.

Early Jury Research

One of the first mock jury experiments ever conducted was performed by Marston in 1924 (Marston, 1968). During class, a confederate entered, and assaulted the teacher. The 18 student witnesses were asked to report the incident in three forms: free narrative—relating the incident, direct examination—answering questions, and cross-examination—defending their answers to direct examination. Marston found that free narrative was more accurate but less complete than either direct

examination or cross-examination, and that subjects were most cautious in cross-examination. The students' reports were then presented to mock jurors, 12 males and 12 females, in either verbal or written form. Jurors' responses to these reports were analyzed to establish the relative validity of jury conclusions based on verbal versus written presentations. It was found that written testimony produced more accurate conclusions than did verbal testimony. Furthermore, females were more accurate than males, although both males and females were overly influenced by one inaccurate witness, whom the jurors thought very sincere. Marston concluded that his jurors were more influenced by the apparent sincerity of a witness than by the logical probability of his testimony.

Although judges instruct jurors not to reach a verdict until all of the evidence has been presented, a study by Weld and Danzig in 1938 (Weld & Danzig, 1968) suggested that this is not the case. In this study, 41 psychology students listened to a mock trial and were asked to give verdicts at 18 points during the trial. At least 25% of the subjects formed their opinions early in the trial, with little change occurring as more evidence was presented. Few subjects altered their personal decisions in the process of jury room deliberations (these data concur with those of James, 1959, see below). To the extent that having to report their verdicts committed subjects to their own predeliberation decisions, Weld and Danzig's group data cannot be generalized to a real jury, which is not requested to make predeliberation decisions. Interestingly, however, Kalven and Zeisel (1966, p. 488) found that in 90% of 225 cases, the verdict was identical to the majority opinion on the first ballot, indicating that the majority of jurors had made up their minds before deliberations began and were able to convince the minority to agree with them.

In summary, the major value of the early jury studies was to highlight some of the problems of trial by jury. Results showed that factors such as the type of testimony (verbal vs. written), sex of jurors, and the apparent sincerity of witnesses may affect the conclusions reached by jurors. Furthermore, such conclusions may be formed prior to hearing all of the testimony. However, due to small sample sizes, lack of systematic statistical analyses, and the methodological problems mentioned above, it is unwise to rely heavily on these findings.

The Jury as a Group

The lack of additional jury research during the 1940s might be traced to political and economic factors that guided the amount and type of research conducted during and after World War II. Only in the mid-1950s did Strodtbeck and his associates decide that the jury was a group worthy of further study (Strodtbeck, James, & Hawkins, 1957; Strodtbeck & Mann, 1956; James, 1959). Their object was not to understand juries per se but rather to evaluate how status works in a group in which status is supposedly unimportant. The methodology for all of these studies was essentially similar. Groups of 12 jurors selected from the actual jury pools of St. Louis, Chicago, or Minneapolis were assembled in real courtrooms and were administered questionnaires that contained questions similar to those of the voir dire.[1] Each group then listened to a recording of a trial and retired to the jury room to reach a verdict. Before discussing the case, each juror was asked to decide privately upon a verdict. They were then instructed to select a foreman and to try to reach a common verdict. In all of these studies, every possible effort was made to maintain high levels of mundane and experimental realism—The experiments were held in court and administered by court officials.

In the first study, Strodtbeck and Mann (1956) presented their jurors with an auto negligence case. Jury deliberations were tape recorded, transcribed, and each juror's statements were classified according to the type of comments he or she made. Four comment categories were employed: positive reactions, that is, expressions of solidarity and agreement; attempted answers; questions; and negative reactions. Data from 12 of the 30 groups tested indicated that males made more comments than females of equal socioeconomic status, and that higher socioeconomic status

jurors made more comments than did those of lower socioeconomic status. Females gave more positive reactions to other jurors than did males, but males exceeded the females in attempted answers. Finally, the jurors described by their peers as most helpful to the group were the ones who had given the most attempted answers. However, an interaction of borderline significance ($p < .07$) was found between asking questions and sex; that is, males who asked questions and females who did not ask questions were rated as more helpful than their respective silent and verbal counterparts. Some combination of sex role expectations and males' greater familiarity with auto negligence may account for these results.

Strodtbeck, James, and Hawkins (1957) elaborated on Strodtbeck and Mann's 1956 work and, in addition to verbal participation rates, reported foreman selection and juror satisfaction patterns. Two civil trials[2] were represented in the 49 cases making up their study, one dealing with an auto accident (29 cases) and the other dealing with an injury that resulted from a defective product (20 cases). The combination of data from these two different civil cases was not justified by the authors and seems questionable because of the possible interactions between type of case and the independent variables. Results showed that higher socioeconomic status (proprietorial and clerical) persons were more often selected as foremen than were lower status (skilled and unskilled) laborers. As in the 1956 report, higher participation rates were found for male and higher socioeconomic status jurors. High status jurors were perceived as most influential, judging by the correlation among the proprietors between individually suggested predeliberation awards and the jury verdict ($r = .50$, $p < .05$). Among clerical, skilled, and unskilled labor status juror groups, there were no significant correlations between predeliberation awards and jury verdicts.

[1] Voir dire is the pretrial process of interviewing potential jurors to determine what biases, if any, they might hold toward the case or defendant.

[2] Civil trials are those in which financial damages are sought by the plaintiffs from the defendants.

Strodtbeck et al. also found that the jurors who participated most also reported the greatest satisfaction with the quality of the deliberation ($r = .52$, $p < .05$). Since those who participated most were also the influential high status members, it is likely that satisfaction is a result of perceived influence. Prior to deliberation, jurors were asked, if they were on trial, whether they would prefer to be tried by a high status person, a low status person, or a member of their family. Most subjects indicated preference for high status jurors. Postdeliberation choices revealed a shift toward more heterogeneous choices, with lower status persons being chosen more often. Strodtbeck et al. suggested that the shift in choice may have reflected a movement away from subjects' reliance on the jurors' status toward consideration of an individual's merits as an indicator of his or her desirability as a juror. This would seem to reflect integration of additional information beyond that available during first impressions.

Rita James Simon (James, 1959) investigated the relationship between juror competence and amount of education. The data were drawn from 10 mock juries, which each deliberated a criminal case. Jurors were classified according to their educational level—grade school, high school, or college. In accord with earlier studies, male and college-educated jurors spoke more. In an improvement over Strodtbeck and Mann's (1956) formal analysis of the verbal data, James used a content approach that classified comments as references to court instructions, references to testimony, opinions on the facts of the case, experiences from personal and daily life, and procedural comments. In addition to the above classification, each comment was also rated on its helpfulness to or detraction from the progress of the jury.

James found that approximately 50% of the jurors' time was devoted to discussing opinions and personal experiences, either directly or indirectly related to the trial; about 25% of their time was spent discussing procedural issues; 15% and 8% of the time was spent on testimony and instructions, respectively. More highly educated jurors placed greater emphasis on procedure and instructions than those with only grade school educations, who, in turn, were more interested in opinions, testimony, and personal experiences. High-school- and college-educated jurors were rated as more accurate in their understanding of court instructions than were grade-school-educated jurors. College-educated jurors also expressed more concern for facilitating group discussion than did less educated jurors. Contrary to findings by Strodtbeck et al. (1957), there were no differences found among the educational groups in their ability to persuade or be persuaded by other jurors, with the following exception: Grade school jurors were overrepresented in the group of reversed jurors, that is, jurors who contributed to hung juries and then changed their verdicts to be congruent with the group after the jury was hung. Nine percent of the grade school jurors, but only 3% of the remaining jurors, were reversed jurors. Finally, in accordance with previous studies, James found that the more a juror contributed to the deliberation, the more positive his evaluation by his fellows, regardless of his educational level.

Hawkins (1962) investigated participation rates of groups of jurors who disagreed with each other (factions). He found that the larger the faction, the less time each faction member spoke and the greater the total length of time the faction used as a group. These data, which suggest that the minority is stifled, lend support to Kalven and Zeisel's (1966) hypothesis that the function of jury deliberation is not to find facts but rather to allow the majority of jurors to persuade the minority to agree with them.

In summary, the study of the jury as a group has revealed that status, measured by either occupational or educational level, and sex are consistently related to the amount and kind of comments that a juror makes during the process of deliberation. High status jurors seem to have higher participation rates and make more procedural comments than low status jurors. Males seem to have higher participation rates than do females. Regardless of status, participation has related positively to a juror's evaluation by his peers, particularly for males. Furthermore, the jury as a whole seems to spend more time discussing personal experience and opinions than facts.

A certain degree of inconsistency among the results of various studies may be noted. Although Strodtbeck et al. (1957) found that high status persons were more persuasive than low status persons, James found no relationship between status and persuasibility. It is possible that this difference was due to the type of case used (civil vs. criminal), the consequent type of dependent measure (the size of a financial award vs. a vote of guilt or innocence), or varied operational definitions of status, as well as the usual procedural, sampling, and time differences.

All of the above studies have a problem in common with the Marston (1968) methodology of repeatedly measuring jurors' opinions. However, whereas Marston made 18 measurements, Strodtbeck and his students made only 3. Since each juror brought a verdict to the formal deliberation, it remains an unanswered question whether expressing this verdict prior to the formal deliberation influenced jurors' commitments to their decisions. Since only the experimenter was aware of predeliberation verdicts, this situation is probably more similar to private than to public commitment paradigms (Kiesler & Kiesler, 1970), allowing jurors to be more open and flexible during deliberation. Some evaluation apprehension toward the experimenter would still be operative, since he or she was aware of personal to group opinion changes. Given the manner in which juries operate, it would seem useful to remove this effect altogether.

Jurors as Individuals

In the above section the major emphasis of the research was on the process and product of the jury as a group. In this section we shall consider studies that have sought relations between characteristics of individual jurors and their verdicts.

Robinson (1950) reported that juries are rarely representative of the population from which they are drawn—a violation of a defendant's civil rights. His data indicated that in California, for the years 1935–1947, professional, semiprofessional, managerial, and proprietorial workers were overrepresented in grand jury nominations, whereas skilled and unskilled laborers were underrepresented.

Robinson suggested that different labor groups hold different opinions on labor and management and that these biases, combined with representative jury selection, might result in biased verdicts. Unfortunately, Robinson did not consider that factors such as World War II and draft exemptions might have accounted for the atypically biased jury selections that he had found. Because of the ease with which professional and semiprofessional workers can be excused from jury duty, one is most likely to find an underrepresentation of such individuals in juries, as did Strodtbeck and his co-worekrs in the 1950's.

More recent and elaborate data regarding personal interests and experimental trial bias were provided by Green (1967). Green used a civil liability case that involved a child falling into a backyard swimming pool, with the owner of the pool as the defendant. There were 16 versions of the case based on all possible combinations of the following 4 dichotomous variables: probability that the accident would occur, degree of injury sustained, extent of precautions taken by the defendant, and the form and content of the instructions given to the jurors. Evaluations for each of the 16 cases were collected from 192 adult subjects interviewed in their homes.

Green found that the degree of injury sustained did not affect the jurors' verdicts. Parents were more sympathetic to the plaintiff than were nonparents, especially if the situation was low risk (that is, the pool was surrounded by a 6-foot fence) and if the parents were in child-oriented occupations e.g., teacher, housewife). However, since all housewives and probably most teachers were females, this latter finding may have been related to the jurors' sex. Green concluded that people who were more likely to identify with the plaintiff voted for the plaintiff and were less influenced by the circumstances of the case. It is unfortunate that the author did not try to verify how similar the subjects perceived they were to the defendant and plaintiff.

Nemeth and Sosis (1973) investigated the relationship between subjects' political and socioeconomic backgrounds, as defined by the type of college they attended, and the severity of penalty they imposed on the defendant.

Half of the sample attended a conservative junior college in Chicago, and the remaining half were undergraduates at the more liberal University of Chicago. An equal number of males and females from each group were studied. Subjects were asked to read a case report of a drunken homicide and answer a number of questions dealing with degree of guilt, severity of sentence, and responsibility of the defendant. The defendant was described as attractive (defined as high status by the authors) or unattractive (low status) and as black or white. The junior college sample gave a harsher sentence to the low status defendant than to the high status one, but the university students did not differentiate between the defendants on this dimension. There was no main effect for the race of the defendant, but junior college students were more severe with the white defendant than were university subjects. When asked to evaluate the defendant's drinking habits,

the unattractive defendant was seen as a more habitual drinker than the attractive defendant; the university sample regarded the defendant, regardless of his personal characteristics, as a heavier drinker than did the junior college sample; and a white defendant was seen to be a heavier drinker than was a black defendant. (Nemeth & Sosis, 1973, p. 226)

Finally, all subjects believed that the high status defendant felt more regret for his actions than did the low status defendant.

The problem with the Nemeth and Sosis study is that factors other than political orientation may covary with the type of college (e.g., educational level, race). In addition, these between-college differences were confounded with different sampling procedures; that is, the junior college subjects were recruited in a cafeteria, and the university subjects were recruited from the psychology of personality class. Although the authors concluded that characteristics of both the defendant and the subjects were important in determining sentencing behavior, it is exceptionally unclear to which factors these differences should be attributed.

The remaining studies in this section investigated the relationship between various personality constructs and evaluations of various aspects of criminal cases. Three personality constructs will be presented: authoritarianism, belief in internal–external control, and belief in a just world.

Mitchell and Byrne (1973) measured subjects' degree of authoritarianism by an acquiescence-free authoritarianism scale and manipulated degree of similarity between the subject and the defendant. A group of 139 college students, about half males and half females, read a case history of a male undergraduate who was accused of stealing an exam prior to its administration. Included in the story was information that led subjects to believe that the defendant agreed or disagreed with them about several aspects of college life and society.

It was found that authoritarians were more influenced by the similarity–dissimilarity manipulations than were egalitarians. In the dissimilar condition, authoritarians recommended a more severe punishment than did any other group in the study. In the similar condition, authoritarians were less certain of the defendant's guilt than were the egalitarians.

Centers, Shomer, and Rodrigues (1970) conducted a field study of 1170 people in which they measured subjects' degree of authoritarianism, their attitudes toward a juvenile defendant, and their willingness to change their recommendations for punishment when presented with an "expert's" views that contradicted their own. Authoritarianism was measured by the Sanford and Older scale (1950). As expected, high authoritarians were more punitive and more likely to change their recommendations than either medium or low authoritarians.

Boehm (1968) constructed a new scale, the Legal Attitude Questionnaire (LAQ) to measure authoritarian attitudes toward the legal system. The scale consists of 10 sets of 3 items each: an authoritarian item, an egalitarian item, and an antiauthoritarian item. Authoritarian items express "right-wing" philosophy, antiauthoritarian items express "left-wing" sentiments, and egalitarian items endorse nonextreme positions. For each set, subjects are asked to indicate the items with which they agree most and least. Responses are summed to yield three scores: authoritarianism, egalitarianism, and antiauthoritarianism. In her study, Boehm used two forms of a manslaughter case, one in which the evidence was prodefense and the other in which the evidence was proprosecution. All of the 151 students who served as subjects were given the LAQ, one version of the case, and a ballot form. It was predicted and found that antiauthoritarians gave less severe verdicts than were warranted in the proprosecution case and that authoritarians gave more severe verdicts than were warranted in the prodefense case. It is not known why the author failed to report the kind and frequency of verdicts made by egalitarian subjects.

Jurow (1971) examined the relationship between subjects' beliefs in capital punishment and their verdicts in capital cases. A group of 55 females and 156 males, recruited from all divisions of a large industrial plant, were required to answer a number of personality and attitude measures, including Boehm's LAQ. They then listened to two different tape recordings of murder trials and voted after each on the defendant's guilt.

For the first case, jurors with a favorable attitude toward capital punishment were more likely to convict than were jurors with less favorable attitudes. This result was not supported by the data from the second case. However, since all of the subjects received the cases in the same order, it is impossible to tell whether this pattern of results was caused by an order effect or by a difference in case content. Despite the failure to replicate the results in the second case, Jurow concluded that the standard exclusion of jurors who are opposed to the death penalty in capital cases biases the jury toward a conviction. Jurow also indicated (without reporting any specific data) that the best predictor of the subjects' decisions to acquit or convict was the authoritarian score on the LAQ, with authoritarians most likely to convict.

Berg and Vidmar (1975) examined in two studies the effects of both subjects' degree of authoritarianism and the defendant's status on two dependent variables, the severity of verdicts and the type of trial information recalled (situational evidence or personal characteristics of the defendant). In the first study, 54 female and 90 male undergraduates responded to the LAQ and were then presented with two cases similar to the one used by Mitchell and Byrne (1973). Results showed that subjects were more certain that the lower status defendant was guilty, and that high authoritarian subjects were more punitive, especially toward the low status defendant.

The authors contacted 90 of the original subjects 7 to 10 days after the experimental session and asked them to recall information about the case. High authoritarian subjects recalled more information about the defendant's character and less information about the evidence than did low authoritarians. Noting that the decision on the verdict may have influenced the recall data, the authors conducted a second study, using a different kind of case (automobile manslaughter), and a different authoritarianism measure (Byrne and Lamberth's scale, 1971), as well as eliminating the part in which subjects had to decide on the defendant's guilt. Again the results showed that high authoritarians remembered more about the defendant's character ($p < .05$) and less about the situational evidence ($p < .10$) than did low authoritarians. Berg and Vidmar suggested that differences between low and high authoritarians in guilt attribution may be paritally based on differences in recall and interpretation of the evidence.

The above results indicate that at least for mock cases, high authoritarians are more severe jurors than low authoritarians. These findings have been applied to jury-selection processes by psychologists such as Schulman, Christie and Tapp (Bermant, 1975) working with the defense in various political trials. The strategy used by Schulman et al. was to exclude jurors who were rated as excessively authoritarian by observers in the courtroom.

Phares and Wilson (1972) studied the relationship between belief in internal–external control (Rotter, 1966), sentencing behavior, and attribution of responsibility to a defendant. Eighty male undergraduates, classified as high internals or externals, read eight auto accident cases in which two independent variables were crossed: severity of the outcome (severe vs. minor damages), and ambiguity of the defendant's guilt (unambiguous vs. ambiguous). Subjects were requested to make decisions about the defendant's responsibility and to recommend degree of punishment. Three main effects emerged: More responsibility was attributed when the case was unambiguous, more responsibility was attributed when the accident was severe, and internals attributed more responsibility than did externals. In addition, there was an interaction such that in the ambiguous cases there was no relationship between responsibility attribution and severity, and in the unambiguous cases responsibility attributions increased with severity of outcome. There was also a triple interaction such that in the severe cases internals attributed more responsibility, but did so only when the evidence was ambiguous.

Sosis (1974) also examined the effects of subjects' beliefs in internal–external control on responsibility attribution and sentencing behavior. Using 70 high school students as subjects, she found that internals were more severe jurors and more likely to hold the defendant responsible for his crime (a car accident) than were externals.

Clearly, the results suggest that internals tend to attribute more responsibility to the defendant in mock trials. Phares and Wilson (1972) and Sosis (1974) explained this tendency in terms of projection. It seems reasonable to assert that internals would apply their self-perceptions of responsibility to their judgments of others.

The third personality construct to be presented here is belief in a just world (Lerner, 1970). This construct refers to an individual's belief that he or she lives in a world where people get what they deserve and deserve what they get. Belief in a just world was used by Lerner to explain the fact that under certain conditions innocent victims are blamed for their misfortunes. His reasoning was that derogating the victim helps the observer maintain his belief that the world is just, because he can see the victim as deserving his fate. Deservingness, according to Lerner, consists of two components: personal worth and behavior. Thus, observers may conclude that a victim is an undesirable person or that he has brought his suffering directly upon himself.

The issue of personality derogation versus responsibility attribution was examined in a study by Jones and Aronson (1973). In this study, 234 undergraduates were administered a case account of a rape. Subjects had to recommend punishment for the defendant and rate the extent of the victim's responsibility. The results showed that the behavior of a victim presented as a married woman or a virgin was faulted more than that of a victim presented as a divorcee. The authors suggested that it is difficult to devalue the character of a respectable woman (that is, a married woman or a virgin). Hence, the tendency was to find her responsible for the crime. There was also a tendency to assign larger sentences to the defendant when the victim was married than in the two other cases.

In a study patterned after that of Jones and Aronson (1973), Zuckerman and Gerbasi (Note 2) presented to 101 male and 93 female undergraduates an account of a rape, together with the Just World Scale (Rubin & Peplau, 1973). This scale differentiates people according to their degree of belief in a just world. In contrast with the Jones and Aronson report, more respectable victims were held less responsible for the crime. It was also found that subjects with high scores on the Just World Scale (high JW subjects) assigned more responsibility to the rape victim than did low JW subjects. These results are consistent with Lerner's (1970) reasoning that people may hold a victim responsible for his fate in order to maintain their belief in a just world.

Derogation of the victim is not the only way available of maintaining belief in a just world. When the victim's suffering is caused by another person, high JW individuals may attempt to restore justice by demanding a harsher treatment of the culprit. Rubin and Peplau (1975) reported a study by Izzett in which high JW subjects who played the role of jurors in a negligent homicide case formed less favorable impressions of the defendant and assigned stiffer sentences than did low JW subjects. Similarly, Gerbasi and Zuckerman (Note 3) presented murder case accounts, along with the Just World Scale, to 62 subjects sampled from a population of real jurors. Again, results showed that high JW subjects gave more severe verdicts than did low JW subjects.

In summary, it has been shown that high levels of authoritarianism, belief in internal control, and high levels of belief in a just world are related to attributions of responsibility to defendants and, in some cases, to more severe verdicts. In view of these results it is not surprising that measures of these three constructs are interrelated. Correlations between various authoritarianism scales and the Just World Scale range from .20 to .56 (Rubin and Peplau, 1975); correlations between the I–E scale and the Just World Scale range from −.32 to −.58 (Zuckerman and Gerbasi, Note 4). However, measures of authoritarianism and belief in internal–external control have not yet been related.

The relationships among these three personality measures raise the question of whether only one true construct is actually related to responsibility attribution. Elsewhere, Zuckerman and Gerbasi (Note 4) have suggested that the relationship between the I–E Scale and responsibility attribution is mediated by the construct of belief in a just world. Obviously, such a question requires further empirical research.

A problem common to most of the studies in this section is that length of punishment rather than verdict was used as the dependent measure. In real trials, jurors usually decide only the degree of guilt. This problem will be discussed in the section dealing with legal issues. A second problem common to all studies presented in this section is that they are based on individual deliberations, and there is not evidence that these functions can be generalized to the product of a group deliberation. However, as Mitchell and Byrne (1973) have suggested, if the goal of the jury is to reach a verdict based on the evidence rather than the personal characteristics of the jurors, it seems at least minimally reasonable to ensure that a group of jurors are heterogeneous with respect to variables that might influence individual decisions.

It is interesting to note that a number of researchers have recently been involved in the process of jury selection for primarily political trials (see Bermant, 1975; Schulman, Shaver, Coleman, Emrich, & Christie, 1973; Wood-

ward, 1952; Shaver, Note 5; and Gould & Gould, Note 6). For most of these cases, which include the Harrisburg conspiracy trial, the Ellsberg-Russo Pentagon papers trial, and Wounded Knee trial, the researchers attempted to select jurors who, based on personal characteristics, would be favorable to the defense. Schulman et al. (1973) were also successful in convincing the Harrisburg judge that, on the basis of survey data, the initial jury pool was not representative of the population in the Harrisburg jurisdiction. As a result, the judge had the pool updated prior to jury selection for the case. In light of the generally unrepresentative nature of juries, this type of procedure might be valuable in most, if not all, judicial districts. (For a discussion of the requirements for admission of survey data into evidence, see Katz, 1975.)

Although the intervention of psychologists in the jury-selection process seems to be spreading, its benefits are questionable. It is obvious that lawyers have long been involved in the same process and perhaps with no less success. This suggestion is supported by data from a study by Diamond and Zeisel (1974). For 10 cases, these investigators compared verdicts of three groups of jurors: randomly selected jurors, jurors chosen by the defense and prosecution, and jurors rejected by the defense and prosecution. The randomly selected jurors found all of the defendants guilty, the lawyer-selected jury found five defendants guilty, and the lawyer-rejected jury found eight defendants guilty. Three judges who also heard the cases found all but one defendant guilty. These data support the notion that lawyers do indeed affect trial outcome through the process of jury selection.

Even if psychologists might be more accurate in predicting the votes of potential jurors, what then? One might imagine a system in which defense and prosecution hire social scientists to help in jury selection. If this were to happen, both the defense and prosecution would recognize each other's "best" jurors and ask for their dismissal. The question is whether a random sample of jurors would render a different verdict than would jurors selected by social scientists (Kahn, 1974). It seems that the answer is unknown and worthy of both extensive future research and ethical consideration.

Characteristics of the Victim and Defendant

Several studies have attempted to gather knowledge of the relationship between characteristics of defendants and trial outcomes. In one of the first studies, Rose and Prell (1955) asked 101 male and 87 female undergraduates to assign fines and prison sentences to defendants of different social classes. Subjects gave larger fines to the higher status defendants; however, there was no clear relationship between the defendant's status and the length of prison sentence assigned. Landy and Aronson (1969) conducted two studies on the effects that characteristics of the defendant and victim may have on trial outcome. In the first study, the victim of a drunken driving accident was presented as either high or low status. Results indicated that subjects tended to give more severe sentences to the defendant who killed the high status victim ($p < .08$). In the second study, Landy and Aronson employed two levels of victim status and three levels of defendant status. Subjects again tended to be more severe with the defendant who killed the high status victim ($p < .09$). In addition, high and medium status defendants were given shorter sentences than those of low status ($p < .05$). However, the degree of guilt attributed to the defendants did not vary as a function of the victim's and defendant's status (degree of guilt was measured on a standard 9-point scale). It should be noted here that Kalven and Zeisel (1966) reported that real jurors tend to find attractive defendants guilty of less serious crimes than unattractive defendants.

Dowdle, Gillen, and Miller (1974) employed modified versions of the Landy and Aronson cases; in addition to replicating the finding that defendants with positive characteristics were treated more leniently than those who were negatively described, they found that the source of the defendants' characterization was a significant determinant of the recommended length of punishment. Defendants who were described by peers received longer sentences than those whose descriptions were given by clinical psycholo-gists or by psychologists and peers. It was also found that the number of traits (three or six) attributed to the defendant did not have a significant effect on the mock jurors' judgments.

Gerbasi and Zuckerman (Note 3) attempted to expand on the relationship between defendant's and victim's status in conjunction with the circumstances of the crime. Ten mock cases (five pairs) were presented to 91 female and 69 male undergraduates. All pairs involved the loss of a life in each of the following situations: euthanasia, auto accident, self-defense, a business disagreement, or a family argument. One case in each pair presented the defendant in a sympathetic light, by virtue of his status, his relationship with the victim, and so forth. The other case was either neutral or unsympathetic. Most of the cases were modified versions of situations that, according to Kalven and Zeisel (1966), had elicited either lenient or harsh verdicts from jurors. Subjects also responded to a number of personality measures, including the Just World Scale and, following each of the 10 cases, answered questions about severity of verdict (not guilty, manslaughter, etc.), length of prison sentence if guilty, and certainty of verdict. After all cases had been read, subjects were asked how similar they felt to the defendant in each case. Two orders of presentation were used, such that no pair of cases appeared adjacent to one another.

For four of the five pairs, the verdicts for one member of a pair were significantly affected by having its partner precede it ($p < .05$). The fifth pair showed a trend to this effect ($p < .09$). These data suggest the operation of a classic order effect (Bieri, Orcutt, & Leaman, 1963; Jones & Goethals, 1971) in which subsequent decisions are influenced by those preceding.

All of the four cases that produced significant order effects also yielded significant differences in verdicts for sympathetic versus unsympathetic cases, with the sympathetic defendants receiving less severe verdicts. No effects were found for belief in a just world. Correlational data indicated a consistent and significant negative relationship between severity of verdict and perceived similarity to the defendant; that is, the more similar the juror perceived himself to the defendant, the less severe his sentence.

Pepitone and DiNubile (1976) predicted and found order effects in judgments of crime severity and defendants' punishment made by 182 male undergraduate volunteers. All subjects read two cases and passed judgment on the second case; however, for half of the subjects, case judgments were also required for the first case (anchored), but the remaining subjects merely read the first case (unanchored). In addition to the anchoring variable, case content was also varied in degree of seriousness. Approximately one quarter of the mock jurors were assigned to each of the following pairs: assault–assault, assault–murder, murder–assault, and murder–murder. When the first case judgments were anchored, the judgments of the assault case that had been preceded by murder and the murder case preceded by assault were respectively less and more severe than when the pairs were matched for type of crime or when the first judgments were unanchored.

Sigall and Landy (Note 7) also varied the defendant's character (likable or unlikable) and the time of the defendant's suffering (either before, during, or after a fight with a male whom he had found visiting his wife). All subjects, 105 male and 79 female undergraduates, were told that the situation between the wife and visitor was truly innocent and that the victim died as a result of the fight. After reading the case accounts, subjects made various evaluations of the defendant's guilt. The unlikable defendant received a longer prison sentence than the likable defendant, but no significant effects were associated with the defendant's time of injury. These findings replicate those of Landy and Aronson (1969) and of Gerbasi and Zuckerman (Note 3), with respect to the relationship between defendant characteristics and trial outcome.

Austin, Walster, and Utne (1976) reported a study similar to that of Sigall and Landy (Note 7). A purse-snatching case, in which the defendant either had only taken the victim's purse or had taken the purse and also beaten the victim, was described to male and female subjects. Further, the defendant was described as having attempted to escape the

police and as having suffered either no harm, moderate harm, or excessive harm in the process. Inspection of the data revealed that females were more severe jurors than males, the defendant who beat his victim was punished more severely than the one who only snatched her purse, and the more the defendant suffered in the attempted escape, the less severe the punishment recommended by the mock jurors.

The effect of a female defendant's physical attractiveness as related to the type of crime perpetrated has been studied by Sigall and Ostrove (1975). They predicted that when the crime (theft) was unrelated to attractiveness, sentences would be greater for the unattractive than for the attractive defendant, but when the defendant's attractiveness facilitated her crime (swindle) the attractive defendant would receive longer sentences. Attractiveness was presented through still photographs, and neutral defendants were presented without pictures. As predicted, the attractive swindler and unattractive thief were assigned longer prison sentences than were their respective unattractive and attractive counterparts. Furthermore, sentences in the unattractive and control conditions were nearly identical, suggesting that being unattractive does not yield discriminatory responses per se, but that being attractive does.

Kaplan and Kemmerick (1974) used a repeated measures design to evaluate the effects of positive, negative, neutral, or no information about the defendant's character on simulated jurors who evaluated auto accident cases containing highly or mildly incriminating evidence. They also instructed the jurors that character information had either great or questionable utility in evaluating guilt, but these instructions had no main effect. Highly incriminating evidence produced higher guilt and punishment ratings than did mildly incriminating evidence. The defendant described in negative terms was attributed the most guilt and punished the most severely, whereas the positively described defendant was treated most leniently. Neutral information, as opposed to no character information, was to the defendant's advantage, especially when the instructions emphasized the utility of character information.

DeJong, Morris, and Hastorf (1976) investigated the effect of an escaped accomplice on the punishment assigned to a criminal defendant by mock jurors. Three independent variables were crossed: The crime was either robbery or murder and robbery, the defendant was described as more or less responsible for the crime, and the defendant's accomplice either was captured or escaped with no possibility of capture. A group of 124 undergraduate subjects were randomly assigned to one of the eight conditions. Significant main effects were found for each of the independent variables: A greater number of years of punishment was assigned for the more serious crime, for the defendant with the greater responsibility, and for the defendants whose accomplice had been caught.

In summary, it has been shown that characteristics of the defendant and, to a lesser extent, the victim play important roles in case evaluations. The main problem is that the studies reported in this section have used subjects working alone rather than interacting as jurors. A study by Izzett and Leginski (1974) suggests that group discussion lessens the effects of the defendant's status on the severity of prison sentences recommended by individuals. In this study, they presented the Landy and Aronson (1969) cases to groups of four to six undergraduates and asked them to individually sentence the defendant. Following the individual sentencing, each group member reported to the group his sentence and the reason for it. Groups then discussed the case for 10 minutes and again rendered individual decisions. It was found that prior to the discussion, longer prison terms were given to the low status defendant. The discussion produced a significant change in the direction of leniency for the low status defendant but did not influence the treatment of the high status offender. Postdiscussion sentences for the two defendants did not differ significantly. These results suggest that group discussion lessens the effects of status, at least for prison sentences made by small groups of jurors.

More recently, Myers and Kaplan (1976) found that group discussion served to polarize the judgments of guilt and severity of sentence recommended by 60 undergraduates. Subjects each read four high- and four low-guilt cases, made prediscussion judgments on all cases, discussed *half* of each type of case and then made postdiscussion judgments on all eight cases. Judgments of the low-guilt discussed cases became less severe and judgments of the high-guilt discussed cases became more severe, when compared with those cases that had not been discussed.

These two studies indicate the methodological importance of group discussion in the execution of jury studies, especially when some degree of generalizability from the laboratory to the courtroom is a desired goal.

Research on Legal Issues

Several aspects of trial procedures, which the judiciary takes as given, have recently been subject to experimental studies. These include (a) the ability of jurors to follow judges' instructions regarding pretrial publicity and evidence; (b) the effects of the number and severity of decision alternatives offered to the jurors; (c) characteristics of the presentation of evidence, such as the order of presentation, adversary versus inquisitorial presentation, and the number of arguments proferred; (d) the ability of jurors to understand and apply various definitions of guilt; and (e) the effect of changing the number of jurors and the decision rule on trial outcomes. Each of these issues will be presented below.

Ability of Jurors to Follow Judges' Instructions

Studies by Simon (1968) and Hoiberg and Stires (1973) investigated the relationship between exposure to pretrial publicity and jurors' verdicts. Simon exposed 97 volunteers drawn from voter registration lists to either a sensational or a conservative newspaper story about a murder case, prior to their hearing a tape of the trial. Subjects who heard the sensational story were more likely to believe the defendant guilty before the trial than were subjects who heard the conservative story. Subjects were then instructed by a judge to disregard any information that they might have heard about the case. Following the judge's instruction, the subjects listened to the case and rendered their verdicts. No differences in verdicts were found between the subjects who had read the sensational story and those who had read the conservative story.

The Simon study is subject to several criticisms. Ideally there should have been two control conditions: one in which subjects did not receive pretrial publicity and another in which subjects received pretrial publicity but not the judge's instruction. In addition, the subjects were self-selected, upper-middle-class, college-educated individuals, and consequently unrepresentative of typical jurors. Furthermore, the demand characteristics of the study were high. Subjects were first handed a newspaper story, and then asked to ignore the information they had read. It should not be hard for intelligent subjects to comply with such a request. In a real and lengthy trial it might be more difficult to sort out trial evidence from news reports.

Hoiberg and Stires (1973) exposed 337 high school students to pretrial publicity that varied on two dimensions: (a) heinousness of the crime, that is, murder (low, as defined by the authors) versus brutal rape and murder (high); and (b) degree of prejudgment, that is, subjects were told that the defendant was questioned (low), or that he had confessed (high). All subjects were divided into low and high IQ groups via a median split. Female subjects exposed to the high heinous pretrial publicity attributed more guilt to the defendant than did low heinous pretrial publicity exposed females. Among low IQ females, high prejudgment exposed subjects attributed more guilt to the defendant than did low prejudgment pretrial publicity subjects. Among males, high IQ subjects attributed more guilt to the defendant than did low IQ subjects. Subjects' self-reports indicated that females identified less with the victim and rated the crime as less heinous than did male subjects. The authors concluded that at least females can be influenced by pretrial publicity. However, it should be noted that, unlike real trials, subjects were not asked to disregard pretrial publicity.

In addition to instructions concerning pretrial publicity, judges also instruct juries on the admissibility of evidence. Kadish and Kadish (1971) indicated, however, that actual jurors are free not to comply with these instructions. Sue, Smith, and Caldwell (in press) hypothesized that if damaging inadmissible evidence were presented to jurors who already had enough evidence for conviction, the effect of the inadmissible evidence would be small. However, if the case were weak and the inadmissible evidence strong, the evidence would increase the likelihood of a conviction. A group of 46 male and 61 female undergraduates were asked to read material that contained a summary of a murder–robbery trial and were then asked to answer questions concerning the defendant's guilt. There were two strength-of-evidence conditions crossed by three additional evidence conditions: admissible, inadmissible, and no additional evidence (control). As expected, subjects exposed to strong evidence were more likely to render guilty verdicts than were those exposed to weak evidence. There were no differences within the strong evidence condition between the control and the two additional evidence groups. However, in the weak evidence condition none of the control subjects rendered guilty verdicts, whereas 26% of subjects in the admissible and 35% of the subjects in the inadmissible conditions rendered guilty verdicts (control versus other, $p < .05$; admissible versus inadmissible, ns). The authors also found that subjects in the strong evidence condition were more confident of their decisions than were weak evidence subjects, and that the length of the sentence assigned to the defendant was positively related to the strength of the subjects' confidence in their verdicts, but was unrelated to the strength of evidence. These data suggest that mock jurors are affected by differences in evidence strength and may rely on inadmissible evidence in spite of a judge's instructions.

Archer and Aderman (Note 8) also conducted a study on subjects' willingness or ability to follow the judge's instructions. A mock trial was staged in which the defense counsel asked the jurors, 72 undergraduates, either to imagine themselves in the defendant's place (empathy condition) or to attend to the evidence (nonempathy condition). These two conditions were crossed by two types of judge's instructions. Half of the subjects received general instructions (nonfact focus), and the other half were additionally instructed to attend only to the facts (fact focus). The counsel's empathic appeal was successful in producing leniency toward the defendant only in the nonfact focus condition. Subjects in this condition attributed less responsibility for the incident to the defendant's personality and considered his behavior as more lawful than did any other group of subjects.

In summary, some of the studies presented in this section are contradictory in their findings. Simon's highly educated jurors were easily able to disregard pretrial publicity, but Hoiberg and Stires' female high school students relied on pretrial publicity in order to make their judgments. It is quite obvious that the type of cases, subject populations, and methodologies used for the two studies make them incomparable. Data gathered by Sue et al. and by Archer and Aderman suggest that factors such as strength of evidence, type of defense appeal and judge's instruction may determine whether or not jurors rely on pretrial publicity, as well as their degree of leniency toward the defendant.

Number and Severity of Decision Alternatives

After jurors have heard all the evidence, the judge instructs them as to the types of verdicts they may render. It has been found in many real trials, such as the Algiers Motel trial in Michigan (Vidmar, 1972), that when jurors are allowed only two extreme choices (e.g., first degree murder vs. not guilty) they will opt for the more lenient choice. Vidmar (1972) and Kaplan and Simon (1972) have experimentally studied this problem.

Vidmar instructed 118 female and 74 male undergraduates to reach verdicts for a defendant being tried for murder and robbery. A pretest prior to the study indicated that manslaughter and second degree murder were the most likely verdicts. There were seven decision alternative conditions in the study: (a) first degree murder or not guilty; (b) second degree murder or not guilty; (c) manslaughter or not guilty; (d) first degree murder, second degree murder, or not guilty; (e)

first degree murder, manslaughter, or not guilty; (f) second degree murder, manslaughter, or not guilty; and (g) first degree murder, second degree murder, manslaughter, or not guilty. Each degree of guilt was attached to a mandatory sentence. An additional group of subjects served as a control and were not asked to decide on a verdict. Vidmar also manipulated the order in which the subjects received pieces of the evidence.

No effects due to sex of the subjects or order of the presentation of testimony were found. The highest percentage (54%) of not guilty verdicts was returned in Condition a. When Condition a (two alternative choices) is compared with Condition g (four alternative choices; 8% not guilty verdicts returned) or with a combination of Conditions b and c (two less severe alternative choices; 13% not guilty verdicts), it is clear that "under conditions of restricted decision alternatives, the more severe the degree of guilt associated with the least severe guilt alternative, the greater the chances of obtaining a not guilty verdict" (Vidmar, 1972, p. 215). In accordance with a consistency model, it was found that after reaching a verdict, subjects' evaluations of the validity of the testimony were congruent with the type of verdict rendered.

In a reanalysis of Vidmar's data, Larntz (1975) found that a proportional weighting model based on jurors' verdicts in the unrestricted conditions, incorporating the severity of the alternatives offered, could account for the distribution of choices in the restricted alternative conditions. Larntz concluded that Vidmar's data "are due necessarily to the constriction of response available to the decision maker and not to any psychological accommodation to that restriction" (p. 125).

Kaplan and Simon (1972) presented a case of a car accident to 307 male and female undergraduates. They manipulated the race of the victim (black or white), the strength of evidence (strong, weak, moderate, or inconsistent), and the latitude and severity of sentencing options offered to the jurors (manslaughter or innocent, second degree murder or innocent, first degree murder or innocent, or a choice of any of the four verdicts). A mandatory sentence was assigned to each verdict. A control group was not asked to reach a verdict, but to indicate their attitudes toward the defendant and victim in the eight Evidence × Race conditions.

The results indicated that the stronger the evidence, the greater the frequency of guilty verdicts (no statistical analysis was reported by the authors). In the case of mixed evidence, the authors reported that subjects tended to be more lenient when the victim was white ($p < .10$). The first degree murder versus not guilty choice produced the greatest percentage of not guilty verdicts (76%), and the choice from all four verdicts produced the lowest percentage of not guilty decisions (43%). The frequency of not guilty verdicts in the remaining two-choice conditions fell between the four-choice and first degree murder/innocent two-choice conditions.

The studies of Vidmar (1972) and Kaplan and Simon (1972) indicate that systematic variations in the decision alternatives offered to jurors can result in predictable variations in jurors' verdicts. They provide direct evidence that judges can influence trial outcomes via the verdict choices given to juries.

Presentation of Evidence

Lawson (1968), in a review of relevant social psychology research, suggested that the order in which evidence is presented may affect trial outcome. Recently, Stone (1969) conducted a study in which 29 male and 36 female undergraduates were presented with one of two orders of case arguments: defense first, prosecution second, or prosecution first, defense second. Following each of the two presentations, anonymous tentative verdicts were elicited from the subjects. All subjects then listened to a strong summary argument by the prosecution and rendered their final verdicts. Results showed that order of presentation did not affect the final verdicts. However, subjects' first tentative verdicts were strongly related to their final verdicts, so that of the 30 subjects initially voting guilty, 21 returned a final guilty verdict. Of the 35 subjects who first voted innocent, 24 rendered the same final verdict. Stone concluded that even private initial commitments can affect jurors' final verdicts.

Walker, Thibault, and Andreoli (1972) also studied the effects of the order of presentation of trial evidence. Two orders of presentation were manipulated: (a) the gross order, that is, whether the defense or the prosecution presented first, and (b) the internal order of the evidence presented by each side, that is, climactic (the most dramatic evidence presented at the end) or anticlimactic (the most dramatic evidence presented at the beginning). A group of 142 undergraduates (their sex was not reported) listened to the presentation of the evidence in a fist fight case. Each side presented five blocks of evidence, and after each block the subjects reported their opinions of the defendant's guilt. The data indicated that the party that presented second had a greater effect on the jury than the party that presented first, regardless of whether it was the defense or the prosecution. The results of the variations in internal ordering were more complicated. Internal order within the first presentation made a difference only for the prosecution—The climactic order was more effective for both defense and prosecution. The authors concluded that the present system, in which the prosecution or plaintiff presents first and the defendant second, is most fair to the defense (that is, gives the defense the greatest opportunity to be found not guilty), especially when both sides present their cases in climactic orders.

Thibaut, Walker, and Lind (1972) attempted to assess differences between adversary and inquisitorial presentation of evidence in relation to trial outcome. In an adversary presentation, evidence is offered by two opposing sides; in the inquisitorial system, the judge assumes a more active role and asks questions for both sides. Three independent variables were manipulated in this study: (a) adversary versus inquisitorial presentation (in the former, two different people presented the prosecution and defense evidence, whereas in the latter, one person presented all of the evidence); (b) biased versus unbiased subjects (half of the subjects were led to believe that the defendant was guilty, and the other half were given no expectation; and (c) order of presentation of the evidence (defense first or prosecution first). The same case and repeated measures procedure was employed as in Walker et al. (1972).

The data were based on the responses of 86 subjects, presumably undergraduates. It was found that (a) evidence presented second had a stronger effect on subjects' verdicts, (b) subjects provided with a pretrial bias towards guilt believed the defendant was more guilty than those who were unbiased, and (c) the inquisitorial method of presentation produced more extreme beliefs in the defendant's guilt, but only among the biased subjects.

In a complex series of studies, Calder, Insko, and Yandell (1974) investigated the relationship between the number of defense and prosecution arguments and mock jurors' perceptions of the defendant's guilt. In four separate experiments, 795 subjects acted as jury members. The data supported the hypothesis that evaluation of guilt would be related to the number of defense and prosecution arguments put forward. For example, subjects who read one defense argument and four prosecution arguments assigned a greater degree of guilt to the defendant than did subjects who read four defense arguments and one prosecution argument.

Despite the problems associated with these studies due to demand characteristics inherent in their repeated measures designs,[3] they do suggest that the order and number of defense and prosecution arguments are important factors in the determination of guilt and that the adversary system is less likely to enhance jurors' biases than the inquisitorial system. It should be remembered, however, that none of these studies employed the elaborate design of the real courtroom, in which two opposing attorneys can interrogate the same witness in succession. Similarly, they did not allow subjects to deliberate in groups to reach verdicts. Clearly the conditions of the studies fell far short of the intercourse and exchange found in a real trial.

Definitions of Guilt

Studies in this section deal with legal and lay conceptions of the meaning of guilt in civil and criminal trials and with the definition of not guilty by reason of insanity. In a study on the meaning of guilt, Simon and

Mahan (1971) presented 69 real jurors and 88 students with a tape recording of a murder trial. Following the tape recording and prior to small group deliberations, half of the subjects were asked to render verdicts and then make probability estimates that the defendant had committed the crime. The remaining subjects made the same decisions in reverse order. At the conclusion of the group deliberations, each group rendered verdicts and made probability estimates in one of the two possible orders of questions. Following the group decisions, all subjects again individually made both decisions in either of the two possible orders.

Predeliberation verdicts showed that the students were more likely to find the defendant not guilty than were the jurors. As expected, subjects who voted guilty were more likely to estimate that the defendant had actually committed the crime. Group verdicts again showed that the students were more lenient. Of the 14 student juries, 11 acquitted and 3 hung, but of the 10 juror juries, 5 acquitted, 4 hung, and 1 convicted. The final individual verdicts indicated that the discussion moved both students and jurors into a stronger prodefendant position than they had held in predeliberation verdicts. The authors also reported that subjects who made probability estimates first tended to render more not guilty verdicts both as individuals and groups.

In a second part of the study, jurors and judges responded to questionnaires about the

---

[3] By having subjects respond to the same questions following the introduction of new information, the intended treatment differences would, in all likelihood, become apparent to subjects. This would suggest to them that they ought to be responsive to these variations, since the experimenter thought them important enough to be included, and lead them to form hypotheses as to the nature of the intended effects. As Greenwald (1976) has noted, the cues that repeated measures are likely to induce often cause subjects to respond to perceived hypotheses rather than to the treatments themselves. The use of these decisions should be limited to those situations in which treatment differences are adequately camouflaged (which does not seem to be the case here) or those in which the apparent contrast is desired (e.g., when similar contrasts occur in real world situations).

meanings of "reasonable doubt" (the criterion in a criminal trial) and "preponderance of evidence" (the criterion in a civil trial), in terms of probability of the crime having been committed by the defendant. For "reasonable doubt" the mean probability necessary for conviction was .89 for judges and students and .79 for the jurors. For "preponderance of evidence" the mean probability necessary for conviction was .61 for judges and .75 for both students and jurors, indicating that judges make a much sharper distinction between civil and criminal convictions than do either students or jurors.

The three groups of respondents were also asked about the probability necessary for conviction for 14 different types of crimes. The judges showed the least range in probabilities over the 14 crimes, with median scores ranging from .92 for murder to .87 for petty larceny. For jurors, probability estimates ranged from .95 for murder to .75 for petty larceny, and for the students, medians ranged from .93 for murder to .79 for petty larceny. For each offense the students' probability estimates were more similar to the judges' than were the jurors'. No statistical analyses were reported for these data. If these results are due to a genuine difference in judges' and jurors' interpretations of legal phrases, it seems important that judges become aware of this difference and insure that juries are given a more concrete criterion than "reasonable doubt" or "preponderance of evidence" upon which to base their verdicts.

In addition to the problem of differences between judges' and juries' criteria for conviction, there are often battles within the courts about which definition of a crime should be applied. Most notable is the debate over the M'Naghten and Durham rules in determining judgments of "not guilty by reason of insanity." The M'Naghten rule, which is the older and more widely used, stipulates that if the defendant could distinguish right from wrong at the time of the crime, then he should not be found not guilty by reason of insanity. The Durham rule, which is reputed to be more psychologically enlightened, says that if the crime is the product of a mental disturbance, regardless of the defendant's ability to distinguish right from wrong, he should be found not guilty by reason of insanity (Simon, 1967). It should be added that the verdict of not guilty by reason of insanity means that the defendant must be institutionalized until authorities deem that he is sane. This procedure has recently come under public criticism by Thomas Szasz, Ralph Nader, and others.

Simon (1967) investigated juries' reactions to these two criteria. Jurors were drawn from real jury pools and were given the Durham (26 juries), M'Naghten (20 juries) or no (22 juries) instructions on the legal meaning of insanity. Juries then listened to a tape recording of an incest trial and deliberated their verdicts. Individual predeliberation verdicts indicated that 36% of the Durham jurors, 34% of the uninstructed jurors, and 24% of the M'Naghten jurors rendered a not guilty by reason of insanity verdict. Following the jury deliberations, 19% of the Durham juries, 18% of the uninstructed juries, and none of the M'Naghten juries voted not guilty by reason of insanity, and 23%, 18%, and 5%, respectively, were hung. Clearly, the M'Naghten juries were more likely to vote guilty than either the Durham or uninstructed juries. Because of the similar responses of the uninstructed and Durham juries, Simon concluded that the Durham rule was closer to the lay public's understanding of insanity than was the M'Naghten rule. In addition the data seem to indicate that although the jurors' conceptions of the not guilty by reason of insanity verdict differed from that of the M'Naghten rule, they were able to follow it when so instructed.

Green (1967), in a study reported earlier, also investigated the effect of different types of instructions. Jurors were given either simple or complicated instructions. The results indicated that jurors' biases were more extreme under the complicated instructions, that is, for complex instructions, subjects whose personal characteristics were similar to the plaintiff's were more proplaintiff, and subjects who were not similar were more prodefendant. Green suggested that the complicated nature of the instructions allowed individuals to easily express their biases through rationalization. It is not clear, however, why the same results could not have been obtained under the more simple, less directive, short instructions.

In summary, data gathered by Simon and Mahan (1971) suggest that jurors and judges make different estimates of the probability of guilt necessary for conviction. Simon (1967) found that guilty verdicts are more likely to be returned by jurors deliberating under M'Naghten than under Durham instructions. In addition, Simon's data suggest that although jurors' conceptions of the not guilty by reason of insanity verdict differ from that of the M'Naghten rule, they are still able to follow this rule when instructed to do so. Finally, Green's data suggest that jurors are more biased under complicated instructions (which they might not understand) than under simple instructions.

Number of Jurors and Decision Rules

In many states, definitions of the number of jurors constituting a jury and of the decision rule (that is, the type of agreement necessary for a verdict to be valid) have been changing (Zeisel, 1971). Changes from 12 to 9 or 6 persons and from unanimity to two-thirds majority rules have fostered much debate and some research. The Supreme Court's position, as expressed in the case of Williams versus Florida (1972), was that given the same evidence, there would be no difference between the verdicts of 6- and 12-member juries. Zeisel and Diamond (1974) critically reviewed the studies upon which the Supreme Court decision was based, concluding that the Court had based its decision on data whose conclusions were laden with artifact.

Saks and Ostrom (Note 9) presented a mathematical probability model to explain the effects of jury size and decision rule changes on verdicts. They argued that it would be easier for small juries to reach a decision, because there are fewer members to convince of the validity of the majority opinion. Similarly, decision rules that do not require unanimity are less likely to result in hung juries than are rules that require all members to agree. The authors suggested that the use of the probability model, as opposed to a reli-

ance on judicial discretion, would result in a more accurate recognition of the impact that the number of jurors and the decision rule will have on verdicts. Additional theoretical models are available to account for differences in verdicts due to the number of jurors and to decision rules (Friedman, 1972; Gelfand & Solomon, 1973, 1974).

Gordon (1968) found no difference in the verdicts of 6-, 9-, and 12-person mock juries that deliberated under a unanimity rule. Similarly, Davis, Kerr, Atkin, Holt, and Meek (1975) studied the decision processes of 6- and 12-person juries deliberating a rape case under unanimous and two-thirds majority rules. A group of 221 female and 499 male undergraduates answered a voir dire, listened to a tape of the case, and made predeliberation, group, and postdeliberation verdicts. In answering the voir dire, males were more likely to indicate that rape is a difficult crime to commit than were females. In accord with this difference, males were also more likely than females to acquit the defendant on both the pre- and postdeliberation verdicts. Twenty-two percent of the pre-deliberation verdicts, none of the group verdicts, and 14% of the postdeliberation verdicts were for conviction. Obviously, neither the size of the jury nor the decision rule affected the groups' verdicts. Postexperimental questionnaires indicated that subjects in the unanimity condition who believed the defendant was guilty were persuaded by the majority to vote not guilty. These data concur with Kalven and Zeisel's (1966) findings that in most cases, the majority opinion becomes a verdict.

Valenti and Downing (1975) noted the failure of the studies by Gordon (1968) and Davis et al. (1975) to find effects for group size and suggested that the evidence was such that most subjects thought the defendant innocent, so that the size of the group became irrelevant. In tying the size of the jury to trial outcome, Valenti and Downing (1975) cited Asch's (1953) conformity studies, as applied by Zeisel (1971) to the judiciary process. Asch found that one person who is faced with a unanimous contradictory group of three or more members is·more likely to go along with the group than is one who has a comrade in dissent. In accordance with Asch's findings, Zeisel suggested that it is not so much the proportion of jurors in the minority as their number that is important to the trial outcome. Valenti and Downing hypothesized that if the evidence were highly incriminating it would be to the defendant's advantage to have a 12-member jury, whereas if the evidence were weak it would be to the defendant's advantage to have a 6-member jury. In the former case, a jury of 12 would maximize the probability that more than one of its members would think the defendant not guilty and hold out for a hung jury; in the latter case, a jury of 6 would minimize the number of jurors who thought the defendant guilty and increase the probability of a not guilty verdict.

In their study, the authors assigned 360 male and female undergraduates to 6- or 12-member juries, who then listened to either a highly incriminating or a mildly incriminating version of the Thibaut et al. (1972) fight case. After hearing the case, subjects rendered individual first ballot verdicts and then deliberated amongst themselves to reach a group verdict. After the groups had decided on verdicts, subjects were asked to indicate if they agreed with the group's decision. The 6-person juries in the highly incriminating condition rendered significantly more guilty verdicts than did juries in any of the other three conditions. Twelve-person juries were more likely to report being hung than their six-person counterparts. The larger groups also took more deliberation time, probably because they were more likely to be hung. Clearly the results indicate that when evidence is strong, it is to the defendant's advantage to have a 12-person jury.

Kerr, Atkin, Stasser, Meek, Holt, and Davis (1976) employed six-member mock juries and manipulated the assigned decision rule (unanimous or majority rule) and the definition of reasonable doubt (any doubt at all—stringent, substantial doubt—lax, or no definition of reasonable doubt). The 359 male and 286 female undergraduate subjects were shown an audio- and videotape of testimony, attorneys' summaries, and the judges' instructions in a rape case that was designed to

maximize juror disagreement. Jurors were asked for predeliberation, group, and postdeliberation verdicts of guilty, not guilty, or hung (no opinion). Thirty minutes were allowed for their group deliberations. In addition to a verdict, the groups were also asked to indicate the probability that the defendant was guilty. Following the postdeliberation verdicts, jurors were asked about their degree of satisfaction with the deliberation and verdict.

The only significant effect on the predeliberation verdicts was the reasonable doubt definition: The largest proportion of guilty verdicts were returned in the lax condition, followed by the defined and stringent conditions. The undefined condition produced more jurors who were unable to reach an opinion than did the other two conditions. Also, females rendered more guilty verdicts than males. For groups the decision rule was significant, with more guilty verdicts in the majority condition; however, when the frequency of hung juries (which was greatest in the unanimous condition) was controlled for, there was no significant effect attributable to the decision rule. The definition of reasonable doubt seemed to have an effect only in the majority decision conditions: There was a trend for more hung juries in the undefined than defined conditions. Finally, there were no significant differences among the treatments in the judgments of the probability of the defendants' guilt. In general, a 5/6 majority rule was able to predict the groups' verdicts, that is, when five of the six group members were in initial agreement, the jury's verdict concurred with that of the majority.

As in earlier studies, the majority rule juries took less time and fewer polls to reach their verdict. Postdeliberation data paralleled the predeliberation verdicts, with subjects being more likely to think the defendant guilty after deliberation than before and also assigning more lenient sentences after than before. In addition, jurors who were minority members of majority rule juries were most likely to indicate that they were unable to make their opinions heard.

The results of this study again highlight the differences in verdicts and the nature of discussion produced by majority versus unanimous decision rules. They also suggest the need for standardization of the meaning of reasonable doubt in judges' instructions. The fact that juries, regardless of their condition, attributed the same probability of guilt to the defendant and rendered verdicts according to their assigned definitions of doubt indicates that they were able to follow the instructions they were given.

In summary, studies presented in this section indicate that when the evidence is weak the verdicts of 6- and 12-person juries tend to be equal, and that juries deliberating under a decision rule of unanimity are more likely to be hung than those assigned a majority rule. Further, these studies appear contrary to the Supreme Court ruling of 1972, which indicated that 6- and 12-person juries would yield equivalent outcomes. When incriminating evidence is strong it is to the defendant's advantage to have a 12-person jury.

Conclusion

What Next?

It is possible to conceive of an almost infinite number of variable combinations that could be investigated in the interest of studying "jury behavior." However, unless it is also possible to demonstrate that the data gathered in the laboratory are at least to some extent generalizable to real juries, these studies will remain without much practical value or external validity. For example, Izzett and Leginski (1974) and Myers and Kaplan (1976) have already demonstrated the importance of including group discussion as part of the mock jury paradigm. Recent efforts by Diamond and Zeisel (1974) and Kerr et al. (Note 1) have attempted to address the overwhelming problem caused by mock jurors' knowledge that their decisions will have no meaningful effect on anyone's life. Diamond and Zeisel compared the verdicts of three different types of juries for 10 real trials. One type of jury was chosen by attorneys, the second type of jury was composed of potential jurors who had been rejected by one or the other attorney (challenged jury: the jurors did not know

which side had rejected them), and the third type was chosen at random (English jury). The three types of juries were treated identically, with the following exceptions: The real juries knew their verdict would decide the cases, and only they were seated in the jury box. The two other kinds of juries knew their verdicts would not count; they were asked for predeliberation verdicts and had their deliberations recorded.

Half of the real juries returned guilty verdicts, whereas all 10 of the English and 8 of the 10 challenged juries voted guilty. The judge in each case was asked for his verdict, and he voted guilty in 9 of the 10 cases. The authors concluded that because the challenged and English juries knew that their verdicts were mock, they assumed a different standard of reasonable doubt. It seems at least as plausible to suggest (especially since these two types of juries produced verdicts more similar to the judges' than to those of the real juries) that the jury selection process was also responsible for the differences in verdicts.

Kerr et al. (Note 1) compared the responses of six-person mock juries and six-person juries who were told that their collective verdicts would determine the outcome of the discipline trial of a college student. A total of 129 male and 114 female undergraduates participated in the study. The subjects were given transcripts of the case to read and were then asked for predeliberation, group, and postdeliberation verdicts (21 of the subjects made only individual decisions, which they were told would break a tie if such occurred in the real juries).

No significant differences were found between the predeliberation verdicts of the mock and real jurors; further, males were more likely to think the defendant guilty than were females. Similarly, the group verdicts of the mock and real jurors did not differ. Postdeliberation judgments revealed that role was important only in the determination of punishment; real jurors (and also females) were more lenient. Despite the overwhelming similarity between the mock and real jurors, the importance of role cannot be ruled out altogether, because the real jurors knew that their verdicts would be only one of several that would be used to determine the defendant's fate. Thus there was ample room for diffusion of responsibility, possibly making real jurors less lenient than they would have been had they alone been deciding the defendant's fate. In addition, of the 18 real juries, none convicted, 10 acquitted, and 8 hung, whereas of the 20 mock juries, 1 convicted, 11 acquitted, and 8 hung. It seems reasonable that a more complete test of the comparability of real and mock juries would use a case slanted less toward either extreme.

In spite of the questions that remain, these studies indicate the direction that jury research must take before its results can be applied to the courts.

However, some degree of generalizability seems cautiously appropriate. It appears that extraevidential factors, such as defendant, victim, and juror characteristics, trial procedures, and so forth, can influence the severity of verdicts rendered by individual jurors. However, the role of these variables in group decisions remains to be experimentally demonstrated, since the studies that have employed groups of interacting jurors have not generally been concerned with these factors. The well-established literature on group versus individual differences in decision making suggests this line of research as a fruitful and necessary next step.

Research reported in the last section of this review is readily applicable to the judiciary. Evidence was presented implying that many procedural differences in courtroom methods have important ramifications for juridic decisions, and consequently, for the realization of justice. These studies suggest, as a beginning, a need for accurately communicating the meaning of guilt to jurors, for judges to be aware of the effect of limiting jurors' decision alternatives, and for courts to recognize meaningful differences in trial outcomes that can result from changes in jury size. Given the rather large variability of trial procedures from state to state, from court to court, and ultimately, from case to case, full investigation of these issues, with an eye toward application, would serve a crucial role.

It seems obvious that a good deal more investigation is necessary for effective and beneficial implementation of the reforms these studies imply. Much of the cited research suffers from methodological and sampling problems, making psychologists and legal professionals justifiably skeptical. However, an additional major frustration to the applied researcher in this area is the preference of the judiciary for the status quo (Simon & Mahan, 1971). It seems likely that if the mundane realism of future studies is increased and if social scientists and legal experts make a greater attempt at working conjointly, then legal practitioners could understand and develop methods of compensating for unwanted biases. Such research will facilitate the development of legal methods that in practice are consistent with their original underlying philosophies and will bring us closer to the ideal of blind justice.

Reference Notes

1. Kerr, N., Nerenz, D., & Herrick, D. *Role playing and the study of jury behavior.* Manuscript submitted for publication, 1976.

2. Zuckerman, M., & Gerbasi, K. C. *Belief in a just world and derogation of victims.* Unpublished manuscript, University of Rochester, 1973.

3. Gerbasi, K. C., & Zuckerman, M. *An experimental investigation of jury biasing factors.* Paper presented at Eastern Psychological Association Convention, New York, 1975.

4. Zuckerman, M., & Gerbasi, K. C. *Belief in internal control or belief in a just world: A reinterpretation of behavioral and attitudinal correlates of the I–E scale.* Unpublished manuscript, University of Rochester, 1975.

5. Shaver, P. *Lessons from the Harrisburg conspiracy trial.* Paper presented at American Psychological Association Convention, Montreal, September 1973.

6. Gould, R., & Gould, R. *Jury selection: Pentagon papers trial.* Manuscript submitted for publication, 1974.

7. Sigall, H., & Landy, D. *Effects of a defendant's character and suffering on juridic judgment: A replication and clarification.* Unpublished manuscript, University of Maryland, 1972.

8. Archer, R., & Aderman, D. *Empathy in the courtroom: The effect of an emotional appeal on the judgments of simulated jurors.* Unpublished manuscript, Duke University, 1974.

9. Saks, M., & Ostrom, T. Laws of probability versus the laws of the land: The possible effects of jury size and decision rules on verdicts. *Social Psychology Bulletin,* Ohio State University, 72-6, 1972.

References

Asch, S. Effects of group pressure upon the modification and distortion of judgments. In D. Cartwright & A. Zander (Eds.), Group Dynamics. Evanston, Ill.: Row, Peterson, 1953.

Austin, W., Walster, E., & Utne, M. Equity and the law: The effect of a harmdoer's "suffering in the act" on liking and assigned punishment. In L. Berkowitz & E. Walster (Eds.), Advances in Experimental Social Psychology. New York: Academic Press, 1976.

Berg, K., & Vidmar, N. Authoritarianism and recall of evidence about criminal behavior. Journal of Research in Personality, 1975, 9, 147–157.

Bermant, G. The notion of conspiracy is not tasty to Americans. Psychology Today, May 1975, pp. 60–67.

Bieri, J., Orcutt, B., & Leaman, R. Anchoring effects in sequential clinical judgments. Journal of Abnormal and Social Psychology, 1963, 57, 616–623.

Boehm, V. Mr. Prejudice, Miss Sympathy and the authoritarian personality: an application of psychological measuring to the problem of jury bias. Wisconsin Law Review, 1968, 734–750.

Brooks, W., & Doob, A. Justice and the jury. Journal of Social Issues, 1975, 31(3), 171–182.

Byrne, D., & Lambreth, J. The effect of erotic stimuli on sex arousal, evaluative responses, and subsequent behavior. Technical Reports of the Commission on Obscenity and Pornography (Vol. 8). Washington, D. C.: U.S. Government Printing Office, 1971.

Calder, B., Insko, C., & Yandell, B. The relation of cognitive and memorial processes to persuasion in a simulated jury trial. Journal of Applied Social Psychology, 1974, 4, 62–93.

Centers, R., Shomer, R., & Rodriques, A. A field experiment in interpersonal persuasion using authoritative influence. Journal of Personality, 1970, 38, 392–403.

Davis, J., Kerr, N., Atkin, R., Holt, R., & Meek, D. The decision processes of 6- and 12-person mock juries assigned unanimous and two-thirds majority rules. Journal of Personality and Social Psychology, 1975, 32, 1–14.

DeJong, W., Morris, W., & Hastorf, A. Effect of an escaped accomplice on the punishment assigned to a criminal defendant. Journal of Personality and Social Psychology, 1976, 33, 192–198.

Diamond, S., & Zeisel, H. A courtroom experiment on juror selection and decision-making. Personality and Social Psychology Bulletin, 1974, 1(1), 276–277.

Dowdle, M., Gillen, H., & Miller, A. Integration and attribution theories as predictors of sentencing by a simulated jury. Personality and Social Psychology Bulletin, 1974, 1(1), 270–272.

Erlanger, H. Jury research in America: Its past and future. Law and Society Review, 1970, 4, 345–370.

Friedman, H. Trial by jury: Criteria for convictions, jury size and Type I and Type II errors. The American Statistician, 1972, 26, 21–23.

Gelfand, A., & Solomon, H. A study of Poisson's models for jury verdicts in criminal and civil trials. Journal of the American Statistical Association, 1973, 68, 271–278.

Gelfand, A., & Solomon, H. Modeling jury verdicts in the American legal system. Journal of the American Statistical Association, 1974, 69, 32–37.

Gordon, R. A study in forensic psychology: Petit jury verdicts as a function of jury size. Dissertation Abstracts, 1968, 29, 1161b.

Green, E. The reasonable man: Legal fiction or psychosocial reality? Law and Society Review, 1967, 2, 241–257.

Greenwald, A. G. Within-subjects designs: To use or not to use? Psychological Bulletin, 1976, 83, 314–320.

Hawkins, C. Interaction rates of jurors aligned in factions. American Sociological Review, 1962, 27, 689–691.

Hoiberg, B., & Stires, L. The effect of several types of pre-trial publicity on the guilt attributions of simulated jurors. Journal of Applied Social Psychology, 1973, 3, 267–275.

Izzett, R., & Leginski, W. Group discussion and the influence of defendant characteristics in a simulated jury setting. Journal of Social Psychology, 1974, 93, 271–279.

James, R. Status and competence of jurors. American Journal of Sociology, 1959, 64, 563–570.

Jones, C., & Aronson, E. Attribution of fault to a rape victim as a function of respectability of the victim. Journal of Personality and Social Psychology, 1973, 26, 415–419.

Jones, E., & Goethals, G. Order effects in impression formation: attribution context and the nature of the entity. In E. E. Jones et al. (Eds.), Attribution: Perceiving the Causes of Behavior. Morristown, N.J.: General Learning Press, 1971.

Jurow, G. New data on the effect of a death qualified jury on the guilt determination process. Harvard Law Review, 1971, 84, 567–611.

Kadish, M., & Kadish, S. The institutionalization of conflict: jury acquittals. Journal of Social Issues, 1971, 27(2), 199–218.

Kahn, J. Picking peers: Social scientists' role in selection of juries sparks legal debate. Wall Street Journal, August 12, 1974, pp. 1, 13.

Kalven, H., & Zeisel, H. The American Jury. Chicago: University of Chicago Press, 1966.

Kaplan, M., & Kemmerick, G. Juror judgment as information integration: Combining evidential and nonevidential information. Journal of Personality and Social Psychology, 1974, 30, 493–499.

Kaplan, K., & Simon, R. Latitude and severity of sentencing options, race of the victim and decisions of simulated jurors: Some issues arising from the Algiers Motel trial. Law and Society Review, 1972, 7, 87–98.

Katz, L. Presentation of a confidence interval estimate as evidence in a legal proceeding. The American Statistician, 1975, 29(4), 138–142.

Kerr, N., Atkin, R., Stasser, G., Meek, D., Holt, R., & Davis, J. Guilt beyond a reasonable doubt: Effects of concept definition and assigned rule on the judgments of mock jurors. Journal of Personality and Social Psychology, 1976, 34, 282–294.

Kiesler, C., & Kiesler, S. *Conformity.* Reading, Mass.: Addison-Wesley, 1970.

Landy, D., & Aronson, E. The influence of the character of the criminal and his victim on the decisions of simulated jurors. *Journal of Experimental Social Psychology,* 1969, *5,* 141–152.

Larntz, K. Reanalysis of Vidmar's data on the effects of decision alternatives on verdicts of simulated jurors. *Journal of Personality and Social Psychology,* 1975, *31,* 123–125.

Lawson, R. Order of presentation as a factor in jury persuasion. *Kentucky Law Journal,* 1968, *56,* 523–555.

Lerner, M. The desire for justice and reactions to victims. In J. Macaulay, & L. Berkowitz (Eds.), *Altruism and Helping Behavior.* New York: Academic Press, 1970.

Marston, W. Studies in testimony. In R. Simon (Ed.), *The Sociology of Law.* San Francisco: Chandler, 1968.

Mitchell, H., & Byrne, D. The defendant's dilemma: Effects of jurors' attitudes and authoritarianism on judicial decisions. *Journal of Personality and Social Psychology,* 1973, *25,* 123–129.

Myers, D., & Kaplan, M. Group-induced polarization in simulated juries. *Personality and Social Psychology Bulletin,* 1976, *2,* 63–66.

Nemeth, C., & Sosis, R. A simulated jury study: Characteristics of defendant and the jurors. *Journal of Social Psychology,* 1973, *90,* 221–229.

Pepitone, A., & DiNubile, M. Contrast effects in judgments of crime severity and the punishment of criminal violators. *Journal of Personality and Social Psychology,* 1976, *33,* 448–459.

Phares, E., & Wilson, K. Responsibility attribution: Role of outcome severity, situational ambiguity, and internal–external control. *Journal of Personality,* 1972, *40,* 392–406.

Reed, J. Jury deliberations, voting and verdict trends. *Southwest Social Science Quarterly,* 1965, *45,* 361–370.

Robinson, W. Bias, probability and trial by jury. *American Sociological Review,* 1950, *15,* 73–78.

Rose, A., & Prell, A. Does the punishment fit the crime? A study in social valuation. *American Journal of Sociology,* 1955, *61,* 247–259.

Rotter, J. B. Generalized expectancies for internal versus external control of reinforcement. *Psychological Monographs,* 1966, *80*(1, Whole No. 609).

Rubin, Z., & Peplau, A. Belief in a just world and reactions to another's lot: A study of participants in the national draft lottery. *Journal of Social Issues,* 1973, *29* (4), 73–93.

Rubin, Z., & Peplau, A. Who believes in a just world? *Journal of Social Issues,* 1975, *31* (3), 65–90.

Sanford, F., & Older, H. *A short authoritarian equalitarian scale.* Philadelphia: Institute for Research in Human Relations, 1950.

Schulman, J., Shaver, P., Colman, R., Emrich, B., & Christie, R. Recipe for a jury. *Psychology Today,* May, 1973, pp. 37–44; 77–84.

Sigall, H., & Ostrove, N. Beautiful but dangerous: Effects of offender attractiveness and nature of the crime on juridic judgment. *Journal of Personality and Social Psychology,* 1975, *31,* 410–414.

Simon, R. *The Jury and the Defense of Insanity.* Boston: Little, Brown, 1967.

Simon, R. The effects of newspapers on the verdicts of potential jurors. In R. Simon (Ed.), *The Sociology of Law.* San Francisco: Chandler, 1968.

Simon, R., & Mahan, L. Quantifying burdens of proof. *Law and Society Review,* 1971, *5,* 319–330.

Sosis, R. Internal–external control and the perception of responsibility of another for an accident. *Journal of Personality and Social Psychology,* 1974, *30,* 393–399.

Stone, V. A primacy effect in decision-making by jurors. *The Journal of Communication,* 1969, *19,* 239–247.

Strodtbeck, F., James, R., & Hawkins, C. Social status in jury deliberations. *American Sociological Review,* 1957, *22,* 713–718.

Strodtbeck, F., & Mann, R. Sex role differentiation in jury deliberations. *Sociometry,* 1956, *19,* 3–11.

Sue, S., Smith, R., & Caldwell, C. Effects of inadmissible evidence on the decisions of simulated jurors: a moral dilemma. *Journal of Applied Social Psychology,* in press.

Thibaut, J., Walker, L., & Lind, E. A. Adversary presentation and bias in legal decision making. *Harvard Law Review,* 1972, *86,* 386–401.

Valenti, A., & Downing, L. Differential effects of jury size on verdicts following deliberations as a function of the apparent guilt of a defendant. *Journal of Personality and Social Psychology,* 1975, *32,* 655–663.

Vidmar, N. Effects of decision alternatives on the verdicts and social perceptions of simulated jurors. *Journal of Personality and Social Psychology,* 1972, *22,* 211–218.

Walker, L., Thibaut, J., & Andreoli, V. Order of presentation at trial. *Yale Law Journal,* 1972, *82,* 216–226.

Weld, H., & Danzig, A. A study of the way in which a verdict is reached by a jury. In R. Simon (Ed.), *The Sociology of Law.* San Francisco: Chandler, 1968.

Williams versus Florida. *Supreme Court Reporter,* 1972, *92,* 1628–1653.

Wolfgang, M., & Reidel, M. Race and the death penalty. *Annals of the Academy of Political and Social Science,* 1973, *407,* 119–133.

Woodward, J. A scientific attempt to provide evidence for a decision on change of venue. *American Sociological Review,* 1952, *17,* 447–452.

Zeisel, H. . . . And then there were none: The diminution of the federal jury. *University of Chicago Law Review,* 1971, *38,* 710–724.

Zeisel, H., & Diamond, S. "Convincing empirical evidence" on the six member jury. *University of Chicago Law Review,* 1974, *41,* 281–295.

Received December 2, 1975 ∎

A Typology of Jury Research and Discussion of the Structural Correlates of Jury Decisionmaking

Robert T. Roper*

This introductory note performs three tasks: (1) It develops a typology of jury research by dividing the research according to whether it focuses on dependent variables–factors representing various aspects of jury and juror behavior–or on the independent variables that potentially explain that behavior; (2) it locates the other articles in this special issue within the typology; and (3) it assesses the literature on the impact of jury size and unanimity requirements. The note concludes by suggesting that despite a significant amount of previous work by researchers, a number of important questions concerning the American jury cannot at present be reliably answered.

Introduction

For almost two hundred years the American jury has served as a cornerstone of the American legal system. Although jury verdicts represent only a small portion of total dispositions in civil and criminal cases in the state courts (Flango and Roper, 1983; National Center for State Courts, 1986), they serve several important functions in the administration of justice. Most basically, juries resolve disputes that litigants are unable to settle themselves; in this sense juries maintain social order and enhance the legitimacy of the courts and, subsequently, the entire political system. The existence of a jury system, however, also serves notice on all potential litigants that failure to resolve conflicts can result in their ultimate resolution being made by others. Some have argued that this "threat" produces a considerable amount of the settlement activity evidenced in civil litigation (see, e.g., Beiser, 1975).[1]

Juries also perform political functions, as reflected in the continuing efforts of judges, court administrators, and legislators to make juries representative of the population. In perhaps their most political (and

---

*Senior Staff Associate, National Center for State Courts.

1. Summary or "advisory" juries are sometimes viewed as yet another method for inducing settlement activity (Lambros, 1986) since they provide parties with a flavor of what might happen in a full-scale trial.

THE JUSTICE SYSTEM JOURNAL, Volume 11, Number 1, 1986

5

controversial) role, juries serve to protect individuals against overzealous legislators and prosecutors through statute nullification—a practice "tantamount to pure judicial legislation" (Becker *et al.*, 1965). In all their various roles lay juries provide one of the last means of direct, efficacious citizen participation in governmental decisionmaking.

Despite their central importance in the American legal system, juries are utilized in only a few countries throughout the world, and debate over their merits even in the United States has often been acrimonious. Most recently, it has been asserted that capricious and unreasonable decisions of juries have created a "crisis" in the insurance industry. This alleged crisis has led to proposals in state legislatures and the U.S. Congress to limit the decisional options of juries, most frequently by limiting the size of monetary awards for particular types of injuries. It should be noted, however, that these sentiments are not universally held. A recent poll published in the *National Law Journal* (Kaplan, 1986) attributes the litigation crisis to groups other than juries. Furthermore, there remains strong support among both scholars and court practitioners for the jury as an institution. For example, at the 1986 Warren Conference on the American Civil Jury at Harvard University, support for the jury among the conferees was virtually unanimous.[2]

The current debate over the jury system necessitates an examination of how juries presently function in the American legal system. The research in this field assumes a variety of forms, ranging from journalistic accounts of selected jury trials (e.g. DiPerna, 1984) to assessments of various dimensions of the institution using historical, anecdotal and case law evidence (e.g. Hans and Vidmar, 1986) to rigorous empirical research on various aspects of the jury (e.g. Kerr and Bray, 1982). This special issue of *The Justice System Journal* provides a critical summary of much of this literature and helps us assess "the state of the art" in jury research. This introductory note first sets out a typology of the issues examined by jury researchers. It then summarizes and evaluates the major research on how the structure of the jury system affects its operation and output.

Developing a Typology of Jury Research

While there may be a variety of ways to organize the literature on juries, the most straightforward has much to commend it. All research on juries attempts to describe or explain particular aspects of jury or juror behavior, usually in terms of one or more explanatory factors. In scientific parlance,

2. *Editor's note:* The role of the jury in the "litigation crisis" will be explored later this year in a special issue of *The Justice System Journal* dealing with trends in civil litigation.

the research describes the *dependent variable* of jury behavior, and often attempts to explain this behavior in terms of one or more *independent variables*. This rudimentary distinction between dependent and independent variables serves as the organizing concept of this review.

The relevant literature in the field is discussed by all the authors in this special issue and, where appropriate, those articles will be cited. The principal independent variable to be discussed in this note deals with the organization and structure of the jury—aspects of juries established primarily by legal standards that mandate jury size and the rule (unanimity or some lesser majority) by which juries reach their decisions. Attention will be paid to the impact of these factors on such dependent variables as verdict, criminal sentencing, and size of civil awards. Extra-legal factors that affect jury behavior, such as racial or social characteristics of jurors, are examined in Marilyn Ford's contribution in this issue; independent variables that concern psychological aspects of jurors are assessed by Valerie Hans; Thomas and Janice Munsterman discuss research on jury representativeness.

Identifying the dependent variables. The first task of any research project is to describe the observation to be explained. Observations about American juries can be classified into at least four groups:

- The outcome of the jury's deliberations
- The behavior of the jury
- Factors related to jury administration and management
- Juror attitudes toward jury service

Without question, the outcome of the jury's deliberations has been the most studied of the dependent variables. This variable has at least three research components: the verdict, the sentence in criminal cases, and the size of the awards in civil cases.

Although jury outcome may be the most studied of the dependent variables, social psychologists are beginning to concentrate on the process through which those outcomes and decisions are reached. The study of outcome alone is increasingly recognized as problematic because researchers and policy makers are unsure of the substantive meaning or policy relevance of observed variance in the decisional output of juries. For example, knowing that twelve-member juries are more likely to convict criminal defendants than six-member juries tells policy makers nothing about the structure that best avoids "judicial error," (i.e. convicting an innocent suspect or acquitting a guilty suspect). One technique for identifying potential problems in the outcomes of jury deliberations is to compare the decisions of judges and juries in similar cases. Several studies

7

have researched this problem of inconsistency; among them is the classic jury study of Kalven and Zeisel (1971) (see also Levine, 1983; Roper and Flango, 1983).

Realizing the limitations of studying outcome alone, jury researchers began to evaluate the processes used to reach verdicts, the assumption being that certain identifiable characteristics of the process are preferred to others. Some of the studied processes include the quality of the deliberations, group interaction and coalition formation, and the role of leadership in jury decisionmaking.

The third major category of dependent variables concerns the efficient administration of justice; the variables studied in this context are various juror management procedures. The basic concern in this area of research is to minimize the cost of jury trials in terms of time and money for the court, the litigants, and the jurors. This area—despite its central importance to court administration—has received relatively little attention in the social science literature.

The fourth category involves public attitudes toward jury service. This area is significant for a variety of reasons. Some observers have suggested that jury service is one of the few modes of entry for lay persons into the judicial process, and that the manner in which such individuals are treated and see others treated may influence their support for the legal system in general (see, e.g., Allen, 1977; Coe, 1976; Richert, 1977; Simon, 1975).

Identifying the Independent Variables. There is a much wider range of variables that serve as explanatory, or independent variables, than are typically examined as dependent variables. This larger set of factors held to influence jury behavior can be grouped into the following four categories:

- Juror selection methods
- Legal factors
- Non- or extra-legal factors
- Organizational and structural factors

The first of these categories, juror selection methods, has three basic dimensions: the development and use of juror source lists, the impact of exemptions, and the voir dire. All of these factors are important because they affect the composition and representativeness of the juries, dimensions that are believed to affect case outcome. For example, it is often argued that different types of jurors are drawn from different source lists (e.g., individuals interested in politics are arguably more in evidence on voter registration lists than on drivers license lists: poor people and minorities are less likely to be on property tax rolls than are the wealthy).

8

The Munsterman article in this issue discusses the considerable progress made in recent years to improve the representativeness of juries and assesses the implications of using different source lists in jury selection.

Exemptions from jury service have long been a potential cause of non-representative juries. Not only are entire groups automatically excluded from jury service by statute in many jurisdictions, but people can also individually plead their case for exemption before a judge, based on an array of additional excuses. The granting of exemptions clearly has implications for the representativeness of juries, especially automatic exemptions which, prior to court rulings in several states, included even "housewives" (see *Duren v. Missouri,* 1979).

Finally, the voir dire serves as the last obstacle to actual jury service. Although most of the case law regarding the voir dire has focused on challenges for cause, especially in the death penalty cases, some attention has been paid to the peremptory challenge. One might expect this literature to grow in light of the Supreme Court's decision last term (*Allen v. Hardy,* 1986) to place some constitutional controls on the use of peremptory challenges to eliminate racial groups from criminal juries. The literature on voir dire is discussed in this special issue in the article by Valerie Hans.

The second category of independent variables involves what can be referred to as legal factors. This category includes the processes that could be termed legally relevant to a jury's decisionmaking: the judge's instructions, the cause of action, the credibility of witnesses, the type of evidence admitted (e.g. oral, physical, video-taped), and the physical ordering of the process. Much of this literature is discussed in Marilyn Ford's article, although her major focus is on the third category of independent variables: non- or extra-legal factors. These variables have been the most heavily researched, and have been studied primarily as correlates of outcome and jury behavior. The group of extra-legal factors assessed in this body of research includes demographic variables, pretrial publicity, witnesses' attractiveness and personality, the previous courtroom experience of jurors, and the occurrence of contemporary political events. The problem with most of this literature, as aptly pointed out by Ford, is that it presents few consistent results that are in a form which provides guidance for policy makers. Unfortunately, as will be seen throughout this special issue, this difficulty is apparent in other areas of jury research as well.

Finally, the fourth group of independent variables focuses on organizational and structural variables. Two basic structures are typically studied in this category: jury size and the unanimity requirements. These two

9

elements will be the principal focus of the remainder of this note.

It must be mentioned at the outset of this discussion that an important component of any jury research is the methodology employed to answer the substantive questions asked. A variety of methods has been used in the study of juries, ranging from simulation, to aggregate statistics, to formal modeling. Additionally, these approaches encompass two units of analysis: the individual juror (either surrogate jurors such as students, or actual jurors) and the jury as a whole. The size of the samples used in the quantitative studies vary enormously, and the conclusions are often equally divergent. Methodology is important here, as in all empirical research, because the utility of the studies rests on the validity and reliability of the methods employed. Bray and Kerr (1982) provide an excellent summary of methodological questions in jury research. Since the Ford article deals with many of these broad methodological questions, and the other articles in this issue refer to methodological concerns where relevant to their particular subject, this note will reference them only as they affect the research being discussed.

Jury Structure and Organization

Jury Size. Until the early 1970s, American courts appeared content with twelve-member juries, despite the fact that the rationale for fixing on the number twelve has never been fully explained. Although the U.S. Supreme Court commented on the jury size question in several cases decided about the turn of the century (see, e.g., *Thompson v. Utah,* 1898; *Rassmussen v. U.S.* 1905), the Court failed to address the issue explicitly in state cases until 1970 in *Williams v. Florida.* Citing a few case studies that evaluated the impact of a jury's size on variance in verdicts (Cronin, 1958; Wiehl, 1968), the Court found "that there is no discernible difference between the results reached by two different sized juries" (*Williams v. Florida,* 1970: 101). This decision allowed states to establish six-member juries in non-capital criminal prosecutions.

The *Williams* holding was extended to federal civil juries by a five to four vote of the Supreme Court in 1973 in *Colegrove v. Battin.* The position of the Court in *Williams* and *Battin* was supported by empirical studies by Mills (1973), Stoever (1972), Kessler (1973), and Bermand and Coppock (1973). In 1978, however, the Court applied the brakes to the shrinking of the jury. In *Ballew v. Georgia* (1978), drawing heavily on social science research, the Court reaffirmed its holding in *Williams,* while at the same time ruling that use of a five-member jury in a criminal case seriously impairs the constitutional right to trial by jury.

10

The issues surrounding jury size have prompted considerable research. Most of the research looks at the impact of jury size on the outcomes of cases. Both quasi-experimental and real world studies have documented that jury size has little effect on verdicts in criminal cases (e.g., Nagel and Neef, 1977; Roper, 1980b). The outcome of jury deliberations is only important from a policy perspective, however, if it can be associated with some measure of its correctness. For example, juries of one size might convict defendants 50 percent of the time, but be incorrect in a substantial proportion of their decisions, while juries of another size might also convict defendants 50 percent of the time, but make mistakes much less frequently. Thus, a conclusion that jury size does not impinge upon the constitutional right to trial by jury, simply because juries of different sizes have similar conviction rates, is erroneous. This problem led researchers to study other aspects of jury behavior.

Researchers have begun to focus on quality of the deliberation process, assuming that some process measures can be clearly identified as preferable in reaching decisions. The most common variable studied is evidence recall (Roper, 1979; Saks, 1977). Others have reviewed the deliberation process itself, using surrogate measures such as changes in pre- and post-deliberation verdicts (Roper, 1980b).

Although there has been a flurry of activity in this area, the findings are generally mixed—a situation that may be attributable to lack of consistency in the methodologies used in the various studies. The one conclusion that has been substantiated by a number of researchers is that twelve-member juries more frequently "hang" (i.e., fail to reach a verdict) than six-member juries.

Unanimity requirements. Prior to the 1970s the U. S. Supreme Court had long required unanimity in jury convictions as a means of insuring maintenance of the reasonable doubt standard in federal criminal cases (see, e.g., *Allen v. United States,* 1896; *Patton v. United States,* 1930). In 1972, however, in the sister cases of *Johnson v. Louisiana* and *Apodaca et al. v. Oregon,* the Court held that provisions of state laws "requiring less than unanimous jury verdicts in criminal cases do not violate the Due Process Clause for failure to satisfy the reasonable doubt standard" (*Johnson v. Louisiana,* 1972: 356). The Court reached this conclusion with no supporting scientific evidence, and suggested that less than unanimous jury decision rules do not inhibit a full discussion by the jury of the relevant issues. In fact, research on this topic strongly contradicts the Court's assumptions (Davis *et al.,* 1975; Hastie *et al.,* 1983; Kalven and Zeisel, 1971; Saks, 1977). These studies found a propensity for more discussion

11

during deliberation in unanimous-rule juries than in majority-rule juries, a finding that is further substantiated by the increased likelihood of unanimous-rule juries to hang (see, e.g., Zeisel, 1982).

The Interaction of Size and the Unanimity Requirement. It was not until 1979, in *Burch v. Louisiana,* that the Supreme Court finally ruled on the validity of less than unanimous, six-member juries. Given the conflicting evidence of social science research in the area, Justice Rehnquist, writing for a unanimous Court, relied on the "line drawing" process expounded in *Ballew* (1978) in holding that a less than unanimous, six-member jury violates the constitutional right to a jury trial. There is not much empirical work on this specific issue; Roper (1980a) found no significant differences between various combinations of jury size and decision rule, and the jurors' abilities to accurately recall evidence.

The United States Supreme Court's use of social science in cases involving jury size and decision rule accurately reflects the status of the research enterprise. In *Williams* (1970) the Court began to use the available data; in *Ballew* (1978) the Court's opinion read almost like an article written for a social science journal; and in *Burch* (1979) the Court fully retreated from using the research. The Court's final position with respect to use of social science data in jury size and unanimity cases would seem to be justified in light of the lack of common findings and methodologies of studies in the area.

Other Aspects of Jury Structure and Organization. In 1980, Flango researched the impact of note-taking on juror behavior. He found that note-taking was especially helpful in understanding instructions and in recalling testimony of expert and character witnesses. The practice also seemed to affect jurors' perceptions of deliberation quality and attitudes toward service. This practice, and its impact on the work of the courts is, except for Flango's work, essentially unresearched.

Two studies of particular relevance to court administrators assessed aspects of jury management. Kasunic (1983) reviewed the implementation of one day/one trial practices, and concluded that this system was successful in meeting its goals of creating more favorable juror attitudes, providing a more representative cross-section of the community, saving money, and increasing the public's exposure to the courts. Stoever (1974) assessed jury management procedures in the federal courts, looking at such strategies as pooling jurors, and seasonal use of jury trials.

Conclusion

Systematic inter-state research on the impact of various structures on

12

jury decisionmaking is lacking. Although the literature abounds with war stories and case studies, our ability to generalize is extremely limited. While the articles in this special issue demonstrate that much progress has been made in furthering our understanding of juries, much more needs to be known. At the most fundamental level, for example, we need to know more about such basic descriptive elements as the number of jury trials in civil and criminal cases in state and federal courts, the final dispositions of those cases (i.e. conviction rates in criminal cases and dollar awards in civil actions), delay measures for jury and bench trials, and the numbers of peremptory and "for cause" challenges requested and granted. In addition, these data should be broken down with as much specificity as possible by case type.

One of the major reasons for the contradictory findings in jury research is the wide variance in methods applied: from use of aggregate statistics, to probability theory, quasi-experimental designs, and simulations. Even across simulation studies, the methods vary significantly: some researchers use students as surrogates for jurors and others do not; some studies involve the use of written text and others use video-tapes or other techniques to recreate courtroom events; some researchers allow deliberation among "jurors" while others simply poll the subjects after conclusion of the "trial." Researchers must agree on some common elements of methodology before replication can substantiate the findings in this area.

Finally, work should focus on investigating and improving jury deliberations themselves. Given the current debate over the very institution of the jury and its alleged contribution to various aspects of the "litigation explosion," the need for reliable social science research is especially pressing.

CASES

Allen v. Hardy, 92 L.Ed. 2nd 199 (1986).
Allen v. U.S., 164 U.S. 492 (1896).
Apodaca et al. v. Oregon, 406 U.S. 404 (1972).
Ballew v. Georgia, 435 U.S. 223 (1978).
Burch v. Louisiana, 441 U.S. 130 (1979).
Colgrove v. Battin, 413 U.S. 149 (1973).
Duren v. Missouri, 99 S.Ct. 664 (1979).
Johnson v. Louisiana, 406 U.S. 356 (1972).
Patton v. U.S., 281 U.S. 276 (1930).
Rassmussen v. U.S., 197 U.S. 516 (1905).
Thompson v. Utah, 170 U.S. 343 (1898).
Williams v. Florida, 399 U.S. 78 (1970).

REFERENCES

ALLEN, James L. (1977) "Attitude Change Following Jury Duty," 2 *The Justice System Journal* 246.

13

AUSTIN, Arthur D. (1984) *Complex Litigation Confronts the Jury System: A Case Study.* Frederick, Md: University Publications of America.

BECKER, T. (1965) "The Influence of Jurors' Values on Their Verdicts: A Courts and Politics Experiment," 46 *Southwestern Social Science Quarterly* 130.

BEISER, Edward N. and Rene VARRIN (1975) "Six-Member Juries in the Federal Courts," 58 *Judicature* 424.

BERMANT, Gordon and Rob COPPOCK (1973) "Outcomes of Six- and Twelve-Member Jury Trials: An Analysis of 128 Civil Cases in the State of Washington," 48 *Washington Law Review* 593.

BRAY, Robert M. and Norbert L. KERR (1982) "Methodological Considerations in the Study of the Psychology of the Courtroom," in Norbert L. Kerr and Robert M. Bray (eds.) *The Psychology of the Courtroom.* New York: Academic Press.

COE, Kenneth (1976) "Juror Utilization in Three Selected Oklahoma District Courts," 29 *Oklahoma Law Review* 65.

CRONIN, P.M. (1958) "Six-Member Juries in District Courts," 2 *Boston Bar Journal* 27.

DAVIS, James, Norbert L. KERR, Robert S. ATKIN, Robert HOLT and David MEEK (1975) "The Decision Processes of 6- and 12-Person Mock Juries Assigned Unanimous and Two-Thirds Majority Rules," 32 *Journal of Personality and Social Pyschology* 1.

DIPERNA, Paula (1984) *Juries on trial.* New York: Dembner Books.

FLANGO, Victor E. (1980) "Would Jurors Do a Better Job If They Could Take Notes?" 63 *Judicature* 436.

FLANGO, Victor E. and Robert T. ROPER (1983) "Rise or Fall of the American Jury," 7 *State Court Journal* 27.

HANS, Valerie P. and Neil VIDMAR (1986) *Judging the Jury.* New York: Plenum Press.

HASTIE, Reid, Steven D. PENROD and Nancy PENNINGTON (1983) *Inside the Jury.* Cambridge, Mass.: Harvard University Press.

KALVEN, Harry Jr. and Hans ZEISEL (1971) *The American Jury.* Chicago: The University of Chicago Press.

KAPLAN, David A. (1986) "What America Really Thinks About Lawyers," 8 *National Law Journal* S-2.

KASUNIC, David E. (1983) "One Day/One Trial: A Major Improvement in the Jury System," 67 *Judicature* 79.

KERR, Norbert L. and Robert M. BRAY (eds.) (1982) *The Psychology of the Courtroom.* New York: Academic Press.

KESSLER, Joan B. (1973) "An Empirical Study of Six- and Twelve-Member Jury Decision-Making Processes," 6 *Journal of Law Reform* 712.

LAMBROS, Thomas D. (1986) "The Summary Jury Trial—An Alternative Method of Resolving Disputes," 69 *Judicature* 286.

LEVINE, James P. (1983) "Using Jury Verdict Forecasts in Criminal Defense Strategy," 66 *Judicature* 449.

　　　(1984) "The Legislative Role of Juries," 1984 *American Bar Foundation Research Journal* 605.

MILLS, Lawrence R. (1973) "Six-Member and Twelve-Member Juries: An Empirical Study of Trial Results," 6 *Journal of Law Reform* 671.

NAGEL, Stuart and Marian NEEF (1977) "The Impact of Jury Size on the Probability of Conviction," 2 *The Justice System Journal* 226.

NATIONAL CENTER FOR STATE COURTS (1986) *State Court Caseload Statistics: Annual Report 1984.* Williamsburg, Va.: National Center for State Courts.

RICHERT, John P. (1977) "Jurors' Attitudes Toward Service," 2 *The Justice System Journal* 233.

ROPER, Robert T. (1979) "Jury Size: Impact on Verdict's Correctness," 7 *American Politics Quarterly* 438.

　　　(1980a) "The Effect of a Jury's Size and Decision Rule on the Accuracy of Evidence Recall," 62 *Social Science Quarterly* 352.

　　　(1980b) "Jury Size and Verdict Consistency: A Line Has to be Drawn Somewhere," 14 *Law and Society Review* 977.

ROPER, Robert T., and Victor E. FLANGO (1983) "Trials Before Judges and Juries," 8 *The Justice System Journal* 186.

SAKS, Michael (1977) *Jury Verdict: The Role of Group Size and Social Decision-Rule.* Lexington, Mass.: Lexington Books.

SIMON, Caroline K. (1975) "The Juror in New York City: Attitudes and Experiences," 61 *American Bar Association Journal* 207.

SPERLICH, Peter W. (1982) "The Case for Preserving Trial by Jury in Complex Litigation," 65 *Judicature* 394.

14

STOEVER, William (1972) *A Comparison of Six- and Twelve-Member Civil Juries in New Jersey Superior and County Courts.* New York: The Institute of Judicial Administration.
_____ (1974) "The Expendable Resource: Studies to Improve Juror Utilization," 1 *The Justice System Journal* 39.

WIEHL, Lloyd L. (1968) "The Six Man Jury," 4 *Gonzaga Law Review* 35.

ZEISEL, Hans (1982) "The Verdict of Five Out of Six Civil Jurors: Constitutional Problems," 1982 *American Bar Foundation Research Journal* 141.

Law and Human Behavior, Vol. 13, No. 1, 1989

Laboratory Simulation and Bias in the Study of Juror Behavior

A Methodological Note*

Geoffrey P. Kramer† and Norbert L. Kerr†

Theoretical speculation and meta-analysis suggest that the strength of treatment effects (e.g., defendant attractiveness) may become weaker as the experimental simulation becomes more realistic and complex. In order to test this hypothesis, various levels of biasing pretrial publicity were combined with both a short and a long trial. Results provided no support for the contention that treatment effects act differently as a function of the length of the stimulus trial in which they are embedded. Rather, it is suggested that treatments used in simplified jury simulations may often show similar effects when examined in more realistic, complex settings *if* the treatments are comparable.

There has been considerable criticism of laboratory simulation methodology in studying juror and jury behavior (see Bray & Kerr, 1982, for a review). A common criticism is that jury simulations often lack complexity and realism. One effect of this lack of complexity, it is argued, is that experimental manipulations loom disproportionately large against the background of simple and unrealistic stimulus trials. For example, Miller, Fontes, Boster, and Sunnafrank (1977) have argued that jurors' evaluation of an independent variable (e.g., defendant attractiveness) is affected by the complexity of the context within which it is presented. If sim-

* This research was supported by NSF Research grant No. SES 8419944 to the second author, John Carroll, and James Alfini. Portions were presented at the Midwestern Psychological Association Convention, Chicago, May 7–9, 1987. Requests for reprints should be sent to either author at the Department of Psychology, Psychology Research Building, Michigan State University, East Lansing, Michigan 48824.
† Michigan State University.

ulated trials are short and artificial, experimental manipulations may have an exaggerated influence on juror judgment.

Kaplan and Miller (1978) suggest that juror judgments are a joint function of two components: extralegal bias toward a defendant and legally relevant evidentiary information pertinent to the judgment (i.e., the verdict). They suggest that as the importance of one component increases, the contribution made by the other tends to decrease. This reasoning implies that if mock jurors are exposed to brief and unrealistic stimulus trials with impoverished evidentiary components, the weight of the biasing component in determining judgment would be atypically prominent while the weight of the evidentiary component would be atypically small.

The issue of whether treatment effects produce differential impact in long/ complex vs. short/simple trials is important because of its implications for external validity. Critics of laboratory simulation trials have argued that the findings of studies that use simple, abbreviated trials may be misleading because the effects they produce on behavior may be much stronger than the effects that would occur in actual trials (see Bray & Kerr, 1982). Linz and Penrod (1982) have suggested that experimenters who use laboratory simulation methodology often neglect external validity while concentrating on internal validity. They argue that researchers often present minimal evidentiary information, thus ensuring that their manipulations will have a significant effect on juror decision making.

In order to investigate whether the impact of treatments changed generally as a function of trial complexity, Linz and Penrod (1982) performed a meta-analysis of 78 simulation studies. They coded various methodological features, such as case completeness (presence or absence of standard trial elements), subject type (student or adult subjects), and presentation form (written summary, audiotape, videotape, or live). These features were then correlated with the effect size obtained in the experiments. Linz and Penrod concluded that treatment effects were generally stronger as the research settings became less realistic when the juror decision task was conviction/acquittal. This is consistent with the argument advanced by Kaplan and Miller (1978). However, Linz and Penrod acknowledged an important limitation in their findings. They were unable to apply multiple regression analysis to assess the independent contributions of the various methodological features. Thus, the influence of one feature (e.g., case completeness) could not be assessed apart from the influence of another (e.g., use of adult subjects). The importance of assessing the independent contributions of each methodological feature is suggested by the results of a multiple regression analysis that used sentencing as the juror decision task. In this analysis, only one feature (use of adult, nonstudent subjects) had a significant impact on effect size. Thus, Linz and Penrod's results are suggestive, but cannot be unequivocally interpreted because the various methodological features they examined tended to be highly intercorrelated across studies.

Other studies have varied the mode of stimulus trial presentation (e.g., video vs. audio vs. written transcript) and thereby simultaneously varied the complexity and realism of the experimental setting (e.g., Bermant, McGuire, McKinley, &

Salo, 1974; Juhnke et al., 1979),[1] but to our knowledge, there have been no direct experimental tests that compare the effects of one or more stimulus trials that differ in complexity or length. The present paper presents such a study.

Before describing this study, it may be useful to distinguish trial length and trial complexity. Trial length is easily measured or manipulated; trial complexity is not. Complexity can be conceptualized in a number of ways. For instance, a trial could be considered more complex by virtue of the sheer volume of information that it contains (e.g., the number of statements or assertions made by witnesses), the number of interconnections involved in deciding what happened in a crime (e.g., the number of composite events that must be considered conjunctively to establish a set of facts), or the number of juror inferences involved (e.g., the sum total of all inferences used in deciding the importance of physical evidence, the credibility of witnesses, and the believability of counsel's arguments). Using these conceptualizations (and there are clearly other possibilities), trial complexity could be manipulated by varying the number of witness statements (volume), the number of related events necessary to establish a given sequence of events (interconnections), and/or the number of mental operations used by jurors (inferences). Obviously, what makes a trial more or less complex is an elusive issue.

Our present concern is not to specify theoretically all the ways in which stimulus trials in simulations might be less complex than actual trials. Rather, our concern is to explore empirically whether stimulus simplifications typical of juror/jury simulation studies systematically distort the impact of experimental treatments, as suggested by several critics of such simulations. Thus, we manipulated trial "complexity" by varying the trial's length and level of detail. We did this by constructing two versions of the same armed robbery trial. The two trial versions contained the same basic factual and evidentiary material and the same standard trial elements, but varied considerably in length and detail. For instance, though both versions contain information that an eyewitness observed a robber for approximately one minute, the shorter version does not include certain nonverbal and paralinguistic features of the eyewitness testimony, nor does it include more detailed information about the conditions of observation—information that is elicited by careful direct and cross examination in the longer trial. Thus, the shorter version is less complex both in terms of the sheer volume of information and in terms of the amount of supporting and nonsupporting information that jurors may use to make judgments of witness credibility or fact.

Both trial versions were presented via videotape. Prior to seeing the trial tapes, however, subjects were first exposed to one of four combinations of biasing pretrial publicity—high or low emotionally biasing publicity combined with high or low factually biasing publicity. Every level of publicity was combined with each level of trial length, creating a fully crossed design. By casting the nonevidentiary pretrial publicity against the two trial versions, we could test whether the

---

[1] Unfortunately, such manipulations may confound the mode of trial presentation with evidentiary content (e.g., defendant appearance).

strength of the experimental manipulations varied as a function of trial length/ complexity.

As Bray and Kerr (1982) have noted, different patterns of results would have different implications for our ability to generalize findings. If there were only a main effect for treatment (e.g., more convictions for either type of biasing publicity) but no interaction with the "realism" factor (here, trial length/complexity), we would be justified in asserting not only the *direction* of the treatment effect (e.g., factually biasing publicity produces more convictions), but could also conclude that the *degree* of the treatment effect is comparable in both the more and less realistic context. A more serious constraint on our ability to generalize would occur if treatment effects and trial complexity interact. For example, an extralegal biasing factor (e.g., emotionally biasing publicity) could produce a strong effect in one setting (e.g., the shorter, simpler stimulus trial) but not in the other. Most serious of all would be the case in which bias publicity produced one effect in one setting and an opposite effect in the other setting. In these cases, the existence, direction, and magnitude of treatment effects would be dependent upon the complexity of the setting, and our ability to generalize results across trial settings would be seriously constrained.

If the criticisms of short laboratory simulations are valid, the effects of either type of prejudicial pretrial publicity should differ as a function of trial length. Kaplan and Miller's (1978) reasoning suggests that weaker or no publicity effects should occur with the longer trial. Interactions between trial length and treatment would undermine the ecological validity of artificial simulation methodology, particularly if it were a cross-over interaction. However, if the effects of the two types of pretrial publicity are unaffected by trial length, concerns stemming from at least one source of simulation artificiality would be reduced.

METHOD

Subjects and Design

Subjects were 529 undergraduate students (362 females, 167 males) at Michigan State University who participated to earn extra credit in an introductory psychology course.

The experimental design was a 2 (trial length: long vs. short) × 2 (factually biasing publicity: high vs. low) × 2 (emotionally biasing publicity: high vs. low) completely crossed factorial.

Materials

The Trial Versions

Two versions of an armed robbery trial (a long version and a short version) were constructed from a videotaped reenactment of an actual armed robbery trial. In both the long and the short version, a young black male was accused of robbing a supermarket of $10,000.[2] The original trial tape was chosen because (a) it was a case to which pretrial publicity could be plausibly added; (b) it was a case which, by itself, produced conviction rates around 40%–50%, thereby avoiding floor/ceiling effects and allowing for the maximum impact of extralegal biasing factors; and (c) it was a highly realistic simulation: actual attorneys and an actual judge played their respective roles, actors portrayed witnesses, and it was taped in an actual courtroom and was based on an actual trial. The long version—lasting approximately 100 minutes—was obtained by minimally editing the original trial tape so that it would be of suitable length for another, larger pretrial publicity project. The short trial version was constructed entirely from the long trial version for the purposes of the present study. The short version—lasting just under 10 minutes—was as brief as possible while still including all the essential information of the trial. The achievement of a factor of 10 reduction in length seemed a fair and reasonable basis for examining trial length/complexity.

Principal characters in this videotape were the defendant, the defense and prosecuting attorneys, and the trial judge. Three witnesses were called during the trial: two employees of the supermarket and the investigating police officer. The prosecution's case was built primarily on the eyewitness identification of the defendant by the supermarket employees. The defense case rested upon demonstrating the unreliability of the eyewitness testimony and upon the unprofessional and biasing nature of the police investigation. All standard trial elements were presented, including opening statements, direct and cross examination of each witness, closing arguments, and judge's instructions to the jury.

The short trial version presented the same characters, factual information, and standard trial elements as the long trial, but in summary form. The chronological order of events and testimony was identical to that in the long trial version. Summaries of each witness's statements—as revealed in direct and cross examination—as well as summaries of closing arguments and judge's instructions were presented on the audio track of a videotape shown to the subjects. Excerpts from the long trial tape were edited onto the video track of this tape to coincide with the portion of the trial being summarized. These excerpts ensured that subjects in both trial length conditions had similar information about the appearances, mannerisms, etc. of all trial participants. As best we could tell, all basic factual evidence from the long trial was included in the short trial; every attempt was made to ensure that the summaries were accurate and representative of the statements or testimony from which they came.

The Publicity Versions

Prior to viewing the trial, subjects were exposed to pretrial publicity. This also was presented via videotape. The pretrial publicity tapes consisted of ostensibly real television and newspaper reports, all designed to relate the defendant to

---

[2] This stimulus trial was produced as part of a National Institute of Justice Research project No. 78-NI-AX-0146. Thanks go to Reid Hastie for supplying the original videotape. These materials are available from the authors upon request.

the armed robbery and to another crime, a hit-and-run that resulted in the death of a child. The television scenes involved actors and actresses playing the roles of newsmen and private citizens. These reports were identified as coming from the files of a small independent television station in the area of the crime (Cambridge/ Boston, Massachusetts). The newspaper reports were stories produced in newsprint and identified as articles from a local newspaper in the area of the crime.

Four separate versions of pretrial publicity were constructed: low factual bias/low emotional bias, high factual bias/low emotional bias, low factual bias/high emotional bias, and high factual bias/high emotional bias. The low factual bias/low emotional bias condition served as a base-line condition in that it contained brief, factual reports with minimal biasing potential. Two television reports (identified as excerpts from evening and late news) and one newspaper article described the robbery and reported that the defendant had been arrested and charged. The reports contained in this version also occurred in the other three versions of publicity. The high factual bias condition added (a) a television editorial that revealed the defendant's substantial past criminal record and (b) a newspaper article that reported that the police had found incriminating but inadmissible evidence at the home of the defendant's girlfriend. The high emotional bias conditions added several television and newspaper excerpts involving a 7-year-old girl. In the first scene, the child was shown in a ''Tuesday's Child'' feature, and an appeal was made for a big brother or big sister. Later segments reported that this same child had been struck and seriously injured in a hit-and-run accident. The license plate and description of the hit-and-run vehicle matched the license plate and description of a car identified at the scene of the armed robbery. Further, the description of an occupant in the hit-and-run vehicle matched the description of the person who had robbed the supermarket. The defendant was described in two separate reports as a prime suspect in the hit-and-run. The final television report in the high emotionally biasing condition was a brief hospital interview with the grieving mother, only minutes after she learned that her child had died. The four publicity videotapes ranged in length from 3 minutes and 8 seconds to 14 minutes and 34 seconds.

It is important to note that none of the biasing information contained in the news reports was included in the armed robbery trial itself. There was no mention in the robbery trial of (a) any prior criminal record of the defendant,[3] (b) the evidence found in the girlfriend's apartment, or (c) the hit-and-run incident involving the child. It is also important to note that the emotionally biasing material had no direct factual or evidentiary relevance for the robbery charge. The fact that this heinous hit-and-run occurred and was very likely done by the robber of the supermarket provided no culpatory or exonerating evidence for the defendant as a suspect and defendant in the robbery. Thus, in this context, the pretrial publicity represents extralegal, nonevidentiary information.

---

[3] Such information can be and is typically revealed during the testimony of the defendant. However, the defendant in this case did not testify at the trial.

Equipment and Procedure

Subjects were randomly assigned to one of four rooms in which identical television monitors had been placed. Attached to each television monitor was a videocassette player. By having experimentors control the videocassette players, all four versions of the publicity could be played simultaneously, but in separate rooms.

The television monitors could also be controlled remotely from a central control room which was situated between the two center rooms. By switching the monitors to the central control room channel, a single version of the trial or instructions could be played simultaneously in all four rooms. In this way each of four groups of subjects could be exposed to one of the levels of prejudicial pretrial publicity. Following this, they could all view either the long or the short trial at the same time.

Because the publicity videotapes were of different length, it was necessary to stagger the starting times for the four rooms/conditions. This was done in order to avoid having subjects who saw shorter pretrial publicity tapes experience delays of several minutes when other subjects experienced no delays.

During the initial instructions, subjects were told that they would act as mock jurors in a case that had been an actual armed robbery trial. They were also informed that, to increase the realism of the simulation, they would see all of the television and newspaper publicity that preceded the trial.

Once the instructions were completed, monitors were switched to the individual videocassette recorders, and a different version of pretrial publicity was played in each of the rooms. Subjects then completed a brief voir dire simulation questionnaire. The primary purpose of this questionnaire was to assess reactions to the publicity (i.e., to check the effectiveness of the factual and emotional bias manipulations). Monitors were then switched back to the control of the central control room. All subjects then viewed either the long or short version of the trial.

A total of four experimental sessions were run, two using the long trial version and two using the short trial version. Within any one session, all four versions of pretrial publicity were represented. At the completion of the trial videotape, several judgments were obtained from the subjects, the most salient of which were the dichotomous verdicts, sentence recommendations, confidence in verdicts, and affective state. Finally, memory for pretrial publicity was tested in a six-item, multiple-choice format. Subjects were then debriefed, thanked, and excused.

RESULTS

Analyses of variance were performed on verdicts, sentence recommendations, and subjects' reports of negative affect (to test the effectiveness of the emotionally biasing manipulation).

Significant main effects for both types of biasing publicity were obtained on individual verdicts ($F(1,525) = 5.31, p < .05$ for factual publicity; and $F(1,525) =$

5.85, $p < .05$ for emotional publicity). Subjects tended to render more guilty verdicts when either the factually biasing publicity or the emotionally biasing publicity was present ($M = 53\%$ vs. 43% guilty for factual publicity and 57% vs. 43% for emotional publicity). In addition, there was a main effect for trial length ($F(1,525) = 3.97, p < .05$). The conviction rate was significantly higher with the short trial version ($M = 53\%$ vs. 44% guilty). The trial length factor, however, did *not* interact with either the emotionally biasing or the factually biasing publicity factors ($p > .3$). Cell means are reported in Table 1.

To further investigate the possibility of interactions between trial length and either type of publicity, several directional tests were conducted. In the emotionally biasing condition, the difference between the high and low bias conditions was greater in the short trial than in the long trial (i.e., in the short trial, the high biasing conditions was 9% greater than the low biasing condition, whereas in the long trial this difference was only 4%). This was in the direction suggested by Kaplan and Miller (1978), but the interaction was far from significant ($t(525) = .51, p > .4$, one-tailed). In the factually biasing condition, the difference between the means was actually greater in the long trial than in the short trial, contrary to the Kaplan and Miller hypothesis (difference of 5% in the short trial vs. 11% in the long trial). Clearly, the effect of either publicity factor was not significantly larger in the short trial than in the long trial version, even by the most sensitive tests of this hypothesis.

Verdict ratings were combined with confidence ratings to form a single, 15-point scale ranging from highly confident of not guilty to highly confident of guilty. Analysis of variance revealed that subjects had higher guilt ratings when emotional publicity was high than when it was low ($F(1,446) = 8.53, p < .01; M = 8.57$ vs. 7.15). The main effect for high vs. low factual publicity was marginal, but not statistically significant ($F(1,446) = 3.21, p < .10; M = 8.31$ vs. 7.25). Subjects had higher guilt ratings in the short trial version than in the long trial version ($F(1,446) = 5.68, p < .05; M = 8.29$ vs. 7.33). There were no interactions between either publicity treatment or trial version on this measure, consistent with the findings for verdict.

Table 1. Conviction Rates as a Function of Trial Length and Pretrial Publicity[a]

Pretrial publicity level	Verdict rating	
	Long trial	Short trial
High emotional, high factual	53%	66%
	(68)	(44)
High emotional, low factual	50%	59%
	(28)	(65)
Low emotional, high factual	49%	52%
	(69)	(54)
Low emotional, low factual	31%	39%
	(64)	(57)

[a] The tabled values are conviction rates (% guilty verdicts). Cell sample sizes appear in parentheses.

In regard to sentencing, subjects tended to be harsher when either level of biasing publicity was high (for factual publicity, $F(1,476) = 14.72$, $M = 159.3$ months vs. 124.9 months; for emotional publicity, $F(1,476) = 17.02$, $M = 160.1$ months vs. 127.0 months, both significant at $p < .001$).

The negative affect measure was included to test the effectiveness of the emotionally biasing publicity manipulation. The high level of emotional publicity produced a highly significant increase in the reporting of negative affect ($F(1,436) = 16.81$, $p < .001$). Parenthetically, this effect was stronger for females than for males ($p < .01$). However, the strength of this effect did not significantly vary as a function of trial length. This result is similar to that for verdict, again suggesting that treatment effects were the same, or at least paralleled one another, in the two versions of the trial.

DISCUSSION

The current study found that trial length affected verdicts. However, we suspect that this effect has less to do with trial length, per se, than with uncontrolled differences in the quality or perceived quality of the evidence against the defendant between the long and short trial. The same basic facts and arguments were included in the short trial version as occurred in the long trial, but in abbreviating one of the trial versions it is always possible that some subtle piece of information (e.g., a comment by an attorney, some gesture by a witness) that influenced jurors in the long trial may have been omitted from the short trial.

We also found that both emotional publicity and factual publicity affected verdicts. Such effects have been observed in several prior studies (see Carroll et al., 1986) and are not particularly surprising in themselves. But the fact that these effects were not influenced by trial length is more surprising. It contradicts the hypothesis made explicitly by some (e.g., Miller et al., 1977) and implicit in Kaplan and Miller's (1978) reasoning, that extralegal biasing effects are greatly magnified by brief stimulus trial materials.

There is an apparent discrepancy between these results and the conclusions drawn by Linz and Penrod (1982) from their meta-analysis. Several explanations for this discrepancy may be advanced. First, in realistic simulations or field studies, experimental control and precise measurement may be sacrificed to achieve greater realism. If realism tends to be accomplished by a lower signal-to-noise ratio in juror/jury research, one would expect weaker effects in more realistic simulations, Linz and Penrod's finding.

Second, treatments used in more complex, realistic studies may be generally less powerful than those used in laboratory simulations. For example, there may be less extreme variations in defendant attractiveness in actual courtrooms than in typical laboratory simulations. Such a situation would, all other things being equal, cause the treatments in realistic studies to produce weaker effects. Some (Miller et al., 1977) view this as a liability. However, it need not be if mundane realism (see Aronsen & Carlsmith, 1968) is not the sole or primary criterion for evaluating research. The need to clarify a theoretical relationship or simply to establish an empirical relationship of interest are valid reasons why a researcher might choose to manipulate an independent variable more powerfully than its typical variation in the natural setting. There are certainly clear precedents in other disciplines (e.g., feeding massive doses of suspected carcinogens to laboratory animals in order to identify *possible* risks to humans under normal levels of intake).

A final possibility for the discrepancy is that the manipulation of trial length in the present study was not strong enough, or that there was too little power to detect Length × Publicity effects. The latter possibility may be reasonably dismissed; with the current sample size (harmonic mean of 51 per cell in the 2 × 2 × 2 design), the estimated power to detect a "small" interaction effect (by Cohen's, 1977 standards) was .64; the power to detect a moderate effect was >.99. In regard to the differences between the trial versions, it is worth noting that the present manipulation was certainly not trivial—the longer trial was approximately 10 times longer and far more complex than the shorter, summarized version. The current manipulation reasonably brackets the range of trial stimuli in current use (see Bray & Kerr, 1982). Of course, the shorter version was also more complex than a one-page written trial summary would have been, but to compare such a trial version with the long videotape version would have been to confound length/complexity with other factors (such as mode of presentation). Neither was the long trial simply a redundant version of the short trial. Though it is true that the shorter version contained the same basic trial facts and elements, it omitted many witness statements and elaborations concerning exact timing and sequences of events, recollections of emotional states, angles of view, etc. Similarly, the basic attorney positions were presented in both trial versions, but many related points, illustrations of points, and arguments made by attorneys were omitted from the short version. Thus, it would be inaccurate to consider the long versions as more complex only by virtue of redundancy. It included more material, and, significantly, more evidentiary material than the short trial version.[4]

Of course, without conducting additional research one cannot rule out the possibility that with more extreme manipulations of trial length and complexity, a Length × Publicity interaction effect might have been obtained. For example, it is possible that variations of trial length/complexity may not matter until trials differ in hours or even days. It is also conceivable that the present results may reflect a restriction in range on the low end. That is, it could be that even our 10-minute trial is sufficiently complex in evidence, volume, number of inferences required, etc. to dilute the influence of the extralegal manipulations, influence that might be much stronger in a skeletal version of our short trial (e.g., a one-paragraph summary). Only additional research with more extreme manipulations will resolve such issues.

It may also be important, in further research, to carefully delineate and test

---

[4] It should be noted that even if there was more evidence in the longer trial version, if its relevance for verdicts was low, or if it was effectively (for verdicts) redundant with the content of the short trial version, our findings would not contradict Kaplan and Miller's (1978) logic.

dimensions of trial complexity. For instance, a trial of several hours could intro-duce juror fatigue, which may be quite different functionally from the number of inferences required or the amount of information that can be held in memory. The former might be manipulated with long, redundant trials, whereas the latter two might be manipulated using either long or short trials packed with information.

We do agree with the moral of much of the criticism of jury simulation research—that such research should not be automatically or carelessly general-ized to actual juror/jury behavior. Questions of ecological validity are ultimately empirical ones. This moral applies with equal force to the current findings. These findings certainly do not establish the irrelevance of stimulus trial length or com-plexity for the magnitude of any (much less all) treatments of possible interest. But they do lend support to the argument (e.g., Bray & Kerr, 1979, 1982) that even highly artificial simulations are not *inherently* distorting and may actually inform us on relationships of real significance for law and human behavior.

REFERENCES

Aronsen, E., & Carlsmith, J. M. (1968). Experimentation in social psychology. In G. Lindzey & E. Aronsen (Eds.) *The handbook of social psychology*. Reading, Massachusetts: Addison-Wesley.

Bermant, G., McGuire, M., McKinley, W., & Salo, C. (1974). The logic of simulation in jury research. *Criminal Justice and Behavior, 1,* 224–233.

Bray, R., & Kerr, N. (1979). Use of simulation method in the study of jury behavior. *Law and Human Behavior, 3,* 107–119.

Bray, R., & Kerr, N. (1982). Methodological consideration in the study of the psychology of the courtroom. In N. Kerr & R. Bray (Eds.) *The psychology of the courtroom* (pp. 287–232). New York: Academic Press.

Carroll, J. S., Kerr, N. L., Alfini, J. J., Weaver, F. M., MacCoun, R. J., & Feldman, V. (1986). Free press and fair trial: The role of behavioral research. *Law and Human Behavior, 10,* 187–201.

Cohen, J. (1977). *Statistical power analysis for the behavioral sciences.* New York: Academic Press.

Juhnke, R., Vought, C., Pyszczynski, T. A., Dane, F. C., Losure, B. C., & Wrightsman, L. S. (1979). Effects of presentation mode upon mock jurors' reactions to a trial. *Personality and Social Psychology Bulletin, 5,* 36–39.

Kaplan, M. F., & Miller, L. E. (1978). Reducing the effects of juror bias. *Journal of Personality and Social Psychology, 36,* 1443–1455.

Linz, D., & Penrod, S. (1982). A meta-analysis of the influence of research methodology on the outcomes of jury simulation studies. Paper presented at the Academy of Criminal Justice Sciences, Louisville, Kentucky.

Miller, G., Fontes, N., Boster, J., & Sunnafrank, M. (1977). Methodological issues in jury research: What can simulations tell us? Paper presented at the meeting of the American Psychological Association, San Francisco.

Psychological Bulletin
1979, Vol. 86, No. 3, 462–492

Models of Jury Decision Making: A Critical Review

Steven Penrod and Reid Hastie
Harvard University

Several models of jury decision making are reviewed. In each instance the model is described and compared with related models, its assumptions are scrutinized, its fit to normative data is evaluated, and possible revisions and extensions of the model are discussed. Models reviewed include (a) multinomial decision schemes designed to adduce implicit decision rules used in jury decision making, (b) binomial models of jury voting that use simplifying assumptions about jury decision making to assess the impact of explicit decision rules and jury size on verdict distributions, (c) Bayesian models that use normative data to estimate prior probabilities of defendants' "convictability" and juror accuracy, (d) models that assess the relationships among jury size, decision rule, and jury accuracy, (e) models that examine the relationship between juror and jury errors, and (f) a computer simulation that uses simple assumptions about group persuasion and individual differences in jurors' resistance to persuasion to model results from empirical studies of jury decision making.

Until quite recently most of our knowledge about juror and jury behavior has been based on survey research such as Kalven and Zeisel's *The American Jury* (1966) and archival data collected in studies of jury utilization. Within the past decade these data have been supplemented by a growing body of experimental jury research (e.g., Boehm, 1968; Davis, Kerr, Atkin, Holt, & Meek, 1975; Landy & Aronson, 1969; Mitchell & Byrne, 1973; Saks, 1977; Simon, 1967; Simon & Kaplan, 1972; Strodtbeck, James, & Hawkins, 1957; Valenti & Downing, 1975; Padawer-Singer & Barton, Note 1); investigators have used simulated, laboratory juries to explore a wide variety of factors that theoretically affect juror and jury decision making. (For reviews of this research, see Davis, Bray, & Holt, 1977; Penrod, Note 2.)

Even more recently a number of researchers have begun using survey and experimental data to develop mathematical and computer models of jury decision making, and these models are the focus of this review. The models can be classified into six categories: (a) *implicit-decision-rule* models that use mathematical techniques to determine the implicit rules that juries appear to use in deliberation, (b) simple binomial probability models that use the binomial expansion to mimic the effects of jury size and explicit decision rules on the distribution of jury verdicts, (c) Bayesian models that use Bayesian and binomial models to estimate the prior probability that defendants are guilty and the probability that jurors can accurately detect guilt or innocence, (d) binomial models of juror accuracy and juror satisfaction and their relationship to jury size and decision rules, (e) models of the relationship between juror and jury errors, and (f) a computer model that uses computer-simulated jurors and data from jury studies to explore the relationships among the initial distribution of individual juror opinions, individual differences in persuadability, rates of juror vote changes, coalition sizes within a jury, deliberation times, and the distribution of jury verdicts.

This research was supported by a grant from the James Marshall Foundation and Grant BNS76-11321 from the National Science Foundation.

The authors would like to thank Dan Stefek for his mathematical and computer programming assistance and Charles Judd and David Kenny for their comments on the manuscript.

Requests for reprints should be sent to Steven Penrod, who is now at the Department of Psychology, University of Wisconsin, Madison, Wisconsin 53706.

60

We examine these models giving particular attention to their structure, the plausibility of their underlying assumptions, their fit to available data, and their generalizability.

Implicit Decision Rules

Of the models reviewed here, the one that is most firmly grounded in empirical data—in the sense that it makes the fewest assumptions about jury behavior—is the model developed by Davis and his colleagues (Davis, 1973; Davis et al., 1975; Davis, Kerr, Sussman, & Rissman, 1974). Davis made a fundamental distinction between two types of decision rules that a jury uses: an explicit decision rule such as the requirement that juries reach a unanimous verdict and an implicit decision rule that describes the method by which a jury actually arrives at a verdict. The assumption, of course, is that juries may in fact operate under a decision rule different from the one given to them in a judge's instructions. To determine the implicit rule Davis has used two sources of data: Simon's (1967) study of the insanity defense, in which 30 12-person mock juries deliberated on a housebreaking case and 68 mock juries deliberated on an incest case, and the Davis et al. (1975) and Davis, Kerr, Stasser, Meek, and Holt (1977) studies of a rape case in which student jurors deliberated individually or in 6- or 12-person juries. These last juries were given either a unanimous or a two-thirds rule as their explicit decision rule.

In all of these studies the researchers asked the mock jurors to reveal their personally preferred verdict before deliberation began. Knowledge of the predeliberation distribution votes combined with knowledge of each jury's final verdict allows one to ask, can final verdicts be predicted by applying a particular decision rule to the initial distribution of individual juror votes? Davis (1973) called such a rule an "*implicit* social decision scheme (p. 99)." To determine the implicit decision rule Davis first examined the set of "distinguishable distributions of member preferences within a group (p. 101)." In general, these distributions can be determined by a multinomial expansion in which the set of initial distributions m equals

$$\binom{n + r - 1}{r},$$

where n equals the number of mutually exclusive outcomes available to each group member and r equals the number of members. For jurors there are, of course, two possible outcomes (guilt or innocence), so $n = 2$. (When $n = 2$ the appropriate expansion is binomial, and the model is much simpler. A detailed discussion of the binomial expansion can be found in the next section of this article.) For 12-person juries ($r = 12$) there are 13 distinguishable initial distributions:

$$\binom{2 + 12 - 1}{12} = 13 = m.$$

These distributions range from 12 votes for guilt and none for innocence (12, 0) to 12 votes for innocence and no votes for guilt (0, 12). Similarly, in a 6-person jury there are 7 possible initial distributions, ranging from (6, 0) to (0, 6).

The question Davis has posed is, given actual data on the frequency of each initial distribution of individual juror verdicts, is there one general decision scheme that will accurately predict the distribution of final jury verdicts? Davis represented various possible decision schemes in the form of an $m \times s$ stochastic matrix in which s corresponds to the available group outcomes (e.g., a verdict of guilt, acquittal, or a hung jury). The entries in the matrix represent the probability that each of the m possible initial distributions will result in one of the s possible group outcomes. Each unique matrix thus represents a distinct decision scheme that may correspond to a jury's implicit decision rule.

Davis et al. (1975) have tested 13 different decision schemes that can be applied to the initial vote distributions for 12-person juries in which final verdicts can be of guilt, innocence, or a hung jury, and Davis, Kerr, Stasser, Meek, and Holt (1977) have tested 15 similar models for 6-member juries. Fortunately, the 3 decision schemes that have provided the best fits can be succinctly characterized verbally. For instance, Decision Scheme 8 from Davis et al. (1975) specifies that if two thirds or more of the jurors agree on a verdict on the initial ballot, this agreement determines the verdict. If two-thirds agreement is not obtained on the first ballot, the decision rule specifies that the jury will hang. For Scheme 7, majorities win,

Table 1
Distribution of Votes for Acquittal on First Ballot and Jury Decisions

Final verdict	No. of votes for acquittal on first ballot										Total n	% of total
	0		1–5		6		7–11		12			
	n	%	n	%	n	%	n	%	n	%		
Not guilty	0	0	5	5	5	50	37	91	26	100	73	32
Guilty	43	100	90	86	5	50	1	2	0	0	139	62
Hung	0	0	10	9	0	0	3	7	0	0	13	6
Total n	43		105		10		41		26		225	
% of total		19		47		4		18		12		100

Note. These data are from Kalven and Zeisel (1966).

otherwise the jury is hung. Scheme 3 reflects a majority persuasion effect in which *persuasion* depends on the size of the initial majority: When 11 or 12 jurors agree (or 5 or 6 jurors agree in a 6-member jury), the verdict is determined; for distributions between (10, 2) and (6, 6) or (4, 2) and (3, 3) in 6-member juries, the juries yield guilty verdicts with probability r_g/r (where r_g is the number of jurors voting for guilt) and not-guilty or hung verdicts with probability $\frac{1}{2}[1 - (r_g/r)]$; and the distributions (5, 7) to (2, 10) [(2, 4) in six-member juries] yield not-guilty verdicts with probability r_{ng}/r and guilty or hung verdicts with probability $\frac{1}{2}[1 - (r_{ng}/r)]$.

Davis (1973) tested 5 different schemes on Simon's (1967) data and found that Scheme 3 made the best predictions for both of Simon's cases. Similarly, he tested 13 decision schemes on his own (Davis et al., 1975) data. The best fitting scheme overall was the two-thirds-majority model (Scheme 8), although other models provided better fits for particular jury sizes and explicit decision rules.

Finally, 15 schemes were tested on the data from Davis, Kerr, Stasser, Meek, and Holt (1977). The study used six-member juries that deliberated with an explicit 4/6 (i.e., four members out of six must agree) decision rule. For these juries a modified two-thirds rule—similar to Scheme 8 except that 75% of (3, 3) juries acquit and 25% hang—best fit the data. Davis et al. concluded that in general juries appear to be operating under an implicit "two-thirds, otherwise hung" decision rule even when the explicit, judge-instructed rule is unanimity.

Davis's approach has been applied by other researchers with similar results. For instance, Saks (1977) studied the effects of explicit decision rule and jury size on the distribution of jury verdicts in two experiments with a total of 85 juries. When Saks tested for implicit decision rules he also found support for Decision Schemes 3 and 8, but he found even stronger support for a power function rule suggested by Latane and Borden (Note 3).

Gelfand and Solomon (1975, 1977) have employed Davis's decision scheme method in their efforts to fit the data on 225 juries supplied by Kalven and Zeisel (1966). (Table 1 reproduces the Kalven and Zeisel data.) Although the first ballot distribution was not given for every possible initial jury split (non-unanimous majorities for guilt and innocence were separately pooled), with minor modifications in Davis's Scheme 3, Gelfand and Solomon estimated the probability of conviction to be .637, of acquittal to be .303, and of a hung jury to be .060—a very close fit to the Kalven and Zeisel data. The Gelfand and Solomon scheme, like Davis's Scheme 3, incorporates a strong majority persuasion effect, but elevates the probability of a hung jury for (10, 2) and (2, 10) initial distributions.

Although these results as a whole support the argument that juries may use something other than their assigned explicit rule, some caution is in order, for the studies reported to date have failed to demonstrate that one particular model consistently makes accurate predictions for all jury sizes and explicit decision rules. Indeed, as Davis et al. (1975) have noted, different implicit rules may apply to different jury conditions; it may be that different implicit rules apply in criminal and civil cases, that different levels of a defendant's apparent guilt elicit different implicit rules, that complex cases involve yet another type of implicit rule, that different types of judge's instructions vary the implicit rule, and so forth. Only further research can resolve these problems.

An even more subtle and potentially more important methodological problem of the decision scheme analysis must be addressed. To date the evidence suggests that the rate of accurate prediction for individual trials is not reliably high. Most of the tests of implicit rules rely on a comparison of (a) the distribution of verdicts predicted from the application of the decision schemes to initial vote distributions with (b) the final distribution of actual verdicts. But without detailed inspection it is not clear that the final verdicts considered individually are consistent with the predictions made by the various decision schemes. Scheme 8, for instance, might predict an overall distribution of verdicts that would resemble the overall distribution of actual verdicts, but the entries in the stochastic matrix associated with the model might do a poor job of predicting actual verdicts on the basis of initial vote distributions. In other words, the model might fit the aggregated data, but for the wrong reasons. There could be an infinite number of matrices that would predict final distributions identical to those of Scheme 8, but only one of them would make the maximum number of correct predictions. Optimally, one would want to take a model and examine the accuracy of predictions for each entry in the matrix. In the case of Scheme 3, for instance, do 83% of the cases with an initial (10, 2) distribution of votes end up with a guilty verdict, 8% with a hung verdict, and 8% with an innocent verdict? Do 50% of the (6, 6) juries vote for guilt while the other 50% divide evenly to acquit or to hang?

The best fitting Scheme 8 (the two-thirds decision rule) is at least partially defective in this regard. One illustration of its failure is that it does not allow either for reversals of initial majorities (cases in which a minority on the initial ballot ultimately prevails) or for hung juries in cases in which eight or more jurors initially agree. And yet there is ample evidence (e.g., Padawer-Singer & Barton, Note 1) that initial majorities are reversed and that juries can hang even when eight jurors initially agree on a verdict. Some of the models allow for such reversals and provide more sources of hung juries, but unless the rules are fitted to actual outcomes on a jury-by-jury basis rather than on an aggregate distribution of outcomes, it is premature to say that one of the schemes accurately reflects the implicit decision rule.

In fact, the initial results obtained from nonaggregated analyses, although mixed, are on the whole disappointing. Grofman (1976) tested the fit of the two-thirds model on the Davis et al. (1975) and Davis, Kerr, Stasser, Meek, and Holt (1977) data and reported that the results were disappointing. We found that the two-thirds rule predicted the verdicts of 66 of 100 juries in the Kerr et al. (1976) study and 59 of 90 juries in the Davis, Kerr, Stasser, Meek, and Holt (1977) study. In fact, even the best fitting Scheme 15 (the modified two-thirds decision rule) mispredicts 10 of 90 juries. On the other hand, the standard two-thirds model predicted 24 of 25 juries in a study by Grofman and Hamilton (Note 4).

In a later section we discuss some of the factors that may contribute to the poor fit of social decision schemes when they are applied to individual juries, but we note briefly at this point that one major source of the problem may be a by-product of the case that Davis and his colleagues have used in their research. The case is one of rape, and it evokes different reactions from male and female subjects. In both Davis, Kerr, Stasser, Meek, and Holt (1977) and Kerr et al. (1976), approximately 60% of the females voted to convict on the first ballot, while only about 50% of the males voted to convict. During deliberation females changed their votes from conviction to acquittal at rather high rates (in the first study, 18.3% of the females shifted from guilt to innocence compared with a 5.5% shift in the other direction, and males shifted relatively little in either direction). As a result of the higher rate of change to acquittal by females, the overall distribution of verdicts is shifted in the direction of acquittal. Since the social decision schemes typically assume that jurors are equally likely to shift in either direction, they fail to account for the bias in female juror behavior and are therefore unable to capture the shift to acquittals. Rape cases may be peculiarly susceptible to this sort of phenomenon, and this observation underscores the fact that case type has a significant impact on the deliberation process.

Probabilistic Models

Earlier it was noted that Davis's jury model is built around the binomial expansion. There are other modeling efforts that also make use of the binomial expansion to mathematically evaluate the effects that jury size and decision rule have on the distribution of jury verdicts. These issues are of practical significance and have been the subject of litigation before the U.S. Supreme Court. In 1970 the Court held that six-member juries did not violate a defendant's right to a trial by jury (*Williams* v. *Florida*[1]), and in 1972 the Court held by a narrow margin that nonunanimous juries were constitutional (*Apodaca* v. *Oregon*[2] and *Johnson* v. *Louisiana*[3]). More recently, in *Ballew* v. *Georgia*,[4] the Court, with Justice Blackmun writing the Court's main opinion, cited a number of empirical and theoretical studies to support the holding that juries with fewer than six members violate a defendant's right to a trial by jury.

The court has not yet reached the question of the constitutionality of nonunanimous six-member juries, but since the issue is likely to be pressed in the courts, empirical research and mathematical models directed to the question have acquired additional importance. The mathematical models that are most relevant are the binomial models of Walbert (1971) and Saks and Ostrom (1975). The binomal expansion is a mathematical expression that facilitates the calculation of the probability that a specified number of successes (or failures) will occur in a given number of trials (in the nonlegal sense), where trials are independent of one another and the probability of success is the same for each trial. More simply (using juries as an example), the binomial theorem applies in situations in which there are two possible outcomes (e.g., a juror can vote for either guilt or acquittal), in which there are a fixed number of trials (e.g., there are 12

jurors who must vote), in which outcomes have identical probabilities (e.g., jurors are randomly drawn from a large jury pool in which a certain percentage of jurors will vote for guilt), and in which trials are independent (i.e., a juror's initial judgments of guilt or innocence are independent).

To apply the binomial theorem to the jury it is clear that several assumptions have to be made. First, it must be assumed that all jurors are prepared to vote for either conviction or acquittal; there can be no undecided jurors. It is not clear how often this assumption is violated in practice, but for statistical purposes it must be assumed that all jurors have at least some inclination—however small—toward conviction or acquittal. Second, it must be assumed that jurors are drawn from a larger pool of jurors, in which a certain percentage of the jurors will vote for conviction or acquittal. Finally, it must be assumed that the jurors have not influenced one another's judgments prior to deliberation (this is probably a fairly reasonable assumption in light of the fact that jurors are typically cautioned not to discuss a case or to form an opinion until they have heard all the evidence).

With these assumptions it is possible to use the binomial theorem to determine the probability that a jury will have sufficient votes to convict a defendant on the first ballot:

$$p(G) = \sum_{i=Q}^{n} \binom{n}{i} g^i (1 - g)^{n-i}, \qquad (1)$$

where $p(G)$ is the probability that a jury will produce sufficient votes to convict on the first ballot, n is jury size, Q is the minimum number of votes required to convict (required quorum), g is the probability that a randomly selected juror will vote for guilt, and $1 - g$ is the probability that a randomly selected juror will vote to acquit.

Note that in the case of a unanimous decision rule, $p(G)$ can simply be written as $p(G) = p^n$. The same theorem can also easily be written to determine the probability that a

---

[1] Williams v. Florida, 90 S.Ct. 1893 (1970).
[2] Apodaca v. Oregon, 92 S.Ct. 1628 (1972).
[3] Johnson v Louisiana, 92 S.Ct. 1635 (1972).
[4] Ballew v. Georgia, 98 S.Ct. 1029 (1978).

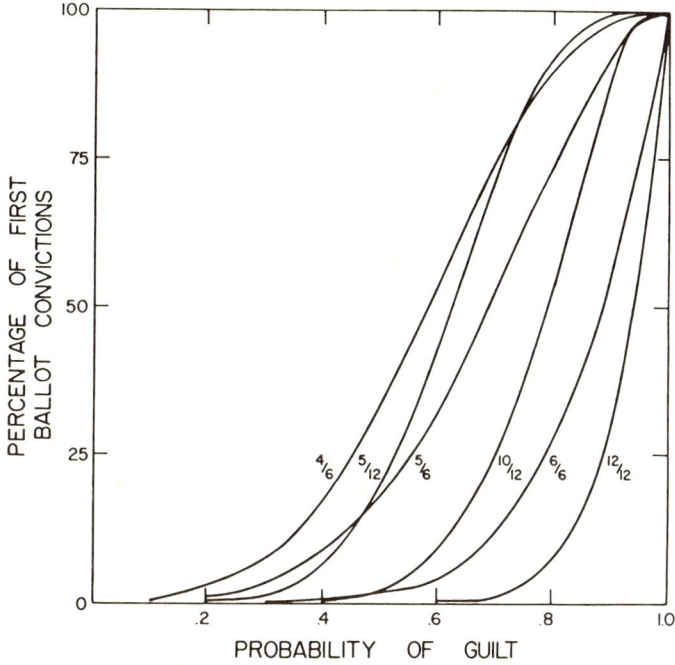

Figure 1. Percentage of first ballot convictions as a function of probability of guilt, according to a single, binomial decision rule model. (Denominator of parameters indicates jury size, and numerator indicates decision rule verdict requirement, i.e., the number of votes needed for a conviction.)

jury will produce sufficient votes to acquit on the first ballot:

$$p(I) = \sum_{i=Q}^{n} \binom{n}{i} g^{n-i}(1-g)^i. \qquad (2)$$

Thus, the probability $p(V)$ that a jury will have sufficient votes to produce either a guilt or an acquittal verdict on the first ballot is the sum of the probabilities from Equations 1 and 2:

$$p(V) = \sum_{i=Q}^{n} \binom{n}{i} g^i(1-g)^{n-i}$$
$$+ \sum_{i=Q}^{n} \binom{n}{i} g^{n-i}(1-g)^i.$$

One can, of course, vary jury size n, the size of the required quorum Q, and the probability that a randomly selected juror will vote for guilt g and use the binomial theorem to determine the probabilities that juries of varying size, drawn from differing jury pools, and who use different decision rules will produce first ballot verdicts for guilt or acquittal (one need only consult appropriate tables of the binomial distribution). Figure 1 summarizes the probabilities of first ballot verdicts for juries of 6 and 12 members who use two-thirds, five-sixths, and unanimous decision rules, where the probability of an individual juror voting for guilt ranges from 0 through 1.0. (Note that the figure also shows the probability of an acquittal—when $1 - g$ is substituted for g, the results are exactly symmetrical.)

Clearly, reductions in the size of the jury and relaxations of the quorum requirements produce similar effects: They heighten the probability that a jury will produce a verdict on the first ballot. Furthermore, if g is in any way an index of a defendant's objective guilt (irrespective of the evidence against the defendant) and juries can accurately detect such guilt on the basis of the evidence presented to them, then it is clear that objectively guilty defendants fare better with larger juries using a unanimous decision rule, for these juries are less likely to convict on the first ballot.

Thus far we have emphasized that by using the binomial theorem with the assumptions made earlier, it is possible to determine the probability that a jury will render a verdict on the first ballot taken during deliberation. Events after the first ballot, when a jury has failed to reach a verdict, have been a recurrent problem for the mathematical modelers, as most juries clearly do not reach a verdict on the first ballot, but typically continue to deliberate until they either reach the required quorum or find themselves hopelessly deadlocked (when a jury finds itself hung, the trial judge is forced to declare a mistrial). Figure 1 shows that in relatively close cases (where g ranges from .3–.7), virtually no 12-person, unanimous juries reach a verdict on the first ballot. What is likely to happen in juries of this sort? Do they hang? Do they divide evenly in their verdicts? Does the majority tend to prevail?

One answer to these questions is provided by Walbert's (1971) analysis. As one has already seen, Davis's (1973) implicit-decision-rule analysis suggests that initial majorities tend to determine final verdicts; Walbert cited additional evidence to support the claim that deliberation after the first ballot is fundamentally irrelevant to the mathematical analysis. He argued as follows: (a) Small-groups research shows strong majority persuasion effects—with complex judgments minorities tend to conform to the judgments of the majority—that are accentuated by external pressures (such as judges' instructions) and are most evident in group discussions with leadership structures resembling those found in the jury room. (b) Empirical evidence indicates (Kalven & Zeisel, 1966) that majority persuasion operates in about 93% of all cases (minorities prevailed in 3%, and 4% ended with a hung jury). (c) Juries in which jurors initially divide evenly (6 to 6) tend to split evenly for conviction and acquittal (Kalven & Zeisel, 1966).

If one takes these data and assumptions as valid and further assumes that the reported discrepancies (i.e., reversals of initial majori-

ties) are of minimal importance (assumptions that we examine below), it is possible to argue that first ballots basically decide almost all cases. With respect to the binomial theorem, these assumptions imply that one need only be concerned with two factors: the probability that a jury will produce a majority of votes for a verdict on the first ballot and the disposition of cases in which the jury splits evenly on the first ballot.

If the initially evenly split cases yield final verdicts divided evenly between conviction and acquittal and the possibilities of hung cases and reversals of initial majorities are ignored, then the binomial theorem can be modified, as in Equation 3, to determine the probability that a jury will render a guilty verdict:

$$p(G) = \sum_{i=(n/2+1)}^{n} \binom{n}{i} g^i + \frac{g^{n/2}(1-g)^{n/2}}{2}. \quad (3)$$

The first term of Equation 3 is identical to Equation 1, except that Q is the majority of jurors and the second term is the probability of an even split in the initial ballot divided by two. A similar expression can be constructed for the probability of an innocent verdict and is analogous to Equation 2:

$$p(I) = \sum_{i=(n/2+1)}^{r} \binom{n}{i} g^{n-i} + \frac{g^{n/2}(1-g)^{n/2}}{2}. \quad (4)$$

Note that by definition the sum of Equations 3 and 4 is 1.00. Furthermore, in these equations the decision rule is essentially fixed at *majority wins*, and only jury size affects the distribution of guilty and innocent verdicts.

Walbert's decision rule is quite similar to Davis et al. (1975) Scheme 7, except that Walbert eliminated hung juries and assigned evenly divided juries equally to guilt and acquittal. However, where Davis examined results by applying his schemes to initial votes from experimental studies to determine their fit to the data, Walbert made a more general argument. Starting from the assumptions outlined above, Walbert calculated the effect of jury size on the distribution of jury verdicts given a wide range of binomially distributed initial individual votes and using (as in Saks & Ostrom, 1975) varying levels of g (the probability that a randomly selected juror will vote for guilt). Walbert's results indicate that a reduction in jury size raises the probability of conviction when $g < .5$: For example, when $g = .4$, the use of a 6-member jury increases the probability of conviction from .25 (for the 12-member jury) to .32. And when $g = .2$, the 6-member jury is six times more likely to convict (6% vs. 1%). Parallel results for acquittals are obtained when $g > .5$.

If one makes the additional assumption that g is a fairly reliable indicator of a defendant's "convictability" (i.e., g indexes the weight of the evidence against the defendant), then Walbert's analysis implies that the more convictable defendants are better off with the smaller juries, whereas relatively unconvictable defendants fare better with large juries.

Furthermore, if one regards convictions of relatively unconvictable defendants or acquittals of relatively convictable defendants as errors, it is clear that the larger jury is preferable. Indeed, it can be argued that the optimal pattern of conviction and acquittal would break sharply at $g = .5$. Juries would always convict when g was greater than .5 and acquit when g was less than .5. With these assumptions, optimality would be achieved with infinitely large juries using majority rule. Coincidentally, this optimality rule also maximizes the likelihood that jury verdicts will accurately reflect the attitudes and values of the community from which the jury pool has been drawn (the representativeness of the pool itself would also be a consideration). Indeed, the binomial theorem can be used to determine the probability that a specified number of jurors (analogous to Q) will be selected from a jury pool in which a specified trait (say, race or sex) occurs at a particular rate (analogous to g). Lempert (1975) discussed this representativeness question at length, and in his article he summarized the probabilities that two, one, or no jurors will be selected with the appropriate trait in 6- and 12-member juries for various rates of trait occurrence in the jury pool.

Given the assumptions made in Walbert's (1971) analysis, it is clear that the 6-member jury is inferior to the 12-member jury: It produces more errors and is less likely to represent the population from which it is drawn.

We note, in passing, that there is yet another way to think about g that could provide a quantifiable definition of *reasonable doubt*. If we were to define g_1 as the probability that a randomly selected juror will say that a defendant committed the charged acts beyond a reasonable doubt and g_2 as the probability that a randomly selected juror will vote to convict the defendant under a more-likely-than-not standard of proof, then we could determine a probabilistic value for RD (the additional certainty required for a reasonable-doubt standard) such that $RD = g_1 - g_2$.

If by empirical methods we found that RD was greater than zero, we could use Walbert's formulation of the binomial decision model to examine the effects of a relaxation in the standard of proof required in criminal cases. If, for example, $g_1 = .6$, $g_2 = .5$, and $RD = .1$, a relaxation from the reasonable-doubt standard to the more-likely-than-not standard would increase the probability of conviction from .5 to .75 in the 12-member jury and from .5 to .68 in the 6-member jury (see Walbert's Figure 1). Similar comparisons can be made for different values of g and RD. In every instance (for $RD > 0$) the relaxation of the standard accentuates the differences in 6- versus 12-member error rates.

To date the empirical evidence regarding the value of RD is mixed. In an experimental study involving a theft case, Cornish and Sealy (1973) found that the probability of a conviction under the reasonable-doubt standard was .50 compared with .51 for the more-likely-than-not standard. Simon and Mahan (1971) asked judges, jurors and, students to rate the chances out of 10 that a defendant committed a crime if convicted beyond a reasonable doubt and if convicted by a preponderance of the evidence. All three groups gave a mean rating of approximately 8.5 out of 10 for reasonable doubt; but whereas judges rated preponderance of the evidence at 5.5, the other two groups gave a rating of 7. Similarly, in Kerr et al. (1976), subjects individually judged a videotaped rape trial using one of three definitions of *beyond a reasonable doubt*. Of the jurors who formed a verdict preference after viewing the trial, 51% of those using a stringent definition (moral certainty), 61.2% of those with no definition, and 66.3% of those using a lax definition (substantial doubt) voted to convict the defendant. When the subjects rated the probability of guilt associated with the standards, the mean rating for the stringent definition was .87 compared with .83 for the other two definitions. Nagel, Lamm, and Neef (Note 5), using a normative decision theory model, reported that student conviction probability thresholds averaged about .55 for various types of criminal cases. Thus, the preliminary evidence indicates that the standards of proof and the definitions of those standards can affect juror judgments, although perhaps not to the extent intended by the legal system. To date there is little research on the factors that may affect the value of *RD*: the quality of judges' instructions, differential experience with legal decision making, individual differences in jurors, differences in types of defendants and indictments, differences in available verdict alternatives, and differences in the types of judgments a jury must make (such as resolving issues of eyewitness identification vs. selecting a verdict or determining whether a defendant is guilty or innocent of any offense vs. determining which offense a defendant has committed).

Before leaving Walbert's (1971) model, it may be useful to note the points at which his analysis appears to be on the weakest ground. Unlike Davis, who attempted to account for reversals of initial majorities and hung juries in some of his models, Walbert assumed that these phenomena are unimportant when compared with the strong majority persuasion effects that he found in empirical data such as Kalven and Zeisel's (1966). However, as Gelfand and Solomon (1974) pointed out, it is not clear that Walbert has properly characterized the Kalven and Zeisel data (see Table 1). These data summarized the relationship between initial ballot distributions and final verdicts for 225 criminal cases tried in Chicago and Brooklyn. On close inspection, it turns out that for all cases in which the jury was not evenly divided (6 to 6), the initial majority ultimately prevailed in 91.5% of the cases (compared with Walbert's 93%), and the jury hung in 6.0% (compared with Walbert's 4%). Even assuming that Walbert's characterization of the Kalven and Zeisel data is the best possible, his model fails to account for

more than 8% of the total cases (six reversals of majorities and 13 hung juries out of 225 cases), and it is not clear what implications these error cases have for his conclusions about the effects of jury size.

Beyond the question of the model's basic fit, one might want to know whether (and in what ways) cases involving reversals of majorities and hung juries differ from cases exhibiting majority persuasion effects. Intuitively, there is good reason to think that such cases are the most difficult for juries to decide; the evidence is not sufficiently compelling in favor of a guilty or an innocent verdict for jurors to be able to readily agree. In other words, these cases may tend to be the ones in which *g* is close to .5. Some evidence for the difficulty of such cases is provided by the results from Padawer-Singer and Barton's (Note 1) study of 92 6- and 12-member mock juries that deliberated after viewing a videotaped murder trial. This case was evidently fairly difficult to decide, for the probability that a juror randomly selected from the pool of jurors who viewed the trial would vote for guilt was ≈ .47. And (summing across 6- and 12-member juries who used both unanimous and nonunanimous decision rules) for the 70 juries with initial majorities for a verdict, the majority prevailed in only 68.6% of the cases, the minority prevailed in 12.9%, and 18.6% were hung. Of the 22 juries that were initially evenly split (6 to 6 or 3 to 3), 54.5% ultimately returned innocent verdicts, 40.9% returned guilty verdicts, and 4.5% returned hung verdicts.

The Padawer-Singer and Barton data suggest that Walbert's model may provide the poorest fit for those cases in which accuracy and representativeness are most critical—the "hard to decide" cases. It would be premature, however, to conclude that the postulated lack of fit for cases with *g* near .5 undermines Walbert's basic arguments about the effects of jury size on jury accuracy and representativeness, for as long as majorities prevail more often than minorities, larger juries should be preferred to smaller juries.

Bayesian Models

One important question that a researcher might ask about juror performance relates to the juror's ability to accurately determine a defendant's guilt or innocence. One would like to know how often, under the best of circumstances, jurors and juries accurately determine a defendant's objective guilt or innocence. But of course there is no reliable method of determining objective guilt and innocence. One can only ask how reliable jurors and juries are at the task of assessing guilt and innocence from the evidence presented to them at trial (and we would hesitate to argue that the quality of trial evidence is necessarily related to a defendant's objective guilt).

The models examined thus far do not attempt to evaluate the acuity of jurors, but assume that the best available index of a defendant's guilt is the proportion of jurors in a jury pool who, after hearing all the evidence and testimony, are prepared to vote for conviction. In this section we examine a jury model that uses a Bayesian analysis to determine both the prior probability that a defendant is convictable and the probability that jurors will correctly assess this convictability.

In a series of articles, Gelfand and Solomon (1973, 1974, 1975, 1977) have developed a model based on Poisson's (1837) application of probability theory to jury verdicts. Following Poisson, Gelfand and Solomon began their analysis by suggesting that with adequate data two important parameters can be estimated:

1. T is the probability that before trial an accused is convictable, that is, the proportion of defendants brought to trial who are convictable or the probability that the weight of the evidence will be against a randomly selected defendant.

2. M is the probability that a juror will not vote for the wrong verdict, the probability that a jury will correctly assess and vote with the weight of the evidence against a defendant. (For the purpose of modeling, Gelfand and Solomon assumed that T and M are independent and that M is a common value for all jurors.)

Gelfand and Solomon made it clear that when they wrote about convictability, they were really discussing the standards of indictment and the community standards for conviction that might prevail in a criminal justice system and were not using convictability (or more loosely, *guilt*) to mean objective guilt.

The specification of these two parameters allows for the construction of a mixed binomial expression similar to Equation 1 in which it is possible to determine $W_{n,i}$, the probability that a jury with n members will cast exactly i votes for acquittal on the first ballot; $Y_{n,i}$, the probability that a jury with n members will cast at most i votes for acquittal on the first ballot; $p_{n,i}$, the probability that the defendant is guilty given exactly i votes for acquittal on the first ballot; and $P_{n,i}$, the probability that the defendant is guilty given at most i votes for acquittal on the first ballot, where

$$Y_{n,i} = \binom{n}{i}[TM^{n-i}(1 - M)^i$$
$$+ (1 - T)M^i(1 - M)^{n-i}]; \quad (5)$$

$$W_{n,i} = \sum_{j=0}^{i} Y_{n,j};$$

$$p_{n,i} = \binom{n}{i}TM^{n-i}(1 - M)^i/Y_{n,i}; \quad (6)$$

$$P_{n,i} = T\sum_{j=0}^{i}\binom{n}{j}M^{n-j}(1 - M)^j/W_{n,i}.$$

Note that Y is the sum of correct and incorrect votes for guilt and innocence and that W cumulates the probabilities of votes for innocence from 0 through i votes. The expression for p is simply the proportion of votes for guilt that are attributable to guilty defendants, whereas P cumulates the proportion of votes attributable to guilty defendants from 0 through i votes.

Gelfand and Solomon (1973) demonstrated that the probability of a verdict is independent of T and that the correctness of a verdict is independent of jury size but does depend on the size of the quorum required for conviction. (This seeming contradiction of Walbert's analysis arises from the differences in the ways that the two models specify *correctness*.)

Using Poisson's (1837) data on French civil and criminal trials of the period from 1825 through 1833, Gelfand and Solomon (1973) obtained estimates of T and M by determining the probability of conviction in criminal cases at times when the required quorum for jury verdicts was either 7 of 12 votes (i.e., $W_{12,5}$ for the years 1825–1830) or 8 of 12 votes ($W_{12,4}$ for the years 1831–1833). With the knowledge that

$Y_{12,5} = W_{12,5} - W_{12,4}$, it was possible for Gelfand and Solomon to estimate the following overall parameter values: $T = .7494$, $M = .6391$, $P_{12,5} = .9406$, and $p_{12,5} = .9943$.

In their second article, Gelfand and Solomon (1974) applied similar methods to Kalven and Zeisel's (1966) data on first ballots and final verdicts in the 225 criminal cases cited by Walbert (1971). (See Table 1 for complete data.) In this instance their estimates of T and M were based on the overall distribution of verdicts reported in Table 1 and the various estimates this distribution provides for different Ys. Thus, 43 of the 225 (19%) juries produced first ballot, unanimous votes for guilt, so that one reasonable estimate of $Y_{12,0}$ is .19. Similar estimates of other Ys produce the following simultaneous equations:

$$Y_{12,0} = .19\,;$$

$$\sum_{i=1}^{5} Y_{12,i} = .47\,;$$

$$Y_{12,6} = .04\,;$$

$$\sum_{i=7}^{11} Y_{12,i} = .18\,;$$

$$Y_{12,12} = .12.$$

In their 1974 article, Gelfand and Solomon used the method of moments approach to find solutions for T and M, whereas in their 1975 article they treated the first ballot results as independent observations from a five-cell multinomial distribution and employed minimum chi-square and maximum likelihood estimation procedures to determine values for T and M. In each instance they also evaluated a three-parameter model in which M_1 is the probability that a juror will vote for guilt given a guilty defendant, M_2 is the probability that a juror will vote for innocence given an innocent defendant, and T is defined as before. The results of the three estimation procedures were roughly similar. The values of M_1 and M_2 clustered around .9 and did not appear to be significantly different (jurors appeared to be equally accurate in detecting guilt and innocence), while the values of T clustered around .7.

As noted earlier, the Gelfand and Solomon model is analogous to Walbert's binomial model, but uses two parameters rather than one. Gelfand and Solomon's model also allows a very simple comparison of the probability of conviction by 6- and 12-member juries for various values of T and M. Assuming majority persuasion and an equal split for guilt and innocence in juries who are initially evenly divided (precisely the assumptions made by Walbert), Gelfand and Solomon set the probability of conviction by a 12-member jury as

$$t = \sum_{i=0}^{5} Y_{12,i} + \tfrac{1}{2} Y_{12,6}$$

and the probability of conviction by a six member jury as

$$s = \sum_{i=0}^{2} Y_{6,i} + \tfrac{1}{2} Y_{6,3}.$$

Table 2 compares the values of t and s for $T = .2, .4, .6,$ and .8 and $M = .2, .4, .6,$ and .8.

Gelfand and Solomon (1974) took the position (one they retreated from in later articles)

Table 2

Probability of Conviction by 12-Man Jury, tw(T, M), and 6-Man Jury, s(T, M), for Values of T and M

T	$tw(T, M)$	$s(T, M)$
	$M = .2$	
.2	.793	.765
.4	.598	.588
.6	.402	.412
.8	.207	.235
	$M = .4$	
.2	.652	.610
.4	.551	.537
.6	.449	.463
.8	.348	.390
	$M = .6$	
.2	.348	.390
.4	.449	.463
.6	.551	.537
.8	.652	.610
	$M = .8$	
.2	.207	.235
.4	.402	.412
.6	.598	.588
.8	.793	.765

Note. Based on Gelfand and Solomon (1974).

that the differences in performance between 6- and 12-member juries are negligible over the full range of values for T and M. In fact, it is clear from Table 2 that whenever jurors vote correctly more than half the time, 12-member juries perform better than 6-member juries (i.e., they vote correctly more often). This is, of course, the same conclusion reached by Walbert (1971). Indeed, when one considers that there are thousands of criminal trials each year, it is also obvious that the otherwise negligible differences in performance may yield quite significant practical consequences, affecting thousands of lives.

Of course, we noted earlier that the Walbert model is less than ideal insofar as it fails to account for reversals of initial majorities and hung juries. In an effort to incorporate these two violations of the simple majority persuasion model, Gelfand and Solomon (1975) proposed that the Kalven and Zeisel data can provide the basis for more refined estimates of M, T, p, and P. Table 1 shows that all the cases with initial unanimous (12 to 0) votes for guilt ultimately returned guilty verdicts, 86% of the cases with between 7 and 11 votes for guilt did so, and half the cases with evenly divided juries did so, whereas 2% of the cases with initial though nonunanimous majorities favoring acquittal were reversed, the minority ultimately prevailing. On the basis of these results Gelfand and Solomon suggested the following equation for the probability that a jury will convict:

$$P_c = Y_{12,0} + .86 \sum_{j=1}^{5} Y_{12,j}$$

$$+ .50 Y_{12,6} + .02 \sum_{j=7}^{11} Y_{12,j}, \quad (7)$$

where, for example, $Y_{12,0}$ is the proportion of juries who begin deliberation with no votes for acquittal. Similarly, they suggested the following equation for the probability of acquittal:

$$P_a = Y_{12,12} + .91 \sum_{j=7}^{11} Y_{12,j}$$

$$+ .50 Y_{12,6} + .05 \sum_{j=1}^{5} Y_{12,j}. \quad (8)$$

The probability of a hung jury is thus $P_h = 1 - P_a - P_c$. Of course, not all acquittals and convictions are correct, but it is possible to determine the probability or proportion of convictions and acquittals that are correct. Thus,

$$P_{g/c} = (p_{12,0} Y_{12,0} + .86 \sum_{j=1}^{5} p_{12,j} Y_{12,j}$$

$$+ .50 p_{12,6} Y_{12,6} + .02 \sum_{j=7}^{11} p_{12,j} Y_{12,j})/P_c;$$

$$P_{i/a} = [P_a - (p_{12,12} Y_{12,12} + .91 \sum_{j=7}^{11} p_{12,j} Y_{12,j}$$

$$+ .50 p_{12,6} Y_{12,6} + .05 \sum_{j=1}^{5} p_{12,j} Y_{12,j})]/P_a.$$

Table 3 compares the results of the three methods of estimating the probabilities of interest for 12-member juries using Walbert's simple majority persuasion model and the more refined equations (7 and 8) proposed by Gelfand and Solomon.

To assess the reasonableness of the refined model, Gelfand and Solomon (1975) computed the values of P_c, P_a, P_h, $P_{g/c}$, and $P_{i/a}$ for different values of M and T and compared the results with the distribution of verdicts from the 225 Kalven and Zeisel cases cited earlier and with the overall distribution of verdicts from the 3,576 trials used in the entire Kalven and Zeisel (1966) study. Again, the best fits were produced with $M = .9$ and $T = .7$.

Finally, as noted above, Gelfand and Solomon (1975, 1977) used their maximum likelihood estimates of M and T in combination with Davis's (1973) social-decision-scheme analysis and by slightly modifying Davis et al.'s (1975) Scheme 3 produced a very good fit to the Kalven and Zeisel data: $P_c = .637$, $P_a = .303$, $P_h = .060$, $P_{g/c} = .9779$, and $P_{i/a} = .9385$—results that compare quite favorably with the results reported in Table 3.

Juror Accuracy and Satisfaction

Grofman (1976, in press) has employed a general binomial model similar to Gelfand and Solomon's for two purposes: to examine the effect of applying several simplifying assumptions to his model and to examine the implica-

Table 3
Comparison of Walbert's (1971) and Gelfand and Solomon's (1975) Jury Decision Models for 12-Member Juries

Study	Probability of outcome				
	Conviction	Acquittal	Hung	Defendant guilty given that jury convicts	Defendant innocent given that jury acquits
Minimum χ^2 estimate					
Walbert (1971)	.6588	.3412	.0	.9986	.9938
Gelfand & Solomon (1975)	.5843	.3433	.0724	.9882	.9092
Maximum likelihood estimate					
Walbert (1971)	.6897	.3103	.0	.9997	.9984
Gelfand & Solomon (1975)	.6189	.3155	.0656	.9918	.9129
Method of moments estimation					
Walbert (1971)	.6999	.3001	.0	.9998	.9993
Gelfand & Solomon (1975)	.6340	.3059	.0601	.9930	.9175

tions for decision rule preferences of jurors' tolerance for verdict errors. We examine these analyses briefly, starting with the analysis of the simplifying assumptions.

Juror Acuity Model

Following Gelfand and Solomon (1973), Grofman (1976) associated a binomial p with the probability that a randomly selected juror will correctly judge innocent defendants to be innocent (P_{II}) and guilty defendants to be guilty (P_{GG}), where P_G is the proportion of defendants who are guilty, P_I is the proportion of defendants who are innocent (by definition, $P_I = 1 - P_G$), P_C is the proportion of defendants convicted by juries, P_A is the proportion of defendants acquitted by juries, P_H is the proportion of defendants whose juries hang, and q is the number of votes required for a verdict (either guilt or innocence) and corresponds to a de facto decision rule (when q votes are not obtained, the jury is assumed to hang). In developing his model, Grofman assumed for simplicity that $P_{II} = P_{GG} = p$ (i.e., that jurors are equally good at correctly determining guilt or innocence).

In some respects Grofman's model is a more general version of the Gelfand and Solomon (1973, 1974, 1975, 1977) model; Grofman's p and P_G correspond to Gelfand and Solomon's T and M.

As the first step in the construction of his model, Grofman examined the probability that a majority of jurors ($q = m$) in a jury with an odd number of jurors (N) will reach a correct verdict:

P (correct verdict)

$$= \sum_{h=m}^{N} \binom{N}{h} p^h (1 - p)^{N-h}. \quad (9)$$

This expression is simply Equation 1 rewritten with $Q = m$ and with p as the probability that a juror will vote correctly. The general implications of this model are that when $p > \frac{1}{2}$, increasing the size of the jury also increases the probability that a majority will reach a correct verdict (while lowering the probability that a verdict will be reached); when $p = \frac{1}{2}$, the probability that a jury will reach a correct verdict is $\frac{1}{2}$ and is independent of jury size; and when $p < \frac{1}{2}$, the larger the size of the jury, the less likely it is to reach a correct verdict.

Equation 9 can also be used to create expressions for P_C, P_A, and P_{II}:

$$P_C = \sum_{h=q}^{N} \left[\binom{N}{h} p^h (1 - p)^{N-h} P_G \right. $$
$$\left. + p^{N-h} (1 - p)^h P_I \right], \quad (10)$$

$$P_A = \sum_{h=q}^{N} \left[\binom{N}{h} p^h (1 - p)^{N-h} P_I \right.$$

$$\left. + p^{N-h}(1 - p)^h P_G \right], \quad (11)$$

$$P_H = \sum_{h=N-q+1}^{q-1} \left[\binom{N}{h} p^h (1 - p)^{N-h} \right]. \quad (12)$$

Equation 12 is a corrected form of Grofman's expression. Note that the first terms of Equations 10 and 11 determine the probability that q or more jurors will correctly vote for guilt or innocence, whereas the second terms determine the probability that q or more jurors will incorrectly vote for guilt or innocence (cf. Equations 5 and 6 in Gelfand & Solomon's, 1973, model). The P_H equation determines the probability that less than q jurors will concur on either guilt or innocence (note that when the decision rule is that the majority wins, P_H is the probability of an even split in juries with an even number of jurors, and $P_H = .0$ with odd-numbered juries). Note that P_H is independent of P_G and P_I.

Table 4

Distribution of First Ballot Votes When the Probability of a Juror Not Erring Equals .88 and the Probability the Defendant Is Guilty Equals .69

No. of votes	Total probability	Correct part	Incorrect part
	Votes to convict		
12	.1488	.1488	.0
11	.2435	.2435	.0
10	.1826	.1826	.0
9	.0830	.0830	.0
8	.0255	.0255	.0
7	.0056	.0055	.0001
	Votes to hang		
6	.0013	.0009	.0004
	Votes to acquit		
7	.0026	.0025	.0001
8	.0115	.0115	.0
9	.0373	.0373	.0
10	.0820	.0820	.0
11	.1094	.1094	.0
12	.0669	.0669	.0

Note. Adapted from Gelfand and Solomon (1975).

Table 4 (based on Gelfand & Solomon, 1975) displays the probabilities of vote distributions from (0, 12) through (12, 0) that obtain from $p = .88$ and $P_G = .69$ and provides some insight into the operation of Equations 10–12. Note that the table is based on a 12-person jury using a majority decision rule. If the decision rule were 8 of 12 votes, the hung portion of the table would consist of the sum of the probabilities of the (7, 5), (6, 6), and (5, 7) distributions.

Grofman (1976) observed that if jurors are very accurate in assessing guilt and innocence, then the values for P_A and p_C are approximated by the first terms of Equations 10 and 11. From Table 4 it is clear that for a 12-member jury with $p = .88$ and a majority decision rule, Grofman's observation is quite correct—deleting the "incorrect" portions of the P_A and P_C terms loses only .02% of the cases.

If one further assumes that the decision rule is unanimity, then the equations simplify even further:

$$P_C \approx p^N P_G, \quad (13)$$

$$P_A \approx p^N P_I, \quad (14)$$

$$P_H \approx 1 - p^N, \quad (15)$$

where

$$P_G \approx \frac{P_C}{P_C + P_A},$$

$$P_I \approx \frac{P_A}{P_C + P_A},$$

$$p \approx (P_C + P_A)^{(1/n)}.$$

Grofman correctly observed that with the appropriate normative data, it is relatively easy to estimate the parameters P_G, P_A, and p, but in making his estimates he assumed that the appropriate data are the distribution of final jury verdicts when, in fact, the appropriate data are the distribution of initial ballots. Grofman assumed that he could treat q as though it were an effective decision rule (similar to the analyses of Davis, 1973, and Walbert, 1971); however, the simplifying assumptions that led him from Equations 10, 11, and 12 to Equations 13, 14, and 15 used restrictions on q that effectively changed the decision rule from a majority decision to unanimity rule. As Saks and Ostrom (1975) demonstrated, the effect of such restrictions is to lower the probability that a jury will produce a verdict on the first ballot. (As can be seen from Table 4, when $p = .88$ and $p_G = .69$, only slightly more than one fifth of the juries can be expected to produce a verdict on the first ballot with a decision rule of unanimity.)

It is, therefore, appropriate to estimate the parameters of the simplified model using data on first ballot distributions. The estimates obtained using the Kalven and Zeisel (1966) data are $P_G = .6232$, $P_I = .3768$, $p = .9062$, and $P_H = .6933$. That the estimates are roughly equivalent to those made by Gelfand and Solomon (1975) should not surprise one, since Grofman's simplifying assumptions allow a straightforward estimation of the same parameters. The estimates are cruder because the simplified equations are based on initial vote distributions at the tails of the binomial distribution—$(12, 0)$ and $(0, 12)$—but the similarity of the estimates produced by the two procedures tends to confirm the validity of Grofman's simplifying assumptions.

One might take this analysis one step further and use the data on final verdicts to assess first ballot parameter values. If, for instance, one regards final verdicts as the best available index of defendants' convictability or "acquittability," then the Kalven and Zeisel (1966) data in Table 1 indicate that 139 (61.78%) of the 225 defendants were convictable, that 73 (32.44%) were acquittable, and that in 13 cases (5.7%) the guilt or innocence of the defendant was ambiguous. One can now ask, what is the probability that a convictable (acquittable) defendant will be convicted (acquitted) on the first ballot? The answer is that 43 of the 139 defendants ultimately convicted were convicted on the first ballot (30.94%), whereas 26 of the 73 defendants ultimately acquitted were acquitted on the first ballot (35.62%).

Thus, the probability that an individual juror will vote to convict a convictable defendant on the first ballot is $.3094^{1/12}$ or .9069, and the probability that an individual juror will vote to acquit an acquittable defendant on the first ballot is $.3562^{1/12}$ or .9176. These results are in close agreement with the Gelfand and Solomon and Grofman estimates and suggest that jurors may be somewhat more reluctant to vote to convict an apparently guilty defendant on the first ballot than they

are to vote to acquit an apparently innocent defendant. As before, of course, this analysis tells one nothing about the deliberation process itself; it merely provides a crude method for assessing first ballot, individual juror accuracy.

Juror Tolerance for Errors

Following the analyses of Rae (1969), Taylor (1969), Curtis (1972), and Badger (1972), Grofman (1976) has used his basic binomial model (Equations 8, 9, and 10) to explore the decision rule implications of various levels of juror tolerance for erroneous jury decisions. He first specified a trade-off ratio R that reflects the number of guilty defendants a juror would be willing to set free to avoid the erroneous conviction of one innocent defendant. Two ratios can be constructed using R: $P_R = R/(R + 1)$ is the relative weight attached to avoiding false convictions (avoiding a Type I error) that Grofman analyzes as the weight attached to assuring correct convictions and $1 - P_R = R/(R + 1)$ is the relative weight attached to assuring correct convictions of guilty defendants (avoiding a Type II error) that Grofman analyzes as the relative weight attached to avoiding false convictions. By way of example, if a juror is willing to set five guilty defendants free to avoid one false conviction, then $P_R = 5(5 + 1) = 5/6$ and $1 - P_R = 1/6$. (For discussions of Type I and Type II errors in legal contexts, see also Feinberg, 1971; Friedman, 1972; Tribe, 1971.)

By weighting the probability of correct voting to reflect the trade-off ratio P_R for Type I and Type II errors, a new equation can be formed for the weighted probability that a quorum q will produce a correct verdict:

$$\sum_{h=0}^{q-1}\left[\binom{N}{h}p^{N-h}(1-p)^h P_I P_R\right]$$
$$+ \sum_{h=q}^{N}\left[\binom{N}{h}p^h(1-p)^{N-h} P_G(1 - P_R)\right]. \tag{16}$$

The second term of Equation 16 corresponds to the first term of Equation 10 and is simply the weighted probability that q or more jurors will correctly vote for conviction. The first term of Equation 16 is related to the first term of Equation 11, but in addition to including all the cases in which q or more jurors correctly vote for acquittal, the first term of Equation 16 also includes the cases in which the jury hangs (from $h = 0$ through $q - 1$). In essence, Grofman's analysis treats hung juries as correct acquittals.

Although Grofman again regarded q as the effective decision rule, his analysis is appropriately treated as an analysis of first ballots rather than of final verdicts. This means, as we have noted before, that the analysis fails to account for those cases in which final verdicts are not characterized by majority persuasion (approximately 5% of the cases reported in Kalven & Zeisel, 1966). Given the limitations on one's knowledge about the deliberation process, Grofman's treatment of q as an effective decision rule is not fatal and has the advantage of simplifying his analysis. The question of interest, of course, concerns what decision rule will maximize the value of Equation 16.

For fixed ns, Grofman determined the values of q that maximize the expression for given levels of p, P_G, and P_R. Of greatest interest are those conditions in which juror accuracy is greater than one half (in which case q should be equal to or greater than a majority m). Grofman noted in particular that when $P_G > 1/2$, the optimal decision rule approaches or equals $q = n$ as P_R approaches 1. Grofman concluded "that it does not require an infinite value of R to justify in normative terms a decision rule requiring unanimity to convict!" (p. 11).

In a similar fashion, Grofman constructed an index of juror satisfaction (D) that reflects the subjective ratio of disappointment a juror experiences when an apparently innocent defendant is convicted compared with the disappointment experienced when an apparently guilty defendant is set free. (Disappointment is *subjective* insofar as a juror can rarely know with certainty that a defendant is objectively guilty or innocent and can only judge on the basis of trial evidence.) The relative disappointment of a Type I error can be denoted by $P_D = D/(D + 1)$ and a Type II error by $1 - P_D = D/(D + 1)$. Thus, if a juror is nine times more disappointed by an

erroneous conviction than by an erroneous acquittal, $D = 9$, $P_D = 9/(9 + 1) = .9$, and $1 - P_D = .1$.

Using the trade-off ratio for disappointment, the weighted probability that a randomly selected juror will agree with a verdict (i.e., the juror's perception of the correctness of other jurors' assessments of the evidence) is expressed by

$$\sum_{h=q-1}^{N-1} \binom{N-1}{h} p^{h+1}(1 - p)^{N-h-1} P_G P_D$$

$$+ \sum_{h=q-1}^{N-1} \binom{N-1}{h} p^{h+1}(1 - p)^{N-h-1} P_I (1 - P_D).$$

$$(17)$$

(This expression includes a correction of a typographical error in Grofman, 1976.)

The first term of the expression is the weighted probability that a juror will join a quorum that will correctly convict, while the second term is the weighted probability that a juror will join a quorum that will correctly acquit. Grofman concluded from his analysis that the value of Expression 17 is maximized when the decision rule corresponds directly to the juror's trade-off ratio P_D (for a related analysis, see Curtis, 1972). Thus, if a juror is as disappointed by seeing two guilty defendants acquitted as by seeing one innocent defendant convicted $(P_D = \frac{2}{3})$, that juror should prefer a two-thirds decision rule. Again, of course, we caution that this analysis is most appropriate for first ballot distribution and would require modification if it were extended to final verdicts.

Both the Gelfand and Solomon and the Grofman analyses of prior probabilities of guilt and juror accuracy are based on data from a wide range of cases. In some of those cases the evidence of guilt was probably overwhelming, in some cases the evidence of guilt was probably fairly weak, and in many cases the evidence was probably relatively balanced. Because the estimates of the parameters used in the models are based on a range of cases, they may not be directly applicable to any particular case. In general, the results suggest that approximately 70% of the defendants brought to trial (in the cases examined by Kalven and Zeisel) are convictable and that jurors are on the average about 90% accurate in their assessments of defendants' convictability. This does not mean that any particular defendant has a 70% chance of conviction, nor does it mean that one can expect 10% of the jurors to err in their judgments of a particular defendant's guilt. The Gelfand and Solomon and Grofman analyses simply are not appropriate for analysis of individual cases. Indeed, it is possible that the convictability and juror accuracy parameters (assumed to be independent in the two models) are in fact interrelated and that juror errors are most likely to occur in cases in which the evidence against and in favor of a defendant is relatively balanced. In cases in which the evidence points unequivocally in one direction or another, it is probably less likely that jurors will err. Existing data on juror behavior are not adequate to the task of determining the relationship between apparent guilt and jury acuity, but the reasonableness of the assumption of independence should be kept in mind when evaluating the parameter estimates provided by the models we have examined.

The aspect of both Gelfand and Solomon's and Grofman's analyses that we find most disturbing is the implication that there are only two distinct types of defendants: defendants who clearly should not be convicted on the weight of the trial evidence ($\approx 30\%$ of all defendants) and for whom the probability that a juror will erroneously vote to convict is $\approx .1$ and defendants who clearly should be convicted on the weight of the trial evidence ($\approx 70\%$ of all defendants) and for whom the probability that a juror will correctly vote to convict is $\approx .9$ (see sample results reported in Table 3).

Although such a view may provide a reasonable characterization of trial evidence and of jurors' assessment of that evidence, we think that this analysis obscures the fact that the evidence presented at trials probably varies widely in the extent to which it indicates a defendant's guilt or innocence. In some cases the evidence may overwhelmingly and unmistakably point to guilt or innocence, and with such evidence we would not be surprised to see unanimous first ballot verdicts. In other instances the evidence may be very close (some of it pointing to innocence and some pointing to guilt), and in these trials we would not be

surprised to find the jury dividing equally for conviction and acquittal on the first ballot.

Basically, we think it misleading to conceive of juror accuracy in Gelfand and Solomon's terms—juror accuracy is, after all, limited by the quality of the evidence presented at trial. Optimal juror performance can probably be attained only under circumstances such as those outlined in the discussion of Saks and Ostrom's (1975) and Walbert's (1971) binomial models: With very large juries, defendants should only be convicted when a majority (or some other critical proportion) of the jurors vote to convict after hearing all the trial evidence. We think it more realistic to assume that the weight of trial evidence (the extent to which the evidence would convince a juror of the defendant's guilt) varies widely across trials and that the best indication of the variability in trial evidence weight is the variability in jurors' first ballot votes for conviction and acquittal.

Judging from Kalven and Zeisel's (1966) data on first ballot votes (Table 1), it appears that the weight of evidence is bimodally distributed and that in approximately 70% of the cases the evidence points to conviction. Because Table 1 provides only summary data on the distribution of votes (i.e., juries produce unanimous verdicts for conviction in 19% of the cases, produce nonunanimous majorities for acquittal in 18% of the cases, and produce unanimous verdicts for acquittal in 12% of the cases), one cannot fix the actual distribution of first ballot votes (or the underlying distribution of evidentiary weight that produces the first ballot distribution of votes). Still, one can test some possible distributions of evidentiary weight across trials (in which such weights represent the probability that a randomly selected juror who has heard the evidence from a particular trial will vote to convict) for their fit to the Kalven and Zeisel first ballot vote distribution.

For example, the Gelfand and Solomon (1975) model that produces the distribution of votes shown in Table 4 assumes a distribution of evidentiary weight in which the probability that a juror will vote to convict is .88 for 69% of the cases and .12 for 31% of the cases. This very simple bimodal distribution of evidence produces a moderately good fit to the Kalven and Zeisel data. We have tested several other types of evidentiary weight distributions (relatively flat but skewed, unimodal, and bimodal) and have assumed in each instance that the weights are distributed in probability intervals of .1. We have found that bimodal distributions of evidence such as the one in Figure 2 produce the best fits to the Kalven and Zeisel data. (We caution that this estimation enterprise is crude; it is subject to the limitations of the data, it is post hoc, and it ignores that the distribution of evidence is probably continuous rather than discrete. Still, the distribution in Figure 2 is psychologically plausible and, as we demonstrate, produces a good fit to the distribution in Table 1.)

To explain our method briefly, one can see that the distribution of weights in Figure 2 implies that in 13% of all cases jurors are expected to judge the evidence against a defendant as unmistakably indicating that the defendant is guilty. In these cases the probability that jurors will vote to convict is equal to 1.0—Each of these juries will return unanimous verdicts for conviction (the expected outcome for a binomial $p = 1.0$ and for $N = 12$). In 8% of the cases Figure 2 implies that all jurors will vote for acquittal ($p = .00$). Similarly, in 16% of the cases the (binomial) probability that a randomly selected juror will vote to convict equals .8.

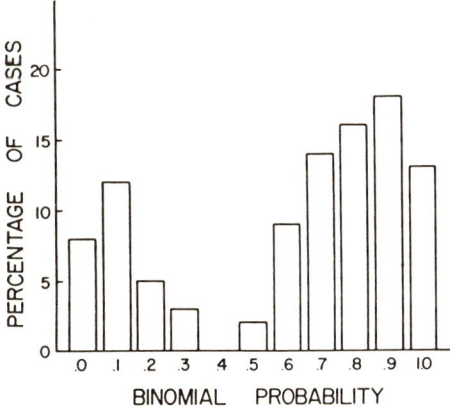

Figure 2. Hypothetical distribution, across cases, of evidentiary weight for conviction (based on data collected by Kalven & Zeisel, 1966).

By consulting binomial tables or using the binomial expansion for $N = 6$ and $N = 12$, one can determine the expected distribution of first ballot votes for the distribution of ps shown in Figure 2.

Figure 3 shows the expected distributions of votes for each of the binomial probabilities for 12-member juries. The figure also shows the cumulative probability of each vote distribution (i.e., if the evidence weight is distributed as shown in Figure 2, then in 12-member juries a unanimous verdict for acquittal should occur in 11.7% of the cases, with the bulk of these verdicts occurring in trials in which the evidence points unequivocally to innocence). The cumulative distribution of first ballot votes in the 12-member jury (shown at the top of Figure 3) provides a very good fit to the Kalven and Zeisel data (11.7%, 18.4%, 3.8%, 46.5%, and 19.4% in the model vs. 12%, 18%, 4%, 47%, and 19% in the respective categories for the normative data).

By making a few simple assumptions, one can also assess the distribution of first ballot votes for accuracy. For example, if one makes the crude assumption that juries should convict whenever the binomial probability of guilt is equal to or greater than .6 (i.e., when 60% or more of all jurors who might hear a case would vote to convict), should hang when $p = .5$, and should acquit when $p \leq .4$, then one can easily determine the number of juries that began deliberation with "errorful" first ballot distributions (e.g., in Figure 3 when $p \geq .6$, all the juries who have produced less than seven votes for conviction have made errors, since one has assumed that defendants with evidentiary weights of .6 or more should be convicted). In Figure 4 we display the proportions of cases in each category of initial votes, ranging from $(0, 12)$ to $(12, 0)$, that would convict, hang, and acquit if one applied the simple rules outlined above. Overall, the probability that a jury will begin deliberations with a majority erroneously preferring acquittal is 1.9% in 12-member juries, while the probability that a jury will begin deliberations with a majority erroneously preferring conviction is .1%. These values can be compared with the much lower error rates produced by Gelfand and Solomon's model (see Table 4). Although the absolute value of the estimates

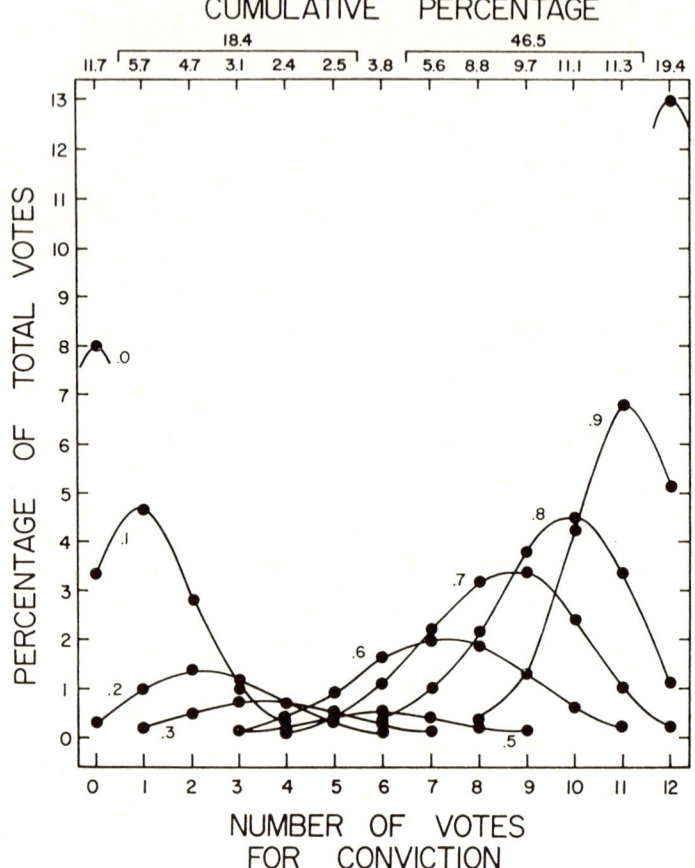

Figure 3. Distribution of first ballot vote percentages for conviction across juries, based on the assumption of a bimodal distribution of evidence such as the one illustrated in Figure 2. (The parameter of the plotted subdistributions in Figure 3 corresponds to evidentiary weight in Figure 2. The cumulative distribution totals, 18.4 and 46.5, correspond to the tabulation of votes for conviction reported in Kalven & Zeisel, 1966, and reproduced in Table 1.)

produced by the model we have developed in this section can be questioned (more complete data on the Kalven and Zeisel juries would heighten our confidence), we think that this model of juror accuracy is superior to Gelfand and Solomon's and Grofman's because it makes more plausible assumptions about the distribution of trial evidence weights. Since the distribution of first ballot votes produced by the model fits the normative data better than Gelfand and Solomon's model, we are also confident that Gelfand and Solomon's model underpredicts first ballot error rates.

Relationship Between Juror and Jury Errors

Ultimately, of course, we would like to know the error rates in jury verdicts (rather than just the first ballot votes); and, in particular, we would like to have some idea of the effects that variations in jury size and decision rule have on these error rates. The problem of finding a satisfactory method of relating first ballots to final verdicts is one we have encountered several times in our discussion of various mathematical models. Although we have criticized all of the proffered solutions to this problem, we think that a decision scheme approach such as Davis's (1973) offers the most promise. Simply for purposes of illustration, we have applied the decision schemes in Table 5 to the initial vote distributions in Figure 2 to acquire a sense of the impact that different decision rules (unanimous vs. two thirds) might have on jury accuracy.

The decision schemes in Table 5 are based largely on the results of a computer simulation of jury decision making that is discussed later in this article (see also Penrod & Hastie, Note 6). These decision schemes are constructed to produce a slight postdeliberation bias toward acquittal, such as is observed in the Kalven and Zeisel (1966) data (in Table 1, more majorities reverse in the direction of acquittal than in the direction of conviction). These decision schemes are also roughly comparable with Gelfand and Solomon's (1975, 1977) version of Davis et al.'s (1975) Scheme 3.

Before discussing the results of this decision scheme analysis, it should be noted that these decision schemes reflect relatively unfavorable views of the deliberation process insofar as they assume that both correct and errorful initial majorities are equally likely to be reversed during deliberation. In other words, these decision schemes do not assume that deliberation serves to correct the errors made in first ballot votes. If deliberations did serve a

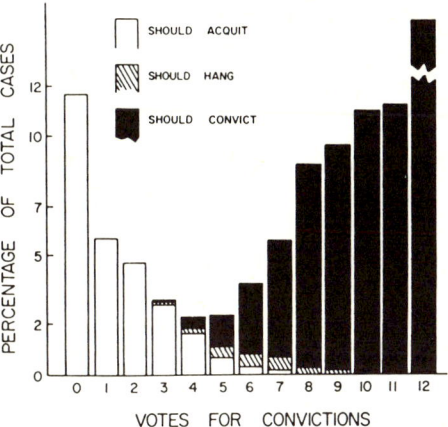

Figure 4. Distribution of percentage of votes for conviction across cases generated by the assumptions of the analysis outlined in Figures 2 and 3 and in the text. (Solid areas represent juries under conditions with evidentiary weights for conviction greater than .50, hatched areas represent juries with weights equal to .50, and clear areas represent juries with weights less than .50.)

correcting function, then one would expect the probability of a reversal in a first-ballot-error case to be higher than the probability of a reversal in an initially correct case. As one will see, our analysis indicates that the selection of optimal jury sizes and optimal decision rules

Table 5
Decision Schemes

Votes for conviction	p of verdict in unanimity (12/12) rule			p of verdict in 8/12 rule		
	Acquit	Hang	Convict	Acquit	Hang	Convict
0	1.0			1.0		
1	1.0			1.0		
2	1.0			1.0		
3	1.0			1.0		
4	.92	.07	.01	1.0		
5	.70	.26	.04	.70	.26	.04
6	.35	.40	.25	.35	.40	.25
7	.14	.26	.60	.14	.26	.60
8	.04	.07	.89			1.0
9			1.0			1.0
10			1.0			1.0
11			1.0			1.0
12			1.0			1.0

Note. In 12/12 and 8/12 rule, the denominator indicates jury size and the numerator denotes the number of votes needed for a decision.

depends on whether deliberation operates to minimize first ballot errors.

The results obtained by applying each of the decision schemes to the initial vote distributions in Figure 2 are summarized in Table 6. (The table also summarizes the results for 6-member juries; for complete details on data and methods see Penrod & Hastie, Note 6.) If one ignores hung juries, it is clear that the 12-member juries produce fewer false acquittals and false convictions than do the 6-member juries: The smaller jury, regardless of decision rule, produces 50% more erroneous acquittals (about 5 in 100 compared with about 3 in 100) and four times as many erroneous convictions (about 6 in 1,000 compared with about 1.4 in 1,000). These same relationships are also evident in the probabilities that a defendant is guilty if convicted ($P_{G/C}$), innocent if convicted ($P_{I/C}$), innocent if acquitted ($P_{I/A}$), and guilty if acquitted ($P_{G/Z}$). (These probabilities can be compared with the 12-member probabilities produced by Gelfand & Solomon's model; see Table 3.)

Somewhat surprisingly, the error rates in nonunanimous juries are lower than the rates in the corresponding unanimous juries. The reason for this is that the decision schemes used to generate the final distributions of verdicts do not use the corrective factor discussed earlier. This point can be illustrated by examining the distribution of error cases in 12-member juries who produce eight votes for conviction on the first ballot. One can see in Figure 4 that most such juries' votes are consistent with the evidence, but a few "should" have begun deliberation with even splits. If these juries use a unanimous decision rule, one can see from Table 5 that 4% of the juries can be expected to reverse the original majority and produce verdicts for acquittals. Since the decision scheme does not distinguish between error cases and correct cases, the result is that 4% of the cases that start with errors will be corrected, while 4% of the cases that begin deliberation with majorities correctly preferring conviction will erroneously acquit. In essence, the decision scheme ultimately creates more errors than it corrects. For juries using an 8/12 decision rule, this problem is avoided—none of the original error

Table 6
Decision-Scheme-Generated Verdicts and Verdict Accuracy for 6- and 12-Member Juries Assigned Unanimous and Nonunanimous Decision Rules for N = 100 Cases

Jury decision rule[a]	Acquittal COR	Acquittal SHH	Acquittal SHC	Hung case COR	Hung case SHC	Hung case SHA	Conviction COR	Conviction SHH	Conviction SHA	Total Convicted	Total Hung	Total Acquitted	Condition[a] $P_{G/C}$	$P_{I/C}$	$P_{I/A}$	$P_{G/A}$
12/12	27.23	.80	3.63	.42	3.51	.46	63.01	.64	.14	63.79	4.39	31.66	.9878	.0021	.8601	.1147
8/12	27.44	.82	3.27	.40	2.87	.45	64.16	.67	.14	64.96	3.72	31.53	.9877	.0021	.8703	.1037
6/6	26.76	.89	5.29	.31	3.74	.70	60.97	.81	.60	62.38	4.75	32.94	.9774	.0096	.8124	.1606
4/6	27.02	.91	4.95	.24	2.68	.48	62.38	.85	.60	63.83	3.40	32.88	.9773	.0094	.8218	.1505

Note. COR = correct, SHH = should have hung, SHC = should have convicted, and SHA = should have acquitted. $P_{G/C}$ = the probability that a defendant is guilty given that the defendant is convicted. $P_{I/C}$ = the probability that a defendant is innocent given that the defendant is convicted. $P_{I/A}$ = the probability that a defendant is innocent given that the defendant is acquitted. $P_{G/A}$ = the probability that a defendant is guilty given that the defendant is acquitted.

[a] The denominator of the decision rule indicates jury size, and the numerator indicates the number of votes needed for a decision.

cases are corrected, but no new error cases are created.

Although we have only limited confidence in the absolute value of the entries in Table 6 (since neither the initial distribution of evidence nor the decision schemes are well-grounded empirically), these results suggest that one's ability to distinguish among optimal decision rules may ultimately depend on one's ability to specify the extent to which jury deliberations serve to correct the "sampling errors" in the distribution of initial votes. Our guess is that a unanimous decision ultimately operates to minimize jury errors: First, it minimizes the probability of an incorrect verdict on the first ballot, and second, it maximizes the opportunities for jurors who have correctly assessed the weight of the evidence to communicate the grounds for their assessments to other jurors, who may then be persuaded to adopt a more accurate view of the evidence. Stated another way, we contend that it is unlikely that reversals of majorities are equally likely for initially correct and incorrect juries. Given the small magnitude of the advantages enjoyed by the non-unanimous juries under the equally likely decision schemes we have used (Table 6 shows that the advantages in the critical false-acquittal and false-conviction categories are very small), it is clear that even a relatively small correcting factor in jury deliberations would give the edge to the unanimous decision rules. As a practical matter, our results indicate that it is important to direct future research to the question of whether deliberation serves to minimize verdict errors. If there is something about the deliberation process that does serve to raise the probability that initial errors will be corrected, then the unanimous decision rule is probably preferable.

To conclude the section on models of juror accuracy we examine a model developed by Nagel and Neef (1975). Nagel and Neef have also tackled the question of the relationship among jury size, decision rules, and error rates, using an approach that is similar to but less general than Grofman's (1976) approach. Perhaps the most important difference between the two lines of analysis is that Nagel and Neef were concerned with defendants' objective or true guilt and innocence rather than the guilt or innocence indicated by the evidence presented at trial (what Gelfand and Solomon called "convictability"). A second important difference is that Nagel and Neef made specific assumptions about the values of the parameters they used in their model and then examined the results obtained with these specific parameter values.

Their analysis proceeded in two stages: First, they analyzed *individual* juror behavior (what we regard as *first ballot* behavior), and then they examined individual plus *collective* behavior (what we would consider to be an analysis of jury verdicts). Nagel and Neef's analysis can most clearly be understood by noting the assumptions about objective guilt and innocence and juror accuracy on which their analysis is based. First, they assumed that the number of truly guilty defendants brought to trial is relatively large (95%), while the number of truly innocent defendants is relatively small (5%). Although we consider the grounds for this assumption rather curious (it is based on an analogy to the .05 significance level used in statistical analysis), we do not quarrel with the reasonableness of the assumption; indeed, we have heard experienced defense attorneys make even lower estimates of the error rate in indictments. (Of course, since only about 10% of all criminal indictments reach trial—most defendants plea bargain—it is possible that truly innocent defendants are overrepresented at the trial stage.) The basic implication of Nagel and Neef's assumption is that it is relatively uncommon to find instances in which evidence sufficient for indictment points to the wrong defendant and that prosecutors are reasonably accurate in their indictments.

Next, Nagel and Neef assumed that 40% of all truly innocent defendants are erroneously convicted by juries (i.e., 2 in 100 cases yield false convictions), compared with a 70% conviction rate for truly guilty defendants (they made this estimate by reference to the Kalven & Zeisel, 1966, data that are presented in Table 1). Disregarding deliberation effects (a point to which we return), Nagel and Neef used the 40% and 70% figures to posit that the probability that an individual juror will erroneously vote to convict a truly innocent defendant is $.4^{1/12}$ or .926, whereas the probability that an individual juror will correctly vote to convict a truly guilty defendant is $.7^{1/12}$ or .971. Finally, Nagel and Neef assumed they could use these individual probabilities in the binomial expansion to determine the weighted probabilities of false convictions and false acquittals for various jury sizes and decision rules (fundamentally the method used in Grofman's, 1976, analysis). For ease of presentation, Nagel and Neef reported their results in terms of 1,000 cases in which 95% (950) of the defendants were truly guilty and 5% (50) were truly innocent. The results of their analysis (in which false convictions were given a weight of 10 compared with a weight of 1 for false acquittals) indicate that with binomial probabilities of .926 and .971, seven-member unanimous juries produce the minimum weighted sum of errors and 11/12 and 10/12 juries produce the lowest weighted sum of errors for nonunanimous juries of various sizes.

Unfortunately, we regard this analysis as faulty at several points. First, by taking the 12th root of the .4 and .7 probabilities, Nagel and Neef implicitly adopted the 12-member unanimous jury as the absolute standard against which all other jury sizes and decision rules are to be evaluated. Nagel and Neef failed to justify using $p^{1/12}$ as a standard individual probability. Second, because they used these probabilities in the binomial expansion to determine the probability that X or more jurors (where X is the decision rule quorum) in a jury with Y members will vote to convict in Y binomial trials, their initial analysis produced the curious result that all juries failing to attain the required quorum in Y binomial trials were treated as acquittals, even though they may have been only one vote short of the necessary quorum for conviction. As one saw before (e.g., in Walbert's, 1971, analysis), for any fixed binomial probability, any reduction in the number of binomial trials (i.e., any reduction in the number of jurors who constitute a jury) increases the probability that all the jurors (or some set proportion of the jurors) will agree on an outcome. Given this fact, the real problem with Nagel and Neef's analysis is that they failed (as did some of the other mathematical modelers we have considered) to make an adequate distinction between individual juror

accuracy (first ballots) and jury accuracy (verdicts).

It is appropriate to say that Nagel and Neef's initial analysis assessed weighted errors in the first ballot verdicts produced by juries of varying size who used various decision rules. Their analysis is comparable with the binomial analysis in Figure 1 and Gelfand and Solomon's (1973, 1974, 1975) analysis. What Nagel and Neef's method potentially adds to these other analyses is the emphasis on weighting errors in first ballot verdicts. With respect to these weights, we note that changes in the relative weights attached to false acquittals and convictions will affect the optimal jury size and decision rules. (For example, if false convictions are given a weight of 14 rather than 10, the advantage in weighted errors on first ballot verdicts shifts to the 12-member jury.)

Although Nagel and Neef failed to mention several of the shortcomings in their model, they were aware that the model does a poor job of accounting for the effects of group deliberation on the accuracy (and even the distribution) of jury verdicts. They attempted to overcome this difficulty by arguing that the final verdict distribution is a product of both individual (or *independent*) factors and collective factors. Thus, that 64% of the defendants in the Kalven and Zeisel trials (see Table 1) were convicted by unanimous juries is taken as an index of the collective factors, whereas $.64^{1/12}$ is taken as an index of the independent factors. The collective factors plus the independent factors are presumed to be reflected in the fact that after deliberation 67.7% of the jurors in the 225 Kalven and Zeisel trials voted to convict (when jurors in hung juries are taken into consideration). This 3.7% difference (67.7% − 64%) is, according to Nagel and Neef, attributable to a weighted combination of individual and collective factors:

$$.677 = \left[\frac{W(.64)^{1/n} + .64}{W + 1} \right],$$

where $W = .13$ and $n = 12$. Nagel and Neef's analysis assumed that this relative weighting of independent and collective factors (11% independent and 89% collective) prevails across all decision rules and jury sizes.

We are troubled by this conception of the deliberation process and the calculations to

Table 7

Jury Verdict Errors for Objectively Innocent and Objectively Guilty Defendants

Jury decision rule[a]	% of total no. convictions		% of total no. acquittals		Unweighted sum of errors	Weighted sum of errors[b]
	Correct	Incorrect	Correct	Incorrect		
12/12	60.60	3.19	1.583	30.07	320.6	619.7
8/12	61.71	3.25	1.577	29.95	332.0	624.5
6/6	59.26	3.12	1.647	31.29	344.1	624.9
4/6	60.64	3.19	1.644	31.24	344.3	631.4

[a] The denominator of the decision rule indicates jury size, and the numerator indicates the number of votes needed for a decision.
[b] The weight ratio was 10:1.

which it gives rise. First, it is not clear what this "combined" model really captures. The relative weight of the independent factor is determined solely by the relative imbalance of juror votes in hung juries (13 of the 225 juries in the Kalven and Zeisel trials) averaged over all 225 juries. (Actually, it is not clear that Nagel & Neef's analysis was based on the distribution of votes in the 13 hung cases reported in Table 1; although they implied that they used these 13 cases, their footnotes indicate they may have drawn on a different sample of 48 hung juries.) Irrespective of their data source, it is clear that Nagel and Neef's analysis depends on the level of disagreement in hung juries—if there were no hung juries (or if in all hung juries the proportion of jurors favoring guilt were the same as the proportion of juries who convicted), there would be no independent probability; the combined probability would be identical to the collective probability, and *W* would equal zero. What Nagel and Neef have done is to take a small bias (toward conviction) in the distribution of votes in a very small number of cases and argue that this bias reflects the individual juror's imperviousness to group influence. Furthermore, by assuming that this independence factor accounts for 11% of the decision making in all jury sizes and decision rules, they have ruled out the possibility that differing jury sizes and decision rules operate directly to affect the extent of group influence on individual jurors (and thereby to affect the distribution of verdict errors). In fact, the evidence that jury size can affect hanging rates (e.g., Kalven & Zeisel, 1966; Padawer-Singer & Barton, Note 1) suggests that the relative impact of independent factors

varies with jury size. (Though it is perhaps a less telling defect, Nagel and Neef did not include the possibility of hung juries being produced by their model.)

In addition to the conceptual problems of the combined model, Nagel and Neef's analysis of verdicts is also based on a binomial model in which the probability of a conviction equals the probability that a quorum will be obtained in *Y* binomial trials. The verdicts of non-quorum juries are once again treated as acquittals, even though the juries may fall only one vote short of a quorum (many such cases end up being added to the error cases for false acquittals).

Although we have chosen not to report the results of Nagel and Neef's verdict analysis (for the reasons enumerated above), we do applaud their efforts and think that with a better formulated verdict model, it would be worthwhile to pursue and test their assumptions about objective guilt and innocence and the effects that different jury sizes and decision rules have on error rates.

One possible approach might make use of the model, developed earlier in this section, that assumes the weight of trial evidence is bimodally distributed. In Figure 2 we used the binomial expansion to generate a distribution of first ballot votes and then applied the decision schemes shown in Table 5 to assess the error rates in final verdicts. If, in common with Nagel and Neef, we are interested in testing inferences about the effects of jury size and decision rule on the weighted probability of false convictions of truly guilty defendants and false acquittals of truly guilty defendants, we can use the same model and, by making

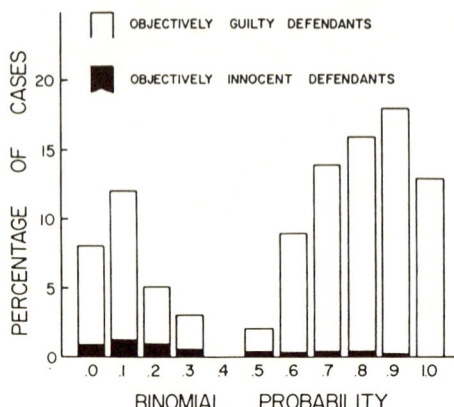

Figure 5. Hypothetical distribution across cases of evidentiary weight for conviction, incorporating the Nagel and Neef (1975) assumption that the distribution of weights is dependent on objective guilt or innocence of the defendant.

reasonable assumptions about the distribution of evidentiary weight against objectively guilty and innocent defendants, assess the probabilities of conviction and acquittal errors for objectively guilty and innocent defendants.

For instance, if we assume (as did Nagel and Neef) that 5% of all defendants are truly innocent and make the further assumption that the evidence against truly guilty and innocent defendants is identically distributed, we can examine the overall distribution of verdicts in Table 6 to assess error rates for different jury sizes and decision rules. As the results in Table 7 demonstrate, with a weight ratio of 10:1, the 12 unanimous juries produced the lowest weighted sum of errors.

A somewhat more complex analysis might incorporate Nagel and Neef's assumption that truly innocent defendants are less likely to be convicted than truly guilty defendants (.4 vs. .7). This assumption can be incorporated into the model by assuming that the evidence against truly innocent defendants is not distributed identically to the evidence against truly guilty defendants, but is skewed in the direction of acquittal. A distribution of evidence such as the one in Figure 5 captures this notion. This distribution of evidence could be used to generate a distribution of verdicts that could then be subjected to an analysis for

errors (including an analysis of the weighted sum of errors).

An analysis such as the one advanced here has the advantage of testing the effects of jury size and decision rule variations on error rates (given a variety of assumptions about the distribution of the weight of evidence against objectively guilty and innocent defendants) in the context of a model that straightforwardly relates jury verdicts to initial votes by individual jurors.

Summary Comments on Mathematical Models

As we have noted above, one of the major shortcomings of the mathematical models of jury decision making is the weakness of their assumptions about the relationship between first ballots and final ballots. As one has seen, Saks and Ostrom (1975) did not confront the problem. Walbert (1971) made the simple assumption that verdicts are governed by majority persuasion, with initially evenly divided juries splitting equally for conviction and acquittal, but his model fails to account for reversals of initial majorities and juries that ultimately hang. Gelfand and Solomon (1973, 1974, 1975, 1977) gave little consideration to the relationship of first ballot distributions to final verdicts, for they were able to estimate their parameters simply by examining post hoc, aggregate relationships between first ballots and final verdicts without making assumptions about the intervening processes.

Grofman's (1976) and Nagel and Neef's (1975) models of juror accuracy also suffer from an inability to treat final verdicts, except under the simplest of assumptions about the relationship of first and final ballots.

Davis (1973) and Davis et al. (1975) addressed the problem of modeling social processes and employed a post hoc analysis of first ballots and final verdicts to find the implicit or effective decision rule that best fits the aggregate data. Although good aggregate fits are obtained, no one decision scheme has consistently provided the best fit. Furthermore, when nonaggregated analyses of initial ballots and final verdicts from individual juries have been made, the predictive accuracy of the best fitting models has proven unreliable (Davis, Kerr, Stasser, Meek, & Holt, 1977;

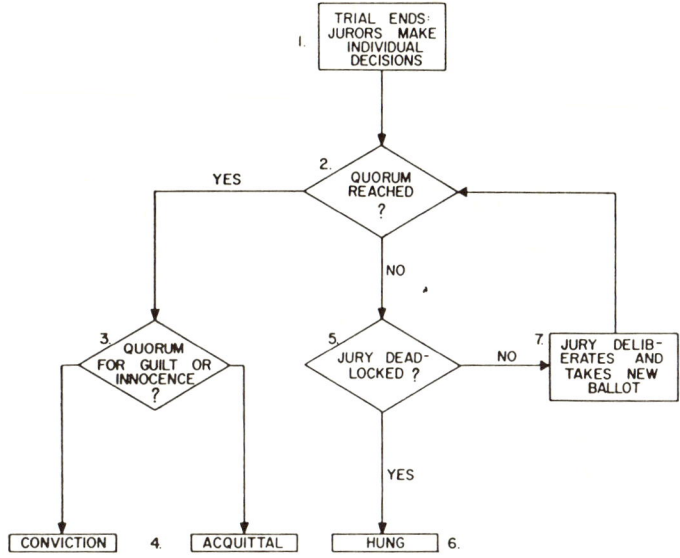

Figure 6. Flowchart summary of our model for jury decision making.

Grofman, 1976; Kerr et al., 1976; Grofman & Hamilton, Note 4).

The binomial model that we have presented avoids some of these problems by introducing more plausible assumptions about the weight of trial evidence and uses a decision scheme approach to determine the distribution of final verdicts. However, its characterization of the deliberation process is still rather barren.

For the present we conclude that the mathematical models built around the binomial theorem are quite adequate for dealing descriptively (and to a lesser extent, predictively) with the relationship between jury size and initial ballot distributions. However, these models are not yet adequate for analysis of jury verdicts. Until we have better knowledge of the actual deliberation process (theoreticians almost universally lament the paucity of relevant data) and this knowledge has been incorporated into the mathematical models, we should be cautious about accepting existing specifications or estimates of the following parameters: the accuracy of juror assessments of guilt and innocence, the prior probabilities of defendants' convictability, the accuracy of jury verdicts, decision rules that maximize

juror satisfaction and performance, and the implications of changes in jury size.

We do not mean to imply that these parameters or even the deliberation processes cannot be mathematically modeled, for we are confident that with better and more extensive data, adequate mathematical models can be specified that will provide reliable estimates of the parameters of interest.

In the remainder of this article we summarize the results of our efforts to develop a multiparameter computer model of the deliberation process (the model is presented in detail in Penrod & Hastie, Note 6) that produces output that fits empirical data at a number of critical points (including, but not limited to, reversal and hanging rates). One major advantage of the computer modeling approach is that it allows analysis of the dynamic aspects of the jury decision-making process (i.e., the computer model can easily represent the process by which a jury moves from an initial vote distribution to a final verdict). Furthermore, the simulation method, although compatible with mathematical models, is more flexible in its ability to represent complex hypotheses about juror and jury behavior (e.g., Abelson, 1968).

Computer Model of Jury Decision Making

The model summarized here is somewhat broader in scope than the mathematical models we have examined, but it addresses similar issues and rests on similar assumptions about juror behavior. The model is named DICE after the Greek goddess frequently depicted wearing a blindfold and holding the scales of justice in one hand and a sword in the other. It rests on the same assumptions made by Walbert (1971) and Saks and Ostrom (1975): that at the conclusion of a trial a certain proportion of the jury pool (consisting of those jurors who are not excluded by the voir dire) will be prepared to vote for guilt (p) or innocence $(1 - p)$ (or in a civil case, for the plaintiff $[p]$ or the defendant $[1 - p]$). Thus, the probability that a randomly selected juror will vote to convict is p.

The model represents the deliberation process in a form that makes it possible to determine the probability that a randomly selected jury of size n, drawn from a pool in which a specified proportion of the jurors will vote to convict (p), and using any specified decision rule question (q) will produce a conviction, an acquittal, or will hang. Furthermore, the model represents the deliberation process in such a way that it is possible to determine the verdict probabilities for any potential first ballot alignment of votes. In the model decision making is largely characterized by majority persuasion, but in a few cases initial majorities fail to prevail in the deliberations and are either reversed (persuaded by the minority) or do not reach a quorum and hang. Similarly (depending on the case), juries who initially divide evenly sometimes reach verdicts and sometimes hang. Hung juries result when juries fail to attain quorums after extended deliberation. Figure 6 is a simplified representation of the deliberation process embodied in the model, but it does capture the basic structure of DICE.

Parameters

DICE is based on six major parameters:

1. Jury size: Although DICE can operate with any jury size, simulations have concentrated on 6- and 12-member juries.

2. Decision rule: DICE can operate with any decision rule, ranging from majority to unanimity. For example, in modeling the results from a major study by Padawer-Singer and Barton (Note 1), the simulations used the two decision rules employed in that study: unanimity (12/12 and 6/6) and five sixths (5/6 and 10/12).

3. Binomial probability for guilty votes: The initial assignment of votes to simulated individual jurors in DICE is accomplished by establishing a probability that a randomly selected juror will vote to convict on the first ballot of the jury simulation. This parameter parallels the Walbert (1971) and Saks and Ostrom (1975) conviction probability parameter. An initial binomial probability of .47 produces a distribution of first ballot votes nearly identical to the distribution produced by the jurors in the Padawer-Singer and Barton study.

By using a random number generator and the binomial value, all the jurors in a simulation are assigned an initial verdict preference (Step 1).

4. Transition probability function: Several methods of modeling the persuasion/deliberation process have already been noted; Walbert (1971) assumed simple majority persuasion and Davis (1973) offered a wide range of decision schemes. In contrast with these models, which make no attempt to model or explain the deliberation processes that occur between the first and last ballots, DICE follows an alternative approach proposed by Rothschild, Klevorick, and McNeil (Note 7). They have suggested that the deliberation process can be modeled as a continuous-time, birth-and-death Markov process in which the probability that the number of votes for conviction (or acquittal) will increase by one from Time 1 to Time 2 is equal to the proportion of jurors who voted to convict (or acquit) at Time 1. A similar approach has been adopted by Stasser and Davis (1977) and Davis (1978). Experimentation with various transition functions has shown that a function exhibiting a group momentum effect best fits the available empirical data (Penrod & Hastie, Note 6). The transition functions used in DICE are shown in Figure 7. Curve A in Figure 7 shows the probability that a coalition of any size

(from 0–12 in a 12-member jury) will remain intact (i.e., none of the coalition members will change their verdict preference) from one ballot (or time period) to the next. Curve B displays the corresponding probability that individual jurors will not change their verdict preference—the probability values are the ith roots of the group probabilities. Briefly, the group transition function (Curve A) captures the following phenomenon: In juries that are roughly equal in size (in which the majority has no more than eight adherents), the majority's persuasive advantage is slight; but as the majority coalition grows in size the probability that it will continue to grow increases exponentially, and single holdouts

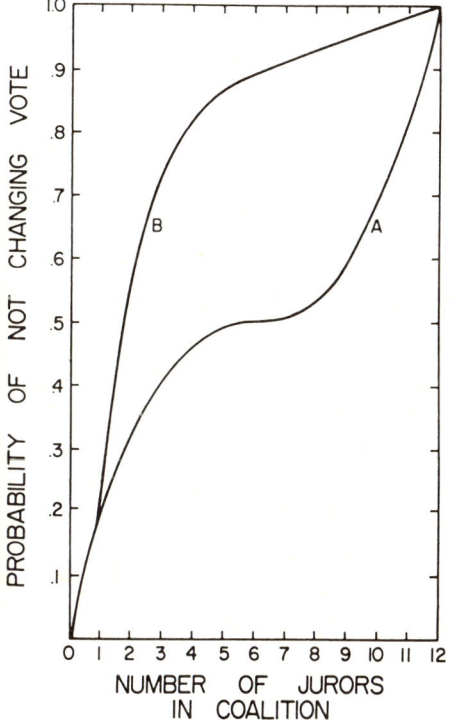

Figure 7. The two functions summarize vote-changing behavior of computer-simulated jurors as a function of coalition size. (Curve A presents the probability that no juror in a coalition of specified size will change votes, and Curve B presents the probability that an individual juror in a coalition will not change votes.)

have a very low probability of not joining the majority (the probability of not changing on any one ballot is .183 for the lone holdout). Readers familiar with early conformity studies (e.g., Asch, 1951; Sherif, 1935) will probably note that these characteristics of the transition function are consistent with conformity research findings. More direct empirical confirmation of the group size effect can be found in research by Godwin and Restle (1974).

5. Individual differences: Padawer-Singer and Barton (Note 1) reported that jurors in juries who ultimately reached a verdict were three times more likely to change their verdict preference during deliberation than jurors in juries who hung. This result and other similar results (e.g., the sex difference in change rates in the Kerr et al., 1976, study and the Davis, Kerr, Stasser, Meek, & Holt, 1977, rape case studies) indicate that some jurors are more susceptible to group persuasion than are other jurors. In DICE all jurors are assigned individual *persuasion resistance scores* that reflect these individual differences.

6. Maximum number of ballots: Not all juries reach a verdict; often members feel that they can no longer make progress toward a verdict because individual jurors are entrenched in their preferred verdict. To simulate hung juries DICE sets a limit on the number of ballots that a jury may take.

Evaluative Criteria

The Padawer-Singer and Barton (Note 1) study provides the widest range of data available on jury deliberations and specifically allows us to test DICE's operation with four different criteria: (a) the distribution of jury verdicts (convictions, acquittals, and hung juries); (b) the number of reversals of initial majorities, that is, juries in which a majority of members initially prefer conviction (acquittal) but the jury ultimately renders a verdict for acquittal (conviction); (c) the difference in the rate at which jurors in verdict-reaching juries change their verdict preferences and the rate at which jurors in juries who ultimately hang change their verdict preferences; and (d) the mean and variance in deliberation times for juries who convict, acquit, and hang.

Table 8
Summary of Simulation Results

Type of jury	12-member jury				6-member jury			
	Unanimous		Nonunanimous		Unanimous		Nonunanimous	
	PSB	DICE	PSB	DICE	PSB	DICE	PSB	DICE
	Verdict							
Guilty	8	7.53	9	7.53	8	7.71	9	7.79
Innocent	10	10.70	9	10.70	11	9.99	14	10.13
Hung	5	4.76	5	4.76	4	5.3	0	5.08
	Reversal of majority							
All juries	2	.8	4	.8	1	.3	2	.3
	% of jurors who changed votes							
Verdict juries	34.0	38.4	26.1	23.0	24.6	31.6	28.3	14.9
Hung juries	11.7	15.1	8.4	15.1	8.3	9.6	—	9.6
	Deliberation time							
Verdict juries	169.3	168.0	177.7	134.6	126.4	104.9	119.0	76.9
Hung juries	327.1	322.6	286.7	322.6	253.0	251.2	—	251.2
All juries	203.6	200.9	201.4	173.6	153.3	138.6	119.9	115.4

Note. PSB refers to Padawer-Singer and Barton's (Note 1) study, and DICE refers to our computer model of jury decision making.

Simulation Results

Table 8 summarizes the results of simulations of Padawer-Singer and Barton's 6- and 12-member juries, who used unanimous and five-sixths decision rules, and compares results produced by the actual juries and those obtained from the DICE simulations. Briefly, the distribution of verdicts is quite satisfactory —the poorest fit is in the 6-member, nonunanimous condition, in which none of the actual juries hung. Without exception the simulation juries produced lower reversal rates than the actual juries. This result suggests that the transition probabilities for juries of nearly equal sizes are probably flatter than is reflected in Curve B of Figure 7.

The rate of vote changing in simulated juries is very close to the empirical rate for unanimous juries, but is too low for nonunanimous juries who reach a verdict. Similarly, the average deliberation times for simulated and actual juries are very close for unanimous juries, but the simulated juries produce lower deliberation times in the nonunanimous conditions. At present, DICE renders a verdict as soon as

the requisite quorum of votes is reached. However, Saks (1977) has found that nonunanimous juries frequently continue deliberating even after they have attained sufficient votes to render a verdict. In fact, between 20% and 31% of the total deliberation time for nonunanimous juries in Sak's study was accounted for by postquorum deliberation. Furthermore, jurors often changed their verdict preferences during this postquorum interval (additional jurors joined in the preferred verdict). If simulated nonunanimous juries were allowed to continue deliberating for similar intervals (i.e., an increase of between 25% and 40% in elapsed time), the average deliberation times and average rates of vote changing in these simulated juries would approach those found in the nonunanimous Padawer-Singer and Barton juries.

The results obtained with DICE suggest that the simulation method may provide substantial insights into the deliberation process by revealing the relationship between group size and persuasion and by providing a method for assessing the relative impact of individual differences on the persuasion process.

The simulation approach can serve as a useful complement to the mathematical models discussed earlier. DICE provides an alternative method for exploring the implicit decision rules that have been studied by Davis and his colleagues and has the advantage of making explicit and testable assumptions about events that occur between the first ballot and final verdicts. The aspect of the deliberation process that most closely approximates Davis's implicit rule is embodied in the transition function and can be summarized by saying that a majority's persuasiveness increases exponentially as the size of the majority increases. This general rule is likely to prevail across juries and cases, but the model will no doubt require modification when a case produces unusual individual reactions (e.g., DICE has produced excellent fits to the Davis, Kerr, Stasser, Meek, & Holt, 1977, rape data when the differential rates of vote changing by males and females are incorporated into DICE's individual differences parameter (see Penrod & Hastie, Note 6).

DICE also complements the binomial models used by Saks and Ostrom (1975) and Walbert (1971), insofar as the initial distribution of votes in DICE is produced by a binomial function. Furthermore, DICE avoids Walbert's simplistic assumptions about majority persuasion effects and uses a number of criteria to evaluate the assumptions about persuasion that are implicit in the transition function.

Finally, DICE promises to provide an empirical basis for the mathematical analyses of juror error rates and juror satisfaction proposed by Grofman (1976) and Nagel and Neef (1975). The principal defect of the existing analyses is that they are unable to make a satisfactory transition from first ballots to final verdicts. DICE makes the relationship between initial votes and final verdicts quite explicit and therefore provides a basis for extending the existing mathematical models.

Reference Notes

1. Padawer-Singer, A., & Barton, A. H. *Interim report: Experimental study of decision making in the 12-versus 6-man jury under unanimous versus non-unanimous decisions.* New York: Columbia University, Bureau of Applied Social Research, 1975.

2. Penrod, S. *Jury simulation research: Defendant and juror characteristics.* Unpublished manuscript, Harvard University, 1976.

3. Latane, B., & Borden, R. *Theory of social impact.* Research proposal submitted to the National Science Foundation, April 1973.

4. Grofman, B., & Hamilton, L. *Group decision-making in three-member and five-member mock juries under unanimous and non-unanimous verdict requirements.* Unpublished manuscript, State University of New York at Stony Brook, 1976.

5. Nagel, S. S., Lamm, D., & Neef, M. *Decision theory and juror decision-making.* Paper presented at the meeting of the International Society for Political Psychology, New York, September 1978.

6. Penrod, S., & Hastie, R. *Computer simulation of jury decision-making.* Manuscript submitted for publication, 1977.

7. Rothschild, M., Klevorick, A., & McNeil, D. Personal communication, November 1975.

References

Abelson, R. Simulation of social behavior. In G. Lindzey & E. Aronson (Eds.), *The handbook of social psychology* (Vol. 2, 2nd ed.). Reading, Mass.: Addison-Wesley, 1968.

Asch, S. E. Effects of group pressure upon the modification and distortion of judgments. In H. Guetzkow (Ed.), *Groups, leadership and men.* Pittsburgh, Pa.: Carnegie Press, 1951.

Badger, W. W. Political individualism, positional preferences, and optimal decision-rules. In R. G. Niemi & H. F. Weisberg (Eds.), *Probability models of collective decision making.* Columbus, Ohio: Charles E. Merrill, 1972.

Boehm, V. R. Mr. Prejudice, Miss Sympathy, and the authoritarian personality: An application of psychological measuring techniques to the problem of juror bias. *Wisconsin Law Review,* 1968, *3,* 734–747.

Cornish, W. R., & Sealy, A. P. Juries and the rules of evidence. *Criminal Law Review,* 1973, April, 208–223.

Curtis, R. B. Decision-rules and collective values in constitutional choice. In R. G. Niemi & H. F. Weisberg (Eds.), *Probability models of collective decision making.* Columbus, Ohio: Charles E. Merrill, 1972.

Davis, J. H. Group decision and social interaction: A theory of social decision schemes. *Psychological Review,* 1973, *80,* 97–125.

Davis, J. H. Group decision and procedural justice. In M. Fishbein (Ed.), *Progress in social psychology.* Hillsdale, N.J.: Erlbaum, 1978.

Davis, J. H., Bray, R. M., & Holt, R. The empirical study of social decision processes in juries. In J. Tapp & F. Levine (Eds.), *Law, justice, and the individual in society: Psychological and legal perspectives.* New York: Holt, Rinehart & Winston, 1977.

Davis, J. H., Kerr, N. L., Atkin, R. S., Holt, R., & Meek, D. The decision processes of 6- and 12-person mock juries assigned unanimous and two-thirds majority rules. *Journal of Personality and Social Psychology,* 1975, *32,* 1–14.

Davis, J. H., Kerr, N. L., Stasser, G., Meek, D., & Holt, R. Victim consequences, sentence severity, and decision processes in mock juries. *Organizational Behavior and Human Performance*, 1977, *18*, 346–365.

Davis, J. H., Kerr, N. L., Sussman, M., & Rissman, A. K. Social decision schemes under risk. *Journal of Personality and Social Psychology*, 1974, *30*, 248–271.

Feinberg, W. E. Teaching the Type I and Type II errors: The judicial process. *American Statistician*, 1971, *25*, 30–32.

Friedman, H. Trial by jury: Criteria for convictions, jury size, and Type I and Type II errors. *American Statistician*, 1972, *26*, 21–23.

Gelfand, A. E., & Solomon, H. A study of Poisson's models for jury verdict in criminal and civil trials. *Journal of the American Statistical Association*, 1973, *68*, 241–278.

Gelfand, A. E., & Solomon, H. Modeling jury verdicts in the American legal system. *Journal of the American Statistical Association*, 1974, *69*, 32–37.

Gelfand, A. E., & Solomon, H. Analyzing the decision-making process of the American jury. *Journal of the American Statistical Association*, 1975, *70*, 305–309.

Gelfand, A. E., & Solomon, H. An argument in favor of 12-member juries. In S. S. Nagel (Ed.), *Modeling the criminal justice system*. Beverly Hills, Calif.: Sage, 1977.

Godwin, W. F., & Restle, F. The road to agreement: Subgroup pressures in small group consensus processes. *Journal of Personality and Social Psychology*, 1974, *30*, 500–509.

Grofman, B. Not necessarily twelve and not necessarily unanimous. In G. Bermant & N. Vidmar (Eds.), *Psychology and the law*. Lexington, Mass.: Heath, 1976.

Grofman, B. Some preliminary models of jury decision making. In C. Tullock (Ed.), *Frontiers of Economics* (Vol. 4). The Hague, Netherlands: Nijhoff, in press.

Kalven, H., & Zeisel, H. *The American Jury*. Boston: Little, Brown, 1966.

Kerr, N. L., et al. Guilt beyond a reasonable doubt: Effect of concept definition and assigned decision rule on the judgments of mock jurors. *Journal of Personality and Social Psychology*, 1976, *34*, 282–294.

Landy, D., & Aronson, E. The influence of the character of the criminal and his victim on the decisions of simulated jurors. *Journal of Experimental Social Psychology*, 1969, *5*, 141–152.

Lempert, R. O. Uncovering nondiscernible differences: Empirical research and the jury-size cases. *Michigan Law Review*, 1975, *73*, 644–707.

Mitchell, H. E., & Byrne, D. The defendant's dilemma: Effect of jurors' attitudes and authoritarianism on judicial decisions. *Journal of Personality and Social Psychology*, 1973, *25*, 123–129.

Nagel, S. S., & Neef, M. Deductive modeling to determine an optimum jury size and fraction required to convict. *Washington University Law Quarterly*, 1975, 933–978.

Poisson, S. D. *Recherches sur la probabilité des jugements en matière criminelle et en matière civile, précédées des règles générales du calcul des probabilités*. Paris: Bachelier, Imprimeur-Libraire, 1837.

Rae, D. Decision-rules and individual values in constitutional choice. *American Political Science Review*, 1969, *63*, 40–56.

Saks, M. J. *Jury verdicts*. Lexington, Mass.: Heath, 1977.

Saks, M. J., & Ostrom, T. M. Jury size and consensus requirements: The laws of probability v. the laws of the land. *Journal of Contemporary Law*, 1975, *1*, 163–173.

Sherif, M. A. A study of some social factors in perception. *Archives of Psychology*, N.Y., 1935, No. 187, p. 60.

Simon, R. J. *The jury and the defense of insanity*. Boston: Little, Brown, 1967.

Simon, R., & Kaplan, J. K. Latitude and severity of sentencing options, race of the victim and decisions of simulated jurors: Some issues arising from the "Algiers Motel" trial. *Law and Society Review*, 1972, *7*, 87–98.

Simon, R. J., & Mahan, L. Quantifying burdens of proof: A view from the bench, the jury and the classroom. *Law and Society Review*, 1971, *5*, 319–330.

Stasser, G., & Davis, J. H. Opinion change during group discussion. *Personality and Social Psychology Bulletin*, 1977, *3*, 252–256.

Strodtbeck, F. L., James, R. M., & Hawkins, C. Social status in jury deliberations. *American Sociological Review*, 1957, *22*, 713–718.

Taylor, M. Proof of a theorem on majority rule. *Behavioral Science*, 1969, *14*, 228–231.

Tribe, L. H. Trial by mathematics: Precision and ritual in the legal process. *Harvard Law Review*, 1971, *84*, 1329–1393.

Valenti, A. C., & Downing, L. L. Differential effects of jury size on verdicts following deliberation as a function of the apparent guilt of the defendant. *Journal of Personality and Social Psychology*, 1975, *32*, 655–663.

Walbert, T. D. Note: Effect of jury size on probability of conviction—An evaluation of Williams v. Florida. *Case Western Reserve Law Review*, 1971, *22*, 529–555.

Received December 30, 1977 ∎

Journal of Applied Psychology
1979, Vol. 64, No. 2, 91–98

Jury Decision Making: An Empirical Study Based on Actual Felony Trials

Diane L. Bridgeman and David Marlowe
University of California at Santa Cruz

Posttrial interviewing was used to examine the possible relationship between a variety of juror characteristics and jury decision making. Sixty-five actual jurors who had participated in 10 felony trials served as subjects. An emphasis was placed on process as well as outcome variables. Demographic characteristics were largely unrelated to both procedural and outcome variables. The findings lend support to the view that jurors are highly involved and responsible people who determine guilt or innocence primarily on the basis of factual evidence.

The past decade has seen a dramatic growth of interest by the social sciences in the criminal justice system. Social psychology in particular has focused on jury selection and jury decision making as areas of special concern. The relevant literature has suddenly expanded, prompting the recent appearance of several reviews (Gerbasi, Zuckerman, & Reis, 1977; Tapp, 1976). These reviews will not be summarized here; in fact, comparison to most other studies is complicated by the fact that other jury research is largely based on simulation.

A considerable unease exists regarding the research strategies used to study jury behavior. This uneasiness stems from problems related to the desire to do socially relevant research while also using rigorous experimental methods. As Tapp (1976) has succinctly stated it, "Clearly the battle to watch

is between the advocates of experimental social psychological models and those who advocate in situ social research" (p. 390). Whatever the final outcome of this controversy, it is apparent that in situ jury research conducted by psychologists is rare and that the convenience and rigor of the laboratory are major considerations that guide the work in this area. This sacrifice of ecological validity is very troublesome in that experimental findings of uncertain relevance to practical sociolegal questions have been used to buttress specific public policy positions. Of course, we do not mean to suggest that laboratory-based jury research is without social utility or scientific value. On the contrary, such work can have considerable heuristic value when it serves to guide or further additional work in natural settings. Unfortunately, this has seldom been the case, and simulation using mock jurors is the preferred mode of investigation. Further, we are convinced that simulation techniques provide information that is at best suggestive (Diamond & Zeisel, 1974; Miller, Fontes, Boster, & Sunnafrank, Note 1). See Miller et al., for an extensive review of simulated jury studies.) The inadequacies of mock jury studies reflect the uncertainty regarding the generality of laboratory-based sociolegal research. To highlight only one problem: The variables typically manipulated in laboratory studies of jury decision making (e.g., victim attractiveness or defendant likability) constitute a minute

This research was funded by a University of California, Santa Cruz, Social Science Patent Fund award to Diane L. Bridgeman and by a University of California, Santa Cruz, Faculty Research award to David Marlowe.

We appreciate the assistance of the Santa Cruz County District Attorney's Office and specifically that of Elizabeth Buck, the county office secretary, and the former and present district attorneys, respectively, Peter Chang and Christopher Cottle.

We also acknowledge the invaluable assistance of Ruth Tebbets for her help with jury interviewing.

Requests for reprints should be sent to Diane L. Bridgeman, Psychology Board, University of California, Santa Cruz, California 95064.

fraction of the total stimulus field to which a real juror is actually exposed in the courtroom. Such truncated experimental settings give undue prominence to factors that are of much less importance when embedded in the more complex courtroom setting.

Are special factors operating to hinder naturalistic research on problems that are so unsuited for exclusively laboratory efforts? Foremost are the legal and ethical constraints that prohibit investigative or experimental intrusion into the trial process. An early and seemingly unique exception was the effort by Strodtbeck (cited in Katz, 1972) to surreptitiously record actual jury deliberations. The storm provoked by this invasion of the jurors' privacy served to prevent any further work of this kind. Another special factor of a methodological nature is the logistical difficulty of locating, enlisting the cooperation of, and then studying real jurors when trials are completed.

Because of the information vacuum that exists, one would be hard put to find any convincing basis for directly linking the findings of simulation research to the processes and outcomes of real trials. It was to this largely unexplored matter that the following modest, descriptive study was addressed. Our research purpose was to find out what actually goes on in the jury room during deliberations.

Method

We interviewed 65 real jurors following the completion of 10 felony trials. Our goals were largely descriptive, and our method was based on a highly structured interview of jurors' perceptions. We devised no specific formal hypothesis but attempted instead to map the jurors' account of the posttrial deliberations.

Our emphasis was on jurors' perceptions of the trial process, and our data consequently are subject to all the limitations of self-report information. In particular we should keep in mind that jurors are likely to learn what is expected of them, and their responses may reflect the operation of a social-desirability response set. Mock jurors in simulated trials, of course, are subject to the same concerns. With these considerations in mind, we made every effort to minimize the jurors' parroting of socially desirable responses (Garfinkel, 1967). We prefaced our interviews with the jurors by assuring them that confidentiality would be maintained, that there was no expected set of "right" or "wrong" answers,

and that the juror's own perceptions of the process constituted the only correct response.

The Interview Format

The basic source of data for this study was a 60-item questionnaire–interview procedure that required about 1½ hours to complete. The juror could answer most of the questions by selecting one of several response alternatives (e.g., "How did you vote on the first ballot?": guilty, innocent, undecided). Some questions were open-ended and served to elicit the juror's extended view on a matter (e.g., "If you could, how would you change the jury system?"). The jurors were encouraged to comment or elaborate on any answer to the questions, especially those that were of multiple-choice format. Several of the questions were repeated with varied wording to check for internal consistency of responses. In our analysis we found strong agreement across these items. In addition to obtaining information of the usual demographic kind, the questionnaire sought to cover a variety of other factors including voting behavior, foreperson selection procedure, perceived effectiveness of lawyers and judge, influence effects, juror activity level, relative importance attached to evidence, lawyers, police, expert testimony, and so forth, and the juror's ability to understand the proceedings and the law. Thus, we were guided by earlier simulation studies while we undertook a virtually unique interview study with a relatively large number of real jurors.

Our first step was to secure the approval and cooperation of local officials in the criminal justice system of Santa Cruz County, California, a coastal community with a population of 160,000, located 85 miles south of San Francisco. We next established that it would be legal to interview jurors at the trial's completion. We also secured permission from the county's district attorney to add his official support to our letter requesting juror cooperation. From the district attorney's office we obtained lists of jurors who served in 10 (1974–1975) felony trials. A letter was sent to these 120 jurors, and their cooperation was solicited for "a study of the jury system." The letter stressed the potential social significance of the project, offered the jurors a token $3 payment for 1½ hours of their time, and provided for home interviews at any convenient hour. Potential volunteers were also assured that strict confidentiality of their responses would be observed.

Results and Discussion

Despite one follow-up letter and at least two phone calls to all reluctant jurors, we were never able to secure the cooperation of more than 7 jurors from any one trial. That figure, however, was considerably better than the 25%–50% typical response to mail solicitation. Of the 55 people who refused to volunteer in response to the mailed request, we were able to persuade 15 to answer some demographic and "process" questions (concerning the deliberation procedure) on the phone. These 15 jurors, who were not included in any of the final analyses in our study, were compared to the 65-member final sample on a number of demographic variables including age, sex, schooling, occupational level, marital status, religious preference, and political party preference. No statistically reliable differences were observed on any of these factors between the 65 volunteers and the 15 telephone interviewees. All 65 jurors had served in a criminal trial within 2–3 months of being interviewed.

A trial-by-trial analysis of our results showed similar juror trends and patterns (i.e., first-ballot results, reliance on evidence, etc.), but due to the limited sample of subjects per trial, the data were pooled across trials and are reported here in summary form.

Trial Characteristics

Of the 10 trials, 1 had 2 defendants, resulting in a total of 11 defendants. The average age of the defendants, all of whom were male, was 23. Five were minority group members (3 Blacks and 2 Chicanos). Of the 11 defendants, 2 faced charges of heroin possession, 1 faced a charge of assault, 2 of rape, 2 of homicide, and 4 faced charges of burglary. They were prosecuted by five different male assistant district attorneys with one attorney prosecuting 4 trials, another attorney handling 3 trials, and with three different attorneys prosecuting the 3 remaining trials. A total of 9 male lawyers provided the defense for the 11 defendants in the 10 trials. Three different judges presided over the 10 trials, with 6 trials presided over by one judge, 3 by a second judge, and 1 by the third judge.

Juror Characteristics

The 65 jurors who volunteered to be interviewed consisted of 36 females and 29 males between the ages of 19 and 71. The mean age was 38; this number included 14 jurors who were 19–25 and 6 jurors who were over 60.

They tended to be well educated: Only 24 (37%) reported attending only grade or high school, whereas 41 jurors (63%) attended college, and this number included 6 who held graduate degrees. Consistent with these educational levels were the reported occupations of the jurors. Only 8 (12%) described themselves as blue-collar workers or laborers. Twelve were housewives; 28 were white-collar workers; 8 were professionals; 3 were retired; and 6 were students. Of the 43 jurors who reported a religious preference, 28 (65%) claimed Protestant and 15 (35%) claimed Catholic. Political party preference included 34 Democrats, 16 Republicans, and 6 Independents. The jurors were also asked to indicate their political orientation on a radical-to-conservative scale. One juror described himself as a radical. Twenty-one (32%) said they were liberal, 32 (50%) claimed to be moderate, 9 (14%) said they were conservative, and 1 juror described himself as extremely conservative. We also asked the jurors to indicate how often they attended church for religious worship. Nine (15%) stated "once a week," 3 (5%) claimed "two or three times a month," 26 (42%) stated "once a month," and 24 (39%) stated "never." Finally, 14 (22%) jurors stated they had served before as jurors, whereas 51 reported this was their first service. Thus, ours is a sample of relatively young, well-educated, middle-class people of moderate to liberal political persuasion who are not active or frequent church attenders. This is somewhat inconsistent with common stereotypes that tend to view jurors in small California counties as older, politically conservative, and relatively poorly educated. One source of this inconsistency with the stereotype is probably the presence in Santa Cruz of a campus of the University of California. Of course, 40 potential jurors out of the original pool of 120 refused to be interviewed or even answer questions on the phone, and it is possible that these 40 were less well educated and politically more conservative than jurors who volunteered. In any event, we cannot conclude that our 65 respondents are fully representative of California or even Santa Cruz County jurors in general.

Process Characteristics

We will begin with the most significant aspect of any trial: How did the jurors vote in the 10 trials? The results were decidedly one-sided. The 11 defendants were found guilty on eight counts and not guilty on three. Only 2 defendants were found not guilty, a conviction rate of 82%. This approximates the overall Santa Cruz County conviction rate in felony trials of about 90%. We would not expect to find correlates of a relatively rare event (verdict of innocence), and our analyses turned up none. Neither the interview nor the demographic data was related to trial outcome. However, the final jury verdict was never the result of a unanimous vote on the first ballot. Consequently, we carried out additional analyses that examined the relationship between our interview data and first-ballot voting behavior. On the first ballot, 42 jurors (65%) voted guilty, 19 (29%) voted innocent, and 4 (6%) voted undecided. Again, as in the prior analysis, neither juror demographic characteristics nor the interview data was related to first-ballot voting behavior. The majority of the jurors, moreover, did not change their vote from their first-ballot decision. Twenty-one jurors (33%) report changing their vote at least once, and only 3 jurors said they changed their vote twice.

The fixity of the jurors' initial judgment is further indicated by the finding that after two ballots, 95% of the jurors had made what proved to be an unalterable decision to vote guilty or innocent. Kalven (1958) similarly reported that the first-ballot vote by jurors has a strong relationship to the final verdict. In no instance did the final trial outcome differ from the majority vote on the first ballot. The minority was never able to persuade the majority to see things its way, and even when numerous ballots were required (25% of the jurors reported that their group took five or more ballots), they served only to convert one or two jurors to the majority view.

The posttrial deliberation proceedings, then, do not appear to be a significant factor in forming juror opinion or in determining final voting behavior. This is confirmed by

the jurors' direct reports during the interview. Only 15 jurors (23%) mentioned "deliberation proceedings" in response to the question, "What was the main reason you finally voted as you did?" And only 11 jurors (17%) stated it was "the opinions of other jurors" that influenced them most during the deliberations. What then do the jurors say they rely on or attend to during the posttrial proceedings? Consistent with another investigative report (Saks, 1976), most jurors (59%) claim that the opportunity to engage in a "review of the evidence" was the most influential posttrial factor. Saks (1976) found that trial evidence is more than three times as powerful as juror attitudes in influencing decisions. He argued that "Jurors' characteristics made a difference, but far less than the characteristics of trial evidence" (p. 56). Of course, the failure to find strong attitudinal or personality correlates of juror decision making is difficult to interpret. There may, in fact, be no such correlates, or it may be that methodological limitations are crucial. We could be studying the wrong personality factors or using deficient assessment strategies.

In our study not a single juror felt that the foreperson's opinion was important in determining how he or she finally voted. It appears, however, that formal information or evidence is important. In fact, in one trial most of the jurors commented that although they felt the defendant was guilty, a not-guilty verdict had to be given because of lack of evidence.

Hence, we might suspect that in the timing of decision making what happens during the trial and before the discussion begins is crucial for most jurors. In fact, the jurors' responses to the interview questionnaire provide direct support for this expectation. When asked, "At what point did you come to feel fairly certain of the defendant's guilt or innocence?" 23 jurors (35%) answered "near the beginning" or "near the middle" of the trial. Another 31 jurors (47%) answered "by the end of the trial" but before deliberations, with only 11 jurors reporting they were still undecided when the trial proper ended. In an early study, Weld and Roff (1938) read scripts of a trial to mock jurors and also found that jurors came to their decisions before the deliberations. The process of making up one's mind, then, starts quite early in the trial process for about one third of the jurors and has moved toward a definite conclusion for the large majority of jurors (82%) before discussion begins.

We do not mean to imply, however, that the process of arriving at a verdict is entirely over for the individual juror before group discussion starts, or that the deliberations serve no important decision-making function. On the contrary, even if the deliberations do not serve to persuade most jurors *how* to vote, they may contribute to the crucial function of convincing the juror that his or her decision was the right one. We have no evidence bearing directly on the argument that follows, and we offer it as a speculation. Some uncertainty must attach to any judgment that has very important consequences and at the same time is not capable of unequivocal personal confirmation. The posttrial discussion, then, can serve a process of "justification" by providing the juror with an opportunity to confirm the validity of a decision that he or she has already made. We might hypothesize a two-stage decision-making process: First, largely on the basis of the evidence and testimony, the juror arrives at a conclusion regarding the defendant's guilt or innocence. A second phase ensues after the trial proper in which the juror seeks consensual validation for his or her judgment by learning the verdicts and arguments of the other jurors. Some jurors must be convinced to change their judgment to that of the majority, but for most jurors (almost 70% in our study) the verdict originally arrived at, before discussion, is also the final one. This validation process might explain the jurors' response to the question, "How confident were you of your final decision?" Fifty-eight jurors (90%) reported "moderately" or "extremely confident," whereas only 7 jurors answered "slightly" or "not confident." Of course, as we noted above, some direct empirical evidence is necessary before we can have confidence in this line of reasoning about the juror decision-making process.

The Decision-Making Process

If it is not the posttrial discussion that forms juror decisions in an important way, what is crucial? As mentioned above, a composite consisting of evidence and testimony seems to be determinative, and this is borne out by responses to the questionnaire.

First, jurors were explicitly asked to "rank in order of importance" the factors that they believed influenced their final decision. The list of factors provided included defendant's appearance; defendant's testimony; defense lawyer; expert testimony; judge; jury discussion; and other witnesses such as friends, parents, co-defendants; police testimony; prosecutor; and an open-ended alternative labeled *other (indicate)*. A rank ordering of the importance ascribed to these factors can be arrived at by simply counting the number of jurors who rated each factor as first or second in importance. Alternatively, a more elaborate ranking procedure can be used that employs a differential weighting system to evaluate the importance attached to the various factors. Since the two methods yielded virtually identical results, we will report the data for the simpler of the two methods. From most to least important, the ranking of the nine factors ("other" is excluded because it includes a variety of disparate considerations) is as follows: police testimony (29), other witnesses (24), defendant's testimony (18), prosecutor (17), jury discussion (11), judge (10), expert testimony (8), defense lawyer (3), and defendant's appearance (0). The numbers in parentheses indicate the number of jurors who ranked that factor first or second in importance. Clearly, the jurors attach much importance to the testimony of police, defendant, and other witnesses. They claim to rely little on the testimony of experts such as doctors and psychiatrists. And although in response to another question, 76% of the jurors rated the defense attorney as moderately or extremely able, only 3 attached much importance to his performance in deciding how to vote.

Anecdotal evidence provided by our jurors indicated that the first view of the defendant was an emotionally toned one. Some jurors mentioned an initial difficulty or reluctance to look at or make eye contact with the defendant. We anticipated that this first view would go hand in hand with a first-impression judgment about a defendant's guilt or innocence, and every juror in our study acknowledged that this was so. They were asked the following question: "At the start of the trial when you first saw the defendant, what was your impression of his guilt or innocence?" Twelve jurors replied "probably guilty," 50 jurors answered "not sure," and the remaining 3 said the defendant was "probably innocent." We are not sure what to conclude about this finding, since the epistemological subtleties are quite real and complex. There are a variety of emphases that can be given to these data. First, only 3 jurors seemed to obey the legal prescription that a presumption of innocence is required by the law until the state has proven otherwise. Alternatively, one might emphasize that almost 20% of the jurors whose first impression was that the defendant is guilty were prejudging in an informed and rational manner consistent with the outcome of about 90% of felony trials. This view is not inconsistent with our speculation that the initial presumption of guilt or innocence has no decisive bearing on the jurors' final judgment, since the jurors reported keeping an open mind and perceived themselves as having only formulated a tentative first hypothesis. This point is supported because only 4 jurors (6%) claimed to have arrived at "a fairly certain" verdict near the beginning of the trial and also because most jurors justify their final verdict largely on the basis of what occurs during the course of the trial.

Selection and Activity of the Foreperson

The literature, though inconsistent, suggests that the jury foreperson exerts an important influence on the decision-making process. Consequently, we included a number of questions that examined the selection of the foreperson as well as questions that concerned his or her activity level and overall influence. There was no uniformly preferred manner of selecting the forepersons (3 of whom were women) from our 10 groups. The jurors were asked, "How was the foreman

selected?" and also, "Do you think he was selected in a fair way?" Their responses clearly indicated that no contest or controversy was involved in the selection process in any of the 10 trials. In fact, 58 jurors (92%) thought that the procedure was a fair one. Our jurors' perceptions revealed that the most commonly used practice was for someone to spontaneously nominate a foreperson and for the others to quickly agree. Twenty-six (40%) of the jurors, representing 7 trials, stated that this was how they proceeded. This finding is consistent with that of Hawkins (1962), who also reported that the first person nominated is generally selected as the foreperson. Twelve jurors (18%) from 4 of the trials claimed that the person selected was the one who said he or she wanted to be foreperson. Other less frequently cited reasons (with the number of jurors who gave that account in parentheses) were: the oldest man (3); where the person sat (5); previous experience as a juror (5); talked a lot (4); general experience (1); and other uncodable statements (8).

The jurors were also asked to rate the foreperson and themselves with respect to activity level ("How active was the foreman?" and influence ("How much influence did you have on the other jurors?"). The foreperson was seen as more active than the jurors. Eighty-nine percent rated the foreperson either extremely or moderately active, whereas 74% made this judgment for themselves. Similarly, with respect to influence, 74% rated the foreperson as extremely or moderately influential, whereas 65% described themselves as extremely or moderately influential. The forepersons were also rated for likability, with 76% stating they liked the foreperson a great deal and the remainder liking the foreperson only a little or not at all. Thus, overall, the foreperson was described as likable, active, and influential. His or her influence, however, does not appear to take the form of directly affecting in an important way the judgmental process or final voting behavior of the jurors. As reported above, in response to the question, "What was the main reason you finally voted as you did?" not a single juror selected the foreman choice from those items provided, nor did they list it in the "other" category. They also did not rank the foreperson as one of the factors that influenced their final decision. Instead, the foreperson was described in terms suggesting that he or she served a function comparable to that of a group facilitator. He or she recognized people who wished to speak, conducted the balloting, recorded the vote, and in general tended to structure and maintain an orderly process. His or her personal views regarding innocence or guilt seemed not to count for more than the beliefs of other jurors.

Juror Reactions and Recommendations

Another group of interview questions sought to assess the jurors' satisfaction with their participation, their understanding of the procedures and law, their willingness to serve again; and these questions also solicited recommendations regarding desirable changes in the jury system. Most of the jurors (87%) reported that the experience was "a generally positive one," with the remaining 13% claiming that it was "a generally negative one." Additionally, many of the jurors also made spontaneous comments regarding the quality of the experience. Their statements clearly indicated that a high level of arousal and interest was associated with their participation. Frequent comments were made illustrating the intensity of their involvement. Remarks such as "This is the most important thing I ever did" were not uncommon. Many explained the importance of the juror function in terms of a citizen's responsibility to participate in the court system. Concepts such as justice, duty, and public responsibility were regularly referred to in the jurors' answers.

When asked whether they understood what was going on during the trial, virtually all (97%) replied "yes," in contrast to mock-jury studies that report jurors having difficulty understanding the judge's instructions (e.g., Forston, 1970). Needless to say, jurors are not likely to emphasize their confusion or ignorance if it existed, and our figure could easily represent a self-serving interest. Similarly, 90% of the jurors reported that the judge was either moderately or extremely helpful, and comparably, 82% said they either completely or mostly understood the judge's instructions to the jury when the trial ended. In a criminal trial then, very few jurors report that they are unable to follow the procedures or understand the law. Consistent with their sense of the importance of the juror function and their perceived ability to perform competently was the jurors' willingness to serve again as a juror. Only 2 jurors stated that they would not want to serve again. Ten jurors (15%) said they would serve again but would do so reluctantly, whereas the rest (82%) said they would very willingly serve again.

Our last set of questions covered jurors' views and recommendations related to changing and improving the jury system. These questions were open-ended and elicited a variety of proposals. Many of the questions could be assigned to a general category, and the final analysis of this material revealed that improving the jury selection procedures was the most frequent (30%) recommendation. The following examples represent the majority of the issues discussed by the jurors when altering the selection process was recommended: (a) better screening of prospective jurors to determine whether the participant would be open-minded and would be able to give sufficient time and attention to his or her jury responsibilities; (b) better consideration of jurors during the selection process and trial with respect to facilities provided and physical needs met. The next most cited recommendation was the desire for more orientation and training for jurors (15%). Twelve percent believed that jurors should be allowed to ask questions of the judge or attorneys, and 14% wanted more opportunity to interact with or talk to the judge regarding the final instructions they received. Many jurors also expressed a strong need for closure to their jury experience. Indeed, some of the jurors acknowledged that participating in the study brought about such closure.

Conclusion

A few of our results deserve further brief comment. Our findings that jurors report a reliance on evidence and seriousness of role seems to show jurors to be reasonable and sensitive. This conclusion corroborates Kalven and Zeisel's (1966) observation that "the jury by and large does understand the case and get it straight, . . . and the evidence itself is a major determinant of the decision of both judge and jury" (p. 162).

The jury system is not without its critics, and the fear that jurors are swayed by bias or incompetence is frequently voiced. Our results concerning juror perceptions suggest the contrary, indicating that jurors appear to be reasonable and are concerned with being fair and just. These jurors relied primarily on the evidence and appeared not to be influenced by subtle sociopersonal considerations such as the defendant's or attorney's personal style or appearance. Overall, they viewed their participation as a civic responsibility and concluded their work with a sense of pride and gratification. We were ourselves greatly impressed with the jurors' ability to embody the collective wisdom and responsibility of the larger community they represent. This point may bear on the lack of direct relevance of mock-jury research to actual trial behavior. If one really wants to know what jurors think, one should begin by asking them.

It seems likely that real jurors succeed at ignoring extraneous or subtle features of a trial (such as a defendant's appearance) because of the significance of their task and the responsibility that it engenders. It is possible that mock jurors attend to extraneous variables because the overriding concerns with justice and responsibility to the community are not present. We cannot claim, however, a compelling scientific basis for the above conclusions and offer them cautiously as personal impressions. It cannot be emphasized too strongly that our sole source of information regarding the jury process was the jurors themselves. Jury service involves, in part, a socialization process wherein the jurors become acquainted with the norms and expectations of the criminal justice system. Admonitions to pay attention only to the evidence, to keep an open mind, to assume the innocence of the defendant, and to withhold final judgment until after the trial are all emphasized throughout the trial procedure, which begins with jury selection. To some extent then our results very likely reflect the jurors repeating what they know to be socially desirable statements. Moreover, it is a social science truism that people are often unaware of the cues or events that influence their behavior. Consequently, our final and strongest conclusion is to again note the limits of phenomenological data and to offer this study as a first effort toward approaching the reality of actual juror behavior.

Reference Note

1. Miller, G. R., Fontes, N. E., Boster, F. Joseph, & Sunnafrank, M. *Methodological issues in jury research: What can simulation tell us?* Paper presented at the 85th annual convention of the American Psychological Association, San Francisco, August 1977.

References

Diamond, S., & Zeisel, H. A courtroom experiment on juror selection and decision-making. *Personality and Social Psychology Bulletin*, 1974, *1*(1), 276–277.

Forston, R. F. Judge's instructions: A quantitative analysis of jurors' listening comprehension. *Today's Speech*, 1970, *18*, 34–38.

Garfinkel, H. *Studies in ethnomethodology.* Englewood Cliffs, N.J.: Prentice-Hall, 1967.

Gerbasi, K. C., Zuckerman, M., & Reis, H. T. Justice needs a new blindfold: A review of mock jury research. *Psychological Bulletin*, 1977, *84*, 323–345.

Hawkins, C. H. Interaction rates of jurors aligned in factions. *American Sociological Review*, 1962, *27*, 689–691.

Kalven, H., Jr. The jury, the law and the personal injury damage award. *Ohio State Law Journal*, 1958, *10*, 158–178.

Kalven, H., Jr., & Zeisel, H. *The American jury.* Chicago: University of Chicago Press, 1966.

Katz, J. *Experimentation with human beings: The authority of the investigator, subject, professions and state in the human experimentation process.* New York: Russell Sage Foundation, 1972.

Saks, M. Scientific jury selection. Social scientist can't rig juries. *Psychology Today*, January, 1976, 48–57.

Tapp, J. L. Psychology and the law: An overture. *Annual Review of Psychology*, 1976, *27*, 359–404.

Weld, H. P., & Roff, M. A. A study of the formation of opinion based upon legal evidence. *American Journal of Psychology*, 1938, *51*, 609–628.

Received August 18, 1978 ∎

Experimental Research on Jury Decision-Making

ROBERT J. MacCOUN

Because trial juries deliberate in secrecy, legal debates about jury functioning have relied heavily on anecdote and speculation. In recent years, investigators have begun to challenge many common assumptions about jury behavior. An important tool in this effort has been the mock jury experiment, in which research participants are randomly assigned to alternative trial conditions and asked to reach a verdict in a simulated case. Researchers have used mock jury experiments to test hypotheses about causal influences on jury behavior and to develop theoretical models of the jury deliberation process.

J URY VERDICTS DIRECTLY AFFECT THE LIVES OF HUNDREDS OF thousands of individuals in the United States every year and serve a broader bellwether function in plea bargaining and settlement negotiations (1). But because jury deliberation is cloaked in secrecy, legal policy-makers have made important decisions about the scope and conduct of jury trials on the basis of untested intuitions about how juries reach their verdicts (2, 3). In this review of research on jury behavior, I will emphasize the use of mock jury experiments to test hypotheses and refine theoretical models of the decision process. Because jury decision-making involves two different phases—cognitive processing during the trial and deliberation in the jury room—I review research on both the trial and deliberation phases of the judgment process. In keeping with the emphasis of most jury research, I focus primarily on decision-making in criminal trials; the extent to which these findings generalize to civil litigation is not clear (3).

Jury Research Methods

In the 1950s, researchers at the University of Chicago covertly recorded the deliberations of several federal juries. Despite the court's cooperation, this endeavor was aborted by a congressional inquiry, resulting in legislation prohibiting attempts to observe or record jury deliberation (4). Since then, researchers have resorted to other strategies to study jury behavior, most notably archival analyses and mock jury experiments. In the archival approach, jury verdicts are sampled from court records or court reporting services and analyzed statistically to describe longitudinal trends and to identify relations between verdicts and case characteristics (5). But archival data sources omit a great deal of potentially relevant information and only document what juries have done, not how or why they did it. Researchers must attempt to infer the latter, which is precarious because one can never completely disentangle the natural covariation among various case and trial characteristics.

In order to better understand the jury decision-making process,

researchers would like controlled experiments with random assignment to conditions under study. In some instances, courts have randomly assigned jury trials to alternative procedures, but manipulations of many variables of interest are not ethically or legally feasible in actual trial settings (6). Mock juries must be used for most experiments; in these, research participants are asked to reach judgments regarding a simulated legal trial. The mock jury approach has the added advantage of permitting replication across juries within the context of a single trial, and there is no legal barrier to observing deliberation (7).

Differences between these experiments and actual trials have led some observers to question whether generalizable conclusions about actual jury behavior can be reached by studying the behavior of mock juries reacting to written, audiotaped, or videotaped trial reenactments (8). The effects of several factors that distinguish mock jury simulations from actual trials have been assessed empirically. Experiments comparing mock jurors with subjects who thought they were actually trying a case have been inconclusive; different studies have found mock jurors' verdicts to be more lenient, less lenient, and no different from those of "actual" jurors (9). Other studies have examined the effects of the frequent use of college students as mock jurors, finding little or no difference in comparisons of verdicts by student and adult jury-eligible respondents for the same cases (10, 11). There is some evidence that simulated trial presentations might artificially exaggerate the impact of experimentally manipulated variables, particularly defendant characteristics (12). But mock jurors do not appear to reach decisions by a fundamentally different process than actual jurors (8, 13). When the objective is to precisely estimate the magnitude of relations among variables in actual jury trials, the archival method is more appropriate. The role of mock jury experimentation is to explain the processes underlying those relations.

Predeliberation Juror Judgment

Evidence evaluation at trial. One of the earliest findings in mock jury research was that despite judges' instructions to the contrary, many jurors form tentative verdict preferences early in the trial (14), a finding that underscores the importance of studying predeliberation juror judgment as an adjunct to research on jury deliberation. Rather than cataloging the dozens of trial and case characteristics that have been found to influence jurors, I will briefly review several theoretical models of individual juror judgment that have proved useful for stimulating research on general principles of juror judgment (15).

The Bayesian and information integration models each represent a juror's evaluation of the evidence as a unidimensional subjective probability judgment. These models are framed in mathematical

The author is a social psychologist in the Behavioral Sciences Department at The RAND Corporation, Santa Monica, CA 90406–2138.

terms, but theorists are not proposing that jurors literally carry out such calculations in their heads: "now I'll divide by 0.5 and carry the 1." Instead, the formulas are a useful way of explicitly predicting the functional relations among a juror's assessment of each evidentiary item and his or her overall judgment. In the simplest Bayesian model (15), the juror's estimate of the odds of guilt given n items of trial evidence is $R_n = R_0(L_1)(L_2), \ldots, (L_n)$, where $R_0 = P(G|e_0)/P(NG|e_0)$, which represents the juror's initial odds estimate of the defendant's being guilty (G) or not guilty (NG) given the fact that the defendant is on trial (e_0), and $L_i = P(e_i|G)/P(e_i|NG)$, a likelihood ratio representing the perceived diagnosticity of item e_i. More sophisticated versions use complex hierarchical chains of inference to account for dependencies among evidentiary items (16). Arguably, Bayesian models depict how a "rational" person would aggregate the evidence, but they generally do a poor job of describing juror judgment (15). For example, relative to Bayesian norms, mock jurors do not adequately adjust their judgments to take into account forensic incidence statistics presented in expert testimony—for instance, the likelihood that the offender and the defendant would have matching hair samples by chance (17). Also, mock jurors have been found to "double count" redundant testimony from corroborative witnesses (16).

The information integration model of juror judgment is grounded in basic research on human judgment (18). According to this model, a juror's evaluation of the evidence, J, can be described by a weighted average of the pretrial opinion, s_0, and the subjective probability of guilt or liability implied by each evidentiary item, s_i. Thus, $J = (w_0s_0 + \Sigma w_i s_i)/(w_0 + \Sigma w_i)$, where w_0 and w_i refer to the weight given to the pretrial opinion and the ith evidentiary item, respectively (15, 19). These weights are postulated to reflect each item's perceived relevance and credibility. Psychologically, this model can be characterized as a process in which the juror's global judgment is continually adjusted so as to fall between its previous value and the value of each new piece of evidence that is presented at trial (20). Mock juror research findings are generally consistent with this averaging model (19), although rigorous tests are rare (15). This model can account for the underuse of incidence statistics and other forms of base-rate evidence; they are simply "averaged in" along with other less statistically reliable items of evidence (20). The model can also explain the impact of redundant testimony; by attenuating the contribution of the pretrial opinion, two items with the same value can produce a more extreme judgment than either one alone (18).

The Bayesian and information integration models represent the juror's judgment on a continuous scale, but jurors are typically required to reach a categorical verdict. Thus, the juror's judgment must be compared to a decision threshold, which should ideally correspond to the assigned standard of proof; for example, the criminal "reasonable doubt" standard. But because legal definitions of these standards are ambiguous, there is considerable variance in the thresholds jurors actually adopt (21, 22). Several theorists (23) have suggested a decision-theory derivation of the juror's threshold. Given the perceived probability of guilt, p, and the expected regret over convicting an innocent defendant, D_{ci}, or acquitting a guilty defendant, D_{ag}, the juror can minimize his or her expected regret by setting a threshold value of $p^* = D_{ci}/(D_{ci} + D_{ag})$. With this model, it is possible to predict jurors' verdicts about 80% of the time by matching their probability-of-guilt ratings to the value of p^* estimated from their expected regret ratings (21, 22). This is a better than chance rate, although it suggests that better models are needed.

The recent "story" model (13, 15, 24) of juror cognition departs from these unidimensional approaches. The model is an extension of basic research on the cognitive representation of narrative information. According to this model, jurors use episode schemata—generic knowledge structures abstracted from prior experience—to remember and organize trial evidence into a plausible story. Jurors then attempt to match the story to available verdict categories, selecting the verdict that provides the best fit. The story model is a psychologically plausible account of juror decisionmaking, and it is the only model in which serious consideration is given to the role of memory processes during the trial, but more research is needed to establish its predictive validity and heuristic value for generating testable hypotheses.

Juror biases. Intuition and courtroom folklore suggest that jurors' personal characteristics might predispose them toward certain verdicts. Attorneys attempt to detect these predispositions during jury selection proceedings, traditionally relying on hunches and stereotypic rules of thumb. In recent years, some defense lawyers have hired social scientists to conduct "scientific jury selection," which usually involves a survey of community knowledge and attitudes regarding the issues in dispute, occasionally supplemented by clinical observation of potential jurors under questioning (25). The relation of survey items intended to serve as a proxy for verdict preference with various demographic, personality, and attitudinal variables is evaluated by regression analysis in order to build a statistical profile of the client's ideal juror.

However, a large body of empirical research calls into question the premise that jurors' votes during deliberation can be reliably predicted from juror characteristics that are observable before trial. In general, jurors' demographic attributes, personality traits, and general attitudes are associated weakly and unreliably with jurors' verdicts (1, 13, 26). For example, in a study of over 800 mock jurors recruited from Boston-area jury pools, jurors' education, occupation, political ideology, gender, age, and trial experience collectively accounted for less than 2% of the variance in their verdict preferences (13). But proponents of scientific jury selection argue that the approach is most effective in trials involving controversial issues. Capital punishment might be one such issue; numerous studies have found that attitudes toward the death penalty in the abstract reliably predict the decision to vote to convict a defendant accused of homicide (27).

A more robust source of bias in juror judgment results from exposure to extralegal information. Studies have documented reliable effects of pretrial publicity, inadmissible evidence, and litigants' physical characteristics on mock juror judgments (1, 28, 29). When seemingly probative information is ruled inadmissible because of due process violations, jurors may nevertheless incorporate it in their probability-of-guilt assessment (29). But other extralegal factors, such as the attractiveness of an automobile theft victim, appear to influence verdicts indirectly by heightening the anticipated regret of either convicting the innocent or acquitting the guilty and thereby raising or lowering jurors' standard-of-proof thresholds (30).

The Deliberation Process

Charting factional movement in the jury. In the 1960s, Kalven and Zeisel (31) used post-trial juror interviews to reconstruct the initial ballots in 225 criminal jury deliberations. Of the 146 juries with a nonunanimous majority on the first ballot, only seven reached the verdict advocated by the minority faction. Kalven and Zeisel suggested that "with very few exceptions the first ballot decides the outcome of the verdict. . . . The deliberation process might well be likened to what the developer does for an exposed film; it brings out the picture, but the outcome is predetermined" (31, pp. 488–489).

In the years since Kalven and Zeisel's analysis, a number of stochastic models of jury decision-making have been developed (32), some of which have been implemented as computer simulations (13,

101

33). A common feature of these models is the use of the group state—the distribution of jurors across distinct verdict factions—as the unit of analysis. For example, an 8:4 state would indicate that 8 jurors favor conviction and 4 jurors favor acquittal in a 12-person jury. These models make a number of assumptions about the dynamics of jury deliberation that have been assessed empirically.

Following Kalven and Zeisel (31), each model has as an assumption that a faction's influence is a function of its relative size. This majority effect is easily the most robust finding in mock jury research (13, 32). Even when a jury is ostensibly operating under a unanimity decision rule, its verdict can be predicted fairly reliably by an implicit two-thirds majority rule. A related phenomenon, group polarization, has been documented in mock jury research and in hundreds of other small group laboratory studies (19, 34). To the extent that a group's average predeliberation opinion deviates from the neutral point on a bipolar scale, the average postdeliberation opinion will tend to be more extreme in the same direction. All other things being equal, polarization does not occur when equal sized and equally opinionated factions are opposed.

However, in criminal juries, all other things are not equal. One might expect influence to be symmetrical within equal-split group states (for example, 6:6) or between equal-ratio group states (for example, 8:4 with 4:8). If so, each faction in a 6:6 group would be equally likely to win, and a two-thirds majority would be as likely to win no matter which verdict it favored. Nevertheless, there is considerable evidence that factions favoring acquittal have more influence than factions of equivalent size favoring conviction (11, 32). This asymmetry effect appears to be a consequence of the asymmetric reasonable doubt standard used in criminal trials. In a recent experiment (11), the asymmetry effect was reproduced when mock juries were assigned the reasonable doubt standard, but influence was symmetrical in mock juries that tried the same criminal case under the symmetrical "preponderance of evidence" standard used in civil litigation. The reasonable doubt standard appears to provide a rhetorical advantage for advocates of acquittal during deliberation, and the effect of the standard is thereby amplified by group discussion.

A common modeling assumption is that influence is proportional to the relative size of a faction, but not its absolute size: for example, that 8:4, 4:2, and 2:1 are functionally equivalent group states. In *Williams v. Florida* (2), the Supreme Court explicitly adopted this proportionality assumption in its decision to uphold the use of 6-person criminal juries in state courts. In an experimental comparison of 12-, 6-, and 3-person mock juries, two different violations of proportionality were observed, both of which agree with replicate basic results in conformity research (35). First, there was more majority influence in the 2:1 state than in the 4:2 or 8:4 states; that is, a lone minority fared more poorly than their proportional counterparts. Second, a minority-of-one was less likely to yield to a 2-person majority than to a 5- or 11-person majority. Nevertheless, the proportionality assumption held up well in comparisons of 6- and 12-person juries, which encompasses the existing range of permissible jury sizes in the state and federal courts.

The transition among group states during jury deliberation can be modeled as a discrete-state Markov process (33, 36) under the assumption that the process is both stationary and path-independent. Minor violations of each assumption have been found in mock jury research. The process would be stationary if the probability of a given transition between group states remained constant throughout the deliberation process, but stronger majority and asymmetry effects have been found during the second half of deliberation (36). The process would be path-independent if the likelihood of a transition between states was independent of the group's history of previous transitions, but there is correlational evidence for a mo-

mentum-like effect in which a jury's next transition can be predicted by the direction of its previous transition (36). Nevertheless, the violations of these assumptions are of relatively small magnitude, and Markov process models have been fairly successful at predicting mock jury behavior (13, 33).

Sources of influence. By comparing the deliberation process to the development of a photograph, Kalven and Zeisel (31) implied that jury deliberation might be a mere vote-counting formality. This is an exaggeration. The strength-in-numbers effect of the majority involves two different sources of influence: normative influence, conformity pressures brought to bear on a minority faction, and informational influence, the number and persuasiveness of arguments generated to support a position (34). In content analyses of deliberation, both types of influence are found and both are correlated with mock jurors' final votes (37). Although a faction's size and its ability to generate arguments are naturally confounded, experiments in which one source of influence is held constant while the other is manipulated indicate that both sources affect voting patterns (34).

Informational influence during deliberation is desirable to the extent that it fosters more complete and accurate recall of trial evidence and corrects errors and biases. Ideally, P_J, the probability that the jury will recall an item of evidence, should equal $1 - (1 - P_j)^n$, where P_j is the probability that an individual will recall it and n is the group's size, but actual group recall tends to fall somewhere between this model and a "majority rule" model—that is, social support is often needed to convince others that a recollection is correct (38). Content analyses of deliberation indicate that in some instances jurors admonish each other to ignore inadmissible evidence (29), but information integration theorists (19) have argued that even without such admonishments, the recollection and discussion of trial evidence should reduce the relative weight given to extralegal biases. Although studies in which imbalanced trial evidence is used show that deliberation attenuates biases (19), studies with very close cases show sustained or even enhanced bias after deliberation (22, 39). Kalven and Zeisel (31) suggested that close cases might "liberate" jurors from the evidence and allow their personal sentiments to influence their judgment.

Effects of Structural Task Variables

During the 1970s, a number of controversial Supreme Court decisions relaxed the traditional requirement that a jury consist of 12 members operating under a unanimous decision rule (2). In doing so, the Supreme Court explicitly assumed that within certain limits, a jury's size and decision rule would not influence its functioning. Since then, a considerable body of research on the effects of these variables has accumulated, much of it too late to dissuade the Supreme Court. Neither of these variables systematically affects verdicts in carefully controlled mock jury experiments, but smaller and nonunanimous juries recall less evidence, deliberate more quickly and less thoroughly, and are more likely to reach a verdict than their traditional counterparts (13, 35). Moreover, rudimentary sampling theory indicates that a smaller jury will be less representative of minority viewpoints in the community, and mathematical simulations suggest that smaller and nonunanimous juries might be more likely to falsely convict the innocent or acquit the guilty (32). Whether these structural changes have increased trial efficiency enough to offset potentially deleterious effects on the performance and perceived legitimacy of the jury remains an issue for public debate (40).

Jury researchers have devoted the most attention to cases in which a jury must render a dichotomous criminal verdict, guilty or not guilty. Several studies suggest that the availability of multiple response options can fundamentally alter the jury's decision. For example, providing mock jurors with a guilty-but-mentally-ill option results in a significant reduction in not guilty by reason of insanity verdicts in insanity defense cases (*41*), and there are similar response option effects in homicide cases (*42*). Juries are occasionally asked to reach multiple verdicts, as when criminal defendants are tried for multiple offenses involving separate incidents. A number of experiments have shown that mock jurors are more likely to convict a defendant of a given charge in a joined trial than when the same charge is tried separately (*43*).

Because jury research has focused almost exclusively on criminal cases, relatively little is known about how juries allocate civil liability among parties and assess compensatory and punitive damages, continuous judgments that might evoke very different decision processes. This is unfortunate because there is currently an active legal debate about the jury's role in resolving product liability, medical malpractice, and other civil disputes. There is also a growing use of special interrogatories and itemized verdicts, which require jurors to disaggregate complex decisions. These topics are ripe for theoretical development and research (*3*).

Conclusions

Empirical research on jury functioning is gradually replacing the reliance on anecdotes and speculation in the legal policy domain. Much is now known about cognitive processing at trial and the dynamics of jury deliberation, and the effects of many key trial variables are generally understood. But in an evaluation of the jury's merit as a legal institution many dimensions must be considered—judgmental thoroughness and accuracy, legal competence, impartiality, representativeness, consistency, efficiency, and perceived legitimacy—only some of which can be assessed by mock jury research (*40*). Although it can be readily shown that jury performance falls short of ideal standards on some of these dimensions, the critical questions for public policy are (i) under what conditions can jury performance be enhanced, and (ii) how does the jury perform relative to other legal decision-makers?

Researchers have begun to address the first question, but less is known about the second one. In a survey of more than 3500 criminal jury trials conducted in the 1950s (*31*), the judge agreed with the jury's verdict more than 75% of the time, but the sources of the judge-jury disagreements are still not understood. It is not clear whether these disagreements indicate that judges and jurors evaluate testimony differently or apply different standards of proof, or whether judges and juries follow completely different judgment processes. Experimental trial simulations that compare the processes by which juries, professional trial judges, and other legal fact finders reach their verdicts may provide answers to this question.

REFERENCES AND NOTES

1. There is an extensive literature on the history and behavior of juries; see, for example, P. Hans and N. Vidmar, *Judging the Jury* (Plenum, New York, 1986).
2. For example, in a series of opinions in the 1970s the Supreme Court asserted that reductions in the jury's size (*Williams v. Florida*, 399 U.S. 78, 1970; *Colgrove v. Battin*, 413 U.S. 149, 1973; *Ballew v. Georgia*, 435 U.S. 222, 1978) and a relaxation of the traditional unanimity requirement (*Apodaca, Cooper and Madden v. Oregon*, 406 U.S. 404, 1970; *Johnson v. Louisiana*, 406 U.S. 356, 1972) would have minimal effects on jury representativeness, performance, and verdicts.
3. R. J. MacCoun, *Getting Inside the Black Box: Toward a Better Understanding of Civil Jury Behavior* (RAND, Santa Monica, CA, 1987).
4. E. Campbell, *Monash Univ. Law Rev.* 11, 169 (1985).
5. D. R. Hensler, M. E. Vaiana, J. S. Kakalik, M. A. Peterson, *Trends in Tort Litigation: The Story Behind the Statistics* (RAND, Santa Monica, CA, 1987); M. A. Myers, *Law Soc. Rev.* 13, 781 (1979); C. M. Werner, M. J. Strube, A. M. Cole, D. K.

Kagehiro, *J. Appl. Soc. Psychol.* 15, 409 (1985).
6. L. Heuer and S. Penrod, *Law Human Behav.* 12, 231 (1988); H. Zeisel, *Stanford Law Rev.* 30, 491 (1978); *Experimentation in the Law* (Federal Judicial Center, Washington, DC, 1981).
7. Posttrial juror interviews are also useful for examining how jurors reach their decisions [C. L. Hinchcliff, *Marquette Law Rev.* 69, 495 (1986); M. Selvin and L. Picus, *The Debate over Jury Performance: Observations from a Recent Asbestos Case* (RAND, Santa Monica, CA, 1987)]. However, jurors' retrospective accounts are vulnerable to memory loss and distortion, and juror interviewing also raises ethical and legal concerns [Note, *Harvard Law Rev.* 96, 886 (1983)]. Another approach is to recruit "shadow jurors," citizens who sit in the courtroom and react to an ongoing trial [D. E. Vinson, *Am. Bar Assoc. J.* 68, 1243 (1982)]. However, the duration of actual trials can make replication across observers or trials prohibitively expensive. Also, since these methods are strictly correlational, neither permits unambiguous causal inferences.
8. Reviewed by R. M. Bray and N. L. Kerr, in *The Psychology of the Courtroom*, N. L. Kerr and R. M. Bray, Eds. (Academic Press, New York, 1982), p. 287; see also E. A. Lind and L. Walker, *Law Hum. Behav.* 3, 5 (1979); D. G. Mook, *Am. Psychol.* 38, 379 (1983).
9. M. F. Kaplan and S. Krupa, *Law Psychol. Rev.* 10, 1 (1986); N. L. Kerr, D. R. Nerenz, D. Herrick, *Sociol. Methods Res.* 7, 337 (1979); D. W. Wilson and E. Donnerstein, *J. Appl. Soc. Psychol.* 7, 175 (1977); H. Zeisel and S. S. Diamond, *Stanford Law Rev.* 30, 491 (1978).
10. R. M. Bray *et al.*, *Soc. Psychol.* 41, 256 (1978); S. Sue, R. E. Smith, R. Gilbert, *J. Crim. Justice* 2, 163 (1974).
11. R. J. MacCoun and N. L. Kerr, *J. Pers. Soc. Psychol.* 54, 21 (1988).
12. R. Juhnke *et al.*, *J. Pers. Soc. Psychol.* 5, 36 (1979); S. Tanford and S. Penrod, *J. Pers. Soc. Psychol.* 47, 749 (1984).
13. R. Hastie, S. D. Penrod, N. Pennington, *Inside the Jury* (Harvard Univ. Press, Cambridge, 1983).
14. H. P. Weld and M. Roff, *Am. J. Psychol.* 51, 609 (1938); H. P. Weld and E. R. Danzig, *ibid.* 53, 518 (1940); P. G. Devine and T. M. Ostrom, *J. Pers. Soc. Psychol.* 49, 5 (1985); S. M. Kassin and L. S. Wrightsman, *ibid.* 37, 1877 (1979).
15. These models are examined in detail by N. Pennington and R. Hastie, *Psychol. Bull.* 89, 246 (1981).
16. D. A. Schum, A. W. Martin, *Law Soc. Rev.* 17, 105 (1982).
17. D. L. Faigman and A. J. Baglioni, *Law Hum. Behav.* 12, 1 (1988); W. C. Thompson and E. L. Schumann, *ibid.* 11, 167 (1987).
18. N. H. Anderson, *Foundations of Information Integration Theory* (Academic Press, New York, 1981).
19. M. F. Kaplan and L. E. Miller, *J. Pers. Soc. Psychol.* 36, 1443 (1978).
20. L. L. Lopes, *Bull. Psychonomic Soc.* 23, 509 (1985).
21. F. C. Dane, *Law Hum. Behav.* 9, 141 (1985); A. W. Martin and D. A. Schum, *Jurimetrics J.* 383 (Summer 1987); R. J. Simon and L. Mahan, *Law Soc. Rev.* 5, 319 (1971).
22. R. J. MacCoun, *Dissertation Abstr. Int.* 46, 700B (1984).
23. J. Kaplan, *Stanford Law Rev.* 20, 1065 (1968); S. S. Nagel and M. G. Neef, *Decision Theory in the Legal Process* (Lexington Books, Lexington, MA, 1979); L. H. Tribe, *Harvard Law Rev.* 84, 1329 (1971).
24. W. L. Bennett and M. S. Feldman, *Reconstructing Reality in the Courtroom* (University Publications of America, Frederick, MD, 1984); N. Pennington and R. Hastie, *J. Pers. Soc. Psychol.* 51, 242 (1986).
25. R. C. Dillehay and T. J. Nietzel, in *The Impact of Social Psychology on Procedural Justice*, M. F. Kaplan, Ed. (Thomas, Springfield, IL, 1986), p. 167; R. S. Tindale and D. H. Nagao, *Org. Behav. Hum. Decision Proc.* 37, 409 (1986).
26. S. Penrod and D. Linz, in *The Impact of Social Psychology on Procedural Justice*, M. F. Kaplan, Ed. (Thomas, Springfield, IL, 1986), p. 135. Research indicates that individual-difference variables are more predictive of broad patterns of behavior than of single behaviors like voting for a verdict [M. Snyder and W. Ickes, in *The Handbook of Social Psychology*, G. Lindzey and E. Aronson, Eds. (Rand McNally, New York, 1985), vol. 2, p. 883].
27. See the Amicus Curiae brief submitted by the American Psychological Association in *Lockhart v. McCree*, 106 S. Ct. 1758 (1986) reprinted in *Am. Psychol.* 42, 59 (1987).
28. Reviewed by F. C. Dane and L. S. Wrightsman, in *The Psychology of the Courtroom*, N. L. Kerr and R. M. Bray, Eds. (Academic Press, New York, 1982), p. 83; J. Carroll *et al.*, *Law Hum. Behav.* 10, 187 (1986).
29. T. R. Carretta and R. L. Moreland, *J. Appl. Soc. Psychol.* 13, 291 (1983).
30. N. L. Kerr, *Pers. Soc. Psychol. Bull.* 4, 479 (1978); *J. Pers. Soc. Psychol.* 36, 1431 (1978); ———, R. Bull, R. J. MacCoun, H. Rathborn, *Brit. J. Soc. Psychol.* 24, 47 (1985).
31. H. Kalven and H. Zeisel, *The American Jury* (Little, Brown, Boston, 1966); M. H. Walsh, *Yale Law Rev.* 79, 142 (1969); A. E. Bottoms and M. A. Walker, *J. Am. Stat. Assoc.* 67, 773 (1972).
32. J. H. Davis, in *Progress in Social Psychology*, M. Fishbein, Ed. (Erlbaum, Hillsdale, NJ, 1980), p. 157; D. A. Vollrath and J. H. Davis, in *The Jury: Its Role in American Society*, R. J. Simon, Ed. (Lexington Books, Lexington, MA, 1980); B. Grofman, in *The Trial Process*, B. D. Sales, Ed. (Plenum, New York, 1981), p. 305; S. Penrod and R. Hastie, *Psychol. Bull.* 86, 462 (1979); G. Stasser, N. L. Kerr, R. M. Bray, in *The Psychology of the Courtroom*, N. L. Kerr and R. M. Bray, Eds. (Academic Press, New York, 1982), p. 221.
33. S. D. Penrod and R. Hastie, *Psychol. Rev.* 87, 133 (1980) with erratum on p. 476; G. Stasser and J. H. Davis, *ibid.* 88, 523 (1981).
34. D. J. Isenberg, *J. Pers. Soc. Psychol.* 50, 1141 (1986); D. G. Myers and H. Lamm, *Psychol. Bull.* 83, 602 (1976).
35. N. L. Kerr and R. J. MacCoun, *J. Pers. Soc. Psychol.* 48, 349 (1985).
36. N. L. Kerr, *ibid.* 41, 684 (1981); ———, R. J. MacCoun, C. H. Hansen, J. A. Hymes, *J. Exp. Social Psychol.* 23, 119 (1987).

103

37. M. F. Kaplan and C. E. Miller, *J. Pers. Soc. Psychol.* **53**, 306 (1987); S. Tanford and S. Penrod, *J. Appl. Soc. Psychol.* **16**, 322 (1986).
38. J. Hartwick, B. H. Sheppard, J. H. Davis, in *Improving Group Decision Making in Organizations*, R. Guzzo, Ed. (Academic Press, New York, 1982), p. 41.
39. J. H. Davis, C. E. Spitzer, D. H. Nagao, G. Stasser, in *Dynamics of Group Decisions*, H. Brandstatter, J. H. Davis, H. Schuler, Eds. (Sage, Beverly Hills, CA 1978); V. P. Hans and A. N. Doob, *Criminal Law* **18**, 235 (1976).
40. Citizens' evaluations of the desirability of judges and different types of juries are examined in R. J. MacCoun and T. R. Tyler, *Law Hum. Behav.* **12**, 333 (1988).
41. C. F. Roberts, S. L. Golding, F. D. Fincham, *ibid.* **11**, 207 (1987); J. C. Savitsky and W. D. Lindblom, *J. Appl. Soc. Psychol.* **16**, 686 (1986).
42. J. C. Mowen and D. E. Linder, in *Social Psychology and Discretionary Law*, L. E. Abt and I. R. Stuart, Eds. (Van Nostrand Reinhold, New York, 1979), p. 219; N. Vidmar, *J. Pers. Soc. Psychol.*, **22**, 211 (1972).
43. K. S. Bordens and I. A. Horowitz, *Law Hum. Behav.* **9**, 339 (1985); S. Tanford, S. Penrod, R. Collins, *ibid.*, p. 319.
44. Supported by NSF grant SES-8796357 and by The RAND Corporation's Behavioral Science Department. I am grateful to L. Dair, D. Hensler, D. Kanouse, N. Kerr, B. Mittman, J. Peterson, J. Rolph, and T. Tyler for helpful comments on an earlier draft.

104

A COGNITIVE THEORY OF JUROR DECISION MAKING: THE STORY MODEL

Nancy Pennington and Reid Hastie*

INTRODUCTION

The goal of our research over the past ten years has been to develop a scientific description of the mind of the juror as it is revealed in the legal decision-making process. Our conclusion is that the juror is a sense-making information processor who strives to create a meaningful summary of the evidence available that explains what happened in the events depicted through witnesses, exhibits, and arguments at trial.

We begin the presentation of our views with a quick survey of the images of the juror that have been significant in modern legal decisions and scholarship. However, we could find no succinct summary of the assumed decision processes of a typical juror in the extensive literature emanating from law schools, courts, and other legal authorities. From clues and fragments appearing in rules of evidence, appellate decisions, and law texts, we can infer a common image of a "reasonable man" who is capable of rough-and-ready logical deductions, but who is also likely to be prejudiced, swayed, or diverted by sentiment-evoking evidence.[1] The psychological literature also lacks any general unified discussion, although an unflattering image of the juror can be discerned in the multitude of references to a bias-prone creature who constructs a decision from a toolbox of prejudices and heuristics.[2]

Probably the most unified descriptions of the juror's thought processes are mathematical models based on Bayesian probability theory,[3] variants of traditional probability theory,[4] and other algebraic

* Psychology Department, University of Colorado. Address all Correspondence to: Nancy Pennington, Psychology Department, Campus Box 345, University of Colorado, Boulder, Colorado 80309-0345.

Research reported in this paper was supported by the National Science Foundation, Law and Social Sciences Program. The authors would like to thank Ronald Allen and Richard Lempert for comments on a previous draft of the paper.

[1] *See* H. KALVEN & H. ZEISEL, THE AMERICAN JURY 193-218 (1966).

[2] *E.g.*, Saks & Kidd, *Human Information Processing and Adjudication: Trial by Heuristics*, 15 LAW & SOC'Y REV. 123 (1980-81).

[3] *E.g.*, Fienberg & Schervish, *The Relevance of Bayesian Inference for the Presentation of Statistical Evidence and for Legal Decision Making*, 66 B.U.L. REV. 771 (1986); Kaplan, *Decision Theory and the Fact Finding Process*, 20 STAN. L. REV. 1065 (1968).

models.[5] However, none of these approaches has dominated legal scholarship or practice and none has been supported as a descriptive model by empirical research on realistically complex juror decision-making tasks.[6] So, the field seems open for a new descriptive model of juror decision making.

We have approached the goal of describing juror decision making with the perspective of psychologists who are interested in how people think and behave. First, we have developed a theory that we believe describes the cognitive strategies that jurors use. We call this theory the Story Model, and it is described in the first section of the paper. Second, we have conducted extensive empirical research to test the theory. This work is summarized in the second section of this paper. The Story Model, as is true for most theories, is not complete in its current form. In the last section of this paper, we discuss directions for future theory development and research.

I. THE STORY MODEL

We call our theory the Story Model because we propose that a central cognitive process in juror decision making is *story construction*.[7] Although story construction is central in our theory, and has been the focus of most of our empirical research, it is but one of three processes that we propose. In overview, the Story Model includes

---

[4] *Eg.*, L. COHEN, THE PROBABLE AND THE PROVABLE (1977); G. SHAFER, A MATHEMATICAL THEORY OF EVIDENCE (1976).

[5] *E.g.*, Kaplan, *Cognitive Processes in the Individual Juror*, in THE PSYCHOLOGY OF THE COURTROOM 197 (N. Kerr & R. Bray eds. 1982).

[6] Pennington & Hastie, *Juror Decision-Making Models: The Generalization Gap*, 89 PSYCHOLOGICAL BULL. 246, 255-57 (1981).

[7] W. BENNETT & M. FELDMAN, RECONSTRUCTING REALITY IN THE COURTROOM: JUSTICE AND JUDGMENT IN AMERICAN CULTURE (1981); Pennington & Hastie, *Evidence Evaluation in Complex Decision Making*, 51 J. PERSONALITY & SOC. PSYCHOLOGY 242 (1986) [hereinafter Pennington & Hastie, *Evidence Evaluation*]; Pennington & Hastie, *Explaining the Evidence: Tests of the Story Model for Jury Decision Making*, 61 J. PERSONALITY & SOC. PSYCHOLOGY (1991) (in press) [hereinafter Pennington & Hastie, *Explaining the Evidence*]; Pennington & Hastie, *Explanation-Based Decision Making: Effects of Memory Structure on Judgment*, 14 J. EXPERIMENTAL PSYCHOLOGY: LEARNING, MEMORY, & COGNITION 521 (1988) [hereinafter Pennington & Hastie, *Memory Structure*]; Pennington & Hastie, *supra* note 6; N. Pennington, Causal Reasoning and Decision Making: The Case of Juror Decisions (unpublished doctoral dissertation, Harvard University 1981) (copy on file with author) [hereinafter N. Pennington, *Causal Reasoning*]; N. Pennington & R. Hastie, Representation and Inference in Juror Reasoning: Two Illustrative Analyses (unpublished paper presented at the second annual meeting of the Cognitive Science Society, New Haven, Conn. 1980) (copy on file at Cardozo Law Review) [hereinafter N. Pennington & R. Hastie, Representation and Inference]; N. Pennington & R. Hastie, Juror Decision Making: Story Structure and Verdict Choice (unpublished paper presented at the annual meeting of the American Psychological Association, Los Angeles, Cal. 1981) (copy on file at Cardozo Law Review) [hereinafter N. Pennington & R. Hastie, Story Structure].

three component processes: (1) evidence evaluation through story construction, (2) representation of the decision alternatives by learning verdict category attributes, and (3) reaching a decision through the classification of the story into the best fitting verdict category (see Figure 1). In addition to descriptions of processing stages, one central claim of the model is that the story the juror constructs determines the juror's decision. As part of the theory, we also propose four certainty principles—coverage, coherence, uniqueness, and goodness-of-fit—that govern which story will be accepted, which decision will be selected, and the confidence or level of certainty with which a particular decision will be made.

In the next sections of the paper we describe the processing stages proposed in the Story Model and the certainty principles that govern them. In order to illustrate our ideas with examples, we will draw on one of the simulated trials that we have used in our research, Commonwealth of Massachusetts v. Johnson.[8] In this trial, the defendant Frank Johnson is charged with first-degree murder.[9] The undisputed background events include the following: the defendant, Johnson, and the victim, Alan Caldwell, had a quarrel early on the day of Caldwell's death. At that time, Caldwell threatened Johnson with a razor. Later in the evening, they were again at the same bar. They went outside together, got into a fight, and Johnson knifed Caldwell, resulting in Caldwell's death. The events under dispute include whether or not Caldwell pulled a razor in the evening fight, whether Johnson actively stabbed Caldwell or merely held his knife out to protect himself, how they got outside together, whether or not Johnson intentionally went home and got his knife, whether Johnson went back to the bar to find Caldwell or went to the bar because it was his habit, *et cetera*.[10]

A. *Constructing a Story*

The Story Model is based on the hypothesis that jurors impose a narrative story organization on trial information. According to the theory, the story will be constructed from three types of knowledge

---

[8] This is a simulated case. *See infra* note 10.

[9] The Story Model has been developed in the context of criminal trials, so it will be presented and discussed in those terms. In the final section of the paper, we discuss its extension to civil trials. *See infra* p. 551.

[10] This trial has been used extensively in mock jury research and has been judged by experienced attorneys and trial judges to be a typical felony trial. *See* R. Hastie, S. Penrod & N. Pennington, Inside the Jury 47-50 (1983); Cowan, Thompson & Ellsworth, *The Effects of Death Qualification on Jurors' Predisposition to Convict and on the Quality of Deliberation*, 8 Law & Hum. Behav. 53, 63-64 (1984).

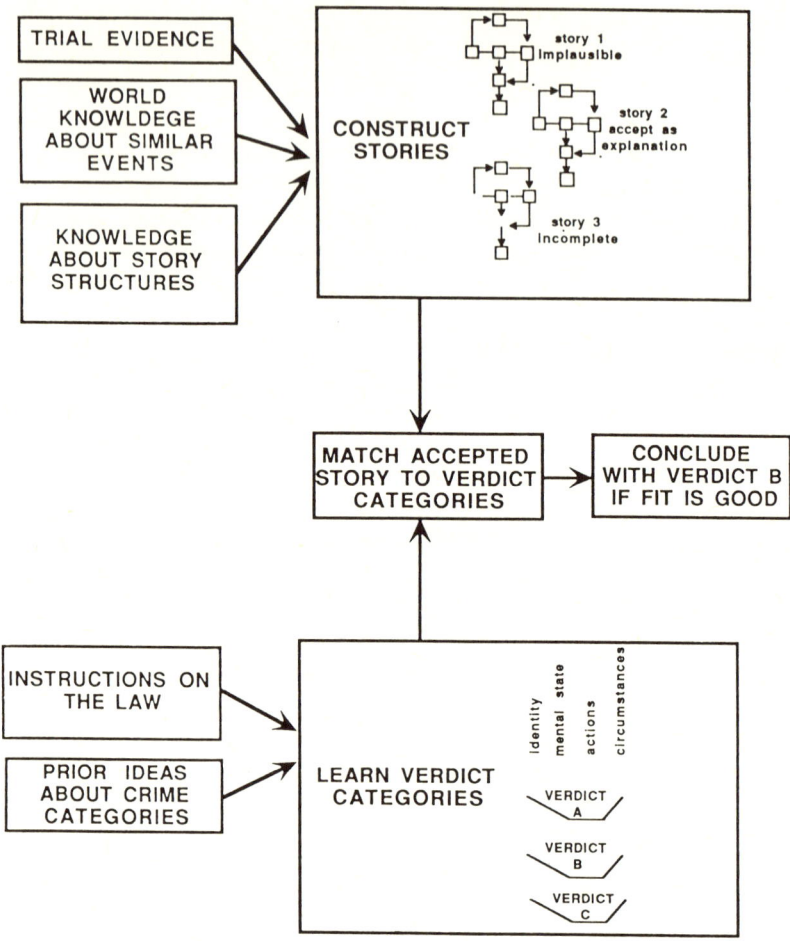

Figure 1. The Story Model for juror decision making.

(Figure 1 top left): (1) case-specific information acquired during the trial (*e.g.*, statements made by witnesses about past events relevant to the decision); (2) knowledge about events similar in content to those that are the topic of dispute (*e.g.*, knowledge about a similar crime in the juror's community); and (3) generic expectations about what makes a complete story (*e.g.*, knowledge that human actions are usually motivated by goals). This constructive mental activity results in one or more interpretations of the evidence that have a narrative story form (Figure 1, top right). One of these interpretations (stories) will be accepted by the juror as the best explanation of the evidence. The story that is accepted is the one that provides the greatest coverage of the evidence and is the most coherent, as determined by the particular juror.

1. Active Story Construction

When we hypothesize that jurors impose a narrative organization on evidence, we mean that jurors engage in an active, constructive, comprehension process in which evidence is organized, elaborated, and interpreted by them during the course of the trial. In part, this activity occurs because comprehension is inherently a constructive process for even the simplest discourse.[11] This is especially true in the context of legal trials in which characteristics of the trial evidence make it unwieldy. First, there is a large amount of evidence, often presented over a duration of several days. Second, evidence presentation typically appears in a disconnected question and answer format; different witnesses testify to different pieces of the chain of events, usually not in temporal or causal order. Witnesses also are typically not allowed to speculate on necessary connecting events such as why certain actions were carried out, or a person's emotional reaction to a certain event.

According to the theory, stories are constructed by reasoning from world knowledge and from evidence. Some potential story elements are accepted as true directly on the basis of their appearance as evidence from one or more credible sources; they are reasonably well established as facts. Which of these events will appear relevant depends upon the interpretation assigned to each fact with respect to its causal relatedness to other events. The inclusion in the story of other

---

[11] E. CROTHERS, PARAGRAPH STRUCTURE INFERENCE 1-13 (1979); W. KINTSCH, THE REPRESENTATION OF MEANING IN MEMORY 105 (1974); Collins, Brown & Larkin, *Inference in Text Understanding*, in THEORETICAL ISSUES IN READING COMPREHENSION 385, 385-89 (R. Spiro, B. Bruce & W. Brewer eds. 1980); Kintsch, *The Role of Knowledge in Discourse Comprehension: A Construction-Integration Model*, 95 PSYCHOLOGICAL REV. 163, 166 (1988).

This is the dominant view in cognitive psychology today. To illustrate, suppose a listener is told a simple narrative: "Billy went to Johnny's birthday party. When all the children were there, Johnny opened his presents. Later, they sang Happy Birthday and Johnny blew out the candles." Many listeners will infer spontaneously, and most will agree when asked, that there was a cake at the birthday party. Yet, no cake is mentioned in the sentences above; indeed, it is not certain that there was a cake. The cake is inferred because we share knowledge about birthday party traditions and about the physical world (the candles had to be on something). Another illustration comes with the comprehension of the sentence, "The policeman held up his hand and stopped the car." Most of us understand this sentence in the cultural context of the policeman's authority, shared signals, a driver watching the policeman but controlling the car, *et cetera*. Indeed, this is a sentence that would be puzzling to a person from a different culture.

evidence, inferred events, and causal relations between them is the result of a wide variety of deductive and inductive reasoning procedures applied to the evidence and world knowledge.[12]

Analyses of inference chains leading to story events reveal that intermediate conclusions are established by converging lines of reasoning which rely on deduction from world knowledge, analogies to experienced and hypothetical episodes, and reasoning by contradiction.[13] A typical deduction from world knowledge in the "Johnson case" consists of the following premise (P1 - P3) and conclusion (C) structure:

P1. A person who is big and known to be a troublemaker causes people to be afraid.
P2. Caldwell was big.
P3. Caldwell was known to be a troublemaker.
C. Johnson was afraid.

In this example, the juror matches features of Caldwell from undisputed evidence (P2) and a previous inferential conclusion (P3) to world knowledge about the consequences of being confronted with such a person (P1) to infer that Johnson was afraid (C).[14]

Confidence in the conclusion drawn from an inference is assessed by analogizing the reasoning to other experiences and by evaluating alternate conclusions that would contradict the initial conclusion. For example, suppose that the same juror who provided the premise-conclusion example just mentioned, continued with, "If someone like Caldwell came up to me in a bar and threatened me, I would be afraid." Alternate reactions were also considered, such as, "I don't

---

[12] Collins, *Fragments of a Theory of Human Plausible Reasoning*, in PROCEEDINGS OF THE CONFERENCE ON THEORETICAL ISSUES IN NATURAL LANGUAGE PROCESSING II 2, 2 (D. Waltz ed. 1978); Collins & Michalski, *The Logic of Plausible Reasoning: A Core Theory* 13 COGNITIVE SCI. 1, 6 (1989).

[13] N. Pennington & R. Hastie, Representation and Inference, *supra* note 7.

[14] It is the certainty of the conclusion C as a function of the levels of certainty of P1, P2, and P3, and the strengths of the relationships between the premises and conclusion that probabilistic (and heuristic) theories of inference were designed to model. It is at this point that Bayesian or Fuzzy Set calculations could be incorporated into the Story Model to yield the level of certainty with which a juror believes in any particular proposition (and consequently in the ultimate decision proposition). However, because of the lack of empirical support for Bayesian calculations as a *description* of human judgment under uncertainty, we have adopted a set of simple assumptions that we believe are closer to actual juror judgment processes and will allow us to perform calculations over a network of relationships. The main assumption is that at the time an inferential conclusion is being considered as a potential story event, it is either regarded as certainly true (and therefore as data; *e.g.*, P2), or as uncertain (and therefore as an hypothesis; *e.g.*, P3, C), or as rejected and therefore certainly untrue. The final level of acceptability of any given proposition is hypothesized to be a function of its role in the story and its relation to relevant world knowledge (we return to the subject of juror confidence in the section on certainty principles, *infra* pp. 527-28).

think Johnson was angry. If he had been angry, he would have gone right back to the bar. He didn't go right back." This alternative is rejected: "No, Johnson was afraid of Caldwell and he took his knife with him because he was afraid."

Different jurors will construct different stories, and a central claim of the theory is that the story will determine the decision that a particular juror reaches. Because all jurors hear the same evidence and have the same general knowledge about the expected structure of stories, differences in story construction must arise from differences in world knowledge; that is, differences in experiences and beliefs about the social world. In contrast to the example inference above, another juror might believe that confrontations by bullies are challenges to manly pride and that, as a result, anger is a more likely response. This particular inference may be a keystone in an evolving interpretation of the evidence that is completely different from that of the previous juror.

2. The Structure of Stories

Stories involve human action sequences connected by relationships of physical causality and intentional causality between events. In its loosest form, a story could be described as a "causal chain" of events in which events are connected by causal relationships of necessity and sufficiency.[15] However, psychological research on discourse comprehension suggests that story causal chains have additional higher order structure both when considering the discourse itself and when considering the listener or reader's "mental representations" of the discourse. Stories appear to be organized into units that are often called *episodes*.[16] We show an abstract episode schema in Figure 2 that depicts a typical configuration of events in an episode; an episode should contain events which fulfill particular roles and are connected by certain types of causal relationships. In stories and episodes, events considered to be *initiating events* cause characters to have psychological responses and to form goals that motivate subsequent *actions* which cause certain *consequences* and accompanying *states*. An

---

[15] Trabasso & van den Broek, *Causal Thinking and the Representation of Narrative Events*, 24 J. MEMORY & LANGUAGE 612, 614 (1985).

[16] J. MANDLER, STORIES, SCRIPTS, AND SCENES: ASPECTS OF SCHEMA THEORY 22-25 (1984); Pennington & Hastie, *Evidence Evaluation*, *supra* note 7, at 243-44; Rumelhart, *Understanding and Summarizing Brief Stories*, in BASIC PROCESSES IN READING: PERCEPTION AND COMPREHENSION 265, 269 (D. LaBerge & S. Samuels eds. 1977); Schank, *The Structure of Episodes in Memory* in REPRESENTATION AND UNDERSTANDING: STUDIES IN COGNITIVE SCIENCE 237, 240-63 (D.G. Bobrow & A. Collins eds. 1975); Trabasso & van den Broek, *supra* note 15, at 625-26.

example of an episode in the Johnson case is the following sequence: Johnson and Caldwell are in Gleason's bar. Caldwell's girl friend, Sandra Lee, goes up to Johnson and asks him for a ride to the race track the next day (initiating events). Caldwell becomes angry (internal response), pulls his razor, and threatens Johnson (actions; note that the goal is missing). Johnson backs off (consequence).

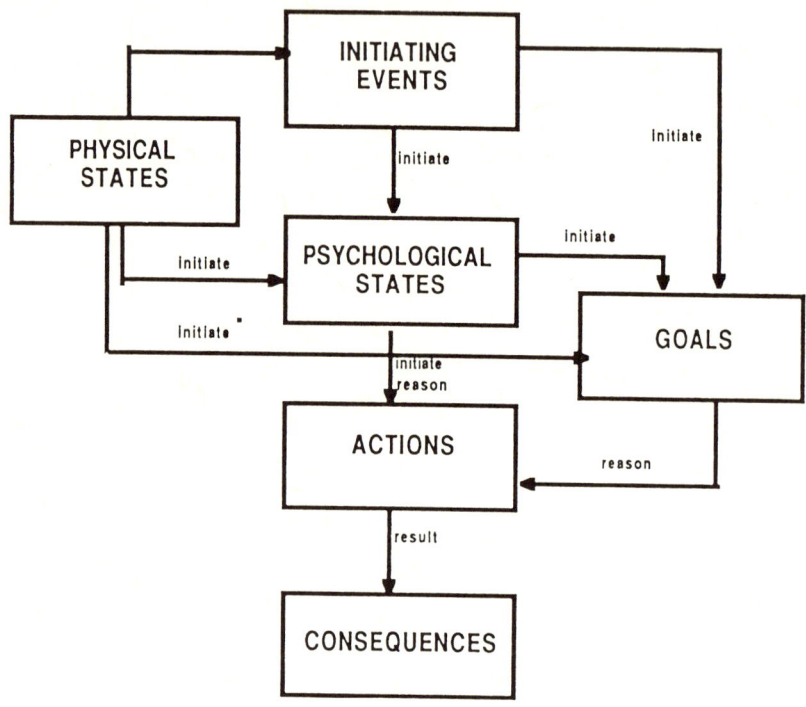

Figure 2. An abstract episode schema.

Stories may have further structure by virtue of the fact that each component of an episode may itself be an episode. For example, the entire episode above (characterized as Caldwell threatens Johnson) is the initiating event in one version of the Johnson story. In this version, the afternoon "threat" episode causes Johnson to be angry and want to pay Caldwell back. Thus, a story may be thought of as a hierarchy of embedded episodes.[17] The highest level episode charac-

---

[17] Rumelhart, *supra* note 16, at 277; Trabasso & van den Broek, *supra* note 15, at 627.

terizes the most important features of "what happened." Components of the highest level episode are elaborated in terms of more detailed event sequences in which causal and intentional relations among subordinate story events are represented.

The structure of stories, according to our theory, plays an important role in the juror's comprehension and decision-making processes. The story constructed by the juror will consist of some subset of the events and causal relationships referred to in the presentation of evidence, *and* additional events and causal relationships inferred by the juror. Some of these inferences may be suggested by the attorneys and some may be constructed solely by the juror. Whatever their source, the inferences will serve to fill out the episode structure of the story. Thus, expectations about the kinds of information necessary to make a story tell the juror when important pieces of the explanation structure are missing and when inferences must be made. Knowledge about the structure of stories allows the juror to form an opinion concerning the completeness of the evidence, or the extent to which a story has all its parts. In addition, the structure of episodes in a story corresponds to the structure of our knowledge about human action sequences in the world; story construction is a general comprehension strategy for understanding human action. Thus, the juror can easily compare the structure that is being imposed on the evidence to prior knowledge that is already encoded. Finally, the hierarchical episode and causal structure of the story provides an "automatic" index of the importance of different pieces of evidence.[18] In the example above, the details of the embedded "threat" episode are subordinate in importance to the details of the top-level episode that reveal what Johnson did in order to pay Caldwell back. However, this indexing of importance is something that emerges from the *structure* of the story.

3. Certainty Principles

More than one story may be constructed by the juror. However, one story will usually be accepted as the "best" story. Furthermore, the juror will have a level of confidence in that "best" story which may be quite high or quite low. The principles that determine acceptability of a story and the resulting level of confidence in the story, are called *certainty principles*. According to our theory, two certainty principles govern acceptance: *coverage* and *coherence*. An additional certainty principle, *uniqueness*, will contribute to confidence.

A story's *coverage* of the evidence refers to the extent to which

---

[18] Trabasso & Sperry, *Causal Relatedness and Importance of Story Events*, 24 J. MEMORY & LANGUAGE 595, 596 (1985).

the story accounts for evidence presented at trial. Our principle states that the greater the story's coverage, the more acceptable the story as an explanation of the evidence, and the greater confidence the juror will have in the story as an explanation, if accepted. An explanation that leaves much of evidence unaccounted for is likely to have a lower level of acceptability as the correct explanation. Poor coverage should lower the overall confidence in a story, and consequently lower confidence in the decision.

A story's *coherence* also affects its acceptability and the level of confidence it induces given that the story is accepted. However, coherence is a concept in our theory that has three components: *consistency, plausibility,* and *completeness.* A story is consistent to the extent that it does not contain internal contradictions either with evidence believed to be true or with other parts of the explanation. A story is plausible to the extent that it corresponds to the decision maker's knowledge about what typically happens in the world and does not contradict that knowledge. A story is complete when the expected structure of the story "has all of its parts" (according to the rules of the episodic structure; see Figure 2 and discussion above). Missing information, or lack of plausible inferences about one or more major components of the story structure, will decrease confidence in the explanation. Thus, the coherence of the explanation reflects the consistency of the explanation with itself and with world knowledge, and the extent to which parts of the explanation can be inferred or assembled. These three ingredients of coherence—consistency, plausibility, and completeness—may be fulfilled to a greater or lesser degree and the values of the three components will combine to yield the overall level of coherence of a story.[19]

Finally, if more than one story is judged to be coherent, then the stories will lack *uniqueness,* which contributes to confidence in a story and in a decision. If there are multiple coherent explanations for the available evidence, belief in any one of them over the others will be lessened.[20] If there is one coherent story, this story will be accepted as the explanation of the evidence and will be instrumental in reaching a decision.[21]

---

[19] Our concept of the coherence of a particular story is closely related to the idea of "persuasiveness" of the evidence.

[20] Einhorn & Hogarth, *Judging Probable Cause,* 99 PSYCHOLOGICAL BULL. 3, 15 (1986); Van Wallendael, *The Quest for Limits on Noncomplementarity in Opinion Revision,* 43 ORGANIZATIONAL BEHAV. & HUM. DECISION PROCESSES 385, 392 (1989).

[21] These principles have been elaborated and formalized. N. Pennington, P. Messamer & R. Nicolich, Explanatory Coherence in Legal Decision Making (unpublished manuscript 1991) (copy on file with author).

4. Summary

Meaning is assigned to trial evidence through the incorporation of that evidence into one or more plausible stories which describe "what happened" during events testified to at the trial. General knowledge about the structure of human purposive action sequences and stories, characterized as an episode schema, serves to organize events according to the causal and intentional relations among them as perceived by the juror. Specific world knowledge about events similar to those in dispute will determine which particular interpretation is constructed or accepted. The level of acceptance will be determined by the coverage, coherence, and uniqueness of the "best" story.

B. *Learning Verdict Definitions*

The second processing stage in the juror's decision, according to the Story Model, involves the comprehension and learning of the decision alternatives, which in criminal trials are the definitions of the verdicts (*e.g.*, first-degree murder, second-degree murder, *et cetera*). Most of the information for this processing stage is given to jurors at the end of the trial in the judge's substantive instructions on the law, although jurors may also have prior ideas concerning the meanings of the verdict categories (see Figure 1, bottom).

The verdict definitions in the judge's instructions are usually abstract and often couched in unfamiliar language. A crime is named and then abstract features are presented that define the crime. Features typically describe requirements of *identity, mental state, circumstances,* and *actions* that constitute the crime.[22] For example, a judge's definition of first-degree murder presented as a feature list is shown in Figure 3.

We hypothesize that the juror's mental representation of this information also takes the form of a category label with a list of features. In all respects, this is a difficult one-trial learning task. If the juror has no prior knowledge of the legal categories, then learning of the abstract information is extremely difficult. In the case where prior knowledge is available, it is equally likely to interfere with accurate understanding as it is to help, because jurors' prior exposures to concepts such as first-degree murder, manslaughter, armed robbery, *et cetera*, are often (mis-) informed by television episodes and other media presentations.

---

[22] J. KAPLAN & J. SKOLNICK, CRIMINAL JUSTICE: INTRODUCTORY CASES AND MATERIALS 4 (4th ed. 1987).

FIRST DEGREE MURDER

IDENTITY:	-RIGHT PERSON
MENTAL STATE:	-INTENT TO KILL -PURPOSE FORMED
CIRCUMSTANCES:	-INSUFFICIENT PROVOCATION -INTERVAL BETWEEN RESOLUTION AND KILLING
ACTIONS:	-UNLAWFUL KILLING -KILLING IN PURSUANCE OF RESOLUTION

Figure 3. Example verdict category represented as a feature list.

C. *Making a Decision*

The third processing stage in our hypothesis regarding the juror's decision making involves matching the accepted story with each of the verdict definitions. In cognitive processing terms, this is a classification process in which the best match between the accepted story's features and verdict category features is determined (see Figure 1, middle).

Because verdict categories are unfamiliar concepts, the classification of a story into an appropriate verdict category is likely to be a deliberate process. For example, a juror may have to reason about whether a circumstance in the story, such as "pinned against a wall," constitutes a good match to a required circumstance, such as "unable to escape," for a verdict of not guilty by reason of self-defense.

Although difficult, the classification process is aided by relatively direct relations between attributes of a verdict category (crime elements) and components of the episode schema (see Figure 4). The law has evolved so that the main attributes of the decision categories suggested by legal experts[23]—identity, mental state, circumstances,

---

[23] *Id.* at 1-4.

and actions—correspond closely to the central features of human action sequences represented as episodes—initiating events, goals, actions, and states. This is not a coincidence; rather, it is a reflection of the fact that both stories and crimes are culturally determined generic descriptions of human action sequences.

The story classification stage also involves the application of the judge's procedural instructions on the presumption of innocence and the standard of proof. If the best fit is above a particular threshold requirement, then the verdict category that matches the story is selected. If some or none of the verdict attributes for a given verdict category are satisfied "beyond a reasonable doubt" by the events in the accepted story, then the juror should presume innocence and return a default verdict of not guilty.[24]

1.   Certainty Principle

A further assessment of confidence occurs in the story classification stage. An evaluation of goodness-of-fit between the story and the best-fitting verdict category is based on the extent to which the story includes instantiations of elements of the category. The more missing element matches between the components of the episode schema and the attributes of the verdict category (see Figure 4), the lower the juror's confidence in the verdict. As we speculated above, if the goodness-of-fit is not sufficient, then a default decision will be made.

D.   *Temporal Relations Between Stages*

The processing stages have been presented as though a story has been constructed, then the verdicts are represented, and then a decision is reached. A fundamental claim of our theory is that the explanation structure is created *a priori* and *causes* the decision. The explanation structure is not a structure that is developed as a *post hoc* justification of the decision. This does not preclude a version of the theory in which there is cycling through the decision phases more than once; in such a case there could be an influence of the tentative decision (initial verdict classification) on an elaboration of the explanation. For example, story construction probably does not stop abruptly at the conclusion of the presentation of evidence. Previous

---

[24] We have no empirical evidence on this point. We are basing this on the assumption that jurors either: (a) construct a single "best" story, rejecting other directions as they go along, or (b) construct multiple stories and pick the "best." In either case, we allow for the possibility that the best story is not good enough or does not have a good fit to any verdict option and, therefore, a default verdict would have to be available. Ronald Allen has suggested another possibility for criminal cases—that the juror will search for any plausible story consistent with innocence. Letter from Ronald Allen to Reid Hastie and Nancy Pennington (Apr. 17, 1991).

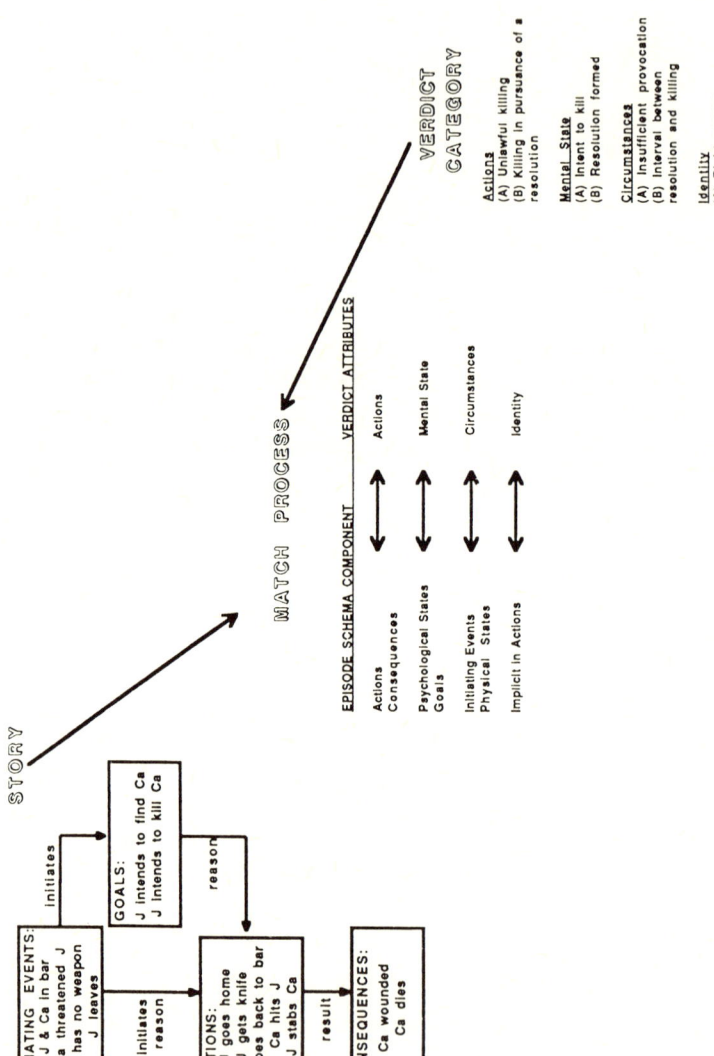

Figure 4. The main elements of a story (Episode Schema) map onto the defining attributes of a verdict definition (Verdict Category Attributes).

research suggests that jurors' judgments involve much sifting and weighing of evidence as well as reflection on the meaning of the verdict categories after the major courtroom events of the trial are concluded.[25] In addition, story meanings are not static structures. Although many causal and intentional inferences are made during the initial comprehension and encoding of events, causal information processing may not be completed during comprehension.[26] Rather, causal reasoning begins then and continues with subsequent attributional inferences influenced by the initial comprehension process. Examining the extent to which processing stages interact is a long-term goal of our research.

II. EMPIRICAL EVIDENCE FOR THE STORY MODEL

The basic claim of the Story Model is that story construction enables critical interpretive processing and organization of the evidence so that evidence can be meaningfully evaluated against multiple verdict judgment dimensions. The Story Model provides a psychological account for the assignment of relevance to presented and inferred information. Precise claims are made concerning the representational form of the evidence, and a mediating role is claimed for stories in subsequent decisions and confidence in those decisions. Uncertainty in the decision is centered in assessments of the coverage, coherence, and uniqueness of the story, and on the goodness-of-fit of the story with reference to the verdict categories. Detailed summaries of empirical studies of the claims of the Story Model are provided in other reports.[27] In this section, we summarize the empirical support for the theory.

A. *Interview Study*

Our initial research on the Story Model[28] was designed to elicit data that would provide a snapshot of the juror's mental representations of evidence and of verdict categories at one point in time. Three questions were the focus of the empirical analysis: (1) Do the mental representations of evidence show a story structure?; (2) Do the mental

---

[25] R. HASTIE, S. PENROD & N. PENNINGTON, *supra* note 10; N. Pennington, Causal Reasoning, *supra* note 7.

[26] W. KINTSCH, *supra* note 11, at 170-71.

[27] Pennington & Hastie, *Evidence Evaluation*, *supra* note 7; Pennington & Hastie, *Memory Structure*, *supra* note 7; Pennington & Hastie, *Explaining the Evidence*, *supra* note 7; N. Pennington, Causal Reasoning, *supra* note 7; N. Pennington & R. Hastie, Story Structure, *supra* note 7.

[28] Pennington & Hastie, *Evidence Evaluation*, *supra* note 7; N. Pennington, Causal Reasoning, *supra* note 7.

representations of verdicts show a category structure?; (3) Are there systematic relationships between an individual juror's verdict decision and that same juror's evidence representation, verdict representation, or classification procedures?

The first study was based on a correlational logic, using an interview to provide structural descriptions of mental representations and then determining whether or not the structures covaried systematically with verdict decisions. According to the Story Model, if story construction is a central determinant of verdict decisions, then we should find that variability in verdict decisions correlates with variability in story structures and is not related to verdict category representations or classification procedures.

Twenty-six adult subjects were sampled from volunteers in the Massachusetts Superior Court jury pool and shown a realistic filmed reenactment of a murder trial (the Commonwealth v. Johnson case described earlier). Subjects were instructed that an actual jury had decided the case and their task was to "be one of the jurors" and to try to reach a decision on the verdict. In the trial, the jurors chose from among four verdict alternatives in reaching a decision. The defendant Frank Johnson could be judged to be not guilty, guilty of manslaughter, guilty of second-degree murder, or guilty of first-degree murder. A sub-sample of sixteen of the twenty-six subjects was chosen for extensive analysis so that a range of verdicts was obtained.[29] The verdict distribution for the sixteen subjects was: five guilty of first-degree murder; four guilty of second-degree murder; four guilty of manslaughter; three not guilty (self-defense). The major source of data was a verbal protocol obtained in an interview with each experimental juror asking each to think aloud while making a decision and to respond to questions about the evidence and about the judge's instructions to the jurors.

Verbal protocols from each juror were analyzed by coding all assertions about events and relationships between events that were claimed to have occurred or not to have occurred within the context of the events referred to in testimony. Many of these assertions referred to events and relationships actually mentioned in testimony and many referred to events and relationships inferred by the juror. This coding was transformed into a directed graph designating interrelations between events.[30] A graph structure was created for each

---

[29] *See* Pennington & Hastie, *Evidence Evaluation*, supra note 7; N. Pennington, *Causal Reasoning*, *supra* note 7.

[30] Goodman & Hedetniemi, *A Descriptive Introduction to Graph Theory and Some of its Applications: Formal Methods*, in COMPUTERS IN LANGUAGE RESEARCH 19 (W. Sedelow & S.

subject in which the nodes represented event codes and the links represented the asserted connections between events. This structure captured part of each subject's conceptual representation of the evidence as indicated by the protocol events mentioned and assertions regarding relations between events.[31] To facilitate economy of presentation and to permit comparisons with other experiments, only the results from the two extreme verdict groups—first-degree murder and not guilty—will be summarized in the present report. Analyses of the data for subjects from all four verdict groups are in agreement with this summary.[32]

Before reviewing evidence that these graphs had a story structure, we should ask what range of plausible structures we might expect. First, evidence could be stored in memory in an unembellished form, as it was presented at trial—in a disconnected question-and-answer sequence, organized by witness and interconnected largely by referential coherence. This is plausible because we know that when judgments are made *on-line*,[33] memory for evidence is unrelated to the judgment. Second, the evidence could be conceptualized in terms of the structure of the legal argument,[34] as analyzed by legal scholars[35] and other theorists.[36] In this conception, evidence is structured in terms of arguments for and against guilt; or, for and against a re-

---

Sedelow eds. 1979). A directed graph is a structure that includes points (nodes) and arcs (links) between points that have direction. In our application, the nodes will stand for an event expressed as a single state or action, such as "Johnson was at the bar," and "Caldwell came over to Johnson's table." The links will stand for relationships between events. An example of one type of directed link would be an enabling causal relationship such as that which might exist between the two events above: Johnson's being at the bar "enabled" Caldwell to come over and talk to him.

[31] *See* A. GRAESSER & L. CLARK, STRUCTURES AND PROCEDURES OF IMPLICIT KNOWLEDGE (1985).

[32] Pennington & Hastie, *Evidence Evaluation, supra* note 7; N. Pennington, Causal Reasoning, *supra* note 7.

[33] Making a judgment "on-line" means incorporating the value of a piece of evidence into a judgment as soon as it is encountered. In a legal trial context, this means that when a witness testifies, "Johnson was carrying a knife," the juror immediately increases his or her belief in guilt. If the witness says, "It was a fishing knife," the juror immediately decreases belief in guilt. Story construction is not an "on-line" decision strategy, but rather a "memory-based" strategy because evidence is organized, elaborated, and interpreted in memory before entering into a judgment.

See Hastie & Park, *The Relationship Between Memory and Judgment Depends on Whether the Judgment Task is Memory-Based or On-Line*, 93 PSYCHOLOGICAL REV. 258, 261 (1986); *see also* Hastie & Pennington, *Notes on the Distinction Between Memory-Based Versus On-Line Judgments*, in ON-LINE COGNITION IN PERSON PERCEPTION 1 (J. Bassili ed. 1989).

[34] For an example of such structure, see Pennington & Hastie, *supra* note 6, Fig. 3, at 256.

[35] *See, e.g.*, T. ANDERSON & W. TWINING, ANALYSIS OF EVIDENCE (1991); J. WIGMORE, THE SCIENCE OF JUDICIAL PROOF (1937).

[36] *See* Schum & Martin, *Formal and Empirical Research on Cascaded Inference in Jurisprudence,* 17 LAW & SOC'Y REV. 105 (1982).

quired element of guilt with respect to a particular charge. A third possibility is that the important evidence revolves around the characterizations of the defendant and victim. In this case, structures emerging from protocols would show character sketches connected to verdicts. A final possibility is our theory—that the juror organizes the evidence into a story that emphasizes the causal and intentional relations among evidence items.

Our first major conclusion from the interview study was that the mental representations of evidence derived from the interview protocols showed story structures and not other plausible structures. There were several features of the conceptual graph structures that support our claim that these structures had story form and not one of the other plausible forms. First, 85% of all the events referred to in the protocols were causally linked. Thus, subjects were primarily making assertions like, "Johnson was angry so he decided to kill him" (here anger initiates the goal to kill), rather than assertions like, "Johnson was a violent man. That makes me think he intended to kill him" (the fact that Johnson was violent leads to an inference of intention to kill). This is strong evidence that subjects were telling stories, and not constructing arguments.[37] Second, only 55% of the protocol references were to events that were actually included in testimony. The remaining 45% were references to inferred events—actions, mental states, and goals—that "filled in" the stories in episode configurations. This data contradicts the image of the juror as a "tape recorder" with a list of trial evidence in memory. Experimental jurors did make character inferences (5.4% of story content), but these were integrated into the story structures as reasons for certain behaviors. For example, an inference that Caldwell was a violent man might be given as a reason that Caldwell pulled a razor when provocation was slight, or as a reason that Johnson was afraid. Finally, the conceptual graphs could be represented as hierarchies of embedded episodes when rules were applied to identify explicit goals linked to actions leading to final consequences.[38] Examples of these structures are illustrated in Figure 5.

The second major conclusion from the interview study was that story structures differed systematically for jurors choosing different verdicts. In order to analyze this phenomenon, a measure of shared

---

[37] *See* Olson, Duffy & Mack, *Thinking-Out-Loud as a Method for Studying Real-Time Comprehension Processes*, in NEW METHODS IN READING COMPREHENSION RESEARCH 253 (D. Kieras & M. Just eds. 1984) (empirical evidence on the psychological differences between narrative forms and argument forms).

[38] *See* N. Pennington, Causal Reasoning, *supra* note 7.

features[39] was used to develop a central story for each verdict group which we call verdict stories. For example, the central story for the jurors choosing first-degree murder is the first-degree murder verdict story. A network was assembled containing only those event codes and links shared in common by 80% of the members of the verdict group. An episode structure was imposed on the causal chains by applying rules to identify explicit goals linked to actions leading to the final consequence.[40] Verdict stories for first-degree murder and not guilty verdict groups are shown in Figures 5A and 5B.

The gist of the first-degree murder verdict story (Figure 5A) is that an argument and threat by Caldwell (the victim) so enraged Johnson (the defendant) that Johnson decided to kill Caldwell. Johnson got his knife, found Caldwell, got into a fight, and stabbed him to death. In contrast, the gist of the not guilty story (Figure 5B) is that Caldwell started a fight with Johnson and threatened him with a razor. Johnson used a knife in order to protect himself and Caldwell ran into the knife.

The episode structures of the two stories map neatly onto their respective verdict category attributes. For example, in the not guilty verdict story (Figure 5B), there are three episodes, two of which are embedded. The main episode is the fight, and the initiating events are all of Caldwell's actions during the fight. The afternoon episode serves to fortify not guilty subjects' conclusions about Johnson's psychological state, leading first to a goal to show the knife and then to actively protect himself. The not guilty story shows the knife going into Caldwell as a consequence rather than as a goal-directed action. These features correspond to the verdict features of not guilty by reason of self-defense: under immediate attack, unable to escape, intent to defend, and reasonable retaliation. First-degree murder requires premeditation; that is, a resolution formed to kill, an interval of time, and a killing in accordance with the resolution. The subjects' emphasis on the initiation of an intent-to-kill goal is expressed through the elaborated afternoon events (Figure 5A). Thus, being hit is not an initiating event, but part of a sequence of acts that follow from behavior directed by a goal to kill.

Verdict representations were coded and compared across different verdict groups. The majority of references to verdicts during the portion of the interview when subjects spoke aloud were to particular

---

[39] *See* Tversky, *Features of Similarity,* 84 PSYCHOLOGICAL REV. 327, 329 (1977); *see generally* Tversky & Gati, *Studies of Similarity,* in COGNITION AND CATEGORIZATION 79 (E. Rosch & B. Lloyd ed. 1978).

[40] N. Pennington, Causal Reasoning, *supra* note 7.

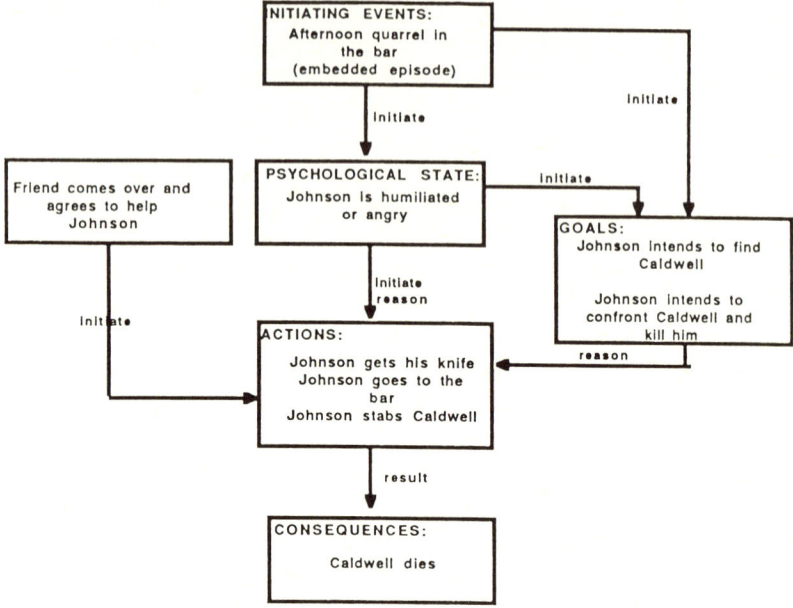

Figure 5A. First-degree murder verdict story (central story for jurors choosing first-degree murder).

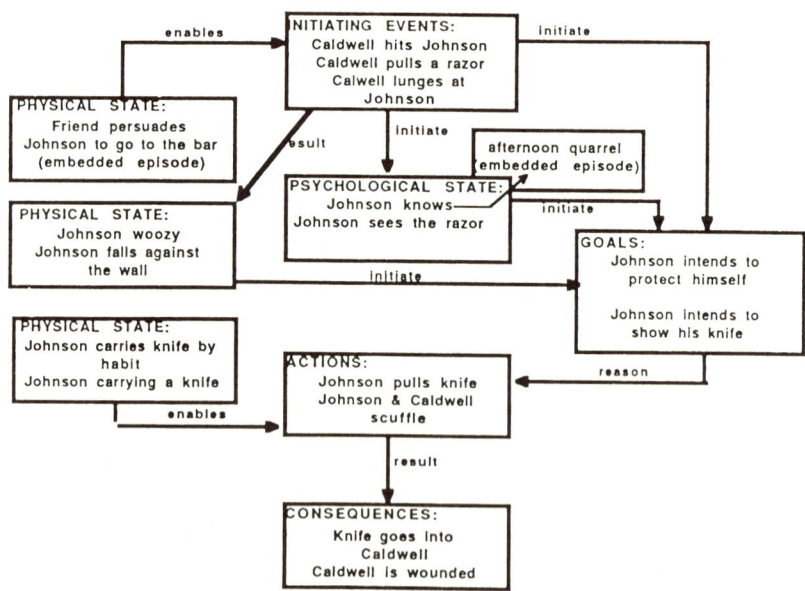

Figure 5B. Not guilty verdict story (central story for jurors choosing not guilty by reason of self defense).

category features such as "premeditation" and "malice." When asked to relate what the verdicts meant, jurors provided lists of features—although they were usually far from complete. Jurors also elaborated their category definitions in some cases by constructing mini-stories to illustrate. An example is, "First-degree murder is premeditated. There is a plan. That would be if he had gone back to the bar looking for him."

There is considerable variation among jurors in the accuracy and completeness of their representations of the verdict category information. If these variations are systematically related to the jurors' verdict choices, then the hypothesis must be retained that differences occurring in the verdict learning stage determine the verdict choice. For example, if jurors favoring first-degree murder verdicts were also jurors who did not remember the judge's instruction concerning premeditation, it would be plausible that the memory failure affected the verdict choice. To the contrary, analyses of the answers to questions about verdict category definitions showed that juror verdict choice was not related to memory for verdict-element relations. Other analyses[41] showed no content differences by verdict choice. Thus, variance in performance in the verdict learning stage of the juror decision does not appear to determine the juror's decision.

The interview study did not obtain information concerning the jurors' notions of presumption of innocence or the "beyond reasonable doubt" standard. However, other research sampling jurors from the same population of jurors and using the same stimulus trial[42] did obtain direct ratings of subjects' estimated values for the "beyond reasonable doubt" threshold and the "presumption of innocence" principle. Analyses conducted on these ratings did not indicate significant differences among the subjects when they were classified by verdict choice. The implication for the present work is that variation in performance in the story classification stage is not associated with variations in verdict choice.

In this research, two key results were established that were necessary conditions for pursuit of the Story Model as a viable theory of decision making in the juror context. First, the evidence structures constructed by jurors had story structure (not other plausible structures) and verdict structures looked like feature lists. Second, jurors who chose different verdicts had constructed different stories. Thus, decisions covaried with story structures, but not with verdict representations or story classification processes.

---

41 Pennington & Hastie, *Evidence Evaluation, supra* note 7.
42 R. Hastie, S. Penrod & N. Pennington, *supra* note 10.

The interview study served its purpose as our initial investigation and played a role in our theory building. Moreover, it provides a strong empirical foundation for the Story Model using a realistic stimulus trial and a range of adult citizen jurors. However, the interview methodology itself may have created a demand for stories as conversational forms or as justifications. Subsequent experiments addressed this issue and tested additional claims of the theory.

B. *Predicting Importance Ratings and Memory for Evidence*

A second empirical study[43] was conducted to test the conclusions of the interview study using conventional laboratory research methods with college student subjects. In this study, subjects' responses to sentences presented in a recognition memory task were used to identify subjects' post-decision representations. The major motivation for this study was to test whether stories were constructed spontaneously in the course of the juror's performance. A second goal of the study was to test our claim that the position of an evidence item in its verdict story would predict the importance rating for that item according to verdict choice.

Stimulus materials were constructed based on the content analysis of interviews from the first study. This yielded a 119 sentence written version of the Commonwealth v. Johnson case. The written case was carefully constructed so that its constituent sentences included propositions from each verdict story that were not also present in any other verdict story. For example, the proposition "Johnson stabbed Caldwell" was a part of the first-degree murder verdict story, but not included in the not guilty verdict story.[44] In addition, sentences were prepared for the recognition test that were not presented in the stimulus case, but which were parts of the verdict stories identified in the interview study; that is, they were frequently inferred by the jurors choosing a particular verdict. Thus, a recognition test could be constructed with old (true) target sentences from each story that had been presented as evidence, and with new (false) lures from each story that had not been presented as evidence (but

---

[43] Pennington & Hastie, *Memory Structure, supra* note 7.

[44] This is an empirical observation. This particular statement could have, in principle, been in any of the verdict stories. We described earlier how verdict stories were determined empirically. The graph of events and links for each juror choosing the same verdict were compared. Those events and links in the stories of 80% of the jurors in the verdict group were retained as part of the verdict story. Some of the constituent events and links were evidence items and some were inferences shared by jurors in the verdict group. A particular verdict story would contain only part of the total body of evidence and only part of the total body of inferences that various jurors drew.

were frequent inferences).[45]

Subjects "recognized" sentences from the story associated with their verdict as having been presented as trial evidence with a higher probability than sentences from stories associated with opposing (rejected) verdicts, for both old and new items. That is, they were more likely to correctly recognize as evidence those evidence items in the verdict story corresponding to their own verdict choices, and they were more likely to falsely recognize as evidence those inferences in the verdict story corresponding to their decisions.

Subjects also rated the importance of trial evidence items. These ratings were strongly related to the causal role of the item in the story associated with a subject's verdict. These results corroborated the conclusions about story structure and story-verdict relationships from the initial study. Furthermore, they implied that story representations were constructed spontaneously as part of the natural decision process, and not artificially elicited by the interview task used in the first study.

Even though we demonstrated with this experiment that causal explanations are constructed spontaneously in the course of decision making, we have still not demonstrated that the story constructed by the juror is a true mediator of the decision. It could still be the case that the juror makes a decision and then constructs a story as a *post hoc* justification. The next experiments address this question.

C. *Predicting Decisions and Confidence in Decisions*

Two experiments were conducted to test our claim that stories cause decisions. We reasoned that if we could manipulate the ease of constructing a particular story and thereby influence the likelihood of the corresponding decision, then this would be strong evidence for our claim of causal mediation. In both studies, we manipulated the case of constructing a particular story by varying the presentation order (but not the content) of the evidence.

In our third study,[46] using the abbreviated Commonwealth v. Johnson stimulus trial, we varied presentation order to influence the

---

[45] Examples of each type of recognition memory test item are as follows:
  I. Old items (presented as evidence) and empirically determined to be a part of:
      A. Not Guilty Verdict Story: Johnson held his knife out in front of himself.
      B. Murder Verdict Story: Johnson stabbed Caldwell in the chest.
  II. New items (not presented as evidence) but empirically determined to be a frequent inference in:
      A. Not Guilty Verdict Story: Johnson was trying to protect himself.
      B. Murder Verdict Story: Johnson was looking for Caldwell.
[46] Pennington & Hastie, *Memory Structure, supra* note 7.

ease with which a prosecution (guilty of murder) or defense (not guilty by reason of self-defense) story could be constructed. Stories were considered easy to construct when the evidence was ordered in a temporal and causal sequence that matched the occurrence of the original events (story order). Stories were considered difficult to construct when the presentation order did not match the sequence of the original events. We based the non-story order on the sequence of evidence as conveyed by witnesses in the original trial (witness order). The logic of the experiment was summarized in our hypothesis that (manipulated) ease of story construction would influence verdict decisions; easy to construct stories would result in more decisions in favor of the corresponding verdicts.

One hundred and thirty college student mock jurors listened to a tape recording of a one hundred-item version of the Commonwealth v. Johnson evidence (50 prosecution statements and 50 defense statements), followed by a judge's charge to choose between a guilty of murder verdict and a not guilty verdict. The 50 prosecution statements and the first-degree murder story were presented either in story order or witness order. Similarly, the defense statements were presented in one of the two orders creating a four-cell factorial design. In all four order conditions the prosecution evidence preceded the defense evidence as per standard legal procedure. After listening to the tape-recorded trial materials, the mock jurors completed a questionnaire indicating their verdict, their confidence in the verdict, and their perceptions of the strengths of the prosecution and defense cases.

As predicted, mock jurors were most likely to convict the defendant when the prosecution evidence was presented in story order and the defense evidence was presented in witness order (78% chose guilty), and they were least likely to convict when the prosecution evidence was in witness order and the defense evidence was in story order (31% chose guilty; see Table 1). Thus, story coherence, as determined by presentation order of evidence, affects verdict decisions in a dramatic way.[47]

Analyses conducted on the strength ratings of the defense and prosecution cases reveal that these ratings were influenced by presentation order, with story order evidence rated stronger than witness order. Furthermore, the perceived strength of one side of the case

---

[47] *See* V. Smith, The Psychological and Legal Implications of Pre-Trial Instructions in the Law, (Ph.D. dissertation, Stanford University 1987) (abstract found in 48 DISSERTATION ABSTRACTS INTERNATIONAL 3451B (1988)) (for a replication of this study with different materials comparing story order with an organization of evidence by *legal issue* rather than by witness order).

Table 1

Percentage of Subjects Choosing a Verdict of Guilty of Murder by Prosecution and Defense Order Conditions

	Defense Evidence		
Prosecution evidence	Story order	Witness order	Means
Story order	59%	78%	69%
Witness order	31%	63%	47%
Means	45%	70%	

depended on the order of evidence for both that side and the other side of the case. This finding supports our claim that the uniqueness of the best-fitting story is one important basis for confidence in the decision. We also examined the verdict confidence ratings and found that, regardless of verdict chosen, jurors who heard both sides of the case in story order were more confident than jurors who heard one or neither side in story order. This result reinforces our conclusion that alternate story strength is also important, although the empirical finding was not predicted.

It should be noted that this experiment was a laboratory experiment designed to test our hypotheses about the presence or absence of certain mental processes and their relationship to the decisions made. The study was not designed to estimate the size of order effects in real trials. In real trials, there are many devices that assist the juror in story construction: opening and closing statements, redundancy in presentation of information, a rich visual environment, and so forth. In this particular experiment, we stripped those enhancements away to reveal the effect of making a story very difficult to construct. In order to estimate the size of order effects in actual trials, this type of experiment would need to be repeated with more realistic stimulus materials.

Our fourth experiment focussed again on the effects of variations in evidence presentation order, allowing us to further examine the relationship between evidence organization, memory organization, recall memory, and judgments.[48] Using case materials developed by Devine and Ostrom,[49] evidence was presented either in story order or

---

[48] *See* Pennington & Hastie, *Explaining the Evidence, supra* note 7.

[49] Devine & Ostrom, *Cognitive Mediation of Inconsistency Discounting*, 49 J. PERSONALITY & SOC. PSYCHOLOGY 5 (1985).

legal issue order. Two cases were used that varied in whether the preponderance of evidence favored guilt or innocence.

Materials were presented to 414 college student subjects in written form. The two evidence organizations resulted in different memory organizations of evidence, as measured by an analysis of clustering in free recall (using an "adjusted ratio of clustering"[50]). Subjects who heard the evidence organized by story showed high story clustering and low issue clustering in free recall; subjects who heard the evidence organized by legal issue showed low story clustering and high issue clustering. However, total amount recalled was not different for the two evidence organization conditions.

The results replicated and extended our previous results. When stories were easily constructed, and therefore represented more coherently in memory, more verdicts were chosen in the expected direction and subjects rated their confidence as higher. Moreover, this effect was obtained in the absence of effects on the overall amount of recall, ruling out the hypothesis that manipulating order merely manipulates memorability of the evidence.

We had predicted and observed sizeable effects of story coherence on verdict choice and confidence that were consistent with the Story Model. Furthermore, the effects appeared in two very different sets of case materials. Alternate algebraic models for juror judgment, derived from the Bayesian approach and primacy-recency principles of information integration, could not account for the particular pattern of order effects we obtained. In our next experiments, we utilized a new set of experimental materials and tested predictions from the Story Model, a Bayesian model, and a Sequential Updating Model.[51]

D. Comparisons With Other Models

Many psychological and legal analyses of the juror's task postulate that the decision depends on the estimation and combination of probabilities. A variety of important legal concepts make reference to the probabilistic nature of evidence at trial. For example, relevant evidence is defined as evidence that has a tendency to make the exist-

---

[50] For a discussion of "adjusted ratio of clustering," (ARC), see Ostrom, Pryor & Simpson, *The Organization of Social Information*, in 1 SOCIAL COGNITION: THE ONTARIO SYMPOSIUM 3 (E. Higgins, C. Herman & M. Zanna eds. 1981).

This is computed by counting the number of times two statements in the same "story" are recalled together and expressing this number as a proportion of total recall, with both numerator and denominator adjusted for the expected number of story items that would occur together by chance if recall order was a randomly scrambled sequence of items. Similarly, an ARC would be computed for items recalled together that referred to the same legal "issue."

[51] Pennington & Hastie, *supra* note 6.

ence of a fact that is of consequence to the determination of the action more probable or less probable than it would be without the evidence.[52]

There is no doubt that the juror's task involves uncertainty, as do all complex decision tasks of the kind we are considering. However, treating the task as a probability assessment task assumes that the uncertainty assessments behave in ways that are consistent with the rules of mathematical probability theory. Within the mathematical (Pascalian) probability system there is a prescription for coherent probability revision in the light of evidence (Bayes' rule). Under this prescription, probabilistic opinion revisions have three basic properties: the combining process is multiplicative, probabilities of alternate hypotheses must sum to one, and a hypothesis that is held at any time with a probability of zero cannot be revived.[53] It is generally recognized that the Bayesian system is an invalid description of human behavior under most conditions.[54]

An alternative probability model has been proposed by Cohen,[55] the inductive probability system, in which probabilities have only ordinal properties. Negation is not complementary, zero probabilities correspond to "no reason to believe" and can therefore be revived with further evidence, and the opinion revision process is not multiplicative. Schum and Martin, in a recent test of the descriptive adequacy of both the Bayesian and inductive probability systems as theories for juror judgments stated, "we can be fairly conclusive in saying that our subjects did not typically respond in accordance with the canons of probabilistic inference in either the Baconian or Pascalian probability systems."[56] In general, features of human uncertainty assessment found across many tasks are inconsistent with the rules of one or more of the traditional probability calculi. For example, the subjective probabilities of complementary hypotheses have been found not to sum to one;[57] if certainty about one hypothesis increases, certainty

---

[52] FED. R. EVID. 401; Lempert, *Modeling Relevance*, 75 MICH. L. REV. 1021 (1977).

[53] D. Schum & A. Martin, Probabilistic Opinion Revision on the Basis of Evidence at Trial: A Baconian or a Pascalian Process? 8-9 (unpublished paper, Rice University, Oct. 1, 1980) (copy on file at Cardozo Law Review).

[54] Fischhoff & Lichtenstein, *Don't Attribute This to Reverend Bayes*, 85 PSYCHOLOGICAL BULL. 239 (1978); Rappoport & Wallsten, *Individual Decision Behavior*, 23 ANN. REV. PSYCHOLOGY 131 (1972); Slovic & Lichtenstein, *Comparison of Bayesian and Regression Approaches to the Study of Information Processing in Judgment*, 6 ORGANIZATIONAL BEHAV. & HUM. PERFORMANCE 649 (1971).

[55] *See* L. COHEN, *supra* note 4.

[56] D. Schum & A. Martin, *supra* note 53, at 77. *See* Einhorn & Hogarth, *Ambiguity and Uncertainty in Probabilistic Inference*, 92 PSYCHOLOGICAL REV. 433, 458 (1985); Pennington & Hastie, *Memory Structure*, *supra* note 7, at 530.

[57] Edwards, *Subjective Probabilities Inferred From Decisions*, 69 PSYCHOLOGICAL REV.

about alternative hypotheses may remain constant, increase, or decrease.[58] Often, hypotheses held with subjective certainty of zero are "revived."[59] The subjective certainty attached to a conjunction of events is frequently overestimated relative to the optimal combination of the component uncertainties;[60] indeed, the subjective certainty attached to a conjunction of events may be assessed to be greater than the certainty of one or more of the component events.[61] Subjective certainty assessments may be too high under conditions where there is a high similarity between the pattern of evidence and a known standard, or when there is high internal consistency of the evidence even though the evidence is known or thought to be unreliable.[62]

The alternative to modeling juror inference as a probabilistic opinion revision process is to consider that the weight of the evidence "accumulates" in some other manner. In this regard, the additive models[63] are more consistent with the anomalies listed above than are the probability formulations.

In our final two experiments on the story construction process, we examined more closely the impact of story completeness on subjects' beliefs in the guilt of the defendant and its effect on evidence evaluation when subjects were asked to respond to the evidence at different levels of aggregation.[64] We expected that more complete stories would produce more verdicts in the direction of the completed story. We also expected that there would be a greater effect of mediating story structures when evidence was evaluated globally at the end

---

109, 130 (1962); Einhorn & Hogarth, *supra* note 56, at 457; Robinson & Hastie, *Revision of Beliefs When a Hypothesis is Eliminated From Consideration*, 11 J. EXPERIMENTAL PSYCHOLOGY: HUM. PERCEPTION & PERFORMANCE 443, 450 (1985); D. Schum & A. Martin, *supra* note 53, at 47; Van Wallendael, *supra* note 20, at 390; Van Wallendael & Hastie, *Tracing the footsteps of Sherlock Holmes: Cognitive representations of hypothesis testing*, 18 MEMORY & COGNITION 240, 240 (1990).

[58] Robinson & Hastie, *supra* note 57, at 450; D. Schum & A. Martin, *supra* note 53, at 47.

[59] D. Schum & A. Martin, *supra* note 53, at 48.

[60] *See generally* Bar-Hillel, *On the Subjective Probability of Compound Events*, 9 ORGANIZATIONAL BEHAV. & HUM. PERFORMANCE 396 (1973); Goldsmith, *Assessing Probabilities of Compound Events in a Judicial Context*, 19 SCANDINAVIAN J. PSYCHOLOGY 103 (1978).

[61] Leddo, Abelson & Gross, *Conjunctive Explanations: When Two Reasons Are Better Than One*, 47 J. PERSONALITY & SOC. PSYCHOLOGY 933, 935 (1984); Tversky & Kahneman, *Extensional Versus Intuitive Reasoning: The Conjunction Fallacy in Probability Judgment*, 90 PSYCHOLOGICAL REV. 293, 298 (1983).

[62] Saks & Kidd, *supra* note 2, at 132-33; Schum & Martin, *supra* note 36, at 134-37; *see generally* Schum, DuCharme & DePitts, *Research on Human Multistage Probabilistic Inference Processes*, 10 ORGANIZATIONAL BEHAV. & HUM. PERFORMANCE 318 (1973); Tversky & Kahneman, *Judgment under Uncertainty: Heuristics and Biases*, 185 SCIENCE 1124 (1974).

[63] For example, the "Information Integration Model" averaging rule and the "Sequential Weighting Model," are reviewed by Pennington & Hastie, *supra* note 6, at 257, 273.

[64] *See* Pennington & Hastie, *Explaining the Evidence*, *supra* note 7.

of all of the evidence compared to judgments rendered after each item of evidence was presented. In addition, we compared these two decision modes, subjects' *global* judgments[65] (the normal decision mode for legal judgments), and their cumulative *item-by-item* judgments,[66] with Bayesian, sequential updating and story models of aggregation.[67]

We directly varied the ease of constructing particular stories by providing or withholding evidence that was of specific relevance to one possible story or another. These "evidence supplements" were designed to instantiate a component of either the defense or the prosecution story by strengthening causal links between certain pieces of evidence and/or weakening others. In this way, we expected to alter the interpretation of the evidence, thus leading to different decisions. The case materials and methods in these two experiments were based on work by Schum and Martin.[68] Three evidence conditions were created for two of their cases involving an embezzlement and a burglary: a *convict* supplements version, an *acquit* supplements version, and the original materials from Schum and Martin (*basic* version).[69] For the first experiment, following methods laid down by Schum and Martin,[70] we had subjects respond to the case materials at three levels: a *global* assessment of the entire collection of evidence; *local* assessments of each block of evidence (essentially each witness's testimony); and an *item-by-item* evaluation where the subject responded after each block of evidence indicating his or her current cumulative judgment. Because the supplements tied evidence together into a more (or less) coherent story, we expected that their effect would be greater when considered in the context of all the evidence (global judgment) than when their impact was incorporated into the judgment as the

---

[65] A *global* judgment refers to the condition in which subjects read through the entire body of evidence and made a single evaluation of the likelihood of guilt at the end of that reading.

[66] Cumulative *item-by-item* judgments refer to the condition in which subjects were asked to read a single block of evidence and then make a judgment of the likelihood of guilt, read the next block, and then make a new judgment (based on all evidence up to that point).

[67] We compared these models to subjects' actual judgments by including a third *local* judgment condition in which subjects were asked to rate the probative value of each evidence block independently. We then applied the three model combination rules to these local judgments and compared the model aggregation result to the subjects' actual global and item-by-item judgments. The Bayes combination rule is well-known; each evidence block was considered to be independent. For a formal analysis of these stimuli, see D. Schum & A. Martin, *supra* note 53; Schum & Martin, *supra* note 36. The sequential updating model was an Anchor-and-Adjust model in which the current judgment (which is a summary of all previous judgments) was weighted .45 and the current evidence block was weighted .55. The model predicts large recency effects. The Story Model combination rule used equal weighing of evidence; that is, the probative evaluation of the item was its effective weight.

[68] Schum & Martin, *supra* note 36.

[69] D. Schum & A. Martin, *supra* note 53.

[70] Schum & Martin, *supra* note 36.

evidence was heard (item-by-item judgment). This prediction was motivated by the assumption that when subjects are asked to make a single *global* judgment after reading the entire body of evidence, they are able to integrate evidence into a unitary summary structure before evaluation; that is, their judgment strategy will be "memory-based."[71] However, when subjects are asked to make a cumulative judgment after each evidence block, the subject is focussed on the adjustment or change in evaluation. This is likely to invoke an "on-line" strategy whereby subjects anchor on the current opinion and adjust for the new evidence confronting them.[72] We also expected that neither the global nor the item-by-item judgments would be well fit by a Bayesian aggregation of the local evidence evaluations; that global judgments were more likely to have involved story construction; and that the item-by-item judgments would be better described by an anchor-and-adjust process.

During the two experiments,[73] our prediction that the addition of story supplements would cause subjects to render stronger evaluations of evidence in the story direction was supported. That is, the convict version of the cases elicited greater odds in favor of guilt than the basic version and the basic version elicited greater odds in favor of guilt than the innocent version.

Next, we tested our assumptions about the strategies that subjects were using at different levels of aggregation. As predicted, the Bayesian model did not fare well as a description of subjects' global or item-by-item ratings in the experiment (also noted by Schum and Martin[74]). First, consistent with a hypothesis of "conservatism," neither the final item-by-item nor the global ratings show the degree of influence of the evidence supplement manipulation that appears in the Bayesian calculation based on local evidence block ratings. *Bayesian aggregates* of the local judgments were about ten times stronger than the global evaluations and about fifteen times stronger than the item-by-item assessments. Thus the subject aggregates (global and item-by-item), consistent with previous research,[75] are extremely conservative with respect to a Bayesian aggregation rule. Second, several

---

[71] Hastie & Park, *supra* note 33, at 259. *See* Hastie & Pennington, *supra* note 33.

[72] Einhorn & Hogarth, *supra* note 56, at 455; Hastie & Park, *supra* note 33, at 261; Robinson & Hastie, *supra* note 57, at 455. *See also* Hastie & Pennington, *supra* note 33; L. Lopes, Toward a Procedural Theory of Judgment (unpublished paper, University of Wis. 1982) (copy on file at Cardozo Law Review).

[73] *See* Pennington & Hastie, *Explaining the Evidence, supra* note 7.

[74] Schum & Martin, *supra* note 36.

[75] Edwards, *Conservatism in Human Information Processing,* in FORMAL REPRESENTATIONS OF HUMAN JUDGMENT 17 (B. Kleinmuntz ed. 1968); Schum & Martin, *supra* note 36.

specific qualitative characteristics of the item-by-item ratings, primarily in the form of non-complementary adjustments, contradict implications of the Bayesian rule.[76] Third, direct comparisons of goodness-of-fit of a Bayesian updating model and an algebraic anchor-and-adjust model,[77] applied to the *item-by-item* ratings, clearly favor the anchor-and-adjust model. The mean difference between item-by-item ratings and the anchor-and-adjust model over evidence blocks is not reliably different from zero for either stimulus case. In contrast, the best fitting algebraic description of the global ratings was neither the Bayesian nor the anchor-and-adjust model (differences between global ratings and anchor-and-adjust predictions were reliably different from zero). A configuration of weights consistent with the Story Model[78] provided the best-fitting model for the global judgments.

We also predicted that story supplements would have greater impact on global judgments than on item-by-item judgments. This was supported by the fact that subjects' global assessments were stronger in force than the item-by-item final evaluation by a factor of about 1.5, and that the predicted interaction between evidence supplement treatments (convict versus acquit) and response modes (item-by-item versus global) on final judgments of guilt was obtained.

In sum, the essential results of the two studies were consistent with predictions from the Story Model and projections from closely related research. The Bayesian model did not provide an adequate description of human performance on either the final ratings of the global judgment task or the ultimate rating of the item-by-item response sequence. Nor did the Bayesian approach provide an acceptable description of item-by-item ratings across the course of evidence presentation. An anchor-and-adjust algebraic updating model did provide a satisfactory fit to the sequence of item-by-item judgments. The final item-by-item judgment was less polarized (as a function of the presence of acquit or convict evidence supplements) than the single global rating in all conditions. As our hypothesis predicted, anchor-and-adjust described the item-by-item judgment process, and story construction best described the global judgment.

E. Summary

The first study used an extensive interview to establish that intervening narrative structures were created by jurors in a realistic mock

---

[76] *See* Schum & Martin, *supra* note 36; Pennington & Hastie, *Memory Structure, supra* note 7; Robinson & Hastie, *supra* note 57.

[77] *E.g.*, L. Lopes, *supra* note 72; Einhorn & Hogarth, *supra* note 56.

[78] *See* Pennington & Hastie, *Explaining the Evidence, supra* note 7.

juror study; that these structures took the form of a story; that jurors who agreed on the verdict decision shared a common story; and that other traces of the decision process (*e.g.*, estimates of standard of proof and knowledge of the verdict definitions) did not vary systematically with the decision. The second study using a recognition memory task reinforced the first study's conclusions and added the finding that the story structures were created spontaneously, without the demands of communication with the experimenter in the interview situation.

The next two empirical studies provided substantial evidence that the story-like evidence summary is a key causal mediator of the verdict decision. In both studies, variations in the order of presentation of a fixed set of evidence had clear effects on verdict decisions. Furthermore, the order manipulations were selected to either facilitate or impede construction of conviction-prone or acquittal-prone stories yielding successful predictions of verdicts from evidence order via the Story Model. The overall pattern of verdict decisions, confidence ratings, and other collateral judgments also supported our hypothesis that completeness, coherence, and uniqueness of the best-fitting story would predict confidence in the correctness of the verdict.

The final empirical studies provided some comparisons of the Story Model to two traditional computation-oriented models, a Bayesian updating model and an algebraic anchor-and-adjust model. At the most general level, we hypothesized that the Bayesian formulation would not provide a satisfactory account of any of the human judgments; that the Story Model would describe global judgments based on all of the evidence; and that the anchor-and-adjust model would describe the sequence of judgments when subjects were prompted for cumulative ratings after each witness's testimony. The general hypothesis and subsidiary hypotheses derived from the Story Model and the anchor-and-adjust model were confirmed.

III.   FUTURE DIRECTIONS FOR THE STORY MODEL

The Story Model is not a "finished" theory. There are some aspects that have only been outlined and others that have not been addressed. We discuss five of these issues here: (1) issues of generalizability; (2) the need to elaborate process components of the model and possible temporal interactions between stages; (3) the need to further elaborate and test the determinants of confidence in decisions; (4) the role of stories as mediators of other influences in legal trials; and (5) the role of stories in group deliberation.

A. *Generalizability*

The issue of the generalizability of the Story Model has two parts. One part concerns questions of the extent to which the cognitive processes and mental structures proposed in the Story Model apply to a large range of legal cases. The second part concerns questions of generalizability of our theoretical principles to actual trial settings, and their implications. Concerning the first issue, our research on the Story Model has used case materials that could be considered especially conducive to story construction. For example, we have concentrated on criminal over civil cases, on cases not reducible to a single issue such as "who-did-it," and on two-sided rather than one-sided cases. There are many other case attributes that we might investigate in determining generalizability, but these three pose obvious challenges to the Story Model. For example, criminal cases almost always involve sequences of goal-directed human activity (perfect for stories) but civil cases may also involve causal models other than stories, such as a mechanical causal model (*e.g.*, Did the mechanic's failure to tighten the lugnuts cause the accident?), an economic causal model (*e.g.*, How much financial damage was caused to the company because of the trademark infringement?), or a biological causal model (*e.g.*, Do the medical studies show that the industrial chemical was the cause of the employee's disability?). There are also additional steps in civil case decisions which are not presently included in the Story Model, such as the need to establish a standard against which actual behavior can be compared to determine negligence, or the processing involved in translating suffering into damage amounts.

Within the criminal case domain, there are also case types that may not involve the central role of stories that we have proposed. For example, a case in which identification of the perpetrator (*e.g.*, based on eyewitness testimony or extensive circumstantial evidence) is the central issue could involve less extensive story construction and more reasoning about non-story events such as police procedures or the abilities of eyewitnesses.

A final concern is that our case materials to date have always provided the material for at least two possible stories. In actual trials, however, the defense may defend by attacking the prosecution evidence and/or story rather than by presenting an alternative version of events. In this case, the juror has only one story to evaluate which may itself be very uncertain. This may alter the processing that occurs as compared to the situation where the juror has a story to reject as well. Investigation of the ways in which these and other attributes influence processing will allow us to begin to formulate principles that define the boundaries of applicability of the Story Model across the domain of legal cases.

The second part of the generalizability question concerns the extent to which the cognitive processing strategies that we have outlined interact with various practices in actual trials. For example, we have shown that the order of evidence presentation can make large differences in the context of case materials that are somewhat difficult to understand. But, what effect does evidence presentation order (as related to stories) have on actual trial outcomes? What effects do strong stories presented by attorneys in the opening and/or closing statements have on the ease of story construction, the number of alternatives considered, *et cetera*? Our research program to date has focussed on the cognitive processing questions and not on the role that evidence presentation plays in actual trials.

B. *Elaboration of Process Components*

The distinction between *mental processes* and *mental structures* (*mental representations*) is an important one in information processing and cognitive science theories of mental activity. Mental representations refer to the form in which information is stored or organized. In our work, we have provided extensive evidence that comprehension, in the context of the juror's decision making, results in a mental representation of the evidence that is a network of beliefs in memory, structured according to a "story schema." However, knowledge about the nature of the mental structure provides only partial information about the nature of the mental processes that constructed that structure. For example, descriptions of the structure do not tell us *when* particular inferences are made, what kinds of knowledge structures are the "premises" of the inferences, or how and when contradictory inferences are resolved. In the legal decision making task, these questions are crucial for understanding how decision making occurs. By understanding the time at which inferences are made *during* the comprehension of evidence, the judge's instructions, and subsequent decision making, we will know whether jurors construct single or multiple stories; what factors influence the point at which alternative stories cease to be considered; and the extent to which processing stages interact to produce a decision.

All of our discussions of the Story Model have assumed that a single "best" story emerges,[79] and have treated the proposed process-

---

[79] For some evidence on this issue, see D. Kuhn, N. Pennington & B. Leadbeater, *Adult Thinking in Developmental Perspective,* in 5 LIFE-SPAN DEVELOPMENT AND BEHAVIOR 157 (P. Baltes & O. Brim eds. 1983).

ing stages (story construction, verdict learning, and story classification) as occurring in sequence. Although the Story Model, as presently formulated, does not include stage interaction, it is possible that the story construction, verdict learning, and decision-making stages interact. For example, there is an indication in our previous data that one way jurors have of trying to understand verdict definitions is in terms of the "stories" they imply.[80] This would be an obvious influence of story construction on verdict understanding. It is also possible that verdict understanding influences story construction by modifying a tentative story to fit more closely the constraints imposed by the verdict definitions. Moreover, we could find that a tentative decision influences further elaboration of the story, leading to a firmer decision. Although the Story Model as it now stands does not predict these interactions, other decision-making research has suggested that there exists a process of "bolstering" in which a tentative decision cycles back and promotes reconsideration and elaboration of the evidence.[81] If this more cyclical view of decision making has merit (or if it is found to be false), it has implications for improving comprehension of the judge's substantive instruction on the law, for the effects of variations in the timing of substantive instructions, and for the effects of including or excluding certain verdict categories as choice options.

C. Determinants of Confidence

A very important direction for development of the Story Model involves elaborating and formalizing the principles that we suggest determine confidence in decisions: coverage, coherence (completeness, consistency, and plausibility), uniqueness, and goodness-of-fit. One part of the puzzle involves examining these principles separately and in interaction. For example, in actual case materials, the coverage of the story and its completeness would often be correlated, although in principle they need not be. Experiments can examine the effects of these variables independently. Our empirical work so far has suggested that there are interactions we did not anticipate. For example, we suggested that uniqueness (the extent to which there is only one coherent story) will enhance confidence. Yet, we found that in one set of case materials, mock jurors were most confident when they were able to easily construct both stories. We suspect this was because one of the stories was less plausible (and thus less coherent) than the

---

[80] See Pennington & Hastie, Evidence Evaluation, supra note 7.

[81] I. JANIS & L. MANN, DECISION MAKING: A PSYCHOLOGICAL ANALYSIS OF CONFLICT, CHOICE, AND COMMITMENT (1977).

other. On the other hand, it could be that knowing both stories will always increase confidence, regardless of plausibility. These are empirical questions that can be addressed through experimentation.

A second goal in pursuing determinants of confidence is to formalize these principles in order to understand how confidence in a decision can result from a computation across semantic features of a mental representation of evidence. Toward this end, we have adopted a formalization of the goodness-of-fit, coverage, coherence, and uniqueness ideas, based on Thagard's model of explanatory coherence, ECHO.[82] We call our modification STORY-ECHO, for the obvious reason that we hypothesize that explanations of the evidence in legal trials take the form of stories.[83] The model is an interactive activation model that represents hypotheses and supporting evidence in a network of interconnected propositions.[84] Similar models have been implemented to describe comprehension processes and representations in non-decision-making tasks[85] and proposed for analogical and deductive reasoning tasks that are similar to our legal judgment task.[86] Although our modeling work is preliminary, we expect to be able to provide more explicit comparisons between our ideas about confidence and uncertainty and those proposed by probability calculi as applied to the legal decision task.[87]

D. *Stories as Mediators*

Finally, there are many aspects of information in trials that we have not specifically incorporated into the Story Model. For example, we have not specified how some kinds of credibility information, such as source reliability and bias (consistency and plausibility aspects of credibility are part of the model) or other kinds of information commonly called "extra-legal," will be processed or enter into story construction.[88]

---

[82] Thagard, *Explanatory Coherence*, 12 BEHAV. & BRAIN SCI. 435 (1982).

[83] For a preliminary report on the work, see N. Pennington, P. Messamer & R. Nicolich, *supra* note 21.

[84] D. RUMELHART, J. MCCLELLAND & THE PDP RESEARCH GROUP, 1 PARALLEL DISTRIBUTED PROCESSING: EXPLORATIONS IN THE MICROSTRUCTURE OF COGNITION 59 (1986).

[85] *E.g.*, W. KINTSCH, *supra* note 11.

[86] Holyoak & Thagard, *Analogical Mapping by Constraint Satisfaction*, 13 COGNITIVE SCI. 295 (1989).

[87] For such a comparison, see P. Thagard, Probabilistic Networks and Explanatory Coherence 11 (rev. ed. Feb. 1990) (unpublished manuscript) (copy on file with author).

[88] In citing extralegal information as a "kind" of information, we are not attempting to join either the descriptive or normative debates concerning rules of admissible evidence. The descriptive debate concerns whether or not such information actually affects decisions. There is ample evidence that it does and the task for our theory is to be able to predict the conditions under which it will or will not. The normative debate concerns whether such information

There is a large literature documenting the influence of information that is available at trial but has been called "extralegal" because it is either not allowed as a consideration in the decision or is allowed for limited purposes.[89] For example, a number of studies have investigated the influence of the defendant's prior criminal record, the moral character of the defendant, attitude similarity between the defendant and the juror or between the victim and the juror, the personal attractiveness of the defendant, and so forth. In general, the effects of these sources of information are complex, depend on the specific cases, and interact with one another. Dane and Wrightsman note: "To date, no single theoretical approach has been successfully applied to the full range of effects. . . . The lack of an integrative approach may well have contributed to the plethora of research findings."[90]

Up to the present, in developing the Story Model, we have not tried to account specifically for these effects of extralegal information. Our basic claim is that story construction mediates the effects of information of all types, when stories can be constructed. Therefore, our predictions are that extralegal information will have substantial effects on decisions under two conditions and not under a third. First, we predict that when it is difficult to construct a story to summarize the evidence, then the extralegal information will have a substantial effect (*i.e.*, not be mediated by a story because a story cannot be constructed). This is equivalent to a situation where there is little "information" on which to base an opinion. Under these conditions, we predict that the effects of particular pieces of information will be direct; especially information, such as extralegal information that can be construed as "bad" or "good" even in the absence of an interpretive framework. Second, we predict that extralegal information will have moderate effects in the direction of the information when it is information that is related to and *consistent* with the story being constructed; when it is contradictory, we expect it to have the opposite effect. Finally, when the extralegal information is unrelated to the story being constructed, but the stories are easy to understand, then the extralegal information will have little impact on decisions.

These complex predictions are speculative but are consistent with

---

should be presented to jurors. Our present goal is only to describe how the information affects jurors, when it is presented.

[89] *See* Dane & Wrightsman, *Effects of Defendants' and Victims' Characteristics on Jurors' Verdicts*, in THE PSYCHOLOGY OF THE COURTROOM 83 (N. Kerr & R. Bray eds. 1982); *see also* V. HANS & N. VIDMAR, JUDGING THE JURY 131-48 (1986).

[90] Dane & Wrightsman, *supra* note 89, at 87.

a model developed by Petty and Cacioppo[91] in which they suggest that persuasive information can be influential via two routes: one in which constructive processing takes place and one in which little "reasoning" at all occurs. In the latter, people are persuaded by superficial aspects of persuasive messages such as the social status of the speaker.

E. *Stories in Group Deliberation*

We have proposed that individuals construct interpretations of evidence that combine the information heard and seen at trial with their knowledge of the world and their understanding of how a "good" story behaves. Jurors who construct different stories will either have brought different bases of world knowledge to the task or will have incompletely processed information presented at trial. It seems obvious that one effect of group deliberation is that different experiences with the world can be shared, thus opening up alternate interpretations for some jurors.[92] An example of this from our videotapes of deliberating mock jurors is the interpretation of what it means to carry a knife. Some jurors (usually from "better" residential neighborhoods) would not at first accept that a person could carry a knife without intending to do specific harm with it. Other jurors pointed out during deliberation that either they or members of their families regularly carried knives because of the neighborhoods they lived or worked in, even though they had no specific intentions of using the knives.

Although sharing knowledge in deliberation is likely to open ways for people to change their stories, we have speculated on conditions that make it difficult for people to alter their accounts of "what happened." For example, there is limited evidence suggesting that once a juror has committed to a decision, it becomes more difficult for that juror to change stories.[93] This suggests that deliberation strategies which combine maximal sharing of information and minimal early commitment to decisions will ensure the broadest coverage of evidence and relevant background knowledge.

CONCLUSION

We have conducted a long series of investigations on the Story Model and believe that it is an excellent method for explaining and

---

[91] Petty & Cacioppo, *The Elaboration Likelihood Model of Persuasion*, 19 ADVANCES EXPERIMENTAL PSYCHOLOGY 123, 125-27 (1986).

[92] *See* R. HASTIE, S. PENROD & N. PENNINGTON, *supra* note 10.

[93] *Id.* at 100.

predicting juror decision making in criminal trials. Clearly there are many areas for further theoretical development and empirical research. Perhaps the most satisfying characteristic of the Story Model approach for us, as cognitive experimental psychologists, is the extent to which it connects important naturally occurring decision-making phenomena to accounts from the mainstream of modern information processing theories of the mind.

Journal of Personality and Social Psychology
1978, Vol. 36, No. 4, 436–450

An Integration Theory Analysis of Jurors' Presumptions of Guilt or Innocence

Thomas M. Ostrom
Ohio State University

Carol Werner
University of Utah

Michael J. Saks
Boston College

An averaging model of information integration was used to (a) identify four conceptions of juror fair-mindedness and (b) provide a quantitative solution for determining weights and scale values in functional measurement. Research is reported that tested the model's appropriateness for analyzing the contribution of jurors' presumptions of guilt or innocence in evaluating sets of trial evidence. The research also established which conception of fair-mindedness was normative for our respondents. Male and female college students ($N = 80$) estimated the likelihood of guilt for 18 different defendants described by stimulus sets that varied with respect to case type, amount of trial evidence, and incrimination value of trial evidence. The data indicated that jurors assumed innocence and that this assumption was averaged with trial evidence to produce the final opinion. An individual difference measure identified subjects who were pro- and antidefendant; antidefendant subjects judged it more likely the defendant was guilty. This difference was found to result from two factors. Surprisingly, antidefendant subjects adopted a more lenient initial disposition than prodefendant subjects. However, the antidefendant subjects more readily abandoned their presumption of innocence when incriminating evidence was presented than did prodefendant subjects.

An American juror is given the task of listening to conflicting testimony from a variety of sources and integrating that information into a single decision to convict or acquit the defendant. The juror presumably arrives at some subjective estimate of the likelihood that the defendant is guilty and decides whether the likelihood is greater than the threshold of reasonable doubt that the defendant is guilty. If we ignore for present purposes the social dynamics that operate during jury deliberations, it is clear that the psychological processes involved in the adjudication task are no different from a multitude of other tasks involving information integration. Thus, it is possible to describe the decision-making process of a juror within the framework of the averaging model of information integration (Anderson, 1974).

According to this model, the juror's final decision is a weighted average of an initial opinion and the trial evidence, or

$$R_k = \frac{w_0 s_0 + k w_i s_i}{w_0 + k w_i}, \qquad (1)$$

where s_i refers to the subjective probability of guilt conveyed by the typical piece of evidence presented to the juror, w_i refers to the weight (relevance, importance, or credibility) given the typical evidence item, and the subscript i refers to the k items of evidence being integrated into R, the final rating of subjective probability of guilt or innocence.

This research was supported by Grant GN-38604 from the National Science Foundation and by the Ohio State University Instruction and Research Computer Center. The assistance of Marcus R. Walker and George Parks in data analysis is gratefully acknowledged.

Requests for reprints should be sent to Thomas M. Ostrom, Department of Social Psychology, Ohio State University, 404C West 17th Avenue, Columbus, Ohio 43210.

Notice that the averaging model provides for an s_0, or initial opinion to be weighted (w_0) into the final judgment. That is, the model allows for the possibility that a juror's final decision regarding the guilt or innocence of a defendant is contingent on his or her initial disposition towards accused people in general. The juror may bring to the trial some prior estimate of the probability that the defendant is guilty, and so it becomes relevant to ask (a) what the estimate is and (b) the degree to which it influences the final judgment. These two questions are represented in the averaging model by the s_0 and w_0 parameters, respectively.

How can a juror be objective yet still incorporate a prior opinion? An analysis of the w_0 and s_0 parameters in the averaging model suggests four conceptions of fair-mindedness. One way for a juror to be fair is to take a middle ground and assume that the chances of a defendant being guilty or innocent are equally likely. That is, the juror assumes neither guilt nor innocence but waits to be swayed by whatever evidence is presented. There is some evidence that people describe their prior disposition in this manner under direct questioning (Anderson, 1959; Saks, Werner, & Ostrom, 1975; Weld & Roff, 1938). In this case, a juror's prior disposition regarding guilt (s_0) would correspond to a probability of guilt of .50.

A second way a juror may define fairness is to try to be as objective as possible in his or her initial opinion. According to a Bayesian analysis of decision making, the prior probability, to be optimal, should be based on the outcome of previous trials. Since more persons brought to trial are found guilty than not guilty (Kalven & Zeisel, 1966, report that the probability of conviction is .643), an accuracy-oriented juror may adopt this Bayesian strategy and set his or her initial probability well above .50. If jurors believe that most trials result in a guilty verdict, they may even put the entire burden of proof on the defense to demonstrate the innocence of the accused ($s_0 \cong 1.0$).

Legal theory in the United States rejects both these notions and instructs the jurors to presume innocence until the facts prove the defendant guilty. Although a variety of interpretations of the "presumption of innocence" can be made, the present model focuses only on its implications for subjective probability of guilt judgments. In this terminology, a presumption of innocence would be represented by an initial subjective probability of guilt near zero (or $s_0 \cong 0$).

A final way for jurors to be fair is to completely ignore their initial dispositions, regardless of what those dispositions may be. To be unbiased is to give zero weight to any possible bias one may possess. Under this definition of fairness, it does not matter whether the initial subjective probability estimate of the jurors is high or low, only that they not allow this predisposition to influence their evaluation of the data presented in the trial (that is, $w_0 = 0$).

In addition to providing a vocabulary and process by which initial dispositions can be analyzed, the averaging model also describes the role of amount of information in the decision process. It predicts that jurors

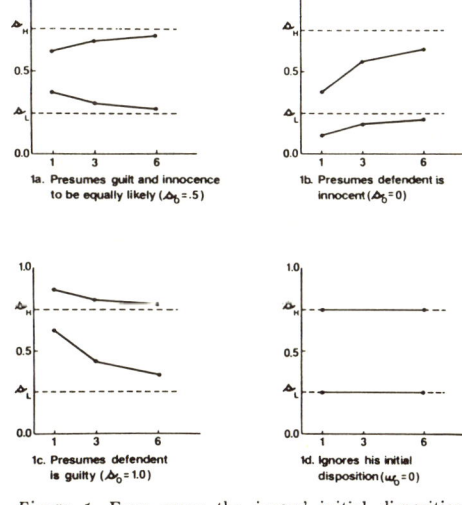

1a. Presumes guilt and innocence to be equally likely ($\Delta_{s_0} = .5$)

1b. Presumes defendent is innocent ($\Delta_{s_0} = 0$)

1c. Presumes defendent is guilty ($\Delta_{s_0} = 1.0$)

1d. Ignores his initial disposition ($w_0 = 0$)

Figure 1. Four ways the jurors' initial disposition could influence probability of guilt judgments based on varying amounts of low- and high-incrimination evidence. (In each panel, the horizontal axis is the number of evidence items [1, 3, & 6] and the vertical axis is subjective probability of guilt [ranging between zero and unity]. The scale value of the high-incrimination items is set at .75 and the low-incrimination items at .25. s_0 = initial opinion; w_0 = weight given initial opinion.)

should revise their initial subjective probabilities more in the direction of the evidence
when the number of evidence items, or set
size (k), is large than when it is small.

When set size is varied, the four conceptions of fair-mindedness should affect final
subjective probability judgments in quite different ways. These differences are described
in the four panels of Figure 1. In each of
these panels, the horizontal axis has three
levels of set size (1, 3, 6) and the vertical
axis describes the judgment of guilt or innocence on a subjective probability scale. The
graphs display set-size functions for evidence
that is located at two different levels of
incrimination (or subjective probability-of-
guilt scale value, s_i): high incrimination evidence ($s_H = .75$) and low incrimination evidence ($s_L = .25$). The solid lines describe
the model's prediction under the four different ways initial disposition might influence
juror decision making. The first three panels
(1a, 1b, 1c) all assume that nonzero weight
is being given the initial disposition. In all
three cases, the shape of the function shows
greater shift from initial position toward the
location of the evidence as set size increases.
Panel 1d describes how the amount of evidence presented should affect jurors who
give zero weight to their initial dispositions;
there should be no effect due to set size.

The four interpretations of fair-mindedness
could be tested qualitatively by seeing which
panel of Figure 1 the data most resemble. It
is preferable, however, to have a quantitative
analysis that provides empirical point estimates of the s_0 and w_0 parameters. We turn
to that problem next.

Estimation of Parameters

In general, two approaches have been used
to estimate parameters in the averaging
model. One involves the exact derivation of
the desired parameter(s) from Equation 1
on the basis of an observed value for R_k and
a priori assumptions about one or more of the
remaining parameters (e.g., Anderson, 1967;
Norman, 1976; Shanteau, 1972). For example, Anderson (1967) obtained empirical estimates of w_0 and w_i in Equation 1 by assigning
commonsense values to the s_0 and s_i terms.

This approach, while appropriate and useful
for some purposes, has certain limitations.
For example, it does not allow an absolute
interpretation of the magnitude of the obtained w_0 and w_i values. Those relative values would differ for different values of s_0
and s_i. It would be preferable to obtain estimates for all four parameters directly from
data.

The second approach provides approximate
values based on computer-aided iterative estimation procedures (e.g., Chandler, 1969).
This has been used successfully in several
studies (e.g., Anderson & Birnbaum, 1976;
Leon, Oden, & Anderson, 1973). One limitation of this procedure is that the reliability of
the estimates decreases as the number of cells
in the experimental design decreases. It proves
not to be useful in small designs.

A third procedure, and the one developed
here, is to identify an experimental design
that allows an exact derivation of all four
parameters from data without having to
assign a priori values to any one of the
parameters. Point estimates of all four parameters can be obtained when subjects make
judgments of factorially constructed stimulus
sets that vary in set size and in scale position
of the information sets, as is the case in the
theoretical graphs portrayed in Figure 1.

Although the formal derivations of s_0, w_0,
s_i, and w_i are given in the Appendix, the
underlying idea can be illustrated in reference
to Panel a of Figure 1. The averaging model
requires the two lines to converge at the left
when set size is zero. The point of convergence corresponds to the subject's initial disposition (s_0). As set size becomes very large,
each line asymptotes at the value of the average item in the information set (s_H and s_L).
The slope of these curves increases as the
ratio w_0/w_i increases.

Set size, as an independent variable, places
a number of useful constraints on interpreting responses in such a design. This is only
possible, however, when stimulus sets are
assembled in a manner that guarantees equality of mean-item scale value for all levels of
set size (note that the values for s_H and s_L
remain constant across set size in Figure 1a).
Fortunately, this presents no problem, since a
variety of stimulus counterbalancing pro-

cedures are available that meet this requirement (e.g., Anderson, 1967).

This assumption of scale value equivalence is central to the derivation of s_0. Estimates can be obtained with an experimental design that has a minimum of two levels of set size and two levels of evidence scale value. Under these conditions, the following equality holds:

$$\frac{s_{BL} - s_0}{s_{BH} - s_0} = \frac{s_{SL} - s_0}{s_{SH} - s_0}. \qquad (2)$$

The first subscript refers to set size (Big/Small) and the second to the value of the evidence (High/Low) on a probability-of-guilt dimension.

If Equation 1 is solved for s_i, the following results:

$$s_i = \frac{R_k(w_0 + kw_i) - (w_0 s_0)}{kw_i}. \qquad (3)$$

The s_is in Equation 2 (s_{BL}, etc.) are replaced by their equivalent from Equation 3 and the resulting equality is solved for s_0. In deriving this solution, one assumption needs to be made: It must be assumed that the weight given the high-incrimination evidence is equivalent to the weight given the low-incrimination evidence (i.e., $w_H = w_L$). Given this assumption, s_0 can be empirically estimated from Equation 4:

$$s_0 = \frac{R_{BH}R_{SL} - R_{SH}R_{BL}}{(R_{BH} + R_{SL}) - (R_{SH} + R_{BL})}. \qquad (4)$$

The computational formulas for the remaining three parameters (for a 2×2 design) are given in the Appendix. One additional assumption was required for their derivation. It was assumed that the ratio w_0/w_i is constant across all set sizes.

Objectives

Two objectives of this article have already been met. It was shown that the averaging model provides a vocabulary (weight and scale values) and an algebraic integration rule (averaging) that allows the identification of four distinct conceptions of fair-mindedness in jurors. The second objective was to establish conditions under which an exact quantitative solution could be obtained for all four parameters in Equation 1.

The final objective, and the one to which we turn next, is to determine which conception of fair-mindedness best describes guiltiness judgments based on sets of evidence items. In the research to be reported, set size and scale value of the evidence sets were varied. The four alternatives can be qualitatively discriminated as in Figure 1. In addition, all parameter values of Equation 1 can be empirically estimated. Of primary concern will be whether w_0 is greater than zero and, if so, what the exact value of s_0 is.

Based on their responses to a brief attitude scale, subjects were assigned to prodefendant or antidefendant subgroups. Separate computation of the four parameters for the two attitude groups allowed a determination of which parameters in the model were affected by this predisposition.

Method

Undergraduate males and females were asked to assume the role of a juror and to decide how likely it was that a defendant was guilty on the basis of trial evidence presented to them in experimental booklets. Each subject evaluated evidence for 18 different cases. The evidence sets were factorially constructed so that each case corresponded to one cell in the experimental design (2 subjective probability scale positions of evidence, 3 set sizes, and 3 case types).

Subjects

Eighty undergraduates from introductory psychology courses at Ohio State University served in the experiment to fulfill a research participation requirement. Forty participated in a first study and 40 participated 3 months later in an exact replication.

Experimental Booklets

The independent variables were scale value of the evidence (high incrimination/low incrimination), set size (1, 3, or 6 items of evidence), and case type (murder, rape, or theft). Each booklet consisted of 18 separate pages, each page presenting a different case and representing a different cell within the design. At the top of each page were the words "Assume all evidence has been judged admissible" and a statement of the type of case being judged. Subjects were asked to read the list of evidence items on each page and to decide, "given *only* this information, how likely is it the accused person actually committed the crime?" The 11-point response scale ranged from 0% to 100%. The 0% endpoint was labeled "Certain he is innocent"; the 100% endpoint, "Certain he is guilty."

Evidence

Approximately 130 evidence statements were gleaned from various law books, television programs, and colleagues' imaginations that related to the murder, rape, or theft case types. To obtain incrimination scale values, the statements were rated by 72 undergraduates who used the same rating scale as was used in the actual experiment. They were told to consider each piece of evidence independently, as though it was all they knew about a single case, and to decide how likely it was the defendant was guilty.

A list of 10 high-incrimination and a list of 10 low-incrimination statements was selected for each of the three case types, resulting in a total of six lists of evidence statements. Clearly redundant or inconsistent statements were excluded from each list. The counterbalancing of scale values across set size was achieved by the method of cyclical replications. Items within each list were randomly ordered from 1 to 10. The 10 items were then partitioned into the three experimental set sizes (1, 3, and 6). The method of cyclical replications requires that this partitioning be replicated in 10 different ways by simply moving the first item to the end of the list and again grouping the rearranged items, in order, into sets of 1, 3, and 6. For example, if (a), (b,c,d), (e,f,g,h,i,j) was the first grouping of 10 items into three sets, then (b), (c,d,e), (f,g,h,i,j,a) would be the second, and so forth. This was done for all six lists of 10 evidence items. Each subject received one of the 10 cyclical replications (that is, 3 different set sizes) for each of the six (2 evidence levels by 3 case types) lists. Four copies of each booklet type were used for a total of 40 booklets in each replication. The pages in each booklet were assembled in a different arbitrary order.

The method of cyclical replications has several advantages over counterbalancing procedures previously used in set-size research (e.g., Anderson, 1967). First, every subject encounters every item exactly once. Thus, all raters are exposed to the same stimuli and the same objective scale values. Second, the subject does not encounter the same item in both large and small sets, thereby reducing subjects' awareness that set size is varying while information items are being held constant. Third, unlike previous methods, each subject sees the same number of small sets as large sets. Finally, this technique provides economically and conveniently a large number of stimulus replications for each set size. It can be used for other set-size combinations as long as the number of items equals the sum of the set sizes (e.g., $1 + 3 + 6 = 10$).

Case Type

There were three types of crimes being judged. One third were murder; one third, rape; and one third, theft. No definitions of these terms were offered. The case type preceded the list of evidence items on each page.

Initial Disposition

One purpose of this article was to show the influence of a juror's initial disposition on his or her juridic decisions. A quantitative estimate of s_0 might be computed for each juror as an index of his or her predisposition. This, however, was not done because the s_0 would be derived from the very data it should predict and so would not be satisfactory for predictive purposes (cf. Kaplan, 1975).

Therefore, subjects responded to five items on a 5-point ("strongly agree" to "strongly disagree") scale that measured their general disposition toward assuming guilt or innocence about a defendant. The scale measured subjects' prior expectation that the typical defendant is guilty (e.g., "Most people who are brought to trial are guilty as charged").[1] A median split within each of the 10 booklet types defined those subjects who seemed disposed to presume innocence and those disposed to presume guilt.

As noted earlier, this experiment was replicated with a second group of 40 subjects. This was undertaken to test the reliability of a tantalizing interaction involving the initial disposition factor that was marginally significant with the first sample. It proved unreliable.

Data Analyses

A log-odds transformation of subjects' probability-of-guilt ratings was used in all data analyses. The transformed score, where p is the untransformed rating expressed in probability terms, is computed as follows:

$$tr = \log_{10} \frac{p}{1 - p}. \qquad (5)$$

This transformation of subjective probability ratings has the effect of stretching out the extremes of the rating scale. Probability ratings between .2 and .8 are relatively unaffected by the transformation.

In general, transformations can be justified either on statistical grounds or conceptual grounds. Both kinds of reasons apply in the present case.

---

[1] The remaining four items were "What we need to halt rising crime are harsher penalties," "Too many criminals are set free by the courts," "Our legal system is set up so that people aren't brought to court unless they are guilty," and "Any jury that fails to convict is made up of people who are just softhearted." The part–whole correlations over 80 subjects ranged from .51 to .68 (median = .60).

When using analysis of variance, it is desirable to minimize any correlation between cell means and variances. When using a logically bounded rating scale as in the present study (probability of guilt cannot be lower than zero or higher than unity), cell variances decrease as their means approach the extremes of the scale. For the present data, mid-scale cell variances were found to average over eight times greater than end-scale variances. This difference was entirely eliminated (and slightly reversed) when the log-odds transformation was used. All analyses were performed on the raw scores as well as the transformed scores, and no statistical decisions relevant to this article were changed by the transformation.

The primary theoretical concern of the present article was to derive and empirically estimate the several parameters of the averaging model applied to subjective probability estimates of guilt. Since this subjective continuum is logically bounded by zero and unity, it follows that the empirical estimates of s_0 and s_1 must fall within these bounds to be meaningfully interpreted as subjective probability values. This condition was not met when the untransformed judgments were analyzed. No such interpretive difficulties arise, however, with the transformed scores, since they range from minus to plus infinity.

The log-odds transformation was selected in preference to other possibilities (e.g., z scores) because of its widespread use in Bayesian analyses (Marshall & Wise, 1975; Schmitt, 1969) with probability rating scales. The Bayesian approach to judgment argues that the relative contribution of two evidence items is a function of their difference on the log-odds transformed scale rather than on the probability rating scale. This implies that the interval property of the subjective probability continuum is better represented by the log-odds transformation than by the direct probability rating.

It is not possible to directly transform the two endpoints, zero and unity, into log-odds terms. Three alternatives were considered, each providing successively closer approximations to the raw score values by setting zero and unity equal to .01 and .99, .001 and .999, and .0001 and .9999. An analysis of variance was done for each of these options; the pattern of significant effects was identical for each. An examination of the s_0s calculated for each alternative indicated few systematic differences. The .001/.999 approximation was chosen for the data analyses presentation in this article. For clarity of exposition, the means of the transformed ratings were converted back to probability units and graphed in the log-odds metric.

Only two levels of set size are needed to estimate the parameters. Three levels were used in this experiment, allowing for three separate estimates of s_0 ($s_{0(1,3)}$, $s_{0(3,6)}$, and $s_{0(1,6)}$) and the other parameters. As explained in the discussion, the reliability of the parameter estimates should increase as the difference between the largest and smallest set size increases. To verify this, all three estimates of s_0 were examined individually. The $s_{0(1,6)}$ was found to provide the most stable estimate of the three across the two

subject-group replications. Consequently, all reported parameter estimates are based on Set Sizes 1 and 6.

Results

Jurors Presume Innocence

Prior dispositions should be reflected in the value of the s_0 and w_0 parameters. Four alternative conceptions of fair-mindedness as defined by an averaging model involving those parameters were illustrated in Figure 1. But before these predictions can be examined, it is necessary to assess whether the averaging model adequately accounts for the obtained judgments.

If subjects were averaging items of evidence with their initial disposition, the interaction between scale value and set size must display one of two patterns. One possibility is that there is no interaction (if $w_0 = 0$). Reference to Figure 2 shows that this is not the case, $F(2, 152) = 25.29$, $p < .001$. Given the presence of an interaction, the averaging model requires that the curves should fan out or diverge to the right. The curves do diverge, and only the linear component is significant ($p < .001$). Furthermore, the pattern of judgments in Figure 2 was comparable for both replications: Set Size × Scale Value ×

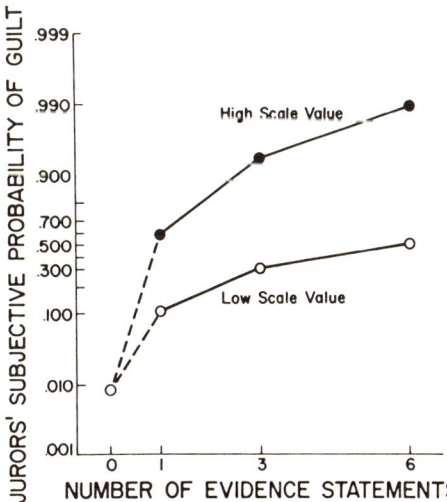

Figure 2. Effects of set size and incrimination value of evidence on jurors' probability-of-guilt judgments.

Replication interaction, $F(2, 152) = .93$. This serves to validate both the applicability of the averaging model to this stimulus domain and the appropriateness of the log-odds response scale transformation.

Parameter estimates. Inspection of the set-size effect in Figure 2 permits certain features of the parameters to be identified. It can be concluded that w_0 is greater than 0, that s_0 is less than .01, that s_L is greater than .50, and that s_H is greater than .99. At this qualitative level, then, Alternative 1b from Figure 1 is supported by these data: People do presume innocence in this study.

The set of equations presented in this article allows exact values to be determined for each parameter. Based on the data in Figure 2, the overall s_0 was equal to .008 (see Table 1). It was not possible to place confidence bounds around this value (or any of the other parameters), since stimulus counterbalancing across set size was accomplished across subjects instead of within subjects. However, separate and independent estimates were obtained for each replication. The two values of s_0 were .005 and .011, indicating fairly small variability (range = .006) in the overall estimate.

The scale value estimates for both the high and low evidence sets were also informative. The scale value for the low-incrimination items ($s_L = .71$) was surprisingly high in that a deliberate attempt was made to use low-incrimination items that had very little

guilt implication. Examples of typical low-incrimination scale value items were, for murder, "He had quarrelled with the victim two weeks before the murder"; for rape, "Several friends testified the accused was a decent man"; for theft, "A friend of the accused said he had left in a hurry the night of the crime and would not say where he was going." It would appear that in the context of a trial, even relatively innocent-appearing acts can convey an implication of guilt.

Items in the high scale-value set conveyed near-certainty of guilt ($s_H = .998$). Examples of these items were, for murder, "The accused had been seen running from the victim's house after a loud argument and gunshots"; for rape, "The victim's hair ribbon was found in the accused's pocket"; and for theft, "Some of the stolen goods were found in the home of the accused." Although these items convey considerably greater implication of guilt than do the low scale-value items, it is interesting to note in Figure 2 that six items of low scale-value evidence led to almost the same guiltiness judgment as did one item of the high scale-value evidence. This is due to the relative weight given an item of evidence compared to the initial disposition.

The typical item of evidence was given slightly less weight than the initial disposition ($w_i = .476$; $w_0 = .524$). This finding is similar to weight estimates obtained in impression-formation studies that used more approximate methods (Anderson, 1967). As

Table 1
Parameter Estimates for Subjective Probability of Guilt Judgments

Experimental condition	Parameter			
	s_0	s_H	s_L	w_i
Overall	.008 (−2.11)	.998 (2.70)	.71 (.39)	.476
Replication				
1	.005 (−2.26)	.999 (2.89)	.71 (.39)	.457
2	.011 (−1.96)	.997 (2.52)	.71 (.40)	.498
Prior disposition				
Antidefendant	.004 (−2.40)	.998 (2.72)	.78 (.55)	.540
Prodefendant	.011 (−1.94)	.998 (2.71)	.64 (.24)	.416
Case type				
Murder	.016 (−1.79)	.998 (2.72)	.68 (.33)	.424
Rape	.016 (−1.80)	.999 (3.51)	.61 (.19)	.354
Theft	.001 (−5.84)	.992 (2.06)	.81 (.64)	.782

Note. Values in parentheses are the parameter estimates based on the log-odds transformation scores. Each subjective probability estimate was retransformed back from its corresponding log-odds value.

can be seen in Table 1, this estimate showed a range of only .041 over the two replications.

Assumption of equal weighting. The parameter derivations assumed that the weight given high scale-value items is the same as that given the low ones ($w_H = w_L$) and the weight given items in a big set size is the same as that given in a small one ($w_B = w_S$). This means that the computed values of the weights under these four conditions are mathematically required to be identical. Consequently, the assumption of equality cannot be tested on the data from the four experimental conditions that entered into the computations. However, since the data for Set Size 3 were omitted from the computations, this set size can be used to test the assumption of equality in weights across high and low incrimination-value evidence. The item-weight estimates for the high and low scale-value conditions of Set Size 3 were .433 and .451, respectively. This small difference appears to be unreliable in that it was reversed in one of the two replication conditions.

No test was made of the assumption of equality of weight across set size. Such a test would have been possible using the above procedure if four or more levels of set size had been used. This assumption has received support in impression-formation judgments (Anderson, 1967). Evidence contradicting both assumptions has been reported, however, for a person-perception task that used an untransformed likelihood (i.e., probability) rating scale (Anderson & Birnbaum, 1976). Conceivably, these assumptions would have held, had a log-odds transformation been used in that study.

Initial Disposition

Subjects were classified as prodefendant or antidefendant on the basis of a brief attitude scale. If the pro- and antidefendant subjects differ only in the location of their initial disposition (s_0), with the antidefendant subject having a higher s_0 than the prodefendant subject, the averaging model predicts a very specific pattern of ratings. First, antidefendant judges should give higher probability-of-guilt ratings than prodefendant judges. Figure 3 shows that this was the case, $F(1, 76)$

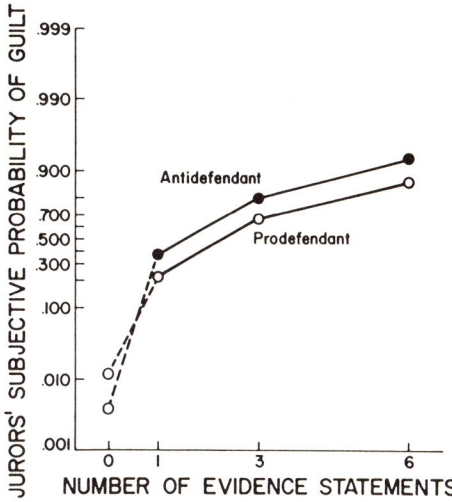

Figure 3. Effects of set size and jurors' predisposition on their probability-of-guilt judgments.

$= 7.59$, $p < .007$. Second, this harshness tendency should interact with set size: The curves should converge to the right, thus affecting the linear component. However, neither the overall interaction, $F(2, 152) = 1.36$, nor its linear component was significant. A final prediction of the averaging model is that the harshness tendency should interact jointly with set size and evidence scale value. Again, neither the overall interaction ($F < 1$) nor its linear component was significant.

The failure of these predictions should not be taken as invalidating the averaging model or the response scale; the results only invalidate the assumption that the anti- and prodefendant subjects differ solely in the value of their initial disposition. Any or all of the four parameters could be affected by this source of individual differences. One advantage of the present approach over previous investigations of initial dispositions (e.g., Kaplan, 1975, in press) is that it allows other parameters in addition to s_0 to be evaluated.

Parameter estimates. The parameter estimates given in Table 1 show that pro- and antidefendant subjects differ substantially [2]

---

[2] Since no test of significance could be meaningfully applied to these values, we only offer an interpretation of differences that are larger than those found between the two replications.

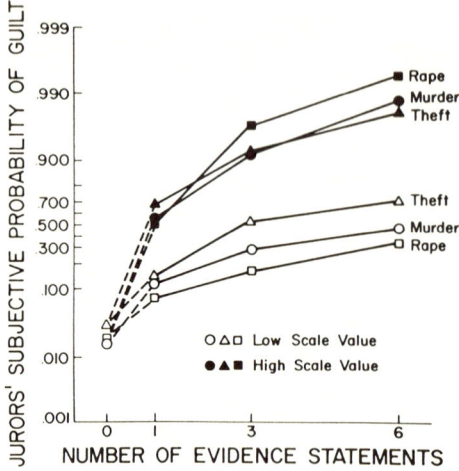

Figure 4. Effects of set size, incrimination value, and case type on jurors' probability-of-guilt judgments.

in three of the four parameters. The most surprising difference appeared in the s_0 parameter. Rather than antidefendant subjects being more harsh in their s_0 than the prodefendant subjects, they actually showed a greater willingness to presume innocence (antidefendant $s_0 = .004$ and prodefendant $s_0 = .011$). However, they accorded greater weight to the evidence, thereby relinquishing that prior disposition much more readily than did the prodefendant subjects (antidefendant $w_i = .540$ and prodefendant $w_i = .416$). Perhaps the prodefendant subjects place less trust in any single item of evidence because they feel the defendant might have an innocent explanation for the fact. Although the two subject groups show no difference in the location of the high scale-value evidence, they do differ in the incrimination value of the low scale-value evidence (antidefendant $s_L = .78$ and prodefendant $s_L = .64$). The low scale-value items, being nearer the middle of the scale, are probably open to a greater variety of interpretations than the high scale-value items. Prodefendant subjects appear to interpret them in more benign ways than do the antidefendant subjects.

Case Types

Three case types (murder, rape, theft) were used in this study. Since no attempt

was made to match the normative scale values of the evidence sets across case type, differences between cases should emerge because of differences in the level of guilt conveyed by the evidence items. Over both levels of evidence, the theft evidence had the highest normative scale value, with the other two cases being lower and roughly comparable. If the cases differ only in the scale value of the evidence (and the s_0 and w_0/w_i parameters remain constant), several predictions would follow from the averaging model. A case type main effect should emerge, with theft receiving the highest ratings. This finding was, in fact, obtained, $F(2, 152) = 4.11$, $p < .007$. Second, case type should interact with set size, with the curves nonintersecting and fanning out as set size increases. This interaction was not significant, $F(4, 304) = 1.79$, $p < .13$, although the linear component was closer to significance ($p < .06$). Contrary to this prediction, the curves intersected and showed a converging instead of a diverging pattern (see Figure 4).

These violations mean that we must reject the assumption that the case types differ only in the scale value of their evidence sets. Analysis at this qualitative level does not allow us to identify whether the case types differ in one or both of the remaining parameters (s_0 or w_0/w_i).

Parameter estimates. Integration theory and functional measurement allow estimation of stimulus scale values from marginal means. This procedure can be seen in Figure 4 to produce inconsistent estimates when the assumptions of the model are not verified. Looking only at the high scale-value data, it can be seen that the theft items would receive a higher scale value than the murder items if the design had contained only Set Sizes 1 and 3. Theft would have received a lower scale value than murder if the design had only included Set Sizes 3 and 6. However, these problems do not arise when the present procedures are used to calculate the theoretical scale value of the evidence items. Table 1 shows that high incrimination-value theft items do have higher s_is than the corresponding murder items.

Subjects did not adopt the same values of s_0 and w_i for all three case types. There was a much greater willingness to presume innocence for the theft case ($s_0 < .001$) than for the murder and rape cases ($s_0 \text{s} = .016$). It is difficult to generalize from only three case types, but it may be that people find it more difficult to presume innocence for more serious crimes that involve irrevocable bodily injury.

The weights given evidence items also differ over the three case types. The value of w_i is three times that given w_0 for the theft cases. We have the anomalous finding that for the type of case in which subjects were most willing to presume innocence, they also were most willing to relinquish this presumption when presented items of evidence. Rape cases received the lowest w_i, indicating that subjects were least willing to relinquish their presumption of innocence in these cases.

Discussion

Do Jurors Presume Innocence in Court Settings?

The present data show that jurors do presume innocence in evaluating sets of evidence under the conditions of the present experiment. The study was designed to establish generality of that conclusion across three different case types, across high and low incrimination-value evidence items, and across 10 different replications of each evidence set. Combined over these factors, this experiment incorporated 60 different stimulus replications within each set size. Consequently, we can feel fairly secure that the present finding was not the result of an idiosyncratic assemblage of evidence items.

The subjects used in the present study were male and female college students. It is possible to argue that college students are more idealistic than typical members of a jury and will more readily comply with the social ideal of presuming innocence. This, however, seems not to be a limitation in the generality of the present findings, as the present experiment was replicated with a heterogeneous sample of adults, all of whom had sat on a jury within the preceding $2\frac{1}{2}$ years, and substantially identical results were obtained (Saks et al., 1975). Since only the s_0 parameter was reported in the article about that experiment, we have computed the remaining parameters from those data and presented them in Table 2. It can be seen that with some minor discrepancies among the parameter values for case type, the values in Table 2 correspond very closely to those of Table 1.

Even though the findings from this approach hold for a variety of stimulus replications and subject samples, the conclusions are not completely general. The three case types selected were all criminal felonies and so did not include any civil suits. What may be perhaps an even more severe limitation is that most of the evidence items were prosecution oriented. The probability-of-guilt scale values of both the high and low incrimination-value evidence sets were above .50. It is conceivable that our subjects only adopted a presumption of innocence because they were encountering one-sided sets of evidence. Had they received

Table 2

Subjective Probability and Weight Estimates for Experienced Jurors

Experimental condition	Parameter			
	s_0	s_H	s_L	w_i
Overall	.003 (−2.54)	.998 (2.72)	.59 (.15)	.496
Prior disposition				
Antidefendent	.002 (−2.81)	.999 (2.88)	.78 (.55)	.556
Prodefendent	.004 (−2.43)	.997 (2.57)	.36 (−.25)	.442
Case type				
Murder	.007 (−2.19)	.998 (2.71)	.53 (.05)	.454
Rape	.003 (−2.62)	.998 (2.80)	.33 (−.30)	.494
Theft	.001 (−3.02)	.997 (2.63)	.83 (.70)	.553

Note. These parameter values were computed from data reported in Saks, Werner, and Ostrom (1975). Log-odds values are given in parentheses.

arguments that were defense oriented (exculpatory) as well as prosecution oriented, they might have adopted an s_0 that was closer to the midpoint (i.e., .50).

It cannot be emphasized too strongly that the present results show only that jurors can presume innocence under the present idealized, abstract conditions. It does not show that jurors do, in fact, presume innocence in the much more complex setting of the courtroom. The subjects in the present experiment were instructed to use only the evidence items in making their judgments, and so the facts of arrest and indictment were presumably less salient to them than would be the case in the courtroom. In addition, they had no information regarding the defendants' appearance, race, sex, or manner of dress. Yet jurors in a courtroom encounter all of these items of information prior to hearing the first item of evidence. One of the strengths of the procedure developed in the present article lay in its ability to detect the contribution of such preevidential influences. Such factors presumably contribute to the value of s_0 and the relative weight given to it. Hence, the contribution of such factors to the integration process can be quantitatively assessed, using the present procedures to investigate the effects of plaintiff and defendant characteristics.

Do Juror Predispositions Make a Difference in Court Settings?

The present study finds that prodefendant jurors give lower probability-of-guilt judgments to evidence sets than do antidefendant jurors. This finding is consistent with other research that has looked at information integration processes in juridical judgment (e.g., Kaplan, in press). However, whereas previous research has interpreted this difference as being due to prodefendant jurors having a lower s_0 than antidefendant jurors, the present study finds just the opposite outcome. This finding was obtained not only for both replications in the present study but also for the heterogeneous adult sample of experienced jurors used by Saks et al. (1975). Both studies showed that the reason antidefendant jurors render more harsh judgments is that they place considerably less weight on their initial disposi-

tion than do the prodefendant jurors. Prodefendant jurors appear to demand more of the evidence before abandoning their initial disposition.

One important implication of the averaging model is that dispositional differences between jurors are predicted to become relatively insignificant as set size increases. Both the prodefendant and antidefendant judges saw the high scale-value evidence as having a theoretical value of approximately .998. This means that as the number of high incrimination-value evidence items increases, the judgment of both subject groups should converge at that probability-of-guilt value. This should be true regardless of any differences that may exist in their s_0s and w_0s. This prediction of the model is consistent with the bulk of research on the relative impact of juror individual differences versus evidence as determinants of trial verdicts (Saks, 1976).

A more serious threat to the criminal justice process lies in the possibility of individual differences in the theoretical scale value assigned to a given item of evidence. Both the present study and the Saks et al. (1975) study (see Table 2) indicated substantial differences between the prodefendant and antidefendant judges when appraising the low incrimination-value evidence. The antidefendant subjects viewed that evidence as conveying a much higher probability of guilt (.78 for both student and experienced jurors) than the prodefendant jurors (.64 for student jurors and .36 for experienced jurors). In this case, the more evidence that is presented, the larger the differences will be between the two groups of subjects. This suggests that juror dispositions would make the greatest difference when the prosecution has a weak case.

The results discussed in this section refer to only one kind of juror predisposition, a generalized prodefendant versus antidefendant orientation. Jurors have a variety of other dispositions toward more specific defendant characteristics (cf. Brooks & Doob, 1975) that also may influence one or more of the model parameters. The role of characteristics such as the defendant's race and physical attractiveness can be assessed with the present approach.

Assumptions of the Model

The parameter derivations involved several important assumptions. We have already examined the assumption that item weights are uninfluenced by set size and by scale value of the evidence sets. It was noted that data internal to the present study indicated that the scale value of the information did not systematically affect the weight given that information. The design of the experiment did not allow a comparable test of the effect of set size on item weight. Some studies in the area of person perception indicate that the more polarized the information is, the greater the weight it is given (Hamilton & Zanna, 1972; Himmelfarb, 1973), and other studies show no such effect (Anderson, 1966). Even if extremity affects the magnitude of item weight in likability judgments, it may not have a similar effect in probability-of-guilt judgments. In one study that used probability judgments, some evidence was obtained for the extremity effect (Anderson & Birnbaum, 1976). In that study, however, the probability judgment scale was not transformed into the log-odds scale used for analysis in the present study. In addition, it may be that extremity effects are maximized when extreme and moderate items are combined in the same information set. In the present study, the information sets were either homogeneously extreme or homogeneously mid-scale.

A second assumption is that the theoretical scale value for each item of evidence is independent of set size. That is, the item's value, s_i, should not change as it is combined with one or more other items. This may, however, be a problem for the model. An item of evidence may imply one level of guilt by itself but take on an entirely different character when it is presented with a second possibly more or less incriminating item of evidence. For example, the testimony that "the defendant was seen running from the scene of the crime" implies a fairly high level of guilt if it is accompanied by testimony that "he was later arrested boarding a plane." It would imply a much lower level of guilt if it is accompanied by testimony that "he brought police to the scene of the crime." The incriminatory value of the first item of evidence may

not be identical in the two different contexts. Although considerable controversy exists (Ostrom, 1977), there is some experimental evidence indicating that such context-induced shifts in meaning can occur (Zanna & Hamilton, 1977; Wyer, 1974).

A final assumption concerns the appropriateness of an averaging model to describe juror decision making. A variety of alternative algebraic integration rules could conceivably be applied. It might be argued, for example, that jurors employ a summative integration rule. Jurors could simply accumulate items of evidence until the total (or sum) passes some "reasonable doubt" criterion.

The averaging model was adopted in the present study for both theoretical and empirical reasons. Theoretically, it provided the necessary vocabulary for analyzing the concept of what it means to be a fair-minded juror and allowed for distinct alternatives to be identified. On the empirical side, a considerable amount of evidence has accumulated favoring averaging over summation in person-perception tasks and in juridic judgment tasks (e.g., Kaplan, in press). However, it has yet to be unequivocally demonstrated that people always adopt an averaging integration rule in juridic judgments.

An entirely different analytic approach to the study of juror decision making is provided by the Bayesian model (Schmitt, 1969). It includes several judgment parameters that are nominally similar to those provided by the averaging model, namely, an index of probability of guilt prior to receiving evidence (the counterpart of s_0) and an index of evidence weight (the counterpart of w_0/w_1). Ideally, these two approaches would lead to a similar description of juror decision-making behavior. However, conclusions at variance with the present findings were reached in a study by Marshall & Wise (1975) that used the Bayesian model. They concluded that antidefendant subjects, compared to prodefendant subjects, had higher initial probability-of-guilt estimates but did not differ in the weight given the evidence items. To resolve these differences, experimental designs should be used that allow both models to be simultaneously tested.

155

Methodological Caveats

Although the derivation of the several parameters was made in the context of examining jurors' prior dispositions, they can be used for estimating parameters on any other judgment continuum that involves an averaging integration rule. Application of the computational formulas requires only that the responses be on an interval scale. Although a log-odds transformation was used in the present case, such a transformation probably would be unnecessary in other judgment domains such as likability impressions. The log-odds transformation stretches the scale out more among the extreme judgments than among mid-scale judgments. This is important when, as in the present study, many of the data points come from the extreme of the scale. The transformation may have been unnecessary if most subject responses had been between .2 and .8 on the probability rating scale.

Obtaining theoretical values that are beyond the bounds of a judgment scale would not always imply a need for a transformation. There are circumstances under which the theoretical scale values (s_i) may receive values beyond the extreme of the scale without implying that the direct rating-scale responses did not have the property of an interval scale. Under some experimental procedures (e.g., when anchor stimuli are not used), single stimuli will sometimes be rated in the most extreme category in the rating scale. When the observed rating is in the most extreme category, it follows from the averaging model that the theoretical value, s_i, must be even more extreme. This would be completely acceptable and not require the adoption of any scale transformation.

One of the difficulties in drawing conclusions in the present experiment is that parameter estimates were obtained on a group-wide basis rather than for individuals. This resulted from the decision to counterbalance stimuli across set sizes on a group basis rather than on an individual basis. If parameter estimates are desired on an individual basis, it would require having each subject see all stimuli in all set sizes. Each stimulus item, then, would be seen more than once by each subject.

Whether this design alteration would change the processes involved in juridic judgments is unknown at present.

The basic design features required to estimate the parameters are two levels of set size and two levels of scale value. The reliability of the estimates for s_0 and s_i is directly affected by the choice of levels for the scale-value and set-size factors. Reliability is enhanced as the difference between the big and small set size increases and the difference between the high and low scale value increases. This is because the equations for those two parameters involve a difference score in their denominators. The absolute value of that difference score increases as the range of set sizes and scale values increases. A fixed amount of error variance in the responses has a less proportional effect on a large difference score than it does on a small difference score. Finally, it would be useful to routinely use a research design that involves at least four levels of set size. This allows the assumption of equality of item weights to be tested across both set size and scale value. This would be done by computing the parameters on the basis of the smallest and largest set size and using those values to estimate the weight given high and low incrimination-value evidence sets for each of the two intermediate set sizes.

References

Anderson, N. H. Test of a model for opinion change. *Journal of Abnormal and Social Psychology*, 1959, *59*, 371–381.

Anderson, N. H. Component ratings in impression formation. *Psychonomic Science*, 1966, *6*, 279–280.

Anderson, N. H. Averaging model analysis of set-size effect in impression formation. *Journal of Experimental Psychology*, 1967, *75*, 158–165.

Anderson, N. H. Cognitive algebra. In L. Berkowitz (Ed.), *Advances in experimental social psychology* (Vol. 7). New York: Academic Press, 1974.

Anderson, T., & Birnbaum, M. H. Test of an additive model of social inference. *Journal of Personality and Social Psychology*, 1976, *33*, 655–662.

Brooks, W. N., & Doob, A. N. Justice and the jury. *Journal of Social Issues*, 1975, *31*, 171–182.

Chandler, J. P. Subroutine STEPIT—Finds local minima of a smooth function of several parameters. *Behavioral Science*, 1969, *14*, 81–82.

Hamilton, D. L., & Zanna, M. P. Differential weighting of favorable and unfavorable attributes in impressions of personality. *Journal of Experimental Research in Personality*, 1972, *6*, 204–212.

Himmelfarb, S. General test of a differential weighted averaging model of impression formation. *Journal of Experimental Social Psychology*, 1973, *9*, 379–390.

Kalven, H., & Zeisel, H. *The American jury*. Chicago: University of Chicago Press, 1966.

Kaplan, M. F. Information integration in social judgment: Interaction of judge and informational components. In M. Kaplan & S. Schwartz (Eds.), *Human judgment and decisional processes*. New York: Academic Press, 1975.

Kaplan, M. F., & Schersching, C. Reducing juror bias. In P. Lipsitt & B. Sales (Eds.), *New directions in psychology and law*. In press.

Leon, M., Oden, G. C., & Anderson, N. H. Functional measurement of social values. *Journal of Personality and Social Psychology*, 1973, *27*, 301–310.

Marshall, C. R., & Wise, J. A. Juror decisions and the determination of guilt in capital punishment cases: A Bayesian perspective. In D. Wendt & C. Vlek (Eds.), *Utility, probability, and human decision making*. Dordrecht, Holland: D. Reidel, 1975.

Norman, K. L. A solution for weights and scale values in functional measurement. *Psychological Review*, 1976, *83*, 80–84.

Ostrom, T. M. Between-theory and within-theory conflict in explaining context effects in impression formation. *Journal of Experimental Social Psychology*, 1977, *13*, 492–503.

Saks, M. J. The limits of scientific jury selection: Ethical and empirical. *Jurimetrics Journal*, 1976, *17*, 3–22.

Saks, M. J., Werner, C. M., & Ostrom, T. M. The presumption of innocence and the American juror. *Journal of Contemporary Law*, 1975, *2*, 46–54.

Schmitt, S. A. *Measuring uncertainty: An elementary introduction to Bayesian statistics*. Reading, Mass.: Addison-Wesley, 1969.

Shanteau, J. Descriptive versus normative models of sequential inference judgment. *Journal of Experimental Psychology*, 1972, *93*, 63–68.

Weld, H. P., & Roff, M. A study in the formation of opinion based upon legal evidence. *American Journal of Psychology*, 1938, *51*, 609–628.

Wyer, R. S., Jr. Changes in meaning and halo effects in personality impression formation. *Journal of Personality and Social Psychology*, 1974, *29*, 829–835.

Zanna, M. P., & Hamilton, D. L. Further evidence for meaning change in impression formation. *Journal of Experimental Social Psychology*, 1977, *13*, 224–238.

Appendix

Derivation of s_0

Since the subjective distance between s_i and s_0 remains constant as set size varies (i.e., $s_{BL} - s_0 = s_{SL} - s_0$), it follows that

$$\frac{s_{BL} - s_0}{s_{BH} - s_0} = \frac{s_{SL} - s_0}{s_{SH} - s_0}. \tag{1A}$$

(Equation 1A is the same as Equation 2 in text.) If s_i is replaced by its equivalent from Equation 3 in the text, and it is assumed that $w_H = w_L = w_i$, Equation 1A becomes

$$\frac{R_{BL}(w_0 + kw_{BL}) - w_0 s_0 - kw_{BL} s_0}{R_{BH}(w_0 + kw_{BH}) - w_0 s_0 - kw_{BH} s_0} = \frac{R_{SL}(w_0 + kw_{SL}) - w_0 s_0 - kw_{SL} s_0}{R_{SH}(w_0 + kw_{SH}) - w_0 s_0 - kw_{SH} s_0}, \tag{2A}$$

which reduces to

$$\frac{(R_{BL} - s_0)(w_0 + kw_{BL})}{(R_{BH} - s_0)(w_0 + kw_{BH})} = \frac{(R_{SL} - s_0)(w_0 + kw_{SL})}{(R_{SH} - s_0)(w_0 + kw_{SH})}, \tag{3A}$$

and since $w_H = w_L$, the weight terms cancel out. Cross multiplying and cancelling leaves

$$R_{SH} R_{BL} - R_{BL} s_0 - R_{SH} s_0 = R_{BH} R_{SL} - R_{BH} s_0 - R_{SL} s_0, \tag{4A}$$

then

$$s_0(R_{BH} + R_{SL} - R_{SH} - R_{BL}) = R_{BH} R_{SL} - R_{SH} R_{BL}, \tag{5A}$$

and Equation 4 of the text follows directly.

(*Appendix continued on next page*)

Derivation of s_i

Equation 1 in the text can be rewritten to determine the ratio of w_0 to w_i as follows:

$$\frac{w_0}{w_i} = \frac{k(s_i - R_{ki})}{R_{ki} - s_0}. \tag{6A}$$

Since the ratio of w_0 to w_i is assumed to be constant over set sizes, it follows from Equation 6A that (for high and low evidence information sets, respectively)

$$\frac{k_B(s_{BH} - R_{BH})}{R_{BH} - s_0} = \frac{k_S(s_{SH} - R_{SH})}{R_{SH} - s_0} \text{ and} \tag{7A}$$

$$\frac{k_B(s_{BL} - R_{BL})}{R_{BL} - s_0} = \frac{k_S(s_{SL} - R_{SL})}{R_{SL} - s_0}. \tag{8A}$$

For a given level of information (either high or low), the mean scale value of the information set is held constant as set size varies. This means, in the example of Equation 7A, that $s_{BH} = s_{SH} = s_H$. Substituting this equivalent into Equations 7A and 8A, we obtain

$$s_H = \frac{R_{SH}k_S(R_{BH} - s_0) - R_{BH}k_B(R_{SH} - s_0)}{k_S(R_{BH} - s_0) - k_B(R_{SH} - s_0)} \text{ and} \tag{9A}$$

$$s_L = \frac{R_{SL}k_S(R_{BL} - s_0) - R_{BL}k_B(R_{SL} - s_0)}{k_S(R_{BL} - s_0) - k_B(R_{SL} - s_0)}. \tag{10A}$$

Derivation of w_0 *and* w_i

Once s_i is obtained, Equation 6A provides the basis for estimating w_0 and w_i. Normalizing so that $w_0 + w_i = 1$, and letting

$$r = \frac{k(s_i - R_{ki})}{R_{ki} - s_0}, \tag{11A}$$

we note that

$$r = \frac{w_0}{w_i},$$

and substituting for w_0,

$$r = \frac{1 - w_i}{w_i},$$

and so

$$w_i = \frac{1}{r + 1}. \tag{12A}$$

By substituting the value of r from Equation 11A into Equation 12A, we find that the two weight parameters are computed in the following manner:

$$w_i = \frac{R_{ki} - s_0}{k(s_i - R_{ki}) + (R_{ki} - s_0)} \text{ and} \tag{13A}$$

$$w_0 = 1 - w_i. \tag{14A}$$

Received July 8, 1977 ■

Law and Human Behavior, Vol. 5, Nos. 2/3, 1981

Another Look at Social Psychological Aspects of Juror Bias

A. Philip Sealy*

Two trials were constructed by tape recording verbatim reports taken in court. One was a case of theft, the other of rape, involving two defendants and varying the amount of incriminating evidence. Subjects were recruited to listen to the trials and reach a verdict after deliberation. The recruitment of subjects was done by door-to-door survey methods aiming at producing a series of juries whose composition was representative of the adult population of Greater London. Thirty-four juries considered the theft case, and 26 the rape case, respectively 319 and 257 subjects. The results indicate that few variables correlate with the verdict, either before or after the verdict. In general, there was a slight tendency for younger (up to 25) and older (above 40) jurors to prefer to acquit. In terms of attitudes and personality, the only general finding was that people with most favorable views towards the jury system tended to wish to convict.

INTRODUCTION

Recent controversies in the British Courts about the "vetting" of potential jurors suggest that it is useful to reconsider the evidence about juror bias and at the same time look at the general problem of identifying bias in social judgements and decisions. Four particular cases have attracted public notice. One involved the vetting and rejection of potential jurors in a case related to the Official Secrets Act, and a second was the so-called "anarchists' trial." Two others involved an application by the defense to remove people from the jury panel and an appeal against conviction on the grounds that the jury had been "vetted."[1]

Four issues are involved. The first is the checking of the jury panel to see that it does not include disqualified persons, that is anyone who has had a conviction leading to a prison sentence of 10 years or more, or who has had one sentence of 3 months im-

---

*Department of Social Psychology, London School of Economics.
[1]For a review, see *The Times*, 4 June 1980.

prisonment or more in the previous five years. The second issue is the checking of jurors for another previous criminal record that might be particularly relevant in a given case. The third aspect of vetting of the jury panel is for people whose general behavior or membership of particularly "sensitive" groups might lead to partiality in a given case. The fourth aspect concerns the challenging of jurors once empanelled, either peremptorily or for cause (see Cornish, 1968).

Looking at these situations from a psychological point of view there are three main themes, granted that the formal disqualification is assumed. First, there is the specific question of whether court convictions, for lesser sentences than disqualifying ones, result in substantial bias. The second is whether other identifiable individual characteristics may produce bias, either generally or in specific cases. The third is whether such bias is normally maintained through deliberation with others who may have equally powerful but different prejudices.

Jurors are selected in the English system from people eligible to vote. The actual mechanism of how names are selected from this list of voters is shrouded in mystery, but it probably has some fairly random basis.[2] Having been summoned for jury service, that is, having in many cases failed to register an acceptable excuse for not attending, juries are then empanelled from a group of people, allowing both defense and prosecution the right to challenge. Challenges may be peremptory (up to three for each side) or with cause. This process is described in more detail elsewhere (Cornish, 1968). The practical implications, in terms of who is invited, chosen and challenged, are unknown. The process of becoming a juror is not altogether clear, either to observers or to jurors (see Hilgendorf, 1980).

The method of jury selection in the United Kingdom is and always has been somewhat *ad hoc*. In the United States the process of challenging jurors either peremptorily or for cause is rather more systematic and has been described by some American writers as a "growth industry." In Britain, prior to the 1972 Criminal Justice Act, juries were selected from a list of rate-payers (that is, by and large, owners of property). Hence they tended to be largely male and, as Devlin (1956) claimed with some satisfaction, "middle aged, middle class and middle minded." Since 1972 juries have been selected from the electoral register and hence become open to a wider range of people in terms of age and social class, as well as becoming equally open to men and women. This legislative change, as well as earlier *de facto* changes (see Cornish, 1968, p. 23) in jury composition, represents a possible "naturally occurring" experiment (Cronbach, 1957), that might establish the effects of changing the criteria of eligibility on the decisions made by juries. No clear evidence exists. Zander (1974, 1975) has examined the general statistical evidence relating to jury verdicts and this shows no particular change in overall verdicts as a result of changing eligibility. His evidence is tangential as far as the question of individual

---

[2]It should be noted that a distinction must be drawn between "random" and "representative" (see Marshall, 1975). A jury drawn randomly from voters in Bournemouth, for example, will be different in composition, in terms of major demographic features, from one drawn randomly from the electorate of Burnley, and neither will probably be representative of the electorate of the U.K. as a whole. Furthermore, seldom will either a randomly chosen or representatively selected jury really mean that a defendant is tried by his peers, whether "peerdom" is defined by age, ethnic affiliation, social status, or whatever. Only in the broadest and most attenuated sense can a representative of the electorate be regarded as a person's "peer."

bias is concerned, but what it seems to say is that if you introduce into the pool of potential jurors a much greater diversity of people in terms of age, sex, occupational status and, presumably, attitudes and personality, you do not detectably alter the patterns of verdicts emerging from the courts.

The problem of juror bias then has two quite separate strands. The first is the relationship between personal characteristics and preference for a particular verdict, and the second is the effect of any such preference on behavior in the jury-room and particularly on the final vote. The first aspect of the problem has some interest for theorists of the psychology of personality. It can be of no help to practical lawyers unless the second question is answered. For example, why bother to exclude obviously biased people from the jury if their bias has little or no effect on the collective decision anyway? There is, however, a third stage to this dilemma. Bias may exist individually (i.e., in terms of prejudicing people to particular decisions), and this bias may be dissipated during interaction with others. However, one wonders what might happen if particular juries were especially loaded with people of particular prejudices,[3] and if so what numerically would constitute a dangerous loading of prejudiced individuals.

There is sufficient research on the first aspect of this problem to encourage Gerbasi, Zuckerman, and Reis (1977, p. 323) to *start* a review article with the sentence "It is beyond argument that a variety of extraevidential factors influence (*sic*) jury decisions."

Bias is but one of these extraevidential factors, but the range of research reviewed is surprisingly limited in terms of them. For instance, the mode or style of presenting evidence as opposed to the evidence itself, the persuasiveness of the presenters, and the local "climate of opinion" have not been studied. Granted that individual bias was the major focus of interest of Gerbasi et al. (1977), the studies quoted as supporting their assertion are remarkably limited in the range of materials used in experiments, subjects recruited as jurors, and psychological variables considered as relevant. Many studies used only students enrolled in semicompulsory experiments, and many used only written synopses of invented trials. In many cases only one measure of personality or attitude was used. A recent review of the literature on the relationship between attitudes and verdicts (Lerner, 1977) is similarly limited. Therefore, a fresh look at this problem seems useful.

THE NATURE OF BIAS

In neither of the reviews cited, nor in most of the literature on the psychological aspects of jurors' decisions, is there much serious consideration of the nature of bias. One review cited (Gerbasi et al., 1977) largely ignores the possible processes involved in biased judgement, the other (Lerner, 1977) simply treats the problem as a special case of attribution theory. The former fails by treating the jury as just another research topic, rather than the unique social institution that it is. The latter fails, in

---

[3]This point has been made more succinctly by Baldwin and McConville (1979, p. 89) who "attached great importance to examining the relationship between the composition of the jury and the verdict it returned," although they, like myself, can offer no substantive evidence.

this context, in its one-sided psychological emphasis and disregard of the variety of real circumstances in which attribution processes might be relevant, as opposed to experimental circumstances in which they are, by definition, relevant.

There is, of course, a vast reservoir of beliefs about the factors that influence jurors in making their decisions, and these beliefs become the basis for the practice of law in courtrooms. Sometimes they are articulated, as in Devlin's (1956) slightly opprobrious description of the jury already quoted. Devlin's idea of the impartial juror of the 1950s, though based, of course, on his experience and opinions, lacked independent supporting evidence. Courtroom practice indicates many assumptions about the nature of juror bias which are manifested in vetting and challenging procedures on the one hand and in preferred tactics in court on the other. These assumptions certainly demand some scrutiny as examples of intuitively based "theories" of personality, not least in terms of the apparent certainty with which they are sometimes held. However, they can be of little assistance to a more systematic and objective analysis of bias.

In order to achieve such an analysis, it is worthwhile classifying the domains of individual variables that might potentially be related to verdicts and to speculate on the types of relationship that arise between them. Five broad areas of personal characteristics might influence a juror's decision: general social background, specific life experiences, education, attitudes, and personality. Such factors may predispose the juror to certain judgements, may make him or her more or less vulnerable to argumentation within the jury room, or may render him or her sensitive to some aspects of the case rather than others. The first of these possible effects can best be seen in the relationship between such personal variables and the verdict prior to any discussion with fellow jurors. The second can be seen in any differences in relationships between first and final (postdiscussion) verdicts, and the third can be judged by looking at different relationships between variables in different types of case. Many other, more subtle forms of relationship between personal variables and verdicts could be hypothesized, but it is sensible to look at the simpler ones first.

The three classes of analyses reported here are relevant to these questions about juror bias. First, are there certain categories of personal characteristics that lead inevitably, though not necessarily strongly, to *some form of bias of judgement?* Secondly, if such bias can be identified, how far is it resistant to group discussion and deliberation to unanimity?[4] Thirdly, are there any special cases or circumstances in which personal factors become a significant feature of the decision?

Before embarking on an analysis of research data it is worth reflecting on optimal strategies for establishing general trends that might become the basis for justifying or refuting bias. One thing is clear. Some rigorous sampling of "jurors" is required, whether they be recruited specifically for experiments or taken from jury panels for research studies. It almost goes without saying that any study claiming to establish bias in jurors' decisions that draws its "jurors" from a very limited population is irrelevant to this issue. This is simply a matter of what conclusions can be drawn from a statistic of covariance when there are artificial limitations on the actual variance of the variables under consideration.[5] A second methodological consideration is the

---

[4]Or in some of our trials to a 10–2 majority (see L.S.E. Jury Project, 1973a).
[5]This is not to say that many studies might not be useful in analyzing the processes of personality, attribution, or whatever.

range and validity of the measures of individual differences used. A third problem concerns the methods used to establish relationships, whether contingency, correlational, or experimental.

METHODS

The first methodological requirement, that of adequate sampling, was met by procedures described in detail elsewhere (L.S.E. Jury Project, 1973b). The aim of such sampling procedures was not just to provide experimental replications of real juries, if that were possible. As pointed out elsewhere (Sealy & McKew, 1981), the procedures adopted in these studies may provide experimental juries that are more rigorously representative of the electorate than real juries are likely to be. The secondary aim was to provide a substantial variance in the attitudinal and personality variables considered, and certainly rather greater diversity of response than one might expect from, say, a particular group of university students. The variance issue is important because of the possibility that, even where there are apparent differences between groups of subjects in terms of general trends, there is also likely to be considerable overlap between them.

The second methodological problem concerns the right balance between correlational and experimental procedures. This will be discussed later. The third aspect of this research on what has come to be known as "extraevidential" factors concerns the sampling of the potential psychological dimensions that might conceivably be relevant to this particular decision. The approach adopted in the present research was a very simple-minded one. Only measures of some known validity were used, and the measures themselves were subject to secondary analysis, in order to see whether other combinations of responses were more relevant to the decisions than the *a priori* scale measurements. This secondary analysis of the personality and attitude scales involved factor analytic procedures.

RESULTS

The data upon which this paper is based will be presented in terms of simple relationships, some of which have been described in previous publications (see L.S.E. Jury Project, 1973a; Sealy, 1975; Sealy & Wain, 1980). The data presented arise from two cases, one of theft and one of rape. The cases themselves have been described at length elsewhere, but involve several kinds of juror bias. The first is the simple bias in favor of or against a defendant, *qua* defendant. This would suggest consistency of relationships between personal variables and verdicts in different cases, and, if the bias was strong, a correlation that occurred with decisions made after deliberation. This might be called the hypothesis of *robust predisposition,* that is one that can be seen in correlations between the variables both before and after deliberation. Following this, it is of interest whether there are any variables that relate significantly to decisions before deliberation, but not afterwards. This might be called the hypothesis of *influenceable predeliction.* These variables might be weak predispositions which, in terms of our analysis of the jury and of our experimental procedures, indicate significant sources of

Table 1. Relationships between Background Information and Verdicts in the Theft Case

Variable	Range		First verdict	Final verdict
Age	21–67 yr	319	$\chi^2_{(4)} = 15.99^a$	$\chi^2_{(4)} = 15.98^a$
Sex		319	$\chi^2_{(1)} = 0.04$	$\chi^2_{(1)} = 0.04$
Occupational status	Levels I–VII Hall–Jones	291	$\chi^2_{(3)} = 2.07$	$\chi^2_{(3)} = 1.52$
Educational level	Secondary to postgraduate	317	$\chi^2_{(4)} = 3.27$	$\chi^2_{(4)} = 2.66$

$^a p < .01.$

variance in individual verdicts which are not sustained in the interpersonal situation.

It is worth reviewing the evidence presented in more detail elsewhere (L.S.E. Jury Project, 1973a). The data refer to two simulated trials played to jurors recruited from the general population. Table 1 shows the relationships between background personal characteristics and verdicts for the first trial. As far as sex, occupational status, and education level were concerned there were no relationships with verdicts, so these variables were neither predisposing nor mediating variables. As for age, both before and after discussion it seemed that the youngest (up to 25) and the oldest (41 or older) showed the greatest inclination to acquit.

Table 2 shows that the most "conviction-minded" group were those between the ages of 31 and 40 years, while the least were those over 40. It is quite possible that differential sampling bias might have contributed something to this result, although precisely how is not clear to us.

Similar results were calculated for the rape case, and it is possible to look at two things: acquittal versus conviction and conviction for the lesser or more serious offense. Regarding the defendant Harrison, who went a long way to incriminate himself in court, and could be convicted of either rape or attempted rape, there was only one significant result. There was a slight ($p < .05$) tendency for jurors whose status was described as Hall–Jones level IV (skilled manual) to prefer, if they finally voted to convict, the lesser charge. The remaining variables (age, sex, and educational level)

Table 2. Percentage of Jurors in Each Age Category Wishing to Convict in the Theft Case

Age	First verdict	Final verdict
19–25	46.7	32.8
26–30	55.4	41.5
31–40	66.7	55.7
41–50	41.9	23.3
51–65	37.2	28.1

Table 3. Relationships between Background Information and Verdicts in the Rape Case, Defendant Bryce

Variable	N	Guilty vs. not guilty		Rape vs. attempted rape	
		First verdict	Final verdict	First verdict	Final verdict
Age	257	$\chi^2_{(4)} = 17.99^a$	$\chi^2_{(4)} = 10.55^a$	$\chi^2_{(2)} = 1.87$	$\chi^2_{(2)} = 0.39$
Sex	257	$\chi^2_{(1)} = 6.02^b$	$\chi^2_{(1)} = 5.63^b$	$\chi^2_{(1)} = 1.46$	$\chi^2_{(1)} = 5.61^b$
Occupational status	230	$\chi^2_{(4)} = 2.05$	$\chi^2_{(4)} = 1.52$	$\chi^2_{(2)} = 3.21$	$\chi^2_{(2)} = 1.13$
Educational level	231	$\chi^2_{(3)} = 5.57$	$\chi^2_{(3)} = 2.35$	$\chi^2_{(2)} = 2.09$	$\chi^2_{(2)} = 1.15$

$^a p < .01.$
$^b p < .05.$

related neither to the guilty versus not guilty dichotomy nor to the subdivision within the guilty decision (between rape and attempt).

Table 3 shows the results for the defendant Bryce, who denied all guilt and against whom no evidence existed beyond the girl's accusation. The significant findings here suggest that younger jurors were more likely to acquit, with this effect being stronger before discussion than after it. Women were more likely to wish to convict the defendant Bryce, though it will be recalled that there was no such bias for the other defendant. This difference is largely accounted for by women who wished to convict Bryce of attempted rape (22% of the women jurors voted this way at the end, whereas only 8% of the men recorded similar intentions).

Before interpreting these results it is worth considering the diverse nature of these background variables. In doing so, perhaps we should ask two questions. First, why should one expect a correlation? Second, if a correlation were found, what should one do with it? The answer to the first question is that we have no scientific reason for expecting a relationship between social class, sex, or education on the one hand and jurors' verdicts on the other. Intuitively based beliefs exist and are likely to continue regardless of any empirical demonstration.[e] There are interesting hypotheses beyond the scope of this paper, concerning for example working-class people's attitudes to cases of fraud, females' attitudes to cases of male homosexual assault, and university-educated people's response to crimes stemming from ideological anarchy.

The answer to the second question, of what one should do with a correlation if it were found, is simple: nothing. Granted the diversity of cases and the diversity of the fact-finders, a correlation in our study relevant to our generalized "types" of case could have no relevance in another situation. Likewise a personality or attitudinal variable relevant in one situation may be irrelevant in another. Vetting and challeng-

[e]Not long ago sex was a variable that figured in these beliefs. Some judges would insist on all male juries in some types of case. One judge (Justice Theisiger in the Cardiff sessions) insisted on an all female jury to try a particular case involving a child, because he thought it was a woman's area of special experience. Likewise, many jokes are made about the empanelled juror carrying a copy of *The Times* or *Guardian* or *Morning Star* newspapers and the likely bias he or she will show.

ing seems to rest on the concept of *generalized bias*. So far, no evidence for this has been found in British work.

In the research presented here we decided to take two fairly humdrum cases, one of theft and one of rape, which though unpleasant was not so serious as to involve major physical injury. Even granted that the cases were unspectacular, it is striking how little evidence there was of juror bias. Social class and educational experience had little relevance to decisions. When there were significant associations, they were not always simple ones. Thus where age was significantly associated with the verdict in the theft case it was the oldest and youngest jurors who were the most lenient. But age, interestingly, was *not* relevant in the rape case where the evidence was conclusive (Harrison's verdict). Where there was no evidence apart from accusation and denial, again younger jurors were more likely to acquit.

Occupational status and education level confer no particular bias in the cases examined here. Of course, the myths that refer to particular circumstances will persist. Women were biased, in the sense of differing from men, in their verdicts only in the case of rape for the defendant Bryce. Here women tended towards conviction, but chose to do so by preference for the lesser charge. In general, it is worth stressing that given such cases and such rigorous sampling of jurors it is undoubtedly true that social variables of the sort used here have little relevance to the verdict. This is not to say that there were no biased individuals,[7] merely that overall bias was dissipated by the group processes.

Attitudes and Opinions

Whatever statistical relationships might exist between background data and verdicts, there clearly have to be putative intervening or mediating psychological variables. Attitudes and opinions have traditionally filled this theoretical role. Personal circumstances produce attitudes which in turn produce either actions or at least intentions (Fishbein & Ajzen, 1975). We developed three attitude scales using Likert techniques, as follows[8]:

(a) Projury scale (12 items)
(b) Legal punitiveness (14 items)
(c) Law and social class (16 items)

In addition a number of single items were devised to cover a number of specific beliefs and opinions about the legal system. Table 4 shows the correlations between attitude measures and verdicts for the theft case. These results show that jurors wishing to vote to convict had attitudes strongly favorable to the jury system, but this correlation was significant *only* for final verdicts, after deliberation. Since most of the direction of change was from an initial vote of guilty to one of not guilty, this suggests that those jurors who held out for a guilty verdict tended to be those with the most favorable attitudes to the jury as a method of administering justice. Perhaps this is evidence for a

---

[7]One juror told us *before* the experiment that he was going to vote not guilty because the law was a "bourgeois conspiracy to keep the workers in their place."
[8]The scales are available from the author.

Table 4. Correlations Between Attitudes and Verdicts in the Theft Case

Scale	N	First	Final verdict
Projury attitudes	132	0.09	0.20[a]
Pro-punitiveness in the law	132	0.12	−0.04
Law unfavorable to working class	132	−0.12	0.02
Benefit of doubt in sex cases	132	−0.25[b]	−0.26[b]
Benefit of doubt in motoring cases	132	−0.11	−0.19[a]
Benefit of doubt in general	132	−0.22[a]	−0.24[b]

[a] $p < .01$.
[b] $p < .05$.

robust predisposition. The second point is that such jurors were *not* necessarily in favor of great punitiveness, such as harsher sentences, nor had they any preconceived ideas about the social fairness of the legal system. Thirdly, jurors who voted to convict had, in general, a less lenient view about where the benefit of doubt should lie in particular types of case. The question was phrased as follows:

> In a case of sexual assault/motoring offense, the benefit of the doubt should always be given to the defendant . . . Strongly Agree to Strongly Disagree (five choices).

The idea was to see whether different views existed about different types of case and if so whether these views correlated with the verdict. Oddly, stringency in applying this "benefit of doubt" in sex cases correlated with verdicts to convict in the theft case, but not in the rape case. Comparable results for the case of rape are presented in Tables 5 and 6 for the two defendants, Harrison and Bryce.

Table 5 shows that jurors wishing to convict Harrison tended to have attitudes favorable to the jury but were not necessarily more punitive in their views. They also tended to be more stringent in their general application of the benefit of doubt to the defendant, although there was no particular tendency for this to apply to cases of sexual assault. As far as final verdicts were concerned, the "convicters" were stricter in their application of the rule to motoring offenses than to sexual ones.

Table 6 shows that the results for the defendant Bryce were very much the same as for the defendant Harrison, and a general pattern seems to emerge across the cases and defendants. Favorability towards the jury as a system of administering justice seems to be positively correlated not only with tendencies to convict but also with sustaining this decision through the deliberation period. On the other hand, punitiveness was unrelated to verdicts; that is, those wishing to convict were no more or less likely to endorse items proclaiming a harsh or punitive attitude in legal matters. Ideological beliefs about the legal system were of no relevance to jurors' verdicts. The single items relating to preferences for awarding benefit of the doubt to defendants suggest that by and large those wishing to convict were more stringent in their application of this

Table 5. Correlations Between Attitudes and Verdicts in the Rape Case, Defendant Harrison

Scale	N	First verdict	Final verdict
Projury attitudes	213	0.17[a]	0.25[b]
Pro-punitiveness in the law	213	−0.05	0.03
Law unfavorable to working class	213	0.12	−0.11
Benefit of doubt in sex cases	213	−0.10	−0.09
Benefit of doubt in motoring cases	213	−0.10	−0.15[b]
Benefit of doubt in general	213	−0.23[b]	−0.21[b]

[a] $p < .05$.
[b] $p < .01$.

Table 6. Correlations Between Attitudes and Verdicts in the Rape Case, Defendant Bryce

Scale	N	First verdict	Final verdict
Projury attitudes	213	0.21[a]	0.18[a]
Pro-punitiveness in the law	213	−0.08	0.06
Law unfavorable to working class	213	0.08	0.06
Benefit of doubt in sex cases	213	−0.10	0.07
Benefit of doubt in motoring cases	213	−0.15[a]	−0.13
Benefit of doubt in general	213	−0.18[a]	−0.13

[a] $p < .05$.

criterion, but not particularly so in cases similar to the one they had heard in the study.

It is worthwhile considering these findings in relation to research on the "Just World" scale of 16 Likert items (see Rubin & Peplau, 1973). Subjects who held negative views about justice were significantly more favorable in their opinions and evaluations of the victim than people who scored highly on the scale. This is consistent to some extent with the present findings that people with a more negative view of the jury system were more likely to acquit, regardless of the type of case and regardless of the amount of evidence against a defendant. Derogation of the victim certainly seems a consistent feature of the rape trial (Sealy & Wain, 1980). There may, however, be two alternative explanations, namely, that people with a favorable view of the jury system differ either in personality or in behavior from those with a less favorable view.

Perhaps those favorable to the jury system are more dominant socially and personally, and perhaps they participate in the deliberation more, thereby ensuring that others participate less.

Personality

In describing an apparent consistency in the relationships between attitudes to the legal system and the verdicts of jurors, two types of explanation were proposed, one concerning individual differences and the other concerning behavior within the decision-making group. The behavioral explanation was briefly that people with strong views about the value of trial by jury would be more dominant in the deliberation and that this dominance would have an important effect on what was discussed and on what was given prominence in the argument. For such a behavioral argument to be sustainable, three things are required or at least desirable. Firstly, the relationship between attitude and verdict should be stronger after deliberation than before. Secondly, juries that produce a conviction should have several dominant members with views strongly favorable to the jury system. Thirdly, the pattern of jurors' deliberations in situations dominated by people with strongly favorable attitudes to the jury should be different from those in which others predominated. The first of these possibilities can be discounted on the basis of data already presented. The second and third require more searching description and analysis of jurors' deliberations than can be reported here and are being examined in a further monograph.

The alternative possibility is that individual personality is the determinant both of attitudes to the legal system and of the preferred decisions made in a jury situation. This was examined using a wide range of personality questionnaires and a variety of methods of analyzing the ensuing results.

Four main areas of personality were selected for analysis: authoritarianism, dogmatism, rigidity, and extroversion. It was never practically possible to apply all scales chosen at one time, so they were put together in various combinations to see what general trends, if any, occurred across the two cases. The choice of these scales was influenced by the need to choose dimensions of personality that might be related to both general evaluations of legal processes and individual factors likely to be relevant to the group dynamics of the jury. So-called comprehensive measures of individual differences, best known by their initial letters, such as MMPI, CPI, 16PF, and GAMIN, were not suitable for our purposes. In their full forms, they were far too long, and their abbreviated forms could be misleadingly invalid. Reasonably well established measures of dimensions were needed that had particular relevance to this situation. A number of scales were selected that seemed both relevant and economical in terms of testing demands. They were as follows:

(a) Authoritarianism: this scale was selected partly because of its historical position in social research (Adorno et al., 1950; Christie & Jahoda, 1954) but especially because it could be broken down into three separate subscales on the basis of factor analyses (e.g., Rubenowitz, 1965):

(i) submissive feelings towards authority;
(ii) intolerant attitudes towards sexual behavior; and
(iii) general aggressiveness and hostility.

(b) Dogmatism: this scale, derived from the work of Rokeach (1960), was used as

169

a balance to the F scale since it suggests a rather similar prejudicial style of thinking about general social and political themes, whether right or left.

(c) Rigidity (Gough, 1957) was chosen because of the search for a scale that might be related to obstinacy or flexibility in dealing with ambiguous material and coping with the group discussion.

(d) Extroversion and neuroticism were introduced as scales that might have special relevance to the evaluation of particular features of the case as well as to reactions in the group situation.

The correlations between these variables and verdicts are easily reported. In the theft case, none of the personality variables correlated with verdict, and in fact all the correlations were below 0.10. The Authoritarianism scale was not applied to the jurors who listened to this case. In the rape case, it is again clear that personality variables had little relevance to verdicts (see Table 7). By and large, those wishing to convict and especially those maintaining this opinion after deliberation were deferential to authority and more dogmatic, but the magnitudes of the correlations indicate that personality variables accounted for a very small proportion of the decision variance.

SUMMARY AND CONCLUSIONS

Two different cases were used, and in one there were two defendants with very different levels of concrete evidence against them. Jurors were sampled in such a way as to optimize the possibility that each jury would be representative of the potential range of jurors. Background, attitudinal, and personality variables had only limited relevance to verdicts in the simulated trial situation. The only recurrent theme across our two cases and three defendants was that the more people claimed to believe in the jury system, the more they were likely to convict and, what is more, to stick by that decision after deliberation. In interpreting even this fairly stable correlation it should be borne in mind that only a small proportion of the variance was actually accounted for. It seems that individual differences, whether defined by personal, social, or psychological variables, are fairly uniformly unrelated to verdicts.

Table 7. Correlations Between Personality and Verdicts in the Rape Case

Variable	N	Defendant Harrison		Defendant Bryce	
		First verdict	Final verdict	First verdict	Final verdict
Dogmatism	197	−0.05	0.04	0.11	0.16[a]
Rigidity	197	0.02	0.01	0.03	0.10
Authoritarianism:					
(a) Submission to authority	197	0.15[a]	0.20[b]	0.14[a]	0.16[a]
(b) Attitudes to sex	197	0.05	0.02	0.02	0.03
(c) Aggressiveness	197	0.01	0.09	0.10	0.17[a]

[a] $p < .05$.
[b] $p < .01$.

One aspect of the background to this paper has never been adequately chronicled, that is, the beliefs held by members of the legal profession about juror bias and the extent to which this bias affects behavior. Discourses on the practice of persuasion and the identification of people's vulnerabilities in these situations exist (cf. Napley, 1970), but they are essentially aids to practitioners rather than surveys of beliefs and tests of their validity. These beliefs exist without a shred of systematic or objective evidence. "Winning" a case on the basis of holding such beliefs does not itself establish their validity. Beliefs about jurors' and judges' behavior and predelictions are widespread. They are, one would hope, treated as they deserve to be, beliefs which may in themselves be entertaining or even plausible, but which no responsible professional uses as the basis for his actions. However, it has to be said that on occasion beliefs about the significance of bias in decisions in courts have been used by naive or unscrupulous advocates in attempts to influence proceedings (Fahringer, 1980). It was, therefore, thought worthwhile to draw attention to this information derived from simulated juries.

Several clear conclusions can be drawn from these studies and can be used, albeit cautiously, in adopting a reasonable approach to evaluating the importance of bias in this social judgement situation. First, it is clear that bias stemming from personal characteristics such as age, occupational status, sex and educational experience is not a particularly significant factor in trial decisions. Secondly, it is clear that, although prejudice did exist amongst our jurors, it again is a relatively unimportant influence. Thirdly, the attitudes that do relate to verdicts are of some interest. The stronger people's beliefs in the value of the jury system, the more likely they are to convict. Perhaps the most important component of this relationship is its converse, namely, that people disliking and not believing in the method tend to acquit more frequently. Finally, it seems that from analysis of tape-recordings of discussions and questionnaires (cf. Sealy, 1975) the consideration of the evidence is of greatest concern to jurors. How they do this may be influenced by their personalities, attitudes, and backgrounds, but their final decisions are not. There were, as far as we could tell, as many dogmatic, inflexible, and prejudiced convicters as there were dogmatic, inflexible, and prejudiced acquitters, and not many of either, anyway.

REFERENCES

Adorno, T.W., Frenkel-Brunswik, E., Levinson, D.J., & Sanford, R.N. *The Authoritarian Personality.* New York: Harper, 1950.

Baldwin, J., & McConville, M. *Jury Trials.* Oxford: Clarendon, 1979.

Christie, R., & Jahoda, M. *Studies in the Scope and Method of the "Authoritarian Personality."* New York: Free Press, 1954.

Cornish, W.R. *The Jury.* London: Allen Lane, 1968.

Cronbach, L. The two disciplines of psychology. *American Psychologist,* 1957, **12,** 671–684.

Devlin, Lord P. *Trial by Jury.* London: Methuen, 1956.

Fahringer, H.P. In the valley of the blind: A primer on jury selection in a criminal case. *Duke University Law Review,* 1980, **43,** 116.

Fishbein, M., & Ajzen, I. *Belief, Attitude, Intention and Behavior: An Introduction to Theory and Research.* Reading, Massachusetts: Addison-Wesley, 1975.

Gerbasi, K.C., Zuckerman, M., & Reis, H.T. Justice needs a new blindfold: A review of mock jury research. *Psychological Bulletin,* 1977, **84,** 323–345.

Gough, H.G. Manual, *California Psychological Inventory*. Palo Alto: Consulting Psychologists Press, 1957.

Hilgendorf, L. Personal communication, 1980.

Lerner, M.J. The justice motive: Some hypotheses as to its origins and forms. *Journal of Personality*, 1977, **45**, 1–52.

L.S.E. Jury Project. Juries and their verdicts. *Modern Law Review*, 1973, **36**, 496–508(a).

L.S.E. Jury Project. Juries and the rules of evidence. *Criminal Law Review*, 1973, 208(b).

Marshall, G. The judgement of one's peers: Some aims and ideals of jury trial. In N. Walker & A. Pearson (Eds.), *The British Jury System*. Cambridge: Institute of Criminology, 1975.

Napley, Sir D. *The Technique of Persuasion*. London: Sweet & Maxwell, 1970.

Rokeach, M. *The Open and Closed Mind*. New York: Basic Books, 1960.

Rubenowitz, S. *Rigidity-Flexibility as a Dimension of Mind*. Stockholm: University of Stockholm Press, 1965.

Rubin, Z., & Peplau, A. Belief in a just world and reactions to another's lot: A study of participants in the National Draft Lottery. *Journal of Social Issues*, 1973, **29**, 73–93.

Sealy, A.P. The Jury: Decision making in a small group. In H. Brown & R. Stevens (Eds.), *Social Behavior and Experience*. London: Hodder & Stoughton, 1975.

Sealy, A.P., & McKew, A. The effects of confession and retraction on simulated juries: A pilot study. In Lloyd-Bostock, S.M. (Ed.), *Psychology in Legal Contexts*. London: Macmillan, 1981.

Sealy, A.P., & Wain, C.M. Person perception and jurors' decisions. *British Journal of Social and Clinical Psychology*, 1980, **19**, 7–16.

Zander, M. Are too many professional criminals avoiding conviction? A study in Britain's two busiest courts. *Modern Law Review*, 1974, **37**, 28.

Zander, M. Juries, decisions and acquittal rates. In N. Walker & A. Pearson (Eds.), *The British Jury System*. Cambridge: Institute of Criminology, 1975.

Law and Human Behavior, Vol. 9, No. 1, 1985

Trial Delay as a Source of Bias in Jury Decision Making

Drury Sherrod*

INTRODUCTION

A jury sits through a lengthy civil trial involving a dispute between two major industrial corporations. Complicated technological testimony is presented on both sides. The jury ultimately finds the defendant liable. A date to assess damages is set, but unforeseen events intervene. A jury member is ill; the judge takes a leave of absence; damage assessment is postponed again and again; two entire years pass. When the jury is finally summoned to reconvene, the defense attorney requests a new trial. After two years, he argues, the jury who will assess damages is no longer the same group of people who decided liability so long ago. Time, he asserts, has changed the jury.

The above case is extreme, but the defense attorney raises a provocative legal and psychological question that pertains to many jurors in lengthy or delayed trials: how would time change a jury? While the jury is composed of the same individuals who heard the case two years earlier, are they still the same people psychologically? Can they recall the facts of the case accurately, or will they reconstruct a distorted version of events? Will they forget mitigating factors in order to justify their prior verdict? Do they have the same attitudes, prejudices and opinions that led them to be selected in voir dire two years before? How will the long delay affect their judgment of damages? Most important, should a new trial be held with a new jury?

A good deal of psychological research, much of it very recent, helps to answer each of these questions. The research comes from different areas of investigation, relating to different types of issues: first, recent research on social cognition has explored how memory functions as human beings note, store, and recall information about other people and events; second, classic work on attitude change has demonstrated how emotional needs motivate people deliberately to reconstruct the past in order to justify their decisions and behavior; and third,

---

* Department of Psychology and Department of Social Sciences, Carnegie-Mellon University, Schenley Park, Pittsburgh, Pennsylvania 15213.

recent research on the biasing effects of attitudes on memory has shown how people misrecall past information to make it more consistent with current attitudes and beliefs. In light of this research, it becomes clear how a jury may change over time.

COGNITIVE BIASES

Research on human memory has a long tradition in psychology (cf. Bartlett, 1932). Only very recently, however, have researchers turned their attention to the specific processes through which people remember and distort information about persons and events in the real world (cf. Hastie et al., 1980; Higgins et al., 1981). The most current perspectives view the human mind much like an active information-processing computer (Hastie & Carlson, 1980). Recalling information about the past involves three distinct stages: first, an acquisition stage in which information from the outside environment is attended to and encoded; second, a retention stage in which the new information is organized or filed according to some meaningful system; and third, a retrieval stage in which the stored information is decoded and acted upon.

These stages are thought to involve three different types of memory: a short-term memory, which can hold up to seven or so bits of information for very brief periods of time (for example, remembering a phone number until dialing is completed); a working memory, in which the information from short-term memory is organized around some "theme" or "schema" for storage (for example, organizing the behaviors of a friendly, outgoing person around the theme of an "extrovert"); and long-term memory, in which the information is stored for later retrieval (for example, recalling that the friendly person from the past is an "extrovert").

The question most relevant to the current case is how do people recall the past? Certainly people are capable of remembering rich details of past events. But according to the above perspective, individuals do not usually *recall* a myriad of specific items; instead, under most circumstances they recall an "organizing theme" and then *reconstruct* the related items of information (cf. Alba & Hasher, 1983). although this is a highly efficient way for memory to proceed—and it results in generally accurate recall—the process is unfortunately subject to several types of errors. Typically, people fail to remember some information that is inconsistent with the organizing theme, and they distort other information to make it fit better with the theme. Also, people "recall' information they have never heard before, simply because it *is* consistent with the theme (a "false alarm" effect). Each of these types of errors are likely to increase over time, as people are less able to recall specific events and come to rely more on their general and thematic knowledge about the events (Alba & Hasher, 1983; Sulin & Dooling, 1974).

A convincing demonstration of how themes distort memory can be seen in recent research conducted by Lingle and his colleagues (Lingle, Geva, Ostrom,

Lieppe, & Baumgardner, 1979; cf. Ostrom, Lingle, Pryor, & Geva, 1980). Experimental subjects read a list of eight characteristics describing a hypothetical individual. Then the subjects were asked to predict the individual's success at a particular occupation, such as "lawyer." Four of the eight characteristics were relevant to the occupation and four were not. Later in the experiment, subjects were asked to recall as many of the original characteristics as they could. The results revealed that subjects recalled significantly more of the characteristics that were relevant to the occupational judgment than traits that were not relevant. In other words, subjects recalled more of the information that was pertinent to their judgments about the individual, and this selective recall happened within *one-half-hour's time*. Other reserach has obtained similar findings (Dooling & Lackman, 1971; Sulin & Dooling, 1974).

The effects are even more striking when short intervals of one day or one week are introduced between the learning phase and the recall phase of the experiment. To test this effect Lingle and his colleagues (Lingle et al, 1979) presented subjects with a photograph and 11 characteristics of a hypothetical individual. Subjects were again asked to make an occupational judgment concerning the individual. For half of the subjects, all 11 of the characteristics were relevant to the occupation; for the other half, all 11 were irrelevant. Half of the subjects in each group returned after one day and half returned after one week. All were asked to recall the occupational judgment they had made previously; then they were asked to pick out the original 11 characteristics from a new list of 33 characteristics, including the original 11 plus 22 additional characteristics they had never seen before. Thus, subjects were allowed to make two types of errors: failing to remember an original item or falsely "recalling" a new item. The results were striking. Subjects misremembered significantly more of the irrelevant details than the relevant details, and the effect increased with the passage of time. These results were obtained with time intervals of only one day and one week. Similar theme-related memory deficits over time have been documented in other research as well (Higgins & Rholes, 1978; Loftus, 1975).

How will these memory biases affect subsequent judgments? Will a previous judgment (such as a verdict of liability) affect a subsequent judgment (such as an assessment of damages) by influencing the recall of information on which the second judgment must be based? Fortunately, research is available that directly addresses this question. In a series of studies conducted by Lingle and Ostrom (1979) subjects were asked to make an initial judgment about an individual based on a set of facts about that person. A short time later, subjects were asked to make a second judgment about the same person, based on their memory of the original information. However, the researchers had varied the number of facts to which subjects were originally exposed. The researchers reasoned that if subjects based their second judgment on the original facts themselves, then subjects who had received more information should correspondingly take longer to make the second judgment; but if subjects based their second judgment on their initial judgment (i.e., the organizing theme) rather than the facts themselves, then all subjects would reach the second judgment in the amount of time, regardless of how varied was the amount or the relevance of the original information. The

175

results showed that despite variations in the original information, subjects took about the same amount of time to reach their second judgments. In other words, in making their second judgments, subjects appeared to be recalling not the original facts themselves, but the organizing theme, which had been shaped by the initial judgment.

Returning to our question of how people recall the past, we can summarize the research findings in three statements: (1) people do not always recall the past accurately; instead, they typically recall an organizing theme and reconstruct "facts" to fit this theme; (2) memory distortions increase over time as the original facts become less vivid; (3) people's subsequent judgments are influenced by their recollections of organizing themes rather than by the original facts themselves.

These research findings are particularly relevant to the case at hand. After returning a verdict of liability, the jury was summoned to reconvene two years later to assess damages. The jury's original verdict is analogous to imposing an organizing theme upon the mass of evidence and arguments presented in court. In this case, the theme is "guilty," and the consequences could have costly implications. After a two-year delay, the jury is likely to recall more facts that are relevant to the theme of "guilty" (i.e., the prosecution's arguments); furthermore, they are likely to forget irrelevant facts (the defense arguments); and they are likely to manufacture and distort additional "facts" (mistaken "recollections" and inferences supportive of the prosecution's case). As a result, the jury may tend to lose sight of mitigating factors that might otherwise moderate their assessment of damages.

MOTIVATIONAL AND ATTITUDINAL BIASES

We have seen that human memory is subject to systematic biases when people seek to recall the past, but in still other ways people may deliberately distort the past in order to satisfy emotional needs. An individual's need for consistency among various attitudes and between attitudes and behaviors is the subject of a whole family of psychological theories (cf. Festinger, 1957; Heider, 1958; Abelson & Rosenberg, 1958). In all of these theories, individuals are seen as desiring consistency and avoiding tension among their attitudes and behaviors. Tension is thought to be greatest when individuals engage in an activity or take a position on an issue that contradicts some of their previous beliefs and attitudes (cf. Aronson, 1969). The easiest and most typical way to resolve this tension is for individuals to change their previous attitudes to correspond with the new behaviors; in other words, people must alter their perceptions, beliefs and feelings about the past (cf. Festinger & Carlsmith, 1959).

To understand how this process pertains to be present case, picture yourself as a member of the jury. You hear a mass of conflicting testimony both for and against the defendant. Most likely, you find some arguments on both sides persuasive. Finally, you retire to deliberate with the other jurors, and after considerable discussion and perhaps some social pressure you commit yourself and declare publicly that the defendant is liable. Presumably this public commitment is inconsistent with at least some of your previous beliefs about the defendant's possible innocence. You now feel some degree of unpleasant tension between your previous belief in the defendant's possible innocence and your declaration that the defendant is liable. To resolve such an unpleasant state of tension, you begin to alter your original attitudes and perceptions regarding the defendant's possible innocence. Factors which originally may have been seen as mitigating or qualifying the case against the defendant must be reevaluated, ignored, or distorted. The more time that passes after your liability verdict, the less salient are your original beliefs and attitudes, and the easier it is to distort your original perceptions of the case.

Each of the reactions described above is based on literally hundreds of experiments that have demonstrated the varieties of attitude change which follow counterattitudinal behavior (cf. Eagley, 1982). In fact, not only do people change their past attitudes to be more consistent with current behaviors, people even appear unable to recall accurately their own previous attitudes before the change (Bem & McConnell, 1970; cf. Fischoff & Beyth, 1975).

A classic experiment, typical of research in this area, presents subjects with two options, choosing between one useful household appliance versus another (Brehm, 1956). Each option has several desirable features, and when subjects are asked to evaluate the two appliances, the two are rated almost equally. Then the subject has to select one to keep, after which the two options are rerated. Surprisingly, whereas both choices were originally rated almost identically, the chosen appliance now becomes more desirable, while the rejected option sinks in value. The amount of time that passes after a decision even increases the discrepancy between two choices that were originally rated almost identically (cf. Walster, 1964).

Research also helps answer the question of how attitudes can bias memory. Regarding the proposition that people are able to recall attitudinally consistent information more fully and accurately than inconsistent information, some studies have found weak support (e.g., Weldon & Malpass, 1981) and others no support (e.g., Greenwald & Sakamura, 1967). However, these studies have tested memory shortly after exposure to the information, when distortions are least likely. The clearest test of this proposition comes from Read and Rossen (1982), who tested subjects' memory for attitudinally consistent and inconsistent information either immediately or after a delay. These investigators measured peoples' attitudes toward nuclear power and then had them read a newspaper article about a fire in an Alabama nuclear power plant. In a subsequent recognition test subjects were shown true items from the article, false items (both pro- and antinuclear) that had never appeared in the article, and exaggerated distortions (both pro- and antinuclear) of items from the original article. Like some of the previous research, the researchers found no evidence of memory biases in the subjects they tested immediately after exposure to the article; however, after delays of one and two weeks subjects "recognized" more items consistent with their own attitudes on nuclear energy, regardless of whether the items were true, false, or distorted. In other words, after a delay attitudes do appear to bias memory of prior information.

Members of a jury are likely to be governed by these same psychological dynamics. Subjects in the above experiments altered their attitudes to justify their behavior, and they misrecalled information in line with their attitudes; in the same way may jurors distort their attitudes and memories to accord with their verdicts. Thus, motivational and attitudinal biases can augment the cognitive biases discussed previously, and all these biases can increase over time. As a result, the jury may further neglect the mitigating factors presented by the losing side— factors that might moderate the assessment of damages if they were accurately recalled.

CONCLUSION

There is good reason to believe that jurors may change during an extended delay between a verdict of liability and an assessment of damages. According to recent research findings on social cognition, memory biases will likely be introduced by the passage of time, as jurors reconstruct the facts of the case around their prior verdict of liability. According to classic and continuing research on attitude change, jurors may be motivated to change their attitudes toward the case in order to justify their former decision. And according to recent research on the effects of attitudes on memory, jurors will be likely to recall more information that is consistent with their attitudes than information that is inconsistent. As a result, when a decision on damages is delayed for two years, this decision will likely be quite different from the same decision that would have been reached immediately after the original verdict. The passage of time may serve to amplify damages. Given the events of this case then, the defense attorney is justified in calling for a new trial with a new jury.

How can such problems be avoided? For one thing, courts should pay special attention when a jury's decision-making process is disrupted by delays. To make sure that jurors do not reconstruct information in a biased way, the court should require an extensive and thorough review of all information presented, regardless of a prior verdict. The court may wish to inform jurors of the biases they are likely to experience so that jurors can take these into account in reaching their final verdicts. Attorneys can also anticipate biases and employ certain strategies to minimize them. For example, research suggests that reconstructive memory errors could be diminished if attorneys repeatedly stressed to jurors the importance of remembering details accurately, if alternative organizational themes were strongly emphasized, and if jurors' likely organizing themes were questioned and refuted in advance. Each of these tactics would lead jurors to rely less on general thematic memory, with its accompanying distortions, and more on memory for specific events, with its greater accuracy (cf. Alba & Hasher, 1983).

Finally, it is important to keep in mind that the analyses and predictions in this report are based on laboratory research extrapolated to the courtroom. It may be that information acquired over the course of a trial and deliberated in a jury will be represented in memory in a very different way than information acquired in the psychologist's laboratory. In addition, a delay of years, or even months, has rarely been studied in laboratory research on memory. And the effects on memory of jurors' experiences during a delay—e.g., conversations with friends, new information, social pressures—have not been studied in conjunction with the cognitive and motivational biases reviewed here. Nevertheless, rather than calling into question the extrapolations based on laboratory research, the effects of these real-world phenomena are more likely to introduce still further biases, confounds, and uncertainties in memory. If so, the question of how people change over time becomes even more significant in the courtroom than in the laboratory.

REFERENCES

Abelson, R. P., & Rosenberg, M. J. Symbolic psycho-logic: A model of attitudinal cognition. *Behavioral Sciences*, 1958, **3**, 1–13.

Alba, J. W., & Hasher, L. Is memory schematic? *Psycholgical Bulletin*, 1983, **93**, 203–231.

Aronson, E. The theory of cognitive dissonance; A current perspective. In L. Berkowitz (Ed.), *Advances in Experimental Social Psychology*, Vol. 4. New York: Academic Press, 1969.

Bartlett, F. C. *Remembering: A Study in Experimental and Social Psychology*. Cambridge, England: Cambridge University Press, 1932.

Bem, D. J., & McConnell, H. K. Testing the self-perception explanation of premanipulation attitudes. *Journal of Personality and Social Psychology*, 1970, **14**, 23–31.

Brehm, J. Post-decision changes in the desirability of alternatives. *Journal of Abnormal and Social Psychology*, 1956, **52**, 384–389.

Dooling, D. J., & Lachman, R. Effects of comprehension on retension of prose. *Journal of Experimental Psychology*, 1971, **88**, 216–222.

Eagley, A. Attitude change. In D. Sherrod (Ed.), *Social Psychology*. New York: Random House, 1982.

Festinger, L. *A Theory of Cognitive Dissonance*. Stanford, California: Stanford University Press, 1957.

Festinger, L., & Carlsmith, J. M. Cognitive consequences of forced compliance. *Journal of Abnormal and Social Psychology*, 1959, **58**, 203–210.

Fischoff, B., & Beyth, R. I knew it would happen—remembered probabilities of once-future things. *Organizational Behavior and Human Performance*, 1975, **13**, 1–16.

Greenwald, A. G., & Sakamura, J. S. Attitude and selective learning: Where are the phenomena of yesteryear? *Journal of Personality and Social Psychology*, 1967, **7**, 387–397.

Hastie, R., & Carlston, D. E. Theoretical issues in person memory. In R. Hastie et al. (Eds.), *Person Memory: The Cognitive Basis of Social Perception*. Hillsdale, New Jersey: Erlbaum, 1980.

Heider, F. *The Psychology of Interpersonal Relations*. New York: Wiley, 1958.

Higgins, E. T., Herman, C. P., & Zanna, M. P. *Social cognition: The Ontario symposium*. Hillsdale, New Jersey: Erlbaum, 1981.

Higgins, E. T., & Rholes, S. "Saying is believing:" Effects of message modification on memory and liking for the person described. *Social Psychology*, 1978, **14**, 363–378.

Lingle, J. H., Geva, H., Ostrom, T. M., Lieppe, M. R., & Baumgardner, M. H. Thematic effects of person judgments on impression organization. *Journal of Personality and Social Psychology*, 1979, **37**, 674–687.

Lingle, J. H., & Ostrom, T. M. Retrieval selectivity in memory based impression judgments. *Journal of Personality and Social Psychology*, 1979, **37**, 180–194.

Loftus, E. F. Leading questions and eyewitness report. *Cognitive Psychology*, 1975, **6–7**, 160–172.

Ostrom, T. M., Lingle, J. H., Pryor, J. B., Geva, N. Cognitive organization of person impressions. In R. Hastie et al. (Eds.), *Person Memory: The Cognitive Basis of Social Perception*. Hillsdale, New Jersey: Erlbaum, 1980.

Read, S. J., & Rossen, M. B. Rewriting history; The biasing effects of attitudes on memory. *Social Cognition,* 1982, **1**, 240–255.

Sulin, R. A., & Dooling, D. J. Intrusion of thematic ideas in retention of prose. *Journal of Experimental Psychology,* 1974, **103**, 255–262.

Walster, E. The temporal sequence of post-decision processes. In L. Festinger (Ed.), *Conflict, Decision and Dissonance.* Stanford, California: Stanford University Press, 1974.

Weldon, D. E., & Malpass, R. S. Effects of attitudinal, cognitive, and situational variables on recall of biased communications. *Journal of Personality and Social Psychology,* 1981, **40**, 39–52.

Sex Role Differentiation in Jury Deliberations[1]

FRED L. STRODTBECK, *University of Chicago*

RICHARD D. MANN, *University of Michigan*

The empirical approach to the study of role behavior which has grown from the application of Bales interaction process categories in different situations is now approaching the phase of development in which the original findings generate new problems (1, 2, 5). The instance being considered in the present paper relates to the carry-over of interaction role specializations from primary groups to a type of *ad hoc* problem solving group—a 12 person jury deliberation.

The subjects in the jury experiments—unlike the students, military personnel and patients on whom so much small group research has been done—were markedly differentiated in age and socio-economic status. In addition, although male and female college students and patients have been subjects in some previous small group research, the men and women drawn as jurors are fully established in their sex and occupational roles. Thus, if conventional structural variables like age and socio-economic status and sex are important determinants of interaction roles in groups, then a subject population of the type provided by the jurors should be maximally favorable to the identification of the relationships involved.

In the search for structural correlates of interaction roles there are effects like age in the adult range for which there are no clear *a priori* expectations; for others, like socio-economic status, expectations growing from empirical studies are available; and for sex role, both empirical and theoretical expectations exist. In general, however, research directed toward the relation of small group performance and conventional structural variables is not extensive (3, p. 351).

In the present instance, age and socio-economic status may be quickly treated. Age does not appear to be an important determinant of interaction role for the persons 21 to 65 involved in the jury deliberations. There is some evidence that middle-aged women and young and old men are more active, but these trends do not emerge clearly. Strodtbeck's prior cross-cultural family study (8) and an unpublished work by Caudill suggested that higher status persons would participate more heavily in the group discussion. This has been confirmed (10). Activity level, which is believed to be the most important determinant of status in the small group, has been

[1] A report of the experimental jury investigation conducted as part of the Law and Behavioral Science Project with funds granted by the Ford Foundation at the Law School, The University of Chicago.

retained as a classification in the present analysis. This offers an approximate means of assessing the contribution of socio-economic status to the differentiation observed in the present data.

Only for sex role differences were there qualitative expectations which might be tested in terms of interaction process categories. Consider the following:

a) Slater (7) has found in small *ad hoc* discussion groups that the member designated by other members as having contributed most to getting the job done is characterized by an interaction profile which is different from the man designated as "best-liked" in the following ways: the task specialist gives a *higher* percentage of his acts in 4) Gives Suggestion, 5) Gives Opinion, and 8) Asks for Opinion, while giving a *lower* percentage of his acts in 2) Shows Tension Release, 3) Shows Agreement, and 11) Shows Tension. These findings have been supported in a study by Mann (4).

b) Strodtbeck (8, 9) has demonstrated that in both father-mother-son and in husband-wife interaction there is a task and social-emotional specialization and, further, that it is the husband or father who preponderantly plays the task role and the mother-wife who plays the social-emotional role.

c) In Parsons, Bales, and Shils (6), the authors suggest two points which exist as a part of their theory and relate a) and c) above. First, task and social-emotional specialization, equated roughly with concentrations of activity in Attempted Answers (categories 4, 5 and 6) and Positive Reactions (categories 1, 2, and 3) is described as arising in all groups (see also 7, p. 306). Therefore, this differentiation may be expected in jury deliberations as well as in groups working on the type of task employed by Slater. Second, the authors state their thesis that the instrumental leadership of the father and the social-emotional specialization of the mother is a pervasive pattern with important implications for such matters as: the effective socialization of the child; the stability of the nuclear family; and the channeling of latent personality patterns of males and females. Task and social-emotional differentiation becomes the central theme of the later book, *Family, Socialization and Interaction Process* (5).

Taken together, the above points suggest the hypothesis that sex role differentiation in the jury will arise, and will result in men more frequently being task, and women, social-emotional specialists. Our objective is to test this hypothesis on a particular set of deliberations.

SOURCE OF DATA

The data employed arises from mock jury deliberations conducted in connection with the Law and Behavioral Science research of the Law School, University of Chicago. The participants in these deliberations are jurors drawn by lot from the regular jury pools of the Chicago and St. Louis courts.

The jurors listen to a recorded trial, deliberate, and return their verdict—all under the customary discipline of bailiffs of the court. The deliberations are recorded with two microphones to facilitate binaural identification of individual participants. The recordings are fully transcribed and these protocols are in turn scored in terms of interaction process categories. The scoring is done by an assistant who listens again to the recording and has available the indications of non-verbal gestures made by the original observer. The level of inter-scorer reliability is checked before the scoring begins and rechecked periodically while scoring is in process.

The 12 protocols utilized in the present paper were the final 12 in a set of 30 in which the jurors considered an auto negligence case. Seventeen of the 144 jurors originated less than 5 acts each and have been dropped from the tabulations. For each of the remaining jurors, the acts originated by category have been expressed as a percentage of their total acts originated. In this form the standard deviation of each category is highly correlated with the percentage of acts in that category, (rho is 0.90). For computational purposes, the percentages have been transformed to log $(x + 1)$, the rank correlation between the mean and standard deviation is reduced to rho equal -0.05 after this transformation.

ANALYSIS

Initial inspection of the data reveals that men originate significantly more acts than women in each socio-economic status level, but category usage and socio-economic status themselves do not seem to be closely related save for the fact that higher status persons originate more acts. The reader is reminded that by expressing the frequency of acts in each category as a percentage of each person's own total, the reflection of the actual number of acts originated has been removed. It is, however, indicated that persons who have been high or low participators be tagged and followed separately in the remainder of the analysis.

The reason for tagging activity level can be made clear by use of a set of 17 comparable deliberations (the first 18 in the series excluding one hung jury). For these deliberations the interaction profile by participation rank was prepared. In Table 1, this result is presented. In order for the interaction profiles to be based upon nearly equal frequencies, adjacent ranks have been collapsed. The trend with decreased activity may be read by comparing the values from left to right. These data are not transformed; each cell entry is a percentage of the base number of acts shown at the bottom of each column.

In Table 1, the rank one participants are high in 4) Gives Suggestion and 6) Gives Orientation but not in 5) Gives Opinion. The lower ranks, in terms of participation, are high on 2) Shows Tension Release and 3) Shows Agreement, but it is the intermediate participation ranks which are highest

TABLE 1

Interaction Profile by Participation Rank

Categories	Rank				Total
	High 1	2 & 3	4, 5, & 6	Low 7 thru 12	
A. *Positive Reactions*					
1. Shows solidarity	.87	1.34	1.26	1.14	1.16
2. Shows tension release	1.64	2.54	3.32	4.60	2.96
3. Agrees	14.38	16.67	18.61	22.49	17.86
B. *Attempted Answers*					
4. Gives suggestion	5.05	4.79	3.27	2.66	4.01
5. Gives opinion	21.23	26.36	27.90	29.32	26.13
6. Gives orientation	46.50	38.11	36.49	31.46	38.32
C. *Questions*					
7. Asks for orientation	4.49	5.12	4.57	4.51	4.69
8. Asks for opinion	3.70	1.83	1.11	1.01	1.93
9. Asks for suggestion	.44	.10	.10	.13	.19
D. *Negative Reactions*					
10. Disagrees	1.29	2.43	2.30	1.87	2.00
11. Shows tension	.33	.42	.90	.71	.59
12. Shows antagonism	.07	.29	.16	.11	.17
Total	99.99	100.00	99.99	100.01	100.01
Base Frequencies	5411	6177	5777	4656	22021

in 1) Shows Solidarity. The close, but not perfect, correspondence between high activity and emphasis upon Attempted Answers and low activity and Positive Reactions suggest that *both* sex and activity may be determinants of task and social-emotional specialization and hence should be viewed as joint effects in the analysis.

One further consideration arises concerning the perceived appropriateness of behavior by persons of each sex and activity level. In each of the juries, the participants were asked to indicate four fellow jurors whom they felt "really helped the group arrive at its decision." This question was phrased in such a way as to permit the respondent to nominate fellow participants for either task or social-emotional contributions. A classification based upon the number of choices received has been retained in the analysis.

In summary, the classificatory designations are:

Sex: M   male
            F   female
Activity: A   active, originated more than the median 80 acts.
            I   inactive, originated less than 80 acts.
Choice: C   chosen, received more than the median 2 votes.
            U   underchosen, received less than 2 votes.

The 127 individuals are distributed as follows:

MAC	32	FAC	8
MAU	13	FAU	10
MIC	16	FIC	8
MIU	25	FIU	15

For a particular category, the acts of the 127 persons can be distributed into a 2 x 2 x 2 factorial pattern. The authors are indebted to Lee H. Hook and John Nadler for adapting generalized formulae for the analysis of variance into a form that would accommodate the unequal frequencies in the cells. It is to be noted that the multinominal character of the full set of Bales' categories causes findings reported for different individual categories to be highly dependent. The reader should understand category by category comparisons to be the equivalent of viewing interrelated data from different perspectives. The comparisons are not independent.

RESULTS

In Table 2, percentage profiles for 127 jurors split into inactive and active males, inactive and active females are presented. The data in this form show women to exceed men in the three Positive Reactions categories and

TABLE 2

Interaction Profile By Sex and Activity

Categories	Male		Female	
	Inactive	Active	Inactive	Active
A. *Positive Reactions*				
1. Shows solidarity	1.14	1.03	1.39	1.45
2. Shows tension release	1.75	1.50	8.49	2.91
3. Agrees	10.50	8.26	16.98	20.59
B. *Attempted Answers*				
4. Gives suggestion	3.50	3.54	2.31	1.52
5. Gives opinion	25.44	19.42	22.07	18.07
6. Gives orientation	41.59	48.49	35.90	34.95
C. *Questions*				
7. Asks for orientation	4.85	5.09	6.33	6.76
8. Asks for opinion	1.08	2.65	.77	1.26
9. Asks for suggestion	.00	.08	.00	.03
D. *Negative Reactions*				
10. Disagrees	6.46	4.99	3.70	9.31
11. Shows tension	1.82	2.61	1.54	2.36
12. Shows Antagonism	1.88	2.36	.46	.77
Total	100.01	100.02	100.00	99.98
Base frequencies	1486	12413	648	3093
Jurors	41	45	23	18

TABLE 3

Significance Tests for Activity, Sex and Choice Effects

Source of Variation	d.f.	Positive Reactions (1, 2 & 3)	Attempted Answers			Questions (7, 8 & 9)	Negative Reactions (10, 11 & 12)
			(4)	(5)	(6)		
Activity	1	—	—	—	A > I*	A > I‡	A > I‡
Sex	1	F > M‡	—	M > F†	M > F*	—	—
Choice	1	—	C > U†	—	—	—	—
Interactions	4	—	—	—	—	—	—
Deviations	119						

* F greater than .05.
† F greater than .01.
‡ F greater than .001.

to be exceeded by men in the three Attempted Answers categories. This finding strongly confirms the hypothesis that there is a continuance in jury deliberations of sex role specialization observed in adult family behavior.

The results of the factorial analyses are presented in Table 3. To conserve space, several conventions have been adopted which require explanation. Since all of the analyses of variance were identical, the detailed breakdown of the degrees of freedom is shown on the left. The order of the two factors involved in instances which were significantly different, and the significance level, are given in the appropriate cells. In the actual computations, each degree of freedom was isolated. Since none of the interactions were significant, they have been pooled for this table. In addition, each category was analysed separately before being combined into the major areas shown in the table. There was an appreciable number of persons with no acts in category 1) Shows Solidarity and 2) Shows Tension Release. While some discrimination has been lost by grouping the three Positive Reactions together, categories with inconsistent trends were not pooled. Similar compressions were made for *Questions* and *Negative Reactions*. In the Attempted Answers categories, the trends for 5) Gives Opinion and 6) Gives Orientation were not identical, and these categories have been analyzed separately. Category 4) Gives Suggestion has a low mean frequency and would have been pooled with adjacent categories if the inconsistent trends had not been present. As a result, it was necessary to check with non-parametric methods the significance tests reported for category 4.

Concerning the substantive information in Table 3, consider the first row of the table. It may be seen that more active persons, A, exceed less active persons, I, in three ways. They have a greater frequency of acts in category 6) Gives Orientation. In Table 1, it may be noted that almost 50% of the acts of the most-speaking person (most frequently, the jury

186

foreman) are directed to non-interpretative orientation remarks. This effect persists after the correction by sex role and choices received involved in the analysis have been made. In addition, more active persons are higher in Negative Reactions—this could not have been anticipated from Table 1, but it is consistent with the conception of the more active person as assuming more responsibility to curb and control activities of others in the meeting.

The finding that more active persons are significantly high in Questions raises an interesting point. Is this the function of the necessity for consensus in the jury, or does it relate to the increased need to use questions to keep low participating members from withdrawing in a group as large as twelve? Comparisons with profiles from 12-man groups engaged on other tasks would be helpful here.

With regard to the male-female differences reported in the second line of Table 3, the apparent trends by sex groups in Positive Reactions forecast by Table 2 have been confirmed—females are significantly higher than males. For the task component as reflected by Attempted Answers, the two larger categories 5) Gives Opinion and 6) Gives Orientation are significantly differentiated by sex—males are higher than females. For category 4) Gives Suggestion, which has a mean incidence rate of less than 2%, the difference is consistent in direction, male being higher than female, but not clearly significant.

Differences in the number of choices received from fellow jurors do not seem to be related to relative category usage, save in one instance. Persons making more suggestions appear to have received more choices.

In the analyses by individual categories, there was just a suspicion of evidence that 2) Shows Tension Release (i.e., laughing and joking) increased the choices received by males but reduced the choices received by females. This interaction disappears in the composite calculation.

, A similar effect occurs in Questions; asking questions increases choices received by men but reduces choices received by women. This interaction effect, which approaches the .06 level, is not shown in Table 3 in which an .05 probability criterion is used. These fragmentary clues involving interaction effects may deserve attention in later research, but for present purposes there is no conclusive evidence that male-female reversal of typical roles result in higher choices received, nor are there other interactions which result in significant effects.

DISCUSSION

To recast our findings slightly, the data suggests that men *pro-act*, that is, they initiate relatively long bursts of acts directed at the solution of the task problem, and women tend more to *react* to the contributions of others.

These important differences, which may be read from the interaction profiles, coexist with similarities arising from the information-exchanging,
consensus-seeking nature of the deliberation problem. By and large, the
jurors' interaction profiles are quite similar. In the face of this similarity
the direction of attention of the differences associated with sex roles should
not be permitted to obscure the determinative influences of the problem
situation.

Concerning the problem-situation, one might be inclined to believe that
women were generally less competent than men to discuss the issues of
negligence and damages involved in the deliberation. This line of reasoning
suggests that social-emotional specialization is a substitute for task competence. While this cannot be proven or disproven with our data, it may be
of value to note the category usage of less active men. If one assumes less
active men were less competent than more active men, then less active men
should also have been higher on social-emotional emphasis. There is little
evidence for this in Table 2. Both the active and the less active men are
clearly distinguished from the women. Thus, the exact role of competence
for the problem is not clear, but it is strongly doubted that it accounts for
a substantial portion of the profile differences here observed.

It should perhaps be stressed that the acts involved in the task and social-
emotional distinction are included in the repertoire of all persons. When
taken in isolation, these acts do not suggest male or female behavior; it
is only in the statistical analysis of aggregates of acts that the sex-typed
connotation emerges. Among the various subjects, there are many individual instances in which men are more social-emotional than women, and
vice versa. The twelve juries reported upon contained from one to six
women, however, in the aggregate profiles there were no discernible trends
associated with the increased number of women in the group.

Parsons has noted that occupations like teacher, social worker, secretary
and nurse, which have a high representation of women, involve large expressive and supportive components, like those associated with the wife-
mother role (see 5, p. 15 fn.). Direct appraisal of the implied hypothesis
that women seek jobs outside the nuclear family similar to their job in the
nuclear family is difficult. It involves both a disentangling of historical and
cultural factors and an empirical study of the quality of relationships in the
jobs in question. While this has not been done, the hypothesis is of interest
as illustrative of a type of reasoning which might plausibly be applied to
the interaction differences found in the present data.

For the small system of social relations involved in a deliberation, the
interaction profile is in many ways analogous to an occupation in the larger
social system. People select, or drift into, their behavior in the group much
as they do their occupation. Training and aptitude requirements foreclose

some roles (or "jobs"), but among the remainder there is a latitude for selection. Insofar as the effects of the differential socialization of boys and girls and their subsequent sex-typed associations have been lasting, it may be reasoned that a latent personality basis has been formed for interaction role selection. As a result, from among the allowable interaction roles in the deliberation, a task emphasis tends to be selected by men and a social-emotional emphasis by women.

Each juror, or more generally, each person, has the ability to play a variety of roles which almost always exceeds the number elicited by the situation in which he operates. Each problem-situation is potentially solvable by a range of role assignments. Each group will tolerate a variety of role combinations. But finally, and this is perhaps the appropriate perspective for viewing the present findings, there are traces of continuity notwithstanding the latitude arising from individual, situational, and group sources. Our data indicates that the structural differentiation of sex role, relating as it does to the nuclear family experience, constitutes a slight, but persistent continuity and that over the range from family problem solving to jury deliberations, sex-typed differentiation in interaction role can be reliably demonstrated.

Manuscript received: August 22, 1955
Revised manuscript received: November 7, 1955

REFERENCES

1. Bales, R. F., *Interaction Process Analysis*, Cambridge, Massachusetts: Addison-Wesley, 1950.
2. Hare, P., E. F. Borgatta, and R. F. Bales, *Small Groups: Studies in Social Interaction*, New York: Alfred A. Knopf, 1955.
3. Katz, D., "Special Review: Handbook of Social Psychology," Psychological Bulletin, 1955, 52, 346–353.
4. Mann, R. D., "The Relation of Informal Status to Role Behavior in Small Discussion Groups," Unpublished honors thesis, Harvard University, 1954.
5. Parsons, T. and R. F. Bales, *Family, Socialization and Interaction Process*, Glencoe, Illinois: The Free Press, 1955.
6. Parsons, T., R. F. Bales, and E. A. Shils, *Working Papers in the Theory of Action*, Glencoe, Illinois: The Free Press, 1953.
7. Slater, P. E., "Role Differentiation in Small Groups," *American Sociological Review*, 1955, 20, 300–310.
8. Strodtbeck, F. L., "Husband-Wife Interaction Over Revealed Differences," *American Sociological Review*, 1951, 18, 141–145.
9. Strodtbeck, F. L., "*Family Interaction, Ethnicity, and Achievement*," to be published in McClelland, D. C. (ed.), *Social Science Research Monograph*.
10. Strodtbeck, F. L., and R. M. James, "Social Process in Jury Deliberations," Unpublished paper presented at the Annual Meeting of the Sociological Society, 1955.

SEX ROLE DIFFERENTIAL
AND JUROR DECISIONS

ELOISE C. SNYDER*
The Pennsylvania State University
University Park, Pennsylvania

ABSTRACT

A comparison of the decisions reached by jurors on all male juries with those reached by jurors on male-female juries shows, among other things, that although the "superior status litigant" won more frequently than the "inferior status litigants," his ability to do so decreased when he confronted a male-female jury. It is suggested that this increase of the inferior status litigants' ability to win juror decisions with the addition of women to juries has broad implications for the society as a whole; particularly in view of the fact that women tend to be playing an increasingly important role in governmental policy making.

The significant role which juries play in resolving conflict in United States society is reflected by the numerous monographs and articles written about juries.[1] Indeed, the recent Task Force Report on Courts composed by the President's Commission on Law Enforcement and Administration of Justice recognizes the importance of juries by discussing the history of the jury's major decision-making functions and by calling attention to the need for improving the conditions under which jurors perform these important functions.[2] Moreover, social scientists have long been interested in studying not only the conditions under which jurors perform their functions but also the impact which the social characteristics of the jurors have upon how these functions are performed. One team of researchers, for example, concerned with attempting to determine the role that unequal social statuses of jurors play in jury deliberations, hypothesized that men participate more than women and that persons with high status occupations participate more than those with lower status occupations in the dynamics of jury decision making.[3] Another study concerned with interaction rates and jury factions found that the smaller the size of the faction, the higher the participation rate.[4]

The present article reports on a study of actual, not simulated, jury decision making and attempts to determine the extent to which certain

190

characteristics of jury composition affect the decisions which jurors render. Specifically it compares the decisions of members of all male juries with those reached by members of mixed-female juries on similar cases.[5] This study was made possible by the fact that prior to 1967, women were not permitted to serve on the juries of the court being studied. However, after that time women were permitted to serve and did. Both jury types were six-person juries and during the period covered by the study in which women were permitted to serve on juries, 59 per cent of the jurors were female and 41 per cent were male. Of course 24 juries, five contained all females, one contained 5 females, six contained 4 females, six contained 3 females, five contained 2 females and one contained 1 female. On several juries women were even appointed by the judge to serve as "foreman" of the jury.

In order to determine the impact which the addition of women to juries had on the decisions reached by the juries, the decisions of the jurors of all male juries for September, October and November of 1966 were compared with those of the jurors on mixed male-female juries for the same time period during 1967; and this comparison was concerned with determining whether any differences occurred between these two jury types in regard to the decisions reached as these decisions related to: (1) the favoring of the plantiff or defendant; (2) the favoring of the "superior litigant" or the "inferior litigant"; and (3) the amount of money awarded to the winner of the case.

Favoring the Plaintiff or Defendant. In each of the cases, one of the litigants, feeling he has been "wronged," brings the case to court and asks for financial redress; this litigant is known as the plaintiff. The other litigant, the defendant, does precisely what his title implies, that is, he attempts to defend himself against the charges being brought against

TABLE I

RELATIONSHIP BETWEEN JURY SEXUAL COMPOSITION AND
ABILITY OF LITIGANTS (Plaintiff-Defendant)
TO WIN DECISIONS*

	All-Male		Male-Female		Totals	
	Per Cent	Number	Per Cent	Number	Per Cent	Number
Plaintiff	50	66	58	84	54	150
Defendant	50	66	42	60	46	126
Totals		132		144		276

* X^2 for table is 1.9 which is not statistically significant at the .05 level.

him by the plaintiff. As is noted in Table I, the combined total of decisions from the all male jury and the male-female jury favored the plaintiff more frequently (54 per cent) than they favored the defendant (46 per cent) ; although the extent to which they did so seems much smaller than might be expected since it is possible that the plaintiff, having brought the case to court, had a better case than the defendant, who had to be brought to court. Nevertheless, according to the figures uncovered by this study, the plaintiff won only slightly more decisions than the defendant. A comparison of all male and the male-female juries, however, shows that the plaintiff's chance of winning decisions does increase slightly from 50 per cent to 58 per cent with the addition of women to the jury. This means that there is a slight but not significant tendency for jurors on the male-female jury to favor the plaintiff nor the defendant. An analysis of the statuses of the litigants, as being superior or inferior to each other, however, uncovers an interesting point concerning differences in the ability of litigants to win decisions from members of these two jury types.

Favoring the Superior or Inferior Litigant. In each of the cases the litigants were compared with each other in order to determine whether they were of relatively equal status or whether a superior-inferior relationship existed.[6] These status determinations were arrived at on the basis of a hierarchy of social positions in which businesses or groups are regarded as being superior to individuals, men superior to women, whites superior to Negroes and adults superior to youths. In all cases, whether concerned with businesses, groups or individuals, the respect accorded the specific litigants by the community was also considered in order to take into account any personal influence factor which might be operating.[7]

In the total decisions rendered by those on the all male jury and the

TABLE II

RELATIONSHIP BETWEEN JURY SEXUAL COMPOSITION AND
SUPERIOR-INFERIOR STATUS OF
LITIGANTS WINNING DECISIONS*

	All-Male		Male-Female		Totals	
	Per Cent	Number	Per Cent	Number	Per Cent	Number
Superior	74	84	50	48	63	132
Inferior	26	30	50	48	37	78
Totals		114		96		210

* X^2 for table is 12.5; $P < .01$; $\phi = .24$

192

male-female jury, the superior status litigant won more frequently than did the inferior status litigant (63 per cent and 37 per cent respectively) although his ability to do so was greater when confronting the all male jury (74 per cent) and lesser when confronting the male-female jury (50 per cent). These figures are shown in Table II.[8] This means that the inferior status litigant's chances of winning are increased when confronting a male-female jury and decreased when confronting an all male jury and the difference is statistically significant. This may be due to any one or a combination of factors, among which are the following: (1) since the all male juries served one year prior to the male-female juries, during this one-year period the inferior litigants may have been able to present increasingly better cases, or (2) during this period the community attitudes toward persons of inferior status groupings (members of minority groups, for example) may have undergone change, or (3) it is possible that the addition of women to the juries was the primary cause of the inferior's ability to win. Although the first two possibilities may be involved, the third explanation cannot be overlooked as a factor in this increased ability of the inferior litigant to win because even with the limited number of cases included in the present study, some increase in the inferior litigants ability to win cases was noted as the number of women jurors on individual cases increase; more data are needed here however before this specific hypothesis can be tested.

It may be that the relationship between the addition of women to juries and the increase in the inferior status litigant's ability to win from such juries is related to the fact that women, often regarded in society as comprising a minority grouping, tend to favor other members of minority groupings more than do men. However, it is interesting to note that analyses of other data concerning jury composition (race, age, occupation and education) indicate that jury members regarded as having superior status show a slight tendency to favor the litigant regarded as having inferior status while inferior status jurors tend to favor superior status litigants.[9] If further research uncovers this same relationship it would mean that women on juries react somewhat differently from other juror classifications regarded as having minority status.

Whatever the reason, however, it appears that in inferior status litigant's chances of winning his case is increased when he confronts a male-female jury rather than an all male jury.

The Amount of Money Awarded to the Winners of Cases. In 1966 (September, October and November) the all male juries were asked to award $62,451, while during the same months in 1967, the male-female juries were asked to award $131,433. Thus, as is noted in Table III, the amount of money asked by litigants more than doubled within a one-year period. And, although from both juries a few litigants received all of what they asked, and others received none of what they asked, the amount

TABLE III

RELATIONSHIP BETWEEN JURY SEXUAL COMPOSITION AND
MONEY ASKED AND MONEY AWARDED LITIGANTS

	All-Male	Male-Female	Totals
Asked	$62,451	$131,433	$193,884
Awarded	32,724	26,811	59,535
Totals			253,419

awarded by the all male jury was approximately 52 per cent of what was asked, while for the male-female juries the winners of cases were awarded only 20 per cent of what they asked. This means that in spite of the much larger amount requested from the male-female juries, these juries actually awarded a great deal less money both in proportion to what was asked as well as in actual money involved. This finding appears to show that although the addition of women to a jury may result in an increased ability for the inferior status litigant to win decisions, as discussed previously, this ability does not guarantee that the inferior litigant will be awarded as much of the money requested as he might have been able to receive from an all male jury. This would seem to indicate that although the presence of women on juries enhances an inferior litigant's chances of winning, it does not enhance his or for that matter the chances of the superior litigant to be awarded money. Such seemingly inconsistent factors as reflected by women's behavior on juries however are not at all unlike the behaviors reflected by women in the United States historically. This is particularly apparent in the political and economic realms. In the political area, women traditionally have displayed vigorous interest in reform movements which were designed primarily to help persons of inferior social status, while at the same time holding most rigidly conservative economic positions.[10] If indeed further research shows that women do tend to be more empathetic toward socially inferior status persons than do men, while at the same time holding more rigid economic conservatism than men, the impact which this has for a society in which women are not only increasing their proportion of the vote but also increasingly being elected or appointed to governmental offices cannot be overstated.

Summary and Discussion. A comparison of the decisions reached by members of all male juries with those reached by members of male-female juries shows that although the superior litigant won more frequently than did the inferior, his ability to do so decreased when he confronted a male-female jury. In fact, the inferior litigant won the same number of decisions (50 per cent) as did the superior litigant when confronting male-female juries; whereas, when confronting an all male jury the inferior won only 26 per cent of the decisions. Several possible explanations were offered for this statistically significant difference in the ability of inferior-superior litigants to win decisions, one of which was that women, being members of a minority group, may tend to be more empathetic toward other members of minority groups. This empathy was found to have very definite limits however, because when financial redress is considered it is noted that the male-female juries although asked for more than twice as much money, actually awarded less money than was awarded by the all male juries. Thus, although the addition of women to juries seems to increase the ability of inferior status litigants to win decisions, the chance of his or any other litigants being awarded financial redress is decreased. This seemingly contradictory position of women on juries in which they display both liberal as well as conservative attitudes, is not totally unlike the position which they have held historically in United States society, however, where traditionally they have lead political reform movements primarily designed to help the "underdog" while at the same time maintaining an essentially conservative economic position. Thus it would appear that the behavior of women on juries is not wholly unlike their behavior historically. And, if further research supports this point, the implications for a society in which women are increasingly playing a greater policy making role are important.

FOOTNOTES

* The author is Associate Professor of Sociology, The Pennsylvania State University, University Park.

[1] See, for example, Harry Kalven, Jr., and Hans. Zeisel, THE AMERICAN JURY, Boston: Little, Brown and Co., 1966.

[2] Task Force Report: The Courts, the President's Commission of Law Enforcement and Administration of Justice, United States Government Printing Office Washington, D.C., 1967, esp. 26 and 90-91.

[3] Fred Strodbeck, Rita James and Charles Hawkins, "Social Status in Jury Deliberations," *American Sociological Review*, 22, (December, 1957), 713-19.

[4] Charles H. Hawkins, "Interaction Rates of Jurors Aligned in Factions," *American Sociological Review*, 27 (October, 1962), Richland 689-91.

⁵ Data for this study were made available by the Richland County Court in Columbia, South Carolina, through the cooperation of Judge Legare Bates and Judge John Mason and members of the court staff; and with the help of Laurens Minson, of The University of South Carolina who served as research aide to the senior researcher. The cases were civil cases involving automobile accidents, employer-employee disputes, etc., in which one litigant, the plaintiff, was suing the other litigant, the defendant.

⁶ These litigant statuses are not meant to imply that the people involved in these cases are, in themselves, superior or inferior but rather that they represent groups which society distinguishes between as being superior or inferior.

⁷ For example, if a case were to involve a woman from a locally prominent family and a man from a relatively unknown background, the inferior status of the woman would be superceded by the prominence of her family and the woman would be considered to be the superior status litigant while the man would be considered to be the inferior; after careful consideration was given to this point, however, it was determined that no case of this type appeared.

⁸ This excludes 14 per cent of the cases heard by the all male jury and 33 per cent of the male-female jury cases because these cases involved litigants of equal status.

⁹ E. C. Snyder, "Portrait of a Judy," paper in preparation.

¹⁰ Robert E. Lane, Political Life: *Why People Get Involved in Politics,* New York: The Free Press, a Division of The Macmillan Co., 1959; William F. Kukes, "Psychological Studies of Values," Psychological Bulletin. 52, (1955), 24-50.

JOURNAL OF RESEARCH IN PERSONALITY 9, 147–157 (1975)

Authoritarianism and Recall of Evidence about Criminal Behavior

KATHLEEN STIRRETT BERG AND NEIL VIDMAR

University of Western Ontario, London, Ontario, Canada

Research by Marshall (1966) suggested that high authoritarian persons might be more accurate at recalling evidence about criminal behavior than low authoritarian persons. Drawing on other research findings, Marshall's hypothesis was expanded to predict that high authoritarians would recall more about evidence relating to defendant character and low authoritarians would recall more about situational evidence. In two jury-simulation experiments the new hypothesis was confirmed.

In conjunction with the recently revived interest in psychology and law, a number of theoretical and empirical studies have investigated the relationship of authoritarianism to judgments about criminals, criminal behavior, and modes of coping with criminals (e.g., see Boehm, 1968; Jurow, 1971; Mitchell & Byrne, 1972; 1973; Oberer, 1961; Vidmar and Ellsworth, 1974). Building upon this literature and a study investigating witness reliability (Marshall, 1966) the present research hypothesized that high and low authoritarian jurors would focus on different aspects of the evidence in simulated criminal trial settings and that these tendencies would be reflected in differential recall of evidence. The findings yield theoretical insights about the concept of authoritarianism and also provide some practical insights for courtroom settings.

Although directed primarily toward examining the accuracy of recall of witnesses to criminal behavior, a study by Marshall (1966) was instrumental in formulating the present research hypothesis. Marshall presented a brief (42-sec) film depicting a scene in which a man showed suspicious and erratic behavior around an unattended baby carriage (possibly attempting to kidnap or molest the child) to groups of law students, police trainees, and low income housing residents. The subjects were then tested for their recall of facts about the incident. Among

This research was supported in part by Canada Council Grant S72-1180 (N. Vidmar, principal investigator). The authors thank William Siegel for helpful advice. Writing of the paper was completed while the second author was a Visiting Fellow at Battelle Seattle Research Center. An earlier version of the paper was presented at the 1974 Eastern Psychological Association Meeting, Philadelphia, Pennsylvania. Requests for reprints should be sent to Neil Vidmar, Department of Psychology, University of Western Ontario, London, Ontario, Canada.

other findings Marshall discovered that subjects who were classified as high punitive were more accurate at recall of evidence than subjects who were classified as low punitive; this relationship, moreover, obtained within each of the three socioeconomic groups. The data also suggested that subjects who assumed they were to be witnesses for the prosecution were more accurate than those assuming they were to be witnesses for the defense. Marshall (1966, pp. 70–81) speculated that the reason for this difference might be that high punitive witnesses (who are likely to be authoritarian, rigid, and extrapunitive) and prosecution witnesses were more "aggressively motivated" to perceive and recall the details of criminal acts. He also observed that the differential recall effect might apply to high and low punitive jurors as well, especially since jurors are not allowed to take notes during the trial itself (Marshall, 1966, pp. 90–91). Thus, aside from whatever biases the two types of jurors may have at the outset, they may enter the jury room with widely different assumptions and inferences about the evidence itself.

Marshall's study used only a single index of recall and did not concern itself with the various types of evidence that might be presented in a trial context. Recent studies on the effects of juror authoritarianism in simulated trial settings, however, yield data which suggest a refinement of the Marshall hypothesis. While studies by Boehm (1968) and Jurow (1971) have shown that high authoritarians are generally more "conviction prone" (i.e., inclined to vote guilty) than low authoritarians, studies by Mitchell and Byrne (1972; 1973) and Vidmar and Crinklaw (1973) have shown that authoritarian tendencies interact with characteristics of the defendant in both guilt attributions and recommended punishment. That is, high authoritarian jurors were more inclined to perceive guilt and/or give more severe punishments when the defendant was described as attitudinally dissimilar from themselves or having a negative character, while low authoritarians did not make any distinction with regard to character. The 1972 Mitchell and Byrne study contained a condition in which jurors were given judicial instructions to disregard any testimony about character. Low authoritarian jurors followed instructions while high authoritarians did not. Two other studies have also found high authoritarians focusing on the criminal's character. Boehm (1968) reported that high authoritarian simulating jurors tended to explain their verdicts with subjective "impressions" of the character of the defendant and Centers, Shomer, and Rodrigues (1970) found that high authoritarians are prone to place personal blame on juvenile delinquents and minimize the role of other contributing factors. In brief, high and low authoritarians may attend to different aspects of evidence during the trial process.

The attentiveness of high authoritarians to defendant character in simulated trial settings is, moreover, supported by research which has varied authoritarianism and character in other contexts. For example, Thibaut and Riecken (1955) and Roberts and Jessor (1958) found high authoritarians were more inclined to express aggression toward a low status source. Other studies have shown a positive relationship between authoritarianism and degree of conformity when the source of incongruous output was high status and a negative relationship when a low status source was involved (Berkowitz and Lundy, 1957; Harvey and Beverly, 1961; Steiner and Johnson, 1963; Vidulich and Kaiman, 1961). Rokeach (1960) proposed that because of his closed-mindedness an authoritarian tends to confuse what an external authority has to say about a situation with who the authority is. Johnson and Steiner (1967) have provided evidence that high authoritarians are "source-oriented" whereas nonauthoritarians are "message-oriented"; that is, whereas nonauthoritarians are concerned with being correct, authoritarians pay comparatively little attention to the position they are asked to accept and instead base their responses on the attributes of the source. Consistent with Steiner and Johnson's findings, Harvey and Beverly (1961) found that authoritarian subjects not only conformed more to the extreme views expressed by a speaker but also showed less evidence of having understood the speaker's arguments.

Thus, consideration of the research on authoritarianism in both simulated jury and other situations led us to an elaboration of Marshall's differential recall of evidence hypothesis, namely that high authoritarians would recall more about evidence relating to the defendant's character and that low authoritarians would recall more about the situational evidence regarding the crime. In two different experiments simulating jurors were presented with cases in which the character of the defendant was varied. Between 7 and 10 days after the experimental sessions subjects were asked a series of questions about the characteristics of the defendants and a series of questions about the situational evidence.

EXPERIMENT I

Method

Subjects

The initial subject population consisted of 144 students (54 females and 90 males) from a teacher's college who volunteered out-of-class time to participate in a brief study of decision-making processes. However, for reasons to be described below, attrition resulted in a final population of 90 subjects for the main dependent variables concerning recall.

Procedure

Upon volunteering the subject was handed a booklet containing a biographical data sheet, the measure of authoritarianism, and two cases involving stealing or cheating on an exam. For each case the subject was asked to make some initial decisions regarding the defendant's guilt and recommended punishment and to express some other attitudes which were intended as a manipulation check. Upon completion of the booklet subjects were thanked and notified that they might be recontacted briefly at some later date. Between 7 and 10 days after this initial session, subjects were contacted by telephone and asked 12 questions about their recall of evidence in the two cases they had read. Six of these questions dealt with defendant character and constituted the Character Recall Index; the other six questions were concerned with the situational evidence and thus constituted the Situation Recall Index. Only 90 of the original 144 subjects were recontacted despite two or three attempts per subject. Subsequent analyses, however, indicated that the final sample was not different from the original sample in terms of sex or authoritarianism.

Measure of Authoritarianism

The measure of authoritarian tendencies was Form II of Boehm's (1968) Legal Attitudes Questionnaire. This scale purports to measure authoritarianism in attitudes toward the legal process, is positively correlated with the California F scale, and has been shown to be a better predictor of juror verdicts than the traditional F scale (see Boehm, 1968; Jurow, 1971). For purposes of analysis the "equalitarian" subscale of the LAQ was subtracted from the "authoritarian" subscale and a median split of the resulting distribution was used to classify subjects as high or low authoritarians.

Tasks and Manipulations

Introductory written instructions informed the subject that the study was concerned with the nature of decision making and its relationship to an appeal system for students charged with violating university regulations. Subjects were then presented with two ostensibly "real" cases, one (case A) concerning a student who was charged with stealing an exam (adapted from Mitchell and Byrne, 1973) and one (case B) concerning a student who was charged with copying other students' answers on the multiple choice part of an exam and with copying from crib notes on the essay part of the exam. Each case consisted of three parts: a summary of the incident, a "personal data" description of the defendant, and finally, the statement made by the defendant at the hearing.

While the summary and defendant statement part of the tasks constituted the situational evidence, the "personal data" constituted the character evidence. There were two character description manipulations, one which described the defendant as essentially low status and one which described him as relatively high status. In the low status condition, the defendant was described as "a second year pass French student [who] reports no plans for the future. He is the son of a . . . factory worker . . . [who] doesn't take the university too seriously and barely manages to pass. He doesn't participate much in school activities, although he did try out for football and quit after the second week of practice. . . [He] is rather unpopular among his classmates and many people find him cold and unfriendly." In the high status condition the defendant was described as "a fourth year honors chemistry student planning to go into medicine. He is the son of a prominent business executive. . . [He] has worked fairly hard through school and maintains very good grades. He plays center for the university football team and was elected captain by his teammates. He is popular among his classmates and has acquired many friends during his four years at the university."

Each subject read both cases and both character descriptions but to control for possible order and character by task effects four conditions were created; (1) case A - high status, case B - low status; (2) case A - low status, case B- high status; (3) case B - high status, case A - low status, (4) case B - low status, case A - high status. The condition which any particular subject received was a result of random assignment.

Dependent Variables

After reading through each case subjects were asked to answer two questions about the defendant's guilt and recommended punishment, which would allow inferences about comparability with previous experiments, and two questions intended as a manipulation check. The guilt question consisted of a seven-point scale anchored from "definitely guilty" to "definitely not guilty." Subjects were allowed eight options regarding punishment which, in order of severity, were as follows: dismissal of the case, a warning, a reprimand, a mark of zero on that test, loss of course credit, a one-semester suspension, a 1-yr suspension, permanent expulsion from the university. Subjects were also asked to indicate their personal feelings about the defendant on a seven-point scale anchored from "extremely negative" to "extremely positive" and to indicate, on another seven-point scale, whether the defendant was of high or low social status.

The main dependent variables were obtained by telephone between 7 and 10 days after the initial session. Subjects were asked to recall information regarding the cases on a standard questionnaire requiring one- or two-word answers which could be readily scored as correct or incorrect. The "Situational Recall Index" consisted of six items, three for each of the two cases: e.g., Who saw the defendant walk out of the duplicating room? What were the clues that indicated the defendant was cheating? Similarly, the "Character Recall Index" also consisted of six items, three for each of the two defendants, which asked about personal characteristics: e.g., What was the defendant's major? What was his father's occupation? How long had he attended university? The answers were scored 1 for correct and 0 for incorrect and then summed for each index. Therefore, subject scores could range from 0 to 6 for each of the two recall indices.

RESULTS AND DISCUSSION

The means for the guilt, punishment, status, and affect variables broken by defendant status and juror authoritarianism are presented in Table 1. To test the statistical significance of these results we collapsed over cases and conducted a 2×2 analysis of variance with status treated as a within-subjects variable and juror authoritarianism treated as a between-subjects variable. Table 1 shows that the status manipulation was successful (F $(1,142) = 176.24$, $p < .0001$). With respect to certainty of guilt only a main effect of status was statistically significant (F $(1,142) = 7.59$, $p < .01$): jurors were more certain the lower status defendant was guilty. On the punishment variable there were significant effects of authoritarianism ($F(1,142) = 3.57$, $p < .001$) and an authoritarianism by status interaction ($F(1,142) = 5.42$, $p < .05$): these effects, however, all reflect the fact that high authoritarians were especially severe on low status defendants. The affect variable appears to reflect the tendency for high authoritarians to be negative toward a low status defendant; the authoritarian by status interaction yielded an F $(1,142)$ of 6.75, $p < .01$. These findings are similar to the effects reported by

201

TABLE 1

MEANS AND SIGNIFICANCE LEVELS FOR GUILT, PUNISHMENT, STATUS, AND
AFFECT VARIABLES

		Independent variables				
	A. Defendant	B. Authoritarianism		Significance levels		
Dependent variable	status	High	Low	A[a]	B[b]	A × B[c]
1 Certainty of guilt	High	5.4	5.7	.01		
(1 = NG; 7 = G)	Low	5.7	6.0			
2 Punishment	High	3.9	3.9	.001	.06	.05
(1 = 0; 8 = severe)	Low	4.4	3.9			
3 Status	High	5.2	5.0	.0001		
(1 = low; 7 = high)	Low	3.1	3.2			
4 Affect	High	3.9	3.7			.01
(1 = Neg.; 7 = Pos.)	Low	3.4	3.8			

[a] Within-subjects variance; $df = 1,142$.
[b] Between-subjects variance; $df = 1,142$.
[c] $df = 1,142$.

Mitchell and Byrne (1972; 1973) and Vidmar and Crinklaw (1974) and thus indicate that authoritarian discrimination in punitiveness extends to social status characteristics of the defendant as well as belief and general character differences.

The data relevant to the main hypothesis, selective recall, are presented in Table 2. Since there were only three questions for each level of status the scores were collapsed over status to yield a more reliable index of recall. Consider first the Character Recall Index. As may be seen in Table 2 high authoritarians remembered an average of 2.91 pieces of information while low authoritarians remembered 2.19 pieces of information. A one-way analysis of variance indicates that this dif-

TABLE 2

DIFFERENCES BETWEEN HIGH AND LOW AUTHORITARIANS IN REMEMBERING
EVIDENCE ABOUT CHARACTER AND ABOUT SITUATION

Variable	Authoritarianism level	Mean[a]	F ratio[b]
1 Character recall index	High	2.91	4.29*
(possible score = 6)	Low	2.19	
2 Situation recall index	High	3.31	9.44**
(possible score = 6)	Low	4.10	

[a] Based on total $N = 90$, 48 high and 42 low authoritarians.
[b] $df = 1,88$.
* $p < .05$.
** $p < .001$.

ference is statistically reliable $(F(1,88) = 4.30, p < .05)$. On the Situational Recall Index high authoritarians remembered an average of 3.31 pieces of information while low authoritarians remembered 4.10 pieces of information and the difference is also statistically significant. $(F(1,88) = 9.44, p < .01)$.

Experiment I, therefore, supports the hypothesis that while high authoritarian subjects would evidence better memory for personal characteristics of the defendant, low authoritarian subjects would evidence better memory for facts about the situational evidence regarding the alleged crime. However, by itself the experiment is susceptible to two interrelated criticisms. First, subjects' recall might have been somehow affected because immediately upon reading through the cases, they made decisions about guilt and punishment. The fact of making such a decision may result in a postdecision rationalizing process which could result in differential recall of high and low authoritarians. Thus, the guilt and sentencing decisions may have confounded the experiment in some way. Second, because of the small number of recall items, the experiment did not consider potential differences in recall about the high and low status character defendants. Moreover, there is also the possibility that there could be a main effect of defendant character on recall; the fact that high authoritarians tended to discriminate against the low status defendant suggests there could be an interaction between juror authoritarianism and defendant character regarding recall.

EXPERIMENT II

Experiment II was designed in a way that would eliminate the ambiguities contained in Experiment I. In addition Experiment II used a different subject population, a different measure of authoritarianism, a different type of case, and a slightly different procedure in an attempt to determine whether the results were generalizeable or were limited to the particular tasks, population, and procedure of Experiment I.

Method

Subjects were 37 students (20 females and 17 males ranging in age between 25 and 55 years) enrolled in two college extension classes who volunteered to participate in a study of decision making outside of regular class time.

In a preliminary session the subjects were given Byrne and Lamberth's (1971) authoritarianism scale and asked to read a summary of an automobile-manslaughter case, modified from Landy and Aronson (1969), ostensibly as preparation for a group discussion which would take place the following week. In addition to the details of the circumstances surrounding the death of a pedestrian, facts about the defendant's age, background, personality, etc. were also built into the case summary. For half of the subjects the defendant was portrayed in such a way as to have a negative or bad character and for the other half he was described as having a positive or good character. Subjects were admonished to not decide on the defendant's guilt or discuss the case with anyone.

The next week, instead of a group discussion, the subjects were given a 17-item written questionnaire that tested their recall of the evidence in the case. Seven of the items pertained to facts about the defendant's character and thus constituted the Character Recall Index. The remaining ten items were used to form the Situation Recall Index.

A median split of the distribution of authoritarianism scores was used to classify subjects as high or low authoritarians. A two-way between-subjects analysis of variance (authoritarianism × defendant character) was conducted on the data for each recall index.

RESULTS AND DISCUSSION

The results of Experiment II are presented in Table 3. Although the data for the Situation Recall Index fell short of the standard set for statistical significance, the results are nevertheless in the expected direction for both recall indices. In comparison to low authoritarians high authoritarians remembered more of the evidence about the defendant's character ($F(1,33) = 4.16$, $p < .05$) and less about the situational evidence ($F(1,33) = 3.87$, $p < .10$). The data do not indicate any effects due to defendant character or to a defendant character by juror authoritarianism interaction.

Despite differences in the substantive and procedural aspects of Experiment II, the data appear to be consistent with the previous findings and do not appear to lend support to the hypotheses that the recall effects of Experiment I were due to (a) jurors making decisions about guilt and punishment or to (b) effects peculiar to only one type of defendant character.

GENERAL DISCUSSION

The present research tested, and confirmed, the hypothesis that in a simulated juror experiment high authoritarian subjects would recall more about evidence relating to defendant character and low authoritarians would recall more about evidence relating to the situation surrounding

TABLE 3
EFFECTS OF JUROR AUTHORITARIANISM AND DEFENDANT CHARACTER IN
REMEMBERING EVIDENCE: EXPERIMENT II

	Independent variables[a]			Significance level		
	A. Defendant	B. Authoritarianism				
Dependent variable	character	High	Low	A	B	A × B
1 Character recall index	Good	3.93	3.32	.05		
(possible score = 7)	Bad	3.83	3.15			
2 Situation recall index	Good	5.03	5.86	.10		
(possible score = 10)	Bad	5.42	5.74			

[a] Total $N = 37$. Cell Ns, reading top across, then bottom across, are 11, 8, 6, and 12.

the crime. These results have some interesting theoretical implications and also provide some potentially practical insights for the courtroom.

One theoretical contribution of the research is the elaboration of Marshall's (1966) hypothesis which appeared to suggest that high authoritarian persons would be more "aggressively motivated" to perceive the details of criminal acts than low authoritarian persons and, therefore, would be generally more accurate at recall. By using two conceptually independent measures of recall, the present experiments indicate that recall is selective, with high authoritarians being more accurate regarding defendant character but less accurate regarding situational evidence. However, because our jury simulation settings were quite different from Marshall's experiment, which examined witnesses' first-hand recall of criminal behavior, the results should not be interpreted as necessarily contradicting his findings. A more direct replication of the latter experiment will be required before we can confidently generalize about authoritarianism and witness reliability.

Another implication of the research is to suggest a different focus for attempts to explain authoritarian punitiveness in jury settings. Previous explanations have tended to center on that stage of the juror's decision-making process after presentation of evidence when the actual decision about guilt and punishment must be made. Vidmar and Crinklaw (1973), for example, have suggested that high and low authoritarians differ in the degree of retributive and utilitarian motives for punishment and that these motives come into play when sanctioning decisions are to be made. Mitchell and Byrne (1972; 1973) hypothesized that high authoritarians cannot separate their affective reactions toward the defendant from their legal decisions. Without negating such explanations the present findings suggest the complementary hypothesis that bias may begin at a much earlier stage in the process, specifically, during the process of evidence presentation. Thus, differences, between high and low authoritarians in guilt attributions and sanctioning behavior may be based on cognitive differences in interpretation of evidence as well as any motivational or affective differences regarding the defendant.

The specific dynamics behind the differences in recall of evidence are, of course, still uncertain and may be rooted in a number of processes. Perhaps high authoritarians have general tendencies to be source oriented instead of message oriented (Johnson and Steiner, 1967) or perhaps they displace aggression onto outgroup members, violators of conventional mores and low status figures (Roberts and Jessor, 1958; Thibant and Riecken, 1955). It may be, as Jurow (1971) suggested, that in jury settings high authoritarians are inclined to make a presumption of guilt rather than innocence; perhaps this presumption causes them to focus more on defendant character than on situational evidence. We should also note that the basic assumption of Marshall's (1966) hypothesis and the present research is that differences in recall are based on differences in selective attention between high and low authoritarians, but both studies only tested recall. It could be that recall is affected by authoritarianism in some other way. Future research might attempt a more direct test of the selective attention assumption by monitoring attention during evidence presentation.

Although we must make the usual, and necessary, caveats about generalizing from the laboratory microculture to the real world, the present study does have some potentially applied aspects. It indicates that persons differing in authoritarianism do respond differently in recalling evidence about criminal behavior. Such information gives insight about the reliability of witness testimony (c.f. Marshall, 1966; Levine & Tapp, 1973), about appropriate strategies in selecting jurors (c.f. Schulman *et al.*, 1973; Rokeach and Vidmar, 1973), and about formulating appropriate strategies of evidence presentation and argument (c.f. Costopoulos, 1972; Lawson, 1970) when faced with a given jury composition. With regard to the last area of application it should be noted that the recent review literature and empirical research on the problem of persuasion in the courtroom (Costopoulos, 1972; Hatton, Snortum, & Oskamp, 1971; Lawson, 1970; Marshall, 1966; Stone, 1969; Thibaut, Walker, & Lind, 1972; Walker, Thibaut, & Andreoli, 1972) has focused on structural characteristics of the evidence or on factors associated with presentation of the message and has more or less ignored personality characteristics of the recipient jurors. The present research indicates that personality characteristics deserve more research attention.

REFERENCES

Berkowitz, L., & Lundy, R. Personality characteristics related to susceptibility to influence by peers or authority figures. *J. Personality*, 1957, **25**, 3-6-316. ·

Boehm, V. Mr. Prejudice, Miss Sympathy and the authoritarian personality. *Wisconsin Law Rev.*, 1968, 734–750.

Byrne, D., & Lamberth, J. The effect of erotic stimuli on sex arousal, evaluative responses, and subsequent behavior. *Technical Reports of the Commission on Obscenity and Pornography*, Vol. 8. Washington, D.C.: U.S. Gov. Printing Office, 1971.

Centers, R., Shomer, R. W., & Rodrigues, A. A field experiment in interpersonal persuasion using authoritative influence. *Journal of Personality*, 1970, **38**, 392–403.

Costopolous, W. Persuasion in the courtroom. *Dusquesne Law Rev.* 1972, **10**, 384–409.

Hatton, D., Snortum, J. and Oskamp, S. The effects of biasing information and dogmatism upon witness testimony. *Psychonomic Science*, 1971, **23**, 425–427.

Harvey, O. J. & Beverly, G. D. Some personality correlates of concept change through role playing. *Journal of Abnormal and Social Psychology*, 1961, **63**, 125–130.

Johnson, H., & Steiner, I. Some effects of discrepancy level on relationships between authoritarianism and conformity. *Journal of Social Psychology*, 1967, **9**, 179–183.

Jurow, G. Y. New data on the effect of a death qualified jury on the guilt determination process. *Harvard Law Review*, 1971, **84**, 567–611.

Lawson, R. Experimental research on the organization of persuasive arguments: an application to courtroom communications. *Law and the Social Order*, 1970, 579–593.

Levine, F., & Tapp, J. The psychology of criminal identification: The gap from Wade to Kirby. *U. Pennsylvania Law Review*, 1973, **121**, 1079–1131.

Marshall, J. *Law and psychology in conflict.* Indianapolis: Bobbs-Merrill, 1966.

Mitchell, H. & Byrne, D. Minimizing the influence of irrelevant factors in the courtroom: the defendant's character, judge's instructions, and authoritarianism. Paper presented at Midwestern Psychological Assn. Cleveland, Ohio, May 1972.

Mitchell, H., & Byrne, D. The defendant's dilemma: Effects of juror's attitudes and authoritarianism on judicial decisions. *Journal of Personality and Social Psychology*, 1973, **25**, 123–129.

Roberts, A. H., & Jessor, R. Authoritarianism, punitiveness and perceived social status. *Journal of Abnormal and Social Psychology*, 1958, **56**, 311–314.

Rokeach, M. *The open and closed mind*, New York: Basic Books, 1960.

Rokeach, M., & Vidmar, N. Testimony concerning possible jury bias in a Black Panther murder trial. *Journal of Applied Social Psychology*, 1973, **3**, 19–29.

Schulman, J., Shaver, P., Colman, R., Emrich, B., & Christie, R. Recipe for a jury. *Psychology Today*, 1973, **6**, 37.

Steiner, I. D., & Johnson, H. H. Authoritarianism and conformity. *Sociometry*, 1963, **26**, 21–34.

Stone, V. A primacy effect in decision-making by jurors. *The Journal of Communication*, 1969, **19**, 239–247.

Thibaut, J. W., & Riecken, H. W. Some determinants and consequences of the perception of social causality. *Journal of Personality*, 1955, **24**, 113–133.

Thibaut, J., Walker, L., & Lind, A. Adversary presentation and bias in legal decision making. *Harvard Law Review*, 1972, **86**, 386–401.

Vidmar, N., & Crinklaw, L. Retribution and utility as motives in sanctioning behavior. Paper presented at the Midwestern Psychological Association, Chicago, Illinois, 1973.

Vidmar, N., & Ellsworth, P. Public opinion and the death penalty. *Stanford Law Review*, 1974, **26**, 1245–1270.

Vidulich, R. D., & Kaiman, I. P. The effects of information, status source and dogmatism upon conformity behavior. *Journal of Abnormal and Social Psychology*, 1961, **63**, 639–642.

Walker, L., Thibaut, J., & Andreoli. Order of presentation at trial. *Yale Law Journal*, 1972, **82**, 216–226.

Journal of Applied Psychology
1982, Vol. 67, No. 5, 629–636

Conviction Proneness and the Authoritarian Juror: Inability to Disregard Information or Attitudinal Bias?

Carol M. Werner, Dorothy K. Kagehiro, and Michael J Strube
University of Utah

Two experiments were conducted to distinguish between inability to disregard information and biased predisposition as explanations for authoritarians' trial decisions. In Experiment 1, 120 mock jurors rendered verdicts and gave probability of guilt estimates for trial evidence involving two levels of admissibility of wiretap evidence (inadmissable and admissible) and two levels of incrimination value of wiretap evidence (exonerating and incriminating). Results supported a pro- and antidefendant bias rather than a differential cognitive ability model. Experiment 2 was conducted to determine whether repeating and emphasizing judge's instructions to jurors to disregard inadmissible evidence would reduce authoritarians' tendency to incorporate it. Authoritarian subjects were more likely to convict, especially in the presence of incriminating evidence, regardless of its admissibility, and regardless of judge's emphasis. The two studies suggest that authoritarians are characterized by an antidefendant bias that influences their responses to trial evidence and that is not easily overcome by emphasizing the judge's instructions.

Renewed awareness of cognitive biases associated with authoritarianism (Adorno, Frenkel-Brunswick, Levinson, & Sanford, 1950; White, Alter, & Rardin, 1965) has resulted in doubts concerning the ability of authoritarian jurors to render impartial verdicts (Bermant & Tapp, 1975; Kaplan, 1977; Rokeach & Vidmar, 1973; Schulman, Shaver, Colman, Emrich, & Christie, 1973). For example, research indicates that decisions by authoritarians are more likely to involve extralegal information, such as defendant–juror attitudinal dissimilarity (Mitchell & Byrne, 1973) and defendant ethnicity (Boehm, 1968).

There are at least two possible interpretations of this incorporation of extralegal in-

formation. One is that authoritarian individuals are simply biased against anyone brought to trial and look for evidence that will permit them to convict the defendant; less authoritarian individuals hold prodefendant biases and look for evidence that will permit them to acquit. For example, unlike less authoritarian individuals, authoritarians have described themselves as being more influenced by prosecution than defense testimony (Sue, Smith, & Pedroza, 1975).

A second interpretation is that authoritarians are less able to disregard extralegal information once it becomes known to them, whereas nonauthoritarians have a greater ability to be aware of extralegal information without utilizing it. This hypothesis assumes no difference in attention to differentially incriminating information, instead suggesting a differential ability to select information from memory. When all information is to be used, there is no problem; only when some information is not to be used (i.e., extralegal information) do inequities occur.

Inadmissable evidence is a good example of extralegal information that authoritarians might incorporate into their verdicts. It provides a useful vehicle for distinguishing between the two suggested interpretations of authoritarian decision making since inad-

This research was supported by a University of Utah Faculty Research Grant to the first author.

We would like to thank B. Jack White and William Johnston for their comments on an earlier draft, Herman Mitchell for providing a copy of the Mitchell-Byrne Authoritarianism Scale, and Gary Damron, Mirelle Davis, and Dan Kenny for their assistance in data collection and tabulation.

Dorothy K. Kagehiro is now at the University of Wisconsin—Parkside. Michael J Strube is now at Washington University.

Requests for reprints should be sent to Carol M. Werner, Department of Psychology, University of Utah, Salt Lake City, Utah 84112.

missable evidence can be either incriminating or exonerating. If authoritarian and nonauthoritarian individuals are characterized by anti- and prodefendant biases, respectively, they should only incorporate evidence that suits those biases. Furthermore, both groups should follow their biases regardless of the evidence's admissibility. These patterns would differ from one characterized by an authoritarian inability to disregard information. If this hypothesis is correct, authoritarian subjects should incorporate exonerating or incriminating evidence, and incorporate it whether admissible or inadmissible. Nonauthoritarian subjects should only incorporate evidence when it has been declared admissable.

Subjects' ratings of the importance of the judge's instructions should also be influenced by authoritarianism. Relative to nonauthoritarians, authoritarians are more submissive to authority figures, and should rate the judge's instructions as more important. More importantly, the ratings might indicate how subjects feel about the judge's instructions. Thus, if subjects are following their pro- or antidefendant biases in making their verdicts, they should attribute less importance to the judge's instructions when those instructions are in conflict with the desired verdict. If subjects believe that they are following the instructions and are unaware that they are not, rated importance of the judge's instructions should not vary with treatment condition.

The first experiment was conducted to compare these two interpretations and supported the bias rather than the inability-to-disregard model. A second experiment was conducted to determine whether one of the mechanisms available in a legal setting to prevent biased verdicts should be useful in overcoming the authoritarians' antidefendant tendencies. It was hypothesized that repeating and emphasizing the judge's instructions to disregard inadmissable evidence would reduce authoritarians' tendency to be influenced by it. Past research suggests that this should be an effective strategy (cf. Harvey & Beverley, 1961; Wagman, 1955). Since it is the judge who instructs the jurors that a particular piece of evidence is inadmissible and should therefore not be a factor in their

decisions, it is possible that the antidefendant bias of high authoritarian jurors might be overcome by the judge's instructions. However, a contrary view has been expressed by Broeder (1959) and Wolf and Montgomery (1977), who believe that reminding jurors of inadmissible evidence only serves to reinstate it in their memory, thereby increasing the likelihood that it could influence verdicts.

In summary, a first experiment was conducted to compare the bias and inability to disregard information explanations of authoritarians' conviction-proneness. The second experiment was conducted to determine if reiteration and emphasis of the judge's instructions to disregard inadmissable evidence would reduce authoritarians' incorporation of inadmissable evidence.

Experiment 1

Method

Subjects. Subjects were 120 male and female students recruited from an introductory psychology course. They were asked to assume the roles of jurors in a robbery/murder trial. Subjects received extra course credit for participating in the study.

Experimental materials. The experimental booklets contained the crime description and trial summary from the weak evidence condition of Sue, Smith, and Caldwell (1973). Only the weak evidence was utilized since the Sue et al. study found that incorporation of inadmissible evidence by jurors occurred only when there was weak evidence against a murder defendant. The description of the robbery/murder was followed by a trial summary of six items of circumstantial evidence presented by the prosecution, and the defense's refutation of them. In some conditions, a seventh item was included that was either highly incriminating or highly exonerating. These items were selected on the basis of a prescaling study in which 44 male and female students established that the exonerating and incriminating inadmissable wiretap evidence items were comparable in: (a) subjects' beliefs that it was indeed the defendant's voice recorded on tape; (b) the plausibility of the alibi/incriminating evidence; (c) the plausibility of the judge's rationale for refusing to admit the wiretap evidence; and (d) the subjects' personal impressions of the defendant's character, apart from the question of his guilt or innocence, (all *F*s, ns). In all conditions where the wiretap evidence was included, it was declared either admissible or inadmissible by the judge within the context of the trial summary, replicating the Sue et al. procedure.

Procedure. Subjects were randomly assigned to conditions in a five-cell between-subjects design. Four cells consisted of a 2 (admissibility of wiretap evidence) × 2 (incrimination value of wiretap evidence) factorial design; the remaining cell was a control group from which the wiretape evidence was omitted. Authoritarianism was measured using the Mitchell-Byrne Authoritarianism Scale (Mitchell & Byrne, 1973). Scores on the scale can range from 22 to 154, with lower numbers indicating more authoritarian responses. The actual range was from 60 to 134, indicating the sample did not contain extremely authoritarian individuals.

After reading the crime description and trial summary, subjects were instructed to review the material if they wished, since they would not be allowed to look back in the booklet after this point. Two dependent measures were collected: Subjects estimated the probability of the defendant's guilt on an 11-point scale from 0 to 100 in intervals of 10, and voted to acquit or to convict. To separate these two measures in the subjects' minds as much as possible, the experimenter removed the first half of the booklet after the subject completed the first measure. The order in which these judgments were made was counterbalanced within each experimental condition. Subjects rated the importance of the judge's instructions on a separate questionnaire at the end of the experimental session. Following the completion of the experimental booklets, subjects were debriefed and dismissed.

Results

The data were analyzed using multiple regression/correlation techniques (Cohen & Cohen, 1975) to capitalize on the full power of analyzing continuous variables (in this case, authoritarianism). (See Cohen & Cohen, 1975, and Kerlinger & Pedhazur, 1973, for extensive treatments of this approach.) Although the statistical analyses are similar, data presentation based on multiple regression is necessarily different from that based on analysis of variance. Thus, we shall provide correlation coefficients rather than group means. Interactive effects will be tests of differences in slopes of the regression lines describing the relationships among authoritarianism, the manipulated variables, and the dependent variable. As a check on the goodness of the fit of obtained frequencies to predictions from the regression equation (see Figure 1), mean values for each condition are presented in Table 1. Technically, because authoritarianism is treated as a continuous variable, we should refer to subjects as more authoritarian and less authoritarian, however, for convenience we shall use the terms *authoritarians* and *nonauthoritarians*.

Probability of guilt estimates and verdicts were analyzed separately. The probability estimates were normalized through the use of a log-odds transformation (see Ostrom, Werner, & Saks, 1978, for a conceptual and statistical justification of the transformation).

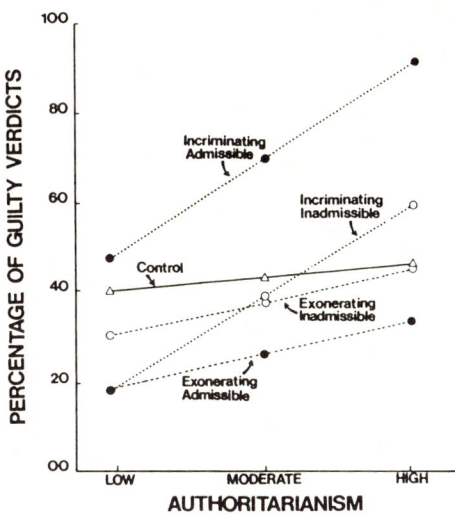

Figure 1. Percentage of guilty verdicts as a function of authoritarianism, evidence admissibility, and evidence favorability. (Points are best fit estimates based on the regression equation as recommended by Cohen & Cohen, 1975. Points along the abscissa are plotted at the mean authoritarianism score [95] and one standard deviation above and below the mean [110 and 80, respectively, on the reversed scale] and hence do not have direct correspondence to the low and high authoritarianism groups represented in Table 1.)

Verdicts were coded 0 (not guilty) and 1 (guilty) for analysis (Lunney, 1970). The use of t tests permitted one-tailed (i.e., directional) analyses of specifically hypothesized relationships.

A significant main effect for authoritarianism was obtained for verdicts, $t(110) = 2.67$, $p < .05$ (see Table 1 and Figure 1), but not so for probability of guilt estimates, $t(110) = 1.39$, $p < .10$. As expected, these results indicated that authoritarian individuals tended to vote for guilt more often ($r = -.24$) than nonauthoritarian individuals (the test was of a linear effect; the curvilinear effect was not significant). Other main and first-order interactive effects will not be presented, since these are qualified by significant effects within evidence type.

Incriminating evidence. Separate a priori contrasts were performed within each favorability condition to assess the role of authoritarianism in these judgments. As can be seen in Figure 1 and Table 1, subjects receiving the incriminating wiretape evidence were more likely to convict when the evidence had been declared admissible than inadmissible. The interaction between authoritarianism and these two conditions (i.e., comparison of the slopes of the two lines) is not significant ($t[110] < 1$ for both verdicts and probability estimates), indicating that evidence admissibility was not differentially important in the decisions of authoritarians and nonauthoritarians. However, the comparison between these two conditions and the control condition is significant for verdict, $t(110) = 1.64$, $p < .05$, though not for probability estimates, $t(110) < 1$, indicating that the presence of the extra evidence had different impacts on authoritarians and nonauthoritarians. Examination of the figure indicates that nonauthoritarians who heard inadmissible incriminating evidence were less likely to convict than those who heard only the basic case. As authoritarism increased,

Table 1

Percentage of Guilty Verdicts as a Function of Incrimination Value, Admissibility, and Authoritarianism (Experiments 1 and 2)

| | Experiment 1 | | Experiment 2 | |
| | Authoritarianism | | Authoritarianism | |
Condition	Low	High	Low	High
Control	41	41	42	43
Inadmissible exonerating	33	41	—	—
Inadmissible incriminating	16	58	41	72
Admissible exonerating	16	33	—	—
Admissible incriminating	58	91	67	80

Note. The data are based on a median split of the authoritarianism scores within each experimental condition. For the low authoritarians, the average overall score on the Mitchell-Byrne Scale was 107.2 ($SD = 9.9$). Mean scores within each condition ranged from 101–110. For the high authoritarians, the average overall score was 82.6 ($SD = 9.4$); mean scores within each condition ranged from 79–88. Note that these results are based on a median split, whereas those in Figure 1 are based on regression estimates ± 1 SD around the mean authoritarianism scores. Thus, there is not direct correspondence between the data points represented here and in Figure 1.

Table 2

Pearson Product-Moment Correlation Between Authoritarianism and Importance in Each Experimental Condition (Experiment 1)

Condition	r
Overall	−.25*
Control	−.26
Inadmissible exonerating	−.45*
Inadmissible incriminating	−.08
Admissible exonerating	−.23
Admissible incriminating	−.34

Note. Low scores on authoritarianism scale indicate high authoritarianism. Low scores on importance scale indicate low importance. $N = 120$ (in each condition, $n = 24$).
* $p < .05$.

so did the likelihood that the inadmissible incriminating evidence would lead to convictions.

Exonerating evidence. Authoritarianism had no influence in the exonerating evidence conditions. The authoritarianism–verdict relation did not differ for the admissible and inadmissible conditions, $t(110) < 1$, for either verdicts or probability estimates, nor did the mean of these two differ from the condition where the wiretap evidence was omitted, $t(110) < 1$, for either verdicts or probability estimates.

Importance of judge's instruction. We had hypothesized that authoritarian and nonauthoritarian biases would be reflected in differential importance attributed to instructions that were compatible with each group's bias. Thus, authoritarianism should correlate negatively with rated importance (high authoritarians have lower scores on the Mitchell-Byrne scale) when exonerating evidence is ruled inadmissible and when incriminating evidence is ruled admissible; authoritarianism should correlate positively with rated importance when exonerating evidence is ruled admissible and when incriminating evidence is ruled inadmissible.

As can be seen in Table 2, only partial support was received for these hypotheses: Only negative correlations were obtained. Authoritarian individuals attributed significantly greater importance to the judge's instructions in the two conditions where authoritarians should be most pleased with the instructions: inadmissible exonerating and admissible incriminating. Authoritarians did attribute greater importance to the judge's instructions, especially when the instructions favored their bias. They did not denigrate instructions, even when the instructions conflicted with their bias. Thus, the bias notion receives partial support from the importance ratings.

Discussion

Results tended to support the hypothesis that high and low authoritarian individuals follow their biases when making decisions about a defendant's guilt or innocence. There was no effect of authoritarianism in the control condition; however, when incriminating evidence was presented, authoritarian subjects thought it more likely that the defendant was guilty and were more likely to convict than the nonauthoritarian subjects. More importantly, the authoritarian subjects incorporated the incriminating evidence almost regardless of admissibility, but did not incorporate the exonerating evidence. Not only did the nonauthoritarian subjects not convict in the presence of inadmissible incriminating evidence, but they became more lenient.

Although the behavior of the authoritarian subjects fits the antidefendant bias explanation best, the behavior of the nonauthoritarian subjects is not so easily interpreted. Although nonauthoritarians were more likely to acquit when admissible exonerating evidence was present, the comparison to the control condition (which conveyed more culpability) was not significant. One explanation is that the exonerating evidence was not sufficiently strong to produce a significant contrast to the basic case. However, the results of prescaling make this an unlikely possibility. It is more likely that the difference between authoritarians and nonauthoritarians is not that one group holds a strong antidefendant bias and the other a strong prodefendant bias, but rather that the nonauthoritarian prodefendant bias is not as strong as the authoritarian antidefendant bias.

Most of the authoritarianism effects occurred when the dependent variable was the verdict; effects were nonsignificant when the dependent variable was probability of guilt. This pattern suggests that individuals with differing degrees of authoritarianism were utilizing different decision criteria when deciding how certain one would have to be in order to convict; that is, the level of reasonable doubt each utilized was different. One method for assessing this possibility would be to use a multiple regression analysis, with verdict, authoritarianism, and the Verdict × Authoritarianism interaction as predictors, and probability of guilt as the criterion. The interaction would be examined to determine if high and low authoritarians differed in probability of guilt estimates associated with guilty verdicts, thus indicating a difference in decision criterion. The analysis indicated no such effect, $F(1, 116) < 1$. It would appear that high and low authoritarians no not differ substantially in their decision criteria.

One mechanism that is utilized in the legal system to reduce the impact of biases is judge's instructions. Jurors are admonished to utilize only information relevant to the case, and to disregard all inadmissible evidence. A second experiment was conducted in which these instructions were emphasized for some subjects but not for others. It was hypothesized that the greater deference of authoritarian subjects to authority figures would increase their responsivity to these instructions and combat their antidefendant bias. Because the bias was most noticeable in the situations in which extra incriminating evidence was presented, only that evidence will be utilized in Experiment 2.

Experiment 2

Method

Subjects. Subjects were 160 male and female university students. Recruitment and procedure were similar to that in Experiment 1, with certain exceptions discussed in the following sections. Subjects' scores on the Mitchell-Byrne Authoritarianism Scale ranged from 56 to 142, indicating, as in Experiment 1, an absence of strongly authoritarian individuals in the sample.

Experimental materials. The experimental booklets were identical to those used in the incriminating evidence condition of the first experiment, with the following addition: For subjects receiving separate judge's instructions, the ruling of admissibility or inadmissibility was reiterated in the judge's instructions following the prosecution and defense summations. The instructions used the standard terminology (Los Angeles County Superior Court, 1970), which instructs jurors to "disregard" the inadmissible evidence rather than instructing them to set aside their biases.

Procedure. Subjects were randomly assigned to conditions in the 3 (admissibility of wiretap evidence) × 2 (reiteration of judge's instructions) between-subjects factorial design. In addition to indicating their estimate of the likelihood that the defendant was guilty and their final verdict, subjects indicated their assessment of the importance of judge's instructions on 11-point scales. The importance of the judge's instructions measure was collected as part of a separate questionnaire at the end of the experimental session.

Results

A significant main effect for authoritarianism was obtained for verdicts, $t(148) = 4.09$, $p < .001$, and for probability of guilt estimates, $t(148) = 1.79$, $p < .04$. Both replicated the first study in indicating that the high authoritarians tended to convict more frequently ($r = -.30$) and to give higher probability of guilt estimates ($r = -.14$) than low authoritarians. (See Table 1 for results based on median split of authoritarianism scores.)

Of greater importance was the finding of a significant Authoritarianism × Admissibility of Evidence interaction for guilty verdicts, $F(2, 148) = 3.92$, $p < .05$. The effect was not significant for probability of guilt estimates, $F(2, 148) = 1.26$, $p > .10$. Examination of the data indicates that the slopes of the regression lines do indeed differ, and that the pattern is similar to that obtained in Experiment 1: Both authoritarian and nonauthoritarian subjects incorporated the admissible evidence; however, although authoritarians were more likely to incorporate the inadmissible evidence, the effect is only marginally significant, interaction $t(148) = 1.42, p < .10$. The interaction between authoritarianism and a contrast of both extra evidence conditions with the control group is once again significant, $t(148) = 2.42$, $p < .01$, indicating that authoritarians are more likely to incorporate any extra evidence than nonauthoritarians, but that the groups do not differ in their opinions about the control case.

Reiteration of the judge's instructions produced no differences either by itself, or in combination with the other variables (all $ps < .10$). Thus, as presented in this study, the judge's emphasis of prior instructions does not offset juror biases. On the other hand, concern that discussing inadmissible evidence as part of the judge's instructions only serves to reinstate that evidence in jurors' memories, appears to be unwarranted. There was no impact of treatment on ratings of importance of judge's instructions; the correlation between these ratings and authoritarianism was $-.02$, *ns*, indicating that, overall, authoritarian subjects did not describe themselves as being more influenced by the instructions.

The analysis of decision criteria indicated, as before, no differences between authoritarians and nonauthoritarians in their levels of reasonable doubt, possibly because of a truncation of range of scores in this study.

General Discussion

Authoritarianism did not influence how subjects evaluated the control case, but it did influence how they responded to the case when extra evidence was included. Authoritarian subjects were more likely to convict in the presence of either incriminating admissible *or* inadmissible evidence. This tendency to incorporate extra evidence did not occur when the evidence could exonerate the defendant.

It is possible to obtain a quantitative estimate of the significance of the combined results of both studies for the Authoritarianism × Admissibility interaction in response to incriminating evidence. The p values obtained from the statistical contrasts in which the two admissible and inadmissible incriminating evidence conditions were compared to the control condition were combined using the Stouffer method (see Rosenthal, 1978). The combined probabilities resulted in a Z of 2.84, $p = .002$; the two experiments clearly suggest that authoritarian individuals are characterized by an antidefendant bias that influences their response to trial information. Moreover, the second experiment indicates that this bias is not easily overcome by emphasizing the judge's instructions.

The present research does not identify the nature of the antidefendant bias. Some possibilities are suggested by Ostrom et al.'s (1978) work on juror decision making. Those authors utilized Anderson's (1974) Information Integration Theory to describe the process by which jurors evaluate trial evidence. Anderson identified four parameters that are combined into an individual's final evaluation: the incrimination value assigned to each evidence item; the weight placed on each evidence item; the initial disposition, or a priori estimate of how likely it is a defendant is guilty; and the weight placed on that presumption. Authoritarians could differ from nonauthoritarians in any or all of these parameters. Because we found no differences in evaluations of the control case by authoritarian and nonauthoritarian individuals, it is unlikely the major difference resides in the initial disposition or its emphasis. The pattern of differences does suggest that authoritarians perceived the extra evidence to be more incriminating and/or gave it greater weight.

The results have implications for the presentation of evidence before a jury. The biased incorporation occurred only for incriminating evidence, and the bias was not reduced by the repeated instructions of a high status figure to disregard it. If there is any doubt as to the admissibility of damaging evidence, that evidence should be screened in the absence of the jury, or testimony videotaped and edited before the trial (Miller, 1975; Bukoff, Moore, Landis, & Klein, Note 1). Another possibility is to screen out authoritarian jurors, but that has equally serious problems, having to do with the legality of such a priori exclusion of certain individuals from jury service and the validity and feasibility of the screening process to be used (VanDyke, 1977).

On the other hand, the problem may be more limited in scope than is presently implied. Although most research suggests that authoritarians are likely to utilize extralegal information to convict, two studies at least have found no support for this hypothesis. Sue et al. (1975) examined the influence of damaging or neutral pretrial publicity on juror decision making. Although denying that they had been biased, jurors exposed to the damaging but inadmissible evidence returned more guilty verdicts than those jurors exposed to the neutral evidence. There was no relationship between authoritarianism of juror and admission of bias, rendering of ver-

dicts, severity of sentence, or rating of the defense case. Kagehiro (1981) also found no impact of authoritarianism on reactions to inadmissible evidence. Both groups of authors speculated that the strength of other factors in the case may have overshadowed the effects of authoritarianism. In the present research, we specifically selected a weak case so that the effects of inadmissibility and authoritarianism could be revealed. It may be that practitioners in the legal system need only be concerned about authoritarian biases when the case is weak and the extralegal information strongly biasing, or when the juror is intensely authoritarian.

We began this article by reviewing evidence that indicated that authoritarian individuals were more likely to incorporate extralegal information into their verdicts. The present research indicates that the problem is one of an antidefendant bias rather than a cognitive deficit. We would be remiss if we did not remind the reader of obvious cautions in generalizing from the present study. Certainly, we cannot say whether the bias is the most appropriate explanation for authoritarians' incorporation of extralegal evidence other than inadmissible evidence (e.g., pretrial publicity, defendant characteristics) or whether we can generalize beyond the particular case and evidence utilized herein. Furthermore, we cannot say that there is no way to overcome these biases. For example, Griffit and Garcia (1979) were able to reverse the authoritarian bias by conditioning their subjects to accept prodemocratic statements. Wolf and Montgomery (1977) demonstrated that strongly worded judge's instructions may arouse reactance that only increases subjects' tendencies to incorporate extralegal evidence; selecting instructions so as to reduce reactivity may have yielded a greater influence of judge's instructions in the present study.

Although we view the results as having possible implications for the presentation of incriminating trial information, care must be taken to avoid generalizing directly and injudiciously from paper-and-pencil tests to the decision-making process of jurors in jury interactions. The primary purpose of this research is to provide additional information about the thought processes of authoritarians; juror decision making is viewed as a vehicle for studying those processes rather than a goal in itself. On the other hand, we are not convinced that one cannot gain any insights about jurors in research such as this. For example, in research that has compared the information processing styles of individuals who have served on juries and the styles of college sophomores (Ostrom et al., 1978; Saks, Werner, & Ostrom, 1975), there were no differences, suggesting that we can make inferences about how actual jurors respond to trial evidence. This does not mean that we would expect the same conviction rates among actual trials and simulated trials, but that the psychological processes underlying convictions would be similar in the two situations. It is only by understanding the psychological processes that we can expand our understanding of juror behavior.

Reference Note

1. Bukoff, A., Moore, C. M., Landis, B., & Klein, R. *The video tape trial experience: Attorney beliefs and satisfaction.* Symposium presented at the biennial meeting of the American Psychology–Law Society, Baltimore, Maryland, 1979.

References

Adorno, T. W., Frenkel-Brunswik, E., Levinson, D. J., & Sanford, R. N. *The authoritarian personality.* New York: Harper, 1950.

Anderson, N. H. Cognitive algebra. In L. Berkowitz (Ed.), *Advances in experimental social psychology* (Vol. 7). New York: Academic Press, 1974.

Bermant, G., & Tapp, J. L. The notion of conspiracy is not tasty to Americans. *Psychology Today,* May 1975, pp. 60–63; 65–67.

Boehm, V. R., Mr. Prejudice, Miss Sympathy, and the authoritarian personality: An application of psychological measuring techniques to the problem of jury bias. *Wisconsin Law Review,* 1968, 734–750.

Broeder, D. The University of Chicago jury project. *Nebraska Law Review,* 1959, 38, 744–760.

Cohen, J., & Cohen, P. *Applied multiple regression/correlation analysis for the behavioral sciences.* Hillsdale, N.J.: Erlbaum, 1975.

Griffit, W., & Garcia, L. Reversing authoritarian punitiveness: The impact of verbal conditioning. *Social Psychology Quarterly,* 1979, 42, 55–61.

Harvey, O. J. & Beverly, G. D. Some personality correlates of concept change through role playing. *Journal of Abnormal and Social Psychology,* 1961, 63, 125–130.

Kagehiro, D. K. *Schema-based information processing of simulated jurors.* Unpublished doctoral dissertation, University of Utah, 1981.

Kaplan, M. F. Judgment by juries. In M. F. Kaplan & S. Schwartz (Eds.), *Human judgment and decision processes in applied settings.* New York: Academic Press, 1977.

Kerlinger, F. N., & Pedhazur, E. J. *Multiple regression in behavioral research.* New York: Holt, Rinehart & Winston, 1973.

Los Angeles County Superior Court. *California jury instructions: Criminal.* St. Paul, Minn.: West Publishing Co., 1970.

Lunney, G. H. Using analysis of variance with a dichotomous dependent variable: An empirical study. *Journal of Educational Measurement,* 1970, 4, 263–269.

Miller, G. R. Jurors' responses to videotaped trial materials: Some recent findings. *Personality and Social Psychology Bulletin,* 1975, 1, 561–569.

Mitchell, H. E., & Bryne, D. The defendant's dilemma: Effects of jurors' attitudes and authoritarianism on judicial decisions. *Journal of Personality and Social Psychology,* 1973, 25, 123–129.

Ostrom, T. M., Werner, C., & Saks, M. J. An integration theory analysis of jurors' presumptions of guilt or innocence. *Journal of Personality and Social Psychology,* 1978, 36, 436–450.

Rokeach, M., & Vidmar, N. Testimony concerning possible jury bias in a Black Panther murder trial. *Journal of Applied Social Psychology,* 1973, 3, 19–29.

Rosenthal, R. Combining results of independent studies. *Psychological Bulletin,* 1978, 85, 185–193.

Saks, M. J., Werner, C. M., & Ostrom, T. M. The presumption of innocence and the American juror. *Journal of Contemporary Law,* 1975, 2, 46–54.

Schulman, J., Shaver, P., Colman, R., Emrich, B., & Christie, R. Recipe for a jury. *Psychology Today,* May 1973, pp. 37–44; 77–84.

Sue, S., Smith, R. E., & Caldwell, C. Effects of inadmissible evidence on the decisions of simulated jurors: A moral dilemma. *Journal of Applied Social Psychology,* 1973, 3, 345–353.

Sue, S., Smith, R. E., & Pedroza, G. Authoritarianism, pretrial publicity, and awareness of bias in simulated jurors. *Psychological Reports,* 1975, 37, 1299–1302.

VanDyke, J. M. *Jury selection procedures: Our uncertain commitment to representative panels.* Cambridge, Mass.: Ballinger, 1977.

Wagman, M. Attitude change and authoritarian personality. *Journal of Psychology,* 1955, 40, 3–24.

White, B. J., Alter, R. D., & Rardin, M. Authoritarianism, dogmatism, and usage of conceptual categories. *Journal of Personality and Social Psychology,* 1965, 2, 293–295.

Wolf, S., & Montgomery, D. A. Effects of inadmissible evidence and level of judicial admonishment to disregard of the judgments of mock jurors. *Journal of Applied Social Psychology,* 1977, 7, 205–219.

Received May 15, 1981
Revision received April 5, 1982 ■

Journal of Personality and Social Psychology
1980, Vol. 38, No. 4, 662–667

Character Structure and Jury Behavior: Conceptual and Applied Implications

Carol J. Mills
Franklin and Marshall College

Wayne E. Bohannon
Johns Hopkins University

A model of character structure, conceptualized in terms of socialization, empathy, and autonomy, was used to analyze jurors' verdict patterns and self-reported perceptions of their role, their performance in that role, and the outcome of the jury process. Measures of character structure were significantly related to voting behavior, juror effectiveness, and perception of duty, as well as outcome. Sex, race, age, and education are shown to be important modifiers of the personality effects.

To what extent a juror's personal decision, as well as the group process of reaching a consensual decision, is influenced by individual differences in personality, attitudinal, and social (demographic) characteristics is an empirical question that has recently aroused interest within the research community. Part of this interest may be attributed to the political trials that have attracted national attention since the latter part of the 1960s (Simon, 1975). The jury selection teams for such trials (Schulman, Shaver, Colman, Emrich, & Christie, 1973) stress the individual characteristics of prospective jurors as determinants of jury behavior. Data from the Chicago Project (Broeder, 1959; Kalven & Zeisel, 1966) indicate that 90% of individual jurors' decisions are made prior to entering the jury deliberation room and that deliberations do not so much decide the case as bring about consensus. Erlanger (1970) points out that personal characteristics of jurors affect both the indi-

vidual's decision and the process through which the jury comes to its collective verdict.

Although the social characteristics of jurors are generally recognized as a determinant of jury behavior (Kalven & Zeisel, 1966; Sealy & Cornish, 1973; Simon, 1967), the effects of personality differences are seldom examined and are therefore poorly understood. As Emerson (1968) stated in the *Kentucky Law Review*, however, "It is essential that we never fall into the error of believing that the group is the smallest unit, as each individual is potentially capable of changing the appearance and overt response of that larger unit . . ." p. 840).

In the present study, three personality variables—socialization, empathy, and autonomy—were chosen for study. These variables have been conceptualized as dimensions of a person's orientation toward the social rules that govern behavior, a reflection of "largely unconscious, typified ways of selecting, using, justifying, and enforcing rules" (Hogan, 1976, p. 4). Hogan (1973, 1976) views this orientation as a person's "character structure," the aspect of personality that organizes one's responses to the ordinary rules and values of conventional society. Character structure has also been implicated in the process of reasoning about legal–moral problems (Hogan & Mills, 1976). The developmental sequence of such legal socialization is seen by some social scientists as involving a series of three stages that closely parallel the development· of

The authors thank Richard Christie, Robert Hogan, Milton Strauss, and Neil Vidmar for their helpful comments regarding an earlier version of this paper, and Scotti Kaminer for her assistance in scoring and analyzing the data. The research was supported in part by a grant from the Spencer Foundation and the city of Baltimore. Special thanks go to Baltimore City Jury Commissioner Frank Sliwka and Dan Lipstein of the Mayor's Coordinating Council on Criminal Justice.

Requests for reprints should be sent to Carol Mills, Department of Psychology, Franklin and Marshall College, P.O. Box 3003, Lancaster, Pennsylvania 17604.

socialization, empathy, and autonomy: (a) attunement to societal rules, (b) sensitivity to social and interpersonal expectations, and (c) the autonomous observance of legal and social rules (Durkheim, 1961; Hogan, 1973; McDougall, 1908; Rawls, 1971). It was believed that an examination of individual differences in character structure would provide insight into the dynamics involved in a juror's behavior during jury deliberations, a supposedly rule-oriented undertaking involving legal–moral reasoning. The primary purpose of the present study, therefore, was to investigate the effects of personality dynamics on jury decision making in terms of actual decisions rendered as well as individual jurors' perceptions of the deliberation process.

Studies of jury behavior tend to use college samples or mock jury trials, but the evidence (Berman, McGuire, McKinley, & Salo, 1974) suggests that the results obtained from such research are questionable. The present study chose to use actual jurors reporting on their behavior and the outcome of real jury trials in which they had taken part. Since the information available on jurors' behavior and the methods used to collect such information are severely limited by the courts (Kalven & Zeisel, 1966), this study relied exclusively on self-reported data. Information on final verdict, however, was available through court records. Although the present procedure is subject to all the problems associated with self-reported data, the advantages in terms of generalizability made it preferable to a procedure with college students playing at being jurors in mock trials.

The following predictions were made for the relationship between each of the three dimensions of character structure (socialization, empathy, and autonomy) and self-reported jury behavior.

1. Since highly socialized individuals are predisposed to follow social rules, values, and prohibitions—an orientation to obey the letter of the law rather than the spirit—they should be predisposed to reach more guilty verdicts. They should also be able to reach their decisions with relative ease and satisfaction, since they understand their duty to society clearly.

2. Highly empathic individuals are inclined to consider the viewpoint of others and thus

should consider the defendant's intentions in making their decisions. They should make more not-guilty verdicts. They should also be effective in influencing the decisions of other jurors, since the high empathy scorer is described as charming, poised, and tactful— qualities that should aid in influencing others.

3. Highly autonomous individuals are described as independent and decisive. They should be able to withstand group influence, influence other jurors, find the decision-making process relatively easy, and experience more satisfaction with their decision.

The relationships between the dimensions mentioned above and the demographic variables of sex, race, education, and age were examined using correlational analyses. It is important to understand these relationships, since high scores on any one of the personality variables may have very different effects on jury behavior, depending on the sex, race, education, or age of the juror. For instance, the possession of various personality characteristics often has very different implications for males and females (Tyler, 1965).

Method

Measures

The three dimensions of character structure in the present study—socialization, empathy, and autonomy —were measured by the following three scales: (a) the Socialization Scale (Gough, 1960) of the California Psychological Inventory (CPI; Gough, 1957), which assesses the degree to which an individual regards the rules, values, and prohibitions of society as personally mandatory; (b) the Empathy Scale (Hogan, 1969), which assesses the ability to take the viewpoint of others and the disposition to consider the implication of one's actions for the welfare of others (the Empathy Scale contains such items from the CPI and the Minnesota Multiphasic Personality Inventory as "I always try to consider the other fellow's feelings before I do something" and "I think I am usually a leader in my group"). It should be noted that the Empathy Scale used here has expanded the traditional concept of empathy. (c) The Autonomy Scale was developed from such items on the CPI as "My parents have generally let me make my own decisions" and "I value being independent of other people" (Kurtines, 1978). The Autonomy Scale assesses the degree to which an individual governs his or her actions by a personal sense of duty.

Information on general verdict patterns and individual juror effectiveness and influence, as well as satisfaction with and ease of decision, was ob-

Table 1
Questionnaire Sent to Jury Study Participants

Directions. Please choose *one* case (trial) you served on as a juror and that you would like to answer questions about. Use that *one* to answer the following questions. Please give only one answer for each question.

1. What was your personal decision in the case? (circle one)ᵃ   Guilty   Not Guilty
2. Were you the foreman in this case?   Yes   No   (circle one)ᵇ
3. Were you personally responsible for changing other jurors' decisions?   Yes   No   (circle one)
4. Did you believe that it was better to reach *some* decision, even if you were unsure of the right decision?   Yes   No   (circle one)
5. Was your personal decision in this case an easy one to make?   Yes   No   (circle one)
6. Were you, and are you now, satisfied with the decision reached?   Yes   No   (circle one)

ᵃ Guilty = 1. Not guilty = 0. ᵇ Yes = 1. No = 0.

tained through a self-report questionnaire (see Table 1). Information on final verdict was available through court records as a check on reliability. Since the purpose of this study was to examine the personality dynamics involved in jury decision making, it was deemed important to look at the final product (the decision reached) and the juror's perception of his or her role in the jury process, as well as effectiveness (and influence) in that role and, finally, the juror's attitude concerning the final outcome. Demographic information (race, sex, age, and education) about each juror was obtained through court records. This information is routinely recorded and kept on file for all prospective jurors.

Subjects

Participants were 117 females and 80 males who responded to a mailing originally sent to 226 males and 324 females randomly selected from the Baltimore city jury panels (i.e., persons who have served on juries) for a 6-month period. Although it is impossible to assess the biases introduced into the study by the nonresponders (there was a 40% response rate), when the present sample was compared with demographic characteristics, it was highly representative of both the general population and the jury population.

Materials and Procedure

Subjects received by mail a packet containing (a) a cover letter explaining the purpose of the study and instructions for completing the material; (b) a questionnaire dealing with the juror's perceptions of the trial experience and deliberations (see Table 1); (c) shortened versions of the Socialization, Empathy, and Autonomy scales; [1] (d) an answer sheet; and (e) a self-addressed, stamped envelope.

Results

Sex and race differences for each of the personality variables are shown in Table 2.

Black males scored significantly higher than black females on empathy. In addition, the socialization scores for black and white females differed significantly, with white females having a higher mean score. Black females had the lowest mean score for both socialization and empathy, whereas black males had the highest mean score for both variables. Black females also had the highest percentage of guilty votes (75%), followed by white females (69%), white males (61%), and black males (50%).

Table 3 presents the correlations for questionnaire items with personality variables for the total sample, as well as correlations for the two sexes. Significant differences between males' and females' correlations are noted in the table.

Socialization

Socialization increased with age ($r = .16$, $p < .05$) but was unrelated to education. A significant relationship between personal decisions (Item 1) and socialization scores was found for both males and females, albeit in different directions. In fact, the two correlations were significantly different from each

[1] The shortened versions of the Socialization, Empathy, and Autonomy Scales correlated with the long versions .89, .89, and .87, respectively. Reliability coefficients for the shortened scales were: Socialization, .79; Empathy, .78; and Autonomy, .75. All items for the three scales come from the CPI and can be scored on that test. For further information regarding these shortened scales, please write to the first author.

other ($p < .05$). For males, higher socialization scores were associated with a greater number of reported guilty verdicts. Higher socialization scores for females, however, were related to more not-guilty verdicts.

Males with higher socialization scores were more likely to believe that their duty was to reach a decision, regardless of their certainty about that decision (Item 4). Females with higher socialization scores found it easier to make a decision (Item 5), whereas males with higher socialization scores were more often satisfied with their decision (Item 6).

Empathy

In the present study, empathy scores increased with education level ($r = .33$, $p < .001$) but decreased with age ($r = -.15$, $p < .05$). For males, only empathy scores were positively correlated with not-guilty verdicts (Item 1), and this correlation was significantly different from that found for females ($p < .05$). Higher empathy scores for males were also related to their personal effectiveness in the role of juror in two ways—serving as jury foreman and influence on other jurors (Items

Table 2

Sex and Race Data for the Three Personality Scales

Sample	Socialization		Empathy		Autonomy	
	M	SD	M	SD	M	SD
Males						
Black ($n = 28$)	20.6	3.9	20.6	3.8	15.9	2.5
White ($n = 52$)	19.2	4.4	19.5	3.7	15.4	3.5
Females						
Black ($n = 55$)	18.3	3.6	18.6	4.2	14.9	4.2
White ($n = 62$)	20.2	3.3	19.7	3.9	15.9	2.8

Note. The number of items in the original personality scales as published and, in parentheses, the number of items in the shortened scales as scored for the present study are as follows: Socialization = 54 items (28 items); Empathy = 64 items (35 items); Autonomy = 38 items (26 items).

Table 3

Correlations for Questionnaire Items With Personality Variables

Scale	Questionnaire item[a]					
	1	2	3	4	5	6
Socialization						
Males	.19	.06	-.01	.20	.13	.18
Females	-.21	.09	-.08	.10	.21	-.02
Total	-.05	.09	-.03	.16	.17	.07
Empathy						
Males	-.23	.18	.22	-.01	.05	-.09
Females	-.03	.06	.13	-.07	.03	.09
Total	-.08	.11	.18	-.03	.03	-.01
Autonomy						
Males	-.21	-.04	.25	-.03	.07	-.09
Females	-.28	.01	.06	.10	.20	-.03
Total	-.25	-.01	.15	.04	.14	-.06

Note. Significance levels are for a one-tailed test. Males, $n = 80$; $r \geq .18$, $p \leq .05$; $r \geq .26$, $p \leq .01$; $r \geq .29$, $p \leq .005$. Females, $n = 117$; $r \geq .15$, $p \leq .05$; $r \geq .21$, $p \leq .01$; $r \geq .23$, $p \leq .005$. Total, $N = 197$; $r \geq .12$, $p \leq .05$; $r \geq .17$, $p \leq .01$; $r \geq .18$, $p \leq .005$.

[a] Questions were: 1. Personal decision: guilty = 1; not guilty = 0. 2. Foreman: yes = 1; no = 0. 3. Influence on others: yes = 1; no = 0. 4. Best to reach *some* decision: yes = 1; no = 0. 5. Easy decision: yes = 1; no = 0. 6. Satisfaction with decision: yes = 1; no = 0.

2 and 3). For the females in this sample, empathy was unrelated to any of the questionnaire items.

Autonomy

Autonomy increased with education ($r = .24$, $p < .001$) but was unrelated to age. The present study found that autonomy scores were positively related to verdicts for both males and females, with higher scores being related to more not-guilty verdicts (Item 1).

Males with high autonomy scores reported believing that they were personally responsible for changing other jurors' decisions (Item 3, a correlation that was significantly different from that found for females on this variable). Females with higher autonomy scores found their decision easier to make than did females with lower autonomy scores (Item 5).

Discussion

In general, the results confirmed predictions for the personality variables. Highly socialized individuals presumably regard society's rules as personally compelling (see Gough, 1960; Hogan, 1973). Consistent with this hypothesis, the present study found that high socialization scores were associated with the belief that the juror's purpose was to reach some decision (males only), even if the person was unsure of the right decision, and with ease (females) and satisfaction (males) in making that decision. Since the jury experience is a highly structured, rule-oriented situation, it is not surprising that well-socialized individuals would exhibit a strong, literal interpretation of their role as jurors and be able to execute this role with ease. Males and females, however, differ qualitatively in their performance of this role. Although a significant relationship was found between socialization scores and guilty verdicts for both sexes, the relation was in opposing directions. Thus, males with higher socialization scores gave more guilty verdicts, whereas females gave fewer.

Empathy reflects sensitivity to social expectations and general social competence. That empathic persons are persuasive and socially effective was partially borne out by the fact that, for males, empathy scores were associated with more not-guilty verdicts, selection as jury foreman, and the belief that the juror was responsible for influencing or changing other jurors' decisions.

Autonomous persons are self-contained and independent; a personal sense of duty governs their actions. High autonomy scores in the present study were correlated with more not-guilty verdicts for both sexes. Consistent with the hypothesis, high autonomy scores were positively related to personal effectiveness for males and ease of decision for females.

As expected, most of the relationships among the personality variables and the questionnaire items were modified somewhat by the demographic variables of sex, race, education, and age. This was particularly true for the demographic variable of juror sex, suggesting a qualitative difference between males and females with regard to the way personality variables are related to jury behavior. For instance, most of the not-guilty verdicts reported by males came from undersocialized but empathic and autonomous male jurors, whereas for females most not-guilty verdicts came from highly socialized but autonomous jurors. Such sex differences in the pattern of variables predictive of juror behavior are theoretically intriguing, but their analysis is beyond the scope of the present paper.

Education was positively related to both empathy and autonomy scores. These findings may indicate that a modicum of intelligence is a prerequisite for developing empathy and autonomy but is less important for simply following the rules.

In the present study, age was positively related to socialization scores but negatively related to empathy scores. A positive relationship has been found between age and maturity of legal–moral reasoning in adolescents (Adelson, Green, & O'Neill, 1969; Daurio & Hogan, Note 1). The nature of the relationship between age and legal–moral reasoning in adults, however, warrants further investigation.

In summary, the present results provide further evidence for the validity of socialization, empathy, and autonomy as measures of an individual's character structure (Hogan, 1969; 1973)—the aspect of personality that organizes one's responses to the rules and values of conventional society. The use of individual differences in character structure as an aid in understanding juror behavior is also supported by the present study. Although personality dynamics involved in the jury process were the primary interest in this study, it is apparent that the results will have implications for anyone interested in jury selection. Although the use of personality tests for selecting prospective jurors is controversial and problematic (Emerson, 1968), it may be preferable to our present system, which is based on intuition, stereotypes, and lawyers' idiosyncratic personality theories. If one considers the "noisiness" of the data and the attenuation effect caused by the elimination of extreme types by the prosecution and defense attorneys, the influence of individual differences in character structure appears worthy of careful consideration in future research.

Reference Note

1. Daurio, S., & Hogan, R. *The development of socio-political reasoning in verbally precocious children.* Paper presented at the meeting of the Eastern Psychological Association, New York, April 1976.

References

Adelson, J., Green, B., & O'Neill, R. Growth of the idea of law in adolescence. *Developmental Psychology*, 1969, *4*, 327–332.

Berman, G., McGuire, M., McKinley, W., & Salo, C. The logic of simulation in jury research. *Criminal Justice and Behavior*, 1974, *1*, 224–233.

Broeder, D. W. The University of Chicago Jury Project. *Nebraska Law Review*, 1959, *38*, 744–760.

Durkheim, E. *Moral education.* New York: Free Press, 1961.

Emerson, C. D. Notes: Personality tests for prospective jurors. *Kentucky Law Journal*, 1968, *56*, 840–854.

Erlanger, H. S. Jury research in America: Its past and future. *Law and Society Review*, 1970, *4*, 345–370.

Gough, H. G. *Manual for the California Psychological Inventory.* Palo Alto, Calif.: Consulting Psychologists Press, 1957.

Gough, H. G. Theory and measurement of socialization. *Journal of Consulting Psychology*, 1960, *24*, 23–30.

Hogan, R. Development of an empathy scale. *Journal of Consulting and Clinical Psychology*, 1969, *33*, 307–316.

Hogan, R. Moral conduct and moral character. *Psychological Bulletin*, 1973, *79*, 217–232.

Hogan, R. *Personality theory: The personological tradition.* Englewood Cliffs, N.J.: Prentice-Hall, 1976.

Hogan, R., & Mills, C. Legal socialization. *Human Development*, 1976, *19*, 261–276.

Kalven, H., & Zeisel, H. *The American jury.* Boston: Little, Brown, 1966.

Kurtines, W. A measure of autonomy. *Journal of Personality Assessment*, 1978, *42*, 253–257.

McDougall, W. *Social psychology.* London: Methuen, 1908.

Rawls, J. *A theory of justice.* Cambridge, Mass.: Harvard University Press, 1971.

Sealy, A. P., & Cornish, W. R. Jurors and their verdicts. *Modern Law Review*, 1973, *36*, 496–508.

Schulman, J., Shaver, P., Colman, R., Emrich, B., & Christie, R. Recipe for a jury. *Psychology Today*, June 1973, pp. 37–44; 77–84.

Simon, R. J. *The jury and the defense of insanity.* Boston: Little, Brown, 1967.

Simon, R. J. (Ed.) *The jury system in America.* Beverly Hills, Calif.: Sage, 1975.

Tyler, L. E. *The psychology of human differences.* New York: Appleton-Century-Crofts, 1965.

Received April 2, 1979 ∎

IMPACT ON SIMULATED JURORS OF TESTIMONY AS A FUNCTION OF NON-EVIDENTIAL CHARACTERISTICS OF WITNESS AND DEFENDANT[1]

VICTOR M. CATANO

Saint Mary's University

Summary.—The impact on jurors' decision making of the non-evidential characteristics of witnesses' and defendant's attractiveness and the agreement of their testimony was explored in a 2 × 2 × 2 between-subjects factorial design. 48 undergraduates read a summary of a courtroom trial in which an eyewitness, who was either a professional (High Attractive) or laborer (Low Attractive), either agreed or disagreed with the testimony of a defendant whose character had been assessed positively (High Attractive) or negatively (Low Attractive). Dependent variables were subjects' verdicts and confidence in the witnesses' and defendant's testimony. Conflict in testimony between the witness and defendant led to higher ratings of guilt but lowered the subject's confidence in the testimony of both. A significant interaction of witness × defendant × testimony showed that ratings of guilt decreased when a witness testified against a defendant who was dissimilar in attractiveness; an unattractive witness supporting an attractive defendant also reduced assessment of guilt but an attractive witness who testified for an unattractive defendant increased findings of guilt. Results were discussed in the context of relevant research involving simulated jurors.

In making its decisions, a jury is expected to evaluate, in an impartial manner, information that has been presented to it. Studies which have investigated decision-making in simulated juries often find a divergence between judicial ideals and social reality; non-evidential variables may substantially affect the jury's verdict.

The attractiveness of the people involved in the courtroom drama is one non-evidential variable that affects jurors' decisions. In this context, attractiveness has been represented by a likable, middle-class, upstanding citizen (Landy & Aronson, 1969; Nemeth & Sosis, 1973; Reynolds & Sanders, 1975) a good looking individual (Sigall & Ostrove, 1973), and positively rated personality traits (Kaplan & Kemmerick, 1974). This research has shown that so described attractive defendants are dealt with more leniently by simulated juries than are unattractive defendants (Landy & Aronson, 1969; Nemeth & Sosis, 1973; Reynolds & Sanders, 1975; Sigall & Landy, 1972). The effect of attractive witnesses is less clear. Garcia and Griffitt (1975) showed that, when testifying against a defendant, the likableness of a witness increased both the witness' credibility and the degree of guilt attributed to the defendant. Ludwig

[1]Requests for reprints should be sent to Victor M. Catano, Department of Psychology, Saint Mary's University, Halifax, Nova Scotia, Canada B3H 3C3. The author would like to thank Ms. Patricia Glenister for her assistance in the data collection.

and Fontaine (1978), in assessing the impact of "expert" testimony delivered against a defendant, indicated that verdicts and sentences were most severe following the expert testimony of a physician and least severe following expert testimony of a police officer. The occupation of physician ranks higher in status than police officer. If one assumes a relationship between status and attractiveness, Ludwig and Fontaine's data are consistent with the previous study's. Attractive witnesses influence the jury's decision to a greater extent than unattractive witnesses.

This study was designed to explore several unanswered questions raised by the previous research. How would attractiveness of a witness and a defendant interact in the same courtroom setting as their testimony agreed and differed? Would a highly attractive witness, testifying on behalf of an unattractive defendant, reduce the chance of conviction? Would a highly unattractive witness, testifying on behalf of an attractive defendant, increase the chance of conviction?

In an attempt to answer these questions, this study employed a $2 \times 2 \times 2$ between-subjects, factorial design, with witness' attractiveness (high/low), defendant's attractiveness (high/low), and the agreement between witness' and defendant's testimony (agree/disagree) as independent variables. The attractiveness of the defendant was manipulated through character descriptions using personality trait words with appropriate likeableness ratings (Kaplan & Kemmerick, 1974). The witness' attractiveness was altered through occupational status; unlike Ludwig and Fontaine's (1978) study, the witness' occupation was not relevant to the testimony. Dependent variables were verdicts and confidence in these verdicts rendered by the individual simulated jurors, as well as their confidence in the accuracy of the testimony given by the defendant and witness.

METHOD

Subjects

Forty-eight undergraduates at Saint Mary's, equally balanced for sex, volunteered to serve as simulated jurors; the students received credit toward a course requirement for their participation. Each student was randomly assigned to one of the eight groups specified by the $2 \times 2 \times 2$ functional design.

Procedure

Subjects were instructed that as part of a study on judicial decision-making they would be given a summary of an actual courtroom trial involving a traffic felony and that they would be asked to act as a juror in assessing the defendant's guilt.

The stimulus case was a modified version of one used by Kaplan and Kemmerick (1974) in which a truck driver is accused of negligent death in the fatal injury of a two-year-old child through failure to blow his horn when leaving a parking space. Character witnesses were reported as describing the highly attractive defendant as "polite and clever," while the low attractive defendant was portrayed as "boring and gloomy." These adjectives were taken from the appropriate end of Anderson's (1968) scale of likableness ratings of personality trait words. The adjectives were chosen so that none reflected characteristics which might foster an aura of negligence on the defendant's part.

The presence of the eyewitness at the scene of the accident was attributed to being on his way home from either "a conference at a nearby professional center" (highly attractive witness) or "a cleaning job at a nearby pool hall" (low attractive witness). The witness' testimony either supported the defendant's (agree) assertion that he had blown his horn in warning or contradicted that statement (disagree).

All subjects were given questionnaires designed to assess the degree of guilt attributed to the defendant, and their confidence in the accuracy of the eyewitness and defendant. Subjects responded on seven-point Likert-type scales anchored from "definitely not guilty" to "definitely guilty" for the first questions and "definitely inaccurate" to "definitely accurate" for the latter two.

RESULTS

The results of the analysis of variance on the question of guilt established a main effect for testimony ($F = 9.81$, $df = 1/40$, $p < .005$). Defendants were generally judged less guilty when their testimony and the witness' agreed ($M = 2.90$) than when they disagreed ($M = 4.30$). Surprisingly, in view of the previous research findings, neither witness' nor defendant's attractiveness produced significant main effects; however, a significant interaction between these variables did occur ($F = 4.42$, $df = 1/40$, $p < .05$). Regardless of testimony, pairing a witness and defendant of like attractiveness produced the highest judgments of guilt ($M = 4.25$; $M = 3.90$) while a witness and defendant who differed in attractiveness produced the least ($M = 3.55$; $M = 2.70$). When nature of the testimony was considered, however, a more complex effect appeared ($F = 6.61$, $df = 1/40$, $p < .025$). If the witness disagreed with the defendant, an effect similar to the interaction occurred: like levels of attractiveness produced higher judgments of guilt of defendant $\times$ witness ($M = 5.5$; $M = 5.2$) than dissimilar levels of attractiveness ($M = 2.8$; $M = 3.7$). This relationship did not hold when their testimony agreed. A highly attractive defendant supported by a low attractive witness was judged less guilty ($M = 1.7$) than when supported by a highly attractive witness ($M = 3.0$). However, a low attractive defendant supported by a highly attractive witness was judged more guilty ($M = 4.3$) than when supported by a low attractive witness ($M = 2.6$).

With regard to confidence in the accuracy of the eyewitness' testimony, a significant main effect was found for testimony ($F = 8.92$, $df = 1/40$, $p <$ .005). The simulated jurors felt more confident in the witness' testimony when it agreed ($M = 5.55$) than when it disagreed ($M = 4.58$) with the defendant's. The effect of witness $\times$ defendant $\times$ testimony was also significant ($F = 14.21$, $df = 1/40$, $p < .001$). When testimony was in conflict and the defendant and witness were of like attractiveness, the simulated jurors had more confidence in the witness' testimony ($M = 6.0$; $M = 4.8$) than when they differed in attractiveness ($M = 3.3$; $M = 4.2$). When their testimony agreed, more confidence was expressed for a low attractive witness supporting a highly attractive defendant ($M = 6.2$), while a highly attractive witness supporting a low attractive defendant ($M = 5.5$) produced about the same level of confidence as when both witness and defendant were of like attractiveness ($M = 5.2$; $M = 5.3$).

When the simulated jurors were asked to consider the question of accuracy of the defendant's testimony a significant main effect for testimony ($F = 17.71$, $df = 1/40$, $p < .001$) was found once more. Confidence in the accuracy of the defendant's testimony was reduced by contrasting testimony (Agree: $M = 5.63$; Disagree: $M = 4.15$). The interaction of the witness' attractiveness and testimony also was significant ($F = 6.25$, $df = 1/40$, $p < .025$). Confidence in the defendant's accuracy was greater supported by a low attractive witness ($M = 6.25$) instead of one who was highly attractive ($M = 5.0$) but that confidence was lower when the defendant was contradicted by a low attractive witness ($M = 3.9$) rather than a highly attractive one ($M = 4.4$).

DISCUSSION

Simulated jurors who were presented with contradictory testimony appeared to be more likely to believe the witness in judging the defendant guilty. Presumably, a witness' supportive testimony raised a reasonable doubt in the jurors' minds and with it, a reluctance to convict. This result changed in an intriguing fashion with the degree of attractiveness of witness and defendant. When a witness testified against a defendant, the jurors were more likely to express verdicts of guilty when the defendant and the witness were similar in attractiveness levels than when they differed. The simulated jurors expressed more confidence in the witness' testimony in the former case and less in the latter. Supportive testimony, however, did not always lead to a decrease in judgments of guilt. An attractive witness who agreed with an unattractive defendant's version of events caused an increase in judgments of guilt while an unattractive witness supporting an attractive defendant led to a decrease. Examination of the jurors' confidence in the accuracy of the witness and defendant substantiated this interaction. An attractive witness reduced the jurors' confidence in the unattractive defendant's testimony; on the other hand, the testimony of the unattractive witness who agreed with the attractive defendant was believed to be more accurate than for any other witness-defendant combination where testimony was in disagreement. The reasons for this are not immediately clear; perhaps, subjects for the group were predisposed to convict, i.e., they were a "hanging jury." They at least exhibited some degree of consistency between their verdicts and their expressed confidence in accuracy of witness and defendant.

The failure to find any major effects of defendant's attractiveness may have been related to the manner in which that variable was manipulated. The defendant was always a truck driver who was characterized as either "polite and clever" or "boring and gloomy." In previous work drinking habits, criminal record, physical attractiveness, and marital status had been used to alter attractiveness, and, generally, they produced straightforward data. The present study suggests that character assessment may affect the juror's decision in a more subtle, but complicated, fashion through interacting with witness' attractiveness and the nature of the testimony.

The non-significance of witness' attractiveness should also be noted, particularly in light of Ludwig and Fontaine's (1978) finding that occupational status of an expert witness affected both verdict and sentence. In the present study in which an eyewitness presented factual evidence, occupational status, professional vs laborer, did not affect judgments of guilt or confidence in the testimony of either witness or defendant. Apparently, the simulated jurors had similar confidence in either type of eyewitness to report accurately on observed events.

Nemeth and Sosis (1973) found that white jurors attributed more drinking to a white defendant than to a black one. They suggested the effect might be due to the subjects "bending over backwards" to avoid ascribing negative stereotyped evaluations to blacks. A similar effect occurred in the present study when an attractive witness testified against the unattractive defendant. The subjects tended to believe in the defendant's innocence ($M = 2.8$) and the accuracy of his testimony ($M = 5.0$) as opposed to that of the witness ($M = 3.3$). This "bend over backwards" attitude may reflect a desire on the part of university students to appear "open-minded," particularly in an abstract situation.

As with any experimental results, extreme care must be taken in the nature of generalizations that are drawn from the data. In research with simulated jury this point cannot be over emphasized. Any effects must be viewed as suggestive rather than definitive in any attempted extrapolation to real-life events. Studies with simulated jury can provide useful information concerning the evidential and non-evidential factors which may influence jury's decision-making procedures and may lead to the incorporation of those factors into theoretical explanations. The models that have been proposed by Calder, Insko, and Yandell (1974), Thomas and Hogue (1976), and Schum (1975) have all recognized the need to account for idiosyncratic juror behaviors that have been identified through simulated jury research.

REFERENCES

ANDERSON, N. H. Likableness ratings of 555 personality-trait words. *Journal of Personality and Social Psychology*, 1968, 9, 272-279.

CALDER, B. J., INSKO, C. A., & YANDELL, B. Relation of cognitive and memorial processes to persuasion in a simulated jury trial. *Journal of Applied Social Psychology*, 1974, 4, 62-93.

GARCIA, L. T., & GRIFFITT, W. Impact of testimonial evidence as a function of witness characteristics. Paper presented at the meeting of the Psychonomic Society, Denver, 1975.

KAPLAN, M. P., & KEMMERICK, G. D. Juror judgment as information integration: combining evidential and non-evidential information. *Journal of Personality and Social Psychology*, 1974, 30, 403-499.

LANDY, D., & ARONSON, E. The influence of the character of the criminal and his victim on the decision of simulated jurors. *Journal of Experimental and Social Psychology*, 1969, 5, 141-152.

LUDWIG, K., & FONTAINE, G. Effect of witnesses' expertness and manner of delivery of testimony on verdicts of simulated jurors. *Psychological Reports*, 1978, 42, 955-961.

NEMETH, C., & SOSIS, R. H. A simulated jury study: characteristics of the defendant and jurors. *Journal of Social Psychology*, 1973, 90, 221-229.

REYNOLDS, D. E., & SANDERS, M. S. Effect of defendant attractiveness, age and injury on severity of sentence given by simulated jury. *Journal of Social Psychology*, 1975, 96, 149-150.

SCHUM, D. A. The weighing of testimony in judicial proceedings from sources having reduced credibility. *Human Factors*, 1975, 17, 172-182.

SIGALL, H., & LANDY, D. Effects of the defendant's character and suffering on juridic judgment: a replication and clarification. *Journal of Social Psychology*, 1972, 88, 149-150.

SIGALL, H., & OSTROVE, N. The effects of the physical attractiveness of the defendant and the nature of the crime on juridic judgment. *Proceedings, 81st Annual Meeting, American Psychological Association*, 1973, 8, 267-268.

THOMAS, E. A., & HOGUE, A. Apparent weight of evidence, decision criteria, and confidence ratings in juror decision making. *Psychological Review*, 1976, 83, 442-465.

Accepted February 6, 1980.

The Role of Extralegal Factors
in Jury Verdicts*

Marilyn Chandler Ford**

Jury verdicts may not always be based on legally relevant evidence. A variety of extralegal factors may intrude in jury decision making. This article reviews the literature on individual juror characteristics, trial processes, and group dynamics that may bias jury verdicts. It is concluded that while some extralegal effects are evident, on the whole American juries perform remarkably well. Two already established procedures, the voir dire and judicial instructions, are discussed as means to mitigate the influence of extralegal factors on jury verdicts.

Introduction

It is commonly assumed that the jury's decision is a public measure of the merits of the prosecution and defense cases (e.g., Saks and Kidd, 1980/81:123). In the logic of legal scholars, facts lead the juror almost inescapably to a certain conclusion. In an almost computeresque fashion the juror marches to the cadence of evidence and logically achieves a verdict. Unhappily, this decisional model may not be appropriate except in the most clear cut cases. A verdict is conditioned by the facts of the case and the value assigned each. In addition, a variety of extralegal factors may intrude. In the adversarial context of a trial, truth often becomes shaded and certainty is frequently replaced by judgment calls.

In such a context extralegal factors such as jury composition, group dynamics, and trial processes may influence the verdict. A different mix of jurors, different evidentiary presentations, and different trial strategies may in fact lead to a different verdict. Jurors interpret evidence within the context of their own unique experiences. Since one's experiential base is in part a function of one's sex, race, age and personality, all of these factors have potential for influencing verdicts. Further complicating the decisional process, juror verdicts may well be moderated or changed by the

---

*An earlier version of this paper was presented at the annual conference of the American Society of Criminology, Cincinnati, Ohio, 1984. Robert E. Ford and several anonymous reviewers provided helpful comments on earlier drafts of this article. However, errors of fact or omission are solely my responsibility.
**Assistant Professor, Criminology and Criminal Justice Program at Niagara University.

THE JUSTICE SYSTEM JOURNAL, Volume 11, Number 1, 1986

group process. Factors inherent in trial, such as evidence presentation or reactions to witnesses' testimony, also may shape jurors' decisions.

This article examines the influence of extralegal factors on jury verdicts. Three questions shape this review. First, in what ways are extralegal factors linked to jury verdicts? Second, are extralegal factors so intrusive that it is necessary to devise legal procedures to limit their influence? And finally, to what extent can legal procedures limit the biasing aspects of such factors?

The literature on juries is voluminous and often repetitive. For brevity, the focus here is on jury research during the past ten years, with occasional reference to older works that made especially significant contributions. While international comparisons are currently very popular, a transnational analysis of juries has not been undertaken. Trial systems and jury usages are sufficiently idiosyncratic to justify a solely American review.

A focus on three areas in which extralegal influences may intrude also limits this inquiry. Individual juror characteristics that may prejudice are considered first. Trial processes that may bias are then analyzed. Group processes that may promote or restrict bias are considered last. The article concludes with a discussion of legal procedures that might be used to limit bias and the methodologies employed in jury research.

Personal Characteristics of Jurors and Their Impacts Upon Verdict

A jury panel is a collection of individuals. The individuals possess unique social and demographic characteristics, temperaments and attitudes. How individual juror characteristics may be related to jury decision making is discussed below.

Social and Demographic Characteristics. Traditionally, gender has been thought to influence verdict. Even Clarence Darrow expressed a definite preference for male jurors (Simon, 1967:103). While conventional wisdom holds that women are more lenient than men, early research indicated no such uniform effect (see Stephan, 1975 for a review). More recent studies have generally supported this finding. The one exception lies in studies of "death-qualified" jurors, which found that those jurors excluded (because of anti-death penalty attitudes) are more likely both to favor the accused and to be female (Fitzgerald and Ellsworth, 1984; Thompson *et al.*, 1984; Winick, 1982).

In fact, the majority of studies indicate that women are *more* conviction prone than men. While such findings have typically been derived from mock rape trials (Davis *et al.*, 1975; Jacobson, 1981; Nagao and Davis, 1980a), there is evidence that females may be conviction prone in other

17

cases as well. Mills and Bohannon (1980b) found gender related to guilty verdicts in robbery cases. Surprisingly, gender and race also interacted for all crime types compared, with black females more likely to convict in murder, rape and robbery (Mills and Bohannon, 1980b). In related work, Constantini *et al.* (1983) and Constantini and King (1980/81) found women more likely to prejudge guilt of three defendants charged in separate cases of murder and rape. The relationship persisted even when amount of information about the case, political attitudes, and level of education were controlled.

While these data suggest that females may be more conviction prone than previously thought, other data suggest that the relationship between gender and conviction orientation is far from clear. No relationship has been found between gender and estimates of guilt (Davis *et al.*, 1981; LaFree *et al.*, 1985; Villemur and Hyde, 1983); between gender and law-fulness ratings, attribution of causality or sentence recommendations (Archer *et al.*, 1979); or between gender and verdict (Bridgeman and Marlowe, 1979; Cowan *et al.*, 1984; Moran and Comfort, 1982; Villemur and Hyde, 1983). Furthermore, the differences in findings do not appear merely attributable to the methodology employed or to the type of stimulus (case materials) used. In summary, there does not appear to be a clear relationship between gender and verdict. However, the data do suggest that there may well be interaction effects between crime type, gender and willingness to convict. There may also be interaction between race, gender and verdict. In the following section we shall also observe interaction effects between gender and age.

Leniency has traditionally been correlated with youthfulness. In fact, jury simulation tests have been questioned on the grounds that the subject populations differ in age from actual jury panels. Some current data confirm the popular wisdom that the young (those under 25 years) are more likely to be lenient in verdict, sentencing, and other assessments (Ackerman *et al.*, 1984; Feild and Barnett, 1978; Hinkle *et al.*, 1983; Mills and Bohannon, 1980b).[1]

However, Mills and Bohannon (1980b) found age effects to be mediated by gender. While guilty verdicts by females remained high across all age levels, male guilty verdicts increased with age. They also report an interaction effect between age and crime type, with older males more likely

---

1. The lone possibly conflicting set of data found younger (17-21 year olds) as well as older (30 years and older) college students to deliver harsher verdicts than the transitional age group (22-29 year olds); see Reed (1980).

18

to convict in the case of rape but less likely to convict in the case of murder. Yet in a study design parallel to Mills and Bohannon's, Moran and Comfort (1982) found age to be uncorrelated with verdict even when controlling for gender or crime type; no significant relationship between age and verdict has been found by others (Bridgeman and Marlowe, 1979; Cowan *et al.*, 1984; LaFree *et al.*, 1985). In sum, the relationship between youthfulness and leniency is less than clearly defined. While a patterning of leniency and age does appear, it may be mediated by crime type and gender.

Tests of the effect of a juror's race upon jury verdict are few. The more common investigation of the impact of race upon jurors' decision making involves consideration of the race of the defendant and/or the victim, since it appears that race effects interact. LaFree *et al.* (1985) found no relationship between the race of the juror and estimates of the defendant's guilt in actual rape trials. Mills and Bohannon (1980b) reported black females were more likely to convict than either black males, white females or white males. Data from the "death-qualified" jury studies suggest a very different relationship, however. Those removed from jury panels because of anti-death penalty attitudes were more likely to acquit the defendant and also more likely to be black (Fitzgerald and Ellsworth, 1984; Thompson *et al.*, 1984).

Education and social class are other characteristics of jurors that might influence their verdicts. The few existing studies achieved mixed findings. No relationship was found between education and verdict in three studies (Bridgeman and Marlowe, 1979; Cowan *et al.*, 1984; LaFree *et al.*, 1985). In contrast, Constantini *et al.* (1983) and Constantini and King (1980/81) found the better educated less likely to report prejudging guilt, and Mills and Bohannon (1980b) found the better educated less likely to convict. Education may interact to some extent with crime type, since Mills and Bohannon also found the less educated to convict more frequently in a rape case than in a murder or robbery case (1980b:29).

Findings with respect to social class mirror the ambiguity of studies examining the impact of education on verdict. Studies have failed to find a relationship between verdict and occupational status (LaFree *et al.*, 1985) or social class (Moran and Comfort, 1982—at least with respect to females). However, Moran and Comfort also found low income males more likely to convict, again suggesting the relationship may be complex, varying by jurors' gender (1982:1057,1058).

In summary, the influence of social and demographic factors on juror behavior is unclear. The relationships appear complex—perhaps mediated by specific case characteristics, other demographic factors or personality

19

variables. While social and demographic effects are ambiguous, the impact of attitudinal or personality types appear more straightforward. The next section considers how individual personality characteristics influence juror decision making.

Jurors' Attitudes and Personality. An individual's outlook on life in general, and on crime in particular, may condition decision making. Prior experiences may also alter subsequent judgments. In general, the effects of personality and attitudes appear more robust and direct than effects of social and demographic characteristics. Persons possessing law and order attitudes or conservative beliefs about crime are more likely to express prosecution biases (Constantini *et al.*, 1983; Constantini and King, 1980/81; Kaplan and Miller, 1978; LaFree *et al.*, 1985). They are also more likely to report prejudging when exposed to pre-trial publicity (Constantini *et al.*, 1983; Constantini and King, 1980/81).

A related body of work explores the relationship between authoritarianism and verdict. Authoritarian personalities have been found more likely to convict (Berg and Vidmar, 1975; Bray and Noble, 1978; Cowan *et al.*, 1984; Moran and Comfort, 1982; Werner *et al.*, 1982). Berg and Vidmar's work suggests that cognitive as well as motivational or affective differences explain verdicts of those rated as "high" and "low" authoritarians. The high authoritarians remembered information about the character of the defendant while the low authoritarians remembered situational information—the facts of the crime (Berg and Vidmar, 1975:152). High authoritarians have also been found especially punitive to low status defendants (Berg and Vidmar, 1975), to rate defendants as unlike themselves (Bray and Noble, 1978), and to be more punitive to those rated as dissimilar (Berg and Vidmar, 1975).

Authoritarianism has also been correlated with attitudes favoring the death penalty (Bray and Noble, 1978; Cowan *et al.*, 1984). Persons favoring the death penalty also tend to possess conservative attitudes toward crime control (Bray and Noble, 1978; Cowan *et al.*, 1984; Fitzgerald and Ellsworth, 1984; Thompson *et al.*, 1984). These latter findings are of particular interest due to Sixth Amendment challenges to jury panel composition in cases in which death is a prescribed penalty upon conviction. The U.S. Supreme Court's ruling in *Witherspoon v. Illinois* (1968)[2] upheld the practice of excluding individuals from jury panels who were categorically opposed to the death penalty, and more recently in *Wainwright v. Witt*

---

2. The state may exclude jurors who make clear "that their attitude toward the death penalty would prevent them from making an impartial decision as to the defendant's guilt."

(1985),[3] the Court permitted exclusion when individuals expressed reservations about such punishment. The resulting "death qualified" jury panels, consisting of those individuals who are not opposed to capital punishment, may well be qualitatively different than jury panels in non-capital cases (but see Finch and Ferraro, 1986).

Death-qualified jurors have been found to be more oriented toward crime control, favoring a swift and efficient criminal justice system and supportive of the prosecution (Cowan et al., 1984; Fitzgerald and Ellsworth, 1984; Thompson et al., 1984). The excluded jurors have been found more sensitive to constitutional protections and to possible defenses (Ellsworth et al., 1984; Fitzgerald and Ellsworth, 1984).

Death-qualified and excluded jurors differ not only in general attitudes on crime and justice, but in perceptions of trial evidence and the level of reasonable doubt necessary to convict (Cowan et al., 1984; Thompson et al., 1984). Death-qualified jurors rated the prosecutor as more competent and credible, and the state's witnesses as more impressive. Ratings of the defense did not differ in the two groups. Further, for death-qualified jurors there was a lower threshold of reasonable doubt. Thompson et al. and Cowan et al. suggest that it is the companion attitudes about crime and justice, and not capital punishment attitudes per se, which result in death jurors' biased interpretations of trial testimony.

Evidence for personality effects have been found in some cases (Archer et al., 1979; Mills and Bohannon, 1980a; Moran and Comfort, 1982) but not in others (Ackerman et al., 1984). The effect of empathy on verdict has been examined most frequently. While empathy leads to greater identification with the accused, it does not necessarily lead to leniency since empathy is also conditioned by similarity between juror and accused (Archer et al., 1979). Further, its effect on verdict also appears mediated by gender (Archer et al., 1979; Deitz et al., 1982; Mills and Bohannon, 1980a; Moran and Comfort, 1982) and type of crime (Deitz et al., 1982). It is also important to distinguish between empathy for the victim as opposed to empathy for the defendant. Female subjects were more empathetic to *victims* of rape and thus, expressed greater certainty in the *defendant's guilt* (Deitz et al., 1982). As with studies of social and demographic characteristics, personality factors appear to interact with a series of case specific and individual traits in affecting judgments of guilt.

Prior Juror Experience. It has often been assumed that those with prior

---

3. The Court extended broad discretion to the trial courts to exclude jurors, based on good sense and intuition, notwithstanding the juror's inability to declare clearly his capacity to impose the death penalty (see also Finch and Ferraro, 1986:62,63).

21

jury experience develop a prosecution bias. Studies employing simulation designs and post-trial surveys of actual jurors provide little substantiation of this assumption (Cowan et al., 1984; Kassin and Juhnke, 1983; LaFree et al., 1985). Yet two archival studies of criminal trials indicate that jury panels containing a larger number of experienced jurors are more apt to convict (Dillehay and Nietzel, 1985; Werner et al., 1985). The discrepancy between these studies is not easily reconciled. On the one hand, differences in methodology, time periods or jurisdictions studied, or units of analysis (jurors versus juries) may account for the source of variation. On the other hand, the literature clearly suggests the group deliberative process affects case outcome only minimally; most jurors do not shift their pre- and post-deliberation verdicts (see e.g., Kalven and Zeisel, 1966).

While jurors' prior case experience becomes a referent in subsequent judgments, the relative patterning of cases may contribute to judgment effects (Kerr et al., 1982; Nagao and Davis, 1980b).[4] Nagao and Davis (1980b) found that jurors who served in trials of serious crimes were less likely to convict in later cases involving minor offenses. Thus, order of cases (strong-weak, weak-strong) may contribute to either lenient or punitive verdicts.

It is important to consider whether trial processes create the opportunity for bias. The next section considers features intrinsic to trial that affect attitude.

Environment and Actors: Trial Processes and Participants

Jurors do not consider trial testimony in a vacuum. The courtroom has its own milieu; each trial has its own ambiance, derived from a variety of factors—from the physical setting of the courtroom to the demeanor of the trial participants. Techniques of communication employed by prosecuting and defense attorneys may influence jurors' judgments. This section reviews, first, those features of trial that are relatively constant from one trial to the next (e.g., order of case presentation). Case factors that may be expected to vary from one case to another (e.g., demeanor of witnesses or defendant) are then considered.

The format of trial is highly structured with prosecuting and defense attorneys following a specific order in presentation. Questions relative to the phenomenon of primacy and recency arise here. The law of primacy

---

4. In both of these studies the mock jurors accumulated their "experience" by responding to successive case stimuli within the time period of the simulation. In the courtroom, prior jury experience is developed over a longer time span. Delay may, therefore, reduce the saliency of prior case judgments in actual trial comparisons.

22

asserts that arguments presented first are more salient than successive ones. The law of recency states a converse effect, that the last word is the best (Lawson, 1969:121,125).

Primacy effects appear under certain conditions. These conditions include: when the prosecutor presents a strong opening statement (Pyszczynski and Wrightsman, 1981), if the information conveyed relates specifically to persons—e.g., to their credibility (Lind, 1982; Linz and Penrod, 1984; Pennington, 1982), or is particularly vivid (Pennington, 1982), and when the listener has been exposed to the message previously (Lawson, 1969). Recency effects are most salient when: the defense attorney's opening statement is stronger than the prosecutor's (Pyszczynski and Wrightsman, 1981), delay occurs between presentation of the state's and defense's cases (Linz and Penrod, 1984), and general or attitudinal information is conveyed (Lind, 1982).

A related body of work compares the persuasiveness of evidence types. The parable, more vivid and concrete, is better remembered over recitals of fact or logic (Bank and Poythress, Jr., 1982:187; Linz and Penrod, 1984:45; Saks and Kidd, 1980/81:137). Others have tested the effects of mediums of evidence presentation: oral descriptions, photographs, modular representations, and videotapes. The body of data support the potency of more visual displays (Wasserman and Robinson, 1980; Whalen and Blanchard, 1982).

The emphasis on visual portrayals to produce greater realism has led to the use of videotapes in civil and criminal cases. Videotapes have been used in personal injury cases to convey the trauma and to recreate accident scenes (Colver, 1981; Perlman, 1981). In the criminal arena they have been used less frequently, to record depositions of witnesses who are elderly or in ill health and to present testimony of expert witnesses. More recently, several jurisdictions have pre-recorded entire trials for later viewing by jurors (Bermant et al., 1975).

Pre-recorded videotapes of civil cases have been rated as objective reproductions of trials (Bermant et al., 1975:994). However, that study also suggests that pre-recorded videotaped trials might promote juror bias. The jurors surveyed believed the black and white tape to be less sensational than a color video and would restrict video usage to civil cases. Kassin's simulation study (1984) found that while most jurors eventually adjust to televised proceedings, television cameras may distract jurors who are especially self-conscious. Effects inherent in the medium, such as camera angle or type of camera shot, might produce subtle—and subliminal—psychological cues. Kaminski and Miller (1984) varied type of witness

23

(strong versus weak) and type of camera shot (close-up, medium, long shot). Interaction between witness type and type of shot employed was evident: the strong (or composed) witness was thought most qualified in the closer range shots and the weak witness was perceived most favorably in the long shot, when nervous body movements (tics, wetting the lips) were less distracting.

Several studies suggest that adversariness may contribute to bias. Vidmar and Laird (1983) found that placing a witness in an adversary role induced juror bias in assessing his later testimony. Kaplan and Miller (1978) found that attacks on the trustworthiness or validity of evidence, characteristic of trial processes, accentuated existing biases in subsequent judgments.

Defendant Characteristics. A substantial number of studies have focused on variable trial features, such as defendants' or witnesses' characteristics. Not surprisingly, the largest number of studies have examined jurors' reactions to defendants, in particular defendant attractiveness and credibility (see Dane and Wrightsman, 1982 for a comprehensive review).

Attractiveness may reference physical beauty. It also may refer to social attractiveness, as measured by an individual's ascribed or achieved characteristics—age, race, social class. In addition, an individual may be considered attractive because he is perceived as being less blameworthy or morally culpable (what has been termed character attractiveness). Attractiveness may influence jurors because it affects liking for the person and estimates of the individual's social worth, or because it affects perceptions of similarity between defendant and juror.

The data generally demonstrate that perceptions of attractiveness are associated with leniency in jury verdicts, and unattractiveness with verdict severity. Physical beauty has generally been found to promote leniency effects (see Berg and Vidmar, 1975; Dane and Wrightsman, 1982; Jacobson, 1981; Weiten and Diamond, 1979). Interestingly, physical beauty may be a double-edged sword for female defendants. Although beauty is generally associated with leniency, it may lead to more punitive judgments if the crime was facilitated by a criminal's good looks (Sigall and Ostrove, 1975; Smith and Hed, 1979 but compare McFatter's study of males, 1978).

Socially attractive individuals may also fare well. Using demographic factors such as employment status, SES or marital status, composite profiles of socially attractive and unattractive defendants have been tested. The socially unattractive tend to be convicted more frequently (LaFree *et al.,* 1985; Meyers, 1980) and to be sentenced to longer terms (Feild and

24

Barnett, 1978).

Only a few demographic factors of the defendant appear to be consistent indicators of verdict severity or leniency. For example, socioeconomic status and race are the characteristics most often cited as influencing jurors' verdicts. However, while many studies report that higher SES individuals are more likely to receive leniency (Feild and Barnett, 1978; LaFree et al., 1985; Meyers, 1980), a number of studies find low SES defendants no more likely to be convicted than acquitted (Dane and Wrightsman, 1982; Hoffman, 1981).

Data on defendants' race are perhaps more persuasive (see Johnson, 1985 for a comprehensive review). Minority defendants appear to be penalized more heavily than white defendants (Denno, 1981; Feild, 1979; Johnson, 1985). Defendants' race also appears to interact strongly with victims' race (Feild, 1979; Meyers, 1980) and jurors' race (Ugwuegbu, 1979). Jurors, both black and white, are more punitive to other-race than same-race defendants (Ugwuegbu, 1979), and more likely to hold a defendant responsible when the victim is the same race as the juror (Miller and Hewitt, 1978; Ugwuegbu, 1979). Jurors are also more punitive if the victim and defendant are of different races and more lenient if victim and defendant are of the same race (Johnson, 1985; Meyers, 1980).

Defendants receiving more favorable character ratings were found more likely to be judged not guilty, although negative character evaluations were not associated with verdict (Howard and Levinson, 1985). Remorseful defendants have also been treated more leniently (Villemur and Hyde, 1983). Prior criminal record might also be interpreted by jurors as evidence of a defendant's moral character. LaFree's et al., (1985) analysis of actual rape trials revealed those with prior records were more likely to be judged guilty, contradicting Meyer's (1980) earlier analysis of archival records of undifferentiated felony trials.

Adverse judgments concerning defendants who were perceived as discreditable or blameworthy have been reported in actual criminal trials (Meyers, 1979) and in simulated civil trials (Whalen and Blanchard, 1982). Jurors rely on nonverbal behaviors in assessing defendants' credibility. The defendant who exhibits few signs of anxiety (good eye contact, few speech errors, few bodily movements) is more likely to be perceived as credible and less likely to be convicted (Pryor and Buchanan, 1984). Credibility might also be imputed from the defendant's willingness to take the stand and testify on his own behalf (Shaffer and Sadowsky, 1979).

Victim and Witness Characteristics. While few studies of victim or witness credibility exist, the results suggest conclusions compatible with

25

findings from studies of defendant characteristics. A defendant accused of raping an attractive woman was thought more likely to be guilty than one raping an unattractive woman (Jacobson, 1981) and assailants of unattractive women received more lenient sentences (Feild, 1979). Meyers (1980) found conviction more likely when the victim was classified as respectable or blameless, based on age and marital status. Disreputable victims or victims whose behavior might have contributed to an attack foster greater leniency for the defendant (Feild, 1979; LaFree et al., 1985; Miethe, 1984). However, these findings are disputed in studies which find no relationship between verdict and victim's attractiveness (physical beauty or social attractiveness) (Villemur and Hyde, 1983) or victim's disreputable behaviors and verdict (Meyers, 1980).

As with studies of a defendant's credibility, a witness' credibility may be enhanced by a strong presentation and composure (Kaminski and Miller, 1984). In Goodman et al.'s study (1984), child witnesses were perceived as less credible than adults, yet the rating of defendant's guilt did not vary substantially by witnesses' ages. Meyers' (1979) findings may or may not be interpreted as supportive of Goodman. On the one hand, Meyer found jurors less likely to convict in cases in which the victim was young, suggesting that the young may be perceived as less credible. On the other hand, she found little evidence that juries were concerned with the evidence offered by victims or their credibility.

Lawyer and Judge Characteristics. While trial manuals advise attorneys about the importance of their behavior in influencing jurors, few studies have manipulated these variables to assess their effect. Furthermore, there is little assessment of whether the trial judge's demeanor may communicate a prosecution or defense bias. The available data, although sparse, suggest that behavior of legally-trained participants does have an effect on jury behavior. In Kaplan and Miller's (1978) simulation study, jurors were biased towards guilt when the defense attorney's behavior was offensive and, to some extent, when the judge's behavior was annoying. Chaney (1983) found jurors reported annoyance with the judge and prosecutor as a result of being sequestered during trial; several jurors also believed they were influenced when the judge or prosecuting attorney spoke sharply. Blanck et al., (1985) document that trial judges' expectations concerning verdict influenced their verbal and nonverbal behavior and were related to actual verdict. Reactance effects to overbearing judges have been demonstrated, with jurors opposing directives given in judicial instructions (Lenehan and O'Neill, 1981). Bridgeman and Marlowe's study (1979) of actual jurors stands in contrast: jurors attached little importance

26

to the effectiveness of the lawyers or judge in reaching their verdicts. Such a finding may well illustrate the hazards of post-trial interviews, since individuals are not particularly adept at distinguishing the factors influencing their judgments.

Pretrial Publicity and Case Characteristics. Hassett, in a historical treatment of pretrial publicity, notes that we should separate prior knowledge that "may have a liberating influence on the mind from that which is fodder for confirming prejudice" (1980:162). Notwithstanding his legitimate distinction, there appears reason to restrict seating jurors exposed to adverse pretrial publicity (Constantini *et al.,* 1983; Constantini and King, 1980/81; Hoiberg and Stires, 1973; Pawdawer-Singer and Barton, 1975). The effects of pretrial publicity may well vary by gender—females have been found more likely to be influenced (Constantini *et al.,* 1983; Constantini and King, 1980/81; Hoiberg and Stires, 1973).

Pretrial publicity need not be case-specific. More general information prominently reported in the media about similar types of crimes, "troublemakers" as a generic group, or other disasters may create adverse impressions transferrable to judgements in criminal cases (Greene and Loftus, 1984; Pawdawer-Singer and Barton, 1975). In sum, it appears that pretrial publicity increases juror bias. However, unfavorable pretrial publicity may not be equally damaging to all cases (Pawdawer-Singer and Barton, 1975).

The nature of a case may also promote bias. The discussion above suggests two types of cases which may be particularly sensitive to such effects: rape and capital offenses. Both gender and attitudes have been found to be related to decision making in sexual assault cases (Deitz *et al.,* 1982; Feild, 1979; LaFree *et al.,* 1985; Meyers, 1980). Death penalty cases present a similar convergence of juror personality type with crime/punishment scenario (Cowan *et al.,* 1984; Fitzgerald and Ellsworth, 1984: Thompson *et al.,* 1984).

Verdicts are not likely to be independent when several charges are adjudicated simultaneously. When offenses are joined at trial, particularly if they are similar, the likelihood of conviction for any offense increases (Bordens and Horowitz, 1985; Tanford *et al.,* 1985; Tanford and Penrod, 1984b). A corollary issue raised in joinder cases is the order in which the charges are decided. By and large, charge order—both absolute and relative positions—influences jurors' decision making (Davis *et al.,* 1984; Nagao and Davis, 1980b). Comparisons of the strength of evidence against the defendant in a joined trial may also occur and bias verdict (Kerr *et al.,* 1982).

27

In summary, trial processes may promote bias. Their biasing influence may vary according to individual jurors' demographics or personality traits. However, such interactions remain unsubstantiated.

Group Dynamics in Jury Decision Making

Some researchers minimize the role of the group in producing jury verdicts (Bridgeman and Marlowe, 1979; Kalven and Zeisel, 1966). Nonetheless, a considerable proportion of research on jury panels has examined the structure and function of the group (Davis et al., 1975; Wasserman and Robinson, 1980).

Many recent studies of jury processes have dealt with size and decision rules (see Roper, this issue). These aspects of jury systems have been regulated to a large extent by court decisions and present legal issues beyond the scope of this article. Therefore, this discussion proceeds by only minimally reviewing some of the more pertinent evidence about group dynamics.

Studies of jury size do suggest that size affects competency. Saks (1977) found smaller juries promoted more equal discussion among members and better recall of other members' arguments. However, he also observed that the members were less likely to recall as much trial testimony. Six-member panels show less consistency between their predisposition and verdict than twelve-member juries, and the reasons for their opinion shifts seemed likely to be caused by factors other than those which would indicate high-quality deliberations (Roper, 1980:992).

Jury size affects verdict in other ways. The power of the initial majority has been demonstrated (Davis et al., 1981; Kerr, 1981). Members are more likely to join rather than defect from the majority view. Majority plus leniency effects are even stronger; a majority favoring acquittal are more likely to win converts than the majority favoring conviction (Davis et al., 1981; Kerr, 1981). Majority effects are also increased by the size of the majority (Kerr, 1981). Kerr and MacConn (1985) suggest that large jury panels are less likely to start near unanimity, lending support for the effect of jury size on decisional shifts. Roper's research on the size of minority contingents is complementary. Jury panels with viable minorities (2 or more individuals holding opinions contrary to the majority) were more likely to hang. Minority views were also more likely to prevail (Roper, 1980:988,989). Minority members would seem less likely to marshall confederates in small panels simply because there are fewer individuals to co-opt. Yet resistance to persuasion and the ability to influence others may be contingent on the size of the group and minority coalitions. Minority

28

members appear to wield more influence than majority members in smaller jury panels (Tanford and Penrod, 1983; Tanford and Penrod, 1984a).

Differences in juror participation have also been analyzed. Females have been found less likely to participate in group deliberations or be selected as foreman (Hastie *et al.*, 1983; Kerr *et al.*, 1982; Strodbeck and Lipinski, 1985), as are lower status persons (Gerbasi *et al.*, 1977; Hastie *et al.*, 1983; Strodbeck and Lipinski, 1985). Some report experienced jurors more likely to participate in deliberations or to be selected as foreman (Kassin and Juhnke, 1983; Kerr *et al.*, 1982; Strodbeck and Lipinski, 1985), while not all find this to be the case (Hastie *et al.*, 1983).

Despite anecdotal accounts of the influence of the foreman or a particular juror (e.g., Brill, 1982), participation or role may not necessarily predict a juror's influence. For example, the opinion of the foreman may not be particularly determinative of verdict (Bridgeman and Marlowe, 1979; Hastie *et al.*, 1983). Similarly, while females may participate less than males in group deliberations, they appear to be no more susceptible to influence (Kerr, 1981). Thus, the process by which deliberations proceed may be more important than any one individual's influence. Alternately, an individual's participation or role may be important only to the extent that the juror is able to steer the course of deliberations.

Group deliberations have been found to heighten anxiety and depression levels of jurors (Goldman *et al.*, 1975; Goldman *et al.*, 1983; Goldman and Casey, 1980), affecting different personality types and leading to tension reduction behaviors during deliberation. As such, jurors who are focused on reducing tension may be less likely to focus on the evidence (Goldman *et al.*, 1983). Jurors also may spend time gathering support for their position rather than considering the evidence (Goldman *et al.*, 1983).

Hastie *et al.* (1983) found early balloting to harden individual differences and to produce "verdict-driven" deliberations. Such deliberations limited full development of trial testimony, as only evidence relating to the verdict positions taken was discussed. In contrast, evidence-driven deliberations led to more thorough consideration of the evidence and the law. Later balloting was also characteristic of evidence-driven deliberations. Hastie *et al.* (1983:230) propose judicial instructions to delay balloting as one mechanism to promote the fullest discussion of the facts (i.e., evidence-driven deliberations). The type of balloting—whether open or secret—might also be relevant in constraining the process of deliberation. In addition, public polling may result in more hung juries in certain size juries (Kerr and MacConn, 1985).

Group deliberations may also serve to inhibit juror bias. It was reported

29

above that authoritarian jurors utilized inadmissible evidence despite judicial instructions to disregard (Werner *et al.*, 1982). Yet group delibera- tions were found to moderate jurors' use of inadmissible evidence (Carretta and Moreland, 1983; Hastie *et al.*, 1983). Kaplan and Miller (1978) re- ported that while group deliberations polarized individuals' opinions in the direction of their initial assessments, it also reduced biases that existed before deliberations. Davis *et al.* (1984) found the biasing effect of joining charges in one trial was not entirely moderated by group discussion, but that bias was more potent at the individual level.

Discussion

Three questions have shaped this review. First, in what ways are ex- tralegal factors linked to jury verdicts? Second, are extralegal factors so intrusive that it is necessary to devise legal procedures to limit their influence? Third, to what extent can legal procedures limit the biasing aspects of such factors?

One may be frustrated by the often tortured nature of this analysis. Clear positive findings were few and often attenuated by juror or case characteristics. Differences in methodologies might account for some of the disparity in findings. With numerous studies surveyed, chance may occa- sion false positives. The outcomes of single studies are also difficult to interpret. Do they reflect the realities of the jury or the enthusiasm of their progenitors?

Is a major overhaul of the American jury system warranted? Interest- ingly, despite all the potential influences discussed, one gains the sense that juries rely primarily upon legally relevant evidence (see also Bridge- man and Marlowe, 1979; Hastie *et al.*, 1983). It is likely that extralegal factors intrude most prominently in truly close cases. If one estimates the number of close cases based on the prevalence of hung juries, their relative frequency is small, approximately 5 percent (Hastie *et al.*, 1983; Kalven and Zeisel, 1966). However, while close cases may occur only infrequently, we nonetheless should consider measures to reduce the effects of extralegal factors.

Collectively the data suggest only limited influence of demographic and personality traits. The obvious exception to this lies in authoritarian personalities and in attitudes toward crime control. Thus, analysis of the impact of attitudes upon verdict suggests the most persuasive of the ex- tralegal factors to be social or ideational. The interrelationship of positive attitudes toward crime control and a prosecution bias suggests that as mores shift from liberal to conservative (at least with respect to crime

30

control), general willingness to convict increases. Willingness to convict may be linked dynamically to crime and fear of crime. From a sociologist's vantage this can be viewed as a societal self-correcting mechanism.

While demographic characteristics appear not particularly predictive of jurors' verdicts, they are related to participation in deliberations and foreman selection. However, too few studies have examined participation and role to conclude that either demonstrates the juror's *influence* in directing verdict.

The data on majority and minority coalitions is provocative, confirming the often asserted weakness of the deliberative process. Yet, as noted earlier, juror characteristics do not appear robust predictors of individual verdicts. Thus, the strength of majority factions in controlling decision shifts during deliberation does not necessarily disturb assumptions about the fairness or accuracy of the deliberative process. Biasing effects in group decision making may, however, arise due to the nature of group discussion and voting. To the extent that a group polls its members early (and often), the evidence suggests bias, or at least rigidity, might more easily intrude.

Certain trial procedures also appear to promote bias. Primacy and recency effects may enhance the persuasiveness of certain communications. The adversarial nature of cross-examination may distort testimony offered by witnesses. Trying multiple offenses simultaneously creates order effects which may impact judgments of guilt.[5] Certain types of cases—sexual assault or death penalty—present more sensitive issues and appear susceptible to unwarranted reactions from specific juror types. Yet characteristics of defendants, victims or witnesses that appear to bias are likely to be irrelevant unless there is convergence of several factors (relative to the juror, crime, and/or litigants).

How may legal procedures limit such biasing influences? Unfortunately, many of the extralegal factors that do appear to bias are "hard-wired." They are not particularly amenable to external control. For example, the order of case presentation is governed by trial rules. Primacy and recency effects that adhere in case presentation are probably unchangeable. Yet in many instances trial features may be variable enough that whatever bias accrues may well be limited in overall impact. Furthermore, many biasing effects of trial processes interact significantly with only a few jurors on any panel.

While we are limited in our ability to eliminate extralegal bias in the courtroom, two established procedures already mitigate these biases: the

---

5. Interestingly, those studying this issue do not recommend immediate revision of court rules for joinder; they call for additional research (Davis *et al.*, 1984).

31

voir dire and judicial instructions. Selection of jurors during the voir dire should receive increased attention from court personnel. While the patently partial are usually removed during the voir dire, other individuals with less overt biases may remain. Clearly the evidence suggests that those exposed to adverse pretrial publicity (both case-specific and general) should be carefully scrutinized. The data also suggest that the practice of death-qualifying juries should be reconsidered in light of the bias of death-qualified jurors towards conviction. Beyond these twin concerns, there are more general considerations.

The jury panel should contain a cross-section of individuals. Diversity of jurors may well ensure impartiality. Cowan *et al.* (1984) compared death-qualified jury panels with mixed juries. They found that those serving on the mixed juries were more critical of all the witnesses, less satisfied with their juries, and better able to remember evidence than those from death-qualified juries (they had controlled for initial death penalty attitudes). Cowan *et al.* concluded that diversity may improve the vigor, thoroughness and accuracy of the jury's deliberations. Diversity may best be accomplished by employing larger jury panels, since the likelihood of drawing a cross-section of individuals is greater. (The process of calling venires also affects the initial respresentativeness of the panel of prospective jurors; see Munsterman and Munsterman, this issue.)

While achieving diversity, and hence balance, in the jury panel is desirable, it does not appear that substantial revision of current procedures is warranted. The data suggest that individual juror characteristics, particularly demographic factors, are not significant predictors of verdicts. In this context scientific jury selection procedures (jurimetrics), heralded by some (e.g., Covington, 1983), appear highly questionable. Scientific jury selection has been used most often in cases that differ from run-of-the-mill criminal trials. Given the selection procedures employed, it is impossible to establish whether the predictions and subsequent use of challenges affected the trial outcome (Moran and Comfort, 1982:1053). Thus, it would appear that the judge need monitor the voir dire only to ensure that a crude balance is achieved. It would also seem useful to advise attorneys and the judiciary on individual juror characteristics so that they may approach the voir dire process more realistically.

There is another aspect of the voir dire to consider. Some argue that the voir dire's importance derives from the opportunity to indoctrinate jurors about the need for impartiality (Hans and Vidmar, 1982:68). Yet the voir dire may also sensitize in other, biasing ways. In a comparison of jurors who had sat through a voir dire in a case involving the death penalty with those who had not been so exposed, death-qualified voir dire jurors were found more likely to believe the defendant would be convicted. Jurors also believed that the prosecutor, defense attorney, and judge were already convinced of the defendant's guilt (Haney, 1984). In short, Haney proposes that whatever biases accrue in seating a death-qualified panel, bias is also amplified through the voir dire process. Court personnel should consider how bias may enter through the voir dire in other types of cases.

A second legal procedure that can be used to check bias is judicial instructions. The law assumes that jurors follow judicial instructions and thus rely only upon the legally relevant information. Some studies suggest that judicial instructions have little effect on jurors (Kassin and Wrightsman, 1981; Thompson et al., 1981; Werner et al., 1982). However, judicial instructions were found more effective if given prior to the presentation of evidence (Kassin and Wrightsman, 1979), and primacy effects were moderated when jurors were informed prior to trial testimony that they would be required to justify their verdict (Tetlock, 1983). Judicial instructions concerning the process of deliberation appear to focus deliberation time on critical issues, discouraging inappropriate statements (Taylor et al., 1981). Further, judges should avoid extreme or inconsistent statements when summarizing trial evidence and charging the jury (Lenehan and O'Neill, 1981). Other research has suggested that clarity in instruction improves jurors' understanding of the task (Charrow and Charrow, 1979; Elwork et al., 1982; Hastie et al., 1983).

In summary, juries appear to perform remarkably well, although we can clearly fine tune the system of jury selection and trial procedures to protect against bias. A final comment is appropriate at this juncture. One difficulty in interpreting jury research lies in often questionable methodological techniques utilized in the studies themselves. As this last section will conclude, jury research needs modification in design and structure. Clarification of relationships and certainly in findings await higher quality methodology.

A Final Note—Methodological Concerns

Most jury research is indirect. Actual observation of jury deliberations is prohibited in nearly all states. As a result, most studies must use a quasi-experimental design, jury simulation. Similarly, researchers denied access to actual trials develop simulated trials. One is never certain that "simulated" trials and jurors adequately mimic actual processes. In social science terms, the problem is one of external validity.

The literature chronicles reoccurring methodological problems in jury studies (Konečni and Ebbesen, 1979; Roper, 1980; Vidmar, 1979; Weiten and Diamond, 1979). To review each problem in detail would require another article. However, several do deserve mention here. Cases used in simulation studies often present insufficient ambiguity to permit diversity of verdict. The jury in actual criminal trials must bring back a judgment of guilt or innocence. Yet it is not unusual to find empirical studies that have required jurors to provide probability of guilt estimates, to award damages in a criminal trial, or to sentence the defendant.

The setting and structure of the simulations often do not resemble actual trials, and research subjects in many cases do not approximate actual jury panel members. Many studies employ the infamous college freshman or other subjects who vary dramatically from actual jury panels (Feild and Barnett, 1978; Hinkle et al., 1983; Weiten and Diamond, 1979). The mode of presentation, whether by transcript, audiotape, videotape, or dramatization, conveys differing levels of realism. Only a handful of studies have been conducted in real courtrooms (Roper, 1980:982). Moreover, the decision-making process (individual verdict versus group verdict), and the length of time allotted for the deliberations cause additional problems of external validity.

Simulations in addition often present abbreviated testimony, thus eliminating the task of extracting information embedded in other contexts that is required of jurors in actual trial settings (Konečni and Ebbesen, 1979:40, 41; Wasserman and Robinson, 1980:102; Weiten and Diamond, 1979:77). Failure to provide judicial instructions to mock jurors prior to deliberations also impairs the validity of the studies.

Functional verisimilitude is another well worn concern (Konečni and Ebbesen, 1979; Roper, 1980; Weiten and Diamond, 1979). Because simulations are not real in their consequences, the information from a study may not correspond to real world processes. There must be a mechanism to trigger conscientious involvement. One such mechanism is to increase correspondence between the structure of actual and simulated trials. Functional verisimilitude is enhanced as structural verisimilitude increases.

Because of the configurations of research design, more subjects are needed in jury panels than is the norm for general research. In an effort to increase sample size researchers sometimes report individual verdicts. However, such compensatory activity impairs conceptual validity.

Jury studies that rely upon surveying impaneled jurors or archival analysis of court records also have problems. Researchers who conduct post-trial interviews enter *after* the event (verdict) has occurred. Such

34

designs rely upon the ability of participants to report accurately the events that transpired and to recall the facts and motivations influencing the verdict. Archival analysis may be restricted by the availability of data for collection, the data collection process, and the analytic strategies employed (see Konečni and Ebbesen, 1979).

While methodological differences and shortcomings restrict what we really know of jury panels and their verdicts, the data taken as a whole suggest the integrity of the American jury panel. The use of higher quality methodologies will surely produce more sophisticated analyses of jurors and jury behavior.

CASES

Wainwright v. Witt, 105 S.Ct. 844 (1985).
Witherspoon v. Illinois, 391 U.S. 510 (1968).

REFERENCES

ACKERMAN, Adele M., Pamela M. McMAHON and Lawrence A. FEHR (1984) "Mock Trial Jury Decisions as a Function of Adolescent Juror Guilt and Hostility," 144 *Journal of Genetic Psychology* 195.

ARCHER, Richard L., H. Clayton FOUSHEE, Mark H. DAVIS and David ADERMAN (1979) "Emotional Empathy in a Courtroom Simulation: A Person-Situation Interaction," 9 *Journal of Applied Social Psychology* 275.

BANK, Steven C. and Norman G. POYTHRESS, Jr. (1982) "The Elements of Persuasion in Expert Testimony," 10 *Journal of Psychiatry and Law* 173.

BERG, Kathleen Stirrett and Neil VIDMAR (1975) "Authoritarianism and Recall of Evidence about Criminal Behavior," 9 *Journal of Research in Personality* 147.

BERMANT, Gordon, Duncan CHAPPELL, Geraldine T. CROCKETT, M. Daniel JACOUBOVITCH and Mary McGUIRE (1975) "Juror Responses to Prerecorded Videotape Trials Presentations in California and Ohio," 26 *Hastings Law Journal* 975.

BLANCK, Peter David, Robert ROSENTHAL and LaDoris Hazzard CORDELL (1985) "The Appearance of Justice: Judges' Verbal and Nonverbal Behavior in Criminal Jury Trials," 38 *Stanford Law Review* 89.

BORDENS, Kenneth S. and Irwin A. HOROWITZ (1985) "Joinder of Criminal Offenses: A Review of the Legal and Psychological Literature," 9 *Law and Human Behavior* 339.

BRAY, Robert M. and Audrey M. NOBLE (1978) "Authoritarianism and Decisions in Mock Juries: Evidence of Jury Bias and Group Polarization," 36 *Social Psychology* 1424.

BRIDGEMAN, Diane L. and David MARLOWE (1979) "Jury Decision Making: An Empirical Study Based on Actual Felony Trials," 64 *Journal of Applied Psychology* 91.

BRILL, Steven (November 1982) "Inside the Jury Room at the Washington Post Libel Trial," 4 *American Lawyer* 1.

CARRETTA, Thomas R. and Richard L. MORELAND (1983) "The Direct and Indirect Effects of Inadmissible Evidence," 13 *Journal of Applied Social Psychology* 219.

CHANEY, Jerry (December 1983) "Survey Finds Jurors' Feelings Mixed About Pluses, Minuses of Sequestration," 11 *Media Law Notes* 1.

CHARROW, R. P. and Veda R. CHARROW (1979) "Making Legal Language Understandable: A Psycholinguistic Study of Jury Instructions," 79 *Columbia Law Review* 1306.

COLVER, C. Phillip (1981) "The Persuasive Impact of Simulation Experimentation," 17 *Trial* 64.

CONSTANTINI, Edmond and Joel KING (1980/81) "The Partial Juror: Correlates and Causes of Prejudgment," 15 *Law and Society Review* 9.

CONSTANTINI, Edmond, Michael MALLERY and Diane M. YAPUNDICH (1983) "Gender and Juror Partiality: Are Women More Likely to Prejudge Guilt?" 67 *Judicature* 120.

COVINGTON, Margaret (1983) "State-of-the-Art in Jury Selection Techniques: More Science Than Luck," 19 *Trial* 84.

35

COWAN, Claudia L., William C. THOMPSON and Phoebe C. ELLSWORTH (1984) "The Effects of Death Qualification on Jurors' Predisposition to Convict and on the Quality of Deliberation," 8 *Law and Human Behavior* 53.

DANE, Francis C. and Lawrence S. WRIGHTSMAN (1982) "Effects of Defendants' and Victims' Characteristics on Jurors' Verdicts," in Kerr and Bray (eds.) *The Psychology of the Courtroom*. New York: Academic Press.

DAVIS, James H., Robert W. HOLT, Craig E. SPITZER and Garold STASSER (1981) "The Effects of Consensus on Mock Juror Verdict Preferences," 17 *Journal of Experimental Social Psychology* 1.

DAVIS, James H., Norbert L. KERR, Robert S. ATKIN, Robert W. HOLT and David MEEK (1975) "The Decision Processes of 6- and 12-person Mock Juries Assigned Unanimous and Two-thirds Majority Rules," 32 *Journal of Personality and Social Psychology* 1.

DAVIS, James H., R. Scott TINDALE, Dennis H. NAGAO, Verlin B. HINSZ and Bret ROBINSON (1984) "Order Effects in Multiple Decisions by Groups: A Demonstration with Mock Juries and Trial Procedures," 47 *Journal of Personality and Social Psychology* 1003.

DEITZ, Sheila R., Karen Tiemann BLACKWELL, Paul C. DALEY and Brenda J. BENTLEY (1982) "Measurement of Empathy Toward Victims and Rapists," 43 *Journal of Personality and Social Psychology* 372.

DENNO, Deborah (1981) "Psychological Factors for the Black Defendant in a Jury Trial," 11 *Journal of Black Studies* 313.

DILLEHAY, Ronald C. and Michael T. NIETZEL (1985) "Juror Experience and Verdicts," 9 *Law and Human Behavior* 179.

ELLSWORTH, Phoebe C., Raymond M. BUKATY, Claudia L. COWAN and William C. THOMPSON (1984) "The Death-Qualified Jury and the Defense of Insanity," 8 *Law and Human Behavior* 81.

ELWORK, Amiram, Bruce D. SALES and James J. ALFINI (1982) *Making Jury Instructions Understandable* Charlottesville, Va.: The Michie Co.

FEILD, Hubert S. (1979) "Rape Trials and Jurors' Decisions: A Psycholegal Analysis of the Effects of Victim, Defendant, and Case Characteristics," 3 *Law and Human Behavior* 261.

FEILD, Hubert S. and Nona J. BARNETT (1978) "Simulated Jury Trials: Students vs. 'Real' People as Jurors," 104 *Journal of Social Psychology* 287.

FINCH, Michael and Mark FERRARO (1986) "The Empirical Challenge to Death-Qualified Juries: On Further Examination," 65 *Nebraska Law Review* 21.

FITZGERALD, Robert and Phoebe C. ELLSWORTH (1984) "Due Process v. Crime Control: Death Qualification and Jury Attitudes," 8 *Law and Human Behavior* 31.

GERBASI, Kathleen Carrese, Miron ZUCKERMAN and Harry T. REIS (1977) "Justice Needs a New Blindfold: A Review of Mock Jury Research," 84 *Psychological Bulletin* 323.

GOLDMAN, Jacquelin and Victoria A. CASEY (1980) "Psychological Aspects of Jury Performance in a Nonviolent Criminal Trial," 8 *Journal of Psychiatry and Law* 443.

GOLDMAN, Jacquelin, Kenneth F. FREUNDLICH and Victoria A. CASEY (1983) "Jury Emotional Response and Deliberation Style," 11 *Journal of Psychiatry and Law* 319.

GOLDMAN, Jacquelin, Karen A. MAITLAND and Pennie L. NORTON (1975) "Psychological Aspects of Jury Performance," 3 *Journal of Psychiatry and Law* 367.

GOODMAN, Gail S., Jonathan M. GOLDING and Marshall M. HAITH (1984) "Jurors' Reactions to Child Witnesses," 40 *Journal of Social Issues* 139.

GREENE, Edith and Elizabeth F. LOFTUS (1984) "What's New in the News? The Influence of Well-Publicized News Events on Psychological Research and Courtroom Trials," 5 *Basic and Applied Social Psychology* 211.

HANEY, Craig (1984) "On the Selection of Capital Juries: The Biasing Effects of the Death-Qualification Process," 8 *Law and Human Behavior* 121.

HANS, Valerie and Neil VIDMAR (1982) "Jury Selection," in Norbert L. Kerr and Robert M. Bray (eds) *The Psychology of the Courtroom*. New York: Academic Press.

HASSETT, Joseph M. (1980) "A Jury's Pretrial Knowledge in Historical Perspective: The Distinction Between Pretrial Information and 'Prejudicial' Publicity," 43 *Law and Contemporary Problems* 155.

HASTIE, Reid, Steven D. PENROD and Nancy PENNINGTON (1983) *Inside the Jury*. Cambridge, Mass.: Harvard University Press.

HINKLE, Andrew Lee, Donald J. SMELTZER, Cynthia A. ALLEN and Glen D. KING (1983) "The Judgments of College Students and Jurors Concerning Sanity and Guilt of An Alleged Murder," 120 *Journal of Social Psychology* 253.

HOFFMAN, Eric (1981) "Social Class Correlates of Perceived Offender Typicality," 49 *Psychological Reports* 347.

HOIBERG, Bruce C. and Lloyd K. STIRES (1973) "The Effect of Several Types of Pretrial Publicity on the Guilt Attributions of Simulated Jurors," 3 *Journal of Applied Social Psychology* 267.

HOWARD, Judith A. and LEVINSON, Randy (1985) "The Overdue Courtship of Attribution and Labeling," 48 *Social Psychology Quarterly* 191.

JACOBSON, Martha B. (1981) "Effects of Victim's and Defendant's Physical Attractiveness on Subject's Judgments in a Rape Case," 7 *Sex Roles* 247.

JOHNSON, Sheri Lynn (1985) "Black Innocence and the White Jury," 83 *Michigan Law Review* 1611.

KALVEN, Henry and Hans ZEISEL (1966) *The American Jury.* Boston: Little, Brown.

KAMINISKI, Edmund P. and Gerald R. MILLER (1984) "How Jurors Respond to Videotaped Witnesses," 34 *Journal of Communication* 88.

KAPLAN, Martin F. and Lynn E. Miller (1978) "Reducing the Effects of Juror Bias," 36 *Journal of Personality and Social Psychology* 1443.

KASSIN, Saul (1984) "TV Cameras, Public Self-Consciousness, and Mock Juror Performance," 20 *Journal of Experimental Social Psychology* 336.

KASSIN, Saul M. and Ralph JUHNKE (1983) "Juror Experience and Decision Making," 44 *Journal of Personality and Social Psychology* 1182.

KASSIN, Saul M. and Lawrence S. WRIGHTSMAN (1981) "Coerced Confessions, Judicial Instruction, and Mock Juror Verdicts," 11 *Journal of Applied Social Psychology* 489.

_____ (1979) "On the Requirements of Proof: The Timing of Judicial Instruction and Mock Juror Verdicts," 37 *Journal of Personality and Social Psychology* 1877.

KERR, Norbert L. (1978) "Severity of Prescribed Penalty and Mock Jurors' Verdicts," 36 *Journal of Personality and Social Psychology* 1431.

_____ (1981) "Social Transition Schemes: Charting the Group's Road to Agreement," 41 *Journal of Personality and Social Psychology* 684.

KERR, Norbert L., Douglas L. HARMON and James K. GRAVES (1982) "Independence of Multiple Verdicts by Jurors and Juries," 12 *Journal of Applied Social Psychology* 12.

KERR, Norbert L. and Robert J. MacCONN (1985) "The Effects of Jury Size and Polling Method on the Process and Product of Jury Deliberation," 48 *Journal of Personality and Social Psychology* 349.

KONECNI, Vladimir J. and Ebbe B. EBBESEN (1979) "External Validity of Research in Legal Psychology," 3 *Law and Human Behavior* 39.

LAFREE, Gary D., Barbara F. RESKIN and Christy A. VISHER (1985) "Jurors' Responses to Victims' Behavior and Legal Issues in Sexual Assualt Trials," 32 *Social Problems* 389.

LAWSON, Robert G. (1969) "The Law of Primacy in the Criminal Courtroom," 77 *Journal of Social Psychology* 123.

LENEHAN, Gregory E. and Patrick O'NEILL (1981) "Reactance and Conflict as Determinants of Judgment in a Mock Jury Experiment," 11 *Journal of Applied Social Psychology* 231.

LIND, E. Allan (1982) "The Psychology of Courtroom Procedure," in Norbert L. Kerr and Robert M. Bray (eds.) *The Psychology of the Courtroom.* New York: Academic Press.

LINZ, Daniel and Steven PENROD (1984) "Increasing Attorney Persuasiveness in the Courtroom," 8 *Law and Psychiatry Review* 1.

McFATTER, Robert M. (1978) "Sentencing Strategies and Justice: Effects of Punishment Philosophy on Sentencing Decisions," 36 *Journal of Personality and Social Psychology* 1490.

MEYERS, Martha A. (1979) "Rule Departures and Making Law: Juries and Their Verdicts," 13 *Law and Society Review* 781.

_____ (1980) "Social Contexts and Attributions of Criminal Responsibility," 43 *Social Psychology Quarterly* 405.

MIETHE, Terrance D. (1984) "The Impact of Victim Provocation on Judgments of Legal Responsibility: An Experimental Assessment," 12 *Journal of Criminal Justice* 407.

MILLER, Marina and Jay HEWITT, (1978) "Conviction of a Defendant as a Function of Juror-Victim Racial Stereotypes," 105 *Journal of Social Psychology* 159.

MILLS, C. J. and W. E. BOHANNON (1980a) "Character Structure and Jury Behavior: Conceptual and Applied Implications," 38 *Journal of Personality and Social Psychology* 662.

_____ (1980b) "Juror Characteristics: To What Extent Are They Related to Jury Verdicts?" 64 *Judicature* 22.

37

MORAN, Gary and John Craig COMFORT (1982) "Scientific Juror Selection: Sex as a Moderator of Demographic and Personality Predictors of Impaneled Felony Juror Behavior," 43 *Journal of Personality and Social Psychology* 1052.

MUNSTERMAN, G. Thomas and Janice T. MUNSTERMAN (1986) "The Search for Jury Representativeness," 11 *The Justice System Journal* 59.

NAGAO, Dennis H. and James H. DAVIS (1980a) "Some Implications of Temporal Drift in Social Parameters," 16 *Journal of Experimental Social Psychology* 479.

_____ (1980b) "The Effects of Prior Experience on Mock Juror Case Judgments," 43 *Social Psychology Quarterly* 190.

PAWDAWER-SINGER, Alice M. and Allen H. BARTON (1975) "The Impact of Pretrial Publicity on Jurors' Verdicts," in Rita James Simon (ed.) *Jury Research in America* Beverly Hills, Calif.: Sage.

PENNINGTON, Donald C. (1982) "Witnesses and Their Testimony: Effects of Ordering on Juror Verdicts," 12 *Journal of Applied Social Psychology* 318.

PERLMAN, Peter (1981) "Seeing Is Believing: Making Proof More Meaningful," 17 *Trial* 34.

PRYOR, Bert and Raymond W. BUCHANAN (1984) "The Effects of a Defendant's Demeanor on Credibility and Guilt," 34 *Journal of Communication* 92.

PYSZCZYNSKI, Thomas A. and Lawrence S. WRIGHTSMAN (1981) "The Effects of Opening Statements on Mock Jurors' Verdicts in a Simulated Criminal Trial," 11 *Journal of Applied Social Psychology* 301.

REED, Robin (1980) "Jury Simulation: The Impact of Judge's Instructions and Attorney Tactics on Decisionmaking," 71 *Journal of Criminal Law and Criminology* 68.

ROPER, Robert T. (1980) "Jury Size and Verdict Consistency: 'A Line Has to Be Drawn Somewhere'?" 14 *Law and Society Review* 977.

_____ (1986) "A Typology of Jury Research and Discussion of the Structural Correlates of Jury Decisionmaking," 11 *The Justice System Journal* 5.

SAKS, Michael J. (1977) *Jury Verdicts: The Role of Group Size and Social Decision Rule.* Lexington, Mass.: D.C. Heath.

SAKS, Michael J. and Robert F. KIDD (1980/81) "Human Information Processing and Adjudication: Trial by Heuristics," 15 *Law and Society Review* 123.

SHAFFER, David R. and Cyril SADOWSKI (1979) "Effects of Withheld Evidence on Juridic Decisions II: Locus of Withholding Strategy," 5 *Personality and Social Psychology Bulletin* 40.

SIGALL, Harold and Nancy OSTROVE (1975) "Beautiful But Dangerous: Effects of Offender Attractiveness and Nature of Crime on Juridic Judgments," 31 *Journal of Personality and Social Psychology* 410.

SIMON, Rita (1967) *The Jury and the Defense of Insanity.* Boston: Little, Brown.

SMITH, Edward D. and Anita HED (1979) "Effects of Offenders' Age and Attractiveness on Sentencing by Mock Juries," 44 *Psychological Reports* 691.

STEPHAN, Cookie (1975) "Selective Characteristics of Jurors and Litigants: Their Influences on Juries' Verdicts," in Rita James Simon (ed.) *The Jury System in America.* Beverly Hills, Calif.: Sage.

STRODBECK, Fred L. and Richard M. LIPINSKI (1985) "Becoming First Among Equals: Moral Considerations in Jury Foreman Selection," 49 *Journal of Personality and Social Psychology* 927.

TANFORD, Sarah and Steven PENROD, (1983) "Computer Modeling on Influence in the Jury: The Role of the Consistent Juror," 46 *Social Psychology Quarterly* 200.

_____ (1984a) "Social Influence Model: A Formal Integration of Research on Majority and Minority Influence Processes," 95 *Psychological Bulletin* 189.

_____ (1984b) "Social Influence Processes in Juror Judgments of Multiple-Offense Trials," 47 *Journal of Personality and Social Psychology* 749.

TANFORD, Sarah, Steven PENROD and Rebecca COLLINS (1985) "Decision Making in Joined Criminal Trials: The Influence of Charge Similarity, Evidence Similarity and Limiting Instructions," 9 *Law and Human Behavior* 319.

TAYLOR, K. Phillip, Raymond W. BUCHANAN, Bert PRYOR and David W. STRAWN (1981) "How Do Jurors Reach a Verdict?" 31 *Journal of Communications* 37.

TETLOCK, Phillip E. (1983) "Accountability and the Perseverance of First Impressions," 46 *Social Psychology Quarterly* 285.

THOMPSON, William C., Claudia L. COWAN, Phoebe C. ELLSWORTH and Joan C. HARRINGTON (1984) "Death Penalty Attitudes and Conviction Proneness: The Translation of Attitudes into Verdicts," 8 *Law and Human Behavior* 95.

THOMPSON, William C., Geoffrey T. FONG and D.L. ROSENHAN (1981) "Inadmissible Evidence and Juror Verdicts," 40 *Journal of Personality and Socal Psychology* 453.

38

UGWUEGBU, Denis Chiameze E. (1979) "Racial and Evidential Factors in Juror Attribution of Legal Responsibility," 15 *Journal of Experimental Social Psychology* 133.

VIDMAR, Neil (1979) "The Other Issues in Jury Simulation Research: A Commentary with Particular Reference to Defendant Character Studies," 3 *Law and Human Behavior* 95.

VIDMAR, Neil and Nancy MacDonald LAIRD (1983) "Adversary Social Roles: Their Effects on Witnesses' Communication of Evidence and the Assessments of Adjudications," 44 *Journal of Personality and Social Psychology* 888.

VILLEMUR, Nora K. and Janet Shibley HYDE (1983) "Effects of Sex of Defense Attorney, Sex of Juror, and Age and Attractiveness of the Victim in Mock Juror Decision Making in a Rape Case," 9 *Sex Roles* 879.

WASSERMAN, David T. and J. Neil ROBINSON (1980) "Extra-legal Influences, Group Processes and Jury Decisionmaking: A Psychological Perspective," 12 *North Carolina Law Journal* 96.

WEITEN, Wayne and Shari S. DIAMOND (1979) "A Critical Review of the Jury Simulation Paradigm: The Case of Defendant Characteristics," 3 *Law and Human Behavior* 71.

WERNER, Carol M., Dorothy K. KAGEHIRO, and Michael J. STRUBE (1982) "Conviction Proneness and the Authoritarian Juror: Inability to Disregard Information or Attitudinal Bias?" 67 *Journal of Applied Psychology* 629.

WERNER, Carol M., Michael J. STRUBE, Allen M. COLE and Dorothy K. KAGHIRO (1985) "The Impact of Case Characteristics and Prior Jury Experience on Jury Verdicts," 15 *Journal of Applied Social Psychology* 409.

WHALEN, Denise H. and Fletcher A. BLANCHARD (1982) "Effects of Photographic Evidence on Mock Juror Judgment," 12 *Journal of Applied Psychology* 30.

WINICK, Bruce J. (November 1982) "Prosecutorial Peremptory Challenge Practices in Capital Cases: An Empirical Study and a Constitutional Analysis," 81 *Michigan Law Review* 1.

39

Law and Human Behavior, Vol. 4, Nos. 1/2, 1980

The Objective Reality of Evidence and the Utility of Systematic Jury Selection*

John R. Hepburn†

Significant relationships between jurors' demographic characteristics, attitudes, and verdicts have stimulated an interest in systematic jury selection. However, critics of this approach argue that verdicts are based on the strength of the evidence presented rather than on the composition of the jury. This analysis of demographic and attitudinal data and the responses to a vignette collected from a jury-eligible sample explores the association between perception of strength of evidence and both case-relevant attitudes and demographic characteristics and then examines the amount of variation in verdict explained by juror characteristics when strength of evidence is already taken into account. The findings point to the inclusion of strength of evidence in systematic jury selection procedures.

INTRODUCTION

There is a growing interest in the possibility that the participation of social scientists in the jury selection process can increase the likelihood of obtaining a jury that is attitudinally unbiased and open-minded, at minimum, or even somewhat biased toward one of the litigants. Referred to as systematic jury selection (Kairys, Schulman, & Harring, 1975) or scientific jury selection (Saks, 1976a), the techniques of social science are actually employed not to select the most unbiased jurors but to exclude from the jury those persons who are least likely to render a fair and impartial verdict (Suggs & Sales, 1978) since the law only allows attorneys to reject potential jurors, not to select them. Despite the misnomer, systematic jury selection has received considerable attention inasmuch as it suggests that rigorous and standardized scientific

---

*The article has benefited from the comments made by Eric Poole to an earlier version.
†Department of Sociology and Center for Metropolitan Studies, University of Missouri, St. Louis.

procedures may be more effective than the individualistic and experiential judgments made by an attorney during voir dire.

Methodological and statistical techniques to select an attitudinally unbiased jury during voir dire have been detailed elsewhere (Berman & Sales, 1977; Kairys, 1972; Kairys et al., 1975; McConahay, Mullin & Frederick, 1977; Schulman, Shaver, Colman, Emrich, & Christie, 1973). Generally stated, the most well known procedure requires a survey of the general population to discover those demographic and other public information variables about which information can be obtained during voir dire that most accurately predict case-relevant attitudes that cannot be ascertained otherwise during voir dire. To the extent that there is little or no measurement error, this technique assumes that the attitudes, opinions, and beliefs of prospective jurors can be predicted with known levels of confidence, thus enabling the prosecution or defense to reject as jurors those persons whose attitudes are least favorably predisposed to their side of the issues in the case. The likelihood of obtaining the desired verdict can then be increased by retaining those jurors whose demographic and background characteristics "predict" the type of favorable attitudes that will predispose them toward a particular verdict.

Demographic Characteristics, Attitudes, and Verdict

Although the relationship between demographic factors and jurors' verdict has been substantiated, it is evident that there is no uniform set of predictor variables that can be applied universally. For example, Simon (1967) reports that mock trial verdict is related to juror's ethnicity and education but unrelated to sex, age, religion, occupation, or income of juror. Yet Bronson's (1970) analysis of "death-qualified" juror's finds that those most in favor of the death penalty are white, male, higher income, lower education, and Republican jurors. In summary, mixed findings have emerged from numerous attempts to assess the relationship between juror's decisions and demographic characteristics (Davis, Bray, & Holt, 1977; Saks, 1976a). Differences are due in part to methodological variations in operationalizations of the "juror" (e.g., actual jurors, jury-eligible residents of an area, and students), the type of case or stimulus (e.g., criminal or civil), presentation of the case or stimulus (e.g., actual trial, video tape, written transcript and vignette), and the nature of the dependent variable (guilt vs. innocence and severity of sanction). In addition, it is possible that the reported differences in the association of demographic variables and jurors' verdicts may reflect such things as regional or cultural differences from one jurisdiction to another.

Similarly, inconclusive relationships have been noted between juror's demographic characteristics and their attitudes (Davis et al., 1977). Racism, for example, is reported to be higher among older, less educated persons in low status occupations who are or have been married and who attend church regularly (Rokeach & Vidmar, 1973). Politically conservative jurors are young, better educated persons with higher incomes who reside in urban areas (Reed & Reed, 1977). Finally, there is a growing body of evidence to substantiate the presumed relationship between juror attitudes and juror decisions. The relationship of authoritarianism to verdict (Boehm, 1968; Bray & Noble, 1978; Mitchell & Byrne, 1973; Rokeach & Vidmer, 1973) and to severity of sanction (Bray & Noble, 1978; Thayer, 1970) is well documented. Juror decisions have been found to be related to such additional attitudes as liberalism (Reed & Reed, 1977), social approval (Buckhout, 1973), punitiveness (Thayer, 1970), and one's belief in the underlying cause (person vs. environment) of the crime (Saks, 1976a).

Although the entire causal linkage remains to be empirically assessed, the existence of bivariate relationships between demographic characteristics, juror attitudes, and verdicts has provided sufficient cause to incorporate the procedure into actual jury selection situations. Demographic data have been used to predict juror decisions in such nationally known trials as Angela Davis (Moore, 1974; Sage, 1973), Joan Little (McConahay et al., 1977) and the Harrisburg Conspiracy Trial (Schulman et al., 1973). The failure to convict in these and other "political" trials has lent credibility to the effectiveness of systematic jury selection, so much so, in fact, that some social scientists (Etzioni, 1973; McConahay et al., 1977; Shapely, 1974), have stated publicly that systematic jury selection procedures are effective.

Others remain unconvinced by the available data, however, and point out that each application of the technique must confront such methodological problems as operationalization, sampling, data reduction, and model building (Berk, Hennessy & Swan, 1977; Berman & Sales, 1977). A prevalent view is summarized by Berk et al. (1977), who state that scientific jury selection will do no worse than the typical attorney in voir dire screening. This view gains credibility when prosecutors, unaided by social scientists, use their peremptory challenges to excuse those rated most highly by the defense on the basis of elaborate jury selection techniques (Schulman et al., 1973).

The Research Problem

The methodological limitations not withstanding, the presumption that attitudes are the predictors of the verdict is criticized for overlooking the importance of a major intervening variable—the evidence. Some trial attorneys and social scientists argue that verdicts are based on the strength or weakness of the evidence rather than jury composition (Saks, 1976a; McConahay et al., 1977). Indeed, Kalven and Zeisel (1966) report agreement, presumably based upon the evidence, between judge and jury in 78 percent of the cases studied. Simon (1967) notes that jurors review each piece of evidence introduced and rely on the record in making their verdict. Finally, Saks (1976a) reports on a study conducted with Werner and Ostrom in which the amount of evidence was more than three times as powerful, and the strength of the evidence was more than seven times as powerful, as were attitudes in determining the verdict of former jurors. This argument suggests that attitudes play a very small part in the determination of guilt or innocence: verdicts are based upon the strength of the evidence, and the evidence is independent of the jurors' demographic characteristics and attitudes. Berk (1976:296) concludes his critique of jury selection techniques by stating that ". . . jury decisions are based on the assessment of empirical facts and that objective reality (or, more accurately, consensual reality) may explain the lion's share of juror decisions. In this context, it is less clear what contribution social science insights can make in jury selections."

To be sure, evidence is an important variable in determining the verdict. At issue, however, is the question of the relationship between juror attitudes and perception of the strength of the evidence. If strength of evidence is an absolute, extraneous to the composition of the jury, then there should be no association of strength of evidence and juror attitudes. If, on the other hand, strength of evidence is relative, then jurors' attitudes may influence their perception of the weight of the evidence. Although Boehm (1968) reports that 62 percent of the verdicts were consistent with the evidence regardless of the juror's level of authoritarianism, it is noteworthy that anti-authoritarians were significantly more likely than authoritarians to render lenient verdicts in the presence of strong evidence. Similarly, Reed and Reed (1977) report that political conservatives were more likely than traditional conservatives to base their decisions on the evidence and less likely to decide the case before deliberations. Finally, Doob (1976) finds that various pieces of evidence introduced by the prosecutor were given more weight by jurors who were informed of the defendant's prior criminal record than by those jurors who were uninformed. These results suggest that juror attitudes affect the interpretation of or weighting assigned to the evidence and, therefore, affect the verdict.

This discussion of the importance of the evidence raises two related questions, the answers to which may suggest severe limitations with the present attempts at systematic jury selection. First, is the perceived strength of the evidence presented during the trial unrelated to the case-relevant attitudes of the jurors? Second, how much added variation in the juror's verdict is explained by case-relevant attitudes when perceived strength of evidence is already taken into account? These two questions focus research attention to the relationship among case-relevant attitudes, perceived strength of evidence, and verdict among a jury-eligible population.

METHOD

During the time of this research, all persons chosen for jury duty in St. Louis County, Missouri, were randomly selected from the roll of registered voters. Data were obtained from a simple random sample of the registered voter list to assure that the research sample was representative of those residents most likely to be called for jury duty. Although 340 names were obtained, only 305 home interviews were completed. As usual, attrition resulted from inability to locate and refusal to cooperate. In addition, however, those who had been notified of future jury duty and those whose occupations would exclude them from jury duty, e.g., police officer, physician, attorney or teacher, were disqualified from the interview. Demographic characteristics, personal history information, and attitudes obtained during the interview were utilized to operationalize the variables under consideration.

In addition, a six-page description of a "hypothetical case" was presented to each respondent. The vignette was based on a transcript of an actual jury trial involving a young, black male charged with murder under the state's felony-murder rule. The transcript revealed that the prosecutor's case was based almost entirely upon police testimony pertaining to the identification of a suspect, the recovery of incriminating physical evidence, and initial statements made by the accused. The defense countered by suggesting that the police, saddened by the death of a fellow officer, were falsifying information in their eagerness to punish the accused. The defense then attempted to highlight inconsistencies in police testimony and interpret the existence of incriminating evidence as due to a police conspiracy. The transcript was simplified to present (1) the description of the crime, victims, and accused, (2) each of the prosecutor's major points of evidence or testimony, and (3) each of the defense's major points of evidence or response to the prosecutor.

Demographic and Background Characteristics

Dichotomous coding (0 to 1) was used for sex (1 = female), race (1 = nonwhite), marital status (1 = married) and religious attendance (1 = at least weekly); interval categories were used for age and years of education, and occupation was grouped according to current U.S. Census Bureau categories. In addition, background information pertaining to prior military service and prior victimization were coded as absent (0) or present (1).

Case-Relevant Attitudes

Two scales were constructed to measure attitudes relevant to the case. A four-item Likert scale of attitude toward the police summed respondent scores on a five-point agree-disagree or likely-unlikely scale to each of the following: (1) "In a situation where it comes down to the word of the accused person against the word of the police, how likely are you to believe the police?" (2) "It is likely that the police would plant evidence on a suspect accused of killing another police officer." (3) "The police today have too much power." (4) "The police discriminate against those who are poor and black."[1]

Similarly, attitude toward punishment was operationalized by a five-item Likert scale consisting of the following case-relevant items: (1) "If the police have arrested an individual and the prosecuting attorney has brought him to trial, there is good reason to believe that the man is guilty." (2) "If a man has been found guilty once but then released by another court, he probably did commit the crime." (3) "The level of violent crime would be reduced if the courts would convict alleged lawbreakers more often." (4) "If the person on trial does not testify at his trial, there is good reason to believe he is concealing guilt." (5) "The courts are far too technical in protecting the so-called constitutional rights of those involved in criminal activity."[2] Designed to differentiate between what Skolnick (1966) refers to as legal guilt and factual guilt, these items assess the respondent's willingness to abridge certain due process considerations and presumptions of innocence in favor of punitive sanctions based on crime control strategies and presumptions of guilt.

---

[1] The attitude toward police scale had a mean value of 14.59 and a standard deviation of 2.38, indicating rather positive attitudes toward the police. The item-to-total correlation coefficients ranged from .39 to .63.

[2] The attitude toward punishment scale had a mean value of 16.06, a standard deviation of 3.71, and item-to-total correlation coefficients ranging from .59 to .66.

The Verdict

After the respondent had read the "hypothetical case" presented during the interview and when the interviewer was assured that the respondent understood the points made in the vignette,[3] each respondent indicated the verdict he or she would make based on the evidence at hand. A small number (13.1 percent) were unable to state a choice, 37.4 percent voted guilty, and 49.5 percent voted not guilty. A followup question to determine the certainty of their decision (very, somewhat, uncertain) enabled the location of each respondent's verdict on a constructed scale of 1 (very certain of innocence) to 7 (very certain of guilt), with the "don't know" respondents at the midpoint.[4]

The Evidence

Only after the respondent's verdict was obtained was each respondent asked to review and rate each point of information and evidence presented in the vignette. Specifically, the respondent was asked to indicate for each of the prosecution's points whether it was unfavorable, irrelevant, mildly favorable, or extremely favorable to the prosecution. Similarly, each element in the defense's case was rated as unfavorable, irrelevant, mildly favorable, or extremely favorable to the defense. Principal component scores without iterations, that is, regression weights, were obtained separately for the prosecution's evidence ratings and the defense's evidence ratings and a scale value was computed by weighting each item in terms of its contribution to the total score. The respondent's scores on the prosecution's evidence and the defense's evidence were expressed as a product of a linear regression equation. The higher the respondent's scores, the greater the respondent's estimation of the strength of the case made by the evidence introduced.

It is noteworthy that perceived strength of evidence was obtained separately for both the prosecution's evidence and the defense's evidence, rather than as a single measure. This permitted the respondent the opportunity to indicate that both the prosecution and the defense had a particularly strong or weak case. Indeed, the correlation coefficient between perceived strength of prosecution's evidence and perceived strength of defense's evidence was $-.27$, indicating that the two may be viewed as independent variables lacking multicollinearity.

RESULTS

A brief examination of the relationships found between attitudes and demographic characteristics among jury-eligible respondents precedes the analysis of

---

[3]The interviewer first inquired whether the respondent had any questions about the points made in the vignette. After answering whatever questions arose, and even in the absence of questions, the interviewer suggested that the respondent read the vignette a second time to focus on details "now that you have the overall picture." Finally, the respondent was asked whether she or he understood the prosecution's case and the defense's case. It was only after an affirmative response that the respondent was asked to render a verdict.

[4]The scale of verdict had a mean of 3.78 and a standard deviation of 2.33, reflecting both the greater frequency of "not guilty" verdicts and the variability in degree of certainty.

perceived strength of evidence to illustrate a problem commonly confronted in systematic jury selection. Also, an understanding of these relationships will be useful in discussing the effect of strength of evidence in the covariation of attitudes and verdict.

Demographic Characteristics, Attitudes, and Verdict

It is evident by the data presented in Table 1 that age, race, and prior military service are significantly related to attitude toward both police and punishment, that marital status is associated with attitude toward police, and that education and prior victimization covary with attitude toward punishment. These relationships would suggest that prodefendant jurors should be young, nonwhite, highly educated, married, with no prior history of military service, and, strangely, with a prior history of victimization.

Yet further examination of the data in Table 1 reveals the presence of two practical problems. First, the combined independent effects of these nine demographic and background variables explain only 9 percent of the variation in attitude toward police and 15 percent of the variation in attitude toward punishment. Much of the variation in respondent attitudes is unaccounted for by the "predictors." This distinction between statistically significant and substantively significant "predictors" is crucial in systematic jury selection (Saks, 1976b).

Second, it is apparent that verdict is associated with only age and prior military service. The other "predictors" of attitudes—race, education, military status, and prior victimization—have no apparent relation to verdict. In addition, the nine independent variables explain only 8 percent of the variation in verdict. Therefore, knowledge of those demographic and background characteristics related to respondent's attitudes does not provide sufficient information to predict the respondent's verdict.

Table 1. Association of Selected Respondent Characteristics
with Attitude toward Police, Attitude toward Punishment, and
Verdict (Pearson Correlation Coefficients)

Respondent characteristics	Attitude toward police	Attitude toward punishment	Verdict
Age	.21[a]	.26[a]	.19[a]
Sex	−.02	.01	−.05
Race	−.19[a]	−.14[a]	−.08
Occupation	−.02	−.02	.03
Education	.01	−.26[a]	−.08
Marital status	.14[a]	.09	.11
Religious attendance	−.01	.06	−.10
Crime victim	.05	−.12[a]	−.02
Military service	.17[a]	.15[a]	.18[a]
R^2	.09	.15	.08

[a] $p \le .05$

Table 2. Zero-Order Pearson Correlation Coefficients among Attitudes,
Strength of Evidence, and Verdict

	Attitude toward punishment	Strength of prosecution evidence	Strength of defense evidence	Verdict
Attitude toward police	.20	.32	−.17	.30
Attitude toward punishment		.24	−.23	.29
Strength of prosecution evidence			−.27	.45
Strength of defense evidence				−.66

Strength of Evidence and Verdict

The bivariate coefficients presented in Table 2 demonstrate the nature of the relationships found among case-relevant attitudes, perceived strength of evidence, and verdict. As anticipated, the more favorable the attitude toward police and toward punishment, the more likely the respondent is to render a verdict of guilty based on the case presented. Similarly, the greater the perceived strength of the prosecution's evidence and the lower the perceived strength of the defense's evidence, the greater the likelihood of a guilty verdict.

The significant zero-order association between case-relevant attitudes and perceived strength of evidence is a preliminary indication that attitudes do influence the interpretation of the evidence. Further exploration by means of partial coefficients lends additional strength to that argument. The bivariate coefficient of .30 between attitude toward police and verdict is reduced to first-order coefficients of .18 and .25 when strength of prosecution's evidence and strength of defense's evidence, respectively, are partialled. When both measures of strength of evidence are controlled, the second-order partial coefficient is .15, indicating that strength of evidence is an intervening variable in the association of attitude toward police and verdict. Similarly, the first-order partial coefficients between attitude toward punishment and verdict are .21 and .18 when prosecution's evidence and defense's evidence, respectively, are controlled. The second-order partial coefficient of .12 is a substantial enough reduction from the observed zero-order partial to suggest that strength of evidence is an intervening variable in the covariation of attitude toward punishment and verdict.

These data suggest that case-relevant attitudes of the jury-eligible respondents are related to and may influence the respondents' perception of the strength of the evidence presented by both prosecution and defense. Evidence is not a completely objective factor introduced into the courtroom; each juror will interpret the strength of the evidence in some degree of concordance with his or her attitudes. The path model presented in Figure 1 sheds further light on this question and addresses the issue of the relative contribution of case-relevant attitudes to the verdict when perceived strength of evidence is taken into account.[5]

---

[5]The value of a path model rests in its ability to present schematically the causal sequence purported to "explain" the variation in the dependent variable. Not only does this enable a diagram of the direct effects or direct causal linkages between each independent variable and the dependent variable, but it demonstrates the degree to which any independent variable affects the dependent variable indirectly by the influence on

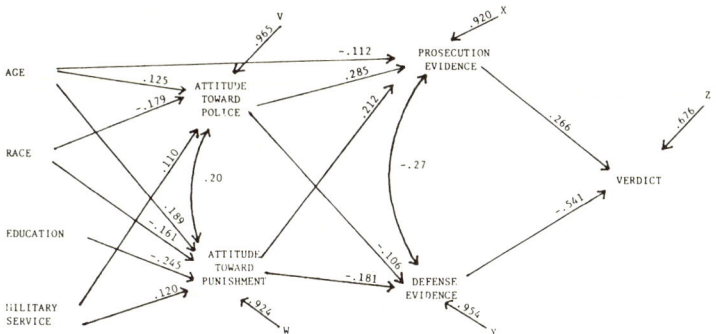

Fig. 1. A model of the causal relationship among case-relevant attitudes, strength of evidence, and verdict.

The path diagram more formally asserts the causal sequence implicit in the findings above: (1) demographic and background factors precede the case-relevant attitude toward police and attitude toward punishment (which are not causally related); (2) these variables causally precede the perceived strength of prosecution evidence and perceived strength of defense evidence (which are not causally related); and (3) verdict is the dependent variable. The model has been trimmed by including only those path coefficients which are twice their standard error, resulting in the omission of several extraneous variables and indicating no direct causal effect of the remaining extraneous variables on verdict.

It is not too surprising to find that strength of prosecution evidence and strength of defense evidence are the major explanatory variables of verdict, but it is interesting to note that neither case-relevant attitude has a significant direct causal effect on verdict. In fact, although the eight independent variables explain 54 percent of the variation in verdict ($F = 36.149, p < .001$), the two case-relevant attitudinal measures account for less than 2 percent of the explained variation once strength of prosecution evidence and strength of defense evidence are entered into the equation.

These results are consistent with those discussed above. Demographic and background characteristics do not significantly explain verdict. The partial correlation coefficients suggest, and the beta coefficients in the path model illustrate, that case-relevant attitudes do not affect verdict independent of perceived strength of evidence.

DISCUSSION

The efficacy and viability of systematic jury selection rests primarily on (1) the existence of bivariate relations found among demographic characteristics, case-

one or more other independent variables that directly affect the dependent variable. Thus, Figure 1 illustrates that defense evidence and prosecution evidence are the only factors to directly affect verdict; the influence of all other variables upon verdict is indirect. The path coefficients indicate the size and direction of the direct effects. Variables V, W, X, Y and Z in Figure 1 represent "unknown" variables, and their path coefficients indicate the direct effect of these unknown variables.

relevant attitudes, and "juror" verdict and (2) the failure to convict in those few trials in which its use is known. Yet, attorneys and others frequently voice the opinion that verdicts are decided on the strength of the evidence, not on the composition of the jury. This sentiment assumes that the strength of the evidence is an absolute rather than relative factor that operates independent of the characteristics and attitudes of the jurors.

The data suggest that the strength of the evidence is relative, influenced by case-relevant juror attitudes. Attitudes toward those issues which constitute the basis for the case and toward those social groups which testify during the trial influence one's perception of the strength of the evidence presented by prosecution and defense. Moreover, it is apparent that these attitudes contribute to the juror's verdict only indirectly. The direct causal effects of case-relevant attitudes do not account for a significant amount of the explained variation in verdict. Verdict is directly affected by the perceived strength of evidence, as Berk (1976) contends, yet the perceived strength of evidence is related to juror's case-relevant attitudes.

These results must be viewed as tentative, however, because of inadequacies in the research. An obvious limitation of the present analysis, as well as many others, is the use of individuals making private decisions rather than groups making public decisions. The degree to which the results are misleading cannot be specified, although at least one experimental study has demonstrated that group decisions are invariably the same as the position initially held by the majority of its individuals (Nemeth, 1976). Until more research becomes available, however, it would be unwise to assume that individual views will not be affected in some way by the dynamics of small group decision-making processes. Secondly, the data are based on interviews with a jury-eligible sample, but not necessarily a sample representative of those most likely to actually sit as jurors. Exclusions of potential jurors due to economic hardship, illness, family needs, and, of course, for "cause" often reduce the heterogeneity among potential jurors to a point where fine discriminations become methodologically impossible. Third, the limitations inherent in correlational analysis render the findings and conclusions tentative. The use of a vignette with no systematic variation produces results that are informative but inconclusive.

Fourth, this analysis is limited to a unique case—a charge of murder, the felony-murder rule, a young, black male defendant, a white male police officer victim, and a defense argument of a police conspiracy. In comparison, Feild (1978) finds that jurors' case-relevant attitudes significantly increased the amount of explained variation in verdict beyond the direct contribution of the evidence in a simulated rape case. It may well be that certain types of demographic information and case-relevant attitudes provide greater predictive utility in some cases than in others. Finally, of course, there is a growing body of literature which indicates that ratings by subject-jurors differ more in comparisons of transcripts to live trials than in comparisons of live trials to audio or video tape presentations (Farmer, Williams, Lee, Cundick, Howell, & Rooker, 1976).

For each of these reasons, the results are only suggestive. Nonetheless, these findings support the earlier work of Boehm (1968) and Reed and Reed (1977), and focus attention on the necessity of further research to explore the relationships among attitudes, evidence, and verdict. Research of this nature is compelling if only because there is little evidence that verdicts can be predicted by demographic data alone. As pointed out initially, the disparities in research findings indicate that no uniform set of predictors is available. What's more, statistically significant associations, which may account for less than 25 percent of the variation, are a far cry from powerful predictors.

These findings also raise issues of interest to jury selection practitioners. Attempts should be made to incorporate specific evidentiary information about the case in the survey of jury-eligible respondents from which "predictors" for the jury selection are to be derived. One obvious utility of data pertaining to perceived strength of evidence lies in its increased predictive power over case-related attitudes. As in any statistical model of etiology, the ability to correctly predict the dependent variable increases as the number of intervening variables between the independent or predictor variable and the dependent variable decreases. While evidentiary questions cannot be raised during voir dire, they can be incorporated into the jury-eligible community survey from which the association of demographic characteristics and case-relevant attitudes is currently obtained. By examining the relationship between strength of evidence and other data obtained in the survey, the voir dire questions may focus on those particular demographics and attitudes found to be predictors of the respondents' perception of strength of evidence. Presently there is an assumption that certain demographics will predict certain attitudes; the inclusion of evidentiary information in the survey changes the assumption to one in which the demographics and attitudes predict a responsiveness to evidence. By moving in this direction, there is an increased probability of correctly predicting the verdict because a major intervening variable—the evidence—is viewed as, indeed, a variable.

A second utility of strength of evidence data relies on the attorney's willingness to incorporate social science techniques into her or his presentation or defense of the case. Each of the prosecution and defense points of evidence can be examined, the opponent's strongest points and one's own weakest points can be identified, and the presentation or rebuttal can be modified to dwell upon those evidentiary points which hamper one's case. In short, a rating of the strength of each piece of evidence, each witness, each cross-examination, and so forth will enable a more selective presentation of the case.

Finally, the relative effects of strength of prosecution evidence and strength of defense evidence should not be overlooked. It was the strength of the defense's evidence that explained the most variation in the verdict. Stated in the contrary, it appears that a weak defense is more important than a strong prosecution in the guilty verdict. This implication that the juror is not so much swayed by the strength of the prosecution's evidence as by the defense's failure to provide some reason to vote for acquittal suggests the presence, at least among those sampled in this analysis, of the presumption of "guilty until proven innocent." The degree to which such a presumption appears in other respondents (see Kaplan & Simon, 1972) may substantially alter the position of the defense or prosecution in the presentation of evidence.

In conclusion, the discussion and debate of the ethical implications of systematic jury selection (Etzioni, 1974; Herbsleb, Sales, & Berman, 1978; Moore, 1974; Saks, 1976a) is premature, if only because the social scientist has yet to elevate the procedure to a predictive science. Such discussions are not irrelevant, however, since increased attention to the juror's receptiveness to evidence may have an impact upon not only the selection of the jury but also the presentation of the evidence during the trial.

REFERENCES

Berk, R. Social science and jury selection: A case study of a civil suit. In Bermant, G., Nemeth, C., & Vidmar, N. (Eds.) *Psychology and the Law.* Lexington, Massachusetts: D.C. Heath, 1976.

Berk, R., Hennessey, M., & Swan, J. The vagaries and vulgarities of 'scientific' jury selection: A methodological evaluation. *Evaluation Quarterly,* 1977, **1**, 143–158.

Berman, J., & Sales, B. A critical evaluation of the systematic approach to jury selection. *Criminal Justice and Behavior,* 1977, **4**, 219–240.

Boehm, V. Mr. Prejudice, Miss Sympathy, and the authoritarian personality: An application of psychological measuring techniques to the problem of jury bias. *Wisconsin Law Review,* 1968, 734–750.

Bray, R., & Noble, A. Authoritarianism and decisions of mock juries. *Journal of Personality and Social Psychology,* 1978, **36**, 1424–1430.

Bronson, E. On the conviction proneness and representativeness of the death-qualified jury. *University of Colorado Law Review,* 1970, **42**, 1–32.

Buckhout, R. Jury without peers. CR-2, Center for Responsive Psychology, 1973.

Davis, J., Bray, R., & Holt, R. The empirical study of decision processes in juries. In Tapp, J., & Levine, F. (Eds.) *Law, Justice and the Individual in Society: Psychological and Legal Issues.* Chicago: Holt, Rinehart and Winston, 1977.

Doob, A. Evidence, procedure, and psychological research. In Bermant, G., Nemeth, C., & Vidmar, N. (Eds.) *Psychology and the Law.* Lexington, Massachusetts: D.C. Heath, 1976.

Etzioni, A. Creating an imbalance. *Trial,* 1974, **10**, 28–30.

Farmer, L., Williams, G., Lee, R., Cundick, B., Howell, R., & Rooker, C.K. Juror perceptions of trial testimony as a function of the method of presentation. In Bermant, G., Nemeth, C., & Vidmar, N. (Eds.) *Psychology and the Law.* Lexington, Massachusetts: D.C. Heath, 1976.

Feild, H. Juror background characteristics and attitudes toward rape. *Law and Human Behavior,* 1978, **2**, 73–93.

Herbsleb, J., Sales, B., & Berman, J. When psychologists aid in the voir dire: Legal and ethical issues. In Abt, L., & Stuart, I. (Eds.) *The Social Psychology of Discretionary Law.* New York: Van Nostrand Reinhold, 1978.

Kairys, D. Juror selection: The law, a mathematical model of analysis, and a case study. *American Criminal Law Journal,* 1972, **10**, 771–806.

Kairys, D., Schulman, J., & Harring, S. *The Jury System: New Methods for Reducing Prejudice.* Philadelphia: National Jury Project and National Lawyers Guild, 1975.

Kalven, H., & Zeisel, H. *The American Jury.* Boston: Little, Brown, 1966.

Kaplan, K., & Simon, R. Latitude and severity of sentencing options, race of victim and decisions of simulated jurors. *Law and Society Review,* 1972, **7**, 87–98.

McConahay, J., Mullin, C., & Frederick, J. The uses of social science in trials with political and racial overtones: The trial of Joan Little. *Law and Contemporary Problems,* 1977, **41**, 205–229.

Mitchell, H., & Byrne, D. The defendant's dilemma: Effects of jurors' attitudes and authoritarianism on judicial decision. *Journal of Personality and Social Psychology,* 1973, **25**, 123–129.

Moore, H., Jr. Redressing the balance. *Trial,* 1974, **10**, 29–35.

Nemeth, C. Rules governing jury deliberations: A consideration of recent changes. In Bermant, G., Nemeth, C., & Vidmar, N. (Eds.) *Psychology and the Law.* Lexington, Massachusetts: D.C. Heath, 1976.

Reed, J., & Reed, R. Liberalism–conservatism as an indicator of jury product and process. *Law and Human Behavior,* 1977, **1**, 81–86.

Rokeach, M., & Vidmar, N. Testimony concerning possible jury bias in a Black Panther murder trial. *Journal of Applied Social Psychology,* 1973, **3**, 19–29.

Sage, W. Psychology and the Angela Davis jury. *Human Behavior,* 1973, **2,** 56–61.

Saks, M. The limits of scientific jury selection: Ethical and empirical. *Jurimetrics Journal,* 1976a, **17,** 3–22.

Saks, M. Social scientists can't rig juries. *Psychology Today,* 1976b, **9,** 48–50, 55–57.

Schulman, J., Shaver, P., Colman, R., Emrich, B., & Christie, R. Recipe for a jury. *Psychology Today,* 1973, **7,** 34–44, 79–84.

Shapely, D. Jury selection: Social scientists gamble in an already loaded game. *Science,* 1974, **185,** 1033–1034, 1071.

Simon, R. *The Jury and the Defense of Insanity.* Boston: Little, Brown, 1967.

Skolnick, J. *Justice without Trial.* New York: John Wiley and Sons, 1966.

Suggs, D., & Sales, B. The art and science of conducting the voir dire. *Professional Psychology,* 1978, **9,** 367–388.

Thayer, R. Attitude and personality differences between potential jurors who could return a death verdict and those who could not. In *Proceedings of the American Psychological Association, 78th annual convention.* Washington, D.C.: American Psychological Association, 1970.

Juror Decision Making

The Importance of Evidence*

Christy A. Visher†

Much of the research on juror decision making is concerned with whether jurors are swayed by irrelevant—or extralegal—issues in their judgments of defendants. Such studies examine whether jurors' attitudes and victims' and defendants' characteristics have a measurable impact on these decisions. Yet, in the typical study, evidential issues are either poorly measured or ignored, hence the effects of extralegal issues may be exaggerated. Moreover, jury simulations are often chosen to study these questions despite critics' concerns about the generalizability of the results. The present study uses data gathered from actual jurors to assess whether the emphasis on juror competence is justified. The results indicate that these jurors' decisions are dominated by evidential issues, particularly evidence concerning the use of force and physical evidence. Jurors were considerably less responsive to characteristics of victims and defendants, although some of these factors significantly affected their decisions.

INTRODUCTION

The jury is the only decision-making body in the criminal justice system composed of laypersons. But recently it has been the center of increasing criticism. Opponents of the jury system argue that persons who lack formal training and knowledge of the law, but control decisions of life and liberty, cannot be expected to render fair and impartial verdicts. Juries, the critics claim, fail to recall the evidence accurately, become confused by complex trials or those involving multiple defendants, and are often swayed by legally irrelevant information (e.g., Kadish & Kadish, 1971; Scheflin & Van Dyke, 1980; Williams, 1963). Thus, the

---

* The research reported here was supported by the National Institute of Mental Health under grant No. R01 MH29727 and the National Institute of Justice under grant No. 82-IJ-CX-0015. The author would like to thank Douglas Smith, Barbara Reskin, and Lowell Hargens for helpful comments on earlier drafts.

† Research Associate, National Research Council, National Academy of Sciences, Washington, D.C.

most serious criticism of the jury system is that jurors are not competent to consider the evidence impartially and to decide issues of fact. These issues are especially serious today as the public and some legislators have been critical of recent jury verdicts involving the death penalty and other publicized cases, such as the trial of John Hinckley, who attempted to assassinate a U.S. President.

Early research on juror behavior was motivated by the question of whether jurors' decisions reflected extralegal (irrelevant) as well as legal (evidentiary) factors (Hoffman & Brodley, 1952; Hunter, 1935; Weld & Danzig, 1940). Later studies have continued this emphasis by examining the potential influences of defendants' characteristics, prejudicial evidence, jurors' attitudes, and jurors' application of judges' legal instructions on juror decision making. In fact, attention to the competence of jurors has been the primary issue in the study of juror decision making (for reviews, see Baldwin & McConville, 1980; Davis, Bray, & Holt, 1977; Gerbasi, Zuckerman, & Reiss, 1977). Unfortunately, in the quest to identify sources of bias in jurors' decisions, researchers have often overlooked the impact of trial evidence which presumably dominates these decisions. Little is known about the types of evidence that may influence jurors or the relative impact of legal and extralegal factors.

This study explores whether the emphasis on juror competence that appears in most studies of jurors and juries is justified by using data on actual jurors' decisions in criminal trials. Specifically, once evidential influences are accounted for, what effect do extralegal factors have on jurors' decisions? Data are available on jurors' personal characteristics, victim's and defendant's attributes, and evidence presented during the trial. After an overview of relevant research on jurors and juries, in particular the extent of knowledge about the role of evidence in jurors' decisions, measures of both legal and extralegal influences are used to estimate a model of juror decision making.

EMPIRICAL ASSESSMENTS OF JUROR DECISION MAKING

After hearing the evidence and closing arguments, most jurors probably have reached a tentative decision regarding the defendant's guilt or innocence. In fact, research on actual jurors has shown that most juries, which typically begin deliberations with an informal poll, decide in favor of the initial majority (Kalven & Zeisel, 1966), and experimental studies of jury verdicts support this finding (Davis, Kerr, Atkin, Holt, & Meek, 1975; Saks, 1977). The final jury verdict is a collective decision based on these individual opinions, and understanding juror decision making prior to the deliberations is important for identifying the salient legal and extralegal factors in those decisions.

The types of factors that affect actual jurors' judgments roughly fall into one of three categories: (1) their personal characteristics; (2) victims' and defendants' characteristics; and (3) evidence and case background. A jury trial is a complex event and these categories of variables represent dozens of possible influences on jurors' decisions. However, most studies of jurors and juries focus on only one group of variables and rarely consider the *joint* effects of these variables. The extralegal influences—jurors', victims', and defendants' characteristics—have received the most emphasis in research on jurors and juries.

Extralegal Influences

Studies of juror behavior typically examine whether jurors' personal attributes—demographic characteristics and attitudes—affect their judgments of the defendant. The assumption that jurors' characteristics do influence verdicts has led to a widespread belief among the legal profession that the composition of a jury can determine the trial outcome (for a review, see Fahringer, 1980). Moreover, the "scientific" jury selection methods used by defense counsel in the last decade rely on correlations between demographic characteristics and case-related attitudes uncovered in community surveys to select jurors who are likely to be favorable to the defendants. There is little evidence, however, that the method makes any difference in trial outcomes (see Hans & Vidmar, 1982; Saks, 1976).

Empirical studies of individual juror behavior occasionally find that jurors' demographic characteristics—age, gender, race, and occupation—are statistically related to jurors' judgments of the defendant. But a careful look at these studies reveals that these factors are not strong enough to be used as predictors and they only account for a small portion of the variance in verdicts (see Hans & Vidmar, 1982; Hastie, Penrod, & Pennington, 1983; Hepburn, 1980; Sealy, 1981). On this point, Hans and Vidmar (1982: p. 57) forcefully argue that "the [jury] literature is plagued with a major conceptual problem" because it assumes that if juror characteristics influence verdicts, these factors will override evidentiary and situational factors.

The only two generally consistent findings about the impact of jurors' characteristics are that (1) *case-relevant* attitudes (e.g., attitudes toward punishment) may influence juror decision making (Hastie et al., 1983: pp. 127–128; Hepburn, 1980), and (2) some demographic factors probably affect deliberation performance and recall of evidence and judge's instructions (Hastie et al., 1983; Strodtbeck & Mann, 1956; Strodtbeck, Simon, & Hawkins, 1957). But neither of these sources of juror bias rival the effects of evidence and case characteristics in the determination of guilt or innocence in the few analyses that have included evidence. In sum, research suggests that jurors' personal characteristics are substantively insignificant in affecting trial outcomes.

In contrast, a variety of studies report that defendants' and victims' characteristics affect jurors' decisions. In simulated trial situations, the defendant's overall "social attractiveness," as revealed in written stimulus materials, has consistently influenced mock jurors' judgments. Occupation, marital status, criminal history, appearance, and personality traits are examples of the types of characteristics that have been included in these studies. Defendants who appeared "attractive" to mock jurors were judged less severely, received more lenient sentences, and were less often thought guilty than their "unattractive" counterparts (e.g., Barnett & Feild, 1978; Landy & Aronson, 1969; Nemeth & Sosis, 1973; for reviews, see Dane & Wrightsman, 1982; Stephan, 1975; Weiten & Diamond, 1979).

In the few studies of actual trials, jurors appeared somewhat responsive to defendants' characteristics. In a study of disagreements between judges and juries carried out by the Chicago Jury Project, Kalven and Zeisel (1966: p. 217) concluded that "sentiments about the defendant" were probably involved in 22% of disagreements. The primary defendant attributes that affected those jurors were prior criminal record, general courtroom appearance, and sympathy-related factors (e.g., repentant attitude, young, supportive family). Defendants' employment status and criminal record also influenced actual jurors' verdicts in two other studies (Reed, 1965; Myers, 1979).

Research on juror decision making that considers the influence of victims' characteristics usually focuses on the "character" of the victim (who is most often female). Typical variables in experimental studies include marital status, previous sexual experience, carelessness, and indicators of a "nontraditional" lifestyle. Many studies report that if the victim in the trial vignette is portrayed with a poor character, then subjects are lenient in their judgments of the defendant (e.g., Calhoun, Selby, Cann, & Keller, 1978; Feild & Bienen, 1980; Jones & Aronson, 1973), although other research shows no relationship (e.g., Burt & Albin, 1981; Kahn et al., 1977).

In Kalven and Zeisel's study, the judge–jury disagreements in sexual assault cases were likely based on the jury's notion of the "contributory fault of the victim" (1966: p. 243). Victims who drank prior to the incident, accepted rides with strangers, or led an untraditional lifestyle apparently influenced jury verdicts. However, the characteristics of defendants and victims were only *partial* explanations of disagreements; differing interpretations of the evidence were the primary reasons for judge–jury differences in verdicts in the Chicago study.

One limitation with much of the experimental research on victims' and defendants' characteristics is that it focuses on either the attributes of the defendant or those of the victim as a source of juror bias (e.g., Jones & Aronson, 1973; Mitchell & Byrne, 1973; Scroggs, 1976), which results in misleading conclusions about juror decision making. It is difficult to imagine how actual jurors could make judgments without information on both the defendant and the victim, but case summaries of this type are often presented to subjects in experimental studies.

A second problem is that studies in which the description of the defendant (or victim) is unusual or prominent[1] may invoke responses particular to the stimulus materials (see Ebbesen & Konecni, 1980; Elwork, Sales, & Suggs, 1981). More generally, experimental manipulations of factors thought to influence jurors may diverge considerably from the way in which this information is actually used by jurors. In one well-designed experiment on juror decision making, experimental manipulations of the victim's and defendant's characteristics and attitudinal scales representing jurors' perceptions of the victim and defendant (mea-

---

[1] For example, in the Landy and Aronson (1969) experiment, the "unattractive" defendant was described as a twice-divorced janitor, unknown to many of his co-workers, previously convicted of breaking and entering and a drug violation; the "attractive" defendant was a friendly widower (whose wife died of cancer), employed as an insurance adjustor.

sured by semantic differential items) were included in a multivariate model (Burt & Albin, 1981). Analyses showed that the *attitudinal* measures had significant effects on subjects' judgments of the defendant's guilt, whereas the factors traditionally manipulated explained virtually none of the variance in the dependent variable. The experimental variables apparently did not capture the mock jurors' reactions to the victim and defendant.

Thus, in many experimental studies, the implications of the manipulated effects for actual juror behavior, particularly for assessing the competence of jurors, may not be clearcut. Features of the experimental design and the lack of attention to evidence in these studies could exaggerate the effects of extralegal factors on jurors' decisions (Weiten & Diamond, 1979; Vidmar, 1979).[2]

Evidential Influences

The research emphasis on extralegal influences and juror competence has created a void in the literature, and research on the role of legally relevant factors—witnesses' testimony and exhibits—in jurors' decisions is lacking. How do jurors perceive evidence in a criminal trial and incorporate it into their judgments regarding the defendant's guilt? Which witnesses have the greatest impact on jurors? Is the evidence presented by the defense and the prosecution evaluated similarly? What weight is given to evidential influences relative to extralegal factors? Several studies have provided fascinating accounts of how jurors discuss the evidence by analyzing the recorded deliberations of simulated juries. The research on individual jurors, however, is much less informative.

As part of the Chicago Jury Project, Simon (1967; see also Strodtbeck et al., 1957; Strodtbeck & Mann, 1956) studied the deliberations of 40 mock juries who heard a 60-minute tape recording of an incest case. After a careful review of the transcripts, she concluded that those juries relied heavily on the details of the case, appropriately weighed the credibility of witnesses, and reached verdicts that were supported by the evidence. Three similar studies—two of which were conducted in England—recruited subjects from local jury pools. These mock jurors either sat in on an actual trial (McCabe & Purves, 1974), listened to an audio tape (Scaly, 1975), or viewed a film reenactment (Hastie et al., 1983) of a criminal trial. Analyses revealed that a high percentage of total deliberation time was spent on relevant evidentiary considerations. Extralegal influences, such as

---

[2] Much has been written about limitations of experimental jury studies, particularly on the issue of generalizability (e.g., Bray & Kerr, 1982; Weiten & Diamond, 1979). In brief, the critics' two primary concerns are that the experimental subjects are often college students, and that the classroom or the "laboratory" is usually the setting chosen for the experiment. The use of student subjects, whose social experiences and attitudes differ from those of actual jurors, may cast doubt on generalizing their decisions to actual jurors (see, e.g., Fried, Kaplan, & Klein, 1975; Simon, 1967). The artificiality of the experimental setting may also impede inferences to the target population because of the brief, written case summaries typically given to experimental subjects, the lack of *voir dire*, and the simplicity of the stimulus materials (Bermant, McGuire, McKinley, & Salo, 1974; Dillehay & Nietzel, 1980; Zeisel & Diamond, 1978).

personal experiences, occasionally entered discussions, but these factors were generally mentioned to help the group resolve conflicts in the evidence.

In the Chicago study of judge and jury verdicts, juries were influenced primarily by legally relevant factors, and in 78% of 3,576 trials the jury agreed with the judge's verdict (Kalven & Zeisel, 1966: p. 58). As mentioned previously, the disagreements usually involved both extralegal and evidential issues. However, Kalven and Zeisel discovered that the influence of factors such as victims' or defendants' characteristics only affected the jury's verdict when the evidence was weak.[3] Interpretations of the evidence clearly dominated jury verdicts in this large study of actual jury decision making.

Since the Chicago Jury Project, experiments involving individual juror behavior have rarely considered how evidence influences jurors' decisions and these studies have been much less realistic than the earlier experimental research. Only a handful of studies include some type of evidence measure in their written summary of a hypothetical case, and usually evidence is dichotomized to represent either incriminating or exonerating conditions (e.g., Kaplan & Kemmerick, 1974; Myers & Kaplan, 1976; Rumsey & Rumsey, 1977), or the number of evidence statements is varied (e.g., Field & Bienen, 1980; Ostrom, Werner, & Saks, 1978). However, these types of evidential measures give subjects the impression that the case against the hypothetical defendant is either strong or weak. In actual trials, jurors must often extract and evaluate relevant information from conflicting testimony, and how they weigh the pieces affects their judgment about the defendant's guilt.

One study is an exception to the pattern of using simplistic evidence measures and the results underscore the importance of including evidential issues in trial vignettes. Tanford and Penrod (1982) used eight pieces of evidence—both trial (e.g., eyewitnesses) and character (e.g., prior criminal record) evidence—in their written summaries of several simulated trials. No previous experimental study has included as wide a range of evidential issues. Subjects rated each type of evidence as to whether it favored or incriminated the defendant. The results indicated that subjects perceived trial evidence to be more incriminating than character evidence. Further, trial evidence differentiated between guilt and innocence judgments more strongly than character evidence.

Thus, with the exception of the Tanford–Penrod study, the impact of evidence on juror decision making has either been poorly measured or been neglected in experimental studies. Jury simulation research does have some advantages over other methods when the focus of study is some aspect of group interaction and its effect on the jury's verdict (e.g., the effects of jury size or different social decision rules on verdict). However, this research method may not be well suited to an examination of the relative weight that jurors give to evidential infor-

---

[3] This possible interaction between evidential strength and the influence of extralegal factors on juror decision making has been empirically examined in many studies (Baumeister & Darley, 1982; Feild & Bienen, 1980; Kaplan & Kemmerick, 1974; Myers, 1979), although the results have been inconclusive. Another analysis of this question using data on actual jurors found some support for Kalven and Zeisel's hypothesis (Reskin & Visher, in press).

mation and extralegal factors. The current study, which uses data collected from post-trial interviews with actual jurors, should provide more detailed knowledge about the importance of evidence for individual jurors' decisions than currently exists in the experimental literature.

DATA AND METHODS

This study is based on post-trial interviews with 331 jurors, 70.4 percent of the 456 jurors who served in the 38 forcible sexual assault[4] trials held in a large midwestern city between July 1978 and September 1980.[5] In three trials jurors were asked to make a judgment on two defendants, which produced a total of 360 juror responses. Missing data on the dependent variable reduced the sample to 340. The 90-minute interviews elicited information on jurors' background characteristics and attitudes about the criminal justice system and rape as well as their reactions to trial participants and proceedings. Additional data were obtained through careful written summaries of trial proceedings by two trained observers. For each trial, observers coded defendants' and victims' characteristics, recorded all evidence presented, and provided a synopsis of the testimony from each witness.

The Juror Sample

Jurors in the midwestern court chosen for this study are randomly taken from lists of registered voters. If their names are selected, they must appear for *voir dire* (jury selection). Both the defense and the prosecution are allotted ten challenges to dismiss prospective jurors without stating a reason. In practice attorneys often dismissed married women with daughters of similar age to the victim, persons who had been recently victimized, and persons who knew police

---

[4] "Forcible sexual assault" encompasses completed and attempted rape and sodomy. Charges against defendants in 34 cases included rape or attempted rape. In four cases, charges included either sodomy or attempted sodomy. Eight cases included both rape and sodomy charges. The similarity in these trials with respect to charges filed also extended to other characteristics. These trials were generally not complex, involved one defendant and one victim (33 trials), and were completed in one or two days (32 trials). Deliberations were completed in four hours or less in all but six cases.

[5] After the jury had reached a verdict and had been dismissed, each juror was given a letter which explained the study, told them that it was being done with the judge's consent, and asked them to return a postcard (with their name, address, and phone number) indicating whether they would consent to an interview. Trained interviewers, matched to jurors on race and sex, followed-up a few days later using phone numbers in court records and interviews were generally scheduled within a week after the trial.

In order to assess nonresponse bias, the interviewed sample was compared with nonrespondents by asking those who refused an interview if they would answer a few questions over the phone. Of the 84 refusals, 31 jurors completed the telephone interview. The contacted nonrespondents did not appear to differ from those interviewed with respect to basic demographic information or attitudes. The 41 jurors who did not participate in this study could not be located because of incomplete or inaccurate address and telephone information in court records.

officers. Prospective jurors may also present an excuse to the court for relief from jury duty. Thus, jurors who decide criminal cases are not a representative sample of all citizens.

Descriptive statistics about the juror sample appear in Table 1. Males and females were equally represented on juries that tried the 38 cases in this sample. Blacks served on these juries in about the same proportion as their population in the large city in which the trials took place (16%). The age of these jurors ranged from 20 to 74, with the average age being about 43 years. The typical juror completed one year of college, was married, and employed. Craftsmen, laborers, and sevice workers represented one-third of the sample. The rest of the sample was divided about equally across the three other occupational status groups—clerical workers, managers, and professionals.

The reader may question whether juror decision making in sexual assault trials is similar to that in other types of criminal trials. Actually, this sample allows an especially strong examination of whether extralegal factors are influential in jurors' decisions. In sexual assault trials the victim's character and behavior are often used by the defense to discredit the victim's testimony (despite increasing legal limitations on this information). Jurors are more likely to hear irrelevant testimony in these emotionally charged cases than in a burglary or robbery case. In addition, jury simulations often use rape as the offense in their hypothetical cases (e.g., Burt & Albin, 1981; Feild, 1979; Jones & Aronson, 1973; Scroggs, 1976), and in one study of prosecutors' decisions sexual assault cases resembled other cases involving violent personal crimes such as assault and robbery (Myers & LaFree, 1982). Thus, this sample would seem to be a good choice for a study of whether jurors are unduly swayed by potentially biasing information.

Dependent and Independent Variables

Table 1 also shows the coding and distribution of the variables. The dependent variable is the individual juror's assessment of the defendant's innocence or guilt at the end of the trial but prior to deliberation. As mentioned previously, the initial majority among the jurors is highly predictive of the final jury verdict. Few studies of individual juror behavior, however, have used jurors from actual trials. This study focuses on the factors influencing individual jurors' judgments rather than the group processes that led to the final jury verdict. The independent variables represent previously mentioned categories of potential influence on jurors' judgments: (1) jurors' characteristics and attitudes, (2) victims' attributes, (3) defendants' attributes, and (4) measures of evidence and case characteristics.[6]

---

[6] Since the jurors were interviewed after the deliberations, it is possible that jurors' recollections of their predeliberation guilt judgments were influenced by the deliberation process. No solution exists to this problem, but the jurors' candor during the interviews concerning their reactions to the jury process increase the validity of the data. During the interviews, about 20% of the jurors expressed less than complete agreement with the final verdict. The interview was also structured to simulate the order of events during the trial: jurors were asked questions in turn about the victim and the defendant, the saliency of several types of evidence, the effect of the closing arguments, their predeliberation judgment, and lastly, their reactions to the deliberation process.

Table 1. Description of Variables

Variable	Correlation with dependent variable	Coding and frequencies	
Dependent variable			
Juror's assessment of defendant's guilt prior to deliberations	—	1 = certainly innocent 2 = probably innocent 3 = probably guilty 4 = certainly guilty	47 44 119 130
Jurors' characteristics and attitudes			
Sex	− .04	0 = male 1 = female	159 181
Race	− .15	0 = white 1 = black	287 53
Age	− .06	Interval (in years)	$\overline{X} = 42.7$
Education	.15	Interval (in years)	$\overline{X} = 13.2$
Occupational status[a]	.12	1 = craftsman, laborer service worker 2 = clerical 3 = manager 4 = professional, technical	112 79 70 79
Tough-on-crime attitudes	.16	Factor scale: high score indicates tough-on-crime attitudes	
Blame-the-victim attitudes	− .22	Factor scale: high score indicates blame-the-victim attitudes	
Victim's characteristics			
Drank, used drugs in general or before the incident	− .33	0 = not mentioned 1 = mentioned by juror	246 94
Victim seemed careless	− .43	1 = careful, 5 = careless	$\overline{X} = 2.85$
Sexual activity outside marriage, illegitimate children	− .36	0 = no or not mentioned 1 = mentioned in court	195(23)[b] 145(15)
Defendant's Characteristics			
Defendant presented negative appearance; unattractive	.06	1 = attractive, 5 = unattractive	$\overline{X} = 3.04$
Defendant seemed uneducated	.28	1 = educated, 5 = uneducated	$\overline{X} = 2.96$
Prior criminal record	.01	0 = no or not mentioned 1 = mentioned in court	232(22) 108(19)
Evidence and case characteristics			
Use of weapon	.34	0 = not mentioned 1 = mentioned by juror	243 97
Physical evidence	.26	0 = not mentioned 1 = mentioned by juror	245 95
Use of force	.37	0 = not mentioned 1 = mentioned by juror	217 123
Eyewitness testimony	.21	0 = not mentioned 1 = mentioned by juror	282 58
Other victim's testimony	.18	0 = none 1 = presented in court	283(31) 57 (7)
Defendant's relatives' testimony	.04	0 = none 1 = presented in court	136(15) 204(23)
Defense claimed victim's story was implausible	− .46	0 = no 1 = yes	176(22) 164(16)

[a] The four occupational status categories follow the divisions used by the U.S. Bureau of Census in coding occupations. Jurors not currently employed were coded for the status of their spouse's occupation.

[b] For the courtroom observation data, values in parentheses are frequencies of the 38 trials, except for defendant's prior criminal record, which is based on all 41 defendants to whom jurors responded. (Three trials had more than one defendant.)

279

The jurors' characteristics are sex, race, age, occupational status, and education, all of which have been included in prior research to assess the impact of personal biases. Factor analysis was used to construct measures of jurors' attitudes that might be relevant to the trial from many attitudinal questions in the interview. One scale taps attitudes toward crime and the criminal justice system. Since rape is often an emotional issue, a measure of attitudes toward rape and rape victims is also included to assess whether these attitudes have any effect on jurors' decisions.[7]

Four measures of victims' and defendants' attributes are taken from jurors' comments about or evaluations of the victim and the defendant: (1) any reference to the victim's use of drugs or alcohol in general or at the time of the assault, (2) how careful or careless the jurors thought the victim was at the time of the assault, (3) an assessment of the defendant's attractiveness, and (4) an assessment of the defendant's educational level. Two additional variables are based on courtroom observations: whether testimony indicated that the victim had been sexually active outside marriage and whether testimony revealed that the defendant had a criminal record.[8]

The last set of variables in Table 1 measure evidential influences and case characteristics. Four variables are dichotomous indicators of types of evidence mentioned by jurors as important in response to a series of open-ended questions: (1) use of a weapon, (2) physical evidence (e.g., torn clothing, items recovered from scene), (3) evidence of force during the assault, and (4) eyewitnesses (either to the incident or to surrounding events). Three additional variables were recorded from courtroom testimony: (1) testimony from other victims involved in the incident or allegedly assaulted by the same defendant, (2) testimony from the defendant's relatives which supported an alibi or provided information about the defendant's character, and (3) testimony and arguments that the victim's story was implausible. Finally, Table 1 also includes the bivariate correlation between the dependent variable and each independent variable.

ANALYSIS AND RESULTS

In the following analyses, multiple regression is used to estimate the relative impact of evidence and extralegal factors on jurors' decisions in a sample of

---

[7] Attitudinal items (coded with five Likert categories) concerning the criminal justice system, sexual assault, and rape victims were entered into a standard principal components factor analysis. The two scales used here achieved reliability scores of .6 to .7, and explained 20%–32% of the variance in the underlying items. Because of the possibility that jurors' attitudes about rape might be influenced by the trial, a separate sample of 87 jurors from trials other than those involving sexual assault cases were selected and interviewed. These jurors were compared with the original sample on demographic information, attitudes toward women and rape, and attitudes towards crime. No significant differences ($p = .05$) were found, which suggests that serving on a sexual assault case probably did not affect jurors' attitudes. For further discussion of the attitudinal questions and scale construction, see LaFree, Reskin, and Visher (1985).

[8] The variables derived from courtroom observations were independently coded by two observers for each trial. Most of these variables had dichotomous choice responses and the observers agreed. In the few instances in which disagreement did occur, the observers and project staff referred to other observations and jurors' comments during the interviews to resolve the differences.

sexual assault trials. An initial equation uses the seven evidential variables to obtain an estimate of their explanatory power for the jurors' predeliberation judgments. In a second equation, victims' and defendants' characteristics and jurors' attributes are added to determine whether these factors significantly affect jurors' judgments after evidence is taken into account. The impact of these extralegal factors, and hence, the issue of juror competence, cannot be assessed accurately unless relevant legitimate influences are controlled.

The Impact of Evidence

Table 2 presents the regression of jurors' judgments of the defendant's guilt on the seven measures of evidence and case characteristics (equation 1). Collectively, these evidence variables explain 34% of the variance in individual jurors'

Table 2. Regression Coefficients and Standard Errors for a Model Predicting Jurors' Predeliberation Judgments of Guilt with Evidential Issues and a Second Model Including Extralegal Influences ($n = 340$)

Variable	Equation 1			Equation 2		
	b	SE	B	b	SE	B
Evidence and case characteristics						
Use of weapon	.405[a]	(.11)	.174	.412[a]	(.11)	.178
Physical evidence	.312[a]	(.11)	.133	.252[a]	(.11)	.108
Evidence of force	.504[a]	(.10)	.231	.355[a]	(.10)	.163
Eyewitness testimony	.222[b]	(.13)	.080	.013	(.13)	.004
Other victim's testimony	.167	(.13)	.059	.051	(.13)	.018
Defendant relatives' testimony	.013	(.06)	.011	− .034	(.06)	− .027
Defense claimed victim's story was implausible	− .588[a]	(.11)	− .280	− .386[a]	(.11)	− .184
Victim's and Defendant's characteristics						
VICTIM						
Sexual activity outside marriage				− .291[a]	(.10)	− .138
Alcohol or drug use				.189[b]	(.11)	− .081
Careless behavior				− .149[a]	(.04)	− .193
DEFENDANT						
Prior criminal record				.028	(.10)	.013
Uneducated				.103[a]	(.04)	.105
Negative appearance				.067	(.04)	.066
Juror's Characteristics						
Female				− .104	(.09)	− .050
Black				− .011	(.13)	− .004
Age				− .002	(.00)	− .028
Education				.020	(.02)	.052
Occupational status				.021	(.05)	.023
Tough-on-crime attitudes				.118[a]	(.06)	.093
Blame-the-victim attitudes				− .028	(.06)	− .022
CONSTANT	2.774			3.380		
ADJUSTED R^2	.34			.44		

[a] $p < .05$.
[b] $p < .10$.

judgments. Corroborative evidence of several types appeared to be especially influential: (1) use of a weapon, (2) testimony that the assault involved force, (3) physical evidence such as torn clothing or defendant's possessions found at the scene, and (4) eyewitness testimony. Conversely, testimony or arguments from the defense that the victim's story was implausible weakened the prosecution's case and resulted in fewer guilty judgments. The testimony of defendants' relatives, however, did not affect initial decisions, probably because jurors did not believe those witnesses. In addition, in a separate analysis (not shown) the defendant's testimony, which was highly correlated with other measures of defense and prosecution evidence, had no effect on jurors' judgments. Eyewitness testimony is much less important ($p = .10$) than physical evidence or evidence of force. The lack of a strong independent effect for this type of testimony is partly attributed to its correlation with the defense tactic measure ($r = -.30$). Defense attorneys are less likely to claim that the victim's story was implausible if an eyewitness was present at the scene.

Evidential and Extralegal Influences on Jurors' Judgments

With the addition of 13 predictors representing measures of jurors', victims', and defendants' characteristics (equation 2), the importance of legal factors and the need for appropriate model specification in studying jurors' decisions is clear. The extralegal factors only explained an additional ten percent of the variance in jurors' predeliberation judgments. Moreover, the evidence measures still have strong effects, with the exception of eyewitness testimony. However, the increase in explained variance between the two estimations is statistically significant[9]; hence, jurors', defendants', and victims' characteristics, as a group, do significantly increase the ability to predict jurors' predeliberation judgments in this sample.[10]

Jurors' personal characteristics, such as age, race, and sex, were not the primary types of extralegal influences. Although other studies have shown that these personal characteristics are related to juror decision making in bivariate analyses, in this multivariate estimation these factors were completely unrelated to actual jurors' judgments of defendant guilt. Jurors' attitudes about rape victims

---

[9] The increase in variance explained is significant at the .05 level with $F(12, 319) = 4.8$. Discussion of this statistic and a standard computational formula can be found in Kerlinger and Pedhauzer (1973: p.71).

[10] In this analysis, 5 of the 20 variables are measured at the jury level (hence, all jurors within a trial receive the same value) and 29 jurors are in the sample twice because three trials had two defendants which these jurors judged separately in the interviews (hence, values on the juror and victim variables for these jurors are counted twice). This raises the question as to whether the statistical assumption of independence of observations has been violated, possibly biasing the results reported here. To test for this possibility, two supplemental analyses were performed. First, in an analysis based on 41 observations (one for each defendant), evidential influences accounted for a much larger share of the variance in aggregate predeliberation judgments (the average value given by jurors within a trial) than extralegal factors; thus, these results support the juror-level analyses. Second, when 29 of the 340 observations were omitted (i.e., the jurors' judgments of the second defendant in the three multiple-defendant trials), the findings paralleled results reported in Table 2.

also had no significant effect, despite a modest zero-order correlation with the dependent variable ($r = .22$). However, jurors' attitudes about crime, such as a belief in the need for harsher sentences and stricter laws, increased the likelihood of guilty judgments.

In contrast to the negligible impact of most jurors' characteristics, both victims' and defendants' attributes exerted some influence on jurors' initial decisions. For the victim, indicators of a "nontraditional" lifestyle—sexual activity outside of marriage and drug use ($p = .09$)—resulted in fewer guilty judgments (see Lafree, Reskin, & Visher, 1985, for a more detailed analysis of these effects). Moreover, perceived careless behavior by the victim was also detrimental to the prosecution's case. As to the defendant, only one of three characteristics—the defendant's educational level—was a significant determinant of jurors' decisions. Knowledge of the defendant's prior criminal history also did not affect judgments. Jurors in this sample seemed to judge defendants on other criteria, especially the evidence concerning the defendant's use of force during the alleged assault and their impressions of the victim.

DISCUSSION

Evidence and case characteristics had a substantial impact on jurors' judgments of defendant guilt in this sample of trials. The seven evidence variables alone explained 34% of the variance in these judgments; victim and defendant characteristics accounted for another 8 percent and jurors' characteristics and attitudes only explained 2 percent. Because most experimental studies highlight biases in decision making rather than the impact of legal factors, the impression they present is that jurors are influenced by irrelevant issues. In the 38 sexual assault trials in this study, the extralegal factors are not the most salient variables affecting jurors' judgments.

Four specific types of evidence significantly influenced jurors' judgments of the defendant. Physical evidence, which often ties the defendant to the scene of the crime, and testimony or evidence of force, including weapon use and victim injuries, are usually difficult types of evidence for the defense to rebut. Eyewitness testimony, however, is often challenged by the defense by claiming that the lighting was poor, the eyewitness was not wearing prescribed glasses, or the incident occurred too quickly for clear identification. Although many simulation studies have found that subjects were strongly influenced by eyewitness testimony (for a review, see Penrod, Loftus, & Winkler, 1982), jurors in these trials clearly gave more weight to other types of evidence. But testimony and evidence presented by the defense in an attempt to discredit the victim's story gave the defendant a significant advantage.

Nonetheless, extralegal factors did enter into jurors' decisions in this study. The results on defendants' attributes weakly support some previous research that sentiments about defendants influenced jurors' decisions. The defendant's educational level did affect their judgments of defendant guilt net of evidential factors. This measure may reflect jurors' attributions about the defendant's character and his propensity for criminal activity. But contrary to other research (Landy & Aronson, 1969; Nemeth & Sosis, 1973; Sealy & Cornish, 1973), knowledge of a defendant's criminal record did not bias jurors against him. Two attributes of the victim also influenced jurors' judgments of the defendant. Not surprisingly, given the nature of the cases, the victim's extramarital sexual behavior and her perceived carelessness appeared to weaken the prosecution's case.

These results also provide some preliminary evidence about the extent to which experimental findings generalize to actual juror behavior. Model specification problems in jury simulations can occur when attention to legal factors is subordinated to an interest in extralegal or irrelevant influences. This focus is, understandably, the result of the growing concern over the viability of the jury in the American criminal justice system. However, these studies may be painting a misleading picture of juror decision making. In the present research, the effects of victim and defendant characteristics accounted for a small percentage of the explained variance in jurors' predeliberation judgments (8% of 44%). In the absence of a properly specified model, these extralegal factors may appear more influential in simulations than they actually are in criminal trials. However, some findings from experimental studies regarding victims' and defendants' characteristics appear to be robust across different research methods.

Finally, a few caveats about this study are warranted. The findings reported here are based on jurors' judgments of defendants in 38 sexual assault trials. The overall impact of extralegal issues on these jurors' decisions is likely an upper bound for the effects of these factors in other serious criminal trials. Characteristics of the victim probably will exert less influence in cases where the victim's behavior is not an issue. Nevertheless, the victim's carelessness, which was *not* highly correlated with her sexual activity, strongly influenced jurors' decisions, and may represent a general impression of the victim. Other studies using different types of trials should explore whether jurors' perceptions that the victim was careless affect their judgments of the defendant. Also, jurors' attitudes about crime, which had a significant impact on the judgments of the defendant in this sample, may be influential in other trials, but the magnitude of the effect may vary with the seriousness of the alleged offense.

In conclusion, the attention given to the competence of jurors in much of the research on jurors and juries has resulted in a large gap in our understanding of juror decision making. Researchers who have incorporated evidential issues into their experimental designs have raised interesting questions about a variety of legal issues that confront jurors (e.g., Hastie et al., 1983; Tanford & Penrod, 1982; Zeisel & Diamond, 1978). More research in this area is sorely needed. The results presented here are only a starting point towards constructing a more complete model of the factors that influence jurors' decisions.

REFERENCES

Baumeister, R., & Darley, J. (1982). Reducing the biasing effect of perpetrator attractiveness in jury simulation. *Personality and Social Psychology Bulletin, 8,* 286–292.

Baldwin, J., & McConville, M. (1980). Criminal juries. In N. Morris & M. Tonry (Eds.), *Crime and justice: An annual review of research* (Vol. 2, pp. 269–320). Chicago: University of Chicago Press.

Barnett, N., & Feild, H. (1978). Character of the defendant and defendant sentencing in rape and burglary crimes. *Journal of Social Psychology, 104*, 271–277.

Bermant, G., McGuire, M., McKinley, W., & Salo, C. (1974). The logic of simulation in jury research. *Criminal Justice and Behavior, 1*, 224–233.

Bray, R., & Kerr, N. (1982). Methodological considerations in the study of the psychology of the courtroom. In N. Kerr & R. Bray (Eds.), *The psychology of the courtroom* (pp. 287–323). New York: Academic Press.

Burt, M., & Albin, R. (1981). Rape myths, rape definitions, and probability of conviction. *Journal of Applied Social Psychology, 11*, 212–230.

Calhoun, L., Selby, J., Cann, A., & Keller, G. (1978). The effects of victim physical attractiveness on social reactions to victims of rape. *Journal of Social and Clinical Psychology, 17*, 191–192.

Dane, F., & Wrightsman, L. (1982). Effect of defendants' and victims' characteristics on jurors' verdicts. In N. Kerr & R. Bray (Eds.), *The psychology of the courtroom* (pp. 83–115). New York: Academic Press.

Davis, J., Kerr, N., Atkin, R., Holt, R., & Meek, D. (1975). The decision processes of 6 and 12 person mock juries assigned unanimous and two-thirds majority rules. *Journal of Personality and Social Psychology, 21*, 1–14.

Davis, J., Bray, R., & Holt, R. (1977). The empirical study of decision processes in juries. In J. Tapp & F. Levine (Eds.), *Law, justice and the individual in society* (pp. 326–361). New York: Holt, Rinehart and Winston.

Dillehay, R., & Nietzel, M. (1980). Constructing a science of jury behavior. In L. Wheeler (Ed.), *Review of personality and social psychology* (Vol. 1, pp. 246–264) Beverly Hills, CA: Sage Publications.

Ebbesen, E., & Konecni, V. (1980). On the external validity of decision-making research: What do we know about decisions in the real world? In T. Wallsten (Ed.), *Cognitive processes in choice and decision behavior* (pp. 21–45). Hillsdale, NJ: Lawrence Erlbaum Associates.

Elwork, A., Sales, B., & Suggs, D. (1981). The trial: A research review. In B. Sales (Ed.), *The trial process* (pp. 1–68). New York: Plenum Press.

Fahringer, H. (1980). In the valley of the blind: A primer on jury selection in a criminal case. *Law and Contemporary Problems, 43*, 116–136.

Feild, H. (1979). Rape trials and jurors' decisions: A psycholegal analysis of the effects of victim, defendant, and case characteristics. *Law and Human Behavior, 3*, 261–284.

Feild, H., & Bienen, L. (1980). *Jurors and rape.* Lexington, MA: Lexington Press.

Fried, M., Kaplan, K., & Klein, K. (1975). Juror selection: An analysis of voir dire. In R. Simon (Ed.), *The jury system in America* (pp. 47–66). Beverly Hills, CA: Sage Publications.

Gerbasi, K., Zuckerman, M., & Reiss, H. (1977). Justice needs a new blindfold: A review of mock jury research. *Psychological Bulletin, 84*, 323–345.

Hans, V., & Vidmar, N. (1982). Jury selection. In N. Kerr & R. Bray (Eds.), *The psychology of the courtroom* (pp. 39–82). New York: Academic Press.

Hastie, R., Penrod, S., & Pennington, N. (1983). *Inside the jury.* Cambridge: Harvard University Press.

Hepburn, J. (1980). The objective reality of evidence and the utility of systematic jury selection. *Law and Human Behavior, 4*, 89–101.

Hoffman, H., & Brodley, J. (1952). Jurors on trial. *Missouri Law Review, 17*, 235–251.

Hunter, R. (1935). Law in the jury room. *Ohio State Law Journal, 2*, 1–19.

Jones, C., & Aronson, E. (1973) Attribution of fault to a rape victim as a function of respectability of the victim. *Journal of Personality and Social Psychology, 26*, 415–419.

Kadish, M., & Kadish, S. (1971). The institutionalization of conflict: Jury acquittals. *Journal of Social Issues, 27*, 199–217.

Kahn, A., Gilbert, L., Latta, R., Deutsch, C., Hagen, R., Hill, M., McGaughey, T., Ryen, A., &

Wilson, D. (1977). Attribution of fault to a rape victim as a function of respectability: A failure to replicate or extend. *Representative Research in Social Psychology, 8*, 98–107.

Kalven, H., & Zeisel. H. (1966). *The American jury*. Boston: Little Brown.

Kaplan, M., & Kemmerick, G. (19;74). Juror judgment as information integration: Combining evidential and nonevidential information. *Journal of Personality and Social Psychology, 30*, 493–499.

Kerlinger, F., & Pedhauzer, E. (1973). *Multiple regression in behavioral research*. New York: Holt, Rinehart and Winston.

LaFree, G., Reskin. B., & Visher, C. (1985). Jurors' responses to victims' behavior and legal issues in sexual assault trials. *Social Problems, 32*, 389–407.

Landy, D., & Aronson, E. (1969). The influence of the character of the criminal and his victim on the decisions of simulated jurors. *Journal of Experimental Social Psychology, 5*, 141–152.

McCabe, S., & Purves, R. (1974). *The shadow jury at work*. Oxford, England: Blackwell.

Mitchell, H., & Byrne, D. (1973). The defendant's dilemma: Effects of jurors' attitudes and authoritarianism on judicial decisions. *Journal of Personality and Social Psychology, 25*, 123–129.

Myers, D., & Kaplan, M. (1976). Group-induced polarization in simulated juries. *Personality and Social Psychology Bulletin, 2*, 63–66.

Myers, M. (1979). Rule departures and making law: Juries and their verdicts. *Law and Society Review, 13*, 781–797.

Myers, M., & LaFree. G. (1982). Sexual assault and its prosecution: A comparison with other crimes. *Journal of Criminal Law and Criminology, 73*, 1282–1301.

Nemeth, C., & Sosis. R. (1973). A simulated jury study: Characteristics of the defendant and the jurors. *Journal of Social Psychology, 90*, 221–229.

Ostrom, T., Werner. C. & Saks, M. (1978). An integration theory analysis of jurors' presumptions of guilt or innocence. *Journal of Personality and Social Psychology, 36*, 436–450.

Penrod, S., Loftus, E., & Winkler, J. (1982). The reliability of eyewitness testimony: A psychological perspective. In N. Kerr & R. Bray (Eds.), *The psychology of the courtroom* (pp. 119–168). New York: Academic Press.

Reed, J. (1965). Jury deliberations, voting, and verdict trends. *The Southwestern Social Science Quarterly, 45*, 361–370.

Reskin, B., & Visher. C. (in press). The impacts of evidence and extra-legal factors in jurors' decisions. *Law & Society Review*.

Rumsey, M., & Rumsey, J. (1977). A case of rape: Sentencing judgments of males and females. *Psychological Reports, 4*, 459–465.

Saks, M. (1976). The limits of scientific jury selection: Ethical and empirical. *Jurimetrics, 17*, 3–22.

Saks, M. (1977). *Jury verdicts*. Lexington, MA: D. C. Heath.

Scheflin, A., & Van Dyke, J. (1980). Jury nullification: The contours of a controversy. *Law and Contemporary Problems, 43*, 52–115.

Scroggs, J. (1976). Penalties for rape as a function of victim provocativeness, damage, and resistance. *Journal of Applied Social Psychology, 6*, 360–368.

Sealy, P. (1975). What can be learned from the analyses of simulated juries? In N. Walker (Ed.), *The British jury system* (pp. 12–21). Cambridge, England: Institute of Criminology.

Sealy, P. (1981). Another look at social psychological aspects of juror bias. *Law and Human Behavior, 5*, 187–200.

Sealy, P., & Cornish, W. (1973). Juries and the rules of evidence. *Criminal Law Review, B*, 208–223.

Simon, R. (1967). *The jury and the defense of insanity*. Boston: Little Brown.

Stephan, C. (1975). Selective characteristics of jurors and litigants: Their influence on juries' verdicts. In R. Simon (Ed.), *The jury system in America* (pp. 95–122). Beverly Hills, CA: Sage Publications.

Strodtbeck, F., & Mann, R. (1956). Sex-role differentiation in jury deliberations. *Sociometry, 19*, 3–11.

Strodtbeck, F., Simon, R., & Hawkins, D. (1957). Social status in jury deliberations. *American Sociological Review, 22*, 713–719.

Tanford, S., & Penrod, S. (1982). Biases in trials involving defendants charged with multiple offenses. *Journal of Applied Social Psychology, 12*, 453–480.

Vidmar, N. (1979). The other issues in jury simulation research. *Law and Human Behavior, 3,* 95–119.

Weiten, W., & Diamond, S. (1979). A critical review of the jury simulation paradigm. *Law and Human Behavior, 3,* 71–93.

Weld, H., & Danzig, A. (1940). A study of the way in which a verdict is reached by a jury. *American Journal of Psychology, 53,* 518–536.

Williams, G. (1963). *The proof of guilt.* London: Stevens Press.

Zeisel, H., & Diamond, S. (1978). The effect of peremptory challenges on jury and verdict: An experiment in a federal district court. *Stanford Law Review, 30,* 491–531.

MR. PREJUDICE, MISS SYMPATHY, AND THE AUTHORITARIAN PERSONALITY: AN APPLICATION OF PSYCHOLOGICAL MEASURING TECHNIQUES TO THE PROBLEM OF JURY BIAS

VIRGINIA R. BOEHM*

Trial lawyers usually develop vague criteria for selecting jurors during voir dire examination. These criteria are based on the lawyers' experience and general knowledge of human behavior. In this article, Dr. Boehm describes her attempt to develop similar criteria based on psychological concepts. Her research indicates that a person's liberalism-conservatism attitudes (as defined by psychologists) have a systematic effect on the way he behaves as a member of a jury.

I. INTRODUCTION

While there is a long-standing social psychology interest in the study of prejudice,[1] few psychological studies of jury prejudice have been done. One reason is the inaccessibility of the jury itself. Another is that the psychologist lacks the proper tools to do such studies in a way that would make the results meaningful to lawyers. Forced to deal with a legal system that is based upon antipsychological, or at least nonpsychological concepts[2] (*e.g.*, reasonable man), the psychologist simply despairs of studies of jury prejudice accomplishing anything worthwhile or contributing anything new to psychological studies of prejudice.

What is an impartial juror? A lawyer might present a common legal definition: "an impartial man, one who extends to his fellow men the humane presumptions of the law, and keeps his mind in such condition with reference to the accused that guilt must be

---

* Research Psychologist, New York State Division of Employment. B.A., 1962, Hanover College; Ph.D., 1966, Columbia University. The author is indebted to Professor Richard Christie, Department of Social Psychology, Columbia University, for his advice in the preparation of the larger study from which this article is drawn.

[1] H. E. Burtt recognized jury bias as an area of study:

> An outstanding psychological problem in connection with the personnel of the jury is the matter of bias. Even when a person is apparently open-minded and trying to be sincere in his judgments, it is quite possible for him to have a distinct bias, owing to some previous experience or some attitude that he has developed.

H. BURTT, LEGAL PSYCHOLOGY 162 (1931).

Judge Jerome Frank put the matter more bluntly: "[P]rejudice has been called the thirteenth juror, and it has been said that 'Mr. Prejudice and Miss Sympathy are the names of witnesses whose testimony is never recorded but must nevertheless be reckoned with in trials by jury.'" J. FRANK, COURTS ON TRIAL 122 (1949).

[2] Louisell, *The Psychologist in Today's Legal World*, 39 MINN. L. REV. 235 (1955).

affirmatively and conclusively shown before he is willing to convict . . . ."[3] The psychologist wonders just how one goes about ascertaining this.

A. *Studies Demonstrating Jury Bias*

During and after the fact bias has been demonstrated. But the tools and procedures used were of a nature that makes these demonstrations of bias more or less meaningless to lawyers. In one of the best studies ever done with mock juries, it was discovered that "early in the trial many jurors reached a fairly definite decision, and that thereafter the effect of the testimony was merely to change their certainty. This happened with at least 25% of . . . [the] jurors."[4] Obviously, these jurors could not be considered impartial. But the finding that the jurors made up their minds prematurely depended on the study procedure used of asking for a tentative verdict. This procedure is avoided during actual trials. Therefore, the experimental situation used was dissimilar from actual trial situations, thus making the study meaningless from a legal point of view.[5]

The work of Hoffman and Brodley[6] avoids this objection. They questioned jurors after they rendered verdicts. Hoffman and Brodley found that the majority of the jurors forgot that stricken testimony was to be disregarded, several thought it was better to draw lots than report inability to decide a case, and two of the jurors in a criminal case thought that an indictment indicated guilt. It should be stressed that these were actual jurors who previously had been selected by *voir dire* examination and who actually had rendered verdicts in the cases being discussed. Unfortunately, this sort of after the fact examination of jurors is useless to practicing attorneys. The general rule is that jurors' testimony is not admissible to impeach their verdict.[7] There is, however, another possibility: the demonstration of before the fact bias.

B. *Legal Challenges to Jury Panels Based on Before the Fact Concepts of Bias*

Challenges have been made to jury panels because members of a race or sex have been systematically excluded, or because the jurors shared some general attitude or opinion that would prevent

---

[3] State v. Beatty, 45 Kan. 492, 502, 25 P. 899, 902 (1891).

[4] Weld & Danzig, *A Study of the Way in which a Verdict is Reached by a Jury*, 53 Am. J. Psychology 518, 535 (1940).

[5] "[T]he weight to be attached to evidence of experiments . . . varies according to the circumstances of similarity existing between the experiments made and the actual occurrence the facts of which are under investigation." E. Morgan, J. Maguire & J. Weinstein, Cases and Materials on Evidence 859 (4th ed. 1957).

[6] Hoffman & Brodley, *Jurors on Trial*, 17 Mo. L. Rev. 235 (1952).

[7] *See e.g.*, Mattox v. United States, 146 U.S. 140, 149 (1892).

them from rendering impartial decisions. And there have been at least two cases in which the United States Supreme Court has ruled on challenges to jury panels based, at least partially, on concepts very similar to psychological concepts of bias.

Thiel v. Southern Pacific Co.[8] was a personal injury action by a passenger against a railroad. The jury returned a verdict for the railroad. Thiel, the petitioner, characterized the jury as "mostly business executives or those having the employer's viewpoint . . ."[9] and claimed that the jurors were "purposely selected . . . thus giving a majority representation to one class or occupation and discriminating against other occupations and classes . . . ."[10] This contention was supported by the uncontradicted testimony of the clerk of the trial court that they usually excluded a variety of blue-collar workers because they simply could not afford to serve for the four dollars per day that jurors were paid. The Court, holding this procedure unjustified, reversed the judgment in favor of the railroad.

The second case, *Fay v. New York*,[11] concerned the conviction of a labor leader by a New York "blue ribbon" jury.[12] "Blue ribbon" juries were challenged on the grounds that they were not occupationally representative of the community, included practically no women or Negroes, tended towards conservatism, excluded labor union members, and were generally prone to convict. These contentions were supported by statistics showing that such juries had higher conviction ratios and comparing the occupational distribution of "blue ribbon" juries with that of the Manhattan labor force. In a five to four decision, the Court upheld the conviction saying that the statute providing for "blue ribbon" juries did not itself exclude any person on the basis of sex, occupation, or race. The statistics showing the occupational discrepancy between the "blue ribbon" juries and the labor force were dismissed because many persons in the labor force were aliens, illiterates, and others who were ineligible for jury service. As for the higher "blue ribbon" jury conviction ratio, the Court pointed out that no statistics had been introduced showing that these convictions were wrongful or that such juries' verdicts were more frequently reversed by the higher courts. The Court also said that no differences in opinions regarding labor unions had been shown between those permitted to serve and those excluded; and even if "blue ribbon" juries could be shown to be more conservative, there was no evidence showing that conservatives are more prone to convict. "It would require large assumptions to say that one's

---

8 328 U.S. 217 (1946).
9 *Id.* at 217, 219.
10 *Id.*
11 332 U.S. 261 (1947).
12 The statute permitting the selection of "blue ribbon" juries in New York State has since been repealed.

present economic status, in a society as fluid as ours, determines his outlook on the trial of cases in general or of this one in particular."[13]

The implicit issue in both these cases is: Do an individual's liberalism-conservatism attitudes have a systematic effect on the way he behaves as a member of a jury?

II. PSYCHOLOGICAL MEASURES OF BIAS

There is currently a growing body of literature concerning the effects of liberalism-conservatism of *judges* on their decisions. Using factor analytic techniques, Shubert[14] examined United States Supreme Court decisions and concluded:

> [T]he justices voted as they did in the set of cases under examination because of their respective individual attitudes towards the liberal values that the cases evoked for decision. . . . The liberalism values so predominated . . . that they can well account for all but a small portion of the variance in the voting behavior of the justices . . . .[15]

This conclusion, which is strengthened by other studies, is the outgrowth of the observation that some justices have more "liberal" voting records than others. However, the conclusions derived from this sort of study can always be criticized on the ground that they are the products of circular reasoning. To avoid this criticism, some criterion of liberalism-conservatism other than the behavior under observation must be used. An outside criterion has been used by Stuart S. Nagel.[16] Using a questionnaire developed by Eysenck,[17] Nagel compared individual judge's decisions in nonunanimous case decisions with questionnaire responses. Nagel sent his questionnaire to all the justices of the highest state courts and to the United States Supreme Court Justices. He found that judges scoring above a mean on the scale (high scores indicate liberalism) were more likely to be on the side of the defense in criminal cases appealed to their courts than judges scoring below the mean. Liberal judges were also more apt to vote for the employee in employment injury cases and to vote for the plaintiff in auto injury cases.

Most decisions made by appellate courts involve questions of law rather than of fact. No direct studies have been made involv-

---

13 Fay v. New York, 332 U.S. 261, 292 (1947).
14 Schubert, *A Solution to the Indeterminate Factorial Resolution of Thurston and Degan's Study of the Supreme Court*, 7 BEHAVIORAL SCI. 448 (1962).
15 *Id.* at 458.
16 Nagel, *Judicial Backgrounds and Criminal Cases*, 53 J. CRIM. L.C. & P.S. 339 (1962); Nagel, *Off the Bench Judicial Attitudes*, in JUDICIAL DECISION MAKING 29 (G. Schubert ed. 1963).
17 H. EYSENCK, THE PSYCHOLOGY OF POLITICS (1954).

ing the conservatism-liberalism dimension on the specific duty of a juror: rendering a verdict on the facts. But existing research provides some clues as to what might be expected, particularly in criminal cases.

A. The Authoritarian Personality

A study by Roberts and Jessor[18] demonstrates that authoritarian persons tend to respond with personal hostility toward lower status persons. Most defendants in criminal cases tend to come from lower social strata.

Conservatism is one of the primary traits of the Authoritarian Personality, while rigidity is another.[19] The latter has been characterized by Frenkel-Brunswick as follows: "[T]here is a reluctance to give up what had seemed certain, a tendency not to see what does not harmonize with an earlier bias; assumptions once made . . . tend to be repeated over and over and not to be corrected in the face of new evidence."[20] Since the prosecution presents its evidence first, the defendant faced with an authoritarian jury may be at a distinct disadvantage because of this trait of the Authoritarian Personality. Also, the authoritarian jury may not even wait for the case to begin before deciding to convict. Such a jury might well enjoy the opportunities for punishment provided by service on a jury. "[M]any of the high scoring men . . . often find themselves in complete agreement with harsh punishment."[21] And finally, the prosecution represents the majesty of the state, a constituted authority: "[T]he typical high scorer remains dependent on the blessing given by external authority . . . primarily those which give license for aggression."[22]

The effects of this channeling of aggression into a legal context is described by Schoenfeld: "[P]rojecting anti-social aggressive wishes onto criminals is a first step in a much-used unconscious technique for curbing one's own aggression. That is, by projecting such wishes and then calling for stiff punishment for their consummation, the public is able to deny the existence of its aggressive striving, and at the same time, to express these strivings in a socially acceptable manner."[23] It would appear from the psychol-

---

[18] Roberts & Jessor, *Authoritarianism, Punitiveness, and Perceived Social Status*, 56 J. ABNORMAL & SOC. PSYCHOLOGY 311 (1958).

[19] T. ADORNO, E. FRENKEL-BRUNSWICK, D. LEVISION & R. SANFORD, THE AUTHORITARIAN PERSONALITY 175-78 (1950). The F (Fascism) scale has been criticized. *See, e.g.*, R. BROWN, SOCIAL PSYCHOLOGY 477-548 (1965).

[20] Frenkel-Brunswick, *Social Tensions and the Inhibition of Thought*, 2 SOC. PROBLEMS 75, 77 (1954).

[21] T. ADORNO, E. FRENKEL-BRUNSWICK, D. LEVISION & R. SANFORD, *supra* note 19, at 351.

[22] *Id.* at 450.

[23] Schoenfeld, *Law and Unconscious Mental Mechanisms*, 28 BULL. OF THE MENNINGER CLINIC 23, 27 (1964).

ogical (if not the legal) point of view that there is some reason for considering it quite possible that conservatives are more prone to convict.

There is also reason to suspect that there are overly-lenient jurors as well as overly-severe ones. Rigidity is not the exclusive property of the right wing authoritarian. Rokeach[24] has studied the closed minded and rigid person irrespective of ideology. Shils[25] has also pointed out that there are authoritarians on the left. Weitman[26] extended this notion and hypothesized that the classic Authoritarian Personality represents only one type of person who has a problem responding to authority. With a sentence completion test, he identified a group he called "Anti-authoritarians."[27] This group consists of persons who may well acquit any defendant merely to thwart authority.

B. *Inapplicability of General Measures to the Problem of Jury Bias*

While there is an arguable case for the hypothesis that liberalism-conservatism attitudes would tend to influence jury verdicts in criminal proceedings, the above studies are not fully adequate for three reasons. First, the measure of authoritarianism used by Adorno and others, the F (Fascism) scale deals with attitudes towards a wide variety of things. Few of the items measure attitudes specifically relevant to the jury decision making process. The same is true of Rokeach's measure, the Dogmatism scale, and the measure used by Nagel. Second, even if opinions about the wide range of topics present in these measures could be used to predict at least the initial verdicts of individual jurors, it would still have to be shown that such attitudes lead to incorrect conclusions. Third, it would have to be demonstrated that persons with biases strong enough to lead to partiality actually do sit on juries. The research to be presented here deals with the first two reasons for the inadequacy of the above studies. To directly investigate the third at the present time would extend beyond the scope of this research.

III.   Development of the Legal Attitudes Questionnaire

If Authoritarian and Anti-authoritarian attitudes are as widespread and influential as research leads us to believe, it should be possible to construct a measure of these attitudes that takes legal

---

[24] M. Rokeach, The Open and Closed Mind (1960).
[25] Shils, *Authoritarianism: Right and Left*, in Studies in the Scope and Method of the Authoritarian Personality 24 (R. Christie & M. Jahoda eds. 1954).
[26] Weitman, *More than one Kind of Authoritarian*, 30 J. Personality 193, 195 (1962).
[27] *Id.* at 203.

issues as its framework. This measure should be correlated with the F and Dogmatism scales and should also predict behavior in a quasi-jury situation. In short it should have psychological and legal validity and relevance.

The measure should allow scores to be derived on three additudinal dimensions: Authoritarianism, Anti-authoritarianism, and Equalitarianism (lack of bias). A measure was constructed with these characteristics. A complex forced-choice ranking format was used in the initial form of the scale. Items were gathered from a variety of sources, including common positions advocating civil liberties, newspapers, the United States Constitution and Supreme Court decisions and conversations with interested persons. Short statements were assembled from these materials.

These items were classified as Authoritarian, Anti-authoritarian, or Equalitarian according to the following loose criteria. Authoritarian items expressed right wing philosophy, endorsed indiscriminately the acts of constituted authority, or were essentially punitive in nature. Anti-authoritarian items expressed left wing sentiments, implied that the blame for all antisocial acts rested with the structure of society, or indiscriminately rejected the acts of constituted authority. Equalitarian items endorsed traditional, liberal, nonextreme positions on legal questions or were couched in a form that indicated the questions reasonably could have two answers. Items that appeared ambiguous or nonclassifiable were discarded. A total of 54 items, 18 representing each attitude, were arranged in nine sets of six items each. Each set contained two items classified as Authoritarian, Anti-authoritarian, and Equalitarian. The subject's task was to rank the items in each set in order of his agreement with the items.

This initial form of what came to be called the Legal Attitudes Questionnaire (LAQ) was administered to a small group of people, the majority of whom were graduate students in social psychology, and item analyses were performed to select the most effective items.

Briefly, the item analysis technique used consisted of summing the ranks each individual had assigned to Authoritarian, Anti-authoritarian, and Equalitarian items. Then this sum was reversed to obtain a score for each person on each of the three attitude dimensions. A high score indicated high agreement with the attitude position. On the basis of the scores on each of the three attitudinal dimensions in turn, the highest and lowest scoring third of the subjects' responses were analyzed on an item by item basis. The t-test procedure used provided a statistical means of seeing whether the scores on a given item were significantly different for subjects in the top third of the total score distribution as compared with those in the bottom third.[28]

---

[28] The t-test is essentially a means for determining whether two sets of scores may be said to be samples from the same population. It is a meas-

As a check on the original classification of the items, similar tests were also run for each item against the two totals to which the item should not relate. This was done to assure that the items were being responded to in an unambiguous fashion. These procedures were followed to assure that the items were measuring something and had some connection to each other. Once this was established, an attempt was made to assure that liberalism-conservatism was indeed being measured.

The ten best items on each attitude dimension were assembled into triads, each containing an Authoritarian, Anti-authoritarian, and Equalitarian item. The subjects were instructed to place a plus (+) beside the item in each triad that he agreed with most and a minus (−) beside the item he agreed with least.[29] A score of 3 was given for a (+) response, 1 for a (−), and 2 for the unmarked item in the triad. The possible range of scores for each of the three attitude dimensions thus ran from 30 (all plusses) to 10 (all minuses). Because a forced-choice format was used, a subject's scores had to sum to 60.

This new form of the questionnaire (Form II) was administered to 50 civil rights workers, mostly Northern college students. They completed the Legal Attitudes Questionnaire (LAQ) along with a form of the F scale and a form of the Dogmatism scale as part of a debriefing session at the conclusion of work in the South in the summer of 1965.[30] This was done to determine if the LAQ was in fact related to these well-established psychological measures of bias and was, therefore, a measure of liberalism-conservatism.

It was hypothesized that the F scale would relate positively to the Authoritarian subscale of the LAQ and negatively to the Anti-authoritarian and Equalitarian subscales, and that the Dogmatism scale would relate positively with both the Authoritarian and Anti-authoritarian subscales of the LAQ and negatively with the Equalitarian measure. These relationships appeared with degrees of statistical significance that were acceptable, though not extremely high, indicating that the LAQ was, to some extent, tapping the same attitudinal dimensions as these established measures.

---

ure based on the normal curve and permits sets of scores to be compared in terms of their means and standard deviations. The significance level of the obtained t is the probability that the result is due to chance, and is determined by considering the numerical t obtained and the size of the sample. The greater the t's deviation from zero in either direction, the smaller the probability that the result is due to chance. *See* A. EDWARDS, STATISTICAL METHODS FOR THE BEHAVIORAL SCIENCES 273-74 (1954).

[29] This revised form (Form II) of the LAQ appears in the Appendix. The attitudinal dimension to which the item pertains is also indicated. An "A" beside the item indicates an Authoritarian item; an "AA," Anti-authoritarian item; and an "E," Equalitarian item.

[30] Dr. Abraham Chaplan was kind enough to administer the materials to this group.

Having a measuring instrument that appeared to be psychologically satisfactory, the next step was to devise materials that could be applied to a quasi-jury situation. In searching for suitable stimuli, I found a number of cases where appellate courts were called upon to decide if jury verdicts had been based upon sufficient evidence. The case finally selected[31] was a manslaughter case where the higher court had overturned the jury's conviction on the ground of insufficient evidence. In its opinion, the court had reviewed the evidence in detail.

Briefly, the case involved an argument between a landlord and tenant over the tenant's overdue rent during which the landlord was shot with his own rifle. It was undisputed that the tenant did the shooting. It was also undisputed that the landlord owned the rifle and kept it in a locked closet to which he alone had access. The issue was whether the landlord had been killed accidently as the tenant struggled to disarm him, or whether the tenant had obtained possession of the rifle, without mortally wounding the landlord, and then fired additional shots which were fatal. The struggle was overheard by another tenant, but there were no other witnesses.

Two versions of the case were prepared based on the court's summary of the facts. In one version, strategic points of evidence were slanted in the direction of guilt; in the other, towards innocence. While the original indictment was manslaughter, alterations in one version were such that second degree murder became a legally possible verdict. So, in the "jury instructions" written to correspond to the judge's charge, this possible verdict was discussed along with manslaughter and not guilty.

A preliminary version of this material was presented to a group of students in the City College of New York and revisions made in line with their comments and suggestions.

IV. APPLICATION OF THE LEGAL ATTITUDES QUESTIONNAIRE

Preliminary work with both the LAQ and the case material having been completed, the following material was presented to 151 psychology students at the University of California (Berkeley) in December 1965:[32] a page of general instructions explaining the study as an investigation of decision making processes on juries, a biographical data form, Form II of the LAQ, an introduction to the case material, one of the two forms of the case, the "jury instructions," and a ballot form. The LAQ was explained to the subjects as corresponding to the *voir dire* examination. Which version of the case a subject received was purely a random result of how the

---

[31] People v. Patterson, 21 App. Div. 2d 356, 250 N.Y.S.2d 715 (1964).
[32] Professor David Marlowe presented the materials to the group at Berkeley.

papers were handed out. Seventy-seven persons received the Not Guilty version and 74 the Guilty version. Approximately one hour was required to complete the materials. Practical reasons made the use of a paper and pencil situation necessary rather than a regular mock trial.

Before determining the relationship between LAQ scores and verdicts rendered, it was first necessary to determine if the subjects as a whole had given different verdicts depending on whether they had the Guilty or the Not Guilty version. These results are presented in Table I.

TABLE I[33]

Verdicts by Form of Case

Form of case	Verdict given					
	Acquittal		Manslaughter		2nd degree murder	
	Number giving	Expected number	Number giving	Expected number	Number giving	Expected number
Not guilty	33	19.91	43	42.30	1	14.79
Guilty	6	19.09	40	40.70	28	14.21

$X^2 = 43.97$ (chance probability less than .001).

As can be seen, the subjects did see the two cases differently. The verdicts they gave had less than one chance in a thousand of being a random result. More tended to acquit on the Not Guilty case and to find the second degree murder verdict if they had read the Guilty case, despite the large numbers of subjects who rendered the manslaughter verdict. The manslaughter verdict was probably chosen by persons who were unsure of the verdict or felt pressed for time.

The subjects were then scored on Authoritarianism, Anti-authoritarianism, and Equalitarianism, as measured by the LAQ to see if those convicting (rendering either a manslaughter or second degree murder verdict) on the Not Guilty case were higher on Authoritarianism than those acquitting, and if those acquitting or rendering a manslaughter verdict on the Guilty case were more Anti-authoritarian than those giving the hypothetically correct second degree murder verdict.

The subjects were further divided into a "younger" (under 21 years of age) and "older" (21 or over) group to see if any obtained

---

[33] The chi-square (X^2) test used here and in Table III is a means of determining whether individuals' responses are distributed in various categories in a way that would be expected by chance. The chi-square obtained can be assigned a significance level by considering the total number of cells in the table. See A. EDWARDS, supra note 28, at 371-73.

attitudinal biases on the verdict would be less pronounced with the older group. The results obtained are given in Table II.

TABLE II

The Effect of LAQ Scores on Verdict Rendered

Group	Num- ber	Average Author- itarianism score	Standard deviation	"t"	Probability difference due to chance
Authoritarianism and conviction on Not Guilty case					
Older group					
Acquittal	15	17.40	3.08		
Conviction	25	19.40	3.65	1.77	.05
Younger group					
Acquittal	18	16.28	3.08		
Conviction	20	18.80	3.67	2.29	.025
Anti-authoritar- ianism and Leniency on Guilty case					
Older group Acquittal or					
manslaughter	22	18.23	2.20		
2d degree murder	11	15.82	2.86	2.68	.01
Younger group Acquittal or					
manslaughter	23	17.58	2.68		
2d degree murder	17	16.41	1.94	1.52	.10

These data clearly demonstrate that while the absolute differences in the obtained scores are relatively small, they are statistically meaningful, except perhaps for Anti-authoritarianism and the younger group's verdict on the Guilty case where there is a 10 percent chance that the result obtained could be due to chance. Those who go against the trend and convict on the evidence presented in the Not Guilty case are more authoritarian than those who follow the trend. Likewise, those who go against the trend of rendering the second degree murder verdict in the Guilty case are more Anti-authoritarian than the trend followers.

The same thing can also be demonstrated by using another method of examining the data. Because of the way the LAQ was scored, to call a person Authoritarian, Anti-authoritarian, or Equalitarian is simply a relative statement. Everyone expresses all three attitudes to some extent. Scores on all three attitude positions were converted to standard scores so that the three scores a person obtained could be directly compared. A subject was then classified as being primarily Authoritarian, Anti-authoritarian, or Equalitarian on the basis of which of his three scores was the highest. In this way, 50 subjects were classified as Equalitarian, 48 as Anti-authoritarian, and 53 as Authoritarian.

This procedure enabled comparisons to be made of over-all "toughness" and "leniency." A "lenient" subject was one who either acquitted or rendered a manslaughter verdict on the Guilty case. There could be no true "leniency" when a person had judged the Not Guilty case, because acquittal was the hypothetically correct verdict. In the same way, a "tough" subject was one who rendered a manslaughter or second degree murder verdict on the Not Guilty case. All "tough" and "lenient" subjects can be considered as having rendered incorrect verdicts in terms of the way the cases were designed and perceived by the subjects as a whole.

If the hypothesis is correct that Authoritarians are overly "tough" and Anti-authoritarians overly "lenient," it would be expected that more persons classified as Authoritarian would be found among those making the "tough" error and more Anti-authoritarians among those making the "lenient" error. The data is presented in Table III.

TABLE III

"Tough" and "Lenient" Errors

Subjects	"Tough" error		"Lenient" error	
	Number making	Expected number	Number making	Expected number
Authoritarians	22	15.72	11	17.28
Anti-authoritarians	5	11.28	20	13.72

$X^2 = 11.21$ (chance probability less than .001).

Using this method, the results are even more clear-cut. When errors are made, the Authoritarians tend to make "tough" errors, and the Anti-authoritarians tend to make "lenient" ones. The probability that the obtained result was due to chance is less than one in a thousand.

Clearly then, the attitudinal biases are operating in some way to influence the verdicts reached by many of the Authoritarians and Anti-authoritarians. The ballot form gave the subjects an opportunity to give the reasoning behind their verdicts. While the material obtained was not quantifiable, there does seem to be a difference in the reasons given by the persons whose biases influenced their verdicts.

The Authoritarians seemed prone to using subjective impressions of the character of the persons involved in the case that they had gleaned in some fashion from the evidence presented as the basis of their verdicts. One Authoritarian commented on the defendant's grammar. Another went so far as to state that while the defendant's guilt was uncertain, the defendant was a "dubious character" and should be removed from society.

The Anti-authoritarians tended to use the same kind of impressionistic evidence to conclude that even if the defendant were guilty as charged, it was not his fault but society's, because he had led a difficult life. One Anti-authoritarian bluntly stated that he did not believe in punishment and acquitted the defendant on that basis alone.

Other Authoritarian and Anti-authoritarian individuals were more subtle in their biases; they gave reasons grounded in carefully enumerated pieces of evidence. But in several cases, there was no evidence available in the case summary that bore any plausible resemblance to the "facts" so carefully listed by the subject.

The greatest weakness of this study, the paper and pencil format, makes it impossible to be certain what effect these systematic attitudinally-predictable errors would have on a *group* deliberation. There is, however, one piece of indirect evidence indicating that the influence of Authoritarians and Anti-authoritarians on a jury might be greater than the influence of Equalitarians on the same jury. The subjects were asked to indicate how confident they were of the correctness of their verdicts. Considering only those subjects who gave hypothetically incorrect verdicts, 72 percent of the Authoritarians and 52 percent of the Anti-authoritarians as opposed to only 42 percent of the Equalitarians expressed a high degree of confidence in their verdict which was in fact hypothetically incorrect. It would appear that if confidence in the correctness of one's position has anything to do with the amount of influence one can exert in a group deliberation, the biased individual, especially the Authoritarian, might exercise considerable influence.

V. CONCLUSIONS

This study was designed to demonstrate that certain measurable attitudinal predispositions that have no obvious legal relevancy can in fact be used to predict how individuals will judge and interpret a criminal case. The results of this study seem to show that these attitudinal predispositions do in fact effect the way jurors respond to evidence.

Are the results of this study applicable to other samples, cases, and situations that are better approximations of an actual jury situation than the one used here? These questions cannot be answered until more studies using this approach are done. But this study, in spite of its limited resemblance to an actual jury situation, was a rather strict test of the hypothesis. The subjects used were college students, who are a select portion of the population. Logically, they might be assumed to be more rational in their thought processes and less biased than the noncollege person. And, in making their judgments, they had the case material before them and could refer back to it as often as they pleased. This would seem more likely to produce accurate judgments than reliance on memory. Yet many of these well educated young people managed somehow to distort the evidence plainly before them in directions that could be predicted from their responses to the LAQ. It seems reasonable to suppose that the degree of bias of less selected, real-life jurors who base their judgments on their memory of oral testimony might be considerably greater.

But all this can yet only be considered conjecture. Strong as the results were, they cannot and should not be considered as providing a definitive answer to the problem of jury bias. This study is a pilot project, the first attempt to bring a new approach to bear on the problem. Perhaps the greatest value of this study is that it demonstrates that it is possible to do research in this area combining psychological and legal concepts in a meaningful fashion.

THE LIMITS OF
SCIENTIFIC JURY SELECTION:
ETHICAL AND EMPIRICAL

Michael J. Saks*

Scientific jury selection was born in the winter of 1971–1972, the child of anti-war activism, social science's re-newed search for social relevance, and the (sometimes) slow pragmatism of lawyers. Philip Berrigan and seven other defendants were the objects of a federal indictment charging them with perpetrating a number of draft board raids, of conspiring to raid draft boards and destroy records, of conspiring to kidnap Henry Kissinger, and conspiring to blow up heating tunnels in Washington. This was another in the government's continuing series of conspiracy trials against anti-war and other activist groups. The jurisdiction selected for the trial—the middle district of Pennsylvania—was one of a number of east coast jurisdictions where the trial could have been held. One can surmise, without much chance of being wrong, that the Justice Department chose the Harrisburg, Pennsylvania, area over Philadelphia, New York City, and Rochester so it would have the advantage of the district's unusually conservative and pro-government citizenry.

Sociologist Jay Schulman, social psychologists Philip Shaver and Richard Christie, psychologist Robert Colman, and rehabilitation counselor Barbara Emrich joined with the team of defense attorneys headed by Ramsay Clark to select from that inordinately conservative population a jury which would be more favorable to the defendants. The social scientists worked without remuneration. They were aided by an army of volunteers who helped gather the demographic and attitudinal data which would make the scientific jury selection possible. In spirit and in style, the first scientific jury selection was another specie of anti-war

---

*Michael J. Saks is a member of the faculties of the Department of Psychology and School of Law at Boston College, Chestnut Hill, Massachusetts 02167.

rally. The trial ended in a hung jury, split 10-2 in favor of the defense, and the prosecution dropped the charges.[1]

The use of social science expertise in jury selection has been growing since the trial of the Harrisburg Seven.[2] So has concern about the long term effects of such technology on the judicial process. Social scientists have helped and are helping lawyers select juries in such trials as the Camden 28, the Gainesville Eight, the Angela Davis trial, the trial of Indian Militants from Wounded Knee, and defendants in the current Attica prosecutions. One of the most publicized uses of scientific jury selection was in the trial of John Mitchell and Maurice Stans. After failing to come to terms with the Christie group, the defense turned to Marty Herbst, a market research consultant, who did the job for them.

Exactly what job is being done is something we will consider shortly. Many concerned people have noted, however, that no defendants who have used scientific jury selection have yet been convicted (except on the most trivial of the charges in their indictments), have interpreted this fact to mean the technology is effective and powerful, and have suggested that its power may be a threat to our system of trial by jury and to justice itself.

Concerned critics are not difficult to find. Writers of letters to the *New York Times* have complained that scientific jury selection is "unquestionably unethical" and makes a farce of justice.[3] Attorneys have questioned whether the infusion of social scientists and their methods into the courts is legitimate.[4] If the outcome of a trial can be manipulated simply by impaneling jurors designated acceptable by social scientists, then trial by jury may cease to function satisfactorily and, ultimately, may be abandoned. Amitai Etizioni, a prominent sociologist, director of the Center for Policy Research, and colleague at Columbia University of Christie and Shaver, has also argued that scientific jury selection threatens the integrity of the jury system, increases the advantages of the rich and celebrated over the poor and obscure, and that it may prompt the state to hire its own social scientists to increase further the government's already sizeable advantages in a criminal proceeding. Etzioni refers to this "sophisticated yet insidious tampering with the jury system" and concludes: "Man has taken a new bite from the apple of knowledge, and it is doubtful whether we will all be better for it."[5]

These criticisms are wrong, I think, on both ethical and empirical grounds. The critics are worried about something which on closer examination shows itself not to warrant such grave concern, while at the same time are failing to worry about something more fundamental which does. Before confronting these issues, though, it may be helpful to understand

---

[1]Schulman, J., Shaver, P., Colman, R., Emrich, B., and Christie, R., "Recipe for a Jury," 6 *Psychology Today* 37 (1963).

[2]The trial became popularly known as the Harrisburg Seven Trial because one of the eight defendants in the original indictment was severed from the cas e and was tried separately.

[3]Gerber, E., New York Times 30:5 (May 18, 1974).

[4]Cristiano, J., Marinaccio, M., and Shortall, J. *Social Science And The Voir Dire: Legalized Jury Tampering?* Public Meeting, Nov. 20, 1974.

[5]Etzioni, A. *Science: Threatening The Jury Trial.* The Washington Post, May 26, 1974. Reprinted as *Creating An Imbalance.* 10 Trial 28 (1974).

how scientific jury selection (or scientific jury *stacking*, as some prefer to call it) works.

The advent of scientific jury selection has come quite late. The necessary attitude scaling technology has been in existence since the late 1920s[6] and the necessary mathematical techniques for a good bit longer than that.[7] By 1950, the development of standardized attitude and personality scales,[8] and studies of the relationships between various demographic characteristics (such things as sex, age, race, religion, etc.) and attitudes were well underway.[9] By the time computers became a common part of the social science arsenal, around 1960, the potential for selecting juries scientifically went from feasible to easy. This extraordinary lag reveals quite a lot about the relationship between social scientists and lawyers.

THE TECHNIQUES[10]

The law provides for a two-stage process for the selection of jurors. From the eligible population, known as the venire, a pool of prospective jurors is drawn. The pool is intended to be a representative cross-section of the population and usually comes from voter registration lists. Persons who would be overburdened by serving or who are not able to perform the juror role competently (such as a person who does not speak English) are "excused". On the other hand, a good many Supreme Court decisions have asserted that no groups of citizens may be arbitrarily denied the opportunity to serve.[11]

From this pool will be drawn the jurors for each jury trial, be it civil or criminal. Jurors are subjected to *voir dire* examination where they are questioned—sometimes by the judge, sometimes by the prosecuting and defense attorneys; sometimes with statutory questions, sometimes with a wider range of questions—in an effort to determine their fitness to serve. Prospective jurors will be impaneled for the trial unless a challenge is made against them. The respective attorneys may challenge for cause,

---

[6]*Thurstone, L. L. and Chare, E. J. The Measurement of Attitude*, (1929).

[7]The development of correlational analysis can be traced through Bravais, A., 9 Mém. l'Acad Roy. Sci. L'Inst. France, Sci. Math, et phys. 255 (1846); Galton, F. *Co-relations And Their Measurement*. 45 Proc. Roy. Soc. 135 (1888); Pearson, K. *Mathematical Contributions To The Theory Of Evolution: Regression, Heredity, And Panmixia*. 187A Philos. Trans. 253.

[8]Relevant collections of such instruments are the following: Robinson, J. P., Rusk, J. G., Head, K. B. (Eds.), Measures Of Political Attitudes (1968, 1973); and Robinson, J. P., and Shaver, P. R. (Eds.), Measures Of Social Psychological Attitudes (1969, 1973, 1974).

[9]See, for example, virtually any issue of the Public Opinion Quarterly over the past three decades.

[10]For detailed descriptions of current techniques see Kairys, D. (Ed.) The Jury System: New Methods For Reducing Prejudice, The National Jury Project and the National Lawyers Guild (1975) or Ginger, A. F. (Ed.) Jury Selection in Criminal Trials: New Techniques And Concepts, Lawpress (1975). The Kairys book is exceptionally informative and inexpensive.

[11]Also, 18 U.S.C. at 243.

where the judge is asked to exclude the prospective juror for reasons put forth by the challenging attorney and if the judge agrees, the juror is excluded from that case. Or the attorneys may use one of a limited number of peremptory challenges with which to exclude a juror without having to state reasons and without requiring the judge's consent. The defense is usually given a larger number of peremptory challenges than the prosecution.[12]

It is through these challenges that attorneys can influence the composition of the jury that is finally impaneled. The purpose of *voir dire* is to eliminate jurors whose biases may interfere with a fair consideration of the evidence, thus insuring—or trying to—an impartial jury. Of course, both advocates try to find and impanel jurors who are most favorable to their side. Literally for centuries, lawyers have relied upon intuition, superstition, past personal experience, old wives' tales, and various combinations of these to try to figure out which prospective jurors will be most favorable to their side.[13] Scientific jury selection allows these decisions to be made with the benefit of knowledge acquired through the use of systematic empirical (i.e., "scientific") methods.

Schulman and his associates have given a lucid account of the procedures they used in the Harrisburg Seven trial.[14] Taking into consideration the issues on which the case is likely to hinge, the social scientists design questionnaires which include:

- scales previously developed and validated to measure attitudes related to the crucial issues of the case, such as a Trust in government measure;
- new attitude and information items written for the particular case at hand, such as knowledge of the defendants and their case;
- measures of background characteristics including:
  ○ personality measures, such as the F-scale[15] (which measures authoritarianism);
  ○ demographic characteristics, such as sex, occupation, race, education, socioeconomic status, etc.;
  ○ media contact and preferences;
  ○ spare time activities, organizational memberships, etc.

Interviewers use these questionnaires to collect data from a sample of the population from which the juror pool is drawn. They do not approach any of the prospective jurors themselves. By correlating the background characteristics with the attitude measures, it is possible to uncover the important predictor variables for the population's attitudes. It might be found, for example, that females are more favorable to the defense than males; young people more than older people; egalitarians more than authoritarians; readers of the New York Times more than readers of the Daily

---

[12]*Louisell, D. and Hazard, G. C. Jr. Pleading and Procedure: State and Federal* (1968) at 976 or *Vanderbilt, A. T., Minimum Standards of Judicial Administration* (1949) at 147.
[13]*Cf. Simon, R. J., The Jury and the Defense of Insanity* (1967) at 98.
[14]*Supra* note 1.
[15]Adorno, T. *et al.*, The Authoritarian Personality (1950).

News; Elks more than Masons; and that level of education, introversion, age, political affiliation, and two dozen other things are not at all related to the critical attitudes.

The reason for surveying the local jurisdiction rather than looking up data on national trends is that each community may have its own unusual circumstances which make, say, women more defense prone in Harrisburg but men more defense prone in Gainesville.[16] It is best to know what is happening in a particular community where the case is being tried instead of relying on general trends which may not hold in that locality. Moreover, these things change not only with geography but with the passage of time or a new case which activates new issues.

Socio-psychological surveys of the population can be useful to defense attorneys for purposes other than jury selection. If the jury venire proves to be unrepresentative of the community, the constitutionality of selection procedures can be challenged. And if the case is lost, the survey data can form the basis for an appeal.

Social scientists can become quite fancy and rather precise with disarming ease, thanks to computers. With about five seconds' extra human effort, the computer can be instructed to perform a "multiple regression analysis." A number of variables can thereby be taken into account simultaneously instead of one at a time, and the relative importance of the several best predictors can be incorporated into a "prediction equation." The best predictor variables are identified, weighted, and combined to maximize predictive power.[17] Should you have to choose between an old female and a young male, the prediction equation would take into account how old is old, and the fact that sex has 31.7 percent more predictive power than age, and tell you which of the two is a safer bet.

One benefit of obtaining demographic correlates of trial-related attitudes is that during *voir dire*, jurors sometimes lie. They may say they are not biased against protesting priests when they actually are and want to be on the jury to punish the defendant. But background characteristics cannot be falsified. If the juror is a 54-year-old male registered Republican who is the proprietor of a sporting goods store, your printouts will tell you what he is likely to believe, even if he won't. On the other hand, your data will tell you only about the probabilities for the population, not

---

[16]*Supra* note 1.

[17]An example of a prediction equation with two predictors is:

$Y = M_1 X_1 + M_2 X_2 + B$. Inserting some hypothetical names and numbers: Vote = .6771 Age + .3934 Conservatism + .1027. This would indicate that the best prediction of a juror's vote for guilt or innocence would be found by multiplying the juror's age by .6771, the juror's conservatism score by .3934, and adding those products together with the regression constant .1027. If this reminds a reader of his or her high school trigonometry, it should. This is built upon the old, familiar $Y = MX + b$ where to predict Y when you know X, you need also to know their relationship, given by the slope (M) and the Y—intercept (b). Further information can be found in most textbooks on research methods and statistics. *See*, for example, *Willemsen, E. W., Understanding Statistical Reasoning* (1974) at 143 or *Kerlinger, F. N., Foundations of Behavioral Research*, 2nd ed. (1973) at 603.

how any particular 54-year-old male Republican entrepreneur will vote. Like a baseball manager deciding on which pinch hitter to use, you cannot know if on *this* occasion player A will outhit player B. But you can know that against this type of pitcher player A, on the average, does better than player B and you play the percentages because in the long run you will come out ahead. And, more important, because there really is no better information available to go on.

Schulman and his colleagues have warned against placing too much faith in such technology as attitude scales and prediction equations. In the courtroom, they also observed the prospective jurors and tried to discern which way each one leaned. They relied on non-verbal behavior, what jurors said and how they said it, on appearance, vibrations, and any other sense data they could muster. The attorneys, of course, did this same thing in their own way, as they would have even without the social scientists, and so did the defendants. The results of these intuitive judgments were compared to the statistical findings and where both agreed, the defense team could be reasonably confident that a favorable juror had been identified. Where the human and computerized indicators did not concur, the juror in question could be skipped over or investigated further.

While such caution agrees with the common sense of most of us, the caution is probably in the wrong direction. Those intuitive, instinctive judgments, when put to the test, have proved notoriously unreliable.[18] Even professional people watchers such as psychiatrists and clinical psychologists (when they engage in these tasks as part of their professional work, it is called "clinical judgment") have produced a surprisingly poor track record. Studies show that professional training, when it has any effect at all on the accuracy of predictions about people, tends to *reduce* judgmental accuracy.[19] Moreover, when the same information is available to a human decision-maker and a mathematical model, almost without exception the mathematical model makes more reliable and accurate predictions. After 60 studies comparing clinical versus statistical prediction, the humans beat the computers only once.[20] These findings were as much of a surprise (and offense to the human ego) to the people who discovered them as to you who read about them. The original intention was to aid human decision makers by providing a floor of statistical accuracy below which they could not fall. But the floor

---

[18] *See, for example, Meehl, P. E. Clinical Versus Statistical Prediction: A Theoretical Analysis And A Review of the Evidence* (1954); Mischel, W., *Personality and Assessment* (1968); Taft, R., "The Ability to Judge People," 52 *Psychological Bulletin* and *infra* notes 23 and 24.

[19] *See, for example,* Danet, B. N. "Prediction of Mental Illness in Colege Students on the Basis of 'Nonpsychiatric' MMPI Profiles," 29 *Journal of Consulting Psychology* 577 (1965); Soskin, W. F., "Bias In Postdiction From Projective Tests," 49 *J. Abnormal and Social Psychology* 69 (1954); and *supra* note 18.

[20] *See* Gough, H. G. "Clinical v. Statistical Prediction in Psychology." In L. Postman (Ed.), *Psychology in the Making* (1962); Livermore, J., Malmquist, C., and Meehl, P. "On the Justification for Civil Commitment," 117 *U. Pa. Law Review* 75 (1968).

turned out to be a ceiling.[21] We are indeed fallible creatures.[22]

Fortunately, we need not choose between trusting the humans and trusting the technology. Both are available for use. If only jurors who are approved by both methods are selected, then many questionable jurors, who would have been picked by one or the other and turned out to be wrong, will be safely excluded. The wisdom of using both and looking for concurrence is obvious.

During and between *voir dire* sessions, the social scientists and attorneys compare notes, classify jurors according to predicted favorableness, and make their selections. The selections are based largely, but not entirely, upon predictions of jurors' predispositions. The defense in the Harrisburg Seven trial also considered the likely dynamics of the group that would become the jury. Since the defendants were mostly Catholic, it would be desirable to place at least one Catholic on the jury so that the expression of anti-Catholic prejudice would be inhibited. Also taken into account was social science knowledge about dominance and marginality in members of small groups—who was most likely to be selected foreman, who would be marginal and therefore least influential but also most resistant to pressure from other jurors—and the effects of possible sequestration on certain jurors. What was the best jury that could be put together, taking all of these factors into consideration? This was the task of the defense in jury selection.

The line between the "scientific" and the not is often a fuzzy one, but the distinction throws some light on the technology we are discussing. Science is one more of many human enterprises. Science is a stance toward knowledge acquisition. Its distinguishing characteristic is that it is obsessed with systematic empirical verification of its hypotheses. That contrasts with the relatively haphazard way most of us most of the time settle on our beliefs, relying upon evidence that does not lend unambiguous support or upon little or no empirical evidence at all. The process of using the findings of social science to select jurors is not in itself science, but rather is the application of findings previously obtained through use of the scientific method. Like engineering and medicine, it is not science, but borrows from science. Almost of necessity, applications themselves cannot be "science." That is why the applications are regarded as scientific and are given the label "technology." Where the borrowings from science combine with other sources of knowledge the resulting enterprise is called an "art."

These distinctions are informative in considering some practices

---

[21]Dawes, R. M., Corrigan, B., "Linear Models In Decision Making," 81 *Psychological Bulletin* 95 (1974).

[22]A moment's reflection might make these findings seem less surprising. Every photographer knows that his or her light-meter will more accurately detect differences in brightness than the photographer's biological light-meter, human visual perception. Why, if such simple perceptual tasks can be improved upon by technology, should more complex perceptual tasks (known to psychologists as person perception or social perception) not also be subject to improvement by science and technology? If sensation and perception can be inaccurate surely the more intricate cognitive processing that follows perception can be inaccurate.

which are often included under "scientific jury selection" but which probably should not be. One distinguishes "modern medicine" from "home remedies" by noting that the former are based upon principles which have been empirically verified in the biological sciences. The latter have not been carefully tested and therefore have a lesser likelihood of being safe and effective. In the Angela Davis trial, psychologists relied upon their observations of prospective jurors. They looked for subtle human characteristics, for hidden antipathies revealed by facial expressions, gestures, and other non-verbal cues as well as the subtle implications of jurors' responses during *voir dire* questioning. Similarly, the courtroom judgments of the Harrisburg Seven team were of this type. In addition, the Angela Davis psychologists had handwriting analysts examine samples of prospective jurors' signatures. These efforts are "scientific" only to the extent that they are based upon principles drawn from careful empirical testing. Otherwise, the social scientists are not adding anything new to what the lawyers have always done or had available.

To the extent that the social scientists rely on their professional and/or clinical experience to "psych out" jurors, to intuit their leanings, they are probably going to be less accurate than trial lawyers who have had more experience in that setting. (Prison officials have been found to make more accurate predictions of dangerousness than psychiatrists,[23] and mental patients were found better able than the institution's staff to detect the true status of researchers who infiltrated mental hospitals.)[24] I am unaware of any empirical studies which have established a relationship between handwriting and attitudes toward defendants. And research on non-verbal behavior shows it to be most subtle and often quite unrevealing. In a lengthy series of experiments, social psychologist Robert Love of American University tried unsuccessfully to establish a consistent relationship between non-verbal behavior and attitudes. He finally found that subjects could display reliable non-verbal patterns, which correlated with attitudes, only when they deliberately sought to do so. And even then it required repeated studies of videotapes of the subjects, counting of eyeblinks, timing of head nods, protractor measuring of body lean.[25] Jurors who wish to conceal their real attitudes are therefore apparently able to do so non-verbally as well as verbally. And we have already mentioned the well established unreliability of clinical judgment to predict attitudes and behavior. Nothing is wrong, of course, with using these techniques. Except that their effectiveness has not been established.

Still, there are verified, reliable techniques and they are being used. These techniques, and others still to be developed, are worrying many lawyers, social scientists, and others concerned with the health of the jury system. What about their concerns that the new jury selection tech-

---

[23]Dershowitz, A., "Psychiatry In the Legal Process," *Trial* (Feb./Mar., 1968).
[24]Rosenhan, D. "On Being Sane in Insane Places," 179 *Science* 250 (1973).
[25]Love, R. "Nonreactive, Nonverbal Measures of Attitudes," Doctoral dissertation at the Ohio State University (1972).

nology raises questions about the integrity of the jury system, and perhaps ultimately will destroy this uniquely democratic institution, and that the only real beneficiaries will be a few wealthy and prominent defendants and many prosecutors, once they hire social scientists to help them?

ETHICAL AND LEGAL CONSIDERATIONS

The defense of scientific jury selection might begin by pointing out that it is thoroughly legal. Prospective jurors are not themselves approached or tampered with. They are merely compared to statistical profiles of the population from which they were drawn. They are questioned only during *voir dire*, and only to the extent permitted by the trial judge, as has been the way for generations. All that has changed is that lawyers can now know the hidden meaning of the answers and of jurors' background characteristics.

The practice of *voir dire* and of challenging jurors was not invented by Schulman and his friends. It has been part of the jury system for centuries. And for those centuries lawyers have sought to impanel the most favorable possible juries for their clients. This has always been widely regarded as a proper goal for the lawyer. Why should the fact that he has finally been given the means to achieve that goal be so objectionable? If the goal was good, why has the ability to actually achieve it become bad? This curious contradiction between the generally positive reaction to a goal and the generally negative reaction to attaining it has emerged in other spheres where psychotechnology has made realities out of dreams. Behavior Modification is a prominent example. For generations and longer people have wished for the power to control behavior— to rid people of their phobias, to reshape the behavior of criminals and delinquents, to make school children stay happily glued to their desks. Now that behavioral scientists have finally made these things do-able, the technology responsible for it has come under much criticism.[26] Behavior Modification's greatest sin has been that it works. Apparently, many of our society's goals are acceptable only as long as they cannot be achieved.

But if a goal is desirable, why should its attainment be undesirable? Moreover, why should it be the fault of the psychotechnology, which merely is making possible the achievement of long standing goals? We may actually have mistaken goals, which becomes obvious to us only after we are about to achieve them. But the problem lies not in the technology but in the goals we have chosen. If we and the generations before us lacked the wisdom to select proper goals, it will not help now to condemn the technology which provides the means to those goals. Had we selected other goals, the technologists would most likely and just

---

[26]See, for example, the brief reviews in *Brown, B. S., Wienckowski, L. A., and Stolz, S. B. Behavior Modifications: Perspective on a Current Issue* (1975) at 12 and *Andrews, L. M. and Karlins, M. Requiem For Democracy?* (1971), especially chapters 2, 3, and 7.

as happily have developed the means to move us toward those ends. Wanting to make children stay fixed in their seats was just as unwise a hundred years ago as it is today. Just because behavioral scientists have made that an easy trick to perform doesn't make the goal their sin. Giving us the realization of our wishes doesn't make them the villains. If there is to be goal reform, we, the society, will have to do it. The social scientists cannot do that for us. Blaming their inventions for the goals implies that their inventions can and should change the goals. Society's goals are and should be the responsibility of society.

But the goal of jury selection is not, I think, an unwise one. The intent is to impanel an impartial jury, that is, a jury whose members do not have biases that would make them unable to fairly weigh the evidence. Jurors are supposed to reach a verdict shaped by the weight of the evidence and not by the decision-makers' biases. The strategy for achieving that goal—allowing both advocates some opportunity to exclude from the jury persons thought to be biased against their side—also seems to me a wise and workable one. Scientific jury selection can add substantially to the achievement of that goal. Instead of guessing at who will be biased and will therefore not respond impartially to the evidence, lawyers can make informed judgments. If both sides have social science help, each will more effectively exclude jurors favorable to the other side, and the final panel will consist of the neutral jurors, the very ones who will be most able to do what a jury is intended to do. Thus, juror attitudes and personality would play a minimal role in determining the outcome of the trial. Evidence would be permitted to play the greatest possible role, which is how it was always supposed to be. Thus, scientific jury selection would make the goal of impartial jury decisions more attainable than has ever before been possible.

But, the critics would interject, the presence of such expertise on both sides is a fantasy which ignores the realities of justice in America. Today only the wealthy and celebrated have such help, and tomorrow the only additional people to have it will be prosecutors, and they will use it routinely. And this criticism is probably entirely true. But it does not demonstrate some evil inherent in scientific jury selection. It points instead to a fundamental inequity in our courts. *All* resources will be unevenly distributed in a system where those with wealth or the right friends can obtain services unavailable to the average citizen. This is not the fault of the resources or their inventors. The rich can hire lawyers who are likely to be better than the prosecutors, and the poor must settle for legal aid attorneys who in many instances will be less able than the prosecutors. It was only as recently as 1963, in *Gideon v. Wainwright*[27], that the defendant's right to have any counsel at all was firmly established. The ability to prepare a strong case is of great importance. In addition to a good lawyer, that depends upon investigators. The prosecution has its investigators. They are called police. And the rich have their private investigators. Investigator's fees can be larger than

---

[27]372 U.S. 335 (1963).

those of attorneys. The evidence they provide is of enormous and often vital importance. The attorney can work only with the evidence available to him. Without Paul Drake, Perry Mason might be just another so-so solo practitioner. The greatest and most serious inequities—differential access to attorneys and investigators—already exist and have for centuries.

Every material and service commodity is systematically more available to one side than it is to the other. And every new invention of social scientists, legal service providers, or anyone else will be too. The problem lies not in each service and invention but in the system in which these things are used. The critics of scientific jury selection, to keep existing inequities from becoming more pronounced, would keep this new technology out of the courtroom or restructure court proceedings to minimize its potential impact. But next year or decade they will have to rally again to ban yet another innovation and then another and another after that. I suggest that these energies would be more efficiently directed at reforming the system which fosters all of these inequities. To do so would eliminate long standing inequities and make future innovations welcome for the benefits they may offer. The alternative is to live with existing imbalances and eternally eschew new developments.

EMPIRICAL CONSIDERATIONS

I have saved for last what is perhaps the most interesting reason for not worrying excessively about scientific jury selection: the empirical reason. No evidence exists to support the apparently widely held belief that scientific jury selection is a powerful tool. What has most people upset about the technique is the fact that no one who has used it has lost a case. By the usual standards for evaluating empirical evidence, the same standards used by the social and behavioral scientists who developed the basic principles for the technique, this seemingly impressive evidence is really no evidence at all. The venerated scientific method usually calls for a control group, that is, a comparison group to tell you what an observation really means. To elucidate, suppose there were a control group. Suppose each of the cases had been tried before two juries—one selected the scientific way and one selected the old way.[28] We could then compare the verdicts delivered by the scientific juries with those delivered by the conventional juries (the control juries.) We know that all of the scientifically selected juries refused to convict. What would the conventionally selected juries have done? The answer to this question is absolutely essential to an assessment of how effective scientific jury selection is or even whether it works at all. Without such comparisons

---

[28]*Cf.* Zeisel, H. and Diamond, S. S. "Convincing Empirical Evidence" on the Six-Member Jury 41 *U. Chicago L. Rev.* 281 (1974); Diamond, S. S. and Zeisel, H. "A Courtroom Experiment on Juror Selection and Decision-Making," *Proceedings of the American Psychological Association Convention* (August, 1974).

it simply is impossible to know. If a significant[29] number of control juries convicted we would know that the use of scientific jury selection techniques helped the defense effort.

If all of the conventional juries also refused to convict, we would know that scientific jury selection offered no help to the defense in those cases.

The focus of controversy on the jury selection process has obscured other critical determinants of trial outcome, such as the nature of the case. If all of our fraternal twin juries refused to convict, it might have been because in none of the trials was a strong enough case made against the defendants. Every one of the trials where the technique was employed could be characterized as political, and nearly every count in every case was a charge of conspiracy. Virtually every recent political trial conducted by the government, *whether the defense used scientific jury selection or not* (such as in the Chicago Seven trial and the Panther 21 conspiracy trial), has failed to result in conviction. (Perhaps prosecutorial judgment falters when ideological fervor wells up.) And conspiracy charges are also very difficult to obtain jury convictions with.[30]

None of this is to say that scientific jury selection did not have an important effect on verdicts in the cases where it was used. It says only that we cannot know what the impact was because the necessary comparisons could not be made. The social scientists at Harrisburg understood all of this and, true to their training, they endeavored to measure the effectiveness of their selections. While the actual jury was deliberating, they re-interviewed a subsample of people from their original survey of the community. Fifty-four percent revealed a high presumption of the defendants' guilt. In contrast, only 17 percent (two of twelve) of the actual jurors voted to convict.[31] The major weakness of these data is that the surveyed citizens differed from the selected jurors in a very important way. The surveyed citizens had not heard the evidence—or lack of it.

More interesting and more complete data are available to help inform our *understanding of the impact* of scientific jury selection.

In popular (i.e., nontechnical) reports of the findings and doings of social scientists working in the jury selection area, you will read, for instance, that females were more favorable to the defense than males. Does that mean that 0 percent of females would vote to convict while 100 percent of males would? Or does it mean that 65 percent of females were conviction prone while 67 percent of males were similarly disposed? The difference is important for a realistic understanding of scientific jury selection. In the first illustration your selections are a certainty. The second shows more correctly how you are really engaged in probabilistic decision-making. You will do better than if you did not have the knowl-

---

[29]"Significant" is used in its technical sense of a finding having a low probability of having occurred by chance (typically, less than .05). For details, see any statistics texts, such as *Willemsen* at 53, *supra* note 17.

[30]Zeisel, H., "Mitchell–Stans Judged," New York Times 15 (May 26, 1974).

[31]*Supra* note 1.

edge, but you will not make flawless selections. This is especially evident when you consider that Male Juror A may be one of the 33 percent of males who would acquit and Female Juror B is one of the 65 percent of females who would convict. You would pick juror B because she was your best bet, but you would lose. Scientific jury selection helps one make educated bets. It is not magic. In fact, it appears to be a relatively weak device, and most social and behavioral scientists would expect it to be. Before explaining why this is so, let's be sure we appreciate how weak the available data show it to be.

Warning to Trial Lawyers: Do not uncritically use the following data to select your juries. The findings may not be applicable in the jurisdiction where you practice.

In one of the most extensive studies of jurors and their decision making behavior, Rita James Simon studied jurors in Chicago, St. Louis, and Minneapolis.[32] She looked at the relationship between a juror's vote and his/her education, occupation, sex, income, religion, ethnicity, and age. Only education and ethnicity were able to predict jurors' votes (in two experimental cases where defendants were pleading Not Guilty by reason of Insanity (NGI).

In one case (the housebreaking case), if you selected your jurors at random, 66 percent would have voted NGI. If you knew that people with less than college education were more inclined that way, and selected only those, you would have a group of whom about 72 percent would vote NGI—an improvement of about six percentage points. Knowing the effect of ethnicity and consequently choosing only blacks, you would increase the likelihood of obtaining an NGI juror to 85 percent—an increase of 19 percentage points. These reductions in uncertainty, incidentally, cannot simply be added together, so that the two pieces of knowledge improve your accuracy by up to 25 percent, because there will be a lot of overlap. Many of the blacks chosen will have less than college education, so that the first cut will already filter out many jurors who are undesirable on the remaining criteria. In the other case (the incest case), a random selection of jurors would consist of people of whom 33 percent voted NGI. Your knowledge of education effects would improve your selection in this case by two percentage points, and ethnicity again would improve it by 19 percentage points. That is not insubstantial improvement. But the most powerful difference of all was the effect of the type of case: the housebreaking case produced 66 percent NGI voters compared to only 33 percent for the incest case—a difference of 33 percentage points. None of the demographic characteristics of the jurors approached that figure.

Looking at the relationship of jurors' attitudes about issues vital to the cases, Simon found even less of importance. She concluded:

> The sharp lack of findings reported in this chapter rival in interest any data we have. Three efforts were made to relate attitudes to verdict and each ended in failure.

---

[32]*Simon, supra* note 13.

Had we reported the responses to the attitude items separately, and not compared them with the jurors' verdicts, we think that most researchers would have expected and would have been prepared to use them as good predictors of verdicts. It may be some comfort to the trial lawyer who is prevented from asking these kinds of questions to learn that such information would give him no advantage.

I studied 480 jurors in Columbus, Ohio. Each was shown the same videotaped trial, deliberated in a jury, and rendered a verdict. Predictor variables examined included many things, from attitudes toward criminals and jurors' personal value systems to their socioeconomic status and level of education to whether they were left or right handed. These predictors were correlated with their degree of certainty of guilt prior to deliberation, and their certainty after deliberation, and there vote to convict or acquit. Out of the 27 predictors, the single best was whether jurors believed crime was mainly the product of "bad people" or "bad social conditions." Those holding the latter belief were more likely to regard the defendant as guilty. (Yes, guilty). This best predictor could account for only 9 percent of the variance[33] in the jurors' judgments. Using a multiple predictor format,[34] the four best predictors in linear combination (belief that crime is caused by bad people versus social conditions, how much they value obedience, how much they value leadership, and political party preference) combined to account for less than 13 percent of the variance. None of the remaining variables could add as much as 1 percent to the predictive accuracy.[35]

Robert Buckhout, director of the Center for Responsive Psychology in New York, studied a sample of municipal court jurors in California. He compared the demographic and personality characteristics of jurors voting guilty to those voting not guilty. He found no significant differences in age, income, education, or on such personality measures as Need for Social Approval,[36] Dogmatism,[37] or Machiavellianism.[38] The only significant discriminator of jurors voting guilty and those voting not guilty was the effective rating of the prosecutor. Those voting guilty liked him more than those voting not guilty. Such an index does not seem likely to be useful in selecting jurors. In court, face to face with the prosecutor and defense attorneys, jurors are not likely to candidly state

---

[33]The amount of variation in a dependent variable can be attributed to certain causes, or "explained" by them. An index of how important an independent variable is or how well it explains the variance is the "proportion of variance accounted for". The more accounted for, in this context at least, the better. For details, see appropriate statistics texts, such as *Willemsen*, at 73, *supra* note 17.

[34]*Supra* note 17.

[35]The data reported were collected in the course of conducting other research reported in Saks, M. J. "Jury Decision-Making as a Function of Group Size and Social Decision Rule" Doctoral Dissertation at the Ohio State University (1975).

[36]*Crowne, D. and Marlowe, D. The Approval Motive* (1964).

[37]Rokeach, M., "Political and Religious Dogmatism: An Alternative to the Authoritarian Personality," 70 *Psychological Monograph* 70 (1956).

[38]*Christie, R., Geis, F., et al., Studies in Machiavellianism* (1970).

16

their preferences even if the judge allowed the question to be asked.[39]

Research by Herman Mitchell and Donn Byrne, fairly often cited of late by social scientists interested in jury behavior, found that measures of authoritarianism did not distinguish conviction-prone jurors from acquittal-prone. They found instead that high authoritarians were more likely to acquit defendants they saw as similar to themselves and convict those they saw as different, while low authoritarians did not respond with such see-saw preferences. The problem for the defendant, then, may not be to select non-authoritarians from the jury pool (because there was no overall difference in the way authoritarians and egalitarians voted). The problem is: do you take authoritarians and hope they'll like you rather than dislike you, or do you go with egalitarians and know that their personal reaction to you will not affect their decision. Even for authoritarians, though, their feelings toward the defendant determined less than 14 percent of the variance in their certainty of his guilt. The effect (on authoritarians' certainty of guilt) of perceiving the defendant as similar rather than dissimilar amounted to only about half a point on a seven-point scale.[40]

All of the findings reported thus far and to be reported are "statistically significant," which means that the effects found are highly unlikely to be the product of chance. That is, they are real. But they are, nevertheless, not strong. What this means is that scientific jury selection can help, but it is not going to come close to absolutely determining the outcome of a trial. If the evidence against a defendant is very strong or very weak, it isn't going to matter who is on the jury. If the evidence is close, then the jury selection could make the difference. You wouldn't be wasting your money or your time if you employed scientific jury selection, but if you did it at the expense of building a strong case out of evidence, you would be making a serious mistake.

Carol Werner of the University of Utah, Thomas Ostrom of Ohio State, and I asked a sample of former jurors to indicate their certainty of a defendant's guilt or innocence in a series of very brief hypothetical cases, each consisting of a set of evidentiary statements. They were given cases in which the crime alleged differed, where the amount of evidence against the defendant differed, and in which the strength of the evidence varied it was either moderately (prescaled to indicate a .44 probability of defendant guilt) or highly (.77) incriminating. We also tested the jurors with a scale of defendant-related attitudes in order to classify them as either favorable or unfavorable to the defense. Our scale did significantly predict how the jurors would respond. Jurors designated as anti-defendant gave an average rating of guilt of 58[41] while pro-defendant jurors gave ratings that averaged −20. That is a spread of 78 points. But the

---

[39]Buckhout, R. *et al.*, "Jury Without Peers," CR-2, *Center for Responsive Psychology* (1973).

[40]Mitchell, H., and Byrne, D., "The Defendant's Dilemma: Effects of Jurors' Attitudes and Authoritarianism on Judicial Decision," 25 *J. Personality and Social Psychology* 125 (1973).

[41]These values have no easily intuited interpretation. They are the product of a complex mathematical transformation. For details, see the original paper, *infra* note 43.

point spread between average certainty of guilt in response to moderately incriminating evidence compared to highly incriminating evidence was 172 points. And presenting one item of evidence compared to six items of evidence produced a difference of 143 points. Looking at the proportion of variance accounted for by each of the independent variables, we find that the amount of evidence was more than three times as powerful, and strength of evidence more than seven times as powerful, as attitudes were in determining a juror's verdict.[42] Juror characteristics made a difference, but far less of a difference than characteristics of the trial evidence.[43]

An article frequently cited by social scientists interested in juries is one published in 1968 by Virginia Boehm,[44] a research psychologist for the State of New York and a former student of Christie. Dr. Boehm's study was on jury bias and the ability of an instrument called the LAQ (Legal Attitudes Questionnaire) to predict which way jurors were leaning. The study found that persons classified by the LAQ as authoritarian were significantly more likely to convict than persons classified as anti-authoritarian. How much more likely? Boehm wisely used two forms of trial evidence—one which favored the defense and one which favored the prosecution. Examining the verdicts of jurors who "erred," that is, who voted guilty when the evidence favored the defense or voted leniently when the evidence favored the prosecution, Boehm found that four-fifths of those designated by the LAQ as anti-authoritarians erred leniently while only one third of the authoritarians did so. What is often overlooked by readers of this research is that only 38 percent of all the jurors erred. And, actually, only 28 percent erred in the direction predicted for them by the LAQ. (Some anti-authoritarians voted guilty in the face of pro-defense evidence and some authoritarians voted leniently on pro-prosecution evidence.) Most important, and most overlooked, is that fully 62 percent of the jurors voted exactly in line with the evidence.

---

[42]Computation of the correlation ratio (eta) can be obviated, since we are interested in the *relative* proportions of variance accounted for, simply by comparing the sums of squares associated with each source of variance. Each of those values will have the same denominator, namely the SS total, which thus cancels out. Following are the sums of squares (SS), degrees of freedom (df), and F-ratios (F) associated with these three sources of variance, plus several key interactions relevant to *infra* note 48.

Source	SS	df	F
Juror attitudes	699520.688	1,36	15.803
Amount of evidence (linear)	2446012.000	1,36	102.910
Strength of evidence	5760546.000	1,36	191.002
Attitudes X Amount	7355.547	1,36	0.309
Attitudes X Strength	1445.057	1,36	0.048
Attitudes X Amount X Strength	12150.383	1,36	1.716

[43]*Saks, M. J. Werner, C., and Ostrom, T., The Presumption of Innocence and the American Juror.*
[44]Boehm, V. R., "Mr. Prejudice, Miss Sympathy and the Authoritarian Personality: An Application of Psychological Measuring Techniques to the Problem of Jury Bias," 1968 *Wisconsin Law Review* 734 (1968).

Probably the best known research on juries is Kalven and Zeisel's *The American Jury*.[45] They found that in 78 percent of a national sample of several thousand cases, the judge and the jury agreed on the verdict—in 64 percent, when the jury believed the defendant was guilty, so did the judge; and in 14 percent both agreed the defendant was not guilty. This substantial agreement is not an accident. By and large, both judge and jury respond to the trial evidence, and thus arrive at the same verdict.

Social and behavioral scientists are generally not surprised by any of this. While in our culture it has been popularly believed for a long time that personal characteristics make the major difference in people's behavior, that apparently is not correct. However important genetics, personality, and attitudes may be, they are generally not as important as situational factors. This realization came only after decades of research on personality variables which turned out to have little relationship to actual behavior,[46] and attitudes measures which were about as bad.[47] Stimulus characteristics of situations account for most of the difference in people's behavior.[48] The old Freudian theory that we have a core personality which manifests itself throughout our behavior, across different situations and circumstances in which we find ourselves, is either inadequate, relatively trivial, or simply wrong. After decades of looking for the core personality types, and finding none, it began to occur to the searchers that perhaps little was there to be found. Behavior changes dramatically from situation to situation. One would therefore be more effective by controlling the key stimulus characteristics of the situation (the evidence) rather than the characteristics of the people in the situation. This is essentially why Skinnerian Behavior Modification[49] has been more effective in producing psychotherapeutic change than psychodynamic-analytic approaches.[50] The former change the situation; the latter try to change the personality. The stimulus of stating these notions is upsetting to many people because they take them to mean that we are not unique individuals with our own autonomous direction in life, that we instead are impotent rats responding to environmental stimuli. The nicer way of stating the case, and the least upsetting to people, is that

---

[45]*Kalven, H., and Zeisel, H., The American Jury* (1971).

[46]*See, for example, Mischel, W., Introduction to Personality* (1971); *Krasner, L., and Ullman, I. P., Behavior Influence and Personality: The Social Matrix of Human Action* (1973); Mischel W., "Continuity and Change in Personality," 24 *Amer. Psychologist* 1012 (1969); Peterson, D. R., *The Clinical Study of Social Behavior* (1968); *Vernon, P. E. Personality Assessment: A Critical Survey* (1964).

[47]Wicker, A. W., "Attitudes Versus Action: The Relationship of Verbal and Overt Behavioral Responses to Attitude Objects," 25 *Journal of Social Issues* 41 (1969).

[48]More important than these main effect differences, it may be, are interactive effects between the two. *See* Hunt, J. McV., "Traditional Personality Theory in the Light of Recent Evidence," 53 *American Scientist* 80 (1965); Mischel, W. "Toward a Cognitive Social Learning Reconceptualization of Personality," 80 *Psych. Rev.* 252 (1973); and Cronbach, L. J., "Beyond the Two Disciplines of Scientific Psychology," 30 *American Psychologist* 116 (1975). Clearly, this was not the case in *supra* note 42.

[49]*E.g.,* Brown et al., *supra* note 26.

[50]*Paul, G. L., Insight Versus Desensitization in Psychotherapy* (1966).

we are all unique individuals, but our differences are vastly overshadowed by our similarities. Moreover, the range of situations we are likely to encounter is far more varied than the range of human beings who will encounter them. Put that way, the Skinnerian view is,[51] I think, a quite humanistic view of human nature. And from the viewpoint of one concerned about the fate of our system of justice and the jury's place in that system, it is optimistic. It means that jurors have been and will continue to be much more responsive to the evidence placed before them than to their own personalities and attitudes.

This state of affairs does not render attitudes irrelevant to the prediction of behavior in all circumstances. If one can take into account the stimuli to which the person will be responding and if the person has a well articulated, well crystallized, well practiced attitude-and-belief system, predictability improves. For example, social scientists such as Ulmer[52] and Shubert[53] have been able to predict the decisions of U.S. Supreme Court Justices with breathtaking accuracy.

I cannot conclude this article without first mentioning some weaknesses in the available studies which leave the question of the relative strengths of juror characteristics and evidence less than satisfyingly answered. While the fact that no defendants who used scientific jury selection lost their cases and the fact that juror's characteristics do bear some predictive relationship to their verdicts do not begin to answer the question, the studies examined in this article do not end the issue.

First of all, the relative contribution of evidence versus juror characteristics to the variance in verdicts depends partly upon the relative range of the two variables. That is, if juror characteristics varied considerably, but evidence did not, that would make the proportion of variance due to juror characteristics increase. If evidence were made to vary markedly from case to case, but juror differences were kept small, then the proportion of variance due to evidence would increase. Ideally, we would like the same range of variation in our studies that exists in the natural world of jury trials. Some of the studies used college student "jurors." Some used trial evidence whose comparability to actual trial evidence variability is unknown. Those studies done on real jurors deciding real trials did not measure differences in evidence, so relative effects of the two could not be computed. It may be then, that the consistent finding in these studies that evidence is more influential than juror bias is an accident of the range of evidence and jurors used. While this is a logical possibility, it seems unlikely. The one study that did measure the

---

[51]E.g., Skinner, B. F., *Beyond Freedom and Dignity* (1971), *Science and Human Behavior* (1953), *About Behaviorism* (1974).
[52]See, for example, Ulmer, S. S., "Supreme Court Behavior in Racial Exclusion Cases: 1935–1960," 56 *Am. Political Science Review* 325 (1962) and Ulmer, S. S., "The Analysis of Behavior Patterns on the United States Supreme Court," 22 *J. Politics* 629 (1960).
[53]See, for example, Schubert. G., "A Solution to the Indeterminate Factorial Resolution of Thurstone and Degan's Study of the Supreme Court," 7 *Behavioral Science* 448 (1962); Schubert, G., "The Study of Judicial Decision-making as an Aspect of Political Behavior," 52 *American Political Science Review* 1007 (1958); Schubert, G., "Ideologies and Attitudes, Academic and Judicial," 29 *J. Politics* 3 (1967).

incriminatory strength of the evidence[54] did not select extremely low and extremely high incriminating evidence for comparison—instead it deliberately used moderate (.44) and fairly high (.77) levels of evidence. Similarly, the Bohem study[55] did not use two forms of the evidence that were extremely divergent. The jurors, on the other hand, probably do represent their populations since they were not selected out to represent a narrow range. Thus, if the researchers wanted to alter the proportions of variance accounted for in their studies by these variables, they would have a difficult time doing so by altering their range of jurors (since they already have the available range,[56] but they could quite easily alter the cases, making the weak ones weaker and the strong ones stronger. It follows, then, that if these studies fail to reflect the true state of affairs, they do so by *underestimating* the impact of evidence relative to juror bias.

A second problem is that perhaps these studies asked the wrong questions of jurors. When social scientists have selected actual juries, they keyed many of their questions to issues unique to that trial. Researchers, on the other hand, tried to use more broad and general measures of juror personality and attitudes. The latter may not be good predictors, but perhaps the former are. Yet another problem is that trials of only a few different crimes have been studied. Perhaps scientific jury selection works better for some crimes than for others. In practice, scientific jury selection has been used only in political/conspiracy trials. In research, other crimes have been studied. If, however, effective scientific jury selection requires tests tailored to each particular trial, rather than standardized tests, that will seriously increase the costs and reduce the reliability of the technique. Again, this adds up to keeping relatively small the impact of scientific jury selection on the judicial system.

CONCLUSION

Studies that have shown that juror attitudes, personality, and demographic characteristics are related to the verdicts rendered by those jurors have led the overwhelming majority of commentators (both proponents and opponents of scientific jury selection) to leap to the conclusion that such juror characteristics are of prime importance in determining the outcome of a trial. A closer look at some of those studies reveals that the data do not support such a conclusion. It is as though a race car designer

---

[54]*Saks et al., supra* note 43.

[55]Boehm, *supra* note 44.

[56]This analysis is relevant to Etzioni's, *supra* note 5, argument that the impact of scientific jury selection could be reduced by increasing the range of citizens who serve: "If fewer persons were allowed to excuse themselves from jury duty ... the universe from which jurors are drawn would be more representative of the community and, to a degree, less easy to manipulate." To the contrary, increasing the range of jurors would *increase* the variability due to jurors and would therefore increase not only the worthwhileness but also the feasibility of manipulating the trial's outcome through selection procedures. You cannot manipulate what is not there; you can manipulate (by selection or deselection) what is.

discovered that tire profiles influenced a vehicle's speed and proceeded to conclude that since that was a real influence it must be the most important influence. As though engines no longer mattered. There is simply no empirical foundation for such statements as the following, offered by its authors as "a very obvious fact: the people who constitute the jury can have as much or more to do with the outcome of a trial as the evidence and arguments."[57] Indeed, the data consistently and directly contradict that conclusion. Evidence is the engine of a trial.

A balanced assessment of the effectiveness of scientific jury selection, based on what is generally known about human decisionmaking and on the data offered by the studies that have been done is, I believe, the following. It is safe to say that scientific jury selection "works;" juror characteristics do influence the decisions they make. But it is evidence that most determines the outcome of trials, rather than the characteristics of the jurors. If the evidence against a defendant is very strong or very weak, it isn't going to matter who is on the jury. If the evidence is close, then the jury selection could make the difference. One wouldn't be wasting money or time if he employed scientific jury selection, but if he did so at the expense of building a strong case out of evidence, he would be making a mistake. In cases where the evidence is close or ambiguous, scientific jury selection would be especially helpful.

No lawyer would be harming his client by taking advantage of scientific jury selection. But if he wanted to have an even greater influence over the outcome of the trial, he ought to hire social scientists to help build and structure the evidence to be presented. Curiously enough, if there is anything social psychologists know about it is the process of persuasion, which they have studied intensively for many years.[58] One has to wonder why no lawyers or social psychologists have thought to consult with each other on that, instead of playing around with the less important matter of jury selection.

---

[57]Kairys, at 1, *supra* note 10.
[58]See absolutely any general textbook on social psychology.

The Effect of Peremptory Challenges on Jury and Verdict: An Experiment in a Federal District Court[*]

Hans Zeisel[†]
Shari Seidman Diamond[‡]

Trial lawyers tell us that they occasionally win their cases at voir dire[1] by the shrewd use of their peremptory challenges.[2] This is the

---

* This experiment was conducted in the United States District Court for the Northern District of Illinois and was supported by Grant GS-33825 from the National Science Foundation. Additional funds were provided by the Nancy G. and Raymond G. Feldman Fund for studies in criminal justice.

† Dr. Jur., 1927, Dr. Pol. Sc., 1928, University of Vienna. Professor Emeritus of Law and Sociology, Research Associate, Center for Studies in Criminal Justice, University of Chicago; Senior Consultant, American Bar Foundation.

‡ B.A., 1968, University of Michigan; Ph.D., 1972, Northwestern University. Assistant Professor of Criminal Justice and Psychology, University of Illinois at Chicago.

1. *Voir dire* is sometimes translated from the French as "see [them] talk," but in fact means "true talk," the word *voir* being a corruption of the Latin *verus*, or "true". *See* WEBSTER'S THIRD NEW INT'L DICTIONARY 2562 (1961).

The earliest known procedure for challenging jurors was found in Roman law. The *Lex Sevilia* (104 B.C.) provided that the accuser and the accused in capital cases could each propose a list of 100 *judices* and that each could reject 50 from the other's list, leaving 100 to try the case. W. FORSYTH, HISTORY OF TRIAL BY JURY 175 (Cambridge 1852). In the year 7 B.C., the Roman emperor Augustus Caesar issued an edict governing the selection of jurors in capital cases in the city of Cyrene on the Lybian coast (the modern Shahhat). II ROMAN CIVILIZATION 37 (N. Lewis & M. Reinhold eds. 1963). The edict provided for the drawing of 50 prospective jurors, one-half of whom had to be Greek, the other half Roman. The edict added: "Of these the prosecutor may, if he wishes, dismiss one from each group, and the accused three out of the total, provided he does not dismiss either all Romans or all Greeks." *Id.*

The modern system of challenges for cause and peremptory challenges originated in the common law of England, which allowed peremptory challenges only in criminal trials for capital offenses; the defendant in such an action could exclude 35 jurors. W. FORSYTH, *supra* at 231. King Henry VIII later reduced this number to 20, where it remained until the mid-19th century. *Id.*

The challenge for cause, allowed by the common law in all cases, was more complex than the present-day system. In Lord Coke's time, the challenge for cause included both the challenge to the array, which led to the exclusion of the entire jury, and the challenge to the polls, which led to the exclusion of individual jurors. *Id.* at 177. Two classes of cause were recognized: The "principal" challenge was allowed as a matter of course upon a showing that

491

report of an experiment designed to discover whether they really do. Normally, this question cannot be answered with precision: Because the excused jurors do not attend the trial, there is no way of knowing how they would have voted had they not been removed. Our experiment attempted to secure this missing information by asking the peremptorily excused jurors to remain as shadow jurors in the courtroom and to reveal at the end of the trial how they would have voted in the case. This allowed us to become retrospectively clairvoyant—to see how well the prosecutor and defense counsel performed in their attempts to eliminate hostile jurors. More important, by combining this knowledge with posttrial interviews of the real jurors, we reconstructed the vote of the jury that would have decided the case had there been no peremptory challenges— that is, if the first 12 jurors in the venire, not excused for cause, had formed the jury. By comparing what the reconstructed "jury without peremptory challenges" would have done with what the real jury did, we were able to gauge the effect, if any, of the peremptory challenges on the composition of the jury and its verdict.

Part I of the Article describes and analyzes the experiment. In Part II, we consider the experiment's significance in the larger framework of the theory and practice of jury selection.

I. THE EXPERIMENT

A. *The Sample of Cases*

The experiment was conducted in 12 criminal trials before three judges of the United States District Court for the Northern District of Illinois.[3] Financial considerations limited the number and size of the cases, and we selected only trials that were expected to last no longer than 2 weeks.[4] Within these bounds, the willingness of the

---

the sheriff, who chose the jury, was related to one of the parties by blood or affinity. A second objection, the challenge "to the favour," was grounded on an allegation of bias and was decided by two court-appointed officers, called "triors." *Id.* at 178-79. By the mid-19th century in England, almost all challenges for cause were decided by the triors. *Id.* at 180.

2. *See, e.g.*, H. BODIN, SELECTING A JURY 8 (1966); I. GOLDSTEIN, TRIAL TECHNIQUE 152 (1935); H. ROTHBLATT, SUCCESSFUL TECHNIQUES IN THE TRIAL OF CRIMINAL CASES (1951); R. TURNEY, COURTROOM PSYCHOLOGY 37 (1924). *See generally* A. AMSTERDAM, B. SEGAL & M. MILLER, TRIAL MANUAL FOR THE DEFENSE OF CRIMINAL CASES § 326 (3d ed. 1974).

3. We would like to thank Judges Hubert L. Will, Philip W. Tone and Frank J. McGarr, and their clerks and marshals, as well as the Clerk of the Court, Stuart Cunningham, and his staff for their assistance and cooperation in this experiment. We also would like to thank Judge Edwin A. Robson, the then-presiding Justice of the Court, for originally authorizing this experiment.

4. Actually, two of the cases in our study lasted somewhat longer than 2 weeks.

judge, prosecutor and defense attorney to cooperate in the experiment dictated the actual selection of cases. We initially planned to look at both criminal and civil cases, but while the parties to the criminal trials generally gave their consent to the experiment,[5] we managed to obtain consent in only three civil cases, too small a sample to integrate into our experimental design. In retrospect, the overwhelming refusal rate in civil cases was a blessing, for it gave us a more homogeneous sample of exclusively criminal cases.

Because of these constraints on their selection, the 12 cases that formed the basis of our study are not a probability sample of anything: They are 12 modestly sized criminal jury cases. Therefore, our experiment should be regarded as only the first step toward an understanding of the effect of peremptory challenges on jury verdicts.

The 12 cases included in our experiment spread across the broad range of modern federal criminal litigation. A brief synopsis of each case follows:

Case 1. The defendant was charged with draft evasion. The judge, persuaded by a lost-mail defense, dropped an added count involving failure to respond to induction notices.

Case 2. The defendant, an accountant accused of doctoring his firm's books, had in his possession $300,000 that supposedly had been removed from the firm for the refund of a downpayment made by another party for purchase of the firm. The formal counts of the indictment were conspiracy and concealing and controlling transferred property in a bankruptcy case. The defense submitted three documents as its case; it called no witnesses.

Case 3. Two defendants were accused of extortion and conspiracy to commit extortion. The prosecution witnesses were the defendant's co-conspirators and the alleged victim. The purported victim, whose business was taking money from individuals in return for fraudulent promises to secure loans for them, was himself under indictment at the time of trial and subsequently was convicted.

Case 4. The defendant, a young man with no previous record, was accused of knowingly purchasing a stolen television set at a bar where he worked. An FBI agent testified that the defendant admit-

---

5. Then-United States Attorney James Thompson, now Governor of Illinois, gave general consent to the experiment. As a rule, the defense lawyers gave theirs. In three of the criminal cases we had wanted to examine, however, we could not obtain consent from both sides. Two of these cases involved extortion charges against policemen, and the prosecutors refused to participate in our experiment despite the prior general consent of the United States Attorney. In the other case, the defense was unwilling to cooperate.

ted knowing that the set was stolen; the defense presented no evidence.

Case 5. The defendant was accused of conspiracy, possession and possession with intent to distribute drugs. The conspiracy charge involved several drugs, including cocaine; the other two counts involved hashish only. The jury did not learn that the alleged ringleader, with whom the defendant lived, already had pleaded guilty. The undercover agent who tried to buy the drugs presented the main testimony; while on the stand, the defendant virtually admitted his involvement in the conspiracy.

Case 6. The defendant was a security guard accused of participating in a scheme to defraud a mail-order house. A roommate and a neighbor of the defendant testified that the defendant received some of the merchandise; a friend of the defendant, however, pleaded guilty and testified that the defendant knew nothing of the fraudulent shipments.

Case 7. The defendant was charged with filing loan applications that contained false information and with selling fake installment contracts to banks. The defense was minimal, and the defendant did not testify.

Case 8. The defendant, a paraplegic, was accused of possession of one stolen automobile and sale of another. He previously had served a prison sentence on a similar charge. The prosecutor produced as witnesses the automobile owners, the person who gave the defendant the automobile referred to in the first indictment, the person who purchased the second automobile, and a person who said he helped to drive the automobiles from where they were stolen. The defendant and his wife, sister and nephew took the stand for the defense.

Case 9. The defendant was accused of possessing seven state checks he knew were stolen and of knowingly passing a forged Treasury check. The defendant purported to make a living by cashing checks for others for a fee, and he claimed that because he had dealt for several years with the people who had given him the checks, he had no reason to believe that the checks were bad.

Case 10. The defendants, a husband and wife accused of several counts of preparation of false income tax forms, allegedly filled out fraudulent forms for people in the community for a $10 fee. Only one of the taxpayers spoke English, and an interpreter was present during the trial. The prosecution's case rested on the testimony of these witnesses and on the obvious uniformity of the deductions claimed on the forms.

Case 11. The defendant was a postal employee charged with detaining or delaying the mail. He allegedly placed one sack of mail inside another and put them in an unusual place. The sack was a "test" bag with a lock, which indicated that it contained money. Postal inspectors watched the defendant from a roof, but did not wait for him to retrieve the sack. Because it was not retrieved, there was no direct evidence of personal gain. The testimony of the inspectors formed the government's case.

Case 12. The defendant was a politician accused of 12 counts of extortion and five counts of income tax evasion. The prosecutor alleged that the defendant took money in return for favors from his office. The two principal prosecution witnesses—the people who claimed they paid the defendant—were given immunity in exchange for their testimony.

B. *Experimental Design*

1. *Voir dire procedure.*

The voir dire procedure in these 12 cases reflected modern federal criminal practice.[6] In each of the cases, the voir dire was conducted in three phases. In the first phase, the judge informed the entire jury panel of the nature of the case and introduced the

---

6. For a general discussion of the practice of voir dire in federal cases, see E. DEVITT & C. BLACKMAR, FEDERAL JURY PRACTICE AND INSTRUCTIONS: CIVIL AND CRIMINAL §§ 3.01-.04 (3d ed. 1977). The manner in which the voir dire is conducted in federal criminal trials is within the trial judge's discretion; the examination of potential jurors may be conducted either by the judge or, with the judge's permission, by the attorneys. FED. R. CRIM. P. 24(a). In practice, most federal judges examine the venire themselves, but allow counsel to submit supplementary questions. C. WRIGHT, FEDERAL PRACTICE AND PROCEDURE: CRIMINAL § 381 (1969). The Judicial Conference Committee has recommended that voir dire questioning be conducted exclusively by the trial judge, on the ground that this procedure will save time and improve the character of the examination. *The Jury System in the Federal Courts*, 26 F.R.D. 409, 424 (1960) (report of the Judicial Conference Committee on the Operation of the Jury System).

Although considerable deference is given to the trial judge's determination of the proper manner of conducting voir dire, an abuse of discretion, such as undue restriction of the scope of voir dire or the inclusion of prejudicial questions, may constitute reversible error. *See, e.g.*, Witherspoon v. Illinois, 391 U.S. 510 (1968); Socony Mobil Oil Co. v. Taylor, 388 F.2d 586 (5th Cir. 1968); Cook v. United States, 379 F.2d 966 (5th Cir. 1967); Progner v. Eagle, 377 F.2d 461 (4th Cir. 1967). *See generally* Babcock, *Voir Dire: Preserving "Its Wonderful Power"*, 27 STAN. L. REV. 545 (1975).

An attorney has available several methods of challenging jurors. The entire array may be challenged because of the manner in which the venire was drawn, summoned, selected, or impaneled. E. DEVITT & C. BLACKMAR, *supra* § 3.02. An individual juror may be challenged "for cause" and will be dismissed if the challenging party can show evidence of bias or incompetence. *See* text accompanying note 7 *infra.*

Peremptory challenges, unlike those for cause, may be made for any reason, or for no reason. Swain v. Alabama, 380 U.S. 202, 220 (1965). The Supreme Court has stated that such challenges are a "necessary part of trial by jury," *id.* at 219, and "one of the most important of the rights secured to the accused," Pointer v. United States, 151 U.S. 396, 408 (1894).

The mechanics of voir dire vary between districts. In some, the jurors are challenged directly by counsel; in others, jurors' names are stricken from a list. Many districts use the method employed by the courts of the state in which the district is located. *See* E. DEVITT & C. BLACKMAR, *supra* § 3.03.

attorneys. The judge then asked the prospective jurors several questions designed to elicit their reactions to the alleged offense in the case. In 4 of the 12 cases, certain jurors' answers to these questions resulted in their being excused for cause from the entire venire.[7]

In the second phase, 12 individuals from the venire were placed in the jury box, and the judge asked them in turn to state their names, addresses, occupations, and the occupations of persons living with them. In most of the cases, the judge also asked the prospective jurors to state their length of residence at their present address, their employment for the previous 5 years, the ages of their children, and all instances of prior jury service. In addition, several judges inquired whether the prospective jurors had a close friend or relative who either was involved in law enforcement or had been the victim of a crime. The judge also posed several questions designed to disclose any close associations between the potential jurors and key elements of the case. For example, the judge in Case 5 attempted to discover whether any of the jurors' friends or relatives ever had used illicit drugs. If a juror had some association with the case, the judge asked whether that association would preclude the juror from making a fair and impartial evaluation of the evidence and merits of the case. Any juror who responded in the affirmative was excused, sent back to the jury room and replaced by a new juror, who was then subjected to the second-phase questioning. All jurors who responded that they had no association with the case, or an association that would not preclude them from fairly and impartially evaluating the case, proceeded to the third phase of voir dire.

In phase three, the prosecutor and defense counsel exercised peremptory challenges.[8] First, the prosecution exercised as many of

---

7. A total of 36 jurors were excused for cause in this phase of the voir dire. Fourteen jurors were excused after the second phase, during which they were questioned individually while seated in the jury box.

8. Rule 24(b) of the Federal Rules of Criminal Procedure governs the number of peremptory challenges in federal criminal cases: "If the offense charged is punishable by death, each side is entitled to 20 peremptory challenges. If the offense charged is punishable by imprisonment for more than one year, the government is entitled to 6 peremptory challenges and the defendant or defendants jointly to 10 peremptory challenges. If the offense charged is punishable by imprisonment for not more than one year or by fine or both, each side is entitled to 3 peremptory challenges. If there is more than one defendant, the court may allow the defendants additional peremptory challenges and permit them to be exercised separately or jointly." FED. R. CRIM. P. 24(b).

State laws vary widely concerning the number of peremptory challenges allowed to either side. Generally, both sides have the same number of challenges, but 20 states allow more challenges to the defense under certain circumstances: Delaware, Maine, New Hampshire, New Jersey (capital trials only); Michigan (when the sentence may be either death or life

its allocated number of peremptory challenges as it desired; the defense was then given the same opportunity. The judge replaced the excused jurors, and the process was repeated with respect to the

imprisonment); Alaska, Arkansas, Kentucky, Maryland, Missouri, Nebraska, South Carolina, Tennessee (all but misdemeanor trials); Alabama, Georgia, Minnesota, New Mexico, North Carolina, Oregon, West Virginia (all trials). The following synopsis summarizes the pattern of allocations of peremptory challenges for 12-member juries in the state courts:

	Capital		Other Felonies		Misdemeanors	
	State	Defendant	State	Defendant	State	Defendant
Highest	26 (Cal.)	26 (Cal.)	15 (N.Y.)	15 (N.Y.)	13 (Cal.)	13 (Cal.)
Mode	10 (11 states)	12 (11 states)	6 (14 states)	6 (12 states)	3 (18 states)	3 (15 states)
Lowest	4 (Va.)	4 (Mont., Va.)	2 (W. Va.)	3 (Hawaii, N.H.)	2 (Ariz., Iowa)	2 (Ariz., Iowa)

Source: J. Van Dyke, Jury Selection Procedures 282-83 (1977).

In April 1976, the Supreme Court proposed a number of amendments to the Federal Rules of Criminal Procedure, which, among other things, would have reduced the number of peremptory challenges available to both sides in all criminal cases and would have equalized the number of peremptory challenges available to the prosecution and defense in noncapital felony cases. 44 U.S.L.W. 4549 (1976). The amendments were scheduled to take effect on August 1, 1976, but Congress delayed the effective date until August 1, 1977. Pub. L. No. 94-349, § 1, 90 Stat. 822 (1976). On July 30, 1977, Congress passed legislation adopting many of the proposed amendments, but specifically rejected the amendment relating to peremptory challenges. Pub. L. No. 95-78, § 2(c), 91 Stat. 319 (1977).

Three arguments were made in favor of the peremptory challenge proposal put forth by the Supreme Court. First, the enactment of the Jury Selection and Service Act of 1968 has led to more representative panels, which have reduced the number of challenges exercised during voir dire and have eliminated the need for the defense to have more challenges than the prosecution. Second, the proposal would make it more difficult for either side systematically to exclude a class of persons from the jury. Third, the proposal would save time and juror costs. S. Rep. No. 354, 95th Cong., 1st Sess 9, *reprinted in* [1977] U.S. Code Conc. & Ad. News 1477, 1482-83.

The congressional rejection was accompanied by a recommendation that the suggestions be studied further by the Judicial Conference of the United States, the body that, pursuant to 28 U.S.C. § 331 (1970), considers proposed rule changes and forwards them to the Supreme Court. S. Rep. No. 354, 95th Cong., 1st Sess. 9, *reprinted in* [1977] U.S. Code Cong. & Ad. News at 1483. The Senate Judiciary Committee noted that the amendments relating to peremptory challenges had stirred more controversy than any of the other proposed rule changes. *Id.*, [1977] U.S. Code Cong. & Ad. News at 1482. The Committee stated that most of the opposition arose from a fear that the proposal was ill-conceived in view of the widespread practice of allowing judges, not counsel, to conduct voir dire: "Witnesses indicated that [not permitting attorneys to question venire members] makes it difficult for counsel to identify biased jurors and develop grounds to challenge for cause." *Id.*, [1977] U.S. Code Cong. & Ad. News at 1483. The Committee concluded that "the Judicial Conference should have the benefit of the comments that have been made on this rule since it was submitted to Congress in deciding whether to make such a change in the future." *Id.*

newly impaneled venire members. Any prospective juror accepted without challenge by both attorneys became a member of the jury and was no longer subject to challenge. The jury finally was filled when the 12th member of the venire successfully completed phase three without being excused.

The experiment introduced one modification into the voir dire procedure in order to avoid the possibility that a peremptorily challenged juror would resent—and therefore vote against—the side that exercised the challenge. In ordinary practice, an attorney wishing to exercise a challenge announces the juror's name in open court. In the experiment, the attorneys simultaneously submitted special challenge sheets to the judge. After reviewing both sheets, the judge announced the names of the challenged jurors without revealing the source of dismissal.

2. *Formation of the experimental juries.*

After the real jury was impaneled and sent to the jury room, the court asked the peremptorily excused jurors and the remaining venire members to participate in the study. The judge emphasized the importance of the study and explained to the jurors that they would be paid for their participation as part of their regular jury service. Almost 90% of those invited agreed to serve in our experiment.

In each case, the judge asked the peremptorily challenged jurors to form a shadow jury and seated them in the first row of spectator seats. The size of these shadow juries varied from case to case depending on the number of peremptorily excused jurors and their willingness to cooperate with the experiment. Although our study required only the pre-deliberation votes of the peremptorily excused jurors, we formed them into "juries" to ensure that they would take their task seriously.[9]

The court then formed a second shadow jury by random selection from the remainder of the venire. This jury was seated without the benefit of voir dire—that is, without questioning and challenges—and therefore was dubbed the "English jury," because challenges, although permitted in England, are almost never exer-

---

9. *See* note 13 *infra* and accompanying text.

cised.[10] Only four of the "English juries" had a full complement of
12 members. One jury (Case 11) required only 6 members to match
the real jury;[11] in another case (Case 12), we were unable to recruit a
jury at all; the remaining six juries varied in size between 7 and 10
members.

Thus, each case actually was tried to three "juries": the real jury,
another composed of peremptorily challenged jurors, and still a
third containing jurors randomly selected from the remainder of
the venire. Table 1 presents the number of persons in each of these
juries for our sample of 12 cases.

TABLE 1

Number of Persons in Each Experimental Jury

Case No.	Real Jury	Peremptorily Excused Jury	"English Jury"
1	12	12	12
2	12	5	12
3	12	9	10
4	12	4	10
5	12	6	7
6	12	7	9
7	12	4	12
8	12	9	9
9	12	8	12
10	12	8	10
11	6	5	6
12	12	8	–
Total	138	85	109

Throughout the trial and even during meal times and recesses,
all three juries were treated as much alike as possible. Both shadow

---

10. "The English tradition is that advocacy should be quite impersonal: . . . [counsel]
should address the jury as an impersonal body of twelve and the less they know about them as
men and women the better." P. DEVLIN, TRIAL BY JURY 34 (1956). But Devlin himself recalls a
trial in which after the verdict was rendered, it was discovered that two of the jurors could not
speak English. *Id.* at 35.   I (H.Z.) once asked the late Chief Justice, Lord Parker of Wadding-
ton, "What if one of the jurors were a cousin of the defendant?" With just the hint of a smile,
he answered, "Wouldn't that be awkward?"

11. Case 11 was tried to a jury of 6, pursuant to FED. R. CRIM. P. 23(b), under which a
case may be tried by a jury of less than 12 upon written stipulation of the parties and approval
of the court.

juries were seated in the front row of the spectator section. When the real jury was removed from the courtroom to keep it from hearing certain testimony, the experimental juries were removed, too; when exhibits were passed out to the real jurors during the trial, the experimental jurors saw them at the first recess. At the end of the trial, the three juries retired to their separate jury rooms to deliberate and reach a verdict. And if the real jury took documents into its deliberation room, the shadow juries received copies, even in the case in which there were some 200 pages of bookkeeping forms.

Before the two shadow juries began their deliberations, we passed each juror a secret predeliberation ballot.[12] During the deliberations, which were tape-recorded, the shadow juries were treated like the real jury. If one of the experimental juries asked a question during deliberations, the judge received it and responded as he would have to a real jury. In one case, this even involved calling a shadow jury back into the courtroom and reinstructing it.

As was to be expected, the shadow jurors took their task seriously. Earlier experiments have indicated that mock juries, even when confronting simulated, tape-recorded cases, become involved quickly and deeply in their tasks.[13] In our experiment, both the substance and length of the deliberations of the shadow juries supported the expectation of serious involvement. The average deliberation time for the real juries was 2 hours, 38 minutes; for the experimental juries, it was 2 hours, 12 minutes. Moreover, the recorded deliberations of the shadow juries revealed many heated arguments—expletives not deleted—and extensive discussions of the evidence and the questions raised during the trials.

3. Reconstructing the "juries without challenges."

Our experimental goal was to reconstruct the juries that would have decided each case had there been no peremptory challenges and to ascertain their verdicts had they been the actual juries. The first part of our task presented no difficulty. The transcribed minutes of the voir dire proceedings provided us with the order in

---

12. We also distributed a questionnaire to the presiding judge in each case, *see* note 3 *supra*, asking him how he would have decided the case had it been a bench trial. This enabled us to measure the extent of judge-jury disagreement on verdicts and its relationship to the exercise of peremptory challenges. For the results of this comparison, see text accompanying notes 27-33 *infra*.

13. *See* R. SIMON, THE JURY AND THE DEFENSE OF INSANITY 175-79 (1967). *See also* S. McCABE & R. PURVES, THE SHADOW JURY AT WORK 4-5 (1974).

which the prospective jurors in each case entered the jury box. To reconstruct the "juries without challenges,"[14] we merely had to read off the names of the first 12, and in one case 6,[15] jurors entering the jury box who were not excused for cause.[16] These groups represented the juries that would have rendered verdicts in the cases had no peremptory challenges been made. Table 2 shows the composition of each of our 12 reconstructed juries.

TABLE 2

Component Parts of the Reconstructed "Juries Without Challenges"

Case No.	Peremptorily Excused			Real Jurors	Total
	Vote Known	Vote Estimated*	Total		
1	5	0	5	7**	12
2	3	0	3	9	12
3	5	0	5	7**	12
4	3	0	3	9	12
5	6	1	7	5	12
6	3	3	6	6	12
7	4	0	4	8	12
8	5	0	5	7	12
9	4	1	5	7	12
10	4	1	5	7	12
11	4	1	5	1	6
12	4	2	6	6	12

*   *See* notes 17-20 *infra* and accompanying text.
**   First ballot estimated. *See* note 20 *infra.*

---

14. Throughout the remainder of this Article, we shall refer to the reconstructed jury as simply the "jury without challenges," even though it did not include any jurors who had been excused for cause, *see* note 16 *infra*, and is therefore technically the "jury without *peremptory* challenges." In contrast, what we have dubbed the "English jury" may have included a few jurors who would have been excused for cause had they undergone the individual questioning during voir dire. *See generally* text accompanying notes 34-35 *infra*.

15. *See* note 11 *supra*.

16. A judge may dismiss for cause any juror believed to be biased or unqualified and has broad discretion in ruling on challenges. Dennis v. United States, 339 U.S. 162, 168 (1950); United States v. Johnson, 401 F.2d 746, 747 (2d Cir. 1968); United States v. Palumbo, 401 F.2d 270, 275 (2d Cir.), *cert. denied*, 394 U.S. 947 (1968). Usually, federal judges liberally dismiss for cause prospective jurors against whom plausible grounds for objection can be stated. *See, e.g.*, United States v. Kline, 221 F. Supp. 776, 780 (D. Minn. 1963). Additionally, the judge may ask the jurors whether they will be influenced by possible prejudicial matters

Our second objective, to ascertain the reconstructed juries' verdicts, required an intermediate step. Because the members of the reconstructed juries never met together or deliberated as a body, their verdicts could not be established directly. To overcome this difficulty, we adopted a 2-step procedure. First, we estimated what the first ballot vote of the reconstructed "jury without challenges" would have been. Then, using an insight from an earlier study, we used this first ballot vote to predict the likely verdict.[17]

In order to ascertain the first ballot vote of each reconstructed jury, it was necessary to establish the first ballot votes of the members of the two groups constituting the reconstructed jury: (1) the peremptorily excused jurors, and (2) those members of the real jury who also would have been on the "jury without challenges." To determine the first ballot votes of the peremptorily excused jurors, we obtained their individual verdicts after they had observed the trial. The votes of the nine excused jurors who declined to participate in the experiment were estimated by assuming that the attorneys followed a consistent pattern in challenging prospective jurors.[18] Consequently, we assigned votes to these jurors in the same proportion as the first ballot votes of the other jurors excused by the same counsel in the same trial.[19]

---

and may give weight to their assurances that they will be fair in evaluating the evidence. *See, e.g.*, Murphy v. Florida, 421 U.S. 794, 800 (1975).

In our experiment, the number of dismissals for cause varied considerably from case to case. In 4 of the 12 trials, the challenges for cause were based upon questions addressed to the entire venire. In one case that involved local politics (Case 12), there were 17 such excuses; in a draft evasion case (Case 1), there were 8; in a drug case (Case 5), 6; and in a misdemeanor case involving the purchase of a stolen T.V. set (Case 4), there were 5. The remaining 8 cases averaged 1.75 challenges for cause: 9 in the case of theft from a mail-order house (Case 6), 3 in the case involving extortion and an alleged use of a gun (Case 3), 1 each in 2 others (Cases 10 and 11), and none in the remaining 4 cases. None of the jurors excused for cause was allowed to serve on either the "jury without challenges" or the "English jury."

17. *See* H. KALVEN & H. ZEISEL, THE AMERICAN JURY 487-91 (1966).

18. This assumption of consistency, though likely to be valid in most situations, does not take into account a factor that may be at work early in the peremptory challenge procedure: Attorneys may decide to accept a somewhat hostile juror rather than risk exhausting all their challenges too quickly and later facing venire members who are even more hostile. This factor, however, should not have affected our assumption in this experiment, because in all the cases except one, the attorneys did not exhaust their allotted peremptory challenges. The one exception was a misdemeanor case (Case 4) in which each side was allotted 3 challenges; the defense used all 3.

19. In one case (Case 9), the only juror excused by the prosecutor declined to participate in the study. We therefore assumed a neutral performance by the prosecutor. *See* notes 45-49 *infra* and accompanying text. Because the prosecutor used only this one challenge, the attorney performance index score would be close to zero regardless of how that juror might have voted. *See id.*

An assumption was also needed to determine the first ballot vote of those real jurors who were part of the reconstructed jury. In 10 of the cases, we learned the overall first ballot votes of the full juries, but not the votes of individual jurors. Thus, although we knew which jurors would have been on the reconstructed jury, we could not learn how each voted on the first ballot. As a result, we had to assume that those real jurors who would have been on the "jury without challenges" voted in the same guilty/not guilty ratio as did the jury as a whole. For example, if there were 8 real jurors who would have been on the "jury without challenges" and the real jury split on the first ballot was 6 guilty and 6 not guilty votes, we assumed that the 8 jurors on our reconstructed jury divided their votes in the same ratio: 4 guilty and 4 not guilty.[20]

By combining these various approaches, we estimated the first ballot votes of all 12 reconstructed juries. As an example, Table 3 illustrates the computation of the first ballot vote of the reconstructed jury in Case 10.

---

20. This procedure assumes that the real jurors on the reconstructed juries were a random sample of the real jurors as a whole. *See* note 18 *supra* and accompanying text. In the remaining two cases (Cases 1 and 3), we were not allowed to learn even the constellation of the first ballot votes of the real juries. In order to estimate the votes of these members of the juries who would have been on the "juries without challenges," we relied on previous studies suggesting that, in an uncomplicated case, lengthy jury deliberations occur most often when a significant minority of jurors disagree with the majority vote on the first ballot. *See* H. KALVEN & H. ZEISEL, *supra* note 17, at 462 ("[J]uries which begin with an overwhelming majority in either direction are not likely to hang. It requires a massive minority of 4 or 5 jurors at the first vote to develop the likelihood of a hung jury."). In both of these cases, the juries deliberated for a considerable length of time before ultimately acquitting the defendant. Therefore, we assumed that a slight majority of the jurors initially believed the defendant innocent, *see* Table 3 and note 23 *infra*, and we assigned each jury a first ballot vote of 5 guilty and 7 not guilty.

We considered two other possible explanations for the lengthy deliberations. First, juries generally deliberate longer in cases involving numerous complex issues than in cases involving only a few simple issues. *See* H. KALVEN & H. ZEISEL, *supra* note 17, at 457. Because the issues in the cases used in the experiment were relatively uncomplicated, however, this first explanation was rejected. The second possible explanation is that in these cases a small minority of recalcitrant jurors prevented a unanimous verdict. There has been considerable research, however, indicating that participants in jury deliberations frequently are influenced to change their votes as a result of the knowledge that an overwhelming majority disagree with them. See the authorities collected in Note, *On Instructing Deadlocked Juries*, 78 YALE L. J. 100 (1968). Consequently, we concluded that the long deliberations indicated that the phenomenon of a few holdout jurors was not in effect here.

TABLE 3

Reconstructing the First Ballot Vote of the "Jury Without Challenges" in Case 10

	First Ballot Vote	
	Guilty	Not Guilty
Seven members of the real jury would have been on the "jury without challenges." The first ballot of the real jury was 11 to 1 (92% to 8%) for conviction. This ratio, applied to the 7 real jurors, yields a vote of	6.40	.60
Four excused jurors whose votes we knew from the experiment	2.00	2.00
One excused juror declined to participate in the experiment. He was dismissed by the prosecutor, who challenged four other jurors. Because their votes were 1 guilty, 3 not guilty, the fifth juror's vote was estimated at	.25	.75
Total	8.65　+　3.35　=　12	
Percent	72%　+　28%　=　100%	

4. *Predicting the likely verdict.*

From the estimated first ballot vote of each reconstructed "jury without challenges," we predicted the likely trial verdict in each case. A study reported by Kalven and Zeisel in *The American Jury*[21] showed that 92% of all jury verdicts are decided by the first ballot vote.[22] Rarely does the minority position become the final verdict; moreover, the greater the degree of agreement on the first ballot, the higher the probability that the majority decision will prevail.[23]

---

21. H. KALVEN & H. ZEISEL, *supra* note 17.

22. *Id.* at 488. *See* notes 23-24 *infra*.

23. H. KALVEN & H. ZEISEL, *supra* note 17, at 489. Kalven and Zeisel conducted interviews with jurors in Chicago and Brooklyn who had participated in criminal trials. By ascertaining the jurors' first ballot votes, the authors were able to determine the relationship between first ballot votes and the jury verdicts in 225 cases. In 31% of the cases the first ballot was unanimous (12% not guilty, 19% guilty). *Id.* at 487. In the remaining cases, the first ballot foretold the final outcome with extreme accuracy. In 86% of the cases in which a majority of the jurors initially voted guilty, the trial resulted in conviction. Similarly, of those cases in which only a minority of the jurors favored conviction on the first ballot, 91% ended in acquittal. In the remaining 4% of the cases, in which the initial vote was split evenly, exactly one-half resulted in acquittal and one-half in conviction. *Id.* at 488. The authors concluded

By extrapolating from this insight into the relationship between the first ballot and verdict, we were able to estimate for each of our trials the probable verdict of the "jury without challenges."

Graph 1 is a freehand interpolation of the relationship found by Kalven and Zeisel between first ballot votes and the likelihood of a given verdict after deliberation.[24]

GRAPH 1

Generalized Relationship Between
First Ballot Vote and Final Verdict

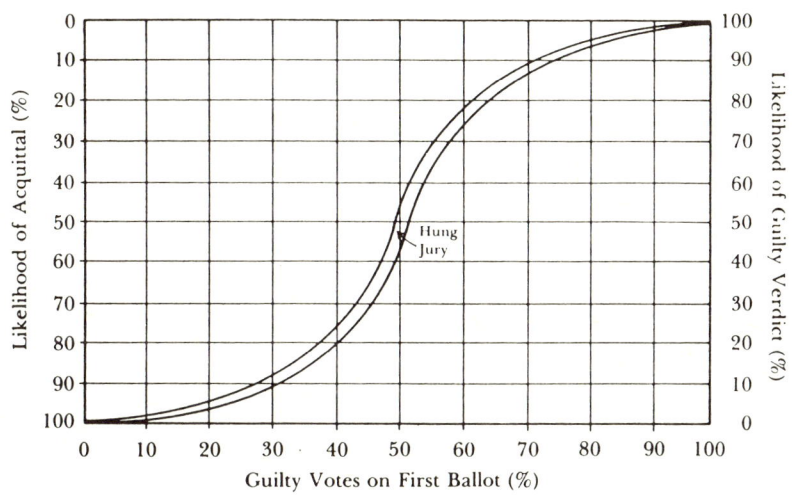

that, with few exceptions, jury verdicts are decided on the first ballot: "The upshot is a radical hunch about the function of the deliberation process. Perhaps it does not so much decide the case as bring about the consensus, the outcome of which has been made highly likely by the distribution of first ballot votes. The deliberation process might well be likened to what the developer does for an exposed film: it brings out the picture, but the outcome is predetermined." *Id.* at 489.

The importance of the first ballot in determining the eventual verdict has been confirmed repeatedly by other studies. *See, e.g.*, Davis, Kerr, Atkin, Holt, & Meek, *The Decision Processes of 6- and 12-Person Mock Juries Assigned Unanimous and Two-Thirds Majority Rules*, 32 J. PERSONALITY AND SOC. PSYCH. 1 (1975).

24. *See* note 23 *supra.* The curves in Graph 1 are based on the data in the following table

The percentage of guilty votes on the first ballot is plotted along the horizontal axis. For any given first ballot percentage, the height of the lower curve (indicated on the rightmost vertical axis) represents the probability that a guilty verdict will be returned; the distance above the upper curve (indicated on the leftmost vertical axis) denotes the likelihood of acquittal; the vertical distance between the two curves represents the probability of a hung jury. For any given first ballot vote, therefore, we can estimate the probabilities of each of the possible trial verdicts.

For example, the first ballot vote of the reconstructed jury in Case 10 was calculated to be 72% guilty, 28% not guilty. Finding the 72% figure on the baseline of Graph 1 and reading vertically, we estimate that the reconstructed jury had an 88% chance of convicting, a 9% chance of acquitting and a 3% chance of reaching no verdict. With these figures, we can compare the estimated verdict of the "jury without challenges" with the verdict of the real jury.

C. *Results of the Experiment*

1. *Impact of challenges on the verdict.*

Table 4 summarizes the results of our experiment. For each case, we have used the relationship pictured in Graph 1 to convert the first ballot votes of the reconstructed and real juries (columns 1 and 2) into the relative likelihood of guilty verdicts (columns 3 and 4). The actual verdict of the real jury is recorded in column 5. Column 6, computed by subtracting column 3 from column 4, represents the shift in the probability of a guilty verdict as a result of the peremptory challenges. A negative score indicates a decrease in the likelihood of a guilty verdict, a positive score indicates an increase, and a score of zero shows that the peremptory challenges did not affect the probability of a guilty verdict.

from H. KALVEN & H. ZEISEL, *supra* note 17, at 488:

First Ballot and Final Verdict in 225 Criminal Jury Trials

Final Verdict	Number of Guilty Votes on First Ballot					Percent of Cases
	0	1-5	6	7-11	12	
Not Guilty	100	91	50	5	-	32.8
Hung Jury	-	7	-	9	-	5.5
Guilty	-	2	50	86	100	61.7
Percent of Cases	12%	18%	4%	47%	19%	100%

TABLE 4

Comparison of the Reconstructed "Juries Without Challenges" and the Real Juries After Challenges

Case No.	Percentage Guilty Votes On First Ballot		Corresponding Percentage Probability That the Verdict Will Be Guilty*		(5)	(4)−(3) Percentage Shift in Probability of Guilty Verdict as a Result of Challenges
	(1) "Jury Without Challenges"	(2) Real Jury	(3) "Jury Without Challenges"	(4) Real Jury	Actual Verdict	
1**	49	42	41	23	NG	− 18
2	88	83	96	94	G	− 2
3***	41	42	22	23	NG	+ 1
4	50	33	42	11	NG	−30
5	77	83	91	94	G	+ 3
6	53	50	55	42	NG	− 13
7	72	83	89	94	G	+ 5
8	100	100	100	100	G	0
9	50	50	42	42	Hung	0
10	72	92	89	97	G	+ 8
11	38	17	17	2	NG	− 15
12	67	33	84	12	NG	−72

*   Percentages are interpolated from Graph 1. *See* note 23 *supra* and accompanying text.
** Assuming an initial vote of 5 to 7. *See* note 20 *supra*. If an initial vote of 6 to 6 is assumed, (1) becomes 54% and (2) becomes 50%; if 4 to 8 is assumed, (1) becomes 44% and (2) becomes 33%.
*** Assuming an initial vote of 5 to 7. If an initial vote of 6 to 6 is assumed, (1) becomes 46% and (2) becomes 50%; if an initial vote of 4 to 8 is assumed, (1) becomes 36% and (2) becomes 33%.

These data provide a preliminary answer to our question of whether peremptory challenges affect jury verdicts. In 7 of the 12 cases, the combined effect of the challenges was minimal and did not produce the expectation that the verdict of the "jury without challenges" would have differed from that of the real jury. In the remaining cases, the probability of a guilty verdict shifted at least 13 points.[25] The most striking shift in probability occurred in Case 12.

25. In Cases 1, 4, 6, 11, and 12, the shifts were -18, -30, -13, -15, and -72, respectively.

The real jury in that case voted for acquittal, while the reconstructed jury almost certainly would have convicted the defendant.[26]

Peremptory challenges changed the expected verdict in Case 6 as well. Although a conviction was the probable verdict of the "jury without challenges," the likely—and obtained—verdict of the real jury was acquittal.

The three other large shifts in probability occurred in Cases 1, 4 and 11. In Case 11, the shift in guilty votes was from 17% to 2%, beginning and ending with the strong expectation of an acquittal. In Cases 1 and 4, the effect of the challenges was to shift the probability of conviction from a value close to the 50% mark, where the expected verdict changes, to a probability substantially below that mark. The probability shifts described here suggest that peremptory challenges had a substantial role in altering the likelihood of guilty verdicts.

2. *Judge-jury disagreement.*

The trial judges' reactions to the verdicts in our sample cases show an intriguing correlation with the findings reported in the previous section. We asked each judge to tell us how he would have decided the case had it been a bench trial. If a judge disagreed with the jury's verdict, he also was asked to disclose the extent of his disagreement by characterizing the jury verdict in one of three ways: (1) a verdict a judge might also reach; (2) a verdict tenable for a jury, though not for a judge; or (3) a verdict without merit.[27] Table 5 presents the results.

---

26. Based on the first ballot votes, the "jury without challenges" had an 84% probability of convicting the defendant. In other words, if the same defendant were tried 100 different times and each time the jury's first ballot votes were the same as those of the reconstructed jury in this case, the defendant would be convicted 84 times. In contrast, the first ballot votes of the real jury indicate that they would have convicted the defendant only 12 times out of 100.

27. Our approach was modeled on a technique developed in *The American Jury. See* H. KALVEN & H. ZEISEL, *supra* note 17, at 428-33. *The American Jury* found that judges agreed with the jury's verdict in over two-thirds of the cases, *id.* at 429 (Table 112), but that when the judges disagreed with the jury's verdict on the issue of guilt, they considered one-third of these jury verdicts "without merit," *id.* at 430 (Table 113). The "without merit" criticism captured such harsh views as "This was an outrageous verdict," or "I felt the result of this case was a clear miscarriage of justice." *Id.* at 428-29.

TABLE 5
The Effect of the Challenges, the Verdicts
and the Judges' Reactions

Case No.	Shift in Probability of a Guilty Verdict Caused by the Challenges (percentage points)*	Verdict of the Real Jury	"Verdict" of the Trial Judge	The Trial Judge's Evaluation of the Verdict of the Real Jury
1	−18	NG	G	"without merit"
2	− 2	G	G	—
3	+ 1	NG	NG	—
4	−30	NG	G	"without merit"
5	+ 3	G	G	—
6	−13	NG	G	"tenable, for a jury"
7	+ 5	G	G	—
8	0	G	G	—
9	0	Hung	NG	(No Comment)
10	+ 8	G	G	—
11	−15	NG	G	"tenable, for a jury"
12	−72	NG	G	"without merit"

* From Table 4, column 6.

Table 5 shows that the judges approved of all 5 convictions but disagreed with 5 of the 6 jury acquittals.[28] In 2 of these cases (Cases 6 and 11), the judges regarded the verdict as "tenable for a jury"; in the other 3 (Cases 1, 4 and 12), the judges considered the verdict to be "without merit." Interestingly, these 5 cases had the greatest shifts in the probability of a guilty verdict as a result of the peremptory challenges. Furthermore, the 3 cases in which the judges felt the jury verdicts were "without merit" were the 3 with the greatest effects caused by peremptory challenges—Case 1 (−18), Case 4 (−30), and Case 12 (−72).

This correlation between the effect of peremptory challenges and the degree of judge-jury disagreement in our sample does not permit us to conclude that peremptory challenges alone caused the severe judge-jury disagreements. In Case 12, the use of peremptory challenges changed the expected verdict from a conviction that the judge would have agreed with to an acquittal he characterized as "without merit," but in Cases 1 and 4, the most likely verdict of the reconstructed juries would have been an acquittal anyway. Thus, the peremptory challenges cannot totally explain why the verdicts reached in these 2 cases were characterized as "without merit" by the presiding judges.

---

28. The judge in Case 9, in which the jury hung, had no comment on the jury's verdict.

A closer look at these 2 cases, however, reveals that both fall into categories that previous research has found foster jury acquittals when the judge would have convicted. The defendant in Case 1 was charged with draft evasion—the type of case in which jurors may have some sympathy with the crime committed.[29] Case 4 was a misdemeanor trial for possession of a stolen television set valued at $50—the type of offense clearly bearing the de minimis stamp that often moves jurors to acquit.[30]

Nevertheless, it is interesting that the judge, when pinning the "without merit" label on the verdicts in Cases 1, 4 and 12, could not have known that these 3 acquittals were brought in by juries whose propensity to acquit was increased by the use of peremptory challenges. Only the "retrospective clairvoyance" we gained through the experiment allowed us to make this connection.[31]

Thus, our experiment suggests that judge-jury disagreements on verdicts must be explained by a combination of factors: the characteristics of the case and the effect of the peremptory challenges. As a result, our theory of why judge-jury disagreements occur must be amended. *The American Jury* found that two influences primarily accounted for these disagreements. Every so often, when the evidence is close to the borderline of reasonable doubt— and even at times when it is clearly beyond the borderline—the jury that does not like the "letter of the law" may be guided by sentiments aimed at dispensing justice in the particular case.[32] In addition, the jurors occasionally set for themselves a lower threshold than would the judge for the level of "reasonable doubt" that warrants acquittal.[33] Both of these factors find their expression in the jury's crucial first ballot vote. Our results indicate that we now must add to these two reasons a third one: an occasional drastic shift in the first ballot constellation caused by the effective exercise of peremptory challenges.

---

29. Previous studies have shown that in such circumstances the jury's antipathy to prosecution of that offense often leads it to a verdict of not guilty even though the judge would have convicted. *See* H. KALVEN & H. ZEISEL, *supra* note 17, at 286-305.

30. *Id.* at 258-85.

31. The coincidence in these three cases of the judge's disapproval and the effectiveness of the peremptory challenges has elements of "triangulation"—an evidentiary convergence that increases confidence in a result. *See* Campbell & Fiske, *Convergent and Discriminant Validation by the Multitrait-Multimethod Matrix,* 56 PSYCHOLOGICAL BULL. 81 (1959). *See generally* Feigl, *Existential Hypothesis: Realistic Versus Phenomenalistic Interpretations,* 17 PHILOSOPHY SCI. 35 (1950).

32. H. KALVEN & H. ZEISEL, *supra* note 17, at 286-97.

33. *Id.* at 182-90.

D.   *The "English Jury" and Experimental Bias*

As mentioned previously,[34] the experimental design included a second shadow jury for each of the trials. Dubbed the "English jury," it was composed of members of the venire of prospective jurors who had watched the voir dire but had not undergone individual questioning. At first glance, the English jury would appear to be another standard against which we could compare the performance of the real jury. As it turned out, the English jurors were significantly more conviction-prone than the other members of the venire who went through the voir dire process and whose first ballot we learned or could estimate.[35] The English jurors would have convicted the defendant in every case, even in the two cases in which the judge would have acquitted.

Table 6 shows that the cumulative first ballot vote of the English jurors differed significantly from that of the other group of jurors that had been randomly selected from the venire—the combined pool of the real jury plus the peremptorily excused jurors who had undergone voir dire.

TABLE 6

Experimental Bias of the "English Jury"

	"English Jurors"	Real and Peremptorily Excused Jurors Combined
First Ballot Vote	%	%
Guilty	80	64
Not Guilty	20	36
Total	100%	100%
Number of Jurors	(109)	(223)

Because the likelihood that a difference as large as this would occur by chance is less than 1 in 100,[36] we concluded that the English

---

34. *See* note 10 *supra* and accompanying text.

35. Even without this increased rate of conviction, the sampling error in such a small group would be too great to allow for a stable benchmark.

36. The Chi-Square statistic for these data is 8.35, indicating a probability of less than .01. Although the English jury did not contain anyone who had been excused for cause, it conceivably could contain some jurors who, had they undergone the voir dire questioning, *would* have been excused for cause. *See* note 14 *supra*. Even when conservative adjustments are made for this possibility, however, the difference presented in Table 6 remains significant.

juries set a different threshold of reasonable doubt—a standard on which jurors are instructed to base their verdicts and which, in the end, jurors must define for themselves. The authors of *The American Jury* found that one of the mechanisms that occasionally contribute to the divergence between the jury's verdict and what the judge would have done[37] is a difference in the respective thresholds of reasonable doubt: Occasionally, the jury sets the demarcation at a lower level and acquits a defendant when the judge would have convicted.[38] It seems that the English jurors in our experiment had a higher reasonable doubt threshold than either the judge or the actual jury.

Although both the English jurors and those in the real jury were selected from the same venire, the English jurors differed in two important respects: None of the English jurors underwent the full voir dire questioning and none of them engaged in the jury deliberations that actually would lead to conviction or acquittal of the defendant. Either or both of these factors may have explained why the threshold of reasonable doubt was set so high by the English jurors. The personal questioning that occurs during the voir dire and the willingness of the attorneys and judge to retain a juror may leave an impact on the sitting jurors that was not experienced by the English jurors. This voir dire process may impress upon the jurors the importance of their task and may enhance their awareness of their duty to decide the case fairly and impartially.[39] Alternatively, simply because the English jurors in our experiment were aware that the defendant's liberty was not in their hands, they may have raised their threshold of reasonable doubt—that is, they may have increased the amount of doubt needed to justify acquittal.

Because we do not know which of these factors may have accounted for the bias of the English jury, we must confront another, more serious question: If the English jury was more prone to convict simply because its verdict would not affect the actual trial participants, might not this same bias also have affected the peremptorily excused jurors who sat as shadow jurors in our experiment? Although the excused jurors were individually questioned, they too

---

37. For a more complete discussion of judge-jury disagreements, see text accompanying notes 27-33 *supra*.

38. H. KALVEN & H. ZEISEL, *supra* note 17, at 182.

39. There is some evidence to support this contention from experiments with simulated juries. *See, e.g.*, Singer, Singer & Singer, *Voir Dire by Two Lawyers: An Essential Safeguard*, 57 JUDICATURE 386, 391 (1974).

were aware that their verdict would not determine the outcome of the trial.

A number of considerations suggest that the excused jurors were not so tainted. The best evidence in support of this position is provided by Table 7, which shows the breakdown of the first ballot votes of the real and the peremptorily excused jurors.

TABLE 7

Average First Ballot Vote of Real and Excused Jurors

	Real Jurors	Excused Jurors	Total
	%	%	
Guilty	61	66	63
Not Guilty	39	34	37
Total	100%	100%	100%
Number of Jurors	(138)	(85)	(223)

The excused jurors produced essentially the same proportion of guilty votes (66%) as the real jurors (61%).[40] By itself, this result is not proof of lack of bias, because the two groups of jurors are not strictly comparable. But it is this very absence of comparability that strengthens the final conclusion. The method of selecting the excused jurors, if anything, should have increased the proportion of guilty votes: The defense excused nearly twice as many jurors (54) as the prosecution (31), and, as we shall show in the next section,[41] the defense on the whole did a better job of finding its target—the jurors who would vote guilty—than did the prosecution. In spite of this twofold expectation of a larger proportion of guilty votes among the excused jurors, Table 7 demonstrates that they differed only slightly from the real jurors in their propensity to convict. We therefore conclude that the excused jurors do not share the higher conviction-proneness of the English jury.

E. *The Attorneys' Ability to Detect Hostile Jurors*

Our data gave us some idea of how well the attorneys used their allotted challenges to excuse jurors who, had they been allowed to sit

40. The Chi-Square value is .57, indicating a chance distribution.
41. *See* Table 9 and text accompanying notes 42-49 *infra*.

on the jury, would have voted against their side. We designed a rough performance index that evaluated the extent to which counsel employed peremptory challenges to dismiss hostile or friendly jurors.[42] Table 8 illustrates the calculation of the index for the prosecutor's performance in Case 10.

TABLE 8

Evaluation of Prosecutor's Use of Peremptory Challenges in Case 10

	First Ballot Vote		Total Number of Jurors (c)	Percent Guilty Votes On First Ballot (a/c)	Prosecutor's Performance Score
	Jurors Voting Guilty (a)	Jurors Voting Not Guilty (b)			
Venire prior to any challenges	22.2	5.8	28*	79%	
Prosecutor's (hypothetical) *optimal* challenge performance	−0.2	−5.8	−6		
Venire after prosecutor's optimal performance	22	0	22	100%	+100
Prosecutor's (hypothetical) *worst* performance	−6		−6		
Venire after prosecutor's worst performance	16.2	5.8	22	73.6%	−100
Prosecutor's *actual* performance	−1.25**	−3.75	−5		
Venire after prosecutor's actual performance	20.95	2.05	23	91.1%	+58

* The members of the venire whom the prosecutor would have had an opportunity to challenge at voir dire if both attorneys had exercised all their challenges.
** The fraction emerged as follows: The prosecutor excused a total of 5 jurors, but we knew the first ballot vote only for 4 of the 5. We apportioned the "unknown" vote in the ratio of 1 to 3 (.25 to .75) according to the known vote of the 4 jurors. *See* Table 3.

---

42. This index provides only an approximate measure of attorney performance because it does not take three factors into account. First, it assumes that all potential jurors are examined at one time, and that the prosecution makes all of its challenges before the defense makes any; in the present trials, potential jurors were examined individually and challenges were made in stages. *See* text accompanying notes 6-8 *supra*. It should be noted, however, that many courts, both federal and state, arrange the challenge procedure so that each side "strikes" jurors from the list, very much as our model assumes. This procedure was used in the Mitchell-Stans trial. *See* note 49 *infra*. Second, our index ignores the possibility that attorneys may be faced with the choice between saving one of a limited number of challenges, and thus accepting a juror who may be unfavorable to their side, or exercising that challenge, thereby risking having later to accept someone who seems even more unfavorable. *See* note 18 *supra*.

Third, our index is calculated as if the attorneys exercised all their challenges. However, because a jury may be impaneled before the attorneys exhaust their peremptory challenges,

The original venire consisted of 28 potential jurors, of whom 22.2 would have voted guilty and 5.8 not guilty.[43] The prosecutor's "best performance," therefore, would have used the allotted 6 peremptory challenges to eliminate all 5.8 jurors voting not guilty; 100% of the remaining jurors would have voted guilty. In formulating our attorney performance index, we would have assigned this optimal performance a score of $+100$. The prosecutor's "worst performance" would have excluded 6 guilty-voting jurors, leaving the proportion of guilty votes at 16.2 out of 22, or 73.6%; this worst possible performance would have been assigned a score of -100. A zero score would represent a performance leaving unchanged the original distribution of the venire, estimated at 79% guilty votes.

In the actual case (Case 10), the prosecutor selected his jurors so as to leave a voting constellation of 91.1% guilty votes. We therefore computed this prosecutor's score as follows: (1) because the prosecutor increased the proportion of favorable jurors, the score was given a positive value; (2) the absolute value then was measured by calculating the difference between the percentage of guilty votes in the original venire (79) and the percentage of guilty votes after the prosecutor's challenges (91.1), a score of 12.1; (3) this value then was normalized by dividing by the maximum possible improvement (the difference between the guilty percentage at a zero score, 79, and the

the attorneys may face fewer potential jurors than is theoretically possible. The justification for this assumption, which was necessary because we needed a common denominator, is twofold. First, in each of the cases used in the experiment, optimally performing attorneys would have used nearly all of their challenges. Second, the attorney performance index has value only as a relative index, and thus, the base standard chosen is not crucial so long as it is applied consistently.

43. We established this distribution of first ballot votes in the standardized 28-person venire by determining the proportion of guilty votes among the potential jurors questioned during voir dire. In Case 10, for example, we were allowed to discover directly the first ballot vote of the actual jury, which was 11 to 1 for conviction. We also knew that all 6 of the potential jurors the defense challenged would have voted to convict, and that among the 5 potential jurors dismissed by the prosecution 1 would have voted to convict and 3 to acquit. The remaining potential juror dismissed by the prosecution did not participate in our study. As demonstrated in Table 3, that potential juror's vote was estimated by the ratio of votes of those potential jurors dismissed by the prosecution who did participate in the study. They voted 1 to 3 to convict, so the missing vote was allocated in a 1 to 3 ratio: .25 to convict, .75 to acquit. By adding the guilty votes of the actual, potential and missing jurors, we determined that 18.25 (11+6+1+.25) or 79% of the actual panel would have voted for conviction. Presumably, any size panel chosen by the same standards would contain the same percentage of guilty votes. We needed to hypothesize a 28-person panel to account for the challenges that were not exercised. Because 79% of 28 is 22.2, we established that figure as the number of guilty votes in the standardized 28-person venire. The difference between 28 and 22.2, 5.8, was designated as the number of not guilty votes in the 28-person venire.

guilty percentage at a +100 score, 100). The resulting ratio, +12.1/21, expressed as a percentage, +58, became the prosecutor's performance score.[44]

To complete the attorney performance index, we performed parallel computations for the prosecution and defense counsel in each of the 12 cases.[45] Table 9 presents the results of these calculations.

TABLE 9

Attorney Performance Index

Case No.	Prosecutor	Defense
1	+23	+46
2	-59	+ 6
3	+44	+30
4	-20	+44
5	+31	+48
6	-61	-11
7	+ 9	-10
8	-32	-62
9	0*	+12
10	+58	+46
11	+62	+36
12	-61	+19
Average (Mean)	- 0.5	+17.0
Average Fluctuation Around the Mean	±38	±25

* The prosecutor exercised only one challenge, and the challenged juror did not participate in the study. *See* note 19 *supra*.

---

44. If the prosecutor in Case 10 had instead *decreased* the proportion of favorable jurors through the use of peremptory challenges, our procedure would have differed in two ways. First, because the peremptory challenges left the prosecutor in a poorer position than if he had not exercised any challenges, he would have been assigned a negative rather than a positive value. Second, we would have normalized the score by comparing the shift away from the configuration of guilty votes at a zero score—the shift caused by the "unwise" exercise of peremptory challenges to exclude favorable jurors—with the *worst* possible result from the prosecutor's point of view (the guilty percentage at a -100 score, 73.6).

45. The basic calculations for the defense differ to the extent that the defense could exercise a minimum of 10 peremptory challenges, whereas the prosecution was limited to 6, except in the one case in which both sides were granted only 3 challenges. Furthermore, the pool of potential jurors to which a defense attorney can be exposed is 22: 28 venire members minus the 6 who might be removed by the prosecutor.

The collective performance of the attorneys is not impressive. The prosecutors' average score is close to zero (-0.5). Thus, in the aggregate, the prosecutors made about as many good challenges as bad ones. The defense counsel's average performance score ($+17.0$) is slightly better, which suggests that, on the average, defense attorneys shifted in their favor the proportion of not guilty votes in the venire. These averages are misleading, however, because the fluctuations around them are so large. The prosecutors' scores fluctuate between $+62$ (Case 11) and -61 (Cases 6 and 12); the defense counsel's scores fluctuate between $+48$ (Case 5) and -62 (Case 8). The average fluctuations around the mean scores are ±38 for the prosecutor and ±25 for the defense, suggesting that in this limited sample of 12 cases, attorney performance was highly erratic. As a result, even though attorneys' scores on the average were around zero, in some cases the attorneys performed very poorly, and in others very well. And if, in a case, one side performs poorly while the other side performs well, such disparity may have interesting results.

There is a correspondence between those cases that Table 4 indicates had the greatest shifts in the probability of a given jury verdict and those cases in which, as Table 9 shows, the difference between levels of attorney performance was greatest. In Cases 1, 4 and 12—the cases in which the effects of voir dire on jury verdicts were most pronounced—the shifts in the likelihood of a guilty verdict are related to differential levels of attorney performance. Case 12, for example, showed the most dramatic shift in the probability of a guilty verdict (-72); it was also the case in which attorney performance differed the most. The prosecutor had a marked negative score (-61), while the defense attorney had a performance score that was noticeably positive ($+19$). In Cases 1 and 4, where the respective shifts in probability were -18 and -30, differences between the performance levels of opposing counsel similarly occur.[46]

---

46. As Case 11 shows, the indices for prosecution and defense are not strictly comparable. Because defense attorneys have more challenges, they may eliminate as many hostile jurors as the prosecutor (in Case 11 each eliminated 2 hostile jurors) yet still receive a lower score because defense counsel *might* have used the extra challenges to eliminate more hostile jurors than the prosecutor.

In Cases 2 and 8, there were noticeable differences in the performance scores of the attorneys as well, yet the probability of guilty verdicts was affected very little. In neither of these cases, however, were there more than 2 potential jurors who would have voted for acquittal. Had both been eliminated, the probability of conviction would have been 100%, but even if the prosecution performed as badly as possible and the defense performed as well as

The present analysis does not take up the complex task of discovering why some attorneys performed better than others. We do not know how much of their performance was the result of superior skill[47] or of luck or simply of easier choices. Nor do we know to what extent the ever-shrinking information that becomes available during voir dire contributes to that differential performance.[48] But whatever the reasons, the generally poor and occasionally disparate performances of the prosecutor and defense counsel raise questions concerning the role of peremptory challenges in furthering the constitutionally prescribed goal of trial by an impartial jury.[49] The following Part of the Article discusses this larger issue.

II. DISCUSSION

The first conclusion emerging from this study is that there are cases in which the jury verdict is seriously affected, if not deter-

---

possible, the first ballot vote still would have been at least 10 to 2 for conviction; Graph 1 reveals that in such cases the jury will convict 95% of the time. Any change in the first ballot vote caused by a realignment of votes in the jury through peremptory challenges can have only a small effect on the ultimate outcome when the venire strongly favors one side.

47. To answer this question, it would be necessary to show whether particular attorneys can eliminate unfavorable jurors, with some consistency.

48. *See* note 66 *infra* and accompanying text.

49. There is a growing body of literature on the methods employed by attorneys to improve their performances at voir dire. *See, e.g.*, A. GINGER, JURY SELECTION IN CRIMINAL TRIALS: NEW TECHNIQUES AND CONCEPTS (1975); THE JURY SYSTEM: NEW METHODS FOR REDUCING PREJUDICE (D. Kairys ed. 1975). Attorneys have attempted to supplement the knowledge about prospective jurors they have gained by their own experience and intuition by using scientific discovery methods, and social scientists have been enlisted to assist attorneys in developing profiles of "good" and "bad" jurors. There are two basic types of juror profiles: personality, or clinical, profiles and demographic profiles. *See* A. GINGER, *supra* §§ 11.9-.11. The utility of such profiles varies, however, depending on the difficulty of establishing distinguishing characteristics in the population and recognizing the criteria in the potential jurors presented for voir dire. For example, personality profiles are found to be less useful in federal trials than in state trials because attorneys in federal trials are less free to direct the questioning of potential jurors to areas that will reveal crucial personality traits. *See* E. DEVITT & C. BLACKMAR, *supra* note 6, § 3.01.

Juror selection techniques, however, can provide only general guidelines and are far from infallible, as was demonstrated in the Harrisburg trial of Father Berrigan, in which the mother of four conscientious objectors surprisingly held out for conviction. *See* J. NELSON & R. OSTROW, THE FBI AND THE BERRIGANS 297 (1972). Included in the list of pertinent literature on this subject are: Schulman, Shaver, Colman, Emrich & Christie, *Recipe for a Jury*, PSYCH. TODAY, May 1973, at 37; Kahn, *Picking Peers: Social Scientists' Role in Selection of Juries Sparks Legal Debate*, Wall St. J., Aug. 12, 1974, at 1, col. 1; McConahay, Mullin & Fredrick, The Uses of Social Science in Trials with Political and Racial Overtones: The Trial of Jo Ann Little (Mimeograph Working Paper, Center for Political Analysis, Duke University). For a critical review of these developments, see Babcock, *supra* note 6, at 559-63; Zeisel & Diamond, *The Jury Selection in the Mitchell-Stans Conspiracy Trial*, 1976 AM. B. FOUNDATION RESEARCH J. 151, 169.

mined, by the voir dire. At times, one attorney will significantly outperform the opposing attorney in challenging hostile jurors. Lawyers apparently do win some of their cases, as they occasionally boast, during or at least with the help of, voir dire.

We have no firm basis from which to estimate how often this occurs. The 12 cases used in the experiment do not constitute a probability sample. Moreover, the unusually low incidence of judge-jury agreement in these cases suggests a biased sample.[50] We have no reason to believe, however, that the method employed to select the trials used in the experiment led to the selection of cases in which the opportunity to influence the verdict by the exercise of peremptory challenges was greater than normal. We are, therefore, tentatively persuaded that cases in which peremptory challenges have an important effect on the verdict occur with some frequency.

In the 5 cases in which we detected significant shifts as a result of peremptory challenges, the shifts benefited the defense. What caused the shifts in favor of the defense? First, the defense attorneys performed better than the prosecutors: Their average score was better—$+17.0$ compared to -0.5 for prosecutors—and they outperformed their adversaries in 8 of the 12 cases. Second, because more challenges are allotted to the defense than to the prosecution, we must explore the extent to which this imbalance is likely to benefit the defense. This question requires a more general explanation of how jury verdicts can be affected by the various combinations of good and poor performance of the two attorneys at voir dire.

A.   *The Potential Impact of the Peremptory Challenge*

In noncapital felony cases, federal rules presently give the prosecution 6 peremptory challenges and the defense 10.[51] Apart from potential jurors dismissed for cause, an attorney therefore can confront as many as 28 veniremen: the 12 who actually serve, the 10 the defense can dismiss and the 6 the prosecution can dismiss. If each of these 28 potential jurors were to sit through the trial and vote on the first ballot, 29 combinations of guilty and not-guilty votes would be possible. These 29 combinations, ranging from 28 guilty votes to 28 not guilty votes, would reflect the strength or weakness of the particular case tried before that jury. In Table 10, we show the

---

50. In 50% of the cases in this experiment, the judge agreed with the jury's verdict. *See* Table 5. Previous research has indicated that, on the average, the judge and jury will agree in 69% of the cases. *See* H. KALVEN & H. ZEISEL, *supra* note 17, at 58; note 27 *supra*.

51. FED. R. CRIM. P. 24(b). *See* note 8 *supra*.

changes in the first ballot voting that would occur if both attorneys performed optimally, challenging as many hostile jurors as their allotment of challenges allows.

TABLE 10

Shift in First Ballot Constellation Through Peremptory Challenges
(Prosecution and Defense Perform Optimally)

First Ballot Constellations in Venire *Before* Challenges			Venire *After* Prosecution Challenges (up to 6 jurors)		Venire *After* Both Prosecution and Defense Challenges (Defense up to 10 jurors)		
Guilty	Not Guilty	Percent Guilty	Guilty	Not Guilty	Guilty	Not Guilty	Percent Guilty
0	28	0	0	22	0	22	0
1	27	4	1	21	0	21	0
2	26	7	2	20	0	20	0
3	25	11	3	19	0	19	0
4	24	14	4	18	0	18	0
5	23	18	5	17	0	17	0
6	22	21	6	16	0	16	0
7	21	25	7	15	0	15	0
8	20	29	8	14	0	14	0
9	19	32	9	13	0	13	0
10	18	36	10	12	0	12	0
11	17	39	11	11	1	11	8
12	16	43	12	10	2	10	17
13	15	46	13	9	3	9	25
14	14	50	14	8	4	8	33
15	13	54	15	7	5	7	42
16	12	57	16	6	6	6	50
17	11	61	17	5	7	5	58
18	10	64	18	4	8	4	67
19	9	68	19	3	9	3	75
20	8	71	20	2	10	2	83
21	7	75	21	1	11	1	92
22	6	79	22	0	12	0	100
23	5	82	23	0	13	0	100
24	4	86	24	0	14	0	100
25	3	89	25	0	15	0	100
26	2	93	26	0	16	0	100
27	1	96	27	0	17	0	100
28	0	100	28	0	18	0	100

At the two extremes, the venire members are unanimous in favoring one side or the other, and any 12 jurors selected from these venires would either all convict or all acquit; peremptory challenges can have no effect in these two situations. When the number of potential jurors who would vote not guilty does not exceed 6, the prosecution has the power to remove all of them, thus leaving a venire with no prospective jurors who would vote not guilty. Similarly, optimal use of the 10 challenges available to the defense serves to eliminate all opposition where the initial venire has no more than 10 jurors who would vote guilty. The effects of optimal use of peremptory challenges on the intermediate constellations vary, but when the venire is closely divided, the present allocation of peremptory challenges offers a significant advantage to the defense. Table 10 reveals that whenever the venire has fewer than 18 individuals who would vote to convict, the defense's 4 extra peremptory challenges allow it to face a jury with proportionately fewer guilty votes than were in the original venire.

The shifts shown in Table 10, however, presume optimal attorney performance, and our experiment suggests that in practice attorneys do not perform optimally.[52] Therefore, Graph 2 illustrates the effects of various combinations of attorney performance on the likelihood of a guilty verdict. We have matched the optimal, neutral and worst possible performances of each of the sides, yielding nine possible pairings: When the prosecution performs optimally (P+), it may meet with the defense's optimal performance (P+D+), its neutral performance (P+Do) or its worst performance (P+D−). Likewise, the neutral performance on the part of the prosecution (Po) may meet with the optimal (PoD+), neutral (PoDo) or worst (PoD−) performance of the defense. Finally, the worst performance of the prosecution (P−) also can meet with the optimal (P−D+), neutral (P−Do) or worst (P−D−) performance of the defense.

The 9 lines in Graph 2 represent different attorney performance combinations. Each line relates the possible first ballot voting constellation in the venire (plotted on the horizontal axis) to the resulting first ballot constellation in the jury (plotted on the vertical axis). As an example, consider the P+D+ performance combination. This line, which represents optimal performance by both attorneys, begins like all the others in the lower left-hand corner of the graph and

---

52. *See* text accompanying notes 45-49 *supra*.

GRAPH 2

Opportunity for Change in the Jury's First Ballot Constellation Under the Present Federal Rules

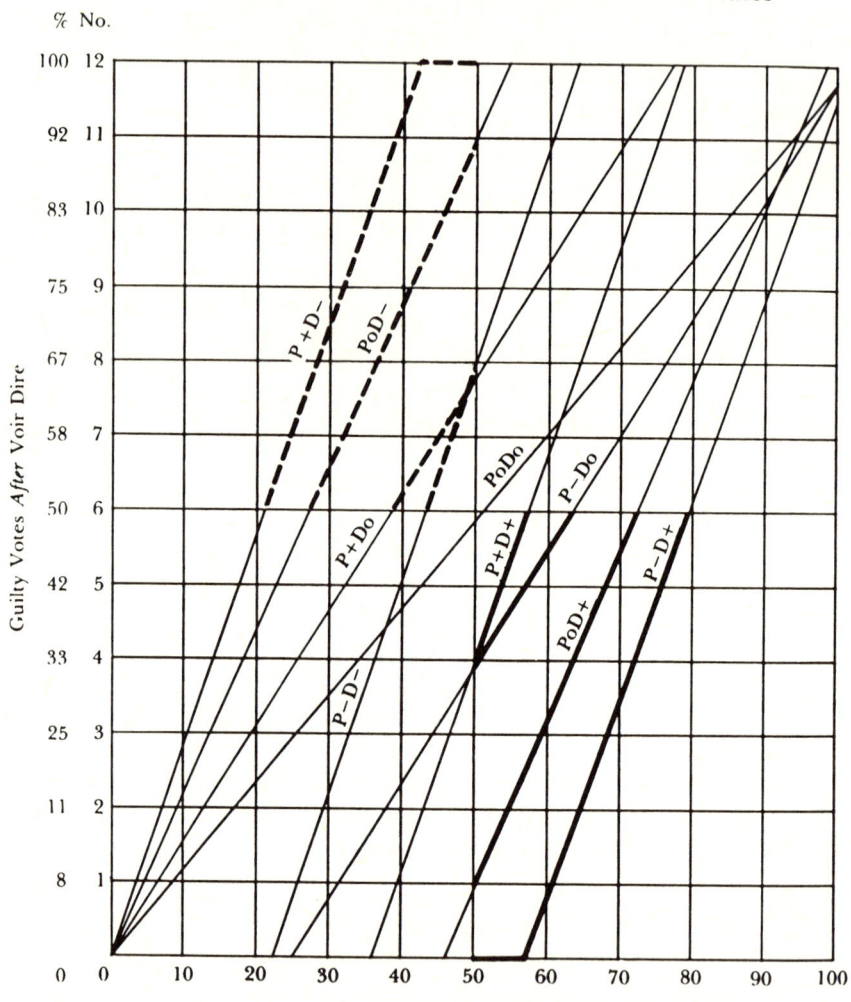

% No.

Guilty Votes After Voir Dire

Jurors in the Venire Who Would Vote Guilty (%)

P = Prosecution   + = Optimal Performance
D = Defense   o = Neutral Performance
                         − = Worst Performance

ends in the upper right-hand corner. The first section of this P+D+ line—that part lying on the horizontal line between the origin and 36—indicates that when there are fewer than 10 persons in the 28-person venire (36%) who would cast guilty votes on the first ballot, the effect of the optimal use of challenges by the defense will be to eliminate all guilty votes from the final jury verdict. The final section of the line begins where 22 or more of those in the 28-person pool (79%) would vote for conviction. Here, the prosecution's optimal use of its 6 challenges would remove all hostile members of the venire from the jury. The middle section of the P+D+ line, the segment sloping upwards from the bottom of the graph, shows the constellation of guilty votes in the final jury in situations in which neither the defense nor the prosecution by optimal use of its challenges can dismiss all hostile members of the venire. Thus, for any first ballot constellation in the venire, we can read the expected first ballot vote in the final jury. For example, if half the venire would vote guilty, we observe that optimal use of peremptory challenges by both sides will result in a jury with only four guilty votes.

Because the defense has four more peremptory challenges than the prosecution, it has a significant advantage when both sides use their challenges optimally or when the defense performs better than the prosecution. The importance of this advantage becomes more apparent when first ballot votes are converted by the use of Graph 1 into the probability of an ultimate guilty verdict. For example, assuming optimal performance, if the venire is split 16-12 in favor of conviction, the relation between the first ballot votes and the verdict indicates that a similarly proportioned jury would find the defendant guilty nearly 70% of the time.[53] After optimal exercise of peremptory challenges by both attorneys, however, the likelihood of conviction decreases to less than 45%. Similarly, if the venire is divided 15-13, the corresponding percentages shift from 60% to less than 25%, and if the venire is split evenly, the percentages change from 45% to 10%.

The dark lines in Graph 2 indicate those areas in which peremptory challenges have changed a probable conviction by the venire into a probable acquittal by the actual jury. The dotted lines, on the other hand, show where probable acquittals become probable convictions. Table 11 extracts from Graph 2 those areas in which various combinations of attorney performance are likely to cause differences in the votes of the final jury and the original venire.

---

53. *See* Graph 1; notes 21-24 *supra* and accompanying text.

TABLE 11

Zones in Which the Peremptory Challenges Reverse the First Ballot Majority Constellations

	Performance Combinations								
	1	2	3	4	5	6	7	8	9
Prosecution (P)	0	+	−	+	−	0	−	+	0
Defense (D)	0	+	−	0	0	+	+	−	−
A *majority for guilty* in the venire will be reversed into a majority for acquittal if the original proportion of votes in the venire was between	—	51%-56% (5 pts)	—	—	51%-57% (6 pts)	51%-70% (19 pts)	51%-77% (26 pts)	—	—
A *majority for acquittal* in the venire will be reversed into a majority for guilty, if the original proportion of guilty votes was between	—	—	43%-49% (6 pts)	39%-49% (10 pts)	—	—	—	21%-49% (28 pts)	27%-49% (22 pts)

Graph 2 and Table 11 address the potential effects of differential attorney performance under a rule that allocates 6 peremptory challenges to the prosecution and 10 to the defense.[54] Table 11 highlights these effects by delimiting those instances in which the attorneys, by use of peremptory challenges, can change the expected verdict. In other words, it shows the range of first ballot constellations in the original venire for which an attorney can use the peremptory challenges to shift what would likely be a losing verdict to a winning one. Table 8 reveals that when both attorneys perform equally (columns 1, 2 and 3), there is little chance of reversing the expected verdict. If the defense counsel performs neutrally (columns 4 and 5), the reversal range is still modest (only 6 or 10 percentage points), regardless of the prosecutor's performance. When the roles are reversed, however—that is, when the prosecutor exercises challenges neutrally—the potential reversal range doubles (to 19 or 22 percentage points). Not surprisingly, the maximum likelihood of changing the expected verdict occurs when the attorneys perform at opposite extremes (columns 7 and 8). Finally, because of the imbalance in the number of available challenges, the performance of the defense counsel (whether good or

---

54. *See* note 8 *supra*.

poor) generally will have a greater potential effect than that of the prosecutor.

In the next section, we examine the arguments for unequal allocation of challenges and, in light of our experimental findings, the utility of the peremptory challenge system in practice.

B.   *Using Peremptory Challenges to Obtain an Impartial Jury*

The primary function of the voir dire is elimination from the venire of those potential jurors prejudiced or biased in favor of either the prosecution or the defense.[55] Graph 3 presents a hypothetical distribution of prejudice in the venire of prospective jurors. In this model, we assume that bias is symmetrically distributed and that it varies from an extreme pro-prosecution orientation, favoring conviction, to a similarly extreme pro-defense predisposition, favoring acquittal; the majority of prospective jurors lie somewhere between the two extremes, around the no-bias point.

Ideally, it is the court's responsibility to excuse for cause those jurors with extreme prejudice—those depicted in the dark areas in Graph 3. And we may see it as a function of the peremptory challenge to remove the less patently prejudiced prospective jurors, those in the shaded areas. The unchallenged jurors remain. They are not free of prejudice, but the level of bias is low. These remaining jurors are the realistic approximation to the ideal of the "fair and impartial jury."[56]

---

55.   *See* Babcock, *supra* note 6, at 549-52. Some authorities suggest that voir dire serves a function in addition to that of qualifying unbiased jurors. Professors Amsterdam and Kaplan, for example, note that because attorneys use the voir dire as a vehicle to speak directly with jurors, it performs the important task of educating the jurors as to the meaning of "reasonable doubt." *See* A. AMSTERDAM, B. SEGAL & M. MILLER, *supra* note 2, §§ 337-39; J. KAPLAN & J. WALTZ, THE TRIAL OF JACK RUBY 91-94 (1965). However, as Professor Kaplan notes, despite this educational role, the "main and, in theory, . . . only legitimate function [of voir dire is] developing sufficient information upon which to select the jurors." *Id.* at 92. Both because of the primary importance of voir dire as a procedure to qualify unbiased jurors and because this study is based upon data from the federal court system (where attorneys are permitted to ask questions during the voir dire only at the judge's discretion), we have not focused on the educational justifications for voir dire. Rather, we have limited our study to an examination of the role of voir dire in altering the distribution of prejudice in a venire and thus affecting the ultimate jury verdict.

56.   The sixth amendment declares that "[i]n all criminal prosecutions, the accused shall enjoy the right to a speedy and public trial, *by an impartial jury* of the State and district wherein the crime shall have been committed." U.S. CONST. amend. VI (emphasis added). The Supreme Court has recognized, however, that requiring that jurors lack any preconceived notions about the trial would set an "impossible standard," Irvin v. Dowd, 366 U.S. 717, 723 (1961), and that a juror's "qualifications as to impartiality" must merely fall within "minimum standards," Beck v. Washington, 369 U.S. 541, 557 (1962).

GRAPH 3

Distribution of Prejudice Within the Venire

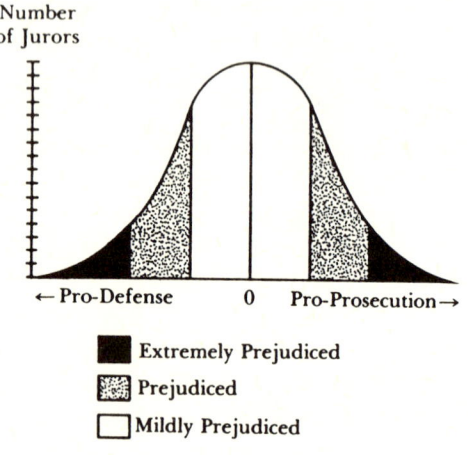

Number
of Jurors

← Pro-Defense   0   Pro-Prosecution →

■ Extremely Prejudiced
▨ Prejudiced
☐ Mildly Prejudiced

For the sake of simplicity, this model assumes that prejudice is distributed symmetrically in the venire. This may well be an unjustified assumption; one-sided pretrial publicity[57] or more firmly rooted community prejudices—against blacks or homosexuals, for example[58]—often may produce asymmetry in the distribution of bias. Furthermore, the distribution is likely to vary in the degree of prejudice that potential jurors may hold. The variance of the distribution may be small, in which case a large proportion of the venire will be grouped around the no-bias point, or the variance may be large, in which case there will be a greater number of potential jurors harboring extreme prejudices.

Graph 4 shows how these two factors—symmetry and variance—combine to form four potential distributions of prejudice in the venire.[59]

---

57. *See* Borcher, *Fair Trial & Free Press: Preliminary Hearing—Gateway to Prejudice*, 1975 LAW & SOC. ORD. 903.

58. *Cf.* Ham v. South Carolina, 409 U.S. 524, 527 (1973) (due process requires interrogation of jurors on subject of racial prejudice when party so demands). *See generally* Blauner, *The Sociology of Jury Selection*, in A. GINGER, *supra* note 49, §§ 10.6–.8.

59. We have assumed for the sake of example in Graph 4 and the following analysis that the asymmetrical distributions are positively skewed towards the prosecution—that is, that a majority of the venire will have a pro-prosecution orientation. An assumption that the underlying population favors the defense, however, would lead to exactly opposite effects of, and solutions to, the skewness.

GRAPH 4
Four Distributions of Prejudice in the Venire

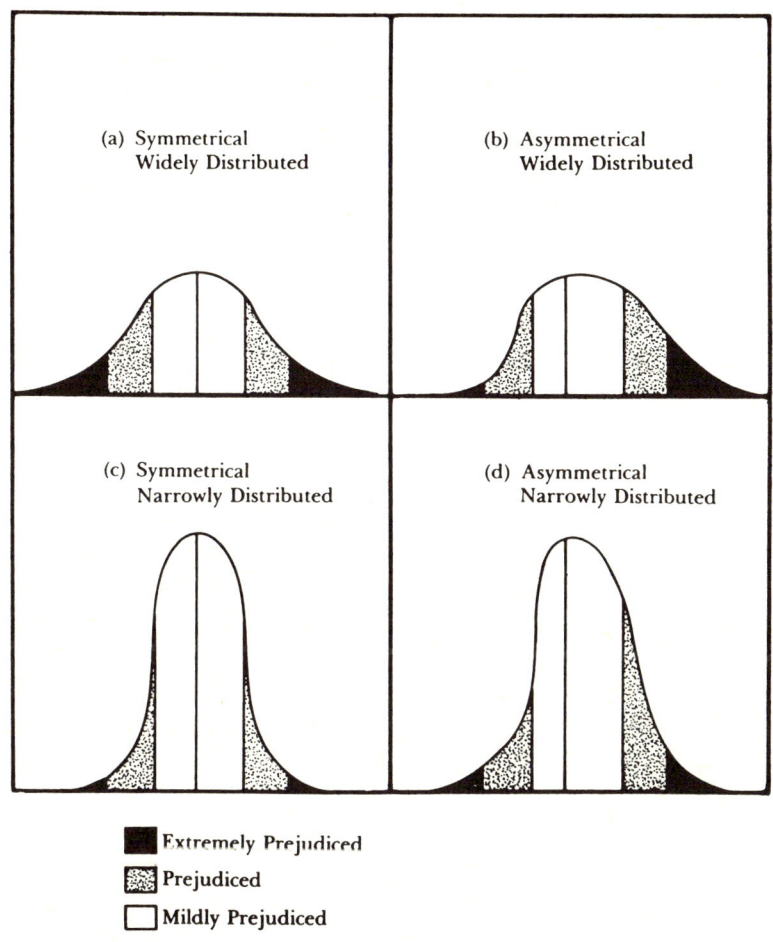

(a) Symmetrical
Widely Distributed

(b) Asymmetrical
Widely Distributed

(c) Symmetrical
Narrowly Distributed

(d) Asymmetrical
Narrowly Distributed

■ Extremely Prejudiced
▨ Prejudiced
□ Mildly Prejudiced

Graph 4 illustrates that if the voir dire process is designed to achieve a jury of low and evenly distributed prejudice, then the distribution of prejudice within the venire will determine the form and extent of juror removal. If prejudice is widely and symmetrically distributed as in Graph 4(a), a relatively large number of prospective jurors will have to be removed, but the same number should be excused from both sides of the spectrum. A skewed distribution like that represented in Graph 4(b) will necessitate the removal of approximately the same number of potential jurors, but more should be removed from one side of the spectrum than from the other. The distributions depicted in Graphs 4(c) and 4(d) will require fewer removals to obtain the same range of bias, because a greater proportion of the venire is closer to the no-bias point. The asymmetrical distribution in Graph 4(d), however, necessitates that the pro-prosecutorial bias be compensated for by removing more potential jurors who are prejudiced in that direction.

The appropriate result can be achieved in each case, provided sufficient challenges are available and are properly allocated, and provided sufficient information is available to identify the prejudiced jurors in the venire.[60] The number and allocation of peremptory challenges available in both federal and state criminal trials vary according to the severity of the offense. Many jurisdictions give an equal number to both parties; some allow a larger number to the defense.[61] The models presented in Graph 4 make it clear that the adequacy of such allocation depends upon the distribution of prejudice in the particular case. But even if the statutory allocation of peremptory challenges does not correspond precisely with the distribution of prejudice in the venire, an additional safeguard remains. The judge can use challenges for cause, which are not limited in number,[62] to compensate for the inability of one side to correct an imbalance in prejudice favoring the opposing side. In order for challenges for cause to operate in this manner and in order for attorneys to identify less-prejudiced jurors who can be eliminated by peremptory challenges, sufficient information on the prejudice of jurors within the venire must be obtained.

Our experiment suggests that, on the whole, the voir dire as conducted in these trials did not provide sufficient information for attorneys to identify prejudiced jurors.[63] The average performance score of the prosecution was near the zero point (−0.5), indicating an inability to distinguish potential bias;[64] defense counsel performed only slightly better (+17.0). Perhaps most significant is the

---

60. This analysis, of course, is conditioned upon positive attorney performance in the exercise of their allotted peremptory challenges. If the attorneys perform neutrally or worse, the number and pattern of allocation of challenges will have no effect on producing the desired result.

61. *See* note 8 *supra*.

62. *See* note 6 *supra*.

63. *See* text accompanying notes 42-49 *supra*.

64. We assume that some initial bias existed in the population of potential jurors in our study.

inconsistent performance of attorneys. Occasionally, one side performed well in a case in which the other side performed poorly, thereby frustrating the law's expectation that the adversary allocation of challenges will benefit both sides equally.[65]

One way of averting the undesirable effects of disparate performance would be to increase the amount of information on which lawyers base their decisions. The more they learn in open court about the prejudice of potential jurors, the less opportunity there is for luck or private knowledge to determine which side benefits from the peremptory challenge process. The current trend is in the opposite direction and has tended to reduce the voir dire's informative power. To an even greater extent than before, judges have reduced the voir dire questioning by counsel and have transferred primary responsibility to themselves, questioning jurors in blocks and restricting the scope of the questions asked.[66]

There is, however, an interesting exception to this trend. In notorious cases with extensive pretrial publicity, the courts have tended to abandon all restrictive rules and have gone to the other extreme. In these cases, the courts apparently have considered it essential that as much as possible become known about each individual juror. They have allowed great latitude in the questioning of jurors, even to the extent of occasionally questioning each potential juror in chambers to assure the most frank and complete response.[67]

One rationale for distinguishing notorious cases from other cases in terms of the kind and extent of the questioning permitted of individual jurors is based on the assumption that the range of prejudice in the venire will exceed that in ordinary cases. Thus, the

---

65. The performance index used in our study is cruder than that required for the task outlined by the model depicted in Graphs 3 and 4. The index gives counsel a positive score for every challenge of a juror on the correct side (that is, for every juror hostile to its side of the spectrum); it gives a negative score for challenges of jurors who would have voted *for* that side. The index does not distinguish the degree of prejudice (that is, the distance from the no-bias point).

66. The move toward restricting the scope of the voir dire suggests that our juror selection process is becoming more closely akin to the English example, in which challenge for cause is limited to "specific" bias—blood relationship or similarly direct association with the parties—and peremptory challenges hardly ever are exercised. As a rule, jurors are not questioned at all, and the court impanels the first prospective jurors who come into the box. *See* note 10 *supra* and accompanying text.

It is difficult to see why the English system should serve as a model for our system. The English jury, unlike the American jury, never confronts the problem of widespread pretrial publicity because English law does not permit it. Moreover, we do not know how well the English model serves the ends of justice.

67. *See, e.g.,* Zeisel & Diamond, *supra* note 49, at 153.

ordinary trial takes on the venire constellations depicted in Graph 4(c), and the extraordinary trial is identified with that of Graph 4(b), in which prejudice is great and asymmetrically distributed. This rationale poses two difficulties.

First, the distinction between the ordinary and the extraordinary trial is often difficult to establish. The two lie on a continuum, and there is no demarcation point at which it becomes clear that different rules should apply. Moreover, the decision as to which trial deserves the mini-voir dire and which the full treatment is left entirely to the trial court's discretion; there are no guidelines for the judge to follow.

Yet another possible justification for reducing the extent of voir dire exists: the desire to obtain a jury that represents as closely as possible the community from which it is drawn. Recent years have seen major reforms designed to achieve this goal, efforts spearheaded by the Federal Jury Selection Act of 1968.[68] A liberal policy of allowing challenges is likely to impair community representativeness.[69] As one critic has observed, first we labor hard to make the juries representative of the communities from which they are drawn, and at the very last moment we allow that representativeness to be destroyed by peremptory challenges.[70]

This rationale for reducing the voir dire also is flawed. First, efforts to make the jury venires representative of their communities have been far from successful.[71] Second, a representative jury nevertheless may be representative of a prejudiced community. To be sure, a change of venue might bring relief, but that is a measure the law grants only in extreme circumstances.[72]

Because we argue for more information on juror prejudice, we should take a closer look at the nature of the "prejudice" we so glibly

---

68. 28 U.S.C. § 1861 (1970).

69. *Cf.* Note, *Limiting the Peremptory Challenge: Representation of Groups on Petit Juries*, 86 YALE L.J. 1715 (1977) (attorneys should be prevented from challenging jurors merely because they are members of certain groups within society).

70. Address by Swedish Judge Mars Molin at the 1974 Cropwood Conference on Jury Trials, held in Cambridge, England, under the auspices of the Cambridge Institute of Criminology.

71. *See generally* J. VAN DYKE, *supra* note 8. Note also that the drawing from the jury wheel may be manipulated to yield a purposefully biased jury. *See* Zeisel, *Dr. Spock and the Case of the Vanishing Women Jurors*, 37 U. CHI. L. REV. 1 (1969).

72. *See* ABA PROJECT ON MINIMUM STANDARDS FOR CRIMINAL JUSTICE, STANDARDS RELATING TO FAIR TRIAL & FREE PRESS 121 (Approved Draft 1968) (not only is there a general reluctance on the part of courts to grant a change of venue, but several states have adopted statutes imposing substantial restrictions on the availability of this remedy).

have located, graded, graphed, and altogether taken for granted. At its extreme, prejudice is easily identified as a predisposition that should not, but is likely to, affect a juror's vote.[73] A close relative of the defendant or the victim safely may be assumed to be prejudiced, as may the drug-using juror in a drug case, or the racist in the trial of a black man. As we move away from these extremes, the identification of undesired prejudice becomes more complicated. If we are intent upon finding the completely impartial juror, we surely shall never find one. All jurors' experiences have shaped their values and attitudes, and these, in turn, are likely to shape jurors' perceptions of the trial evidence and hence their votes. In this sense, "prejudice" is not only ineradicable but often indistinguishable from the very values and attitudes of the community that we expect the jurors to bring to the trial.[74]

The law recognizes that jurors cannot perceive and evaluate the evidence before them without being affected by their attitudes and beliefs, and thus it insists that the differing values held by the jurors be adequately mixed. This insistence that the values of the jury be reflective of the distribution of values that exist in the community provides the law with an objective standard against which the "fairness" of the jury can be measured: A representative jury, then, is the first approximation to the ideal jury.

As its second approximation, the law, through the voir dire, tries to improve the selection process by removing the strongly biased jurors and by preventing whatever prejudice remains from being one-sided. This second approximation is more difficult to achieve. Potential jurors may hide their prejudices from the examiner, either consciously or unconsciously. In the end, it is difficult to define and describe the borderline between prejudice and value differences with any precision. Perhaps that is why the law in its wisdom does not require reasons for the peremptory challenge.

---

73. Psychological research has demonstrated that such prejudices can even distort perceptual abilities. *See* Note, *Did Your Eyes Deceive You? Expert Psychological Testimony on the Unreliability of Eyewitness Identification*, 29 STAN. L. REV. 969, 981 (1977).

74. "All people have biases and opinions that will inevitably influence their decisions and perceptions, including those on jury duty. The Supreme Court has recognized this in cases in which it finds that jury selection procedures must assure a 'fair possibility for obtaining a representative cross section of the community.' The reason for a cross section, stated explicitly in the opinions, is that it assures that a range of biases and experiences will bear on the facts of the case." Babcock, *supra* note 6, at 551 (footnote omitted).

USING COMMUNICATION CUES TO EVALUATE PROSPECTIVE JURORS DURING THE VOIR DIRE*

David Suggs**
Bruce Dennis Sales***

The selection of a jury is one of the most important parts of a jury trial and is often central to the final outcome.[1] Consequently, the effective use of voir dire is a crucial part of any trial lawyer's skills. There are a number of purposes the voir dire may serve. For example, the attorney may use it to ingratiate himself or to indoctrinate prospective jurors.[2] Although attorneys engage in both strategies, neither are judicially sanctioned.[3] The acceptable purposes of voir dire are to determine whether prospective jurors should be eliminated from the jury for cause and to allow the attorneys to obtain information upon which they can base their peremptory challenges.[4]

Considering the acceptable purposes only, the attorneys' task during the voir dire is to obtain sufficient information from the prospective jurors to identify those individuals that the attorneys feel are prejudiced or biased against their client or who will not be receptive to

* The research for and preparation of this Article was partially supported by a grant from the National Institue of Mental Health, Center for Studies of Crime and Delinquency (MH-13814).
** Research Assistant, Law-Psychology Graduate Training Program, University of Nebraska-Lincoln.
*** Director, Law-Psychology Graduate Training Program, Professor of Psychology and Associate Professor of Law, University of Nebraska-Lincoln.
1. *See* Hauwrish & Tate, *Determinants of Jury Selection*, 39 SASK. L. REV. 285, 285 (1974-75).
2. *See* A. CONE AND V. LAWYER, THE ART OF PERSUASION IN LITIGATION, §§ 8.2, 8.4, 8.7, 8.10, 8.12 at 256-58, 260-62 (1966); Blunk & Sales, *Persuasion During the Voir Dire*, in PSYCHOLOGY IN THE LEGAL PROCESS 39, 43-44 (B. Sales ed. 1977); Broeder, *Voir Dire Examinations: An Empirical Study*, 38 S. CAL. L. REV. 503, 521-28 (1965); Rothblatt, *Techniques for Jury Selection*, 2 CRIM. L. BULL., No. 4 at 14, 14-17, 21-22 (1966).
3. *See* BLUNK & SALES, *supra* note 2, at 40.
4. *See* Hare, *Voir Dire and Jury Selection*, 29 ALA. LAW. 160, 160 (1968).

the arguments they wish to raise in the trial. The attorneys must then exercise their challenges for cause or peremptory challenges in order to remove these undesirable prospective jurors. Ideally, when this process of elimination is carried out by counsel for both sides of the lawsuit, a fair and impartial jury is secured.

In order to make an intelligent use of the challenges at their disposal, the attorneys must know how each prospective juror feels in regard to: (1) counsel for both sides; (2) the opposing litigants; and (3) the legal and factual issues that will be raised at trial. Unfortunately, the attorneys will usually encounter obstacles that prevent them from acquiring much of the information they desire. In the federal courts, and in an increasing number of state courts, for example, the trial judge will usually conduct most of the questioning and may not probe into desired areas of information or may not probe deeply enough to satisfy the attorney. The attorneys may also be hampered in acquiring information from prospective jurors by the constraints of time—either by the time limits imposed on the voir dire by the trial judge or by self-imposed limitations adopted to avoid antagonizing prospective jurors with lengthy questioning. Furthermore, the practice of questioning prospective jurors in open court and in the presence of other jurors may inhibit their self-disclosure and encourage socially desirable, conforming responses. As a result of these limitations, the attorney is frequently forced to exercise his challenges on the basis of incomplete information and inference.

To assist the attorneys in their predicament, a number of writers have advocated systems to guide the attorney in his evaluation of prospective jurors. These systems employ various methods ranging from stereotypic notions based on ethnicity and occupational backgrounds to using criteria generated by a sophisticated demographic and attitudinal survey of the community in which the trial is to be held.[5] The present Article will focus on a new method that can be used to evaluate prospective jurors on the basis of their communicative behaviors. Unlike some other methods, this procedure focuses on the particular individual in the courtroom rather than abstract socio-economic groups in the community. It relies solely on behavior observed during the voir dire.

WHAT ARE THE COMMUNICATIVE BEHAVIORS OF JURORS?

Communicative behaviors can be classified in terms of three dimensions: verbal, paralinguistic, and kinesic. The verbal dimension consists of the words which are actually spoken and their syntactical

---

5. For a review of these systems, see Suggs & Sales, *The Art and Science of Conducting the Voir Dire*, 9 J. PROFESSIONAL PSYCH. 367 (1978).

arrangement. The paralinguistic dimension consists of aspects of speech—such as breathing, pauses and latencies, pitch and tone of voice, and speech disturbances—that are not actually concerned with words or sentences.[6] In other words, when we look at paralinguistics, we are interested in *how* something is said rather than *what* is said. Kinesic behavior, or body language, consists of such behaviors as facial expressions, body movements, body orientation, eye contact, and hand movements.

The legal training of attorneys most probably enables them to be particularly astute at analyzing the verbal component of an individual's communicative behaviors. But it is doubtful that they consciously and systematically attend to the prospective juror's paralinguistic and kinesic behaviors. This omission is unfortunate because, for the purposes of the voir dire, the nonverbal cues may be the most important part of a prospective juror's behaviors. This is so because psychological and communication research indicates that verbal behavior is used for communicating about events external to the speakers (a function which is appropriate in the examination of witnesses), while nonverbal cues are used to establish and maintain interpersonal relationships, to communicate interpersonal attitudes, to express emotion, and to make a presentation of the self.[7]

Furthermore, Ekman and Friesen have demonstrated that through their nonverbal behavior people "leak" their true feelings and provide clues that deception is taking place.[8] This latter point is particularly important in light of Broeder's conclusion that "jurors often, either consciously or unconsciously, lie on voir dire."[9] Since emotions, attitudes, and clues of deception are transmitted primarily through the nonverbal channels of communication, a systematic analysis of the nonverbal behaviors presented during the voir dire should be a fruitful method by which the attorney could determine a prospective juror's suitability to serve.

The analysis of nonverbal communicative behaviors discussed here is *not* of the type proposed by the popular literature. Much of that literature advances the notion that particular gestures and movements

---

6. *See generally* Pittenger & Smith, *A Basis for Some Contributions of Linguistics to Psychiatry*, 20 PSYCH. 61, 69-74 (1957).

7. *See generally* M. ARGYLE, SOCIAL INTERACTION (1969); Hunt & Kan Lin, *Accuracy of Judgements of Personal Attributes from Speech*, 6 J. PERSONALITY & SOCIAL PSYCH. 450, 453 (1967); Mehrabian & Ferris, *Inference of Attitudes from Nonverbal Communication to Two Channels*, 31 J. CONSULTING PSYCH. 248, 248-49, 251 (1967); Mehrabian & Wiener, *Decoding of Inconsistent Communications*, 6 J. PERSONALITY & SOCIAL PSYCH. 109, 113-14 (1967).

8. Ekman & Friesen, *Nonverbal Leakage and Clues to Deception*, 32 PSYCH. 88, 88 (1969); Ekman & Friesen, *Detecting Deception from the Body or Face*, 29 J. PERSONALITY & SOCIAL PSYCH. 288, 294-297 (1974).

9. Broeder, *supra* note 2, at 528.

have very specific meanings. This may be so within individuals, but the research literature indicates that different people will exhibit different communicative behaviors, and that the meaning of the various nonverbal behaviors exhibited is idiosyncratic rather than universal in nature.[10] The literature also reveals, however, that there are some common nonverbal indicators of emotion and situational anxiety; it is these behaviors that are important to the attorney and on which we will focus our attention in succeeding sections of this Article.

The Rationale for Analyzing Communicative Behaviors

Consider again the plight of attorneys during voir dire. They need to determine whether the prospective juror is more favorably disposed toward one side than another and whether the juror is making truthful responses to the questions proposed. There are several assumptions we can make. First, it is reasonable to assume that the prospective juror will feel relatively more anxiety when being questioned by an attorney whom the juror regards with disfavor or who represents a client toward whom the juror has a negative bias. Second, anxiety also should manifest itself when the juror is being questioned about sensitive issues on which he has strong feelings (e.g., racial prejudice, death penalty, "law and order"). Finally, it is reasonable to assume that a juror will feel anxiety, unless he is a pathological liar, when he is being deceptive in in response to questioning. The anxiety which the juror feels in each of these cases is situational anxiety—that is to say, the anxiety is generated by the particular situation at hand rather than being a stable personality trait of the individual. Research indicates that it is precisely this situational-type anxiety that is made manifest in the individual's communicative behaviors. Thus, a careful and systematic analysis of these behaviors could yield valuable insights into the individual's feelings and dispositions toward the various sides of the lawsuit, the issues, and the litigants. This is especially true when counsel can question jurors within each of these areas.

The balance of this Article will describe the various behaviors that are indicative of emotional affect and situational anxiety and will then conclude by presenting a systematic method for analyzing those behaviors (i.e., evaluating a juror's desirability).

---

10. Krause, *Anxiety in Verbal Behavior: An Intercorrelational Study*, 25 J. Consulting Psych. 272, 272 (1961).

COMMUNICATIVE BEHAVIORS INDICATIVE OF EMOTION AND/OR
SITUATIONAL ANXIETY

Paralinguistic Cues

Speech disturbances. One of the manifestations of situational anxiety is in the area of speech disturbances. These phenomena have been studied by numerous investigators. Dibner found that the speech patterns of unfinished sentences, breaking in with new thoughts, self-interrupted sentences, repeating words or phrases, stuttering, saying "I don't know" not in answer to a question but as in resignation or disgust, sighing or taking deep breaths, inappropriate laughter, voice changes, questioning the interviewer, and blocking (unusual hesitation) are clearly related to situation anxiety and not to anxiety as an overall personality characteristic.[11] This finding has been substantiated by many other investigators.[12]

The increase in speech disturbances under anxious conditions for the interviewee is substantial. Mahl found that during anxious phases of interviews, the average increase in speech disturbances was twenty-nine percent.[13] Cook found that when the areas of interviews generating anxiety were identified and pursued by further questioning, the speech disturbances increased markedly even though the severity of questioning was mild.[14]

Not only is there an increase in speech disturbances when the interviewee feels anxious, but the whole character of speech changes. For example, Price and Eldred found that when an interviewee feels anxious, his speech becomes more stilted and stereotyped with less differentiated word usage.[15] Thus, if a prospective juror had been responding to questioning in an informal manner and switched to a more formalistic and pompous style when questioned about his attitudes toward racial minorities, it could well be that the juror feels some anxiety about the subject matter and is perhaps being deceptive in his answers.

Amount of speech. A number of investigators have found that people tend to talk longer with people toward whom they have positive

11. Dibner, *Cue-Counting: A Measure of Anxiety in Interviews*, 20 J. CONSULTING PSYCH. 475, 477 (1956).
12. *See, e.g.*, Eldred & Price, *A Linguistic Evaluation of Feeling States in Psychotherapy*, 21 PSYCH. 115, 115-21 (1958); Kasl & Mahl, *The Relationship of Disturbances and Hesitations in Spontaneous Speech to Anxiety*, 1 J. PERSONALITY & SOCIAL PSYCH. 425, 430 (1965); Mahl, *Disturbances and Silences in the Patient's Speech in Psychotherapy*, 53 J. ABNORMAL & SOCIAL PSYCH. 1, 11-13 (1956); Pope & Siegman, *Interviewer Warmth and Verbal Communication in the Initial Interview*, 2 PROCEEDINGS OF THE 75TH ANNUAL CONVENTION OF THE APA 245, 246 (1967).
13. *See* Mahl, *supra* note 12, at 7.
14. Cook, *Anxiety, Speech Disturbances, and Speech Rate*, 8 BRIT. J. SOC. & CLINICAL PSYCH. 13, 19-20 (1969).
15. *See* Eldred & Price, *supra* note 12, at 117-20.

emotions.[16] By examining the amount of verbal output of the prospective jurors to questions posed by the attorneys, observers could determine with which side the prospective juror feels more comfortable.

Speed of speech and breath rate. Goldman-Eisler found that people talk noticeably faster after they have been asked an anxiety-arousing question, and that the interviewee's breathing is inhibited when he feels anxious or fearful.[17] This increase in the speed of speech and the inhibition of breathing could lead to noticeably labored breathing and indicate anxiety in reaction to the particular areas probed.

Pauses and latencies. A pause refers to a prolonged silence within a spoken sentence or phrase. Latency refers to the time between a question and the beginning of the interviewee's response to the question. Cassotta found that pauses and long latency periods are positively correlated with induced state anxiety and not with a personality trait type of anxiety.[18] This would be another fruitful approach for aiding in the analysis of a prospective juror's responses.

Kinesic Cues

Eye contact. The variable of eye contact as it relates to state anxiety has been researched by a number of investigators. Day maintains that when an interviewee is anxious, there is a marked increase in the frequency of lateral eye movements.[19] Kanfer felt that the average eye-blink increased when anxiety-arousing topics were discussed, although this increased rate declines with time.[20] Even more impressive is the work done in three studies, where it was discovered that when individuals are being deceitful, there is a decrease in the amount of visual interaction with others.[21]

The variable of eye contact, in addition to indicating anxiety and

---

16. *See generally* Howeler & Vrolijk, *Verbal Communication as an Index of Interpersonal Attraction,* 34 ACTA PSYCHOLOGICA 511, 514 (1970); Pope & Siegman, *supra* note 12, at 296; Wiens, Jackson, Manaugh & Matarazzo, *Communication Length as an Index of Communicator Attitude: A Replication,* 53 J. APPLIED PSYCH. 264, 264-65 (1969); Worthy, Gary & Kahn, *Self-Disclosure as an Exchange Process,* 13 J. PERSONALITY & SOCIAL PSYCH. 59, 61 (1969).

17. Goldman-Eisler, *Speech-Breathing Activity—A Measure of Tension and Affect During Interviews,* 46 BRIT. J. PSYCH. 53, 60-62 (1955).

18. Cassotta, *The Stability and Modification of the Vocal Behavior of Individuals in Stress and Nonstress Interviews,* 27B DISSERTATION ABSTRACTS 2867, 2868 (1966).

19. Day, *An Eye-Movement Indicator of Type and Level of Anxiety: Some Clinical Observations,* 23 J. CLINICAL PSYCH. 438, 439 (1967).

20. Kanfer, *Verbal Rate, Eye Blink, and Content in Structured Psychiatric Interviews,* 61 J. ABNORMAL & SOCIAL PSYCH. 341, 345-46 (1960).

21. Ekman & Friesen, *Nonverbal Leakage and Clues to Deception,* in NONVERBAL COMMUNICATION 269, 279 (S. Weitz ed. 1974); Exline, Thibaut, Brannon & Gumpert, *Visual Interaction in Relationship to Machiavellianism and an Unethical Act,* 16 AM. PSYCHOLOGIST 396, 396 (1961); Mehrabian, *Nonverbal Betrayal of Feeling,* 5 J. EXPERIMENTAL RESEARCH IN PERSONALITY 64, 70-73 (1971). An exception to this general proposition is the finding by Exline et al., *supra,* that people high in machiavellianism maintain as much eye contact when they are lying as when they are telling the truth.

deceitful behavior, can also be used to define the type of relationship which exists between two people. A number of investigators have found that increased eye contact indicates a positive feeling toward an individual.[22] Closely related to this finding are the results of Efran's work in which he found that individuals maintain more eye contact with people of whom they have a high expectancy of approval.[23] Efran's work is particularly important because of the nature of the voir dire. The average prospective juror enters the voir dire knowing none of the parties concerned, and thus should have no feelings, either positive or negative, toward any of the participants. His relative eye contact with the different attorneys, however, will indicate from whom he *expects* approval and a positive relationship. It is reasonable to assume that such an expectation of approval from an attorney representing a particular side is indicative of bias in favor of that side.

Facial cues. All of us, to some extent, attempt to read facial cues when we are trying to understand a person's true feelings. It is difficult to verbally specify exactly which expressions are indicative of which emotions, but there is considerable evidence to indicate that our common sense opinions of what constitutes negative or positive emotions in the face are indeed valid.[24] Ekman did a cross-cultural study and found that people universally attribute similar facial expressions to the emotions of happiness, sadness, anger, surprise, disgust, and fear.[25] These facial expressions arise spontaneously when people are involved in verbal behavior.[26]

The utility of using the facial cues of prospective jurors during the voir dire to analyze their responses is underscored by the work of Mehrabian and Ferris, Mehrabian, and Zaidel and Mehrabian. These investigators found that facial cues are much more effective in communicating a person's attitudes than either the verbal or paralinguistic portions (pitch, tone of voice, etc.) of the communication.[27] Some in-

---

22. *See generally* Argyle & Dean, *Eye Contact, Distance and Affiliation,* 28 SOCIOMETRY 289 (1965); Mehrabian, *A Semantic-Space for Nonverbal Behavior,* 35 J. CONSULTING & CLINICAL PSYCH. 248, 249 (1970); Mehrabian, *Some Referents and Measures of Nonverbal Behavior,* 1 BEHAVIOR RESEARCH METHODS & INSTRUMENTATION 203, 205 (1969). A word of caution is in order here. Ellsworth & Ross, *Intimacy in Response to Direct Gaze,* 11 J. EXPERIMENTAL SOCIAL PSYCH. 592, 608-10 (1975), have noted that a direct linear relationship between eye contact and intimacy appears to hold true only for women subjects. Males tend to view continuous eye-contact from another (particularly from other males) as threatening.

23. Efran, *Looking for Approval: Effects on Visual Behavior of Approbation from Persons Differing in Importance,* 10 J. PERSONALITY & SOCIAL PSYCH. 21, 24-25 (1968).

24. EKMAN, FRIESEN & ELLSWORTH, EMOTION IN THE HUMAN FACE 101 (1972).

25. Ekman & Friesen, *Constants Across Cultures in the Face and Emotion,* 17 J. PERSONALITY & SOCIAL PSYCH. 124, 128-29 (1971).

26. Ekman, *Body Position, Facial Expression, and Verbal Behavior During Interviews,* 68 J. ABNORMAL & SOCIAL PSYCH. 295, 301 (1964).

27. *See* Mehrabian, *Nonverbal Communication,* 19 NEBRASKA SYMPOSIUM ON MOTIVATION 107, 139-140 (1971); Mehrabian & Ferris, *Inference of Attitudes from Nonverbal Communication in Two Channels,* in NONVERBAL COMMUNICATION 291, 295-296 (S. Weitz ed. 1974); Zaidel &

vestigators have pointed out that facial cues show *what* emotion the individual is feeling whereas body cues show the *intensity* of a felt emotion.[28]

A note of caution must be made, however, in regard to facial cues. Ekman and Friesen have pointed out that while the face is the major site of affect displays, it is also the site which is under the most control of the individual.[29] Thus, if a person wished to disguise his true emotions, he could fairly easily display false emotions on his face. Body postures and movements are not as easily controlled, however, and also should be watched for signs of emotion. Fortunately, researchers have found that when the use of facial cues is precluded, body cues can be used effectively in perceiving emotional cues.[30] If the body cues contradict those given by the face, one must suspect deception by the prospective juror.

Body postures and movements. Body postures and movements are used by everyone whenever they interact with other individuals. Mehrabian has demonstrated that the concepts of immediacy and relaxation of body posture indicate an individual's attitude towards another person.[31] His concept of immediacy refers to the distance between individuals, forward lean, eye contact and whether or not an individual squarely faces the person with whom he is interacting. The more immediate a person's body orientation to another the more positive is the regard shown. A person's postural relaxation is indicated by arm position asymmetry (such as one hand in the lap and the other draped over the back of a chair), side-ways lean, leg position asymmetry, hand relaxation, neck relaxation, and a slight reclining angle. The more relaxed a person's body posture when interacting with another, the more positive is the regard shown. One exception to this description must be made, however. A slight reclining angle indicates positive regard for another while an extreme reclining angle indicates a hostile or more negative attitude.

Investigators have found that body movements are indicative of

Mehrabian, *The Ability to Communicate and Infer Positive and Negative Attitudes Facially and Vocally*, 3 J. EXPERIMENTAL RESEARCH IN PERSONALITY 233, 240 (1969).

28. Ekman, *Differential Communication of Affect by Head and Body Cues*, 2 J. PERSONALITY & SOCIAL PSYCH. 726, 734 (1965); Ekman & Friesen, *Head and Body Cues in the Judgement of Emotion: A Reformulation*, 24 PERCEPTUAL & MOTOR SKILLS 711, 717-22 (1967).

29. *See* Ekman & Friesen, *supra* note 22, at 280.

30. *See* Dittmann, Parloff & Boomer, *Facial and Bodily Expression: A Study of Receptivity of Emotional Cues*, 28 PSYCH. 239, 243-44 (1965); Ekman & Friesen, *supra* note 22, at 281.

31. *See* Mehrabian, *Significance of Posture and Position in the Communication of Attitude and Status Relationships*, 71 PSYCH. BULL. 359, 359-71 (1969); Mehrabian, *Relationship of Attitude to Seated Posture, Orientation and Distance*, 10 J. PERSONALITY & SOCIAL PSYCH. 26, 28-29 (1968); Mehrabian, *Orientation Behaviors and Nonverbal Attitude Communication*, 17 J. COM. 324, 330-31 (1967). Mehrabian & Friar, *Encoding of Attitude by a Seated Communicator via Posture and Position Cues*, 33 J. CONSULTING & CLINICAL PSYCH. 330, 335-36 (1969).

emotional arousal.[32] Still body positions occur either when there are low levels of arousal or when an act is inhibited and a tense position results. It could be safely assumed that if a prospective juror was trying to be deceptive, he would be emotionally aroused and this emotional arousal would become manifest either in an observable increase in body movements or in a tense, still body posture. Scheflen feels that postural changes serve as communication markers and can indicate changes in emotions and attitudes.[33]

Hand movements. Hand movement is another variable which could be used to detect deception on the part of prospective jurors during the voir dire. Freedman and Hoffman felt that body-focused activities such as finger-tapping, wringing of the hands, and manipulating various parts of the body with the hands function to modify sensory experience and may effect the state of body tension by relieving or intensifying it.[34] Ekman and Friesen examined the same type of hand movements and concluded that body-focused hand activities occur when an individual is in psychological discomfort or anxiety.[35] An increase in the frequency of body-focused hand movements by a prospective juror could indicate that the juror feels uncomfortable with a particular attorney or that he feels anxious because he is being deceitful.

Verbal Cues

Immediacy of language. Mehrabian's concept of immediacy in interaction was first introduced in regard to body posture. He also used the concept in regard to language as a measure of the directness and intensity of interaction between the communicator and the object of his communication.[36] Examples of the concept of non-immediacy in language are such things as: the speaker referring to the object of communication by using demonstrative pronouns such as "that" and "those"; referring to the object in past or future tense instead of the present tense; indicating that the relationship between the communicator and the object is imposed; referring to the relationship as possible rather than actual; indicating that only one aspect of the communicator is involved with the object; indicating that a group of people, including the

32. *See* Ekman, *supra* note 28, at 733-34; Ekman & Friesen, *supra* note 28, at 717-22.
33. Scheflen, *The Significance of Posture in Communication Systems*, 27 PSYCH. 316, 319-21 (1964).
34. Freedman & Hoffman, *Kinetic Behavior in Altered Clinical States: An Approach to Objective Analysis of Motor Behavior During Clinical Interviews*, 24 PERCEPTUAL & MOTOR SKILLS 527, 532-33, 537-38 (1967).
35. Ekman & Friesen, *Hand Movements*, 22 J. COM. 353, 359-63 (1972).
36. Mehrabian, *Immediacy: An Indicator of Attitudes in Linguistic Communication*, 34 J. PERSONALITY 26, 28 (1966).

communicator, is related to the object; and indicating that a group of objects including the object is related to the communicator.

Mehrabian and others have concluded that communications about affectively or evaluatively negative people or events contain more non-immediacy than communication about positive events or people.[37] The essential point which Mehrabian is making is that a style of language which places distance between the speaker and the topic of conversation indicates that the speaker feels negatively toward the topic of conversation. As an example of non-immediacy in language, consider the situation where two prospective jurors are questioned about any bias they may have against blacks. Juror 1 responds, "No, I don't think I'm prejudiced against blacks," while Juror 2 responds, "No, I don't think I'm prejudiced against those people." Mehrabian would assert that Juror 2 is exhibiting more non-immediacy (and thus, probably more negative emotions towards blacks) than Juror 1.

Applying the Kinesic, Paralinguistic and Verbal Measures During the Voir Dire

If it is observed that a prospective juror's communicative behavior indicates that he is feeling situational anxiety, such a result may be because: (a) he is anxious about being questioned by anyone in such a public forum; (b) he is anxious and has a negative emotional response to the particular person who is questioning him at the time; (c) he has some strong emotional feelings related to the particular subject matter being discussed at the time; or (d) he is being deceptive in his responses and is anxious about being found out.

By isolating the cause of the juror's anxiety (or lack of anxiety), a better impression of his suitability can be formed. One method of isolating the source of the anxiety is as follows. During the initial questioning by the judge and the attorneys, the interviewers invariably start out by asking the prospective juror questions to elicit background information such as his occupation, marital status, and where he lives. These questions are unlikely to evoke emotional and deceptive responses, and thus, this phase of the questioning may be used to obtain a baseline of the juror's repertoire of kinesic, paralinguistic, and verbal behaviors in response to questioning by the particular interviewer. During this questioning, the observers rate the communicative behavior of the juror in terms of being positive or negative toward the inter-

---

37. Mehrabian, *Attitudes Inferred from Neutral Verbal Communications*, 31 J. Consulting Psych. 414, 416-17 (1967); Mehrabian, *Attitudes Inferred from Non-Immediacy of Verbal Communications*, 6 J. Verbal Learning & Verbal Behavior 294, 294-95 (1967); Mehrabian & Wiener, *Non-immediacy Between Communicator and Object of Communication in a Verbal Message: Application to the Inference of Attitudes*, 30 J. Consulting Psych. 420, 424-25 (1966).

viewer. The following grid is an example of how the juror's responses may be coded.

Name	J	P	D
Eye Contact	+	+	+
Facial cues	0	+	−
Body orientation	+	+	0
Body movements	0	0	−
Body posture	0	+	−
Hand movements	+	+	+
Speech disturbances	0	0	0
Pauses & latencies	0	0	0
Speech output	0	+	0
Style of language	0	+	+

Column J = Juror's responses to baseline phase of questioning by the Judge.

Column P = Juror's responses to baseline phase of questioning by the Prosecuting or Plaintiff's Attorney.

Column D = Juror's responses to baseline phase of questioning by the Defense Attorney.

The authors have found it most convenient to use the 3-point (*i.e.*, negative, neutral and positive) scaling of communicative responses illustrated above. The ratings are guided by the criteria outlined in the previous sections, but a certain degree of subjectivity is invariably introduced in assigning a particular rating. To reduce the effects of subjectivity, it is best to have at least two observers independently rate each juror.

The juror's responses on these same dimensions are again rated when the interviewer asks attitudinal questions which are relevant to the case.[38] These questions will vary from case to case, but, in general, will deal with the prospective juror's dispositions toward the attorneys, litigants, and the legal and factual issues of the case.

The observers compare the juror's responses *within* each interview in an attempt to determine whether the juror has positive or negative feelings toward the attitudinal issues which were discussed. In other words, the observers attempt to determine whether and at what point in the interview the juror becomes positively or negatively aroused in his communicative behavior by comparing his baseline responses with his later responses. As an example, suppose that a prospective juror had emitted favorable responses toward the interviewer (the prosecuting attorney) during the baseline phase (i.e., direct eye contact, direct body orientation, relaxed body posture, an absence of body-focused hand ac-

---

38. Although the observers attend to the same behavioral dimensions during questioning relating to attitudes, the authors have found that it is impractical to employ a separate grid for the coding of responses to each line of questioning. The impracticality arises from the speed with which the voir dire is conducted and because attorneys frequently do not address the same questions to each juror. Our procedure during the attitudinal phase of questioning has been to note on a separate sheet of paper only the particularly revealing responses of jurors in regard to important attitudinal questions.

tivities, etc.), but when the interviewer asked him if he had formed an opinion about the guilt or innocence of the defendant, the juror said, "No," and averted his eyes, oriented his body away from the interviewer, became more tense in his body posture, and began to play with his ring. Given this large discrepancy between the juror's baseline response and his later response, it would seem fairly safe to conclude that the juror may well have an opinion as to the defendant's guilt or innocence, and that he was being deceptive in his response to the latter question. Further questioning would then be needed to probe the reason for this deception.

The observers also compare the juror's kinesic, paralinguistic and verbal behaviors *across* interviewers in an attempt to determine the juror's affective responses to the respective sides of the case. This determination merely involves a comparison of the juror's baseline behavior in response to questioning by each interviewer. Since the content of the baseline phase of questioning by each interviewer is usually very similar, differences in the juror's baseline behavior between interviewers is most probably reflective of the juror's affective response to the interviewer on an interpersonal level or as a representative of a particular viewpoint in the case.[39] From the observations within and across interviewers, the observers can rate the juror's suitability for either side.

PRACTICAL CONSIDERATIONS

Since the attorney who is actually conducting the voir dire must attend to his or her own performance, it will be next to impossible for him or her to make a systematic evaluation of the jurors' nonverbal behavior. Therefore, it will be necessary for the lead attorney to use other observers to make the evaluations. These observers should be seated as closely as possible to the prospective jurors and positioned so that they may have a head-on view of the jurors. If the observers are seated too far away or at an angle, it will be difficult for them to distinguish between a smile and a grimace or to determine with whom the prospective juror is making eye contact. It has been the authors' experience that the best place from which to make the observations is at the counsel table. If the observers are attorneys, their placement presents no problem. If the attorney chooses to employ psychologists or psychiatrists to make the observations, a frequently raised question is whether

---

39. As an example, the figure reproduced earlier, at page 639, *supra*, indicates that the juror is most responsive to the prosecuting attorney and least responsive to the defense attorney. By comparing the P and D columns it is easily seen that the juror's responses to the defense attorney were less favorable on the dimensions of facial cues, body orientation, body movements, body posture and speech output. On none of the dimensions were the juror's responses more favorable to the defense attorney than to the prosecuting attorney.

and how the social scientists should be introduced; the fear being that the jurors will react negatively toward psychologists or psychiatrists. It is our position that the presence of social science observers should be fully disclosed and explained to the jurors. In post-trial interviews conducted with numerous jurors in both civil and criminal cases, we have never encountered a juror who objected to or resented the presence of social scientists during the voir dire. Furthermore, it is possible that the announced presence of social scientists may have tactical advantages. One set of researchers has speculated that the visible use of social scientists during the voir dire may give the side using them a psychological boost and demoralize the opponents.[40] They also note that it is possible that the use of an unusual technique to pick a fair jury may create a bond between the jurors and the side which has used the technique to "certify" them as fair jurors.

If the observers elect to use the rating form which was presented earlier, we recommend that twelve to fourteen rating boxes be placed on a single legal size page. Given the usual rapid pace of voir dire and the number of ratings to be made on each juror, it is easier to make the ratings on four to five large pages than to be shuffling fifty or more single rating forms.

Finally, it should always be remembered that the use of this technique involves the evaluation of communication cues. The maximum use of the technique will be achieved when jurors are questioned with a view toward eliciting as much communication as possible from them. Open-ended questioning should be used whenever possible—i.e., "What are your feelings about the death penalty?" rather than "Do you have any negative feelings about the death penalty?" If a juror expresses an opinion which is antagonistic toward the position to be taken by the attorney, the attorney should refrain from using the juror's statement as a springboard to "educate" the jury until after the remaining jurors have been questioned on the same subject. If the jurors are "educated" too early, the remaining jurors may not disclose their true opinions out of fear of giving the "wrong" answer.

CONCLUSION

During the voir dire, lawyers typically seek to evaluate the suitability of prospective jurors by analyzing the verbal content of their responses to questioning. Psychological and communications research indicates, however, that the bulk of information communicated by an individual about his or her attitudes and emotions is transmitted

---

40. McConohay, Mullen & Frederick, *The Use of Social Science in Trials with Political and Racial Overtones: The Trial of Joan Little*, 41 LAW & CONTEMP. PROB. 205, 225 (1977).

through nonverbal behavior. Since the object of the voir dire is to determine the prospective jurors' attitudes and emotions in regard to the litigants and issues in the particular case at hand, the attorney would be well advised to focus his or her attention on the prospective jurors' nonverbal behavior in response to questioning. This Article has attempted to give a description of relevant communicative behaviors and a method by which those behaviors can be analyzed to determine a juror's suitability.

The behavioral criteria described above have been derived from a considerable body of prior research. This research has consistently demonstrated that there are common nonverbal indicators of interpersonal preferences, situational anxiety, and deception. It must be remembered, however, that these empirical findings have been obtained in the context of either clinical or experimental settings. The application of these findings to the context of the voir dire rings true at an intuitive level, yet there are potential problems. Because of the public nature of voir dire and the penalties involved for testifying falsely under oath, prospective jurors may be more circumspect about revealing themselves through their nonverbal behaviors than were the experimental subjects from whom the behavioral criteria for evaluation were derived. Thus it may be that prospective jurors are so guarded in their responses that use of the behavioral criteria will be ineffective. It is also possible that the stress generated by the setting of voir dire may increase the production of nonverbal behaviors indicative of anxiety and deception to the point that the behaviors may not be properly interpretable. The heightened stress may even change the quality of the relevant behaviors as well as their quantity. On the other hand, it is possible that the stress associated with voir dire works to the advantage of a systematic evaluation of nonverbal behavior in that the prospective jurors' defenses may be so taxed that they are less capable of disguising or controlling their nonverbal behaviors. Until these questions are rigorously evaluated through empirical research, this technique must still be considered as experimental.

Juror Self-Disclosure in the Voir Dire: A Social Science Analysis†

DAVID SUGGS*

BRUCE D. SALES**

The term "voir dire" has been translated as "to speak the truth"[1] or "to see them talk."[2] It refers to the preliminary examination of a potential witness or juror when his competence is in issue. It has also taken on the colloquial meaning of referring to the entire stage of trial in which jurors are empaneled. To convey this latter meaning, many people use the term "jury selection" rather than voir dire, which incorrectly implies that the jury is actively selected. In fact, the jury is not "selected," but is composed of persons who were not rejected through a process of exclusion.[3] During voir dire, questions are put to prospective jurors by the attorneys or judge or both; after this time, the attorneys may exercise challenges to remove particular jurors from the panel. Those remaining after the exercise of these challenges comprise the jury.

There are two types of challenges which may be made to remove prospective jurors—challenges for cause and peremptory challenges. A challenge for cause is successful whenever it is shown that the juror does not satisfy statutory requirements for jury service[4] or that the

† Preparation of this article was partially supported by a grant from the National Institute of Mental Health, Center for Studies for Crime and Delinquency.

* B.A. 1975, J.D. 1979, Ph. D. 1980, University of Nebraska at Lincoln. Associate of Donovan, Leisure, Newton & Irvine, New York, NY.

** B.A. 1966, Ph. D. 1971, University of Rochester; J.D. 1973, Northwestern University. Professor, University of Nebraska College of Law and Department of Psychology; Director of Law-Psychology Graduate Training Program.

[1] BLACK'S LAW DICTIONARY 1746 (4th ed. 1968).

[2] Zeisel & Diamond, *The Effect of Peremptory Challenges on the Jury and Verdict: An Experiment in a Federal District Court*, 30 STAN. L. REV. 491, 491 n.1 (1978) (noting that this is an incorrect translation).

[3] "The right to challenge is the right to reject, not the right to select." 1 F. BUSCH. LAW AND TACTICS IN JURY TRIALS § 74 (encyc. ed. 1959).

[4] A person does not become eligible for jury duty until he has reached the minimum age prescribed by statute. *See, e.g.*, ALA. CODE § 12-16-60(a)(1) (Supp. 1980) (19 years); CONN. GEN. STAT. ANN. § 51-217 (Supp. 1980) (18 years). Nonresidents are usually excluded from jury duty, *see, e.g.*, IND. CODE § 33-4-5-7 (1976), and some states exempt various government officials, *see, e.g.*, CONN. GEN. STAT. ANN. § 51-219 (Supp. 1980), and attorneys, *see, e.g., id.*, from serving as jurors. In addition, grounds for challenges for cause commonly provided for by statute include: conviction of a felony, *see, e.g.*, ALA. CODE § 12-16-150(5) (1975); indictment for a similar offense within a fixed time, *see, e.g., id.* § 12-16-150(3); having scruples against capital punishment, *see, e.g.*, IND. CODE § 35-1-30-4(3) (Supp. 1980); relation by blood or affinity to a party in interest, *see, e.g., id.* § 35-1-30-4(4), or to any attorney in the case, *see, e.g.*, ALA. CODE § 12-16-150(4), (11) (1975); previous jury service within a year, *see, e.g.*,

juror is so biased or prejudiced that he cannot render a fair and impartial verdict based on the law and evidence as presented at trial.[5] Attorneys may make an unlimited number of challenges for cause during voir dire. When a challenge is made, it is up to the judge to determine its validity. In addition, the judge may remove a juror for cause *sua sponte*.

For several reasons, the use of challenges for cause is inadequate to remove those jurors who may have significant biases or prejudices. First, assuming that the juror is willing to admit to being biased or prejudiced, the judge may decide that the juror is not so biased or prejudiced as to be incompetent to serve on the jury as a matter of law. Second, if the juror admits that he has formed an opinion about the case, it is standard procedure to ask if he can set aside that opinion and decide the case on the basis of the evidence to be presented.[6] Since all of us like to think we can be fair, it is the rare juror indeed who will admit to being unable to set aside an already formed opinion. Nevertheless, challenges for cause are rarely sustained when the juror maintains that he can be impartial. Third, the problem of using challenges for cause to eliminate jurors is further complicated by the fact that "[j]urors often, either consciously or unconsciously, lie on *voir dire*."[7]

Since challenges for cause are so infrequently sustained, the exercise of peremptory challenges remains the chief means for securing an impartial jury. Unlike challenges for cause, the number of peremptory challenges allowed is limited by statute.[8] No explanation need be given for the use of a peremptory challenge, and attorneys may use their allotted challenges for whatever tactical reasons they desire.[9] Theoretically, after the attorneys have exercised their peremptory challenges, those jurors who were most biased will have been eliminated, and the resulting jury will be relatively impartial.

In order to exercise their peremptory challenges intelligently, at-

---

IND. CODE § 35-1-30-4(15) (Supp. 1980); and solicitation of service as a juror, *see, e.g., id.* § 35-1-30-4(10).

[5] *See, e.g.*, CONN. GEN. STAT. ANN. § 51-240 (Supp. 1980).

[6] *See, e.g.*, IND. CODE § 35-1-3-4(2) (Supp. 1980).

[7] Broeder, *Voir Dire Examinations: An Empirical Study*, 38 S. CAL. L. REV. 503, 528 (1965).

[8] *See, e.g.*, IND. CODE § 34-1-20-7 (1976); *id.* §§ 35-1-30-2 to -3. Peremptory challenges are regarded as a privilege granted by legislative authority and a litigant may exercise them as a matter of right only to the extent authorized by the legislature. *See* Kunk v. Howell, 40 Tenn. App. 183, 189, 289 S.W.2d 847, 877 (1956).

[9] Note, *Limiting the Peremptory Challenge: Representation of Groups on Petit Juries*, 86 YALE L.J. 1715, 1715, 1718 (1977). A few recent cases, however, have held that some uses of peremptory challenges may be impermissible. *See, e.g.*, People v. Wheeler, 22 Cal. 3d 258, 583 P.2d 748, 148 Cal. Rptr. 890 (1978) (systematic use of peremptory challenges by prosecutor to eliminate blacks from jury denied defendant the right to jury representing a fair cross-section of the community).

torneys must gain information through voir dire regarding jurors' attitudes toward the opposing litigants, counsel for both sides and the legal and factual issues which are relevant to the case. Yet attorneys do not receive adequate information through voir dire upon which to base their peremptory challenges. One study concludes that "[*v*]*oir dire* was grossly ineffective not only in weeding out 'unfavorable' jurors but even in eliciting the data which would have shown particular jurors as very likely to prove 'unfavorable.'"[10] Another study summarizes:

> [O]n the whole, the voir dire, as conducted in these trials did not provide sufficient information for attorneys to identify prejudiced jurors. The average performance score of the prosecution was near the zero point . . . , indicating an inability to distinguish potential bias; defense counsel performed only slightly better . . . . Perhaps most significant is the inconsistent performance of attorneys. Occasionally, one side performed well in a case in which the other side performed poorly, thereby frustrating the law's expectation that the adversary allocation of challenges will benefit both sides equally.[11]

Given that the typical voir dire does not produce sufficient information to identify prejudiced jurors, the question becomes why this is so. This article will answer this question by first asserting that voir dire may be ideally characterized as a self-disclosure interview because it purports to obtain background and attitudinal information which might affect a juror's decision in the case. The balance of this article will then demonstrate that the procedures used during voir dire and the psychological atmosphere in which it takes place are virtually guaranteed to inhibit rather than facilitate such self-disclosure. To support this thesis, a number of variables will be examined: first, whether the voir dire is conducted by the attorneys or by the judge; second, whether the potential jurors are questioned as a group, as individuals within a group or individually; third, the interaction distance between the prospective jurors and the interviewer; and fourth, the environmental characteristics of the room in which the questioning takes place. For each of these variables, the current legal practice and its rationale will be examined. Research from social science literature tending to indicate that the current legal practice discourages self-disclosure during voir dire will then be presented. The research presented is not specifically addressed to the issue of juror self-disclosure. Rather, it is basic social science research which has been undertaken to explore the determinants of self-disclosure in clinical and experimental settings. Although application of the conclusions of this research to the setting of the courtroom involves extrapolation, the extent of the research and the consistency of its

---

[10] Broeder, *supra* note 7, at 505.
[11] Zeisel & Diamond, *supra* note 2, at 528-29.

results are great enough to raise serious questions as to the validity of current voir dire practices. Finally, a number of recommendations will be made for modifying the current practices to enhance self-disclosure by jurors and, thus, facilitate the intelligent exercise of peremptory challenges by attorneys.

THE PURPOSES OF VOIR DIRE

There are three judicially sanctioned purposes for voir dire. The first two are related to causal challenges while the third is related to the exercise of peremptories. First, voir dire may always be used for the purpose of determining whether the juror satisfies statutory requirements for serving on a jury.[12] Second, jurors may also be questioned to determine if they can impartially participate in the deliberation on the issues of the case based solely on the law and evidence as presented at trial.[13] This second purpose is mandated by the sixth amendment guarantee of the right to trial by an impartial jury.[14] Nevertheless, the extent of questioning allowed for this purpose is restricted to determining if the juror is biased or prejudiced as a matter of law.[15] Often, when the judge conducts questioning of this type, it will simply take the form: "'Can you be fair?' Once the juror has answered 'Yes,' everything else is considered irrelevant and the judge passes on to the next juror, even though Adolph Hitler himself would have answered that question in the affirmative."[16]

The third, and final, judicially sanctioned purpose of voir dire is to provide the attorney with a procedure by which he may obtain information to exercise the peremptory challenges intelligently.[17] The scope of

---

[12] 2 A. AMSTERDAM, B. SECAL & M. MILLER, TRIAL MANUAL FOR THE DEFENSE OF CRIMINAL CASES § 328 (1967).

[13] Hare, *Voir Dire and Jury Selection*, 29 ALA. LAW. 160, 173 (1968).

[14] *See* Witherspoon v. Illinois, 391 U.S. 510, 518, 521 (1968).

[15] A prejudiced juror is one who has actually decided how he will rule in the case before the trial. A biased juror, on the other hand, has an inclination to favor one side over the other. If the juror admits that he has already decided on what the outcome of the case should be, the juror may be excluded as a matter of law. In order to be successful in challenging a prospective juror for cause on the ground of bias, however, it is necessary to show that the bias is of such a magnitude as to lead to the natural inference that the juror will not act impartially. *See generally* Flowers v. Flowers, 397 S.W.2d 121 (Tex. Civ. App. 1965).

[16] Garry, *Attacking Racism in Court Before Trial*, in MINIMIZING RACISM IN JURY TRIALS xv, xxii (A. Ginger 1969).

[17] *See* Evans v. Mason, 82 Ariz. 40, 46, 308 P.2d 245, 249 (1957); ABA PROJECT ON MINIMUM STANDARDS FOR CRIMINAL JUSTICE, STANDARDS RELATING TO TRIAL BY JURY § 2.4 (1968). *See also* MacGutman, *The Attorney-Conducted Voir Dire of Jurors: A Constitutional Right*, 39 BROOKLYN L. REV. 290 (1972); Van Dyke, *Voir Dire: How Should It Be Conducted to Ensure that Our Juries Are Representative and Impartial?*, 3 HASTINGS CONST. L.Q. 65 (1976); Comment, *Court Control over the Voir Dire Examination of Prospective Jurors*, 15 DE PAUL L. REV. 107 (1965).

Some jurisdictions, however, do not sanction this purpose, and allow only questions

questioning for this purpose is much broader than that associated with challenges for cause. For example, under this rubric questioning is often allowed to probe the juror's occupation, marital status, number of children, past jury service, residence, exposure to news coverage of the case, attitudes toward the death penalty, degree of belief in the concept that the defendant is innocent until proven guilty and attitudes toward racial minorities.[18]

The broader scope of permissible questioning for this purpose results from the importance of peremptory challenges, and the courts have frequently recognized this importance. In *Swain v. Alabama*,[19] for example, the United States Supreme Court stated: "The persistence of peremptories and their extensive use demonstrate the long and widely held belief that peremptory challenge is a necessary part of trial by jury."[20] This use of voir dire to gain information for peremptory challenges is based on the recognition by the law that

> the rules of evidence can only partly limit the extent to which a juror's bias affects his deliberation. The tests which the law furnishes to the jury for weighing evidence are crude and imperfect and provide few internal checks on jury prejudice. There is a critical area in every case, where a juror must rely on his own experience to reach a decision. If bias permeates a juror's thinking, it may distort the importance of evidence consistent with it. . . . Bias may, therefore, be a fact of singular importance in the case.[21]

The notion that verdicts are frequently affected by the jurors' values and biases is supported by a report that "in about two-thirds of all cases the jurors are likely to differ over the significance of the evidence presented to them in the trial. In only about one-third of the trials is the jury unanimous on the first ballot; in two-thirds of the cases the jurors differ in their vote."[22]

In addition to the above three approved purposes, voir dire is often used for reasons which are not judicially sanctioned. Some attorneys

---

which might uncover legal grounds for challenges for cause. 2 A. AMSTERDAM, B. SEGAL & M. MILLER, *supra* note 12, § 334. In these jurisdictions, "any enlightenment given by the answers which serves to inform counsel's judgment on the intelligent exercise of peremptory challenges is at best a by-product, and often one suspiciously regarded." *Id.* See also Van Dyke, *supra*, at 89-90.

[18] For general discussions of the proper scope of voir dire, see 2 A. AMSTERDAM, B. SEGAL & M. MILLER, *supra* note 12, §§ 334, 336; 1 F. BUSCH. *supra* note 3, § 84; Bodin, *Selecting a Jury*, in CIVIL LITIGATION AND TRIAL TECHNIQUES 211, 225-62 (H. Bodin ed. 1976).

[19] 380 U.S. 202 (1965).

[20] *Id.* at 219.

[21] *See* MacGutman, *supra* note 17, at 303-04. The concept of bias used here is the same as that referred to in the challenge for cause, *see* note 15 *supra*, with the exception that the attorney does not have to prove that the juror will not act impartially before exercising a peremptory challenge.

[22] Zeisel & Diamond, *The Jury in the Mitchell-Stans Conspiracy Trial*, [1976] AM. B. FOUNDATION RESEARCH J. 151, 173 (footnote omitted).

abuse the voir dire by using it as a means to ingratiate themselves with the jurors and to indoctrinate the jurors to their version of the case before the presentation of evidence.[23] Attempts at ingratiation may take a variety of forms. The "grandstand play" occurs when the attorney declines the opportunity to question the prospective jurors, announcing his faith in the jury system and in that particular panel.[24] This method is not often employed, however, and jurors tend to regard an attorney who uses this method as careless in his treatment of the case.[25] More commonly employed methods of ingratiation include such obvious strategies as exaggerated courtesy extended to members of the panel, concerned but polite questioning as to the health of the older members, joking with the panel and making it known that the jurors and the attorney have mutual acquaintances or associations. Attorneys also use voir dire to attempt to indoctrinate the prospective jurors. For example, one author recommends that attorneys use voir dire to teach jurors important facts, to expose damaging facts in the case in order to reduce their impact, to instruct jurors as to the law involved and to force jurors to face their own prejudices.[26]

A minimum level of rapport between the person conducting voir dire and the jurors is necessary for a productive dialogue. However, at the point at which the establishment of effective rapport becomes an attempt at ingratiation, it becomes unacceptable and should be guarded against. Likewise, while the jurors must be given some minimum level of introduction to the facts of the case during voir dire since the questioning cannot take place in a vacuum, this introduction should not be allowed to become indoctrination in the pejorative sense. The concern of the judiciary over these two unacceptable purposes of voir dire seems to be somewhat justified. A study of a number of cases in a midwestern federal district court concludes that attorneys use about eighty percent of voir dire time indoctrinating the jury panel.[27] The study adds, however, that such indoctrination attempts by the attorneys often do not appear to succeed.[28]

ATTORNEY-CONDUCTED AS OPPOSED TO JUDGE-CONDUCTED VOIR DIRE

Traditionally, the questioning of jurors during voir dire was left to at-

---

[23] *See* Blunk & Sales, *Persuasion During the Voir Dire*, in PSYCHOLOGY IN THE LEGAL PROCESS 39 (B. Sales ed. 1977); Field, *Voir Dire Examinations—A Neglected Art*, 33 U. MO. KAN. CITY L. REV. 171 (1965).

[24] *See* M. BELLI, MODERN TRIALS § 121, at 803 (1954).

[25] *Id.* at 804.

[26] *See* A. GINGER, JURY SELECTION IN CRIMINAL TRIALS §§ 7.18-.21 (1975).

[27] Broeder, *supra* note 7, at 522.

[28] *Id.* at 522-23.

torneys.[29] In recent years, however, there has been a move away from attorney-conducted and toward judge-conducted voir dire. At present, only nineteen states allow attorneys to exercise primary control over the conduct of voir dire in both civil and criminal cases.[30] In fifteen states, the judge has unfettered control, although attorneys may submit questions for the judge to ask.[31] The judge, in his discretion, may or may not ask the questions or, alternatively, may allow the attorneys to directly question jurors after he has questioned them. The remaining jurisdictions divide the responsibility for conducting voir dire between the judge and the attorneys. Usually this means that the judge will begin by asking standard questions and then the attorneys will be allowed to ask their own questions concerning particular matters important to the case at hand.

In the federal system, judges may allow attorneys to conduct voir dire, but are not obligated to do so.[32] In the event the judge elects to conduct the voir dire himself, he is required to allow the attorneys to supplement the examination or to submit further questions to be asked by the judge. Nevertheless, the scope of supplemental questioning lies in the discretion of the judge. In fact, by 1977, "approximately three-fourths of federal judges conduct voir dire examinations without oral participation by counsel."[33] It would seem that the trend toward increasing judicial control over the conduct of voir dire is continuing; a 1970 report revealed that at that time only fifty-six per cent of the federal district judges reported that they conducted the voir dire without oral participation by counsel.[34]

One of the justifications given for this recent shift is that it prevents attorneys from abusing the voir dire process. Those who support judge-conducted voir dire argue:

> [It] saves time, promotes respect for the court, brings the judge into greater prominence at the very outset, reveals that an impartial court can obtain an impartial jury better than partisan counsel, that extended individual questioning by counsel may embarrass or even

[29] *See* McGuirk & Tober, *Attorney-Conducted Voir Dire: Securing an Impartial Jury*, 15 N.H. B.J. 1, 4 (1973).

[30] *See* Van Dyke, *supra* note 17, at 95-97.

[31] *See id.*

[32] *See* FED. R. CIV. PROC. 47(a); FED. R. CRIM. PROC. 24(a).

[33] G. BERMANT, CONDUCT OF THE VOIR DIRE EXAMINATION 6 (Federal Judicial Center Pub. 1977).

[34] *See* COMMITTEE ON THE OPERATION OF THE JURY SYSTEM, JUDICIAL CONFERENCE OF THE UNITED STATES, REPORT ON VOIR DIRE PROCEDURES (1970). There are regional differences in the degree of counsel participation allowed. G. BERMANT, *supra* note 33, at 5-20. Federal district courts sitting in states which allow attorney participation in the state courts are more likely to allow a greater degree of attorney involvement in the federal voir dire. *Id.* at 10-13.

insult the juror, or that he may become brainwashed and committed by counsel before any evidence has been heard.[35]

There is no question but that abuse by attorneys of voir dire through ingratiation and indoctrination attempts will be completely eliminated by judge-conducted voir dire. In addition, the assertion that judge-conducted voir dire saves time is supported by data. In a direct comparison of voir dires conducted by attorneys and judges, one study finds that judge-conducted voir dire results in a significant savings of time.[36] Yet, there is no objective data to support the assertion that a judge is more likely than partisan counsel to obtain an impartial jury. It is also doubtful that any attorney would intentionally embarass or insult a prospective juror, since such conduct would alienate not only that particular juror, but also the remaining jurors who witness the event.

Those who support the attorney-conducted voir dire argue that inquiry into the biases of jurors requires the interviewer to have a thorough knowledge of the legal issues involved in the case and of the evidence to be presented by both sides. Because the trial judge does not, and should not, have such knowledge at the time of voir dire, it has been argued that he is not as competent as the attorneys to question the jurors.[37] In addition, some commentators argue that judges do not ask pressing or probing questions about the jurors' attitudes and that, "[e]ither because of institutional pressures to keep their calendars moving or because of their lack of sympathy to one or both of the litigants, many judges question prospective jurors without much interest or enthusiasm, hoping that a panel can be quickly assembled and that the trial can begin."[38] Studies which report that judge-conducted voir dire saves time have been criticized because, if the studies are examined as a whole, no conclusive proof exists one way or the other. Even though some studies do show a statistically significant savings of time through the use of judge-conducted voir dire, the time differences are not dramatic when compared to the overall length of the trial.[39]

Finally, supporters of attorney-conducted voir dire argue that it is unnecessary to eliminate attorney participation simply because attorneys

---

[35] Braswell, *Voir Dire—Use and Abuse*, 7 WAKE FOREST L. REV. 49, 54 (1970); *see* Levit, Nelson, Ball & Chernick, *Expediting Voir Dire: An Empirical Study*, 44 S. CAL. L. REV. 916 (1971); Note, *Judge Conducted* Voir Dire *as a Time-Saving Trial Technique*, 2 RUT.-CAM. L.J. 161 (1970).

[36] *See* Levit, Nelson, Ball & Chernick, *supra* note 35, at 946-49.

[37] *See* MacGutman, *supra* note 17, at 327-28; Padawer-Singer, Singer & Singer, *Voir Dire by Two Lawyers: An Essential Safeguard*, 57 JUDICATURE 386, 391 (1974); Comment, *The Jury Voir Dire: Useless Delay or Valuable Technique*, 11 S.D. L. REV. 306, 317-18 (1966).

[38] Van Dyke, *supra* note 17, at 76.

[39] *See id.* at 88-89 (noting that what little court time was saved by judge-conducted voir dire was made up for by additional pretrial conferences).

have been known to abuse it. A number of commentators point out that the conduct of the voir dire has always been subject to the judicial discretion of the courts.[40] Thus, the judge has the power to curtail any attorney abuse of the voir dire.

Social Science Research Relevant to a Determination of Who Should Conduct Voir Dire

There is a considerable body of basic research investigating how status differentials and reinforcement techniques affect self-disclosure in interview situations. There is also a considerable body of research which illustrates how attitudes may be communicated to others through nonverbal communication. This research indicates that attorneys are probably better suited to conduct the voir dire.

Status Differentials Between the Judge and Attorneys

The judge obviously has the highest status of anyone in the courtroom. He is physically separated from and elevated above everyone else, and is addressed by jurors and attorneys alike as "your honor." One psychological study seems to indicate that the judge would be the more appropriate interviewer to elicit juror self-disclosure.[41] It finds that both males and females disclose more to a high-status male interviewer than to one of low status.[42] On the other hand, the status level of female interviewers does not appear to affect the amount of self-disclosure from either male or female subjects. Since there are currently more male judges and attorneys than there are female judges and attorneys, the judge, having a higher status than the attorney would appear to be the more appropriate interviewer in most cases.

Other studies, however, indicate that there is a curvilinear relationship between the status of the interviewer and interviewee and the amount of self-disclosure; too great a status differential between the interactants may lead to an interviewing bias effect.[43] One study on bias in information interviews states:

> [B]ias is likely to occur in the interview when there is social distance between interviewer and respondent. Status distance and threatening questions may create a situation in which the respondent feels pressure to answer in the direction he believes will conform to the opinions or expectations of the interviewer. . . .

---

[40] *See, e.g.,* Comment, *supra* note 17, at 110; Comment, *supra* note 37, at 318.

[41] *See* Brooks, *Interactive Effects of Sex and Status on Self-Disclosure,* 21 J. COUNSELING PSYCH. 469, 473 (1974).

[42] *Id.*

[43] *See, e.g.,* Williams, *Interviewer Role Performance: A Further Note on Bias in the Information Interview,* 32 PUB. OPINION Q. 287 (1968).

> It would seem likely that the role performance of the interviewer could either enhance or mitigate the biasing effects of status characteristics and potentially threatening questions.[44]

Furthermore, another study finds that liking for a person will vary as a function of perceived similarity.[45] A large status differential between the interactants will most likely reduce perceived similarity and, in turn, the degree of self-disclosure. Finally, it has been found that such interviewer biasing effects are greatest when the respondent perceives the social distance between himself and the interviewer to be either very large or very small.[46] When social distance is very large, the respondent may hedge opinions out of fear of retaliation from a more powerful interviewer. On the other hand, when the social distance is very small, he may hedge opinions so as not to alienate an equal.

While the lawyer is in a higher status position in the courtroom as compared to the prospective jurors, he is at an intermediate social distance from the jurors as compared to the judge. It is probable that attorneys will be seen by the jurors as more similar to themselves than is the judge. Given these circumstances, it appears that attorneys would be better suited than the judge to interview prospective jurors and elicit self-disclosure.

Role Differentials Between the Judge and Attorneys

The judge has an extremely difficult role to fulfill, both intellectually and emotionally. He must be the arbiter of fine points of law, coordinate the activities of all parties to facilitate a just result and remain above interparty rivalries, all of which require that he remain aloof and emotionally detached. In fact, the judge's physical placement in the courtroom and the use of somber black robes probably evolved to foster such detachment. The attorneys, on the other hand, are free to modulate openness and familiarity with prospective jurors without compromising role requirements. Indeed, the flamboyant and expansive lawyer is a part of American folklore. Thus, attorneys are capable of interacting with prospective jurors either in a warm and friendly manner, or in an aggressive manner, depending on what the situation requires.

Common sense dictates that people prefer to talk to and will reveal more of themselves to warm and friendly people, than they will to those who are aloof and emotionally detached. This view is supported by a

---

[44] *Id.* at 287-88 (footnotes omitted).

[45] *See* Knecht, Lippman & Swap, *Similarity, Attraction, and Self-Disclosure,* 8 PROCEEDINGS OF THE 81ST ANNUAL CONVENTION OF THE APA 205 (1973).

[46] Dohrenwend, Colombotos & Dohrenwend, *Social Distance and Interview Effects,* 32 PUB. OPINION Q. 410 (1968).

number of psychological studies.[47] Since an attorney can manipulate his behavior to appear warm and friendly to prospective jurors, whereas the judge runs the risk of compromising his role performance if he acts in that way, it would seem that attorneys are better suited for the role of the interviewer.

Furthermore, because of the greater flexibility in behavior allowed to the attorney in his role as the interviewer, he is in a better position to positively reinforce the prospective jurors' self-disclosure. For example, it has been shown that nonverbal stimuli, such as head-nodding and mm-hmming which indicate interest in what the interviewee is saying stimulate longer speech.[48] Increased eye contact, less physical distance, relaxed posture and a direct orientation of the interviewer's body toward the interviewee all serve to reinforce the interviewee and, thus, elicit more verbalization and presumably more self-disclosure from him.[49] A word of caution is in order, however, in regard to eye contact. Another study indicates that a direct linear relationship between eye contact and intimacy appears to hold only for women subjects: males view continuous eye contact, especially from other males, as threatening.[50] Other research reveals that increased body motion on the part of male therapeutic counselors generates more self-disclosure from subjects, while low levels of body motion on the part of female counselors enhances subject self-disclosure.[51]

The judge would not be at a disadvantage, as compared to the attorneys, in rendering the nonverbal types of positive reinforcement to prospective jurors. But his role requirements and physical placement within the courtroom preclude him from administering some of the other types of reinforcement. For example, the judge's placement behind the bench may prevent him from directly facing the jurors and the fact that he wears a robe may obscure expressive body motions and relaxed body posture. Attorneys, on the other hand, can get out from behind the table, approach the jury[52] and engage in all of the nonverbal

---

[47] *See, e.g.*, Pope & Siegman, *Interviewer Warmth and Verbal Communication in the Initial Interview*, 2 PROCEEDINGS OF THE 75TH ANNUAL CONVENTION OF THE APA 245 (1967); Simonson, *The Impact of Therapist Disclosure on Patient Disclosure*, 23 J. COUNSELING PSYCH. 3 (1976); Worthy, Gary & Kahn, *Self-Disclosure as an Exchange Process*, 13 J. PERSONALITY & SOC. PSYCH. 59 (1969).

[48] *See* Matarazo, *The Interview*, in HANDBOOK OF CLINICAL PSYCHOLOGY 403, 443-44 (B. Wolman ed. 1965).

[49] *See* Mehrabian, *A Semantic Space for Nonverbal Behavior*, 35 J. CONSULTING & CLINICAL PSYCH. 248 (1970); Reece & Whitman, *Expressive Movements, Warmth and Verbal Reinforcement*, 64 J. ABNORMAL & SOC. PSYCH. 234 (1962).

[50] Ellsworth & Ross, *Intimacy in Response to Direct Gaze*, 11 J. EXPERIMENTAL SOC. PSYCH. 592 (1975).

[51] *See* Gardner, The Effects of Body Motion, Sex of Counselor, and Sex of Subject on Counselor Attractiveness and Subject's Self-Disclosure (1973) (unpublished manuscript on file at Univ. of Wyo.).

[52] Some judges, however, may restrict the attorneys' movements by requiring, for example, that they remain behind a podium.

methods of reinforcement without appearing artificial or out of character.

As noted above, in addition to an ability to interact with the jurors in a warm and empathic manner, attorneys are better able to interrogate them in an aggressive style without compromising their role. If the interviewer suspects that a juror is lying and is unable to confirm this through friendly questioning, resort to aggressive tactics may be called for. This tactic is supported by the results of a study on the effects of induced anxiety which concludes that individuals tend to regress in stressful situations and respond to stimuli as they have done in the past.[53] Thus, a prospective juror with long-held prejudices might be more likely to admit them in a stressful situation engineered by the attorney's aggressive questioning. A further advantage of the occasional use of aggressive questioning is found in research on psychiatric interviews, which concludes that high anxiety questions produce a higher verbal output than do neutral questions.[54]

From a psychological viewpoint, it appears that more self-disclosure from prospective jurors would be produced by allowing attorneys, rather than the judge, to conduct voir dire. Attorneys are at a moderate social distance from the jurors thus minimizing interviewer biasing effects and they are able to modulate their interviewing behavior to positively reinforce or attack juror responses as necessary.

Ability to Prejudice Jurors Through Nonverbal Communication

In the preceding sections, it was concluded that attorneys are better suited to conduct voir dire because they are in a position to facilitate the jurors' self-disclosure. This section illustrates that exclusion of attorneys from the voir dire process may lead to bias on the part of jurors resulting from the judge's unintentional communication of whatever biases he may have. To explain this point, it is first necessary to refer to Kalven and Zeisel's classic empirical study[55] of the jury's decisionmaking process. The study, in comparing juries' actual decisions with judges' opinions of how the juries should have decided the cases, finds that juries and judges concur in their decisions about seventy-five percent of the time.[56] This level of concurrence persists even when the juries are confronted with difficult evidentiary and legal issues, which leads to the conclusion that juries are capable of understanding difficult cases.[57] There is, however, an alternative explanation for the high

---

[53] See Beier, The Effect of Induced Anxiety on Flexibility of Intellectual Functioning, 65 PSYCH. MONOGRAPHS, Whole No. 326, at 17-18 (1951).

[54] Kanfer, Verbal Rate, Eye Blink, and Content in Structured Psychiatric Interviews, 61 J. ABNORMAL & SOC. PSYCH. 341, 347 (1960).

[55] See H. KALVEN & H. ZEISEL, THE AMERICAN JURY (1966).

[56] Id. at 56, 63.

[57] Id.

degree of concurrence between jury and judge decisions: "[J]udge/jury concurrence may result, at least in part, because the judge subtly and unintentionally conveys to the jury his feelings about the parties and participants in the case and because the jury is influenced by his cues."[58]

The judge may communicate feelings and attitudes about the litigants to the jury through kinesic and paralinguistic behavior. Kinesic behavior, or body language, includes: facial expressions, body posture, body movements, body orientation and hand movements. Paralinguistic behavior includes aspects of speech such as: pitch and tone of voice, pauses and latencies, loudness, tempo and breathing patterns. Both types of behavior are normal components of communicative behavior. Indeed, these behaviors constitute well over half of an individual's total communicative behavior and operate to communicate interpersonal attitudes, express emotions, indicate mutual attentiveness, provide feedback and provide illustrations for speech.[59] Furthermore, these behaviors are for the most part beyond the individual's control. Thus, even if one actively attempts to hide feelings, research indicates that the attitudes and emotions will continue to escape through nonverbal behavior.[60] Not only are nonverbal cues sent by everyone, but nonverbal messages are received and interpreted by others; even untrained observers are able to accurately decode a sender's nonverbal cues.[61] The decoding process is, like the sending of cues, largely unconscious.

The significance of this communication research is enhanced when its findings are coupled with the findings of research concerning experimenter biasing effects. In the last fifteen years, there has been a considerable concern among psychologists that experimenters might be subtly influencing their subjects' responses. In fact, research shows that experimenters will often unintentionally influence the subject to make a "correct" response.[62] This phenomenon is explained by the fact that the experimenter's unintentional actions seem to be reciprocated by attempts on the part of subjects to search for and respond to the experimenter's influence. Research on evaluation apprehension demonstrates that this phenomenon is enhanced when a subject is confronted

---

[58] Note, *Judge's Nonverbal Behavior in Jury Trials: A Threat to Judicial Impartiality,* 61 VA. L. REV. 1266, 1267 (1975).

[59] *See* M. ARGYLE, SOCIAL INTERACTION 110-14 (1969).

[60] *See, e.g.,* Ekman & Friesen, *Nonverbal Leakage and Clues to Deception,* 32 PSYCH. 88 (1969).

[61] P. EKMAN, W. FRIESEN & P. ELLSWORTH, EMOTION IN THE HUMAN FACE: GUIDELINES FOR RESEARCH AND AN INTEGRATION OF FINDINGS 77-108 (1972).

[62] *See* Duncan, Rosenberg & Finkelstein, *The Paralanguage of Experimenter Bias,* 32 SOCIOMETRY 207 (1969); Masling, *Differential Indoctrination of Examiners and Rorschach Responses,* 29 J. CONSULTING PSYCH. 198 (1965); Rosenberg, *The Conditions and Consequences of Evaluation Apprehension,* in ARTIFACT AND BEHAVIORAL RESEARCH 279 (R. Rosenthal & R. Rosnow eds. 1969); Rosenthal, *Interpersonal Expectations: Effects of the Experimenter's Hypothesis,* in ARTIFACT AND BEHAVIORAL RESEARCH, *supra,* at 181.

with an ambiguous situation and is apprehensive about performing well.[63]

When these various research findings are combined, they militate against a wholly judge-conducted voir dire. When a prospective juror is brought to the voir dire, he has been removed from a daily routine and subjected to a novel and ambiguous situation. The prospective juror "wants to serve and do his duty for society . . . . To be selected to judge his fellow man is indeed serious business, and he knows that he will likely be called upon for decisions that are much deeper than daily expressions of opinion."[64] Individuals placed in novel situations will often look to individuals of higher status for guidance as to the appropriate behavior.[65] Since it is obvious that the judge has the highest status of anyone in the courtroom, the jurors may well look to him for such guidance. If the judge conducts the voir dire and has negative feelings toward the parties or their counsel, the communication research indicates he will almost surely convey these feelings to the jurors through nonverbal communication. Research also indicates that the jurors will be able to interpret these nonverbal cues. Furthermore, studies on experimenter bias indicate that jurors may well adopt the attitudes and emotions of the judge as appropriate. Thus, a voir dire conducted solely by the judge may lead to a subtle inculcation of bias in the jurors toward the parties or counsel.

To be sure, attorneys are even more likely than the judge to have biases and prejudices regarding the case. They also lack compunctions against revealing their beliefs and even attempt to do so on the verbal level rather than merely on the nonverbal level. But it is precisely because attorneys are open about their biases that they should be allowed to conduct the voir dire. Jurors are aware that the attorneys are acting as advocates, and, therefore, jurors are less liable to accept their biases as absolute truth. Furthermore, the persuasive attempts of one attorney will be counterbalanced by the other. The judge, on the other hand, is presumed to be impartial and the attitudes which he conveys are more likely to be readily accepted. Also, if a judge conveys negative attitudes toward one side during the voir dire, counsel has no effective way to counter the resulting impact of such conduct on the jury.

THE METHOD OF ADDRESSING QUESTIONS TO THE PROSPECTIVE JURORS

In most jurisdictions, at least some portion of the voir dire consists of

---

[63] Rosenberg, *supra* note 62, at 324-29.

[64] Brown, *A Juryman's View*, in SELECTED READINGS — THE JURY 102, 102 (G. Winters ed. 1971).

[65] Rosenthal, *On Not So Replicated Experiments and Not So Null Results*, 33 J. CONSULTING & CLINICAL PSYCH. 7 (1969).

questions addressed to the group as a whole.[66] In some voir dires, this is the predominant mode with individual questioning taking place only when a juror has affirmatively responded to a question put to the group and follow up questions are required. Many voir dires, however, start with some brief group questioning on general topics, followed by an extended period of questioning addressed to specific individuals seated within the group as a whole. Occasionally, prospective jurors are questioned out of the presence of the other members of the panel—particularly when there has been massive publicity surrounding the trial and the judge concludes that this form of voir dire is required to determine the extent to which prospective jurors have been "tainted" by the media without further biasing the other prospective jurors.[67] Individual questioning outside the presence of the other jurors may not be allowed, however, if the judge feels that it will unduly lengthen the voir dire process.

In general, the conduct and scope of voir dire is within the discretion of the judge. Determining whether the questioning should be done individually or collectively is also within the discretion of the judge, and most cases hold that a judge does not abuse that discretion by refusing to allow individual examinations.[68] Inherent in the rationale of these cases is the justified belief that group questioning will render a considerable savings of time and the questionable belief that in most cases collective questioning is capable of revealing biases and prejudices.

Social Science Research Pertaining to the Mode of Questioning

Both the group and the individual-within-a-group styles of questioning are grossly inadequate for producing honest self-disclosure because they engender conformity of responses. It seems intuitively obvious that when people are called for jury duty by a judicial summons, they feel a certain degree of anxiety at being removed from the context of their ordinary lives and ordered to perform a role which will have a significant effect on the lives of others. A variety of investigators find that anxious individuals have an increased need for affiliation while they are awaiting a threatening event.[69] Many prospective jurors perceive interroga-

---

[66] *See* 2 A. AMSTERDAM, B. SEGAL & M. MILLER, *supra* note 12, §§ 331-332.

[67] The American Bar Association has advocated this practice. *See* ABA PROJECT ON MINIMUM STANDARDS FOR CRIMINAL JUSTICE, STANDARDS RELATING TO FAIR TRIAL AND FREE PRESS § 3.4(a) (1968).

[68] *See, e.g.*, United States v. Tropiano, 418 F.2d 1069 (2d Cir. 1969), *cert. denied*, 397 U.S. 1021 (1970); *cf.* United States v. Addonizio, 451 F.2d 49, 66 (3d Cir. 1971), *cert. denied*, 405 U.S. 936 (1972) (trial court's refusal to examine jurors individually was not an abuse of discretion; noting, however, in dicta, that if there has been extensive pretrial publicity, jurors should be examined individually).

[69] *See* Gerard & Rabbie, *Fear and Social Comparisons*, 62 J. ABNORMAL & SOC. PSYCH. 586, 588-89 (1961); Helmreich & Collings, *Situational Determinants of Affiliative Preference Under Stress*, 6 J. PERSONALITY & SOC. PSYCH. 79 (1967); Sarnoff & Zimbardo,

tion in a public forum to determine their suitability as jurors to be such an event. In addition, conformity increases as the need for affiliation increases.[70] Thus, even before the voir dire begins, there are socio-psychological factors at work which encourage group cohesiveness and conformity of response, thereby militating against honest self-disclosure.

In the group questioning method of conducting voir dire, the entire group of prospective jurors is asked a question such as, "Would any of you be unable to be fair and impartial toward the defendant because of the media coverage which has surrounded this case?" If no one from the group responds to this question, the interviewer moves on to other areas. This technique is hardly fitted for a self-disclosure interview. Since no response is required of any particular individual and factors of group conformity are at work, it is highly unlikely that a prospective juror will respond to such a question, particularly when it would discredit him as a fair person. Even when relatively mundane questions are addressed to the prospective jurors as a group, researchers have observed that they squirm in their seats and look around to see if anyone else is going to volunteer information; if they discover that no other hands are raised, they settle back in their chairs and refuse to respond. In contrast, responses were forthcoming when attorneys later addressed the very same questions to particular individuals.

The technique of questioning an individual within a group is an improvement over group questioning but it still closely resembles the paradigm used by psychologists to study conformity. In one study on independence and conformity, it was found that when an individual was called upon to state his opinions in public after hearing the opinions stated by the majority of the group, over one-fourth of the minority individuals covertly changed their private opinions and stated their public opinions so that they matched those of the majority.[71] When the individual was not required to state an opinion in front of the group, the degree of conformity was markedly lower. Other research in this area, while differing in methodology and emphasis, supports the same conclusion.[72] This research also supports the conclusion that an individual in-

---

Anxiety, Fear, and Social Affiliation, 64 J. ABNORMAL & SOC. PSYCH. 356 (1961); Zimbardo & Formica, *Emotional Comparison and Self-Esteem as Determinants of Affiliation,* 31 J. PERSONALITY 141, 161 (1963).

[70] *See* Hardy, *Determinants of Conformity and Attitude Change,* 54 J. ABNORMAL & SOC. PSYCH. 289 (1957); McGhee & Teevan, *Conformity Behavior and Need for Affiliation,* 72 J. SOC. PSYCH. 117 (1967).

[71] Asch, *Studies of Independence and Conformity: A Minority of One Against a Unanimous Majority,* 70 PSYCH. MONOGRAPHS, Whole No. 416, at 11 (1956).

[72] *See, e.g.,* Deutsch & Gerard, *A Study of Normative and Informational Social Influences Upon Individual Judgment,* 51 J. ABNORMAL & SOC. PSYCH. 629, 635 (1955); Sherif, *Group Influences Upon the Formation of Norms and Attitudes,* in READINGS IN SOCIAL PSYCHOLOGY 219, 224-25 (E. Maccoby, T. Newcomb & E. Hartley eds., 3d ed. 1958); *cf.* A.

terview which takes place away from the group is the best way to determine a person's opinions on a given issue[73] because "in the interest of bolstering the opinions of others, [individuals within a group] may make statements that deviate from the truth as they see it."[74]

The conformity experiments demonstrate a sizeable conformity effect when individuals are required to state their opinions in front of members of a group, even under such nonthreatening conditions as requesting each individual to judge line length.[75] This effect is likely to be even more pronounced under the conditions of anxiety which arise when an attorney challenges a juror in the courtroom. For example, when an attorney challenges a juror for cause, he may publicly accuse the juror of being biased or prejudiced because of the opinion he stated.[76] Often the judge will initially reject such a challenge and require the attorney to further question the prospective juror. This questioning can be quite brutal to a novice in the courtroom. If the individual is being questioned within a group, the other prospective jurors witness what can happen to one who makes the "wrong" response. Thus, in an attempt to avoid such close scrutiny, they may alter their responses so as not to give "wrong" answers.

Both of the predominant questioning techniques create a group situation which tends to foster conformity in the expression of personal opinions. If the goal of voir dire is honest self-disclosure, the most effective way to facilitate the achievement of that goal is to interview prospective jurors out of the presence of their fellows, thus eliminating the conformity-generating aspects of group voir dire. Collective questioning is the method least likely to encourage self-disclosure and should be avoided whenever possible.

INTERACTION DISTANCE DURING VOIR DIRE

The interaction distance between the person conducting the voir dire and the prospective jurors is usually quite large. For example, it is not uncommon to observe a distance of twenty to thirty feet between the interviewer and the prospective jurors. This large interaction distance is most prevalent when questions are addressed to the jurors as a group, probably because such a distance fosters a loud speaking voice from all

---

HARE. HANDBOOK OF SMALL GROUP RESEARCH 361-62 (1962) (discussing small group dynamics).

[73] *See* Chandler, *An Evaluation of the Group Interview*, 13 HUMAN ORGANIZATION 26 (Summer 1954).

[74] *Id.* at 28.

[75] *See* Asch, *supra* note 74.

[76] Most commentators, however, suggest that the attorney politely request the juror be "excused," without making it seem like an accusation. *See, e.g.,* M. BELLI. *supra* note 24, § 120.

parties, thus allowing everyone to hear the questions and answers. Although some assume a closer interaction distance when questioning prospective jurors in an attempt to establish closer rapport with them, such attempts generally are not satisfactory because, in order for everyone in the courtroom, including the court reporter, to hear what is being said, the interactants must still speak very loudly. The result is that the two interactants who are positioned fairly close together speak in stentorian voices for the benefit of others—a result which enhances the artificiality of the interaction and may even hinder the establishment of rapport. Only two voir dires where the interactants were able to maintain a social distance[77] and speak at a normal conversational level have been observed. In one of these, jurors were examined individually, out of the presence of the other jurors, and in a courtroom cleared of spectators. In the other, jurors were questioned individually in the privacy of the judge's chambers. The attorneys involved in both of these cases indicated that in their experience such procedures were extremely rare.

The issue of interaction distance between the interviewer and interviewee has not been addressed in either case law or legal literature. This is probably because whoever conducts voir dire theoretically has the option of assuming a close interaction distance with the prospective jurors. If the judge conducts the voir dire, he may ask prospective jurors to take the witness stand next to the bench while they are being questioned individually. Attorneys may approach the prospective juror whether the person is sitting in the jury box or in the witness stand. As already noted, however, the practicalities of current voir dire procedures require the interactants to speak very loudly, even if they are physically very close, and this is not conducive to self-disclosure. Thus, the issue of interaction distance during voir dire is closely tied to the issue of the appropriate environmental characteristics of the room in which voir dire is to take place. If voir dire is to take place in a large public room designed and decorated to reflect a formal atmosphere, the interaction distances which people adopt will also be formal.

Social Science Research Concerning the Effect of Interpersonal Distance on Self-Disclosure

Four main categories of interpersonal distance are used to define and maintain interpersonal relationships: intimate distance (contact to one and one-half feet); personal distance (one and one-half to four feet); social distance (four to twelve feet); and public distance (twelve or more feet).[78]

---

[77] *See* E. HALL, THE HIDDEN DIMENSION 114-16 (1966); text accompanying note 78 *infra*.
[78] E. HALL, *supra* note 77, at 113-20.

Most voir dires take place with a public distance between the speakers. There is some evidence to suggest that this public distance is most conducive to persuasion, the primary function of the attorneys during the trial.[79] It is doubtful, however, that a public distance is conducive to eliciting self-disclosure during voir dire. At the close phase of public distance, around twelve feet, speakers adopt a formal style of speaking and at the more distant phases, speaking style becomes positively frozen. The frozen style of speech is for people who expect to remain strangers. Both the verbal and nonverbal aspects of the communicative process must be exaggerated at this distance with the result that communication tends to assume stereotypic forms.

It is argued that the extent to which the behavior of an interviewee is affected by the interviewer is inversely proportional to the distance, both physical and psychological, which separates one from the other.[80] This hypothesis is supported by a number of research studies on interpersonal attraction in general,[81] and self-disclosure interviews in particular.[82] These studies show that closer physical distance facilitates communication and the formation of a positive feeling. The self-disclosure studies find that when interviews are conducted at distances ranging from three to six feet, the interviewee feels more comfortable, speaks significantly more and reveals more of himself to the interviewer. In addition, one study on interaction distance indicates that interviewers are able to form much stronger impressions of the interviewee's personality at interview distances ranging from four to six feet than they are at closer and farther distances.[83] Thus, the relationship between distance and self-disclosure is not a linear function. If the interview distance is decreased to less than approximately three feet, the interviewee becomes anxious and self-disclosure decreases. A height differential between the interactants at close interpersonal distances would generate even more discomfort in the person at the lower level.

---

[79] *See* Albert & Dabbs, *Physical Distance and Persuasion*, 15 J. PERSONALITY & SOC. PSYCH. 265 (1970).

[80] Kleck, *Interaction Distance and Non-verbal Agreeing Responses*, 9 BRIT. J. SOC. & CLINICAL PSYCH. 180 (1970).

[81] *See* Cook, *Experiments on Orientation and Proxemics*, 23 HUMAN RELATIONSHIPS 61 (1970); Willis, *Initial Speaking Distance as a Function of the Speakers Relationship*, 5 PSYCHONOMIC SCI. 221 (1966).

[82] *See* Jourard & Friedman, *Experimenter-Subject "Distance" and Self-Disclosure*, 15 J. PERSONALITY & SOC. PSYCH. 278 (1970); C. Lassen, Interaction Distance and the Initial Psychiatric Interview: A Study on Proxemics (1969) (unpublished dissertation, Yale Univ.); J. Weber, The Effects of Physical Proximity and Body Boundary Size on the Self-Disclosure Interview (1972) (unpublished dissertation, Univ. S. Cal.); *cf.* Knight & Blair, *Degree of Client Comfort as a Function of Dyadic Interaction Distance*, 23 J. COUNSELING PSYCH. 13 (1976) (noting client comfort is highest at midrange distances).

[83] *See* Patterson & Sechrest, *Interpersonal Distance and Impression Formation*, 38 J. PERSONALITY 161 (1970).

Thus, if the interviewer approaches the interviewee in order to enhance self-disclosure, he should also adjust his height so as not to arouse anxiety in the interviewee. For example, if the interviewee is seated, the interviewer can adjust his height by also sitting. The evidence supporting the notion that there is an optimal interpersonal distance of three to six feet for self-disclosure interviews is substantial and consistent. The legal system should take advantage of this research and modify the voir dire procedure to allow the interviewer to question the prospective juror at this distance.

The issue of optimal interview distance also has ramifications for some of the other issues regarding voir dire procedures. Use of the optimal distance is not possible if the jurors are questioned in the traditional group or individual-within-a-group manners. Unless the individual being questioned is placed in the witness stand, it is physically impossible to approach the prospective jurors at the optimal distance in those interview contexts. The evidence concerning distance also has a bearing on the determination of whether the attorneys or the judge should conduct voir dire. When the judge does the questioning, he generally remains at the bench and is not able to approach the jurors; even if a prospective juror is brought closer to the judge and placed in the witness stand, the judge and juror will still not directly face one another. In addition, the judge looks down at the prospective jurors, further hindering juror self-disclosure. Thus, the findings on the subject of optimal interview distance add further weight to arguments in favor of individualized attorney-conducted voir dire.

Environmental Aspects of the Courtroom and Their Impact on Juror Self-Disclosure

While the exact environmental characteristics of particular courtrooms will vary, in general, the courtroom may be described as a very large, public room charged with a ritualistic atmosphere and staged with props that clearly demarcate the roles assigned to the various participants. Courtrooms are devoid of any props which denote warmth and informality. When group questioning is employed, the prospective jurors are often seated in the spectator section. In such a situation, the "bar" literally acts as a physical barrier between the interviewer and prospective jurors. Frequently, a small subgroup of the prospective jurors is randomly selected to come before the bar and sit in the jury box. Although these jurors may be questioned as individuals, it is usually in the presence of the surrounding group, and, once again, there is a physical barrier created by the jury box between the interviewer and the prospective jurors. Even though the judge directs and controls the events taking place, he is physically removed from the proceedings. The judge sits in an elevated, enclosed box which allows only his upper torso and head to be seen. Moreover, the upper torso is somewhat obscured by a voluminous, ceremonial black robe. Thus, a double set of physical barriers separates the judge and the prospective jurors — those which isolate the jurors and those which surround, elevate and obscure the judge.

Very little has been written about the environmental aspects of the courtroom from a legal perspective. Presumably, the ritualistic atmosphere is encouraged for the same reasons which support the practice of requiring witnesses to take the oath; ritual is presumed to impress upon the individual the gravity of the events which are about to transpire and, therefore, encourage candor.[84] The legal view regarding the appropriate atmosphere in which to conduct voir dire may be illustrated by considering an experiment involving an unusual voir dire practice conducted largely without a judge being present.[85] In this method of empanelment, voir dire takes place in an ordinary room which seats twenty-five prospective jurors, as well as the judge, attorneys, clerk and court reporter. When all of the parties have been assembled, the prospective jurors are sworn in. The judge explains the purpose of voir dire and the procedures to be followed and asks only a few very general questions. The judge then leaves the room and the rest of the voir dire is conducted by the attorneys. If one of the attorneys objects to the nature of the other attorney's questioning, the procedure is halted and the judge returns to resolve the dispute. Once the jury has been selected, it is then transferred to a courtroom for trial.

This procedure is highly unusual not only in the degree of latitude afforded to the attorneys, but also in that it takes place in a room which is much smaller than the courtroom and presumably does not have all of the trappings which normally furnish a courtroom. Attorneys who have participated in this type of voir dire generally approve of it.

> All say that the atmosphere allows them to become acquainted and develop a degree of rapport with the jurors that is normally not possible irrespective of whether the voir dire is conducted primarily by the judge or primarily by counsel. Every attorney stated that the system is a fair one. All agreed that it allows sufficient latitude in the examination of prospective jurors.[86]

Despite the fact that the attorneys praised the method in part because of its less formal atmosphere, the study concludes that voir dire should not be regularly conducted in an informal room.

> For a juror to respect the process it must be unmistakably "judicial" in order to convey an official and formal air. . . . Especially because

---

[84] See Levit, Nelson, Ball & Chernick, supra note 35, at 939, 950.
[85] See id. at 931-36.
[86] Id. at 938 (footnotes omitted).

the voir dire comes at the very beginning of the trial, all care must be taken to assure that the tone is not one of excessive casualness.[87]

Thus, the legal community takes the position that excessive casualness is an evil which must be guarded against in order to insure the integrity of the trial. The legal community should also be aware, however, that excessive formality during the voir dire will inhibit juror self-disclosure and thus hinder the exposition of bias and prejudice.

Social Science Research Relevant to the Environmental Aspects of the Courtroom and Their Effect on Juror Self-Disclosure

The large size of the courtroom appears to have an effect on preferred interpersonal distance which may in turn affect the amount of self-disclosure generated in the voir dire. One study proposes that an inverse relationship exists between room size and preferred interaction distance between subjects.[88] Thus, in a large room, subjects assume a close interpersonal distance, whereas in a small room, subjects tend to assume larger interaction distances. Another study suggests that interaction distances decrease in large rooms because both auditory and visual sensations diminish with the increase in room size:[89] "Screaming across a void does not make for comfortable conversation; rather than increase the volume, most people choose to decrease the void."[90] The implication for voir dire taking place in a large courtroom is that people prefer to have a fairly close interaction distance. This preference is blocked, however, either because of the physical barriers in the courtroom or because of the necessity of everyone in the courtroom being able to hear the exchange of questions and answers. The blocking of these preferred distancing patterns probably generates discomfort and anxiety for the prospective juror, thus reducing self-disclosure. If this is indeed the case, two solutions come readily to mind: either remove the voir dire from the context of the large, open courtroom or remove the physical barriers between the participants to allow closer interaction distances, thereby eliminating the necessity of loud speaking voices by the participants during the exchange.

In addition, environmental aspects may affect the jurors independently of their relation to the attorneys. Specifically, although there is a considerable distance between the interviewer and the interviewee in the typical voir dire, the distance between the various interviewees is

---

[87] *Id.* at 939.

[88] *See* Sommer, *The Distance for Comfortable Conversation: A Further Study*, 25 SOCIOMETRY 111, 115 (1976).

[89] *See* White, *Interpersonal Distance as Affected by Room Size, Status, and Sex*, 95 J. SOC. PSYCH. 241, 248 (1975).

[90] *Id.*

minimal. When prospective jurors are seated in the spectator section, as is the case in most group-style voir dires, they are usually in actual physical contact with those on either side of them. Even when prospective jurors are brought into the jury box for questioning, the distance between jurors does not exceed several feet. In studying the effects of room size and crowding on stress and self-disclosure, one researcher concludes that, under conditions of crowding as, for example, where subjects are shoulder to shoulder, the subjects are significantly less comfortable, exhibit more nonverbal indicators of stress such as manipulating objects and frequently changing positions and are less willing to discuss intimate topics.[91] Thus, the seating of prospective jurors in a compact grouping probably leads to reduced self-disclosure.

It has long been the common sense view that reduced privacy leads to reduced self-disclosure. A study finding that self-disclosure in a dyad increases under conditions of isolation[92] supports this view. Other research, also supporting the common sense view, concludes that reduced privacy decreases client self-disclosure in a counseling setting and this occurs even when partial barriers such as desks or bookcases are employed to encourage the client's perception of privacy.[93] From this research, it would seem that one way to encourage self-disclosure among prospective jurors is to conduct voir dire in the most isolated setting possible, for example, in the judge's chambers. To be sure, the complete isolation of a client-counselor setting cannot be achieved since the voir dire must include, at a minimum, the juror, judge, both litigants in a civil case or the defendant in a criminal case, counsel for both sides and the court reporter. Yet, a small group setting is much more conducive to self-dislcosure than a voir dire which takes place in front of fifty or more spectators.

The final aspect of the environment considered here is the degree of warmth or coldness of the room in which voir dire takes place. "Hard architecture" is described as that which is unyielding, impervious and impersonal, and it is argued that such architecture tends to foster isolation and estrangement among people.[94] The courtrooms in which voir dire is conducted can typically be characterized as "hard" rooms. Empirical data from a counseling analogue demonstrates that subjects disclose significantly more in a "soft" rather than a "hard" room.[95] This result

---

[91] *See* Sundstrom, *An Experimental Study of Crowding: Effects of Room Size, Intrusion, and Goal Blocking on Nonverbal Behavior, Self-Disclosure and Reported Stress*, 32 J. PERSONALITY & SOC. PSYCH. 645 (1975).

[92] *See* Altman & Haythorn, *Interpersonal Exchange in Isolation*, 28 SOCIOMETRY 41 (1975).

[93] Holahan & Slaikeu, *Effects of Contrasting Degrees of Privacy on Client Self-Disclosure in a Counseling Setting*, 24 J. COUNSELING PSYCH. 55 (1977).

[94] R. SOMMER. TIGHT SPACES *passim* (1974).

[95] Chaikin, Derlega & Miller, *Effects of Room Environment on Self-Disclosure in a Counseling Analogue*, 23 J. COUNSELING PSYCH. 479 (1976).

might occur because hard architecture makes status differences between client and counselor more salient, because a soft environment is
similar to that in which friends interact or because a soft environment is
more conducive to a feeling of relaxation and ease.[96] Whatever the
reason, both common sense and empirical data clearly demonstrate that
more self-disclosure is forthcoming in a warm and intimate room than in
a cold and impersonal one. Therefore, voir dire could be improved by
removing it from the courtroom and into the judge's chambers or into
some other room especially designed for the voir dire of prospective
jurors.

RECOMMENDATIONS FOR THE LEGAL SYSTEM

The courtroom functions as a public forum in which society determines the civil and criminal liabilities of its members through the use of
an adversarial system. The structure of the courtroom and the procedures which are used in the courtroom setting have evolved to further that function. Although voir dire is nominally a part of the adversary system, it should be conceptualized as a separate part of the trial
process. Since the purpose of voir dire is to obtain information from prospective jurors regarding their qualifications and attitudes toward
issues in the case at hand, it can best be conceptualized as a self-disclosure type of interview. The research which has been reviewed above
demonstrates that self-disclosure is markedly affected by situational factors. Thus, the voir dire situation needs to be tailored to facilitate self-
disclosure. Present voir dire practices are not designed to encourage
self-disclosure and indeed seem almost intended to discourage open,
honest self-revelation.

There are several specific recommendations for revising the procedures used in conducting voir dire which could encourage self-
disclosure among prospective jurors. First, emphasis should be placed
on individual rather than group or individual-within-a-group questioning. Second, questioning should be conducted by attorneys rather than
by the judge. Third, the interviewer should conduct the interview from
a distance of three to six feet from the jurors. Fourth, the questioning
should take place in a smaller room than is traditionally employed, but
should not result in crowding. And finally, the room where voir dire
takes place should have a warmer and more intimate atmosphere than
that of the cold, hard, ritualistic settings where it is presently conducted. Essentially, these recommendations urge the legal system to
de-emphasize the adversarial approach to voir dire and to transform it
into a more relaxed proceeding where free and open self-disclosure can
take place.

---

[96] *Id.*

Once voir dire is moved to a more open setting, there are four other recommendations derived from the psychological literature which could be employed to facilitate disclosure. First, positive reinforcement should be given to the juror when he makes self-disclosing statements. Second, the interviewer should make self-disclosing statements about himself to the prospective juror. Third, a model of self-disclosure should be offered to the juror prior to the voir dire. And finally, jurors should be instructed to disclose information about themselves.

The first of these recommendations, the giving of positive reinforcements to increase self-disclosing statements by the juror, was mentioned previously in dealing with the issue of who should conduct voir dire. These reinforcements could take the form of verbal praise or nonverbal indicators of interest, such as increased eye contact, direct body orientation, relaxed posture, head-nodding and mm-hmming.

The second recommendation, that the interviewer disclose himself to the prospective juror during the voir dire, is based upon a considerable body of research indicating that interviewer disclosure appears to facilitate self-disclosure in interviewees.[97] There are three theoretical explanations for this phenomenon. One explanation is that the interviewer's example of self-disclosure tends to lessen the interviewee's inhibitions concerning self-disclosure.[98] In addition, there is evidence indicating that the phenomenon might be the result of the modeling aspect of the situation.[99] In other words, the interviewees use the interviewer's behavior as a discriminative cue to guide their own behavior. Finally, the phenomenon may be viewed as a social exchange process in which the disclosures follow a norm of reciprocity.[100] Whatever the cor-

---

[97] Davis & Skinner, *Reciprocity of Self Disclosure in Interviews: Modeling or Social Exchange?*, 29 J. PERSONALITY & SOC. PSYCH. 779, 779 (1974). There is, however, other research indicating that when subjects view interviewer self-disclosure as inappropriate to the interviewer's role, they may actually withdraw and disclose less of themselves when confronted by the interviewer's disclosures. *See* Derlega, Lovell & Chaikin, *Effects of Therapist Disclosure and Its Perceived Appropriateness on Client Self-Disclosure*, 44 J. CONSULTING & CLINICAL PSYCH. 866 (1976). Further research needs to be done to determine which interviewee personality variables are associated with this phenomenon. Empirical research is also needed to determine whether most prospective jurors would view voir dire as an inappropriate social situation for interviewer self-disclosures thereby rendering this strategy of generating juror self-disclosure untenable.

[98] *See* A. BANDURA, PRINCIPLES OF BEHAVIOR MODIFICATION 192-96 (1969). There is, however, some data indicating that interviewees maintain elevated levels of self-disclosure only if the interviewer also continues to disclose, *see* Davis & Sloan, *The Basis of Interviewee Matching of Interviewer Self-Disclosure*, 13 BRIT. J. SOC. & CLINICAL PSYCH. 359 (1974), thus militating against this disinhibitory theory.

[99] *See* Marlatt, *Exposure to a Model and Task Ambiguity as Determinants of Verbal Behavior in an Interview*, 36 J. CONSULTING & CLINICAL PSYCH. 268 (1971). However, there is also evidence indicating that interviewees do not model the content of interviewers' disclosures. *See* Davis & Sloan, *supra* note 98. This tends to negate the modeling theory.

[100] *See* Worthy, Gary & Kahn, *supra* note 47, at 59-60.

rect explanation,[101] the principle of interviewer disclosure can get out of hand. For example, one study finds that an intermediate level of interviewer self-disclosure, such as four disclosures during a thirty minute interview as opposed to none or twelve, leads to greater self-disclosure by the interviewees.[102] Thus, if the interviewer makes too many self-disclosures, the results may be counter-productive. This finding has an implication for the decision whether to question prospective jurors individually or within the group context. If individuals are questioned with the entire group present, the attorney may not be able to safely employ the self-disclosure technique since he may have overexposed himself. Thus, interviewer self-disclosure should only be employed in conjunction with a truly individual voir dire. The type of disclosure made by the interviewer also needs to be considered. Interviewees respond more to a warm therapist making demographic disclosures than to a warm therapist making personal disclosures.[103] Thus, the voir dire interviewers should not disclose information which is too personal. It is doubtful that the parties involved in voir dire would consider personal disclosures appropriate on the part of the judge or attorney anyway.

It is also recommended that a model of self-disclosure be provided to prospective jurors prior to the voir dire. In a study in which the subjects witnessed an interview of a self-disclosing stooge and were then asked how much they would be willing to disclose in the interview, it was discovered that subjects exposed to high disclosing stooges are significantly more willing to disclose information about themselves than are those exposed to low disclosing stooges.[104] There was no interaction between the interviewer and the subject or between the stooge and the subject, so that willingness to disclose in this instance must be a function of modeling rather than of a social exchange process. In addition, another study demonstrates that a model for self-disclosure on videotape can increase subject self-disclosure in subsequent interactions.[105] In some jurisdictions, prospective jurors are exposed to movies which attempt to explain the functions of the trial and the role of the juror in a trial. These movies could be adapted to include a segment showing a voir dire in which prospective jurors are highly disclosing. Based on the

---

[101] It seems that self-disclosure follows a norm of reciprocity, *see* notes 97-98 *supra*, and that, therefore, self-disclosure on the part of the interviewer on a fairly continuous basis throughout voir dire would facilitate self-disclosure on the part of the prospective jurors.

[102] *See* Mann & Murphy, *Timing of Self-Disclosure, Reciprocity of Self-Disclosure, and Reactions to an Initial Interview*, 22 J. COUNSELING PSYCH. 304 (1975).

[103] Simonson, *The Impact of Therapist Disclosure on Patient Disclosure*, 23 J. COUNSELING PSYCH. 3 (1976).

[104] *See* Thase & Page, *Modeling of Self-Disclosure in Laboratory and Nonlaboratory Interview Settings*, 24 J. COUNSELING PSYCH. 35 (1977).

[105] *See* Annis & Perry, *Self-Disclosure Modeling in Same-Sex and Mixed-Sex Unsupervised Groups*, 24 J. COUNSELING PSYCH. 370 (1977).

research findings described above, this should lead to increased self-disclosure in the real voir dire.

The final recommendation for altering voir dire procedures is that the jurors be instructed to disclose information about themselves. Two studies demonstrate that descriptive instructions by themselves will significantly increase subject self-disclosure in interviews.[106] Although such instructions are sometimes given, they are frequently mentioned almost as an afterthought or in an offhand manner. The research indicates that self-disclosing instructions should always be given and emphasized prior to voir dire.

CONCLUSION

The voir dire is an important part of the trial process in which the constitutional right to an impartial jury is at stake. In order to protect that right, it is essential that attorneys obtain as much information about prospective jurors as possible so that they may challenge for cause those who are biased or prejudiced as a matter of law. Juror self-disclosure will also allow the attorney to protect his client's legal interests by permitting him to exercise his peremptory challenges on the basis of solid information rather than on speculation and guesswork. Unfortunately, current voir dire practices are not conducive to promoting juror self-disclosure. Thus, in order to further the goals of voir dire, research from the social sciences on the subject of self-disclosure interviews, should be implemented to change current voir dire practices and increase self-disclosure.

---

[106] *See* McGuire, Thelen & Amolsch, *Interview Self-Disclosure as a Function of Length of Modeling and Descriptive Instructions*, 43 J. CONSULTING & CLINICAL PSYCH. 356 (1975); Stone & Gotlib, *Effect of Instructions and Modeling on Self-Disclosure*, 22 J. COUNSELING PSYCH. 288 (1975).

The Conduct of Voir Dire:
A Psychological Analysis*

Valerie P. Hans**

The voir dire process in jury selection, in which prospective jurors are questioned about their possible biases in the case, has come under increasing scrutiny in recent years. This article discusses psychological research and its implications for the conduct of the voir dire. The research indicates that individual, sequestered, open-ended questioning on issues directly relevant to the trial is the superior method for uncovering bias in prospective jurors. Furthermore, adversary attorneys appear to have a modest edge over judges in the detection of prejudice. The author notes that these findings must be balanced against other interests served by the voir dire process.

Introduction

Although the right to trial by jury is an important aspect of our contemporary legal system, many procedural features of the jury trial vary across jurisdictions. The voir dire process, through which prospective jurors are examined concerning their possible prejudices in the case, is no exception to this rule. Some countries, such as Canada and Great Britain, do not even regularly provide for questioning of prospective jurors (Baldwin and McConville, 1979; Vidmar and Melnitzer, 1984). In the United States, a voir dire questioning period is routine, but the manner in which it is conducted varies tremendously. In some jurisdictions, the judge alone conducts the voir dire, while in others, attorneys participate in some or all of the questioning of prospective jurors (Bermant, 1977). The scope of questioning also varies. Depending upon the nature of the case and the trial judge's discretion, the pretrial examination of jurors may be restricted to relatively narrow issues such as knowledge of the case or witnesses, or may contain more expansive questions about a potential juror's attitudes, general experiences, and preconceptions of the case.

In recent years, the conduct of the voir dire has come under increasing scrutiny. Courtroom critics have charged that lengthy voir dires are use-

---

*The author would like to thank Gordon Bermant and Sam Gaertner for helpful comments on a draft of this article.
**Associate Professor of Criminal Justice and Psychology, University of Delaware.

less and a waste of valuable court time. They have alleged that the questioning period is used not simply to ferret out prejudice but also to begin indoctrinating the jurors (see, e.g., Balch *et al.*, 1976). Some scholars have argued that the manner in which the voir dire is typically conducted discourages self-disclosure by prospective jurors (Suggs and Sales, 1981); others have claimed that jurors make deliberate falsehoods on the stand so they will not be challenged (Broeder, 1965; Schulman, as cited in Ginger, 1975).

In some courts, judges have restricted the number and type of questions posed to prospective jurors. Appellate decisions have upheld the constitutionality of such judicially imposed limits (*Ristiano v. Ross*, 1976; *Rosales-Lopez v. United States*, 1981). Attorney involvement has also become more limited. By one estimate, the number of judges conducting the voir dire without attorneys increased about 20% during the 1970s (Bermant, 1982). On the other hand, within the last few years, at least two bills have been introduced in the United States Senate to expand the oral participation of attorneys during voir dire in civil and criminal cases (Bermant, 1985).

With considerable variability in the manner of conducting the voir dire, and continuing debate about its proper conduct, it is of interest to assess the voir dire from a psychological perspective. In some ways, the task of judge and counsel in voir dire inquiry is very much like the task facing the psychological researcher studying the more general issue of prejudice. Both tasks aim to detect prejudice and gauge its likely impact. Therefore, psychological insights derived from research could provide suggestions for the conduct of the voir dire. Yet there are important differences that limit the analogy. The voir dire occurs in a highly formal setting, and its conduct is bound by legal history, tradition, the judge's past practices, and appellete court opinions. Its purpose is not only to detect prejudice that would justify a challenge for cause, but also to provide information to attorneys on which they can base their peremptory challenges, and to contribute to the "appearance" of justice. The voir dire must thus be evaluated against the fulfillment of these multiple purposes. In contrast, the psychological researcher is bound only by imagination and ethical principles for the treatment of subjects. Hence, psychological methods for uncovering prejudice may not be completely applicable to the voir dire setting.

Nevertheless, there are a number of essentially psychological issues to be explored in evaluating arguments and trends in the conduct of the voir dire. These include the following: Is a judge or an attorney better equipped to conduct the voir dire examination? What types of questions would best

41

elicit conscious or unconscious prejudices on the part of prospective jurors? What is the impact of questioning jurors individually or in groups? And what about the "appearance of justice?" Do certain methods of voir dire conduct encourage it? Before considering these questions, it is important to address a broader issue that underlies the existence of the voir dire: the extensiveness of prejudice in jury verdicts.

The Problem of Prejudice

Some practitioners believe that the personal characteristics of jurors are important determinants of the verdict. In the words of one trial tactics manual, it is "a very obvious fact: the people who constitute the jury can have as much or more to do with the outcome of a trial as the evidence and arguments." (Kairys et al., 1975: 1). And consider the following quote from a past president of the American Trial Lawyers' Association: "After decades of trials—and tribulations—I am convinced that the major factor determining the outcome of a jury trial is the prejudice that jurors bring with them to court" (Kelner, 1983: 48). Indeed, jury simulation studies and research on actual jurors indicate that people routinely differ in their orientation to cases, and that these differences are translated into different initial preferences for verdicts (e.g., Kalven and Zeisel, 1966). Simply because jurors possess differing attitudinal orientations, however, does not mean that they are prejudiced, or that they should be eliminated from the jury.

The courts have long struggled with the definition of prejudice. In the leading case of *United States v. Wood* (1936), Chief Justice Hughes stated that the impartiality of jurors is not a "technical conception." Instead, it is a "state of mind," a "mental attitude of appropriate indifference" (pp. 145-146). Partly as a consequence of the definition, there are no specific tests for assessing exactly when a juror holds an attitude of appropriate indifference. There has been a historical shift in our judgments of juror impartiality. Whereas in the past only blatant interests or biases were recognized, in recent years subtler forms of bias have been cause for the removal of prospective jurors (Hans and Vidmar, 1982).

If we define prejudice as the inability to decide a case "impartially," on the evidence, just how widespread a problem is it? Scholarly research on jury decision making suggests that prejudice plays only a modest role. One way of estimating the impact of prejudice in juries is to calculate how often other expert decision makers, such as judges, would agree with the verdict. The presumption is that judges, because of their legal training and experience, are less affected by extralegal biases. In their classic study of judges' agreement with jury verdicts, Kalven and Zeisel (1966) found that judges would have reached the same verdict that the jury reached in four cases out of five. Jury verdicts in the fifth case, where disagreement took place, tended to occur in cases in which the evidence was close, and when either a conviction or an acquittal could be supported by the trial evidence. Furthermore, the disagreements appeared most often to be based on the jury's distinctive sense of justice rather than outright prejudice. The overwhelming majority of disagreements occurred when juries were more lenient than judges would have been, suggesting that if juror prejudice exists it most often favors the defendants who take their case before the jury. More recent research in England indicated similarly that judges supported the majority of jury verdicts (Baldwin and McConville, 1979; but see Roper and Flango, 1983).

Another way of examining the potential impact of prejudice is to determine the extent to which jury verdicts can be predicted from the evidence or from jurors' characteristics or attitudes. This research approach has shown that the jury's verdict is most strongly linked to the weight of the evidence presented in the case; by contrast, individual characteristics of the jurors play a negligible role (Myers, 1979; Penrod, 1979). Hence, experts have concluded that the overwhelming majority of verdicts is decided not by extralegal factors or jury prejudice but rather by the strength and credibility of the evidence presented at trial (Kassin and Wrightsman, 1985: 8).

Nevertheless, scholars might point to specific cases or types of cases in which the jury's verdict appeared to result from prejudice rather than the strength of the evidence. For instance, Carter (1975) and Wolfgang and Riedel (1973) have documented the negative reactions of jurors to interracial rape cases. There is also the problem of defendants who have been subject to extensive pretrial publicity. While the importance of prejudice in these and other cases cannot and should not be dismissed, there are some surprising instances of jurors putting aside their preconceptions and following the evidence and the judge's instructions. Examples include the cases of John DeLorean and John Hinckley, Jr. Before DeLorean's trial, a poll indicated that 70% of the community had prejudged his guilt. Many of the jurors who served on the case admitted during voir dire that they believed DeLorean was probably guilty. Yet, after hearing the evidence, they acquitted him of all charges (Brill, 1984). Similarly, interviews with the Hinckley jurors after the trial indicated that a number of them wanted to see Hinckley punished for his behavior. Nevertheless, they followed the judge's instructions and found him Not Guilty by Reason of Insanity

43

because the prosecution had not met its burden of proof. (United States Congress, 1982).

While prejudice is certainly a factor to be contended with in juries, our best evidence suggests that it is not nearly so pervasive as some commentators believe. In the majority of cases, juror prejudice appears to play only a minor role. As odd as it may seem, we can often trust jurors when they say they can decide a case on the evidence. Even some people who bring fairly strong preconceptions with them to the jury box, can occasionally set them aside. While these assessments are reassuring, the search for jurors whose attitude is one of "appropriate indifference" is nonetheless complicated.

How Can We Best Detect Prejudice?

The legal system's search for prejudice is typically conducted within the context of a single case. Prospective jurors are asked to reflect on their own mental states, and to estimate whether they will be able to weigh impartially an as yet unknown set of facts. The juror's own assessment is deemed to be the best standard. In a leading case on voir dire questioning, Chief Justice Hughes approvingly quoted another judge's rationale for this standard:

> As the juror best knows the condition of his own mind, no satisfactory conclusion can be arrived at, without resort to himself. . . . [T]o ask a person whether he is prejudiced or not against a party, and (if the answer is affirmative), whether that prejudice is of such a character as would lead him to deny the party a fair trial, is not only the simplest method of ascertaining the state of his mind, but is, probably, the only sure method of fathoming his thoughts and feelings (*Aldridge v. United States*, 1931:313-314, citing *People v. Reyes*).

Other legal commentators have reacted less favorably to the standard. Defense attorney Charles Garry, noting that judges often simply ask jurors if they can be fair, has remarked, "Once the juror has answered 'Yes,' everything else is considered irrelevant and the judge passes on to the next juror, even though Adolph Hitler himself would have answered that question in the affirmative" (Garry, 1969).

Many psychologists believe that reliance on an individual's judgment of his or her own prejudice is unwarranted. Indeed, over thirty years of research on prejudice and racism have amply illustrated the weakness in people's own assessments of their prejudice (Adorno *et al.*, 1950; Allport, 1954; Gaertner, 1976; McConahay *et al.*, 1981; Sears and McConahay, 1973). Survey methods for assessing prejudice, in which respondents are

44

asked to judge their own level of prejudice, typically underestimate the extent of bias, and psychologists have become increasingly dissatisfied with the approach (Crosby *et al.*, 1980). Nisbett and Ross (1980) have convincingly documented people's inability to estimate the impact of various factors on their own behavior.

Rather than asking subjects directly, psychologists have developed experimental designs that permit them to detect the existence of a subject's prejudice. For example, to determine whether people are biased by a defendant's race or criminal record, a psychologist might design a study in which different groups of subjects read slightly different case transcripts. In one version, the defendant might be described as an Hispanic or as possessing a criminal record, while in the control version, no such information would be presented. A comparison of responses to the two versions would allow an assessment of the impact of race or criminal record on judgments. While it is difficult to imagine how these methods might be adapted to courtroom jury selection, the more general point holds: Exclusive reliance on the juror's admission of bias is bound to give only a partial picture of a jury panel's views. However, even within the practical limits imposed by the voir dire, some questioning methods are, from a psychological perspective, likely to be superior to others.

Should Judges or Lawyers Conduct the Voir Dire?

The most heated aspect of the debate over the conduct of the voir dire concerns whether attorneys should be involved in the questioning of prospective jurors. In approximately three-fourths of federal district courts, judges conduct the voir dire alone, although they sometimes consult with attorneys and accept suggestions about questions to ask the panel. Federal judges' practice of permitting attorney participation is related to the judges' attitudes about whether adversary attorney involvement is appropriate during voir dire, and to the prevailing tradition in the local state courts (Bermant, 1977). In state courts, attorney participation varies; in some, attorneys are restricted from participation, while in a small minority of jurisdictions such as New York, the judge may actually leave the courtroom during the attorneys' often lengthy and basically unrestricted voir dire questioning.

Attorneys, including representatives of the American Bar Association, the National Association of Criminal Defense Lawyers, and the Association of Trial Lawyers of America, have urged broader attorney participation in voir dire. In contrast, judges associated with the Judicial Conference of the United States have argued against providing attorneys the

45

right to participate in voir dire in federal cases (see Bermant, 1985, for a comparative summary of their respective views).

Table 1 displays the major arguments on both sides of the debate over attorney participation in voir dire. As Table 1 shows, central to the debate are many issues of psychological import. Attorneys say that they should have the right to question prospective jurors because judges botch the job. Judges ask leading questions, indicate to prospective jurors what the proper answer is, and fail to ask follow-up questions even if initial responses are suggestive of bias. These attorneys charge that judges unquestioningly accept jurors' claims of impartiality. Some attorneys also say that the judge's role prevents him or her from being an effective questioner, claiming that prospective jurors are so intimidated by the judge's superior status that they hide their true feelings from the judge (Begam, 1977; Bermant and Shapard, 1981; Kairys *et al.*, 1975).

Judges have countercharges: that attorneys abuse the privilege of questioning prospective jurors to indoctrinate the jurors; that they invade juror's privacy; and that attorney involvement will result in unnecessarily long voir dires. Judges argue that they are perfectly competent to conduct voir dire, that jurors are not so awed by judges that they do not admit their prejudices, and that there are two lawyers to watch what they do and object to any shortcomings (Stanley, 1977; Bermant and Shapard, 1981). Both sides claim that their control over the voir dire will contribute most to the appearance of justice: the judges, because jurors and the public are spared the sight of endless probing into prospective jurors' private lives and thoughts, and the attorneys, because defendants and the public will be more secure that every effort has been advanced to select an impartial jury.

Several overarching factors emerge from a consideration of Table 1: the benefits or drawbacks of adversary involvement in the questioning; the roles of judge and attorney and their impact on prospective jurors; and the nature of questions asked by judges and attorneys. Yet, in contrast to voluminous arguments on both sides (more voluminous, it must be admitted, on the attorneys' side), there is little, if any, research that directly tests the respective claims of judges and attorneys. However, more general psychological research on three central issues—the impact of adversary procedures, role differences, and question format—bears on the debate and can be of some use in evaluating the arguments.

The effects of adversary involvement. Consider first the issue of adversary involvement in questioning. Scholars have explored the impact of different procedures in the justice process, and, more specifically, the benefits and drawbacks of adversary versus nonadversary procedures. The

46

Table 1.
Arguments For and Against Attorney Involvement in Voir Dire

Arguments in Favor of Attorney Involvement
1. Judges ask leading questions and indicate appropriate answers.
2. Judges fail to ask probing, follow-up questions when early answers indicate possible bias.
3. Jurors are so awed and intimidated by judges that they have difficulty being frank in their answers.
4. The pressure for jurors to appear socially desirable and impartial is greater when judges do the questioning.
5. Jurors are more likely to self-disclose to a person of intermediate social distance (e.g., an attorney) than to a person of extreme social distance (e.g., a judge).
6. Attorneys have greater incentive to question prospective jurors thoroughly.
7. Attorneys have better knowledge of the case and can thus tailor questions to the specific facts jurors will have to decide.
8. The longer time attorneys as opposed to judges take to question prospective jurors indicates that attorneys are doing a better job.
9. If attorneys do "indoctrinate" prospective jurors, what is wrong with indoctrinating them to be fair and impartial?
10. Any abuse of the voir dire questioning by over-eager attorneys can be easily controlled by the judge.
11. Attorney involvement will contribute to the appearance of justice.

Arguments Against Attorney Involvement
1. Attorneys ask leading questions.
2. The longer time attorneys as opposed to judges take to question prospective jurors indicates that attorneys are wasting the court's time.
3. Attorneys use the voir dire for inappropriate didactic purposes.
4. Judges are more objective in the types of questions they ask.
5. Judges are less likely to invade the jurors' privacy.
6. The opportunity for judicial discretion now allows judges to permit worthy attorneys to question prospective jurors and to forbid questioning by those attorneys who typically abuse it.
7. Judicial control of questioning will contribute most to the appearance of justice.

Sources: Begam (1977); Bermant (1985); Bermant and Shapard (1981); Kairys *et al.* (1975); Stanley (1977); Suggs and Sales (1981)

47

prime assumptions underlying the adversary character of our legal system are that such a system will reduce the bias of the decision-maker, will best protect the rights of the parties, will result in the greatest discovery of evidence, and will be most satisfying to the parties (see Thibaut and Walker, 1975; Lind, 1982). A number of research projects have tested these assumptions; some of the findings validate the presumed superiority of adversary procedures in the development and presentation of evidence. For instance, simulation experiments by Thibaut, Walker, and Lind compared presentations of evidence in an adversary format (with two attorneys presenting the evidence) to a nonadversary format (with only a single attorney presenting the evidence). The researchers discovered that when subjects were initially biased against a particular side, the adversary presentation actually reduced their bias in the decision at hand (Thibaut *et al.*, 1972; Lind *et al.*, 1976). According to the researchers, the adversarial presentation did a better job of combatting the decision maker's pre-existing biases. To the extent that voir dire questioning is similar to the presentation of testimonial evidence at trial, this research suggests that adversary questioning would be better able to reduce any predispositions the judge might have in making decisions about whether a prospective juror is impartial.

Research on procedural justice also hints that adversary involvement in voir dire could contribute to the appearance of justice. A large number of studies (see Lind, 1982, for a review) have found that most people believe that adversary procedures are fairer. They are more satisfied with verdicts reached after adversary presentation of evidence, even when the verdicts are not in their favor. Furthermore, when they are asked to choose a method, people usually select one that allows for adversary representation. If this research can be extended to the voir dire portion of the trial, it suggests that the individual parties in a case, as well as the public at large, may consider jury selection to be fairer if adversary involvement occurs.

There may be distinct differences, though, in perceptions of the fairness of adversary procedures during jury selection as opposed to the trial. Bermant (1977) discovered, for instance, that the majority of federal judges believed that jury selection should be independent of the adversary process. Only one judge in twenty agreed that "Just as the adversary process is a good method for arriving at the truth of testimony, so is it a good method for the selection of impartial jurors."

A survey by Vidmar, Driver, and Tassi (1985) also suggests some limits in approval of adversary methods in jury selection. These researchers conducted an opinion poll immediately after the controversial trial of

48

Canadian abortion rights champion Dr. Henry Morgenthaler. Dr. Morgenthaler stood trial in Toronto on charges of operating an abortion clinic in defiance of Canadian laws prescribing that abortions could only be performed in a limited number of hospitals. Social scientists helped to pick the jury, which later acquitted Morgenthaler on all charges. Vidmar and his colleagues discovered that the extent to which the respondents approved of the "scientific" jury selection depended on their views of the correctness of the jury's verdict and their attitudes toward abortion. Those who were more sympathetic to Morgenthaler and abortion rights were more supportive of the jury selection process. Thus, especially in cases which sharply polarize the community, support for adversary involvement in jury selection may depend on attitudes toward the issues and parties in a specific case.

On the negative side, the literature indicates that adversary procedures create some information biases in the development of evidence by attorneys. In one simulation study, the researchers asked law students to investigate a mock case in which the evidence was either weighted against one or the other client or evenly balanced. Half of the law students were assigned an adversary role to work for one of the disputants, while the other half were assigned to work for the judge. The adversary role attorneys worked harder and discovered more facts only when the case was biased against their "client." Because their counterparts representing the favored side did not work any harder, there resulted an imbalance in the final presentation of facts before the judge (Lind, 1982).

Research by Sheppard and Vidmar (1980) revealed a similar information bias. Subjects in that study watched a slide-tape presentation of a bar-room incident and later gave their "eyewitness testimony" to a judge. After they had seen the slide-tape show but before they testified, they were interviewed by another student, who prepared them for the delivery of their testimony. Half the subjects were interviewed by students who had been assigned an adversary role, and who had been told that if their side won they would be financially compensated. The other half were interviewed by students who had been assigned a nonadversary role, and who had been told that they would be compensated if they came up with the most accurate and complete version of the facts. Sheppard and Vidmar found that those witnesses who had been interviewed by the adversary role students gave, under some circumstances, more biased testimony. Again, if we can extrapolate this pattern to adversary involvement in the voir dire, we should find that attorneys work harder to detect or to demonstrate bias against their clients, especially if their clients are severely disadvan-

49

taged. Adversary involvement in the questioning could thus result in more truly prejudiced people being challenged off the jury, but it could also result in the removal of impartial jurors. The assiduous efforts of the adversary attorney to prove bias might also violate other interests, such as the privacy rights of prospective jurors, or the speediness of the trial.

To summarize, the bulk of the work on procedural justice, if generalizable to the voir dire selection process, suggests that adversary involvement in questioning may have some benefits. It could enhance perceptions of justice by clients and the public, it could reduce any pre-existing sentiments on the part of the judge in ruling on challenges for cause, and, especially when the facts of the case are strongly against a client, it should result in more facts about prospective jurors coming to the attention of the court. On the other hand, it may well result in a biased selection of facts about prospective jurors, it may interfere with privacy rights, and it may produce in judges and some members of the public a sense that justice was not done. A final note: Future research might explore whether judges, who have considerable experience with the adversary system, react to adversary and nonadversary processes in the same manner as the public.

The Roles of Judge and Attorney. Another theme in the debate over judge-attorney conduct of the voir dire concerns how their respective roles might affect the ability to detect prejudice in prospective jurors. As a glance back at Table 1 will show, attorneys claim that because they know more about the case, they can ask better questions; and because attorneys are less intimidating than the judge, jurors will be frank with them. Judges have countered that by the time the case goes to trial, they already know a lot about the case by ruling on pretrial motions, and that jurors are more apt to be frank with them than an adversarial attorney.

Suggs and Sales (1981) analyzed the research literature on self-disclosure and concluded that attorneys have the edge in stimulating jurors to reveal their prejudices. Likening the voir dire to an interview situation, they discuss the factors that encourage people to reveal information about themselves during an interview. One variable is the status of the interviewer: There is a curvilinear relationship between an interviewer's status and the willingness of a person to disclose, such that extremely high and extremely low status interviewers tend to decrease people's self-disclosure. With high status interviewers or threatening questions, people feel pressure to answer in a way that will conform to the expectations or views of the interviewer.

Suggs and Sales argue that this research suggests that attorneys, who are at an "intermediate" social distance from the jurors (compared to the

50

judge, who is much more distant), will be better able to encourage jurors to disclose prejudice. Furthermore, attorneys can be warmer and friendlier than the judge and stay within their role boundaries, whereas the judge must remain aloof and "objective." Because people typically disclose more to friendlier interviewers, attorneys may again have an advantage in detecting prejudice.

The roles of judge and attorney differ along a number of dimensions, however, and these multiple dimensions complicate the application of the self-disclosure research to the voir dire setting. First, both judge and attorney are likely to be of higher social status than the majority of jurors; many jurors enter the courtroom very apprehensive and nervous about their task. Is the somewhat lesser social distance between attorney and juror enough to encourage self-disclosure under these circumstances? In addition, if threatening questions inhibit self-disclosure, who is more likely to ask such questions, the attorney or the judge? Anecdotally, expert witnesses have confided that they are much more wary about questions that come from adversary attorneys than from the judge, who they presume is less likely to try to slant answers in a way that undermines their testimony. A similar process could operate with jurors during voir dire.

Research evidence on role differences between judge and attorneys is thus inconclusive in its implications for the conduct of the voir dire. While it tends to indicate a modest advantage for attorneys in voir dire questioning, such advantage may be negated by jurors' perceptions of the lack of objectivity of the questioner.

Type and Method of Questioning Prospective Jurors

In contrast to the somewhat ambiguous evidence on judge versus attorney questioning, the evidence is quite straightforward in indicating the superiority of extensive, open-ended, sequestered questioning of prospective jurors for the discovery of prejudice. The voir dire is now conducted by a variety of methods which can be located on a continuum from least expansive to most expansive questioning. There are several relevant dimensions along which the questioning may vary. Jurors may be questioned as a group or individually, and may be questioned outside the presence of other jurors (referred to as sequestration). They may be asked a small number of questions directly related to the trial or, at the other extreme, a large number of questions more peripherally related to the case. They may be asked to respond to questions with a simple "Yes" or "No", or, in contrast, be asked to relate their views in an open-ended format. Thus, on the most expansive end of the continuum, the judge and both attorneys might question each juror at length and outside the presence of other jurors about attitudes toward the case. They might employ not only questions requiring yes-no answers, but also open-ended questions. The other end of the continuum might consist of brief judicial questioning of the jury panel as a group, where jurors would be asked to identify themselves if they believe they may be prejudiced. Psychological research indicates that the expansive voir dire questioning methods are more likely to reveal existing prejudices than the limited methods (Hans and Vidmar, 1986; Nickerson *et al.*, forthcoming; Suggs and Sales, 1981).

Several observational studies of voir dire suggest that the limited method of conducting voir dire makes it difficult to detect prejudice. Broeder (1965) interviewed 225 jurors after their trials had ended. Apparently, most of them had been asked about their possible prejudices by general questions posed to the panel in open court. Broeder discovered a number of instances in which jurors concealed their true feelings during voir dire. Broeder concluded: "[v]oir dire was grossly ineffective not only in weeding out 'unfavorable' jurors but even in eliciting the data which would have shown particular jurors as very likely to prove 'unfavorable' " (Broeder, 1965: 505). Zeisel and Diamond (1978) studied the use of peremptory challenges in a federal district court and similarly concluded: "[O]n the whole, the voir dire, as conducted in these trials did not provide sufficient information for attorneys to identify prejudiced jurors" (Zeisel and Diamond, 1978: 528). These studies did not explore the efficacy of different methods of conducting the voir dire, so by themselves they do not speak to the issue of whether other methods might be superior.

Analysis of jury selection in a notorious Canadian case of a child killing does suggest the advantages of more extensive and individualized questioning (Vidmar and Melnitzer, 1984). In Canada, the challenge for cause procedure is conducted only in exceptional cases, and the decisions about whether specific jurors are impartial are made not by the judge but by members of the jury panel ("triers"), who rotate in a round-robin fashion. In the child killing case, the judge first requested any persons who could not be impartial to come forward. Just four jury panel members did so. Then, the defense attorney and the Crown questioned the jurors individually about their knowledge of and possible prejudices in the case. The triers ultimately judged that only 38% of the prospective jurors who were individually questioned were impartial enough to sit as jurors. Thus, the judge's general query was ineffective in detecting many jurors who later turned out to be biased.

Vidmar and Melnitzer offered several possible explanations for this

52

discrepancy. First of all, some of the jurors apparently did not know what the judge meant by his general question about being biased. The jurors began to understand more about the problem of prejudice only after they were questioned individually and thought about their own views more deeply. Jurors may also have been reluctant to step forward and admit to the socially undesirable characteristic of prejudice. There are obvious pressures to remain quiet; and prospective jurors who believe that they are prejudiced are protected by the anonymity of the group setting. Some jurors might also have deliberately withheld information because they wanted to be on the jury, but their stance was more difficult to maintain under individual questioning by counsel.

Another field of study of voir dire questioning supports the superiority of individual and sequestered questioning in uncovering certain types of biases. Nietzel and Dillehay (1982) compared four different types of voir dire methods employed in thirteen capital murder cases in Kentucky. Voir dire procedures in each of the thirteen trials were classified as one of four types: (1) questioning of individual jurors sequestered from one another; (2) questioning en masse (in a group), followed by questions to sequestered individual jurors on specific topics; (3) questioning of the panel en masse, supplemented with individual questions to nonsequestered jurors on certain topics; and (4) questioning of the panel en masse in open court. In each type of voir dire, the judge and both attorneys participated in the questioning. Nietzel and Dillehay then calculated the percentage of potential jurors who were eliminated for cause by the judge for defense reasons (pretrial publicity, prior knowledge of the parties, opinions about the case, unwillingness to follow the judge's instructions or presume innocence) and those eliminated for cause by the judge because of their opposition to the death penalty.

They discovered that the type of voir dire questioning had a significant impact on the rate of successful challenges. The judges eliminated a greater percentage of jurors for defense reasons when jurors were questioned individually and out of the presence of the other jurors. Apparently, this method provided considerably more information that convinced the judges that many prospective jurors were prejudiced against the defendant.

Interestingly, far *fewer* jurors were challenged for cause on the basis of their opposition to the death penalty when voir dire was done in a sequestered fashion. In open court, defense attorneys were much less able to "rehabilitate" those prospective jurors who indicated some opposition to the death penalty. The presence of some jurors with feelings against the death penalty could make a difference in the verdict and the sentence the

53

jury ultimately recommends. Research studies have demonstrated that support for the death penalty is associated with more prosecution-prone attitudes and a greater willingness to convict defendants (Haney, 1984; but see *Lockhart v. McCree,* 1986, in which Justice Rehnquist, writing for the majority, criticized the studies). It is of interest to note that just one of the four juries in the Nietzel and Dillehay study that had experienced the most extensive form of sequestered voir dire returned the death sentence, compared to seven of the nine juries that had experienced other forms of voir dire. Thus, the collected research indicates that private questioning tailored to individual jurors is better able to detect prejudice, and the Nietzel and Dillehay study hints that it may work to the advantage of some criminal defendants.

A final psychological aspect of voir dire questioning of prospective jurors pertains to the subject matter of the questions. What types of questions should be asked to assess possible prejudices? Judges and attorneys often have different views on the matter, with attorneys usually preferring more numerous and more general questions. Attorneys who do not participate in direct questioning may submit voir dire questions to the judge, but a judge who believes a question is inappropriate may refuse to ask it. Appellate courts have generally upheld such judicial discretion, although they have indicated specific types of cases in which the defendant is entitled to some voir dire questions. For instance, in cases involving interracial violence, the courts have deemed it necessary to include at least one question about prospective jurors' attitudes toward minority races (*Rosales-Lopez v. United States,* 1981).

Nickerson, Mayo, and Smith (forthcoming) analyzed a pool of questions defense attorneys had submitted in cases with black defendants, to determine what types of questions judges accepted and rejected. They discovered that the accepted and rejected questions differed in two main ways. Judges were most likely to accept questions that bore directly on the law and legal issues, and they tended to reject questions that dealt with more general experiences prospective jurors had with blacks. Furthermore, the law-related questions were most often posed in a close-ended way, for example, "Do you realize that the presumption of innocence applies to a black defendant as well as a white defendant?", whereas the more general questions were more likely to be open-ended, for example, "How would you describe your experience with black people at your job?" Thus, judges tended to reject open-ended questions, and those that dealt with matters outside the courtroom.

The more general questions have the advantage of exploring the multidimensional nature of attitudes (Nickerson *et al.*, forthcoming). However, the judges' assessment of their limited relevance comports with at least some psychological research on the attitude-behavior link (Ajzen and Fishbein, 1980). That research indicates that fairly precise questions about a person's behavioral intentions are better predictors of what the person will actually do than more general questions about liking or affect. At the least this research suggests that wide-ranging questions that delve into many aspects of prospective jurors' lives are usually unnecessary and may be misleading in judging whether jurors can decide a case impartially. It would be much more fruitful to ask questions specifically related to details of the case jurors are about to hear.

The judges' apparent preference for close-ended as opposed to open-ended questions, however, is likely to hinder the search for prejudice. A yes-no answer format often results in the development of automatic patterns of response. Particularly if the socially appropriate answers are obvious, such responses tell us little about respondents' attitudes. It is preferable to intersperse close-ended and open-ended questions.

Research on the impact of different types of questioning has some implications for the judge-attorney questioning debate. If attorneys routinely engage in a different sort of questioning than judges, and their preferred methods are better at detecting prejudice, then they may have the edge in the detection of prejudice. The reverse, of course, could also be the case. In contrast to some of the other differences between judges and attorneys, any present superiority of one or the other parties is not immutable. With knowledge of effective questioning techniques, judges and attorneys could no doubt develop comparable levels of effectiveness (cf. Bermant, 1982, Appendix F: Recommendations for the Conduct of the Voir Dire Examination and Juror Challenges).

Conclusion

This review of psychological aspects of the voir dire provides some grist for the debate over its conduct. While the problem of jury prejudice is likely to be important in only a minority of cases, its assessment remains problematic. The typical judicial query to the panel at large about the existence of prejudice is likely to be insufficient, and the court's insistence on relying on prospective jurors' admissions that they are biased is at odds with decades of psychological research delineating the influence of unconscious biases on behavior.

Better methods for the detection of prejudice exist, even within the constraints posed by the voir dire. Psychological research indicates that individual and open-ended questioning of prospective jurors out of the presence of other panel members is most likely to detect biases if they exist. Furthermore, adversary attorneys may have a slight advantage over judges in detecting prejudice in prospective jurors.

These psychological aspects of voir dire questioning must, of course, be considered along with the other varied functions of the voir dire. While extensive questioning may be better able to detect prejudice, this need must be balanced against jurors' rights to privacy or the interests of a speedy trial. The desirability of expansive voir dire may also depend on whether the case is an exceptional one which engenders great hostility in prospective jurors, or a less extraordinary case in which prejudices are not likely to dominate. The balancing of these multiple interests is more properly a judicial concern than a psychological one. In this context, it is fitting to quote Judge Learned Hand, who, while recognizing the inadequacies of limited voir dire questioning, and revealing considerable psychological insights into the nature of prejudice, nevertheless justified such limits:

> It is of course true that any examination on the voir dire is a clumsy and imperfect way of detecting suppressed emotional commitments to which all of us are to some extent subject, unconsciously or subconsciously. It is the nature of our deepest antipathies that often we do not admit them even to ourselves; but when that is so, nothing but an examination, utterly impracticable in a courtroom, will disclose them, an examination extending at times for months, and even then unsuccessful. No such examination is required . . . . If trial by jury is not to break down by its own weight, it is not feasible to probe more than the upper levels of a juror's mind (*United States v. Dennis,* 1950: 221).

One might well disagree with Judge Learned Hand's pessimism about the fruitfulness of the voir dire examination in uncovering prejudice, and even about the relative importance of the speediness of the trial and the detection of prejudice. Nonetheless his statement illustrates that, in contrast to the psychologist's leisurely exploration of prejudice in the laboratory, the court's search for bias is often tempered by other concerns.

CASES

Aldridge v. United States, 283 U.S. 308 (1931).
Lockhart v. McCree, 106 S. Ct. 1758 (1986).
Ristiano v. Ross, 424 U.S. 582 (1976).
Rosales-Lopez v. United States, 451 U.S. 182 (1981).
United States v. Dennis, 183 F. 2d 201 (1950).
United States v. Wood, 299 U.S. 123 (1936).

REFERENCES

ADORNO, Theodore W., Else FRENKEL-BRUNSWIK, Daniel J. LEVINSON, and R. Nevitt SANFORD (1950) *The Authoritarian Personality.* New York: Harper.

AJZEN, Icek and Martin FISHBEIN (1980) *Understanding Attitudes and Predicting Social Behavior.* Englewood Cliffs, N.J.: Prentice-Hall.

ALLPORT, Gordon W. (1954) *The Nature of Prejudice.* Cambridge, Mass.: Addison-Wesley.

BALCH, Robert W., Curt T. GRIFFITHS, Edwin L. HALL, and L. Thomas WINFREE (1976) "The Socialization of Jurors: The Voir Dire as a Rite of Passage," 4 *Journal of Criminal Justice* 271.

BALDWIN, John, and Michael McCONVILLE (1979) *Jury Trials.* London: Oxford University Press.

BEGAM, Robert G. (1977) "Who Should Conduct Voir Dire? The Attorneys," 61 *Judicature* 71.

BERMANT, Gordon (1977) *Conduct of the Voir Dire Examination: Practices and Opinions of Federal District Judges.* Washington, D.C.: Federal Judicial Center.

_____ (1982) *Jury Selection Procedures in United States District Courts.* Washington, D.C.: Federal Judicial Center.

_____ (1985) "Issues in Trial Management: Conducting the Voir Dire Examination," in Saul M. Kassin and Lawrence S. Wrightsman (eds.) *The Psychology of Evidence and Trial Procedure.* Beverly Hills, Calif.: Sage.

BERMANT, Gordon and John SHAPARD (1981) "The Voir Dire Examination, Juror Challenges, and Adversary Advocacy," in Bruce D. Sales (ed.) *The Trial Process.* New York: Plenum.

BRILL, Steven (1984) "Inside the DeLorean Jury Room," December, *American Lawyer,* pp. 1, 94-105.

BROEDER, Dale W. (1965) "Voir Dire Examination: An Empirical Study," 38 *Southern California Law Review* 503.

CARTER, Dan T. (1975) *Scottsboro: A Tragedy of the American South* (rev. ed.). Baton Rouge, La.: Louisiana State University Press.

CROSBY, Faye, Stephanie BROMLEY, and Leonard SAXE (1980) "Recent Unobtrusive Studies of Black and White Discrimination and Prejudice: A Literature Review," 87 *Psychological Bulletin* 546.

GAERTNER, Samuel L. (1976) "Nonreactive Measures in Racial Attitude Research: A Focus on Liberals," in Phyllis Katz (ed.) *Toward the Elimination of Racism.* New York: Pergamon Press.

GARRY, Charles (1969) "Attacking Racism in Court Before Trial," in Ann F. Ginger (ed.) *Minimizing Racism in Jury Trials.* Berkeley, Calif.: National Lawyers' Guild.

GINGER, Ann F. (1975) *Jury Selection in Criminal Trials.* Tiburon, Calif.: Law Press.

HANEY, Craig (ed.) (1984) "Special Issue: Death Qualification," 8 *Law and Human Behavior,* Numbers 1/2.

HANS, Valerie P. and Neil VIDMAR (1982) "Jury Selection," in Norbert L. Kerr and Robert M. Bray (eds.) *The Psychology of the Courtroom.* New York: Academic Press.

_____ (1986) *Judging the Jury.* New York: Plenum Press.

KAIRYS, David, Jay SCHULMAN and S. HARRING (eds.) (1975) *The Jury System: New Methods for Reducing Prejudice.* Cambridge, Mass.: National Jury Project and National Lawyers' Guild.

KALVEN, Harry and Hans ZEISEL (1966) *The American Jury.* Boston: Little, Brown & Company.

KASSIN, Saul M. and Lawrence S. WRIGHTSMAN (eds.) (1985) *The Psychology of Evidence and Trial Procedure.* Beverly Hills, Calif.: Sage.

KELNER, Joseph (1983) "Jury Selection: The Prejudice Syndrome," 19 *Trial* 48.

LIND, E. Allan (1982) "The Psychology of Courtroom Procedure," in Norbert L. Kerr and Robert M. Bray (eds.) *The Psychology of the Courtroom.* New York: Academic Press.

57

LIND, E. Allan, John THIBAUT, and Laurens WALKER (1976) "A Cross-Cultural Comparison of the Effect of Adversary and Inquisitorial Processes on Bias in Legal Decisionmaking," 62 *Virginia Law Review* 271.

McCONAHAY, John B., Betty B. HARDEE, and Valerie BATTS (1981) "Has Racism Declined in America? It Depends on Who is Asking and What is Asked," 25 *Journal of Conflict Resolution* 563.

MYERS, Martha A. (1979) "Rule Departures and Making Law: Juries and their Verdicts," 13 *Law and Society Review* 781.

NICKERSON, Stephanie, Clara MAYO, and Althea SMITH (forthcoming) "Racism in the Courtroom," in John F. Dovidio and Samuel L. Gaertner (eds.) *Prejudice, Discrimination, and Racism: Theory and Research.* Orlando, Fla.: Academic Press.

NIETZEL, Michael T. and Ronald C. DILLEHAY (1982) "The Effects of Variations in Voir Dire Procedures in Capital Murder Trials," 6 *Law and Human Behavior* 1.

NISBETT, Richard and Lee ROSS (1980) *Human Inference: Strategies and Shortcomings of Social Judgment.* Englewood Cliffs, N.J.: Prentice-Hall.

PENROD, Steven D. (1979) *Study of Attorney and "Scientific" Jury Selection Models.* Doctoral dissertation, Harvard University.

ROPER, Robert T. and Victor E. FLANGO (1983) "Trials Before Judges and Juries," 8 *Justice System Journal* 186.

SEARS, David O. and John B. McCONAHAY (1973) *The Politics of Violence: The New Urban Blacks and the Watts Riot.* Boston: Houghton-Mifflin.

SHEPPARD, Blair H. and Neil VIDMAR (1980) "Adversary Pretrial Procedures and Testimonial Evidence: Effects of Lawyer's Role and Machiavellianism," 39 *Journal of Personality and Social Psychology* 320.

STANLEY, Jr., Arthur J. (1977) "Who Should Conduct Voir Dire? The Judge," 61 *Judicature* 70.

SUGGS, David and Bruce D. SALES (1981) "Juror Self-Disclosure in the Voir Dire: A Social Science Analysis," 56 *Indiana Law Journal* 245.

THIBAUT, John and Laurens WALKER (1975) *Procedural Justice.* New York: Erlbaum/Halstead.

THIBAUT, John, Laurens WALKER, and E. Allan LIND (1972) "Adversary Presentation and Bias in Legal Decisionmaking," 86 *Harvard Law Review* 386.

UNITED STATES CONGRESS (1982) Limiting the insanity defense. Hearing before the Subcommittee on Criminal Law of the Committee on the Judiciary. United States Senate, 97th Congress, 2nd Session. (Testimony by Hinckley jurors: June 24, pp. 155-201.)

VIDMAR, Neil, Pam DRIVER, and Filomena TASSI (1985) "Introduction of Social Science to the Canadian Trial Process: Scientific Jury Selection," Unpublished manuscript, University of Western Ontario.

VIDMAR, Neil and Julius MELNITZER (1984) "Juror Prejudice: An Empirical Study of a Challenge for Cause," 22 *Osgoode Hall Law Journal* 487.

WOLFGANG, Marvin E. and Marc RIEDEL (1973) "Race, Judicial Discretion, and the Death Penalty," 407 *American Academy of Political and Social Science* 119.

ZEISEL, Hans and Shari DIAMOND (1978) "The Effect of Peremptory Challenges on Jury and Verdict: An Experiment in a Federal District Court," 30 *Stanford Law Review* 491.

FEATURES

JURY BEHAVIOR AS A FUNCTION OF THE PRESTIGE OF THE FOREMAN AND THE NATURE OF HIS LEADERSHIP[*]

William Bevan, Robert S. Albert, Pierre R. Loiseaux, Peter N. Mayfield, and George Wright[†]

*The following article describes the results of two experiments
on the behavior of juries conducted by a team of psychologists
and a lawyer. The chief inquiry was on the extent to which the
personality of the foreman of the jury influenced the decisions
reached by individual members of the group. But wider questions were also explored. The factual data set out below should
be of interest to anyone concerned with the judicial process,
even though the tests were carried out in a moot court recon-
struction rather than on juries in actual trial courts.*

I. Introduction

HUMAN PERSONALITY has been traditionally described in Western thought
in terms of three independent facets—the cognitive, the conative, and the
affective. Thus any man, if established to be of sound mind, is held to be
rational and hence fully responsible for any legal transgression he com-
mits. Similarly, any verdict rendered against him is assumed to be the
consequence of the same sort of rational thought.

In contrast, the modern behavioral sciences all treat the human personality as the resultant of a complex of interacting processes, and behavior, both acceptable and unacceptable, as the predictable end product
of both personal and situational forces. A voluminous literature supports
this view for even the simplest kinds of human response.

A. The Psychology of Testimony

The implications of the psychological point of view confront the legal
specialist in at least two important areas: The reliability of testimony
and the rationality of verdicts. Faulty testimony results from errors of
perception, judgment and memory, and from the manner in which reports

* This study was supported by grants from the Social Science Research Council and
the University Center in Georgia. The data of Experiment I were collected during the summer of 1956; those of Experiment II, the following fall.
† R. S. Albert is at Massachusetts Mental Health Center; P. R. Loiseaux is at School
of Law, University of Texas; P. N. Mayfield is at Department of Psychology, University of
North Carolina, and George Wright is at Department of Psychology, Washington University. William Bevan, Emory University, served as project leader and assumed the major
responsibility for the preparation of this report.

are obtained. Inaccuracies in perception are attributable in turn to the several characteristics of the stimulus situation, sensory defects of the observer, the presence or absence of certain attitudes and expectancies in the observer, his activity at the time of observation, and his motivations. For example, the alteration of certain facial features in photographs influences the judgment of features not retouched. Properties of visually-presented material (i.e., color) are more widely recalled when the viewers have been forewarned that they will have to recall the features. The apparent duration of a temporal interval depends upon the nature of activity engaged in by the observer during the interval. The apparent size of objects is a function of their personal value to the observer, the more highly valued tending to be overestimated. And judged physiognomy varies with the racial attitudes of the judge.[1]

The relation of fallibility of memory to testimony is so clearly recognized that it requires little comment. The accuracy with which a narrative is reproduced, for example, decreases as the time between initial presentation and reproduction increases and the reported consistency of reports by observers of staged "crimes" is alarmingly low. Recall of pleasant events is better than of unpleasant; memory of emotionally toned experiences better than of neutral. Faces associated with occupations highly valued by an observer tend to be better remembered than those associated with low values.[2]

Meanwhile, less clearly recognized, by the lay public at least, is the fact that the reliability of testimony greatly depends upon the manner in which it is obtained. Use of the definite article in questions reduces caution, suggestibility and reliability in answers, while introduction of a negative term reduces both caution and reliability as it increases suggestibility. Asking whether or not certain events have occurred rather than whether or not they were observed reduces answers in all three properties. Meanwhile, the most reliable responses tend to follow positive questions related to the seeing or hearing of an event. Direct examination and cross-examination produce more information than free recital, but it is considerably less accurate. Sworn testimony is, of course, more accurate than

---

1 Consult for more detailed information, Stritch and Secord, Interaction Effects in the the Perception of Faces, 24 J. of Personality 272-284 (1956); Guilford, General Psychology (1939); Gulliksen, The Influence of Occupation upon the Perception of Time, 10 J. of Experimental Psychology 52-59 (1927); Dukes and Bevan, Size Estimation and Monetary Value. A Correlation, 34 J. of Psychology 43-53 (1952); Secord, Bevan and Katz, The Negro Stereotype and Perceptual Accentuation, 53 J. of Abnormal and Social Psychology 78-83 (1956).

2 Dallenbach, The Relation of Memory Error to Time-Interval, 20 Psychological Review 323-337 (1913); Vickery and Brooks, Time-Spaced Reporting of a "Crime" Witnessed by College Girls, 29 J. Crim. L. & Criminology 371-382 (1939); Jersild, Memory for the Pleasant as Compared with the Unpleasant, 14 J. of Experimental Psychology 284-288 (1931); Carter, Emotional Correlates of Errors in Learning, 27 J. of Educational Psychology 55-67 (1936); McGinnus and Bowles, Personal Values of Determinants of Perceptual Fixation, 18 J. of Personality 224-235 (1949).

unsworn and trained observers, like detectives and journalists, are more accurate than the "man in the street."[3]

B. *The Psychology of Judge and Jury*

Less thoroughly studied than testimony, but certainly as important, is the psychology of juridical decision-making.

Though the institution of the trial is justified by classical assumptions concerning the rational mind, it is generally accepted that judges maintain differences in their patterns of sentencing and that the strategy of counsel is guided by this knowledge. Similarly, it is widely recognized that trial lawyers make and juries respond to emotional appeals, their attitudes on an issue oscillating as opposing appeals are made. Furthermore, the personality of an examining lawyer appears to greatly influence the effectiveness of a witness' testimony. At the same time, the moral and ideological biases held by an observer clearly affect how he actually perceives an opinion presented to him. If the divergence between the observer's own and the presented position is small, the opinion is seen as factual and fair. If it is great, the view is held to be propagandistic and unfair. Where divergence is small, differences in position are underestimated. Where it is great they are exaggerated.[4]

Within recent years, many social scientists have directed their attention to the analysis of group structure and the identification of the variables influential in group problem-solving and decision-making. An interesting body of data—some expected, some surprising—is accumulating. The effectiveness of communication in producing agreement between individuals increases as interpersonal liking increases. At the same time, lack of confidence in another individual is associated with reluctance to express a conflicting opinion. As the size of a discussion group increases from five to twelve, discussion produces less consensus, and, although the leaders of small groups tend to control the group decision, their individual skills as leaders are of minor importance. In large groups, members are less inclined to express their view; at the same time they are more inclined toward dissatisfaction with the group decision and tend toward more factionalism. In addition there is a negative relationship between a participant's self-oriented needs (i.e., dependency, status, dominance, aggression, catharsis) and his satisfaction with the results of group discussion and the amount of work done; there is a positive rela-

---

[3] Muscio, The Influence of the Form of a Question, 8 British J. of Psychology 351-389 (1916); Marston, Studies in Testimony, 15 J. Crim. L. 5-31 (1924).

[4] Gaudet, Individual Differences in the Sentencing Tendencies of Judges, 230 Archives of Psychology (1938); Weld and Danzig, A Study of the Way in Which a Verdict is Reached by a Jury, 52 American J. of Psychology 515-536 (1940); Hovland, Harvey and Sherif, Assimilation and Contrast in Reaction to Communication and Attitude Change, 55 J. of Abnormal and Social Psychology 244-252 (1957).

tionship between these needs and the amount of conflict generated within the group.[5]

A research team at the University of Chicago Law School is investigating group decision-making in the jury setting. They are especially interested in the manner in which the jury handles the matter of damage awards. While full reports have not yet appeared, their data appear to be in many ways provocative. Two basic findings stand out. First, there is no single decision or solution to a jury problem. When a case is presented to a number of panels, a variety of verdicts appear. And secondly, in deciding equitable damages, the panel is inclined less to systematically analyze the damage components, more to strive for a single sum acceptable to all jurors. Their results also indicate the importance of the judge's charge—the ease with which it is understood, and the ease with which it can sensitize the jury to certain aspects of the case. The jury meanwhile is able to compensate for the inflexibility of the law by the type of decision it renders. It can, for example, get about the "either-or" requirement of the judgment of liability by adjusting the amount of damage awarded. Furthermore, juries appear to be less sensitive to the claim of pain and suffering than is generally believed. Where information on insurance is available, the jury tends to place the full loss on the defendant rather than increase the damages for the plaintiff. Finally, a juror's attitude toward damages is clearly related to cultural background, social and economic status.[6]

But to the psychologist, of greater interest and significance in an understanding of jury behavior than demographic variables are those of personality and personal experience. Classic studies of the group behavior of children have shown that it varies with the type of leadership provided. Laissez-faire leadership produces less work, and work of poorer quality than does democratic. Democratic produces less, but work of better quality than autocratic. And in the autocratic setting, the participants display more hostility and aggression, less independence and individuality. Similarly, a participatory leader is more effective than a supervisory leader in influencing group decisions of college students. Meanwhile, the airing of minority views is more effective when a leader is present than when not.[7]

---

[5] Borgatta and Bales, Interation of Individuals in Reconstituted Groups, 16 Sociometry 302-320 (1950); Mellinger, The Relationship between Communication and Consensus as Conditioned by Interpersonal Attitudes (unpublished manuscript, Research Center for Group Dynamics, University of Michigan, 1954); Hare, Interaction and Consensus in Different-Sized Groups, 17 American Sociological Review 261-267 (1952); Fouriezos, Hutt and Guetzkow, Measurement of Self-Oriented Needs in Discussion Groups, 45 J. of Abnormal and Social Psychology 682-690 (1950).

[6] Consult Kalven, Report on the Jury Project, Conference on Aims and Methods of Legal Research 155 (1957); and 2 Kalven, The Jury, the Law and the Personal Injury Damage Award, The Law School Record 6-8, 55-64 (University of Chicago, 1958).

[7] White and Lippit, Leader Behavior and Member Reaction in Three "Social Climates," in Cartwright and Zander, Group Dynamics, Research and Theory 584-611 (1953); Preston and Heintz, Effects of Participatory v. Supervisory Leadership on Group Judgment, 44 J. of Abnormal and Social Psychology 345-355 (1949); Maier and Solem, The Contribution of a Discussion Leader to Quality of Group Thinking: The Effectiveness of Minority Opinion, 5 Human Relations 277-288 (1952).

The aim of the present study is to explore the relationship of leadership to group behavior in the jury context. More specifically, it is directed toward explicating the relationship between two leadership qualities, leader prestige and type of leadership, on the formal properties of group structure, upon the manner in which group decisions are made, on the efficiency with which the decision is reached, and, of course, on the nature of the decision itself.

II. The Experimental Situation

The investigation described in this paper consisted of two experiments, the second essentially a repetition of the first, with certain improvements in procedure and additional data collection. During the second study, the complete deliberations of each panel were recorded on audio-tape.

The experimental design is indicated in the following diagram:

Leader's Prestige

Type of Leadership	High Prestige Democratic	Low prestige Democratic
	High prestige Autocratic	Low prestige Autocratic

Each block represents one jury panel, the legend within the block indicates the type of leadership provided. The foreman in each case was a confederate trained by the experimenters to behave in either an autocratic or democratic fashion. He was identified for his panel in such a way that he was presumed to have either high or low prestige. The remaining eleven panel members were, of course, unaware of the foreman's relation to the experiment and his appointment was handled deceptively in order to minimize the detection of his true identity. The membership of the panels was matched person by person, according to criteria to be described, in order to insure equivalent groups. Each panel heard the same case, under equivalent conditions, in a courtroom setting. Immediately upon presentation of the case, the jurors were asked to complete a questionnaire dealing with important aspects of it. They then retired to the jury room, and after discussion, rendered a verdict. After this decision had been reached, they were again asked to complete a questionnaire, and dismissed.

A. Membership of the Panel

For Experiment I the panel members were volunteers, drawn from the university community and from the middle and upper class residents of Atlanta, Georgia. They were organized into four matched groups in the ratio of seven men to four women. Their mean age was 38.5 years (range 21-64). Their average educational level was 15.4 years (range 5-18). They represented the following occupations: teacher, 13; student, 10; business executive, 3; salesman, 3; engineer, 2; librarian, 2; housewife, 2; accountant, 2; banker, 2; secretary, 1; telegraph operator, 1; public relations specialist, 1; telephone company employee, 1; and retired Army Officer, 1. Prior to assignment to a particular panel, they were given the Guilford-Zimmerman Temperament Survey. This is a self-evaluative personality inventory, from which estimates may be derived of ten basic personality traits. The juror's responses were scored for four traits which it was thought might be significantly related to behavior in the jury group. The traits selected were: A (aggressiveness), the tendency to speak up, exert leadership, be persuasive and conspicuous in a group; E (emotional stability), the capacity for being optimistic, composed, even-tempered; F (friendliness), the tendency to be agreeable, accept domination, show tolerance and respect of others; and P (personal relations), the capacity for cooperation with faith in people and social institutions. These test scores plus sex, age, and educational level provided the criteria for the matching of the groups. The adequacy of the matches was checked by statistical tests and the means of the four groups on each criteria were not found to differ reliably among themselves.

For Experiment II, the panel members were recruited from evening Community Education classes at Emory University. These four panels were organized in exactly the same ways as those of Experiment I, except that the California F-Scale was used in place of the Guilford-Zimmerman E-Score. The California F-Scale measures the need for dependence and authority with an unrecognized hostility toward it, with the result that "out-groups" (i.e., groups with which the person does not identify) are seen as threatening and the world generally as an evil place. The mean age of the Experiment II panels was 35.5 (range 19-58). Statistical tests again indicated the groups not to differ reliably on the matching criteria. These jurors represented the following occupations: mechanic, 6; salesman, 6; teacher, 5; business executive, 4; housewife, 3; secretary, 2; student, 2; nurse, 2; social worker, 2. The following were represented by one person each: engineer, missionary, sales analyst, accountant, personnel manager, insurance underwriter, bank clerk, psychometrist, electrician, factory foreman, and service representative. Table 1 describes the groups in terms of the criterion data. While these groups are probably representative of actual juries in age, they are perhaps of generally higher educational level.

TABLE 1

MEAN AGE, EDUCATIONAL LEVEL, AND PERSONALITY TEST SCORES
FOR THE MATCHED PANELS OF EXPERIMENTS I AND II

A.   Experiment I

Group	Age	Yrs. of Education	Factor A	Factor F	Factor P	Factor E
Low-autocratic (LA)	34.3	16.3	14.0	16.9	22.5	18.9
Low-democratic (LD)	35.9	14.8	15.9	13.4	18.5	17.5
High-autocratic (HA)	37.2	16.1	13.3	16.8	20.6	19.5
High-democratic (HD)	46.9	14.3	15.7	19.2	22.4	19.6

B.   Experiment II

Group	Age	Yrs. of Education	Factor A	Factor F	Factor P	California F
Low-autocratic (LA)	34.0	14.4	17.1	17.0	20.8	-2.5
Low-democratic (LD)	35.2	15.0	15.4	17.4	21.0	-18.9
High-autocratic (HA)	38.7	14.5	15.5	17.8	20.6	-12.6
High-democratic (HD)	34.2	13.5	13.1	16.2	18.0	-15.0

B. The Jury Foreman

The twelfth member of each panel was specially selected by the experimenters to serve as jury foreman so that some control might be exercised over the jury discussion without the remainder of the panel being aware of the foreman's particular relationship to the experiment. In Experiment I, he was formally appointed, this procedure being rationalized as a timesaving device. In Experiment II, his designation was accomplished through the subterfuge of drawing lots. The four leaders of Experiment I were each assigned a different role. These were duplicated in Experiment II. Two foremen were identified as persons of high prestige, two of low. Two were trained to conduct their jury session in a directive, autocratic fashion, two in a more permissive, democratic way. All leaders were men in their late twenties or thirties, either graduate or professional students or faculty members. The low-prestige autocratic leaders were both introduced as shoe salesmen. The low-prestige democratic leaders were introduced as a night club musician and an encyclopedia salesman respectively. The high-prestige autocratic foremen were given their true identities: a professor of political science who is an expert on legal procedure, and a professor of sociology who is an expert on group processes. The high-prestige democratic leader for both experiments was the same person, a professor of applied psychology. All leaders were requested to set as the goal of the jury discussion a verdict of negligence on the part of the defendant with $40,000 compensation for the plaintiff. The training of the leaders was based on criteria formalized by White and Lippitt.[8]

C. Staging the Trial

Each jury met on a different evening to hear testimony in the same civil suit for damages and to render its judgment. The trial was conducted in the courtroom of the Lamar School of Law at Emory University. It was enacted by a group of amateur actors, selected to match in age and sex the individuals involved in the actual trial. The roles of judge and opposing attorneys were portrayed by senior law students. The entire court proceedings from the swearing of the jury to the charging of the jury by the judge were presented. After the charge, but prior to retiring to the jury room, each juror completed a questionnaire dealing with important aspects of the case. After the jury decision had been reached, each again completed a questionnaire dealing both with the case and his own decision-making behavior. The jury deliberations of Experiment II were monitored and tape recorded by means of microphones concealed in the jury room.

The case heard by the several panels faithfully followed, with several minor exceptions, the transcript of a case actually tried in a nearby county several years prior to the experiment. Material held to be irrelevant was stricken and the testimony of certain minor witnesses omitted in the interests of time. Names of all persons involved in the actual case were, of course, altered and, at certain points, the transcript was changed to reduce ambiguity.

The substance of the case was as follows: The plaintiff, an elderly, physically infirm woman, was seriously injured in a collision while a passenger in the car of a neighbor. The defendant, a middle-aged woman of doubtful skill as a driver, had verbally contracted with the plaintiff to provide transportation in exchange for baby-sitting services. The accident occurred when the defendant's car emerged rapidly from a parking lot into a busy thoroughfare, striking a truck and then careening into a store front on the opposite side of the street. It was the plaintiff's claim that the defendant, engrossed in conversation, entered her parked car, the engine of which had been left running by a parking attendant, and, with no regard for the moving traffic, stepped on the accelerator. Negligence was alleged and damages of $50,000 plus medical expenses asked. The defendant claimed that she was not negligent, but that the brakes of her

---

[8] White and Lippit, op. cit. supra note 7.

car failed to hold as she attempted to enter the street. (The jury hearing the actual case found in favor of the plaintiff and awarded $15,000 compensatory damages.)

D. The Questionnaires

The predeliberation questionnaire administered to the panel members of Experiment I consisted of the following questions, all but two of which were answered with "yes" or "no." These exceptions required specifying a monetary sum and a person's name.

1. Was the defendant negligent in the operation of her car?
2. If the defendant was negligent, what amount of compensation should be given to the plaintiff?
3. Was the defendant accurate in her testimony given on the witness stand?
4. Was the plaintiff accurate in her testimony given on the witness stand?
5. Were the doctors who testified for the plaintiff impartial in their testimony?
6. Which witness did you find most believable?
7. Do you understand the Judge's instructions?
8. Do you thing the plaintiff was well represented by her attorney?
9. Do you think the defendant was well represented by her attorney?
10. Do you feel that you have heard enough of this matter to make a fair and accurate decision?

The post-deliberation questionnaire was exactly the same as the predeliberation except that an additional question was included: 11. If your answers to items 1 and/or 2 differ from answers given before deliberation, briefly state why you changed your mind.

The questionnaires administered to the panels of Experiment II were more elaborate. The predeliberation questionnaire consisted of fourteen questions. These, for the most part, involved making a judgment of degree, using from four to six scale categories. (For example, in the case of Item 3: 4. very much responsible, 3. responsible, 2. slightly responsible, 1. not responsible.) In the following presentation of the items the number of categories presented and the labels of the two extreme categories are indicated.

1. Do you find the defendant negligent in the operation of her car? (Yes/no).
2. If yes, how negligent do you think the defendant was? (five categories from "extremely negligent" to "not negligent").

3. How responsible do you think the plaintiff was for the accident? (four categories from "very much responsible" to "not responsible").

4. If you regard the defendant to be negligent, what compensation (zero or more dollars) do you think the plaintiff should receive?

5. How accurate do you think the defendant's testimony was? (five categories from "almost 100% accurate" to "almost completely inaccurate").

6. How accurate do you think the plaintiff's testimony was? (five categories from "almost 100% accurate" to "almost completely inaccurate").

7. How accurate do you think the first doctor's testimony was? (five categories from "almost 100% accurate" to "almost completely inaccurate").

8. How accurate do you think the second doctor's testimony was? (five categories from "almost 100% accurate" to "almost completely inaccurate").

9. How accurate do you think the automotive expert's testimony was? (five categories from "almost 100% accurate" to "almost completely inaccurate").

10. Attached is a list of the witnesses. Please rank 1, 2, and 3, the three witnesses you found most accurate. Put an "X" by their names. Next rank 1, 2, and 3 the three you regard most inaccurate. Put an "O" by their names.

11. How well do you think the plaintiff was represented by her attorney? (six categories from "execeptionally well" to "extremely poorly").

12. How well do you think the defendant was represented by her attorney? (six categories from "exceptionally well" to "extremely poorly").

13. Do you feel that you have heard enough of this case to make a fair and accurate decision? (Yes/no).

14. If your answer to No. 13 is "no," indicate what other information you feel you should have had.

The post-deliberation questionnaire of Experiment II was a modified and expanded version of the predeliberation form. Questions 1-9, 11, 12 were again used unchanged. Items 13 and 14, general evaluations of the amount of available information were not expected to change appreciably with deliberation and were omitted. Item 10, included as a check on the consistency of ratings of key witnesses, was replaced by the following more comprehensive item:

12. Rank 1, 2, and 3 the factors among this list which were most help-ful to you in reaching your final decision: (a) The defendant's tes-timony, (b) the plaintiff's testimony, (c) extent of the plaintiff's injuries, (d) the testimony of the first doctor, (e) the testimony of the second doctor, (f) the automotive expert's testimony, (g) the defendant's lawyer, (h) the plaintiff's lawyer, (i) the judge's final words to you, (j) other factors (please list).

In addition six items were added to secure information on the structure of each jury and on the interpersonal relations that obtained between panel members.

13. If you could choose, how much would you like to work with this group again on other problems? (five categories from "very much" to "definitely not at all").

14. If you could choose, how regularly would you like to continue meeting with this group socially? (five categories from "weekly" to "never again").

15. If you had your way, whom of your fellow jurors would you like to get to know better? (a) Person I'm most eager to know, (b) person I'm next most eager to know, (c) third person I'd like to know better, (d) there was no one I'd like to know better.

16. Which three persons in your group do you feel positively influ-enced your final decision. If they were equal in influence write the word "equal," (a) most influential, (b) next most influential, (c) third most influential, (d) none were influential.

17. Which three persons do you feel negatively influenced your final decision? If they were equal in influence, write "equal," (a) most negatively influential, (b) next most negatively influential, (c) third most negatively influential, (d) no one was negatively in-fluential.

18. Next to each name listed in item 15, 16, and 17, put an "X" if you think this person reacted in the same way toward you. Put an "O" if you think they reacted oppositely toward you.

E. The Transcripts of the Jury Discussions

The tapes of the deliberations of the Experiment II panels were put into typewritten form and the source of each comment identified. These were then submitted to Bales' interaction process analysis.[9] This involves classifying each verbal response into one of twelve categories, which Bales regards as constituting an "interaction system" operating in conference situations. This analysis is concerned less with the content of the dis-cussions and more with the general lines along which the discussion

---

9 Bales, Interaction Process Analysis (1950).

moves. Six may be identified: (1) orientation, finding a common basis for discussion of the problem at hand; (2) evaluation, setting up criteria for arriving at a common judgment; (3) control, attempting to influence the participation of other group members; (4) reaching a common decision; (5) patterns of interpersonal tension; (6) integration and planning. Analysis involves a frequency count of the responses for each of the twelve Bales categories. Since comparisons were being made across groups in this study, relative frequencies were computed.

F. Statistical Evaluation of the Data

The responses of the several panels were compared and the differences obtained were evaluated by means of certain widely used statistical procedures. Since certain of the present readers may be unfamiliar with the rationale of these procedures, a few general orienting comments are in order.

If a series of observations of natural events are made, it is seen that they are not all exactly alike. If, for example, one measured the body's temperature repeatedly one would find that the thermometer did not always read 98.6. Sometimes it would be above and sometimes below. If these variations cannot be demonstrated to be the result of some consistently operating factor, these are said to be chance variations. Chance variations have certain mathematical properties. They are said to describe a bell-shaped or Gaussian distribution. Small variations occur most frequently, the larger less frequently. Furthermore they are symmetrically distributed about the average of the observations. Not only do individual observations distribute themselves randomly about a sample mean (the average of a set of observations), but it is also assumed that sample means distribute themselves about a population mean (the average of all the observations that might be made under a prescribed set of conditions), and the random differences between sample means are similarly distributed. The statistical tests employed allow one to state at a given level of confidence that an observed average or average difference belongs or does not belong to a random distribution of sample means or differences among sample means. If the statistic is extra-chance or non-random, it is said to be reliable or significant. Statements of significance are probability statements. It is conventional in the behavioral sciences to accept as significant a statistic that might be expected to occur by chance less than five in one hundred times. There are two kinds of statistical tests: parametric tests and non-parametric tests. In order for parametric tests to be performed, the scores used to represent the observation must have certain mathematical properties, the major one being that the numbers used be cardinal numbers amenable to arithmetic manipulation. Non-parametric methods are used with data that do not have these properties. For example, where rating scale judgments were obtained, we made the common assumption that these were equal-interval data and could be averaged. They were subjected to parametric tests. Where "yes" or "no" was gotten, we had only frenquency data, and had to use a non-parametric test. The parametric tests used were the F and t tests; the non-parametric was X^2. In later sections the results of statistical evaluations will be presented at F- or t-ratios, or as X^2's. Accompanying each will be a probability equivalent: P<.05 or .01; P>.05. Since the 5 precent level was chosen to indicate significance, P could be >7.01 and still be significant. When the P value is <.05 or <.01, the statistic under consideration is significant; when the P value is >.05, it is not.

III. RESULTS AND DISCUSSION

The present report concerns itself with answers to the following questions: Do the processes of jury deliberation have any systematic influence upon juror opinions? Do differences in the type of leadership provided by the foreman affect jury behavior and jury decisions? Does the foreman's prestige within the jury influence jury behavior and decisions? Do the variables of leadership and prestige influence group structure and the patterns of interaction, and do these in turn, relate to jury decisions? A number of other interesting questions (i.e., is there a relationship between personality characteristics of jurors and their predeliberation decisions, their deliberation behavior and their post-deliberation responses?) will be examined at a later time.

A. The Verdict of the Juries

TABLE 2

NUMBER OF PANEL MEMBERS JUDGING THE DEFENDANT
NEGLIGENT BEFORE AND AFTER JURY DELIBERATION.
DATA FOR EXPERIMENTS I AND II

Group	Experiment I		Experiment II	
	Before	After	Before	After
LA	8	10	10	10
LD	10	10	10	11
HA	10	11	9	9
LD	10	10	10	11

Table 2 reports the number of members on each panel judging the defendant to be negligent. Inspection indicates that the predominant opinion of all panels, both before and after deliberation was that the defendant had been negligent. Deliberation, furthermore, had no effect upon this opinion.[10] This gains support from the Experiment II panel ratings of degree of negligence (Item 2). There were no interpanel differences on either the prediscussion or the postdiscussion responses.[11] Nor was the over-all prediscussion mean of 3.55 (somewhat negligent) reliably different from the postdiscussion mean of 3.75 (somewhat negligent).[12] There were, similarly, no significant interpanel differences in the ratings of the plaintiff's responsibility (Item 3),[13] and no reliable changes produced by deliberation (Pre=1.16 [slightly responsible]; Post=1:11 [slightly responsible]).[14]

These particular results may be reasonably attributed to the circumstances of the case and to the fact that the experimenter had edited out much of the ambiguous dialogue from the transcript. It is interesting to note, meanwhile, that although all panels announced a unanimous verdict in favor of the plaintiff, there were individuals in certain of the panels who maintained a private opinion to the contrary. The reasons presented for this involved a desire to avoid a hung jury, a desire to complete the deliberations and be released, and concern for the advanced age and financial status of the plaintiff.

B.   The Matter of Damages

TABLE 3

MEAN ESTIMATED JUSTIFIED COMPENSATION, BEFORE AND AFTER DELIBERATION, AND ACTUAL JURY AWARDS MADE. FIGURES REPRESENT THOUSANDS OF DOLLARS

	Experiment I			Experiment II		
Group	Pre	Post	Award	Pre	Post	Award
LA	16.4	25.9	30.0	14.4	17.1	20.0
LD	19.2	25.9	28.5	11.2	14.0	14.0
HA	11.8	17.9	21.0	14.4	20.2	27.0
HD	21.0	19.5	20.0	11.3	11.4	12.0
Mean	17.1	22.3	24.9	12.8	15.9	18.3

[10] Exp. I: $X^2 = 2.20$, df $=1$, P>.05; Exp. II: $X^2 = .152$, df $= 1$, P>.05.
[11] Pre: F= 1.75, df = 1/40, P>.05; Post: F = 1.16, df = 1/40, P>.05.
[12] t = 1.74, df = 43, P>.05.
[13] Pre: F = 1.00, df = 1/40, P>.05; Post F = .24, df = 1/40, P>.05.
[14] t = .34, df = 43, P>.05.

Table 3 presents the average of the individual estimates of justified compensation, both pre- and post-deliberation, as well as the actual damages awarded by each panel. It would appear from the results of both experiments that group discussion under the direction of a leader, irrespective of the type of leader or leadership, results in a shift in the individual juror's estimate of equitable damages. That this change is produced by the leader is strongly suggested by the fact that the shift in amount, with one exception, is upward toward the leader's stated preference of $40,000. Statistical analysis indicated that this average increase was clearly significant for four panels (Experiment I: LA, HA; Experiment II: LD, HA), very suggestive for two (Experiment I: LD; Experiment II: LA) and not reliable for two (Experiment I: HD; Experiment II: HD).[15] The apparent reversal in Experiment I, in Group HD, is not significant. Nor are the over-all per cent increases for the two experiments reliably different.[16] Meanwhile, analysis, performed to evaluate the relative importance of type of leadership and leadership prestige in bringing about the general shift upward, produced opposite results. In Experiment I, the low-prestige panels displayed a *relatively* greater change than did the high prestige.[17] At the same time, type of leadership did not have a consistent influence upon the damage award[18] nor was there a reliable interaction between prestige and type of leadership.[19] In contrast, in Experiment II, the autocratic leader produced a greater relative shift than did the democratic,[20] while level of prestige appears not to have been systematically influential.[21] Again the interaction was not reliable.[22]

It is not possible, at present, to account for the difference in the results of the two experiments. It is tempting to speculate, following the recent results of Stotland, concerning the rejection of the high-prestige foreman as "outgroup figures" with less influence than low-prestige "ingroup" leaders.[23] But this is not allowable in the face of the Experiment II data. Similarly it is not appropriate to explain the greater effectiveness of the Experiment II authoritarian leaders in terms of the over-dependence of groups upon their leader in the light of the Experiment I data.

Methodological differences between the two experiments may be presented as reasons, but these are difficult to identify. Since the subjects of Experiment II were procured from somewhat different sources than those

---

[15] Exp. I. LA: t = 2.76, df = 10, P<.02; LD: t = 2.21, df = 10, P<.06; HA: t = 3.09, df = 16, P<.02; HD: t = .42, df = 10, P>.90. Exp. II. LA: t = 2.10, df = 10, P<.07; LD: t = 2.66, df = 10, P<.05; HA: t = 2.73; df = 10, P<.05; HD: t = 1.88, df = 10, P<.10.

[16] t = 1.00, df = 43, P>.05.

[17] X² = 5.70, df = 1, P<.02.

[18] X² = 1.84, df = 1, P<7.05.

[19] X² = .20, df = 1, P>.05.

[20] F = 5.21, df = 1/40, P<.05.

[21] F = .04, df = 1/40, P>.05.

[22] F = .56, df = 1/40, P>.05.

[23] Stotland, Peer Groups and Reactions to Power Figures (unpublished manuscript, Research Center for Group Dynamics, University of Michigan 1954).

of Experiment I, this may account for the differences. Table 3 suggests that panels of the second experiment were, on the average, somewhat less generous in their awards, even before deliberation, than were those of Experiment I. This was, however, not confirmed by statistical test.[24] Indeed the $12,800 average award of Experiment I and the $17,000 of Experiment II both compare favorably with the $15,000 of the actual case. The reader will recall that, with the exception of the high-prestige democratic leader, different individuals served as leaders in the two experiments. In addition, the leaders of Experiment II received more thorough predeliberation training. It is thus possible that the differences between the two experiments may reflect these differences in personnel. Meanwhile, it is probably more than coincidence that for both experiments the high-democratic foreman was, with respect to his assigned task of achieving a high monetary settlement, the least effective of the four leaders, achieving no increase at all.

What these results—both the inconsistency between Experiments I and II and the differential in the effectiveness of various leaders—do demonstrate is the extent to which situational and otherwise circumstantial factors influence what is assumed to be a completely rational activity—how the plaintiff fares depends not only upon the merits of his case, but upon the jury that hears it, and upon the personality and behavior of the jury foreman. As Kalven has pointed out there is a range of possible verdicts for a single case, the relativity of jury law being obscured by the fact that actual trials are single instances. At the same time this same variability provides average decision-tendencies which probably become the *shifting standards,* over the longer time-span, for what is acceptable as equitable arbitration. Variability reflects the jury's capacity for circumventing the inflexibility of the legal machinery. At the same time it means that obtaining an optimal decision is a matter of probability.

When we reported a failure to demonstrate a difference between, for example, the judgments of the autocratic and democratic panels of Experiment I, we of course, mean a difference in a statistical sense, i. e., the individual pre- and post-deliberation differences in judgment upon which the average difference is based, vary to such an extent among themselves that the average can not be said to reliably represent them. In another sense—the size of the check received in settlement—the difference between the awards, for the plaintiff, at least, is very real. The lack of clearcut significance for several large average differences is probably in line with Hare's report that as the size of a group increases from five to twelve, the degree of consensus in a decision decreases. It suggests that the problem of what number constitutes an optimum jury size should be examined.[25]

Table 3 also indicates the damages formally awarded by the several

---

[24] t = 1.26, df = 43, P>.05.
[25] Hare, op. cit. supra note 5.

panels. Inspection reveals differences in amount and further suggests that the amount awarded in all but one instance exceeds the average post-deliberation evaluation. This would imply that panels (or large proportions of panels) are sensitive to the leader's pressure. Meanwhile, the fact that the group awards fell far short of the $50,000 goal indicates that the sensitivity was not complete. Tests of significance, however, indicate that in all but one case (Experiment II: Group HA) the differences between the group award and the mean of the post-deliberation evaluations were not reliable.[26] This single instance of a clear-cut difference, the high-prestige authoritarian group, is in line with expectation, if Hare's data on consensus is valid. The general lack of a statistically reliable difference between award and post-deliberation opinion as to what it should have been suggests not only that the group decisions lack unanimity of opinion, but also that the technique by which the sum presumed to constitute equitable compensation is determined is, as was indicated earlier, one of pooling individual opinions and averaging, either consciously or unconsciously. Discussions with the foremen after the deliberations and examination of the Experiment II transcriptions indicated the process to be indeed one of averaging—both conscious and deliberate.

C. The Role of the Leader in Controlling the Group Decision — Experiment II

If leader control can be defined in terms of the extent to which the foreman dominates the group discussion and the speed with which agreement is achieved, we have several sources of information on this factor in the data of Experiment II. We can calculate the number of statements made during each deliberative session, the per cent of the total made by the leader, and the number of ballots taken prior to unanimous agreement. Judging from these criteria, it would appear that the high-prestige autocratic leader was most influential, having brought his group to unanimous agreement after one ballot, after making 32% of the 500 statements that comprised the discussion. The second most effective was the low-prestige autocratic leader who effected agreements with 32% of a total of 837 statements. He, however, took seven ballots to reach a unanimous decision. The high-prestige democratic leader stood third, with 19% of 812 statements and three ballots, and the low-prestige democratic foreman ranked last with 17% of 1165 statements and four ballots. It is interesting to note the close correspondence between this order and the rank order of the awards in the right-most column of Table 3. The highest award was obtained by the HA leader, the next by the LA leader, the third highest by the LD leader, and the lowest by the HD leader. This is clear

---

[26] Exp. I: LA: t = .94, df = 10,P>.05; LD: t = 1.00, df = 10, P>.05; HA: t = 1.80, df = 10, P>.05; HD: t = .02, df = 10, P>.05. Exp. II. LA: t = 1.16, df = 10, P>.05; LD:t = .10, df = 11, P>7.05; HA: t = 3.24, df = 10, P<.01; HD: t = 1.05, df = 10, P>.05.

evidence for a point made earlier, that group opinion reflects to a significant degree the view of an effective leader—or in broad terms, that reason may in large measure be persuasion.

D. Interaction Process Analysis—Experiment II

TABLE 4

RESULTS OF THE BALES CATEGORY ANALYSIS PERFORMED ON THE FOUR
GROUPS OF EXPERIMENT II, EXPRESSED AS SIMPLE
FREQUENCIES AND AS PERCENTS

	LA		LD		HA		HD	
Category	f	%	f	%	f	%	f	%
1. shows solidarity	38	4.54	50	4.29	28	5.60	29	3.57
2. shows tension release	31	3.90	13	1.12	25	3.00	33	4.06
3. agrees	72	8.60	166	14.25	50	10.00	80	9.85
4. gives suggestion	58	6.93	69	5.92	17	3.40	32	3.94
5. gives opinion	289	34.53	328	28.16	149	27.80	385	47.42
6. gives orientation	150	17.92	273	23.43	161	32.20	128	15.77
7. asks for orientation	34	4.06	96	8.24	30	6.00	35	4.32
8. asks for opinion	23	2.75	46	3.95	16	3.20	45	5.54
9. asks for suggestion	5	.60	2	.17	0	.00	4	.49
10. disagrees	25	2.99	76	6.52	16	3.20	16	1.97
11. shows tension	20	2.39	28	2.40	7	1.40	12	1.48
12. shows antagonism	92	10.99	18	1.55	11	2.20	13	1.60
	837	100.00	1165	100.00	500	100.00	812	100.00

From the results of the analysis performed on the transcriptions of the Experiment II jury deliberations, two things become immediately apparent: (1) The primary activity of group members, as a whole, involved making statements of orientation and giving personal opinions; and (2) the profile of activities is highly similar for all groups. To get a quantitative expression of this last conclusion, product-moment coefficients of correlation were computed between all combinations of groups in pairs.[27] The

---

[27] A coefficient of correlation is a statistical index which expresses *degree* of positive or negative relationship between two variables. Coefficients between .90 and 1.00 indicated an extremely high relationship; between .70 and .90, a marked relationship; between .40 and .70 a substantial relationship; between .20 and .40 a small but definite relationship; and less than .20 only a negligible relationship.

coefficients obtained vary between .83 and .96, and indicate the high degree of similarity among the profiles. Comparisons among the groups on individual categories were made. A high criterion—P< .001—was deliberately set so that only markedly reliable differences would be identified. The groups with the autocratic leaders differed from those with the democratic foremen on only one category—No. 12, the autocratic groups displaying antagonism reliably more frequently.[28] This agrees with Preston and Heintz's report that supervisory leadership makes for less satisfying, less enjoyable group problem-solving.[29] It is also seemingly in line with Hare's finding that factionalism is much more apparent in groups the size of juries than in smaller discussion groups.[30] Differences in response related to prestige level are seen for two categories, 12 and 5. In the case of the former we surprisingly note that there was a strikingly more frequent expression of hostility among the low-prestige autocratic leader panel than among the others. We had expected, as Stotland reports, that peer support would have produced greater antagonism toward the high-prestige leader, especially in the autocratic environment.[31] Instead, the data appear to agree with Hurwitz, Zander and Hymovitch's claim that low-status group members are inclined to behave ego-defensively toward a high-prestige discussant.[32] Meanwhile, the generally great influence of all leaders is indicated by high correlations between the Bales profiles for the foreman and the average profiles for the remaining eleven panel members (LA = .95, LD=.65, HA=.82, HD=.89). In only one case (LD) is this relationship less than marked, and here it is substantial and probably reflects a greater over-all flexibility within the group. Such flexibility, however, did not, as was indicated above, result in greater influence of the leader. The second difference related to prestige level reflects substantially more frequent expression of opinion in the high-democratic group. This suggests again the ego-defensive identification of low-prestige members with high-prestige participants described by Hurwitz, Zander, and Hymovitch, which should be maximized with the more permissive atmosphere of the democratic group.

The Bales categories may be combined to give a clearer schematization of the discussion activity: Evaluation (categories 5, 8); orientation (categories 6, 7); control (categories 4, 9); positive reactions (categories 1, 2, 3); and negative reactions (categories 10, 11, 12). Averaged for the four panels of Experiment II, the relative frequencies for these criteria are respectively 39.0%, 27.4%, 5.5%, 18.2%, and 9.9%. As mentioned earlier, the greatest proportion of the discussion was directed toward clari-

---

[28] $X^2 = 74.42$, df = 1, P<.001.
[29] Preston and Heintz, op. cit. supra note 7.
[30] Hare, op. cit. supra note 5.
[31] Stotland, op. cit. supra note 23.
[32] Hurwitz, Zander and Hymovitch, Some Effects of Power on the Relations among Group Members, in Cartwright and Zander, Group Dynamics, Research and Theory, c. 32 (1953).

fying and evaluating, with the atmosphere more positive than negative. These proportions compare quite favorably with a similar set presented by Bales and Strodbeck as representative of conference and committee discussion: 34%, 30%, 7.5%, 25%, and 7.5%.[33] What is especially striking when one takes an overview of the transcription is that the problems of negligence and damages appear to have been solved in all juries less by a systematic piece-by-piece analysis of the problem, and more by a trading of opinions until a satisfactory compromise was reached.

E. The Social Structure of the Panels — Experiment II

TABLE 5

The data on social structure were gleaned from the final five items of the post-deliberation questionnaire. By social structure we mean the complex of relationships that develop among group members that become translated into preferences for one another along a variety of social dimensions, like those of personal influences and of personal likes and dislikes. It should be kept in mind that the present groups, unlike families, groups of close friends, work associates, schoolmates, etc., had an extremely short organizational history. Our data suggest that even under the present circumstances a network of mutual supports and antagonisms can develop. In addition, the nature of the task set for juries probably greatly influences their structure and makes it different from the structure of groups in other situations.

THE EXTENT TO WHICH POSITIVE AND NEGATIVE ATTRACTIONS AND INDIFFERENCE WERE JUDGED TO BE PRESENT IN THE SEVERAL GROUPS

	Total No. of choices	% of possible judgments	No. of positively reciprocated influences	Relative No. of positively reciprocated influences
LA	61	.921	43	.705
LD	57	.878	34	.596
HA	46	.696	22	.478
HD	51	.772	29	.570

	No. of negatively reciprocated influences	Relative No. of negatively reciprocated influences	No. of nonreciprocated responses	Relative No. of nonreciprocated responses
LA	16	.262	2	.033
LD	11	.182	12	.222
HA	11	.239	13	.283
HD	3	.058	19	.372

---

[33] Bales and Strodtbeck, Phases in Group Problem Solving, 46 J. of Abnormal and Social Psychology 488-495 (1951).

Table 5 summarizes the information on group structure. Column 1 indicates the total number of choices made by each group. Column 2 indicates the proportion this value represents of the total possible number. (Since each juror was required to indicate as many as three of the eleven remaining panel members who had a positive and three who had a negative influence on his decision, the total possible number of choices for each panel was sixty-six.) Column 3 indicates the number of positively reciprocated influences judged by the panel members to exist in each panel.

Column 4 indicates what proportion of the choices made this represents. Columns 5 and 6 provide the same information for the estimates of negatively reciprocated influence. Column 7 indicates the number of nonreciprocated influences judged to be present. Column 8 presents the relative number of such influences. Inspection suggests that the group members with the high-prestige authoritarian leader were the most apathetic of the four panels and saw themselves as rather emotionally isolated, for they made relatively the fewest judgments of influence, held these to be positively reciprocated the least frequently, and judged a considerable number of their felt influences to be nonreciprocated. One possible reason for this lies in the monopolization of the jury deliberation by the foreman in the expression of his views. In contrast the group with low-prestige authoritarian leadership appears to have seen itself as more vigorous and with a more clear-cut group structure. It showed the highest degree of felt influence, making sixty-one out a possible sixty-six choices, showed by far the greatest amount of assumed positive reciprocity of influence, and assumed nonreciprocity to be practically nonexistent. In all, this suggests that the presence of an authoritarian leader, if he is not too strong, facilitates the identification of group members with each other for emotional support. The differences between the two democratic groups are, in contrast, less pronounced. In both, there is a strong expression of influence and this is presumed, to a large extent, to be either positively or not reciprocated at all.

If we look at the over-all effects of the two major variables, level of prestige and type of leadership (Table 6), we note that the low prestige groups display a more pervasive feeling of interaction, since they utilized an average of 90% of their total possible choices of influence as contrasted with 71% for the high-prestige groups, where, it would appear, the panels were more passively oriented toward the foreman-leader.

TABLE 6

EXTENT OF POSITIVE AND NEGATIVE ATTRACTION AND INDIFFERENCE IN
PANELS AS A FUNCTION OF LEVEL OF PRESTIGE AND TYPE OF LEADERSHIP

	% of possible judgments	Relative No. of positively reciprocated influences	Relative No. of negatively reciprocated influences	Relative No. of non-reciprocated influences
High	71	53	15	33
Low	90	66	22	13
Autocratic	81	59	25	16
Democratic	83	59	12	30

This influence is further supported by the relatively small number of assumed nonreciprocated and the greater number of assumed positively reciprocated influences in the low-prestige groups. Meanwhile, type of leadership did not affect an overall difference in the amount of participation (proportion of possible choices) nor in the relative number of positively reciprocated influences, the authoritarian, as might be expected, provoking more negatively reciprocated and nonreciprocated responses than the democratic.

F.   Identification With the Group

The panel members of Experiment II were asked how much they would like to work with their respective groups on similar problems in the future and to associate on a purely social basis. In the latter matter there were no significant differences between groups, the overall mean (cf. Table 8) suggesting an interest in occasional social gatherings. Meanwhile, all panels indicated an interest in working together again at group decision making, those with high-prestige leaders showing a reliably higher preference than those with low-prestige foremen.[34]

G.   The Credibility of the Witnesses

[34] F = 5.13, df = 1/40, P<.05.

TABLE 7

JUDGMENTS OF PANEL MEMBERS ON THE CREDIBILITY
OF WITNESSES

Item of comparison	Groups			
	L.A.	L.D.	H.A.'	H.D.
1. No. of jurors, before deliberation, regarding plaintiff's testimony to be accurate (Exp. I)	3	9	3	8
2. Mean rating, before deliberation, of accuracy of plaintiff's testimony (Exp. II)	2.00	2.27	2.55	2.64
3. No. of jurors, after deliberation, regarding plaintiff's testimony to be accurate (Exp. I)	5	9	4	8
4. Mean rating, after deliberation, of accuracy of plaintiff's testimony (Exp. II)	1.64	2.82	2.64	2.64
5. No. of jurors, before deliberation, regarding defendant's testimony to be accurate (Exp. I)	7	7	5	6
6. Mean rating, before deliberation, of accuracy of defendant's testimony (Exp. II)	2.82	3.09	2.90	2.82
7. No. of jurors, after deliberation, regarding defendant's testimony to be accurate (Exp. I)	6	6	4	7
8. Mean rating, after deliberation, of accuracy of defendant's testimony (Exp. II)	2.73	2.90	2.73	2.82
9. No. of jurors, before deliberation, regarding doctor's testimony to be accurate (Exp. I)	7	10	10	9
10. No. of jurors, after deliberation, regarding doctor's testimony to be accurate (Exp. I)	6	9	10	9

11. Mean rating, before deliberation, of accuracy of first doctor's testimony (Exp. II)	3.73	3.55	3.82	3.82
12. Mean rating, after deliberation, of accuracy of first doctor's testimony (Exp. II)	3.27	3.27	3.62	3.45
13. Mean rating, before deliberation, of accuracy of second doctor's testimony (Exp. II)	3.64	4.00	3.73	3.64
14. Mean rating, after deliberation, of accuracy of second doctor's testimony (Exp. II)	3.45	3.91	3.45	3.36
15. Mean rating, before deliberation, of accuracy of automotive expert's testimony (Exp. II)	3.45	3.45	3.55	3.00
16. Mean rating, after deliberation, of accuracy of automotive expert's testimony (Exp. II)	3.18	3.64	3.36	2.73

TABLE 8

JURORS' JUDGMENTS CONCERNING THE EFFECTIVENESS OF COUNSEL,
READINESS TO RENDER JUDGMENT, AND GROUP IDENTIFICATION

	Groups			
	L.A.	L.D.	H.A.	H.D.
1. No. jurors per panel regarding plaintiff to be well represented by counsel (Exp. I)	9	11	10	11
2. No. jurors per panel regarding defendant to be well represented by counsel (Exp. I)	6	5	5	5
3. Mean rating of effectiveness of plaintiff's counsel: before deliberation (Exp. II)	4.73	3.72	4.45	4.36
4. Mean rating of effectiveness of plaintiff's counsel: after deliberation (Exp. II)	4.45	4.09	4.00	4.09
5. Mean rating of effectiveness of defendant's counsel: before deliberation (Exp. II)	4.00	3.18	3.82	3.00
6. Mean rating of effectiveness of defendant's counsel: after deliberation (Exp. II)	3.82	3.36	3.18	3.27
7. Mean rating of clarity of charge (Exp. I)	1.45	1.55	1.36	1.64
8. No. jurors per panel, before deliberation, who felt capable of rendering a fair decision (Exp. I)	9	11	10	11
9. No. jurors per panel, after deliberation, who felt capable of rendering a fair decision (Exp. I)	6	5	5	5
10. Mean rating of individual juror's preferences for serving with particular group again (Exp. II)	2.36	2.81	3.00	3.45
11. Mean rating of individual juror's preference to know the members of his group socially (Exp. II)	1.72	1.65	1.27	1.45

Table 7 presents information on the juror's opinions concerning the credibility of the several major witnesses. Inspection indicates that for Experiment I, a large proportion of the membership of two panels had some doubt concerning the credibility of the plaintiff.[35] Yet opinion in all four panels was predominantly on her side and every panel found in her favor. It would thus appear that her credibility is not a consistent factor in influencing the verdict. Informal questioning of the jurors after the trial suggested that considerations such as her age and financial insecurity were of great consequence in determining their decision. (In this connection, it is significant to point out that *every* panel considered at length the matter of expenses and possible insurance compensation in their discussion, one group going so far as to instruct their foreman to determine from the court officers whether or not the defendant was insured—he was told, of course, that this information could not be supplied. It is quite clear from a study of the transcript of Experiment II that the decisions of all panels were influenced not only by the extent of the plaintiff's injuries, but also by their impressions of the plaintiff's capacity to meet damage claims). The picture is similar for Experiment II. Prior to deliberation, all panels judged her to be between 50% and 75% accurate. This was not appreciably changed after deliberation, although the low-autocratic group showed a drop and the low-democratic a shift upward (prestige by leadership interaction was significant at < .05). These differences, however, appear not to be related to the jury awards.

Opinions of the defendant's credibility are essentially the same. In Experiment I there is approximately an even split,[36] and, in Experiment II, all panels, both before and after the jury session, regarded her to be about 75% credible. This suggests a fundamental weakness in the logic of all panels. While the principals in the case present conflicting accounts of what occurred, they are regarded to be equally credible and the issue must inevitably be resolved on other grounds.

On the other hand, the credibility of the doctors was accepted by the majority of all panels. In Experiment I, no panel had less than seven of the eleven subjects judging the medical testimony to be accurate.[37] In Experiment II, the physicians were judged to be 75% or more accurate, and this estimate did not vary with group membership or with deliberation. When the jurors of Experiment I were asked to indicate the most accurate witness, the doctors stood at the top of the list, well separated from all the others—the two combined drew votes from 48% of the forty-four jurors, while the remaining eight witnesses drew 52%. This indicates the operation of a halo effect contributed by professional status, for this high

---

[35] Deliberation had no effect on evaluations of the plaintiff's credibility: $X^2 = .38$, df = 1, P>.05.
[36] Again, deliberation had no effect on opinion: $X^2 = .18$, df =1, P>.05.
[37] Deliberation did not affect this: $X^2 = .28$, df = 1, P>.05.

opinion was held despite the fact that each doctors' testimony made it quite clear that he had a considerable financial interest in the case. The next highest vote went to the automotive expert (16%), the only other expert witness appearing in the trial. He also constituted a vested interest since he represented the automobile firm which manufactured the car involved in the accident.

H. Effectiveness of Counsel

A predominant number of each Experiment I panel regarded the plaintiff's counsel to have performed adequately in the prosecution of her case—this, despite considerable doubt that she herself was an accurate witness (Table 8). In contrast, the panels of Experiment I were about equally divided on the effectiveness of the defendant's counsel. These data thus suggest confirmation of the widely held assumption that the manner in which an issue is presented to the court is a major determinant of court decisions.

This is corroborated in the results of Experiment II. The mean ratings for the four panels do not differ significantly on either the pre- or post-deliberation evaluations of the opposing attorneys. Meanwhile, while the differences between the two are not so striking, perhaps, as those of Experiment I, they are nonetheless highly reliable.[38] Again, in all instances, the decision went to the party with the counsel judged the more effective by the jury hearing the case.

I. Confidence of the Juries in Their Own Readiness to Render a Competent Decision

The panels of Experiment I were asked if they felt that they understood the judge's charge administered just prior to entering the jury room. Their responses were rated on a three-point scale: 1. completely; 2. reasonably well; 3. not very well. The mean rating for all groups was 1.50—between reasonably well and completely. There were no significant differences among the panels. This means that all groups felt that they understood very well the issues they were to deliberate. Similarly, before deliberation, a predominant number of each panel felt they had heard enough of the matter to be capable of rendering a fair and accurate decision. At the same time, it will be recalled that many also indicated doubt concerning the credibility of certain key witnesses. In contrast, after deliberation there was a marked reduction in the number of panel members in all panels who expressed confidence in being able to reach a fair and competent

---

[38] For example, for the difference between the mean rating of the two opposing attorneys, t = 3.47, df = 43, P<.01.

decision.[39] This suggests that one important effect of discussion in group problem solving is to make the individual participant sensitive to the subtle and complex factors that influence his judgments concerning human conduct.

In Experiment II responses were more evenly divided (affirmative answers: LA, 6; LD, 6; HD, 5; negative answers: LA, 5; LD, 5; HD, 6) in all except the high-prestige autocratic group where eight persons expressed the opinion that they had adequate information for reaching a fair decision.

J. Factors Influencing the Individual Juror's Decision

Item 12 of the Experiment II post-deliberation questionnaire required each juror to rank fifteen factors from highest to lowest in influence on his final decision. Group profiles of these factors were then constructed for each panel.[40] Finally, rank-order coefficients of correlations were computed to determine the extent of resemblance existing between the profiles of each panel.

TABLE 9

RANK-ORDER COEFFICIENTS OF CORRELATION EXPRESSING DEGREE OF SIMILARITY BETWEEN RANK-ORDERS OF FACTORS INFLUENCING JURORS' DECISION ON EACH PANEL. COLUMN THREE PRESENTS CORRESPONDING STANDARD ERRORS. ASTERISK INDICATES STATISTICAL SIGNIFICANCE

Panels compared	rho	rho
LA - LD	.34	.25
LA - HA	.52*	.21
LA - HD	.46*	.23
LD - HA	.33	.26
LD - HD	.20	.28
HA - HD	.69*	.15

Table 9 represents the results of these comparisons.[41] Only three comparisons reveal reliable similarity: LA - HA; HA - HD; and LA - HD. In

[39] $X^2 = 25.20$, df $= 1$, P<.001.
[40] The profile was constructed by first determining the frequency over all panels with which each factor was listed first, second, or third. Arbitrary weights (intensive values) of 3, 2, or 1 were then assigned to the frequency scores. Next the products of frequency and weight were obtained and summed together for each factor in each panel. The rank order of these sums constituted the panel's profile.
[41] For these coefficients to be significant, they were required to be at least 2.16 times

one case, both groups have autocratic leadership in the second, both have high-prestige leaders, and in the third, they differ in both types of leadership and prestige. It would appear impossible to explain similiarity—or lack of it in the three remaining comparisons—in terms of the systematically varied conditions of this experiment. The items occupying the top three and bottom three ranks in the orders are as follows for each panel. LA: high: extent of the plaintiff's injuries, the judges's charge, a miscellaneous collection of reasons—including the plaintiff's age and the length of the jury session; low: the plaintiff's lawyer, the testimony of the automotive expert, and the defendant's lawyer; LD: high: extent of plantiff's injuries, the judge's charge, and the second doctor's testimony; low: the foreman, the juror's own experience as a driver, and miscellaneous factors; HA: high: the juror's experience as a driver, the extent of the plaintiff's injuries, and the judge's charge; low: the defendant's lawyer, miscellaneous factors, and the automotive expert's testimony. HD: high: extent of the plaintiff's injury, the views of the rest of the jury, and the juror's own experience as a driver; low: the defendant's lawyer, the automotive expert's testimony, and the testimony of the first doctor.

It would thus appear that the factors most consistently of great influence in forming individual opinion are the extent of the plaintiff's injuries and the judge's charge—neither directly concerned with the specific circumstances of the accident. Only two of the four groups listed a factor (the juror's own experience as a driver) which might be assumed to be related to the latter and thus the charge of negligence. Concern with the plaintiff's injuries reflect the effectiveness of the plaintiff's lawyer, who emphasized these in his presentation. Most frequently listed among the least influential factors was the defendant's lawyer, although it was earlier indicated that he was rated slightly better in effectiveness. This suggests that since he lacked extreme effectiveness, the circumstances of the case mediated against his having an effect at all. The automotive expert similarly lacked influence. This might suggest that his inevitable bias in the case was recognized and his testimony discounted. In contrast, the medical witnesses, it would appear, were assumed to be free of bias.

K. Overview

If one skims across the mass of detail of the present report, certain general impressions are gained. First, the jury decision, far from being a simple rational matter, is a complex phenomen involving emotional attitudes of the individual jurors and, quite probably, general situational factors. The importance of personal factors is seen in the fact that the jury foremen, with one exception, were able to reliably change the opinions of individual jurors concerning what constitutes equitable damages. Reason

as large as their standard errors. This last statistic is presented in the right-most column of Table 9.

was thus conditioned by persuasion. Meanwhile, the effects of two personal characteristics of the foreman which were assumed to have been experimentally manipulated, his prestige with other jury members and the mode of leadership which he provided, did not exert consistent effects from the first experiment to the second. The experimenter can only rationalize this by saying either that subtle and thus unspecified considerations in the design rendered experimental control inadequate or that strong variables of a different order—i.e., situational—militated against the consistent effect of the specified variables. Certainly it is not presumed the heuristic procedures used in organizing the jury panels and selecting leaders exhausted the personality dimensions which might produce significant interactive effects when given an opportunity to meet in a particular panel setting. Meanwhile, this inconsistency does suggest a relativity of truth as the jury defines it.

The second impression of importance concerns the manner in which the jury reached its decision on damages. Instead of a logical establishment of criteria for measuring damages and a systematic businesslike assessment of what was reasonable in these terms, panel members began by presenting to the group overall impressions, and by a process of give and take, arrived at a damage figure formally acceptable to all. The actual amount appears to be obtained, in some cases at least, through a deliberate arithmetic averaging of individual opinions. Again, persuasion tempers reason.

Thirdly, the formal structure of the legal process forces a degree of solidarity upon jury opinion that is only phenotypic. The circumstances of the case made for a generally rapid judgment of negligence—although even here there were individual panel members who held an opposite opinion even after their jury service was over. Meanwhile, the real feeling of the jury is seen in their prolonged discussion of the matter of damages, where their freedom of decision is greater. But even here, the requirement of unanimous agreement results in certain individuals voting against their convictions. At the same time, the jury is able to compensate for the either-or requirement on the negligence charge and closely approximate their real opinion by adjusting the amount of damages awarded.

Finally, a word on method is in order. The results were obtained in a moot court and it is not yet possible to confidently state the extent to which they may be generalized. The panel members represented a range of occupations and educational and economic levels. How they compare in their composition to actual juries is undetermined. Furthermore, in every case they were volunteers, and the significance of this is not known. Finally, the fact they knew they were in a moot court situation may have added a degree of latitude to their discussion that may not be present in actual cases. But despite the tentativeness of these and any other current experimental results in this field, the application of the experimental method to the study of behavior of interest to the legal profession holds promise, for by allowing for the replication of trials, it provides a more confident notion of what the range and variety of jury behaviors is like; and by providing the techniques of control, it makes possible the eventual identification and regulation of the factors that produce these behaviors

IV. Summary

Two sets of four jury panels each sat on a case involving a charge of negligence resulting from an automobile accident in which the plaintiff, a passenger in the defendant's car, was seriously injured. The panels differed in type of leadership provided by and the prestige held by the foreman.

All eight panels agreed on a verdict of negligence. Three of the first four panels (Experiment I) increased their estimates of what constituted adequate compensatory damages following jury deliberation, during which the foreman (a confederate trained by the experimenter to behave in certain ways) attempted to reach a high settlement. All four panels of Experiment II showed a similar increase. Meanwhile, differences in the type of leader and leadership did not provide generalizable results. In Experiment I panels with low-prestige foremen showed greater relative increases than those with high-prestige foremen. Type of leadership, autocratic versus democratic, had no systematic effect on the amount awarded. In contrast, for Experiment II the results were reversed: the autocratic leaders produced a greater relative increase in awards than did the democratic, and leader-prestige was found to have no systematic influence. Meanwhile, the general correspondence between the averages of individual estimates of equitable damages and the damages awarded by each group suggests that such values are arrived at by pooling, consciously or unconsciously, the individual estimates of the panel members. Analysis of tape recordings of the jury deliberations of Experiment II indicated that this was consciously and deliberately done. Interaction process analysis of these same transcripts indicated the action-structure of all panels to be highly similar and to consist primarily of discussion providing orientation or evaluation.

Although there was persistent and prominent doubt concerning the credibility of the plaintiff, opinion generally favored her. This would appear to be primarily a function of the effectiveness of her counsel and the extent of her personal injuries, highly dramatized in the presentation of her case. Prior to deliberation, the panels of Experiment I consistently indicated confidence in their capacity, with the information provided, to reach an equitable decision. After deliberation this confidence was decreased.

THE IMPORTANCE OF THE SCAPEGOAT IN JURY TRIAL CASES: SOME PRELIMINARY REFLECTIONS

DALE W. BROEDER*

INTRODUCTION

This is a strategy piece about juries. The data which follow are based on the constant and uninterrupted study of a series of twenty-three jury trials in a single federal district court in the Midwest. The writer's usual introductory apologia will here be foregone. It has been repeatedly stated elsewhere.[1] At the same time, it must unequivocally be noted that the data herein and such messages as may be derived therefrom were all made possible by a Ford Foundation grant to the University of Chicago Law School.[2] In other words, what follows is merely a small portion of the author's extremely small contribution to what is now popularly known as the *University of Chicago Jury Project*.

The topic chosen is minor and intentionally so. The *Jury Project* data as a whole are enormous and multi-faceted; it would be extra-ordinarily presumptuous of this writer to begin reporting it by a full-blown and supposedly definitive essay, for example, one dealing with a matter such

---

* Visiting Professor of Law, University of New Mexico. The author is deeply indebted to Professor Harry Kalven, Jr., of the University of Chicago Law School for his always sage advice and encouragement.

1. See generally Kalven, *Report on the Jury Project of the University of Chicago Law School*, Pam. Conference on Legal Research, University of Michigan Law School (Nov. 5, 1955); Kalven, *A Report on the Jury Project of the University of Chicago Law School*, 24 Ins. Counsel J. 364 (1957). See, also Meltzer, *A Projected Study of the Jury as a Working Institution*, 287 Annals 97 (1953).

As regards the author's own published *Jury Project* work see Broeder, *The University of Chicago Jury Project*, 38 Neb. L. Rev. 744 (1959); Broeder, *The Jury Project*, 26 S.D.B.J. 133 (1957); Broeder, *The Negro in Court*, 1965 Duke L.J. 19 (1965); and Broeder, *Previous Jury Trial Service Affecting Juror Behavior*, 506 Ins. L.J. 138 (1965).

For other *Project* publications, see, Zeisel, Kalven & Buchholz, Delay in the Courts (1959); Zeisel, *Split Trials and Timesaving: A Statistical Analysis*, 76 Harv. L. Rev. 1606 (1963); Kalven, *General Analysis of and Introduction to the Problem of Court Congestion and Delay*, 1963 ABA Sect. Ins. N. & C.L. 322 (1963); Zeisel, *Splitting a Liability and Damage Issue Saves 20% of the Court's Time*, 1963 ABA Sect. Ins. N. & C.L. 322 (1963); Kalven, Zeisel & Buchholz, *Delay in the Court*, 15 Record 104 (Mar., 1960), as reprinted in 8 U. Chi. L. Rev. 23 (1959); Zeisel, Kalven & Buchholz, *Is the Trial Bar a Cause of Delay?*, 43 J. Am. Jud. Soc'y 17 (1959); Kalven, *The Jury, The Law and the Personal Injury Award*, 19 Ohio St. L.J. 158 (1958), reprinted in 7 U. Chi. L. Rev. 6 (1958).

2. The data in question are based, not only on the twenty-three jury trials mentioned in the text, all of which trials were observed from beginning to end, but likewise on interviews with the judge, the law clerk, and other court personnel. Likewise, in the twenty-three jury cases studied, 225 jurors, all of those consenting to be interviewed, were interrogated at their homes, the average interview running about two and one half hours. Some of the interviews ran in excess of four hours.

as the jury room behavior of various socio-economic groups. Yet that which follows, hopefully at least, may provide some worthwhile insights concerning at least one aspect of the institution of jury trials as a viable, operative force in our society.

A "scapegoat," as the term is employed here, is someone other than plaintiff or defendant upon whom some or all of the responsibility for the happening complained of can or might conceivably be placed. Defendant's fellow tortfeasor, who might or might not also be a defendant, would be a typical negligence-case scapegoat. Defendant's accomplice, who might or might not also be on trial, would be a typical scapegoat in criminal cases. The purpose here is to show the role played by the scapegoat in the cases studied and, as far as possible, to chart his impact upon the juror's thinking and behavior.[3] The question is clearly of importance, for three of the seven criminal and four of the sixteen civil cases involved scapegoat situations, and the scapegoat left his mark in each case.

CRIMINAL CASES

Of all the cases studied, civil as well as criminal, the scapegoat rose to his—actually her—greatest heights in *Cooper*,[4] a Mann Act case. Defendant was charged with transporting his wife, Sue, from State X to State Y for the purpose of placing her in a house of ill-repute. Defendant was thirty-six years of age, fairly handsome, and very articulate; Sue, a tired-looking twenty-nine, often very inarticulate, and apparently

3. Recognition was afforded the effect that "scapegoat" reasoning may have upon the ability of one of several plaintiffs in a consolidated action to prove his injuries in *Moss v. Associated Transport, Inc.*, 344 F.2d 23 (6th Cir. 1965), where Judge O'Sullivan stated at 25-26:

> In support of his claim of prejudice, appellant asserts that because of the separation [of liability and damage issue] prevented him from showing the severity of his own injuries, he was denied a weapon with which to combat the natural sympathy that a jury would feel for the two plaintiff widows who had, in effect, been made Moss' opponents by the consolidation. Without a record containing the proofs on the point, we have no basis for speculating whether the issue of liability was so close that sympathy for the widows might have tipped the scales in their favor. The material before us, however, does disclose that the appellant Moss was present in the courtroom and there is no challenge to the District Judge's statement that 'the mental impairment and total disability of the plaintiff was for all practical purposes stipulated by the parties, as it was stated as a fact both in the opening statement and in the argument and never disputed.' The extent of his injuries could also have been established in explanation of the failure to put him on the stand to testify on the issue of liability. From our review of all the material made available to us, we cannot say the District Judge's discretion was abused by his order of separation.

4. Necessarily, all names and places referred to in this article have been changed. It goes without saying that this is likewise true of other pieces I have written which are based on data garnered while I was a member of the *Jury Project* team.

not very bright. The evidence, as regards Sue, established the following: (1) that she had been a prostitute since the age of sixteen, ten years before defendant came into her life, and that she had plied her trade in many parts of the United States and, particularly, in Alaska; (2) that she had, by a man (or men) other than defendant, two illegitimate children whose care had for many years been entrusted to her mother in State X; (3) that she was the owner and "resident manager" of a house of ill-repute in a remote corner of the United States when she married defendant in 1950; (4) that she began working as a prostitute in State Y almost immediately after the trip from State X in 1953 and continued to do so until shortly before defendant's indictment; and (5) that she had not worked as a prostitute since defendant's indictment, but had instead begun "making a home" for defendant and her two children whom defendant was supporting.

Defendant, the evidence showed, had both "bad" and "good" sides to his personality. The "bad" side consisted of: (1) association with prostitutes for most of his adult life not spent in the military; (2) a previous marriage to one Bess, a prostitute, who, at the time of trial, was working in Los Angeles; (3) the selling of "trick suits," garments employed by prostitutes, to houses of ill-fame in the Southwest and along the Pacific seaboard; and (4) the transporation for hire of prostitutes from the United States to Mexico.

The "good" side was defendant's lack of a serious criminal record, his devotion to the Allied cause in World War II, and his obvious initiative and enterprise, which, when properly channeled, could produce much that was worthwhile. His previous record consisted merely of a conviction for petty theft and assault when he was twenty. He had enlisted in the Royal Canadian Air Force in September, 1939, at the outbreak of World War II, had served several years as a pilot, and was decorated for bravery in action. He was then transferred to the USAF in 1943 where he served with distinction in a similar capacity until his honorable discharge in 1945. In 1948, he had established an apparently successful taxicab business in a far corner of the United States which he continued until 1953, when he and Sue left for the central section of the United States. There he had obtained a job as a salesman for a prominent national advertising concern within five days after the trip from State X, held onto the job and made it pay over $400 per month, placed second among two-hundred and twelve salesmen in a recent selling contest and had so endeared himself to his company that its vice president testified on his behalf at the trial and announced that defendant would, if acquitted, be continued in the company's employ.

The government's case rested chiefly on defendant's prior association with prostitutes, on Sue's admission that she had begun working as a prostitute shortly after coming to State Y, and upon the testimony of several witnesses that defendant was instrumental in transporting Sue to and from the house of ill-fame where she was employed.

The defense stated that defendant had always opposed Sue's involvement with prostitution, that Sue had promised him that she would give up prostitution and begin life anew when they arrived in State Y, and that his only purpose in coming to State Y was to find work, in which he was successful. Defendant's attorney further stated that defendant left Sue when she returned to and refused to give up prostitution and rejoined her only when assured that she would thenceforth make him a "good wife" and would properly care for her two children whom defendant would support and bring up "in the ways of the Church." Sue, who appeared for the government as well as defendant, supported defendant's story in every particular. The only other circumstance to be noted is that Sue had not and apparently would not be prosecuted for her obvious violation of State Y laws. The decision of the Supreme Court in *Gebardi v. United States*,[5] establishing that the female "immorally transported" cannot, simply because of her consent to a journey interstate suggested by her husband, be found guilty either of a substantive Mann Act offense or of conspiracy, made federal prosecution impossible. The jury, however, was unaware of the decision, and no explanation was offered at the trial for the government's failure to take action against Sue. Defendant was acquitted after a deliberation of approximately six hours.

The "anvil chorus" of the deliberation and the personal interviews was that acquittal became necessary because Sue was "more guilty" than defendant and yet was allowed to go unpunished. The following comment was representative: "The government was trying Sue, not Bob (the defendant). She was the one who was really guilty. Compared with her, he was a paragon of virtue. Yet they let her go free and wanted us to convict him. It would have been a different story if she had been on trial, too; everyone seemed to agree on that. But how could we convict him on such weak evidence when she was getting off scot-free?" The uniformly-held view of the jurors that defendant was "comparatively (*i.e.*, with reference to his wife), free from fault" coupled with their irritation at the government's failure to proceed against Sue were undoubtedly the two factors most responsible for defendant's acquittal.

This is perhaps best and certainly most dramatically shown by the juror's responses to a question phrased substantially as follows: "Supposing everything in the case were the same except that Sue had been indicted for conspiracy to violate the Mann Act and was being tried right along with her husband. Would that have made any difference?" Only two of the twelve jurors responding, both of whom strongly favored

5. 287 U.S. 112 (1932).

defendant in the deliberations, said that it would not have. Their response was: "The fact that she was obviously guilty wouldn't make him guilty; everybody is entitled to be judged separately. But it would have made a big difference to a lot of the jurors; I know that from what was said in the deliberations."

The remaining ten jurors, on the other hand, three of whom had originally voted to convict—the other seven having consistently voted for acquittal—took a markedly different view. The former stated that they would have hung the jury rather than to have acquitted either Sue or defendant, the latter that they would "undoubtedly" (as in the case of five jurors), or would "probably" (as in the case of two jurors), have voted to convict both. The theory, of course, was that the presence of Sue, the "primary wrongdoer," as a defendant would remove the central reason for acquitting her husband; *viz.*, that the husband was comparatively less at fault and that it was unfair to convict him while his "more guilty" wife was allowed to go free. Whether these jurors would also have voted to convict defendant if they had been told the reason for the government's failure to prosecute Sue, if they had thought that she was under indictment for a Mann Act violation but had not yet been tried or that she had been tried but acquitted, or that she had been or would be in the future punished by state authority, is not known. This is especially unfortunate, as data bearing upon such questions would have cast some much needed light upon several important aspects of criminal procedure and particularly the prevailing trend towards trying many defendants jointly rather than separately, as was our practice in earlier times.

While defendant in *Cooper* was only arguably the "less culpable" of the two persons involved in the interstate journey, the defendant in *Johnson* was clearly so. So far, then, the scapegoat theory would dictate an acquittal in *Johnson a fortiori.* However, the two cases differed in their scapegoat aspects by the circumstances that the "more guilty" party in *Johnson*, the jury was informed, had pleaded guilty and was imprisoned at the time of the trial. This feature of *Johnson*, with reference to *Cooper*, would appear to cancel defendant's advantage or even to put him at a disadvantage. That it did not seems certain: scapegoat reasoning again triumphed.

The situation was as follows: Defendant, a twenty-three year old male Negro, was charged under the Dyer Act with "aiding and abetting" the interstate transportation of a stolen Cadillac automobile, known by him to have been stolen. The principal defense was that defendant did not know that the Cadillac was stolen. It was uncontradicted at the trial that one James, defendant's "more guilty" accomplice and the government's chief witness, had stolen the car by himself in Madison, Michigan, for the purpose of going to Parma, Illinois, in order to avoid capture by the Madison police for a series of robberies, burglaries, and car thefts he had previously committed. James, a mentally retarded and almost wholly inarticulate twenty-year old male Negro, had been in jail almost continuously since the age of fourteen. His criminal record was extensive.

James testified that he drove to defendant's home in Madison after stealing the car and invited defendant to accompany him to Parma to visit some girls and his (James') brother for a few days and then return to Madison. James stated that he merely wanted defendant's company and, since defendant had no money, was willing to finance the entire trip; that defendant accepted the offer and that the pair started immediately for Parma, with James driving. However, James insisted that he had not told defendant that the car was stolen until some point where defendant, who was then driving, stopped to permit a hitchhiker whom he had previously picked up to get out of the car. The police, who had by this time been informed of the theft, arrived upon the scene shortly thereafter. The government impeached James by reading his signed and sworn out-of-court statement—which James denied making—that he had told defendant that the car was stolen at the inception of the journey in Madison. The government's case rested upon James' out-of-court statement, upon testimony that the glass in the car's right front vent window was broken, and that the car had to be started and stopped by crossing and uncrossing the ignition wires. The prosecution mentioned that it was unreasonable to suppose that James could have acquired a Cadillac by lawful means. Defendant did not take the stand and introduced no evidence. The only suggestion that defendant had a previous criminal record was the testimony of James—ordered stricken upon defense counsel's objection—that he and defendant had first met as cellmates. Defendant was acquitted after a heated deliberation of more than six hours.

At the outset, the jury divided seven to five in favor of acquittal, the principal argument of the majority being that the government, instead of trying defendant, had tried James. James, the hardened criminal and perjuror, was the primary culprit. Defendant had played but a minor and incidental role. Defendant was the sheep, the follower; James, the evil shepherd. Defendant had merely been led astray. The government had "got" James and should be satisfied. Social policy did not demand a second and less palatable sacrifice. Reversing the pattern found in *Cooper*, the fact that the "more guilty" was being punished now became a factor favoring defendant. Society was entitled only to so much blood. The central point to be noted, however, is that the jurors vented their spleen on James, as Sue "took the rap" for her husband in *Cooper*. All but two of the ten jurors personally interviewed stated that defendant's role as a follower, *i.e.*, his comparative freedom from fault with reference to James, was one of the major factors causing them either originally to vote for defendant or to change their votes from guilty to not guilty. The two exceptions were jurors who had strongly favored a conviction and who merely consented to an acquittal in order to end the deliberations and avoid a hung jury.

The scapegoat aspect of *Williams*, the last of the criminal cases to be considered, is extremely marginal, though this feature of the case, oddly enough, becomes for the present purpose its primary virtue. *Williams* involved an accomplice (actually, someone resembling an accomplice), who was "less guilty" than defendant. Without more, of course, scapegoat theory as developed in *Cooper* and *Johnson* would dictate a conviction. *Williams*, however, like *Cooper* and unlike *Johnson*, involved a situation where the "accomplice" was apparently allowed to go freé. What happened with this combination?

Defendant, a good-looking and articulate thirty-year-old male Negro, was charged under the Mann Act with transporting one Jane Walter from State X to State Y in order to place her in a house of prostitution. Jane, a Negro of twenty-three, was fairly articulate, beautiful, and extremely well-dressed. The government's evidence that defendant had attempted to place Jane in a house of prostitution shortly after his arrival in State Y was overpowering. Defendant, however, contended that Jane had not accompanied him on the interstate journey, but had followed him to State Y separately and voluntarily and without the slightest encouragement.

The government's evidence to the contrary consisted merely of the testimony of Jane. Jane's story was that she first met defendant in a tavern in a small State X town, that she fell in love almost immediately, and that defendant, without telling her that he was already married, had seduced her under promise of marriage and had taken her to a large State Y city where he said they would be married. Prior to meeting defendant, Jane lived with her grandfather, a convicted murderer, and periodically with the father of her one-year-old illegitimate child. The child was entrusted to the grandfather when Jane left the small town with defendant for a large State Y city.

The promised marriage never took place. However, Jane and defendant took up housekeeping in the large State Y city where they were soon joined by defendant's wife, Connie, a professional prostitute. With the assistance of defendant, Connie taught Jane the "trade" while the three of them were living together in Connie's one-room apartment. "Neither of us would give him up and there was no sense in having two apartments." Jane claimed that defendant forced her into prostitution by threats of physical violence and, later, when she wanted to quit, beat her and stabbed her in the leg. Defendant, she said, supported himself for nearly two years on the money she and Connie derived from prostitution. Jane's only criminal record was a soliciting conviction, though she admitted having worked as a prostitute in several cities in State X and State Y.

Defendant claimed that Jane, knowing that he was married, had sexual relations with him on the night of their first meeting. He denied that he had ever proposed marriage, saying that he was for many months unaware that Jane and Connie were engaging in prostitution. He further testified that he had taken none of their earnings, but instead had supported them from his earnings as a jewelry salesman. He knew that Jane and Connie both loved him and accordingly saw no reason for giving up either. Defendant, who was extremely cocky while testifying, had previously been convicted of several gambling charges and of selling jewelry without a license. He admitted having stolen a car and having bought another with no intention of paying for it. He had also served two years in the stockade for desertion in wartime—he was a.w.o.l. for approximately a year and a half, having deserted the day after his induction—and been dishonorably discharged from the Army. Neither Jane nor Connie, the jury was informed, were under federal indictment, though no explanation for this was given; neither would apparently be prosecuted under state law. At the time of the trial, Connie, most of whose testimony tended to exonerate the defendant, was working as a prostitute in State X; Jane, on the other hand, claimed to have given up prostitution several months prior to the trial.

Though defendant was convicted in less than thirty minutes, the deliberations evidenced considerable dissatisfaction among the jurors concerning the government's failure to take action against Jane and Connie. Jane's testimony that defendant had coerced her into prostitution was viewed with utter disbelief. Nor did the jurors believe that defendant had seduced Jane under promise of marriage or that she had given up prostitution. "It was an ugly, sordid mess; she (Jane) was almost as much to blame as he was." Indeed, this notion, coupled with the government's failure to charge Jane and, to a lesser degree, Connie, was the principal basis for the original position taken by one juror that defendant should be acquitted.

"It's difficult to put my feelings into words. I guess it comes down to this: They were all in it together; their values, though different from ours, were held by them in common. Who were we, speaking for only one class of society, to punish them for acting in accordance with those values? They probably felt that they had done nothing wrong. It was one class of society sitting in judgment on another and that's not as it should be. And then she (Jane), and his wife also, nothing was going to happen to them. They would go on just as before. I had no use for him—you couldn't help but dislike him and he was guilty as sin—but I couldn't see what jailing him would accomplish, especially when nothing was being done to the others (Jane and Connie)."

This comment was that of an extremely intelligent and articulate housewife whose performance on other cases where she served—and particularly one criminal case where her understanding of a technical rule of law and her ability to explain it to her fellow jurors prevented a serious miscarriage of justice—does credit to the highest and best of our jury traditions. Though she rapidly abandoned her original position— "he was, after all, clearly guilty"—it was not without serious misgivings. "I have considerable doubt about the justice of the verdict." Similar doubts, based upon identical grounds, were also expressed by an intelligent elderly social worker and librarian whose deceased husband had been a prominent member of the Bar. Scapegoat theory, it would appear, must sometimes tend to operate even in cases where defendant is "more guilty" than his associates, assuming, of course, that the associates are not also being prosecuted.

CIVIL CASES

The civil cases studied—to the extent that they involved scapegoat situations—reflect patterns of behavior very similar and, in important respects, identical with those observed in the criminal cases. Such situations were presented in four cases, *Turner*, *White*, and the two *Phillips* cases.

Turner resembles *Cooper* in that the "more guilty" party was apparently allowed to go free. Plaintiff, a paying-passenger in an automobile owned and operated by defendant, sought recovery for personal injuries sustained in a head-on collision with a car driven by one Fuller. Fuller was intoxicated at the time and was driving on the wrong side of the road. While conceding Fuller's "primary negligence," plaintiff charged that defendant was also negligent in failing to get out of the way. Fuller was not joined as a defendant and did not testify at the trial; nor had his deposition been taken. The jury was not given any explanations for this and was not told whether plaintiff had already or would in future recover from Fuller. The only related remark was the court's instruction that the jury should in no way concern themselves with the question. Fuller, then, was substantially like the jurors' conception of Sue in *Cooper*.

Fuller, like Sue, "took the rap," though the way in which he did so, to be sure, was closely connected with the jurors' consideration of whether plaintiff had already recovered against him, a question upon which there was a sharp division of opinion. The point to be noted, however, is that all six of the jurors personally interviewed felt that plaintiff should have sued Fuller rather than defendant and, because of this feeling, either had originally voted against liability or had made substantial reductions from their personal estimates of the amount of damages that should be awarded. Defendant's negligence with reference to Fuller's was extremely marginal, and the verdict had to be made to reflect this. And it undoubtedly did: $1500, the amount of the award, was palpably inadequate with regard to the evidence as to damages. The reasoning pattern thus bears a close resemblance to that present in *Cooper*. The analogy to *Johnson* is even more telling. Plaintiff in *Turner*, like society in *Johnson*, was only entitled to so much blood (damages), and should be satisfied with his right to go against (or, as some jurors thought, the damages he secured by going against), Fuller, just as society should be content with having punished the "more guilty" James in *Johnson*.

The data from *White* is extremely inadequate because, among other things, the case was settled just after the judge instructed the jury. This was an action to recover for personal injuries sustained when a car which defendant was towing with ordinary rope broke loose and shot over onto the highway's right shoulder. There the plaintiff, an eighty-five-year-old woman, was walking, and was allegedly so frightened that she fell. Her hip was broken in an effort to escape the car's path. The car which broke loose was driven by defendant's fifteen-year-old son. The defense was that plaintiff was "unreasonably" frightened and that any negligence other than plaintiff's was that of defendant's son for which defendant, under applicable state law, would not be responsible. As plaintiff's counsel sarcastically characterized it, "they're trying their best to blame everything on this helpless old woman and this young schoolboy." In the judgment of the court, the law clerk, and the jury project observer, the son's negligence was about equal to that of defendant, and plaintiff was not contributorily negligent.

The number of jurors taking the above view, however, is unfortunately not known. There were no personal interviews; the mailed questionnaire distributed within a few days of the trial was defective. However, it can at least be stated that six of the ten jurors responding to the questionnaire indicated that they would have reduced damages on account of the negligence of plaintiff and defendant's son. The question, of course, is whether the other four jurors, all of whom favored recovery, felt that plaintiff and/or defendant's son were free from fault and accordingly saw no reason to reduce damages; or whether their failure to reduce damages was motivated by other considerations. Nevertheless, inadequate though they are, the data seem clearly to suggest that scapegoat theory would have operated to a considerable degree had the case been submitted to the jury. At least half of the jurors favored giving defendant the benefit of his son's negligence. The son, and the plaintiff, as is probably true in many cases involving a question of contributory negligence, were made scapegoats.

The two *Phillips* cases present a scapegoat situation markedly different from any of those involved in the cases heretofore considered. The litigation arose out of a three-vehicle highway accident, occurring about midnight in the winter of 1950. In brief, the driver of a tractor-trailer, one Fox, hit a car parked partly in the lane in front of him. His rig, then out of control, shot across the highway into the path of another tractor-trailer driven by plaintiff. Plaintiff's tractor struck Fox's tractor on its right side, causing personal injuries to plaintiff and damage to his tractor-trailer and cargo. A fourth vehicle, belonging to the scapegoat, while not directly involved in the collision, was a remote contributing factor, in technical tort parlance, a "condition" without which the mishap would never have occurred. The highway in question, which ran in an east-west direction and had three lanes, was to some degree icy. The scapegoat's vehicle had veered off the highway into a ditch to the north and had become mired in soft mud. Its headlights shined up out of the ditch towards the southeast.

Scapegoat, a woman, was unable to extricate the car and flagged down a passing motorist, one Rodgers, who stopped and agreed to render assistance. His parked car was soon struck by Fox's tractor-trailer. While Rodgers was up to his knees in mud, Fox approached the scene from the east, traveling in the outside lane partially obstructed by Rodgers' car. Plaintiff, driving in the opposite outside lane, approached from the west. The center lane remained clear. Both vehicles were traveling at a moderate rate of speed. Fox saw the headlights of plaintiff's tractor and also those of the car in the ditch to the north. "The lights from the woman's car were very bright." While not blinded by the lights, Fox still did not see Rodgers' car behind them until within ten or fifteen feet of where it was parked. It was then too late. His tractor struck the car on its left side, glanced diagonally across the highway towards the south shoulder and into the path of the tractor-trailer driven by plaintiff, who had no opportunity to avoid the collision. The confusion following the accident enabled the woman to escape. Neither Fox nor "Samaritan" Rodgers, who was then rendering assistance to plaintiff, got her name; she was successful in eluding all subsequent efforts to locate her. Plaintiff brought suit against Fox, Fox's employer, the XYZ Motor Co., and Rodgers. Fox, plaintiff charged, was negligent in failing to maintain a proper lookout; Rodgers, in parking on a traveled portion of the roadway and in failing to have his taillights working. Rodgers, however, was clearly free from fault, the evidence establishing that he was reasonable in parking where he did and that his taillights were on. Plaintiff was, likewise, clearly free from fault and, indeed, the court so ruled as a matter of law in the second trial. The serious and only liability issue in both trials was whether Fox was negligent in view of the semi-icy condition of the highway, the icy rain, and the lights from the woman's car, the headlamps of which, according to some of the evidence, shined towards him out of the ditch. The first jury rendered a verdict in favor of all three defendants. This was later set aside because of inconsistent answers to certain special interrogatories. The second jury, while exonerating Rodgers, found against Fox and his employer for substantial damages.

The defendants' verdict in the first trial undoubtedly resulted in material part from the fact that the jurors blamed the accident upon the woman. This appears, first of all, from an affidavit filed by one of the jurors within a week of the trial which sets out the deliberations at length and indicates that this was one of its central themes. In addition, all six of the nine jurors interviewed at the time of the second trial—two and a half years later—who could recall anything of the case likewise in part attributed the verdict to such a feeling. "The woman was the one primarily to blame. If she hadn't been negligent in keeping her headlights on, the accident wouldn't have happened. She was the one who should have been on trial. It wasn't . . . (defendants') fault that she couldn't be found. Besides, there was something fishy about the fact that she disappeared right after the accident." The "something fishy" apparently was the notion—totally without foundation—that the woman and plaintiff may have conspired to defraud defendants and/or their insurance companies.

Similar—indeed, virtually identical—reasoning was engaged in by all four of the *Phillips #2* jurors originally taking the position that Fox and his employer were not liable: that the woman was "primarily to blame" on account of her "negligence" in sliding off the road (which caused Rodgers to stop) and in failing to turn off her headlights and that there was "something fishy" about the fact that she disappeared so suddenly after the accident. Two of these jurors strongly argued this during the deliberations. Fortunately, however, such arguments, though never objected to as legally improper, were not convincing. Of the eight jurors originally voting that Fox was negligent, only three took the view that the woman was in any way at fault, and even they did not feel her to be very much at fault. The remaining five jurors simply stated that she "just didn't matter" and that "she was out of the picture altogether."

The jurors' own explanations for placing blame upon the woman, *i.e.*, the casual connection between her acts, the accident and the "fishiness" thought to be involved in her sudden disappearance, have a very hollow ring. A more accurate explanation, it is submitted, is this: The jurors in question, having decided not to hold Fox liable for a variety of reasons (*e.g.*, a desire to protect his reputation as a truck driver, a feeling that his negligence, if any, was "very slight," a feeling that plaintiff was not seriously injured and had already sufficiently been compensated by his insurance companies), nevertheless felt a need to pin the responsibility upon someone, thus avoiding the unsatisfactory feeling which arises if they conclude that no one was responsible. Plaintiff was clearly not at fault; neither was Rodgers. Holding Fox was psychologically difficult. In this posture of affairs, it became very easy to blame everything on the thankless, ungrateful woman who had not even possessed the decency to remain after the accident. This alternative, of course, possessed the added psychological advantage that since the woman was not in court, the jury did not have to face her when they filed in to render a verdict. The suggestion, in sum, is that the chances for a defendant's verdict are enhanced by an absent third-party even though responsibility can only be placed upon such party by strained reasoning.

*   *   *   *   *   *

A conclusion will be foregone except to state that, if the data contained herein are any criteria, it may be well for any jury trial lawyer to consider carefully potential scapegoats and to count or discount the strength of his case accordingly.

469

SOCIOECONOMIC FACTORS INFLUENCING JURY VERDICTS*

FREDA ADLER**

I. INTRODUCTION

The legal and philosophical basis of our jury system requires that the jury be an impartially drawn group of the defendant's peers.[1] No attempt will be made in this discussion to challenge the desirability of such a jury system. Our purpose is simply to focus on our jury system as it presently operates and to examine the implications of this operation for the execution of justice.

The roots of the American jury system can be traced to the Norman customs of the ninth century.[2] Originally a jury was made up of local people selected because they had knowledge of the facts.[3] Until the late seventeenth century an accused who felt he was denied a fair verdict could have the verdict tested by the process of attaint.[4] A second panel of twenty-four would rehear the evidence. If the verdict of the second panel differed from that of the first, members of the previous jury were fined and imprisoned or had to forfeit property on the ground that they had sworn falsely. Such a procedure was meant to serve as an inducement to impartiality.[5]

The United States Constitution established the English practice of trial by jury as a fundamental right for criminal proceedings.[6] The sixth amendment explicitly stipulates that the jury be impartial, but the selection of jurors to that end represents a problem that has been part of the jury system since its inception. The United States Supreme Court has established the principle that a jury ought to be a representative cross-section of the community.

> The American tradition of trial by jury, considered in connection with either criminal or civil proceedings, necessarily contemplates an impartial jury drawn from a cross-section of the community. . . . [This means] that prospective jurors shall be selected without systematic and intentional exclusion of . . . [economic, racial, political, and geographic] groups.[7]

---

* The data for this study were collected while the author was at the Center for Studies in Criminology and Criminal Law, University of Pennsylvania.

** Ph.D., 1971, University of Pennsylvania (sociology); Assistant Professor of Psychiatry, Medical College of Pennsylvania; Regional Coordinator, Section on Drug & Alcohol Abuse, Medical College of Pennsylvania; Consultant to the Criminal Law Education and Research Center, New York University School of Law.

1 Magna Charta, par. 39 (McKinney vol. 2, 1969). See Note, Trial by Jury in Criminal Cases, 69 Colum. L. Rev. 419 (1969); Note, Economic Discrimination in Jury Selection, 1970 Law & Soc. Order 474, 474-78; Note, The Jury: Is It Viable?, 6 Suffolk U. L. Rev. 897, 897-904 (1972); Comment, Challenging the Juror Selection System in New York, 36 Albany L. Rev. 305, 305-07 (1972).

2 W. Forsyth, Trial by Jury 4-5 (2d ed. 1878).

3 Id. at 134-35; R. von Moschzisker, Trial by Jury § 59 (2d ed. 1930).

4 W. Forsyth, supra note 2 at 149-55; R. von Moschzisker, supra note 3 at § § 290, 364.

5 Kean, Quandry in the Law: The Not So Impartial Pennsylvania Juror, 9 Vill. L. Rev. 645, 647 (1964).

6 U.S. Const. amend. VI: "In all criminal prosecutions, the accused shall enjoy the right to a speedy and public trial, by an impartial jury of the State and district wherein the crime shall have been committed. . . ."

7 Thiel v. S. Pac. Co., 328 U.S. 217, 220 (1946).

1

In *Thiel v. Southern Pacific Co.*[8] this principle of representation was extended to cover the status of those on the jury.

Wage earners, including those who are paid by the day, constitute a very substantial portion of the community, a portion that can not be intentionally and systematically excluded in whole or in part without doing violence to the democratic nature of the jury system. Were we to sanction an exclusion of this nature we would encourage whatever desires those responsible for the selection of jury panels may have to discriminate against persons of low economic and social status. We would breathe life into any latent tendencies to establish the jury as the instrument of the economically and socially privileged; that we refuse to do.[9]

Many of our present jury selection methods raise serious questions about the extent to which this principle of representation has been put into practice in our courtrooms.[10] But, if we are to argue with any degree of persuasion that this particular failure to implement a policy articulated by the Supreme Court represents an important problem for the administration of justice, it seems crucial that we first establish the extent to which a jury verdict is actually dependent on the representativeness of the jury.

II. PREVIOUS STUDIES

Previous studies of jury composition and jury deliberation have identified some of the factors, other than the specific legal issues in question, which are involved in jury decision-making. Not surprisingly it has been found that the nationality, the race and the religion of the jurors all play a part in the rendering of a verdict. One study found that jurors of German and British backgrounds were more likely to favor a guilty verdict, whereas Negroes and people of Slavic and Italian origin were more likely to favor a not guilty verdict.[11] Another study concluded from mock jury

---

[8] 328 U.S. 217 (1946).

[9] Id. at 223-24.

[10] See, e.g., Kuhn, Jury Discrimination: The Next Phase, 41 S. Cal. L. Rev. 235 (1968); Lindguist, An Analysis of Juror Selection Procedure in the United States District Courts, 41 Temp. L. Q. 32 (1967); Note, The Jury: A Reflection of the Prejudices of the Community, 20 Hastings L. J. 1417 (1969); Note, Economic Discrimination in Jury Selection, 1970 Law & Soc. Order 474; Voter Registration Lists — Do They Yield, 5 U. Mich. J. L. Ref. 385 (1972); Note, Jury Selection: The Need for Statutory Reform in Minnesota, 53 Minn. L. Rev. 977 (1969); Note, Jury Composition — The Purposeful Inclusion of American Indians, 16 S.D. L. Rev. 214 (1971); Note, Jury Selection Procedures, A Reform, 6 Suffolk U. L. Rev. 865 (1972); Comment, Challenging the Juror Selection System in New York, 36 Albany L. Rev. 305 (1972).

[11] Broeder, The University of Chicago Jury Project, 38 Neb. L. Rev. 744, 748 (1959). The data upon which Broeder's article is based were generated by the University of Chicago Jury Project, a study of the American jury system conducted in the late 1950's [hereinafter Jury Project].

For Jury Project data generally see Kalven, A Report on the Jury Project of the University of Chicago Law School, 24 Ins. Counsel J. 368 (1957). See also Meltzer, A Projected Study of the Jury as a Working Institution, 287 Annals 97 (1953).

As regards Broeder's own published Jury Project work see Broeder, Occupational Expertise and Bias as Affecting Juror Behavior: A Preliminary Look, 40 N.Y.U. L. Rev. 1079 (1965); Broeder, The Jury Project, S.D.B.J., Oct. 1957, at 133. See also Broeder, The Negro in Court, 1965 Duke L.J. 19; Broeder, Plaintiff's Family Status as Affecting Juror Behavior: Some Tentative Insights, 14 J. Pub. L. 131 (1965); Broeder, Previous Jury Trial Service Affecting Juror Behavior, 1965 Ins. L.J. 138; Broeder, Voir Dire Examinations: An Empirical Study, 38 So. Cal. L. Rev. 503 (1965); Broeder, Jury, 13 Encyclopedia Britannica 205 (1963 ed.); Broeder, The Functions of the Jury: Facts or Fictions?, 21 U. Chi. L. Rev. 386 (1954).

2

experiments with insanity pleas that Negroes are more likely to acquit on grounds of insanity than any other ethnic group.[12] Clarence Darrow, writing on the subject of religion and nationality, stated:

> In criminal cases, I prefer Catholics, Episcopalians, and Presbyterians to Baptists and Methodists, because the tenets held and disciplines practiced by the latter set higher standards of human conduct and make them less tolerant of human frailty.
> The Irishman and the Jew, because of their national background, will put a greater burden on the prosecution and prove more sympathetic and lenient to a defendant, than an Englishman or a Scandinavian whose passion for the enforcement of the law and order is stronger.[13]

The education and the sex of the jurors are also factors which enter into jury decision-making. Grade school educated jurors have been found to put more emphasis on testimony, personal life experiences and opinions based on the trial, whereas persons with higher education emphasize procedure and instruction.[14] Men tend to *act* more and women to *react* more to the contributions of others.[15] It has been suggested that the verdict which a male juror reaches often is based not on his assessment of whether the facts justify a verdict of guilty or innocent but on whether or not he wants to see the accused punished.[16] In certain types of cases (e.g., those involving mechanical problems) women are prone to leave it "entirely up to the men" because "men know more about such things than women do."[17]

Previous jury experience has been shown to have effects on the attitudes of those recalled. The Jury Project concluded that jurors with previous jury experience tend to use past experiences as a basis for premature conclusions about all future trials in which they might be involved.[18] For example, one of the jurors in the Project who had served on three prior occasions, stated that she had watched jurors divide into factions according to their socioeconomic backgrounds and was convinced from her past experience that cases were decided primarily according to this background. Believing that her fellow jurors would be *for* the defendant and *against* the plaintiff on account of their high socioeconomic level, she stopped listening during the trial.[19] Another juror had recently served three times and was too emotionally exhausted to fight for what she believed was right.[20] Confirmation of the principle that previous jury experience influences the decision-making process was found in the fact that previous jury experience was often the sole reason for the exercise of pre-emptory challenges.[21]

For other Project publications see Kalven, A General Analysis of and Introduction to the Problem of Court Congestion and Delay, 1963 A.B.A. Ins., Neg. & Comp. Section 322; Kalven, The Jury, the Law, and the Personal Injury Damage Award, 19 Ohio St. L.J. 158 (1958); Zeisel, Splitting Liability and Damage Issues Saves 20 Per Cent of the Court's Time, 1963 A.B.A. Ins., Neg. & Comp. Section 328; Zeisel & Callahan, Split Trials and Time Saving: A Statistical Analysis, 76 Harv. L. Rev. 1606 (1963); Zeisel, Kalven & Buchholz, Delay in the Court (1959); Zeisel, Kalven & Buchholz, Is the Trial Bar a Cause of Delay?, 43 J. Am. Jud. Soc'y 17 (1959).

[12] R. J. Simon, The Jury and the Defense of Insanity 111 (1967).

[13] Id. at 104, quoting F. Busch, Law and Tactics in Jury Trials 198 (1958).

[14] James, Status and Competence of Jurors, 64 Am. J. of Soc. 565 (1959).

[15] Strodtbeck & Mann, Sex Role Differentiation in Jury Deliberations, 19 Sociometry 9 (1956).

[16] Devons, Serving as a Juryman in Britain, 28 Modern L. Rev. 561, 564 (1965).

[17] Broeder, Occupational Expertise and Bias as Affecting Juror Behavior: A Preliminary Look, 40 N.Y.U. L. Rev. 1079, 1082 (1965).

[18] Broeder, Previous Jury Trial Service Affecting Juror Behavior, 1965 Ins. L.J. 138.

[19] Id. at 140.

[20] Id. at 142.

[21] Id. at 139.

3

The influence of pre-trial publicity on jurors has for many years been the subject of much debate.[22] Even though jurors are asked whether their opinions will yield to evidence, it is suggested that either unconscious mechanisms come into play or that jurors simply do not reveal they will be influenced.[23] Evidence indicates that publicity causes partiality because of the strong resistance to change.[24]

Metacommunication holds a place in any discussion of extra-legal factors which influence jurors. Metacommunication is the conveyance of messages which cannot be understood simply in terms of the words used, through which we judge and understand people in a dimension which cannot be conveyed by the court stenographer's record alone. For example, the jurors respond not only to what is said but the manner in which it is said and the gestures which accompany it, and they interpret these in the context of the emotional impact of the speaker. There is much juror anecdotal material relating to sincerity and courtesy of lawyers, dress of people involved, how "objections" are voiced and the like.[25]

Finally we turn our attention to that bias which appears to be the most important single extra-legal factor associated with jury deliberations: the bias related to socioeconomic levels. In our stratification system individuals are perceived by each other as occupying a position in a power-prestige hierarchy.[26] Furthermore, this stratification generally coincides in our modern industrial society with the division of labor.[27] Even in a society with a fluid class system, values are not homogeneous; the position a person occupies influences his values and has a profound influence on his understanding of, and judgment toward, people of other ranks.[28]

In 1946 a representative sample of the national population was asked: "Suppose you had been acting as a referee in labor-management disputes during the past three months, do you think your decisions would probably have been more often in favor of labor's side, or more often in favor of management's side?" Preferences tended strongly to follow occupational lines, with workers favoring labor and executives siding with management.[29] These general predispositions exert themselves when members of the public are called to jury duty.

The importance of such a socioeconomic bias becomes apparent when we look at the composition of juries in the United States. A statistical analysis of the occupations of the jurors sitting in the United States District Court of the District of Maryland from 1958 to 1961 placed 1515 jurors into their occupational categories as defined by the Bureau of the Census.[30] In comparing the jurors with the population from which they were chosen (Baltimore Standard Metropolitan Area), it was found that professional, managerial and sales occupations were overrepresented whereas craftsmen, operatives, service workers and laborers were underrepresented. Professionals, technicians, managers, officials and proprietors equaled less than 20 per cent of the eligible labor force but over 50 per cent of the classified jurors while craftsmen, foremen, operatives, service workers, farm workers and laborers constituted 59 per cent of the eligible labor

---

[22] See, e.g., Goggin & Hanover, Fair Trial v. Free Press: The Psychological Effect of Pre-Trial Publicity on the Juror's Ability to be Impartial; A Plea for Reform, 38 S. Cal. L. Rev. 672 (1965); Kaufman, Judges and Jurors: Recent Developments in Selection of Jurors and Fair Trial — Free Press, 41 U. Colo. L. Rev. 179 (1969); Stanga, Judicial Protection of the Criminal Defendant Against Adverse Press Coverage, 13 Wm. & Mary L. Rev. 1 (1971); Note, Criminal Law: Pretrial Publicity — Threat to Trial by Jury, 22 Okla. L. Rev. 165 (1969).

[23] Goggin & Hanover, supra note 22, at 675.

[24] Id. at 679.

[25] See, e.g., M. Bloomstein, Verdict: The Jury System (1968); M. Gleisser, Juries and Justice (1968); S. McCart, Trial By Jury: A Complete Guide to the Jury System (2d ed. 1965); F. Wellman, Gentlemen of the Jury; Reminiscenses of Thirty Years at the Bar (1936).

[26] R. Simon, supra note 12, at 99.

[27] Id.

[28] Id.

[29] Robinson, Bias, Probability and Trial by Jury, 15 Amer. Soc. Rev. 78 (1950).

[30] Mills, A Statistical Study of Occupations of Jurors in a United States District Court, 22 Md. L. Rev. 205, 208-13 (1962).

4

force, but only 24 per cent of the classified jurors.[31] In *Fay v. New York*[32] the defendants contended that laborers, craftsmen, operatives, foremen and service workers were unconstitutionally and systematically excluded from a panel of jurors from which the trial jury had been chosen. Proprietors, managers and officials make up 43 per cent of the jurors but only 9.3 per cent of the Manhattan labor force.[33]

The Jury Project presents several cases where a juror's background clearly affected his judgment and influenced his verdict.[34] Cited is a civil case[35] where, in general, the proprietor jurors sided with the defendant (railroad) and the laboring jurors with the plaintiff (railroad worker). The conclusion reached by the study was: "[O]ccupational bias was the central characteristic of the *Thomas* deliberations and of the thinking of the *Thomas* jurors with regard to the case."[36] In the case, out of the eight jurors favoring the plaintiff (a laborer), six belonged to the laboring class.[37] This "identification" process is not limited to the juror's identification with the defendant and/or plaintiff. For example, a particular juror had sold advertising in his youth, knew how hard it was to succeed, and "was not, therefore, going to convict defendant, who had made a success in advertising and particularly when defendant's employer, with whom Tobin [juror] identified, continued defendant in his employment knowing all of the circumstances."[38] Occasionally a juror will judge a case on the basis of identity with one of the witnesses.[39] The type of crime may also be considered by juries e.g., in a crime against property jurors who have accumulated more wealth may feel more threatened by the accused.[40]

In addition to this identification process which individual jurors undergo there are other ways in which socioeconomic standing, and resulting bias, may influence jury decision-making. For example, the foreman of the jury is expected to be a male, preferably a man of higher occupational level.[41] Datum from the mock jury trials indicates that proprietors are strongly overrepresented among those chosen to be foremen.[42] The foreman accounts for about 25 per cent of the total interaction acts.[43]

---

[31] Id. at 211-12.

[32] 332 U.S. 261 (1947).

[33] Id. at 275 n.15.

[34] Broeder, supra note 17; See also Hermann, Occupations of Jurors as an Influence on Their Verdict, 5 Forum 150 (1970).

[35] The question in the case was whether defendant railroad had provided plaintiff, a railroad engineer, with a reasonably safe place in which to make emergency repairs on a defective locomotive boiler-check valve claimed to have been negligently packed. The evidence showed that plaintiff had climbed up the side of his locomotive without asking for his foreman's assistance and had slipped on some ice formed from steam emanating from the boiler-check valve. Plaintiff had filed a report some weeks prior to the accident informing defendant of a defect in the engineer's water pump which, according to plaintiff's experts, could have been caused by an improperly packed boiler-check valve. Defendant took no action on this report. Broeder, supra note 17, at 1083.
Typical remarks of the businessmen on the panel were: "99 per cent of all industrial accidents are solely caused by employee negligence;" and "[t]hese laboring people here have all got the same idea; the working people on the jury were as bad as ... [plaintiff] ... Soak the rich; make business pay for everything." Id. at 1091. In contrast the typical reaction of the laborers included: "plaintiff was injured 'in the line of duty;'" and "[plaintiff] had given many years of loyal service to defendant prior to the accident." Id. at 1092.

[36] Id. at 1090.

[37] Id. at 1091.

[38] Id. at 1099.

[39] Id. at 1085.

[40] R. Simon, supra note 12, at 106.

[41] Strodtbeck, James & Hawkins, Social Status in Jury Deliberations, 22 Amer. Soc. Rev. 715 (1957).

[42] Strodtbeck & Hook, The Social Dimensions of a Twelve-Man Jury Table, 24 Sociometry 401 (1961).
"[I]ndex values relating to frequency of choice by occupation are as follows: Proprietor, 1.95; Clerical, 0.81; Skilled, 0.92; and Labor, 0.63." Id.

[43] Id.

5

In the deliberation period, higher status males tend to rise to prominence.[44] What they have to say is perceived as being more important. This may be realistic or it may be that the status cues — dress, speech, etc. — differentiate the group by expectation rather than real performance.[45] Jurors were also asked who they believed contributed most toward the decision; the votes paralleled the status levels in society.[46]

Thus far an attempt has been made to establish that a bias exists which is related to socioeconomic level and that this bias influences verdicts. Most of the evidence presented in this paper has come from mock jury trials or post-trial interviews with jurors. It remains to be demonstrated empirically that socioeconomic level influences actual jury decision. To this end it is hypothesized that there is a greater socioeconomic discrepancy between a defendant found guilty and his jury than between a defendant found not guilty and his jury.

III. METHOD

To test the aforementioned hypothesis fifty not guilty defendants (for whom a guilty match could be found) were selected from the records of the Montgomery County Criminal Court of Pennsylvania covering the period from January, 1965 through May, 1967. From the same time period a group of guilty defendants was selected who were matched individually with the not guilty group.

The following four variables were drawn into the matching process: age, sex, race, and offense.[47] The defendants were individually matched within the following age groupings: 18-29, 30-49, 50 and over. Offense matching was done by specific

---

[44] Strodtbeck, James & Hawkins, supra note 41, at 718.

[45] Id. at 719.

[46] Strodtbeck, Social Process, the Law, and Jury Functioning, in Law and Sociology 144, 154 (W. Evans ed. 1962).

[47]
TABLE I

Breakdown of Offense Categories into Specific Offenses

1. Traffic violations
   a) Operating a motor vehicle while under the influence of liquor and/or drugs.
   b) Failure to stop at the scene of a motor vehicle accident.
   c) Failure to exhibit operator's license and give identification at the scene of a motor vehicle accident.
   d) Failure to render assistance.
   e) Operating a motor vehicle after suspension or revocation of operating privilege.

2. Malicious use of telephone

3. Violation of the Pennsylvania Liquor Code

4. Violation of the Uniform Firearms Act

5. Assault and battery

6. Involuntary manslaughter

7. Burglary and larceny
   a) Burglary
   b) Larceny
   c) Receiving stolen goods
   d) Conspiracy to commit burglary
   e) Conspiracy to commit larceny

8. Sexual offenses
   a) Open lewdness
   b) Rape

6

offense, not the general class.[48] Ideally the caliber of the lawyer and the nature of the evidence should have been included, but this information either could not be ascertained or could not be compared from case to case.

Each of the 100 defendants was scored according to the NORC Prestige Scale.[49] Individual jurors were scaled for occupation and a mean score was computed for each of the 100 juries. Women were scored by their husbands' occupation, unless they were unmarried. Fifteen occupations were found among the jurors which were not included in the NORC Scale. Three independent researchers were asked to rate these fifteen occupations according to the Scale, and a mean score was taken of the three ratings.

The following comparisons were made:

1. Not guilty defendant *group* with guilty defendant *group.*

2. Not guilty jury *group* with guilty jury *group.*

3. Discrepancy scores between each guilty defendant and his jury with the discrepancy score of his counterpart not guilty defendant and his jury.

4. Direction of discrepancy.

---

c) Corrupting morals of children
d) Indecent assault
e) Assault with intent to ravish
f) Fornication
g) Bastardy
h) Incestuous fornication

TABLE II

Breakdown of Entire Defendant Population by Age, Sex, Race and Offense

	1	2	3	4	5	6	7	8
White Male								
18-29	8	2	—	—	—	—	6	10
30-49	28	—	2	—	2	2	6	6
50 and over	10	—	—	—	—	—	—	—
Negro Male								
18-29	—	—	—	2	2	—	—	4
30-49	2	—	—	—	—	—	2	—
50 and over	—	—	—	—	—	—	—	—
White Female								
18-29	—	—	—	—	—	—	2	—
30-49	2	—	—	—	2	—	—	—
50 and over	—	—	—	—	—	—	—	—
Negro Female								
18-29	—	—	—	—	—	—	—	—
30-49	—	—	—	—	—	—	—	—
50 and over	—	—	—	—	—	—	—	—

The numbered categories above correspond to the numbered categories of offenses listed in Table I.

48 For example, failure to stop at scene of an accident paired with like offense rather than one from general traffic offense category.

49 The NORC Prestige Scale is based upon a survey where participants are asked to rank the prestige of a large variety of occupations according to the following ratings: excellent, good, average, below average, poor, don't know. From the percentage of responses in each rating category, a score is computed and a rank assigned to each occupation. For example, in a 1963 survey, the highest scores achieved were, in descending order, U.S. Supreme Court Justice (94), physician (93), nuclear physicist (92) and scientist (92). The bottom four categories were sharecropper (42), garbage collector (39), street sweeper (36), shoe shiner (34). For the original reference to this scale, see Hatt & North, Jobs and Occupations: A Popular Evaluation, Opinion News, Sept. 1947 at 3-13.

7

IV. RESULTS

1. The Mann-Whitney U test[50] was used to determine whether there was a significant difference between the socioeconomic level of the not guilty defendants and the guilty defendants as groups. The mean score of each group was used for comparison.[51] No significant difference emerged between score values of guilty and not guilty defendants.[52]

2. The Mann-Whitney U test was used to determine whether there was a significant difference between the socioeconomic level of the not guilty juries and the guilty juries as groups. The mean of the individual jury means was used for comparison. Juries who found defendants guilty are significantly higher on the prestige scale than those who found defendants not guilty.[53]

3. The sign test[54] was used to determine whether there was a greater socioeconomic discrepancy between a defendant found guilty and his jury than between a defendant found not guilty and his jury. Comparing the discrepancy score between each guilty defendant and his jury with the discrepancy score of his counterpart or not guilty defendant and his jury, it was found that in 41 of the 50 cases there was a greater discrepancy between a defendant found guilty and his jury

---

[50] The Mann-Whitney U Test is a statistical method which can be used to compare two groups (here guilty and not guilty defendants) which have been ranked for prestige by one authority (here by the NORC Prestige Scale). The test begins by making the assumption that the two populations are identical. Then, by a mathematical analysis involving differences between summations of the ranks involved (or in a related process, the means of the ranks), a statistic (U) is arrived at which will indicate whether the original (null) hypothesis of identical populations should be rejected. Whether the numerical size of this statistic is so unusually large or so small as to require rejection of the hypothesis is determined by referring to tables grouped according to a level of significance (here p = .05). Here, where there was a large amount of data, we used a normal curve, and the statistic Z to obtain the sampling distribution of U. This applicable significance level is indicative of the particular statistical accuracy attained. For a more detailed mathematical discussion of this method, see H. Blalock, Jr., Social Statistics 197-203 (1960).

[51]

TABLE III

Mean and Standard Deviations of NORC Scores of Defendant and Jury Groups

	Mean	Standard Deviation
Guilty Defendants	59.3	16.57
Not Guilty Defendants	62.78	12.78
Guilty Juries	71.16*	3.69
Not Guilty Juries	69.26*	3.53

*This mean represents the mean of the 50 jury panel means.

[52] Z = .6963, p = .05. For a definition of these variables, see note 50 supra. Here, Z is not so large as to require rejection of the hypothesis that there is no difference between the socioeconomic level of not guilty and guilty defendants.

[53] Z = 2.5526, p = .05. For a definition of these variables, see note 50 supra. Here, Z is large enough to indicate a significant difference between socioeconomic levels of not guilty and guilty juries.

[54] The sign test is based upon the signs of the differences between paired values. Here the values are the two sets of discrepancy scores between defendant and his jury. The test begins with the null hypothesis that plus and minus differences occur with equal probability. A mathematical equation is used to determine the validity of this hypothesis. If there is a significant difference in the occurrence of plus vis-a-vis minus differences, the null hypothesis is rejected, and one discrepancy will be considered greater than another. For a discussion of the sign test, see R. Steel & J. Torrie, Principles and Procedures of Statistics 400-02 (1960).

8

than between a defendant found not guilty and his jury. The results of the sign test tend to support the hypothesis.[55]

4. One other question relates to whether the discrepancy scores, supporting the hypothesis, indicate that the guilty juries consistently had a higher socioeconomic standing than the defendant, or indicate that the discrepancy for the guilty defendants was generally greater, irrespective of whether the jury had a higher or lower socioeconomic status. These data were compared to arrive at an answer.[56]

There were 30 matched pairs for which the jury of both the guilty and not guilty defendants was higher in socioeconomic level than the defendant. In 27 of the 30 instances, the hypothesis is substantiated, which suggests that significantly more frequently than would be expected by chance, if a not guilty jury had a higher socioeconomic level than the respective defendant, a guilty jury would still have a socioeconomic level higher than both.

There are 5 pairs in which both juries of the matched defendants had a socioeconomic level lower than that of the defendant. The data indicate that in 4 of the 5 instances the guilty jury was more discrepant than its matched not guilty jury. The suggestion made before is that the hypothesis tends to be substantiated even in the opposite direction; that is, when the jury had a lower socioeconomic status than the defendant. Unfortunately, there were only 5 instances with both juries of matched pairs of defendants having lower socioeconomic levels than their respective defendants. Nevertheless, the suggestion is that in 4 out of 5 instances when a not guilty defendant had a jury with a lower socioeconomic level than himself, his matched guilty defendant had a jury whose socioeconomic level was even lower (i.e., more discrepant).

There are two other possibilities. The data indicate that in the 9 instances in which the not guilty jury had a higher socioeconomic level than its defendant, and the matched guilty jury had a socioeconomic level lower than its defendant, in 6 of the 9 cases the guilty case still has a more discrepant score than its matched not guilty case. In the reverse combination in which the not guilty jury had a lower socioeconomic level than its defendant, and the matched guilty jury had a socioeconomic level higher than its defendant, the hypothesis is supported in 4 of the 6 cases.

---

55 The mathematical formula used here is as follows for the .05 significance level. If the sum of plus differences added to the negative of minus differences (D) is greater than twice the square root of the total number of cases, there is a significant difference. In the instant case,

$$D=\overset{+}{41}-\overset{-}{9}=32, N=41+9=50; D>2\sqrt{N}; 32>2\sqrt{50}; 32>14.14.$$

56

TABLE IV

Direction of Discrepancy Related to Trial Outcome

	Mean occupational status of jury higher than both guilty and not quilty defendants	Mean occupational status of jury lower than both guilty and not guilty defendants	Mean occupational status of jury higher than not guilty but lower than guilty defendants	Mean occupational status of jury lower than not guilty but higher than guilty defendants
	n = 30	n = 5	n = 9	n = 6
Matched cases in which discrepancy between occupational status of convicting jury and defendant is greater than discrepancy between occupational status of non-convicting jury and defendant	n = 27 (% = 90)	n = 4 (% = 80)	n = 6 (% = 67)	n = 4 (% = 67)

9

These data indicate that the hypothesis is not only supported with the matched cases in which both juries exceed the defendants in socioeconomic level, but in other instances as well. While there are too few cases in each one of the other three instances, all trends are in the same direction and are consistent with the initial discrepancy hypothesis.

V. SUMMARY

We have found that discrepancy in occupational status between juror and defendant is related to trial outcome. High discrepancy between defendant and jurors is more likely to lead to a conviction than a trial situation in which low status discrepancy occurs. This relationship holds under various configurations of occupational level among jurors and defendants.

VI. CONCLUSION

The study presented in this paper provides further evidence as to the critical importance of the methods used in the jury selection process. At the very least an effort must be made to find that method or those methods which will insure a randomly selected cross section of the community. In theory, the jury system is designed to dispense substantial justice, but no system is any better than the conditions under which it operates, and under the present conditions of its operation the jury selection process sometimes results in juries which are almost totally drawn from nonpeer groups. Randomization would at least provide a cure for the extreme cases where as a matter of course certain classes of defendants would be subject to trial by a jury composed entirely of people of a different socioeconomic level.

Courts frown on any attempt to discover what transpires during jury deliberations.[57] A broad ban on post-trial questioning of jurors stems from an attempt to implement two policies. The first of these is the protection of the jury system and, more specifically, the protection of the finality of jury verdicts.[58] The second is the protection of the jury members.[59] But, since each day the lives and liberties of so many are at stake, more research is needed into the questions which have been raised in this paper. So far the law has done its best to avoid finding answers.

---

[57] See e.g., Northern Pac. Ry. v. Mely, 219 F.2d 199 (9th Cir. 1954); United States v. Driscoll, 276 F. Supp. 333 (S.D.N.Y. 1967); Primm v. Continental Cas. Co., 143 F. Supp. 123 (W.D. La. 1956). See also Sinclair v. United States, 279 U.S. 749 (1929).

[58] McDonald v. Pless, 238 U.S. 264 (1915).

[59] Rakes v. United States, 169 F.2d 739 (4th Cir.), cert. denied, 335 U.S. 826 (1948).

Another consideration which applies to questioning of jurors by attorneys is the ethical requirements of bar membership. However, such ethical requirements represent an ideal standard born of these two policies mentioned above.

10

Social Psychology Quarterly
1980, Vol. 43, No. 2, 190–199

The Effects of Prior Experience on Mock Juror Case Judgments*

DENNIS H. NAGAO
JAMES H. DAVIS
University of Illinois

The effects of prior experience on case judgments were investigated by asking mock jurors to decide defendants' guilt in either a rape-vandalism or vandalism-rape case presentation order. Mock jurors with prior experience on the rape case were found to favor conviction in the vandalism case significantly more often than jurors without such experience. However, jurors with prior experience on the vandalism case were significantly less likely to convict the defendant in the rape case than those judging that case without experience. Various explanations along with the two major hypotheses motivating the study are discussed, and the implications of effects from repeated experience are considered in light of recent proposals to reduce the required term of jury service.

The terms of jury service required by the federal government and certain states mean that jurors often sit for more than one case. For example, jurors sitting in federal courts are on call for four months and report for duty up to 30 separate court days. However, only 4% of the trials in federal courts during the period 1 July 1976 to 30 June 1977 exceeded nine days, while 69% lasted three days or less (Administrative Office of U.S. Courts, 1978). In the extreme, a juror might sit on as many as ten different trials, but such strings would be rare.

Whether or not jurors' prior experiences bias them in determining a defendant's guilt is a question of considerable import, and has been the subject of several recent court rulings. In general, it has been assumed that prior experience which was unrelated to a later case did not unduly bias the juror's ability to render a "fair" verdict. Where prior and present duties were closely related (e.g., several defendants are charged with the same crime but tried separately), it was held

* This research was supported by Grant BNS-7715216 from the National Science Foundation to the University of Illinois, James H. Davis, Principal Investigator. We would like to thank Patrick Laughlin, Blair Sheppard, Verlin Hinsz, Dave Vollrath and Scott Tindale for their comments on an earlier draft of this paper. The assistance of Kathleen Y. Sasamoto and Barbara Skyer in collecting the data is greatly appreciated. This research is based upon an MA thesis submitted by the first author to the University of Illinois. Address all communications to Dennis H. Nagao, Dept. of Psychology, Univ. of Illinois, Champaign, IL 61820.

that such prior service did not necessarily disqualify a juror (*Virgin Islands* v. *Williams*, 1973; *U.S.* v. *DeMaris*, 1976). Furthermore, it was ruled that prior service of almost all jurors on a criminal panel did not "taint" (through conversations with "old hands" concerning previous cases) new jurors (*U.S.* v. *Demet*, 1973).

However, the little empirical evidence available suggests that jurors' prior experience may lead to an increased disposition to vote for conviction (Reed, 1965; Jurow, 1971; Skolnick, 1966; Dillehay & Nietzel, Forthcoming). For example, Reed (1965) surveyed former jurors in the East Baton Rouge Parish (Louisiana) over a two-year period and found that jurors with prior experience exhibited a predisposition to vote for conviction. Similarly, Jurow (1971) noted that individuals with actual prior juror experience were more prone to vote for conviction on a mock case involving capital punishment than those lacking such experience.

Many lawyers also seem to believe that experienced jurors are more likely to vote guilty. Skolnick (1966) has noted that prosecutors prefer to try their cases before experienced jurors while defense attorneys prefer a naive panel. He suggested that this preference was due to a commonly shared belief among lawyers that the greater a juror's trial experience, the more likely an inclination towards guilty, on the presumption of regularity in law enforcement (i.e., the courtroom experience with all its formalities and order may lead jurors to believe that the authorities usually apprehend guilty persons). Skolnick's observations essentially describe what we will call a "guilt-bias" explanation of prior juror experience, where prior experience is seen as predisposing the juror towards a verdict of guilty.

The above evidence, while quite suggestive, involves inferences from surveys of actual trial records (with the exception of Jurow). Such research, while having the attractiveness of dealing with the "real thing," also has disadvantages, such as confounded variables (observations were aggregated over various trials and there is no way to determine whether one kind of case or another predominated, etc.) and lack of replication for any one case. Hence, the experience of any one juror is likely to differ from that of another on a variety of dimensions (type of crime involved, the number of cases previously judged, etc.). Without further information about the relationship of types of case experience, juror populations, and other contextual or subject variables with judgments of guilt, we cannot rule out the possibility that certain types of prior experience might even serve to increase a juror's disposition towards voting for acquittal. These problems suggest that a more systematic inquiry would be valuable at this point. The investigation presented here focuses on the effect of the type of prior case experience on mock jurors' guilt judgments.

Perhaps the simplest tactic for investigating prior experience effects is for mock jurors to render judgments on different cases, with order carefully controlled across subjects.[1] The comparison of guilt preferences among orders could yield useful information, when coupled with a knowledge of particular case content. An examination of the mock trial literature revealed only one study (Pepitone & DeNubile, 1976) in which more than one case was presented to mock jurors *and* where the effect of order of judgment was explicitly examined.

However, the subjects in this study did not assess the guilt of a defendant (they were instructed that the defendant in each case had been found guilty), but instead rated the seriousness of the incident described in a case summary. The data, though relevant, do not directly address the effect of prior experience on mock jurors' preferred verdicts.

Pepitone & DeNubile's (1976) subjects each read two cases and made judgments on the second (either a murder or an assault). Half of the subjects were also required to judge the first case (anchored condition) while the other half were only required to read it (unanchored condition). In addition, half of each group was assigned to either a matched (i.e., assault-assault or murder-murder) or discrepant (i.e., murder-assault or assault-murder) crime order condition. Based on social judgment theory, Pepitone and DeNubile predicted and subsequently found that when the first case was anchored, subjects' ratings of the seriousness of the second case in the discrepant order conditions were contrasted, relative to the judgments of the same case by subjects in the unanchored or matched crime conditions. That is, subjects who judged the murder case first gave *less severe* ratings to the seriousness of the assault case than those who rated the same case in the unanchored or matched crime conditions. Correspondingly, judgments of the murder case by subjects who had first judged an assault case were *more severe* than in the unanchored or matched crime conditions. The same pattern also characterized subjects' punishment recommendations. These findings suggest that experienced jurors may perceive both the seriousness and appropriate punishment of a particular crime differently than naive jurors (i.e., those who have never judged a case before).

Kerr (1978) has recently proposed two hypotheses linking penalty severity to verdict choice. He likened the juror's task of reaching a verdict to the testing of a statistical hypothesis, an analogy proposed earlier by Feinberg (1971) and others. That is, the juror decision-maker must choose between the null hypothesis and an alternative (innocence or guilt of

---

[1] We shall in this paper, however, only consider those instances where a naive juror's responses are contrasted with those of a juror who has had experience on only one previous case.

the defendant, respectively). The subject must evaluate the likelihood of the evidence (x) given the null hypothesis and compare it to a decision criterion of reasonable doubt (y). The decision rule would then be: If $x > y$ choose guilty, otherwise not guilty.

From this model it is clear that verdict choice may be affected by changes either in the criterion of reasonable doubt, or in one's estimate of guilt likelihood given the evidence, or both. On the basis of this analogy and a review of the relevant literature, Kerr (1978:1432) proposed two related hypotheses: (a) The more severe the penalty prescribed for an offense, the more evidence of guilt necessary for conviction (the severity-criterion hypothesis); and, as a result, (b) the lower the likelihood of conviction (the severity-leniency hypothesis).

Kerr's hypotheses in conjunction with Pepitone and DeNubile's contrast results suggest what will be called a "contrast" explanation of prior juror experience. First, we assume that, all other things being equal, the more serious a crime is perceived to be, the greater the degree of punishment likely to be associated with it as an appropriate penalty.[2] However, the more serious the potential consequences to a defendant are perceived to be, the higher the juror's perception of the cost of convicting an innocent person (making a Type 1 error) is also likely to be.[3] This, in turn, may lead to a greater burden of proof

being required for conviction and, ultimately, a more lenient verdict (Kerr's severity-criterion and severity-leniency hypotheses, respectively).

Given the above, Pepitone and DeNubile's contrast results suggest that the effect of prior experience on verdict choice will depend on the pattern of contrast effects resulting from differences in the seriousness of the cases judged by a juror. For example, if jurors judged two cases, a murder and an assault, we would expect jurors who had previously judged the assault case to rate the murder case as *more* serious and deserving of *greater* punishment than would naive jurors judging the murder case. In this situation the experienced juror is likely to perceive the cost of convicting an innocent person (i.e., making a Type 1 error) as being greater than that of acquitting a guilty person (a Type 2 error). Given the severity-criterion hypothesis, we would then expect experienced jurors to require a greater burden of proof to establish guilt relative to naive jurors and, consequently, to convict less often (the severity-leniency hypothesis). Jurors who had judged the murder case first, however, are likely to rate the assault case as *less* serious and deserving of *less* punishment than naive jurors. These jurors are thus likely to require less proof of guilt than naive jurors and, consequently, are more likely to convict.[4] If the perceived seriousness of two cases is equivalent, however (e.g., two similar assaults), we would have no reason to expect any contrast effects to occur. Consequently, we would have no basis for expecting any corresponding differences in the conviction rates of experienced and naive jurors. This contrast explanation of the possible effects of prior juror experience differs from the guilt-bias explanation described earlier, and is the major focus of this research.

---

[2] Pepitone (1975) has suggested that the primary basis for this correlation between seriousness and punishment is a normative value of justice in the sense of equity. Some supporting evidence for this view is provided by Horai & Bartek (1978).

[3] Reducing the probability of a Type 1 error, of course, raises the likelihood of committing a Type 2 error (i.e., setting a guilty person free). While instances can be imagined where the cost of making a Type 2 error may be high, we assume for the most part that the juror or judge is generally much more apprehensive about committing a Type 1 error (and thus adopts a "defendant protection" norm) and will seek to protect against that possibility (and thus require a greater degree of evidence to convict). Such an orientation is consistent with admonitions to presume innocence on the part of the defendant. Evidence for the existence of an apparent norm of defendant protection in the mock jury setting has been reported in other studies (e.g., Davis, Kerr, et al., 1977; Davis et al., Forthcoming).

[4] The juror's perception of penalty severity can also be directly manipulated independently of the seriousness of the crime. For example, Kerr (1978) independently manipulated both the seriousness of the charge and the severity of the prescribed penalty. He found that as the severity of the penalty increased, mock jurors adjusted their conviction criteria upwards (i.e., required more proof of guilt for conviction), which resulted in a reduced probability of conviction.

Overview

Mock jurors were required to study each of two case summaries which differed in an obvious way as to the seriousness of the crime committed (i.e., rape and vandalism), but not in the likelihood of the defendant's guilt. Indeed, pretesting confirmed an approximately even split between guilty and not guilty verdicts preferred by individual subjects independently in each case.

Half of the sample judged the cases in the order rape-vandalism while the others received the reverse order. Subsequently, subjects were assigned to six-person juries, which were required to deliberate to a unanimous verdict on each of the two cases. If the guilt-bias explanation is correct we would expect the initial (personal preference) conviction rate for the case presented second in the sequence to be greater than that of the same case judged by mock jurors without any prior experience. However, if the contrast explanation based on the severity-criterion and severity-leniency hypotheses is valid we would expect that: (a) mock jurors who judged the vandalism case first should convict at a lower rate on the rape case than those without such experience; whereas (b) mock jurors with experience on the rape case should convict at a higher rate on the vandalism case than those without. Although both explanations make the same prediction with respect to the guilt judgments on the vandalism case (i.e., that the second case judgments will be harsher), they generate opposing predictions for the rape case.

METHOD

Subjects

The subjects were 144 male undergraduates at the University of Illinois at Urbana-Champaign who participated in partial fulfillment of a course requirement for introductory psychology. The participants were randomly assigned to 6-person mock juries, which were in turn randomly assigned to experimental conditions.

Design

There were twelve juries assigned to each order of cases (rape-vandalism or vandalism-rape). Within this particular design, each order condition served as the naive (no prior experience) comparison group for one case (e.g., R-V order for the rape case) and as the experienced group on the other case (e.g., R-V order for the vandalism case).

Case Summaries

The rape case was an adaptation of a videotaped rape trial used in previous research (see Davis, Kerr, Stasser, Meek & Holt, 1977) and the vandalism case was composed for this study. Rape was found to be considered the second most serious crime in a study by Coombs (1967), while vandalism, although not tested in the Coombs study, is very similar to those crimes rated least serious (those involving little injury to others).

Each case summary was approximately three pages long and consisted of a specification of the crime with which the defendant was charged, descriptions of defendant and complainant, and summaries of the testimony from both prosecution and defense witnesses.

Procedure

Participants were seated in sets of six persons in small, experimental rooms equipped with one-way mirrors and an intercom system. Subjects were instructed to consider themselves members of a six-person jury whose task would be to deliberate and reach a final verdict of guilty or not guilty for each of two cases. Case A was the rape case for half of the subjects, and the vandalism case for the others; this was the only procedural difference between the two orders. All participants individually completed a preliminary "voir-dire" questionnaire (which called for general opinions about crime and punishment), read the case summary, and responded to a personal opinion questionnaire which elicited judgments of guilt, certainty of verdict, and other characteristics of the case they had just read.

Upon completion of the personal opinion questionnaire, participants began their deliberation as soon as the foreman (randomly selected) was identified and polling instructions given. Once a verdict had been recorded for Case A, the jury members were instructed to complete Case B using the same procedure.

After completing the second case, all subjects individually completed a post-session questionnaire containing items from the earlier personal opinion questionnaire as well as sociometric ratings of fellow jurors' influence and participation, and judgments of characteristics of the case that influenced their verdict. Finally, subjects were debriefed, thanked and excused.

The small number of groups available in each condition prevented analysis at the group level. Consequently, the focus of this report is at the level of the individual juror.

RESULTS

Task Checks: Initial Differences between Cases

Initial differences between the rape and vandalism cases were assessed by comparing the responses of mock jurors who judged the rape case first with those of jurors who judged the vandalism case first. The proportion of guilty preferences in the two cases did not differ significantly ($\chi^2(1)=.11$), nor did the mean judgment on a 10-point, guilt-likelihood scale ($F(1,142)=.77$). Relative frequencies and means for each of these items are given in Table 1 (POQ items 1 and 2). The convic-

tion rates for both rape (.45) and vandalism (.48) were close to the desired level (.50) (necessary to avoid floor and ceiling effects).

Mock jurors also completed several other items about (a) the seriousness of the crime (rape or vandalism) *in general* (Voir Dire Questionnaire [VDQ] items 1–3), and (b) the seriousness of the *particular incident* portrayed in the summaries (POQ items 3 and 4). Mean responses to these items appear in Table 1. Each set of items may be regarded as defining a space within which responses to the two cases may differ. Consequently, the vandalism and rape cases were compared separately on each item set by means of multivariate two-sample tests (Tatsuoka, 1971). Rape was judged significantly more serious than vandalism in general (multivariate $F(3,138) = 60.70$, $p<.001$) and significantly more serious for the particular instance (multivariate $F(2,140) = 8.80$, $p<.001$, respectively). Inspection of the relevant items in Table 1 shows that this pattern occurred for each of the measures.

Prior Case Experience and Mock Juror Judgments

We consider next our major point of interest, the effect of prior experience on mock jurors' guilt judgments. Then we shall examine two variables relevant to the contrast explanation: (a) the perceived

Table 1. Mean Juror Ratings of Each Mock Trial: Initial Case Differences

	Rape	Vandalism	F(1,142)
General Crime Items (VDQ)			
1. Seriousness of the crime[a]	7.72	5.32	82.42*
2. Severity victim aftereffects[b]	2.24	4.06	75.97*
3. Defendant consequences[b]	2.94	4.03	30.04*
Case Specific Items (POQ)			
1. Likelihood of guilt[c]	5.36	5.67	<1
2. Verdict (guilty, not guilty)[d]	32,39	34,37	$\chi^2=.11$
3. Severity victim aftereffects[b]	3.79	4.42	8.63**
4. Defendant consequences[b]	2.62	3.25	12.94*

Note: VDQ and POQ refer to the Voir Dire and Personal Opinion Questionnaires, respectively. For each case $n = 72$. The superscripts index the range of values each item score could take.

[a] 1 = not serious at all to 9 = extremely serious.

[b] 1 = extremely bad to 9 = extremely good.

[c] 0 = 0–10% likely to 9 = 90–100% likely.

[d] For this item only, the values presented are frequency counts.

* $p < .001$.

** $p < .005$.

Table 2. Frequency of Juror Personal Verdict Choices for Each Case as a Function of Order Condition

Order	Rape		Vandalism		Total	
	G	NG	G	NG	G	NG
Rape-Vandalism	32	39	43	29	75	68
	(.45)	(.55)	(.60)	(.40)	(.52)	(.48)
Vandalism-Rape	24	48	34	37	58	85
	(.34)	(.66)	(.48)	(.52)	(.41)	(.59)
Total	56	87	77	66		
	(.39)	(.61)	(.54)	(.46)		

Note: Numbers in parentheses are relative frequencies (row) for each case.

seriousness of the rape and vandalism cases, and (b) the criterion of reasonable doubt.

Predeliberation guilt judgments. Mock jurors' guilty/not guilty verdict choices and mean judgments on the 10-point likelihood scale are given in Tables 2 and 3.

Responses to the verdict choice item were summarized by means of an Order (rape-vandalism, vandalism-rape) by Case (rape, vandalism) by Verdict (guilty, not guilty) multidimensional contingency table. In this analysis the first two dimensions are "explanatory" variables and the last a "response" variable. The approach (fitting log-linear hierarchical models in turn) described by Bishop, Fienberg & Holland (1975) was used to assess main effects and interactions.[5]

The results indicated that the log-linear model incorporating only the main effects of Order and Case was adequate to describe the observed data (i.e., the addition of the interaction parameter did not contribute significantly to the fit of that

[5] The procedure is analogous to that used in fitting linear regression models. Parameters are added to a given log-linear model to improve its power in generating predicted tables that accurately describe the observed data tables. The goodness of fit between the predicted and observed data tables can then be assessed by the likelihood ratio chi-square statistic, G^2. A small, non-significant value of G^2 indicates that the model being tested is adequate to describe the observed data tables. As in the fitting of regression models, many constructions may be adequate to describe the data; however, a "best-fitting" model may be selected from among those that fit the data by repeated applications of the procedure. In our case, it was feasible to test all possible models and assess the significance of each effect. For a discussion of the hierarchical principle and the fitting of log-linear models see Bishop, Fienberg & Holland (1975), Fienberg (1977), or Goodman (1972).

model). The main effects of case and order are evident from an examination of the respective marginal totals shown in Table 2. Both of these main effects can be accounted for by the differences that occurred in the second case judgments of each case (recall that first case judgments for each case did not differ significantly). That is, jurors with prior experience (i.e., those in the V-R condition) voted for conviction on the rape case at a lesser rate than did naive jurors (.34 and .45, respectively). However, on the vandalism case this pattern was reversed; experienced jurors (those in the R-V condition) were more likely to favor conviction than naive jurors (.60 and .48, respectively). This is exactly the pattern predicted by the contrast explanation and is inconsistent with the prediction of the guilt-bias explanation that prior experience would result in an increased predisposition towards guilt.

The effect of prior experience on the guilt likelihood ratings was assessed by an Order X Case ANOVA (where the latter was a repeated measures factor). The results indicated that none of the differences shown in Table 3 were significant. It is interesting to note that the two guilt items do not yield similar results. We will discuss below this apparent lack of correspondence.

Seriousness judgments. After reading each case summary, mock jurors rated the seriousness of the aftereffects they per-

Table 3. Mean Likelihood of Guilt Rating For Each Case as a Function of Order Condition

Order	Rape	Vandalism
Rape-Vandalism ($n = 69$)	5.36	5.67
Vandalism-Rape ($n = 71$)	5.24	5.69

Note: 0 = 0–10% likely and 9 = 90–100% likely.

ceived the victim to have suffered as well as the consequences they thought the defendant might incur if convicted. Mean responses to each of these items are presented in Table 4 as POQ items 3 and 4, respectively. The effect of prior experience for each item was assessed by an Order X Case ANOVA (where the latter was a repeated measures factor). A significant effect of prior experience would be indicated within these analyses by a statistically significant interaction. For *victim* consequences, only the effect of case attained statistical significance, $F(1, 142) = 28.29$, $p < .001$. This reflects the fact that jurors perceived the victim of the rape to have suffered more serious consequences than the vandalism victim. For *defendant* consequences both case and order were statistically significant, $F(1,141) = 86.76$, $p < .001$ and $F(1,141) = 7.12$, $p < .01$, respectively, as was their interaction, $F(1,141) = 4.05$, $p < .05$. Inspection of the mean responses shows that experienced mock jurors perceived the possible consequences to the defendant in the rape (vandalism) case as being more (less) serious than those without such experience. This pattern of mean responses reflects the expected pattern of contrast effects according to the predictions of the contrast explanation.

Reasonable doubt criterion. After reading each of the case summaries, but prior to deliberation, mock jurors indicated the level of "likelihood that the defendant committed the crime" required for them to judge the defendant in that case "guilty beyond a reasonable doubt." According to Kerr's (1978) analysis, a juror's verdict choice may be affected by

Table 4. Mean Juror Seriousness Ratings For Each Case as a Function of Prior Experience

Case Specific Ratings (POQ)[a]	Rape		Vandalism	
	R-V[b]	V-R	R-V	V-R
3. Severity victim aftereffects	3.77	3.33	4.35	4.42
4. Defendant consequences	2.66[c]	2.07[d]	3.43	3.25

Note: Row entries with subscripts c, d differed significantly at the $p < .05$ level.
[a] The ranges of these items are given in Table 1.
[b] R-V and V-R represent the rape-vandalism and vandalism-rape order conditions, respectively.

changes in either the apparent weight of the evidence or the criterion for reasonable doubt. However, no shifts as a function of prior experience were observed in subjects' ratings of the apparent weight of the evidence, as measured by the likelihood of the defendant's guilt item (see Table 3). Perhaps the observed lack of correspondence between the two guilt measures (i.e., guilty/not guilty, and likelihood of guilt) can be accounted for by shifts in the criterion of reasonable doubt. The results of an Order X Case repeated measures ANOVA, however, revealed no significant differences.

DISCUSSION

The primary purpose of this investigation was to test two explanations of prior experience on mock jurors' subsequent judgments. The results indicate that mock jurors with prior experience on the rape case voted to convict the defendant in the vandalism case at a significantly *higher* rate than did jurors without such experience (60% to 48%, respectively)—as predicted by both explanations. Mock jurors with prior experience on the vandalism case, however, voted to convict the defendant in the rape case at a significantly *lower* rate than jurors without such experience (34% to 45%, respectively). This latter finding is consistent with the contrast explanation, and is inconsistent with the guilt-bias proposal.

The logic of the contrast explanation is further supported by the pattern of mean responses of mock jurors' ratings of the seriousness of the consequences if the defendant were convicted. As expected, experienced mock jurors perceived the possible consequences to the defendant in the rape (vandalism) case as being more (less) serious than those without such experience and subsequently convicted the defendant at a lower (higher) rate.

Despite the success of the contrast hypothesis in explaining the pattern of seriousness judgments and juror verdict choices, the lack of a similarly interpretable pattern in the mean choice of a reasonable doubt criterion is puzzling. One possibility is that mock jurors misunderstood the reasonable doubt item. An informal examination of the distribution of responses, however, reveals relatively few obviously ''inappropriate'' responses—criterion choices of less than 50–60% likely on either case.

Another possible explanation is that mock jurors may have consistently over- or underestimated the criterion of reasonable doubt they actually used. For each case mock jurors estimated the likelihood of the defendant's guilt, indicated their reasonable doubt criterion (on the same scale as the guilt item) and gave their verdict choice. Given this set of items it was possible to assess mock jurors' consistency in responding. A predicted verdict for each juror for each case was generated on the basis of the following rule: If the likelihood value exceeded (was less than) the reasonable doubt criterion, a guilty (not guilty) verdict was predicted.[6]

Note that two types of inconsistencies were possible: the juror was (a) predicted to say guilty but chose not guilty or, (b) predicted to say not guilty and chose guilty. Interestingly enough, approximately the same percentage of inconsistencies occured for rape (26%) as for vandalism (27%). In addition, the percentage of each type of inconsistency, (a) vs. (b), was approximately the same for rape (22% vs. 4%) as it was for vandalism (24% vs. 3%). Apparently, the type of case, as represented here, was not an important factor.

The preceding pattern of inconsistencies in mock juror responses to the reasonable doubt item might be due to social desirability. Concern for protecting the defendant seems to be a fairly strong normative principle in the trial setting, perhaps in keeping with Blackstone's familiar admonition that "it is better that ten guilty persons escape than one innocent suffer" (1789[1962:420]). Jurors may have indicated, perhaps unintentionally, a criterion in line with such a principle (e.g., 80–90% likely), in order to avoid appearing too unconcerned over the possibility of convicting an innocent person. If such a

response bias did occur then the pattern of inconsistencies obtained is not surprising. That is, an artificially inflated reasonable doubt criterion necessarily means there would be a smaller range of likelihood of guilt scores that could exceed the criterion value and, hence, a decreased likelihood of the error of falsely predicting a guilty verdict. Note that this simultaneously raises the probability of erroneously predicting an innocent verdict. If such response biases occur for jurors' self-estimates of the reasonable doubt criterion, then more indirect methods of measuring the criterion may be preferable (e.g., techniques suggested by Thomas & Houge, 1976, and Fried, Kaplan & Klein, 1975).

However, the important finding was that prior experience affects the verdict preference of subjects reacting to a later, ostensibly separate event. The pattern of effects is consistent with our contrast hypothesis, but considerably more research will, of course, be required to map out the limits of applicability.

Implications

Within the past decade or so the mock trial paradigm has become a popular vehicle for investigating issues of concern to both psychology and the law (see Davis, Bray & Holt, 1977 and Gerbasi, Zuckerman & Reiss, 1977 for critical reviews of the literature). The use of such controlled settings generally allows for a greater degree of internal validity, but at the cost of some generalizability (external validity). (See Bray & Kerr, Forthcoming, for a discussion of the relative merits and drawbacks of the simulated mock trial paradigm.) Consequently, it is important to avoid recommending any particular action or social policy as a result of a single study.

Nonetheless we can explore some implications in light of our results. Perhaps the most important implication of this research lies not in the particular manner in which prior experience affected mock jurors' later judgments, but rather that such effects occurred at all. The results of this study, in conjunction with the field studies cited earlier and lawyers' informal

---

[6] In those cases where jurors' estimates of the reasonable doubt criterion and the likelihood of the defendant's guilt were equal, they were categorized as being consistent with their verdict choice.

observations, all suggest that jurors might be influenced by prior experience.

If prior experience does indeed incline the juror to one verdict or another, some provision to counteract this effect might be useful—e.g., a reduction in the length of jury service. In fact, there have been two recent recommendations to do just that: the Uniform Jury Selection and Service Act limits jury service to ten court days, and the Model Act, prepared by the National Conference of Metropolitan Courts, recommends a further reduction to five days (cited in Van Dyke, 1977). Our results are certainly consistent with such trends.

However, the results of this study suggest that a reduction to only one trial may be worth considering. Such a system has been in operation in Texas since the early 1970s when legislation established that a juror's tour of duty ended whenever that juror had sat for one trial to a verdict, or had been challenged peremptorily or for cause during the selection process. As a result the average juror in Texas now serves for only one or two days (Van Dyke, 1977).

A reduction in the required length of jury service to one trial would have several additional benefits, besides eliminating any biases resulting from prior juror experience. For example, the granting of excuses from jury service on grounds of financial burden or nature of employment (e.g., physician) could be partially eliminated since jurors would on the average (given the Texas experience) serve for only one or two days. Since fewer sub-populations would be consistently excused, juries would become more representative of the community.

REFERENCES

Administrative Office of U.S. Courts
1978 1977 Juror Utilization in United States Courts. Washington, D.C.: Government Printing Office.

Bishop, Y. M. M., S. E. Fienberg, & P. W. Holland
1975 Discrete Multivariate Analysis: Theory and Practice. Cambridge, MA: MIT Press.

Blackstone, W.
1962 Commentaries on the Laws of England of
[1769] Public Wrongs. Boston: Beacon Press.

Bray, R. M., & N. L. Kerr
Forth- "Use of the simulation method in the study
com- of jury behavior: Some methodological
ing considerations." Law and Human Behavior.

Coombs, C. H.
1967 "Thurstone's measurement of social values revisited forty years later." Journal of Personality and Social Psychology 6:85–91.

Davis, J. H., R. M. Bray & R. W. Holt
1977 "The empirical study of decision processes in juries: A critical review." Pp. 326–361 in J. L. Tapp and F. J. Levine (eds.), Justice, and the Individual in Society: Psychological and Legal Issues. New York: Holt.

Davis, J. H., R. W. Holt, C. E. Spitzer & G. Stasser
Forth- "The effects of consensus requirements
com- and multiple decisions on mock juror pref-
ing erences." Journal of Personality and Social Psychology.

Davis, J. H., N. L. Kerr, G. Stasser, D. Meek & R. W. Holt
1977 "Victim consequences, sentence severity, and decision processes in mock juries." Organizational Behavior and Human Performance 18:346–365.

Dillehay, R. C. & M. T. Nietzel
Forth- "Conceptualizing mock jury/juror research:
com- Critique and illustrations." In K. S. Larsen
ing (ed.), Psychology and Ideology.

Feinberg, W. E.
1971 "Teaching the type I and type II errors: The judicial process." The American Statistician, June:30–32.

Fienberg, S. E.
1977 The Analysis of Cross-Classified Categorical Data. Cambridge, MA: MIT Press.

Fried, M., K. J. Kaplan & K. W. Klein
1975 "Juror selection: An analysis of voir dire." Pp. 49–66 in R. J. Simon (ed.), The Jury System in America: A Critical Overview. Beverly Hills, CA: Sage.

Gerbasi, K. C., M. Zuckerman, & H. T. Reis
1977 "Justice needs a new blindfold: A review of mock jury research." Psychological Bulletin 84:323–345.

Goodman, L. A.
1972 "A modified multiple regression approach to the analysis of dichotomous variables." American Sociological Review 37:28–46.

Horai, J. M. & M. Bartek
1978 "Recommended punishment as a function of injurious intent, actual harm done, and intended consequences." Personality and Social Psychology Bulletin 4:575–578.

Jurow, G. L.
1971 "New data on the effect of a 'death-qualified' jury on the guilt determination process." Harvard Law Review 84:567–611.

Kerr, N. L.
1978 "Severity of prescribed penalty and mock jurors' verdicts." Journal of Personality and Social Psychology 36:1431–1442.

Pepitone, A.
1975 "Social psychological perspective on crime

and punishment." Journal of Social Issues 31:197–216.

Pepitone, A., & M. DeNubile
  1976 "Contrast effects in judgments of crime severity and the punishment of criminal violators." Journal of Personality and Social Psychology 33:448–459.

Reed, J. P.
  1965 "Jury deliberations, voting and verdict trends." The Southwestern Social Science Quarterly 45:361–370.

Skolnick, J. H.
  1966 Justice Without Trial: Law Enforcement in Democratic Society. New York: Wiley.

Tatsuoka, M. M.
  1971 Multivariate Analysis: Techniques for Educational and Psychological Research. New York: Wiley.

Thomas, E. A. C., & A. Houge
  1976 "Apparent weight of the evidence, decision criteria, and confidence ratings in juror decision making." Psychological Review 83:442–465.

U.S. Court of Appeals, 1st Circuit
  1976 U.S. v. DeMaris. 531 F.2d 632.

U.S. Court of Appeals, 3rd Circuit
  1973 Virgin Islands v. Williams. 476 F.2d 771.

U.S. Court of Appeals, 7th Circuit
  1973 U.S. v. DeMet. 486 F.2d 816.

Van Dyke, J.
  1977 Jury Selection Procedures. Cambridge, MA: Ballinger.

Law and Human Behavior, Vol. 9, No. 2, 1985

Juror Experience and Jury Verdicts*

Ronald C. Dillehay* and Michael T. Nietzel†

Most trial attorneys believe that repeated jury service produces several effects in jurors, one of the most important of which is an increased disposition toward conviction of criminal defendants. However, case law reveals a reluctance to accept the proposition that prior service per se would disqualify a juror from sitting on an instant case because of actual or implied bias. The need for direct empirical investigation of the effects of prior jury service prompted the present study, which examined a complete docket of 175 consecutive criminal trials across one calendar year in a state circuit court which required a 30-day term of its venire. The results indicated that as the number of jurors with prior jury experience increased there was a modest, but significant, increase in the probability of a conviction. Analysis of the relationship between initial verdicts and subsequent service disconfirmed the alternative hypothesis that attorneys deselected jurors on the basis of their first verdicts. Several parameters of experience were also related to foreperson selection. Implications for legal practice and for additional research are discussed.

INTRODUCTION

Criminal trial attorneys tend to believe that experienced jurors are conviction prone. For example, Bailey and Rothblatt (1971, p. 107) assert that "All other things being equal, new jurors are desired over experienced jurors. The principles of reasonable doubt and presumption of innocence will be received more readily by a new juror." This preference for novice jurors (see also Belli, 1954; Ginger, 1977) is shared by some jury selection consultants and researchers (Nietzel & Dillehay, 1979). If experienced jurors are more likely to convict, there are implications for bias in jury trials as well as implications for the jury selection strategies of the prosecution and defense. As a theoretical matter a documented effect of juror experience on verdicts should elicit efforts to test the plausible perceptual, cognitive, attitudinal, and interpersonal process explanations of the phenomenon.

* Support for this research was provided, in part, by National Science Foundation grant No. SES-8209479. A portion of this work was conducted while the senior author was a James McKeen Cattell Foundation Fellow.

† Department of Psychology, University of Kentucky, Lexington, Kentucky 40506-0044.

The courts generally have not been willing to disqualify jurors with prior experience even when by psychological standards juror bias seems likely. Prior jury service in the same term of court is not sufficient to warrant a challenge for cause (see, e.g., *U.S. v Riebschlaeger*[1]; *U.S. v. Stevens*[2]; *U.S. v. Williams*[3]) even if jurors have sat on an earlier trial of the same defendant which involved a different transaction from the current one.[4]

In *Casias v. United States*[5] an equally divided Tenth Circuit Court of Appeals affirmed the conviction of the defendant who claimed that jurors were biased because 43 of the 44 venirepersons had prior service in one or more of eight similar cases (narcotics) presented by the same prosecution witnesses testifying in the defendant's case. In addition, ten of the current jury had deliberated together. The affirming judges stated that an "inference of prejudice in such a situation is based on nothing more than suspicion, speculation, and conjecture" (p. 617); the three dissenting judges argued that the array should have been discharged for an "implied bias."[6] Although subsequent decisions (e.g., *U.S. v. Garza*[7]; *U.S. v. Riebschlaeger*) have rejected the dissenting theory of implied bias in *Casias*, the language of *Garza* suggests the possible importance of appropriate data on the question of whether prior service prejudices jurors (*U.S. v. Garza*, p. 303). At the moment, however, the conditions of juror experience required to meet case law precedents are extreme.[8]

The courts are divided in their opinions about the extent to which counsel should even be able to inquire about a venireperson's prior jury service. Some courts have ruled that it is proper for the trial judge to deny defense counsel's posing questions to jurors about their previous jury service (*Viramontes-Medine v. U.S.*[9]; *U.S. v. Ruggiero*[10]) or verdicts (*U.S. v. Ochoa*[11]). Other courts have decided that counsel must be permitted to inquire about prospective jurors' prior experience (*U.S. v. Montelongo*[12]), especially if that experience has occurred after the jury has been struck but prior to the actual trial (*State v. Holmes*[13]; *U.S.*

---

[1] 528 F.2d 1031 (5th Cir. 1976).

[2] 444 F.2d 630 (6th Cir. 1971).

[3] 484 F.2d 176 (8th Cir. 1973). *cert. denied*, 414 U.S. 1070, 94 S. Ct. 381, 38 L.Ed. 2d 475 (1973).

[4] 47 Am. Jr. 2d 475 (1973).

[5] 315 F.2d 614 (10th Cir.), *cert. denied*, 374 U.S. 845, 83 S. Ct. 1901, 10 L.Ed.2d 1065 (1963).

[6] See *U.S. v. Casias, op. cit.*

[7] 574 F.2d (C.A. Texas 1978).

[8] A juror who had served earlier on the trial of a different defendant charged with a crime arising out of the same transaction as the one currently at trial would be disqualified [*Kleindienst v. U.S.*, 48 App. D.C. 190 (1918)]. Likewise, jurors may be properly challenged if they were members of a jury which tried a civil suit involving the same factors as the criminal trial for which they are now part of the venire [*Shumate v. State*, 19 Ala. App. 340, 97 So. 772 (1923)]. In one of the most unusual cases in this area a defendant's conviction was reversed because eight members of his jury had served on the jury that convicted his wife for the same offense on the same day as his trial [*Lett v. U.S.*, 15 F.2d 690 (8th Cir. 1926)].

[9] 411 F.2d 981 (C.A. Cal. 1969).

[10] 472 F.2d 599, *cert. denied*, 93 S. Ct. 2772, 415 U.S. 939, 37 L.Ed. 2d 598.

[11] 543 F.2d 564 (5th Cir. 1976).

[12] 507 F.2d 639 (5th Cir. 1975).

[13] La., 347 So.2d 221 (1977).

v. Mutchler[14]). Prosecutors routinely keep "jury books" which show how jurors voted on previous trials (*Hamer v. U.S.*[15]), and there is case law supporting the right of a defendant to look at prosecution dossiers on prospective jurors (*People v. Aldridge*[16]).

As the above cases indicate, the courts have been reluctant to rule that prior jury service, in general, introduces an implied bias against defendants, though some decisions suggest that research might be substituted for current conjecture.

Survey and Archival Research on Actual Jurors

Broeder (1965) explored the relationship between juror experience and verdicts by conducting post-trial interviews with 225 jurors who had served on 23 trials in federal court. In his nonstatistical report he concluded that juror experience has an impact on verdicts. Reed (1965) sent questionnaires to 432 jurors who had served on 36 criminal trials in Louisiana. Among his findings was the result that jurors with previous jury experience were' significantly more likely to vote guilty than were novice jurors. However, only 56% of the jurors who were sent questionnaires returned them, introducing a possible sampling bias.

Three studies of the relationship between jurors' prior experience and verdicts used archival data from actual jurors. Werner, Strube, Cole, and Kagehiro (1982) studied 206 criminal trial juries over an 18-month period in Salt Lake City, Utah and found no significant relationship between the number of experienced jurors and jury verdict. However, the conviction rate for four-person juries with no experienced jurors was 50%, while that for juries with one or more repeaters was 73%, a difference which was not statistically significant. Kerr, Harmon, and Graves (1982) studied 210 criminal trial juries from the Superior Court of San Diego, California. The index of experience for a jury was the number of jurors with one or more previous trials during the 20-day term. Kerr (1981) reports that the number of experienced jurors did not predict jury verdicts. Nietzel, Dillehay, and Rogers (1976) analyzed data for 28 months of felony trials in the Lexington, Kentucky Circuit Courts, by comparing the verdicts for the first trial of each month with that held last in the month. While a sizable difference in percentage of not guilty verdicts did result—43% for first trials and 25% for last—the difference was not statistically significant for the small number ($N = 56$) of trials examined.

Experiments with Mock Jurors

In one experiment focusing on death-qualified juries rather than juror experience per se, Jurow (1971) compared 66 mock juror volunteers who reported previous actual jury experience with 124 subjects who had not previously served

---

[14] 559 F.2d 955 (5th Cir. 1977), *modified,* 566 F.2d 1044 (5th Cir. 1978).
[15] 259 F.2d. 274 (9th Cir. 1958).
[16] 209 N.W.2d 796 (1971).

as jurors. On a number of individual difference variables, the subjects with prior experience did differ significantly from those without it. Experienced subjects were older, more often male, more in favor of capital punishment, more inclined to apply it in a hypothetical instance, more authoritarian, and more conservative. They also gave higher penalties on 14 actual, previous capital cases which they were asked to judge.

These differences may reflect psychological processes activated by juror experience. But other interpretations are possible. Jurow's view was that conservative persons are picked from the venire, producing the relationship between personality and prior service. Another alternative is that people with authoritarian personalities and jury experience are more likely to enjoy jury experience and thus to volunteer for an experiment that entails a mock trial (or make themselves available readily to the court for subsequent actual jury duty). Even if Jurow's interpretation is right, prior experience serves as an indicator of conviction proneness, and the constellation of traits found in his subjects with prior jury experience might provide one basis for increased proclivity to convict following actual service.

Kerr et al. (1982) asked 239 students to provide verdicts for five hypothetical cases. They also included a control so as to compare subjects who had and those who had not judged previous cases in the same experimental session. Subjects who had the experience of reading several cases and making judgments about each were not different from those who lacked that experience.

Overall, research results on the relationship between juror experience and jury verdicts are mixed. In discussing some of this research, Kerr (1981) concludes that there is some indication that experience does lead to a greater likelihood of conviction. He called for more clarifying research.

Selection or Experience? Competing Interpretations

Our major hypothesis is that experienced jurors are conviction-prone, evidence for which is to be sought in an association between indices such as the number of experienced jurors on a jury and guilty verdicts. However, competing with the explanation that experienced jurors are more likely to convict is the hypothesis that conviction-prone jurors are more likely to serve. The possibility that acquitting jurors in particular are selectively eliminated by prosecutors during voir dire needs to be taken seriously as an explanation for an experienced juror phenomenon should it occur. Concern about defense attorneys eliminating jurors who have previously convicted does not arise largely because defense attorneys rarely accumulate as much information about a venire as does the prosecutor.

Foreperson Experience

Since the juror elected foreperson occupies a position of greater potential influence than other jurors during deliberations, we were interested in whether those elected as forepersons were more likely to have served as jurors previously. We also assessed the possibility that once selected as a foreperson, a juror is more likely to be picked again as foreperson on subsequent juries on which he or she serves. Werner et al. report that in 10 of the 34 trials in which an experienced juror was selected to be foreperson, that juror had been a foreperson before. Finally, one feature of experience on the jury is the number of jurors who have previously served as forepersons. We analyzed the data to determine whether there is a relationship between verdict and the number of jurors with foreperson experience.

METHOD

The sample consisted of all criminal trials ($N = 175$) in the Circuit Court of Fayette County, Kentucky for the period January through December, 1973. All were felony cases except for 20 that came up on appeal from the lower court. Information on each trial, obtained from the Court's trial summary, included data of the trial, charges in the indictment, names of the jurors, identity of the foreperson in all but hung juries, verdicts on each count, and penalty assigned for each guilty verdict. The coding was done first by a graduate assistant, and then independently by the authors. Instances of discrepancy or ambiguity were rare and were resolved by examining the case file, which contained more detailed information.

In this jurisdiction, a juror is typically on call for one month and then not recalled for jury duty for some time, usually much longer than one year. We found no juror in our sample of 175 trials who served in a trial remote in time during the year of data analyzed. All of the juror experience assessed was on criminal juries. Civil jury experience likely occurred for some of the jurors because of the administrative practices in the courts of Fayette County, in which members of concurrent civil jury panels might be borrowed to fill out a criminal jury on a given case, and vice versa. Because we believed such borrowing was infrequent, we did not assess any influence of civil juror experience.

Juror Experience

Juror experience was defined as occurring within the 30-day jury term and was indexed by five variables: (1) number of experienced jurors on the trial, (2) total amount of juror experience represented, (3) prior jury experience of the foreperson, (4) number of jurors who had previously served as a foreperson, and (5) previous foreperson experience of the foreperson. A juror was considered experienced if he or she had served on one or more prior trials on which the jury was sworn and the trial commenced. Thus, if after the swearing but before deliberation a trial was terminated either by a directed verdict or a change of plea, the jurors on that trial were credited with trial experience. This decision contrasts with a decision to credit juror experience only if there was deliberation in the trial, and is based on the recognition that juror experience begins when a person reports for jury duty and progresses through many steps before a verdict is attempted. Also, the literature suggests that predeliberation factors determine jury verdicts to a greater degree than do deliberation effects (see Dillehay & Nietzel, 1980; also Kalven & Zeisel, 1966). The number of trials in our data in which juries were sworn but took no action is small (12 of 175).

Using trial dates and juror names we determined for each trial the number of experienced jurors. This index is predicated on the hypothesis that prior experience is a threshold phenomenon, that one trial is sufficient to produce the effects to be observed. The second index of experience is based on the alternate possibility that the psychological effects of experience are best regarded as cumulative over trials. For this index the number of previous trials for each juror was determined and summed over jurors. This variable represents the aggregate juror experience on each trial and is termed "total juror experience."

The number of jurors previously a foreperson was a simple count over the 12 jurors of each trial. The prior jury experience of the foreperson was a count of previous trials for that person. Previous foreperson experience for the current foreperson was treated dichotomously (yes, no).

Trial Verdicts

The measure of jury verdicts was our best linear ordering of the court's actual outcome categories of jury decisions. These are: (1) not guilty, (2) hung jury, (3) guilty of a lesser included charge, (4) guilty on some but not all of the charges, and (5) guilty as charged in the indictment. This represents a dimension of favorableness to the defendant (or to the state). In cases with multiple charges (several charges for a single defendant or multiple defendants) the verdict was coded according to the most unfavorable outcome for the defendant(s). Since 12 of the 175 juries did not deliberate, the number of cases with jury outcomes is 163.

RESULTS

The means and standard deviations for the experience measures are shown in Table 1 for each variable overall and for types of jury verdicts. The average trial in the study contained a mean of 6.83 experienced jurors. Eighty-two percent of the trials had at least one experienced juror, and 54% of the trials contained eight or more jurors with experience during the term. Twenty-six of the 163 trials (16%) contained 12 experienced jurors.

Table 2 displays the number and percent of jurors serving on various numbers of cases. By the end of the term 44.3% of the jurors who had served at least once had served on only one trial, while more than one in five (21.5%) had served on four or more trials. In all, counting deliberating jurors and alternates, there were 902 jurors who made 1990 appearances during their one-month terms of service.

With regard to verdicts, Table 1 indicates that 26% of the trials yielded an acquittal, 16% were hung, and 58% produced a conviction of some sort.

Table 1. Means and Standard Deviations of Experience Factors for Trial Outcomes[a]

Verdict	N	%	Number of experienced jurors		Total juror experience		Number of previous forepersons		Juror experience of the foreperson		Forepersons previously a foreperson	
			M	SD	M	SD	M	SD	M	SD	M	SD
Not guilty	42	26	5.33	4.29	11.69	13.16	.60	.91	1.24	1.66	1.83	.38
Hung	26	16	6.66	4.17	14.92	14.07	1.04	1.00	—	—	—	—
Guilty, lesser charge	22	13	6.86	4.51	14.18	12.36	.50	.60	1.50	1.63	1.77	.43
Guilty, on some charges	9	6	7.00	4.85	16.67	15.42	1.11	1.17	1.56	1.88	1.78	.44
Guilty, on all charges	64	39	7.88	4.13	18.19	14.58	1.00	1.05	1.75	1.62	1.81	.39
Totals	163	100	6.83	4.34	15.37	13.99	.84	.98	1.54	1.65	1.81	.39

[a] Note: Total juror experience is the sum of all prior service during the term for all jurors on the jury. $N = 137$ for Juror Experience of the Foreperson and for Foreperson Previously a Foreperson. The foreperson on hung trials was not identified. Scores for Foreperson Previously a Foreperson were 1 = yes, 2 = no.

Juror Experience and Jury Verdicts

Pearson product moment correlations among verdict and experience variables appear in Table 3. As would be expected because of the way the variables are defined and derived, the experience measures intercorrelated moderately to substantially among themselves, with values ranging from .32 to .83.[17]

The correlations between verdict and the experience variables are shown in the first row of Table 3, where it can be seen that two experience variables are significantly correlated with verdict. The number of experienced jurors on the trial shows a slightly higher correspondence with verdict ($r = .23$, $p < .01$) than does total juror experience ($r = .18$, $p < .05$). The former accounts for just over 5% of the variation in trial outcomes. Thus, as juror experience increases, so does the tendency to convict. Experience associated with foreperson status, however, was not significantly correlated with jury verdicts.

A stepwise multiple regression procedure was used to determine the best combination of experience variables for the prediction of trial outcomes. The sex of the foreperson (discussed below) was also entered with the experience variables as a predictor. In this procedure (*SAS User's Guide*, 1979) the best single predictor is identified, using the amount of variance accounted for in the criterion (verdict) as a basis for the choice. Then the best two-variable model is selected, and so on. The number of experienced jurors on the trial was the best single predictor [$R^2 = 0.062$, $F(1, 131) = 8.71$, $p < .004$]. Adding variables beyond the

[17] Note while the correlations nonetheless depict the relationships indicated, interdependencies are reflected in some of these correlations so that for some purposes other statistics may be more suitable for the information desired. For example, the correlation of .45 between the number of jurors who have been a foreperson and having a foreperson on the instant jury who has previously served in that role should not be used as the best indication that jurors experienced as forepersons are selected for that task beyond a chance level. A chi-square analysis utilizing chance-level expectations is more appropriate for that determination (see below).

Table 2. Extent of Juror Service

Number of trials served on	Jurors	
	Number	%
1	400	44.3
2	182	20.2
3	126	14.0
4	85	9.4
5	48	5.3
6	33	3.7
7	14	1.6
8	12	1.3
9	0	0
10	2	0.2
Totals	902	100

number of experienced jurors reduced slightly in each case the significance of the regression obtained. For this data set the best predictor, then, is the number of experienced jurors, and other significant individual relationships do not contribute new information.

A graphic view of the percentages of not guilty, hung, and guilty (lesser charge, some but not all charges, and guilty as charged combined) verdicts for juries with different numbers of experienced jurors is shown in Figure 1. For purposes of grouping the trials in terms of the number of experienced jurors we selected the cutting points that gave us a reasonably even distribution of trials on the experience variable while separating out those trials which contained all ex-

Table 3. Intercorrelations for Verdict and Juror Experience Variables[a]

	Number of experienced jurors	Total juror experience	Number of previous forepersons	Juror experience of the foreperson	Forepersons previously a foreperson
Verdict	.23[b]	.18[c]	.14	.13	− .04
Number of Experienced Jurors		.83[b]	.61[b]	.64[b]	− .32[b]
Total Juror Experience			.73[b]	.77[b]	− .36[b]
Number of Previous Forepersons				.55[b]	− .45[b]
Juror Experience of The Foreperson					− .52[b]

[a] Note: $N = 137$ for Jury Experience of the Foreperson; $N = 146$ for Forepersons Previously a Foreperson, which was coded 1 = yes, 2 = no.
[b] $p < .05$.
[c] $p < .01$.

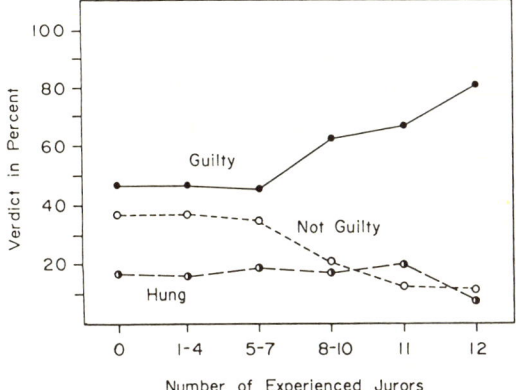

Fig. 1. Verdict changes as a function of the number of experienced jurors. Note: Guilty includes guilty of a lesser included charge, guilty of some but not all of the charges, and guilty as charged.

perienced jurors. We were interested in the latter as a special category. As the figure shows, the deviation toward more guilty verdicts and fewer not guilty verdicts occurs past the point of a majority of experienced jurors on the trial. The percentage of hung juries varies little across categories of experience.

Initial Verdict and Subsequent Service

To test the hypothesis that jurors who acquit or hang are less likely to serve on subsequent trials, we examined frequencies of service as a function of initial verdicts. If jurors who acquit are struck through the exercise of prosecution peremptories, they should show a lower frequency of service than jurors who return guilty verdicts initially. Table 4, which includes all juries sworn during the period studied (the no deliberation group consists of mistrials, changes of plea, and directed verdicts), displays the overall relationship between initial verdict and one vs. more jury services for the 902 jurors studied. The association between

Table 4. Frequency of Subsequent Jury Service as a Function of Initial Verdict

	Trials on which served				
	One only		More than one		Totals
Initial verdict	N	%	N	%	N
Not guilty	107	38.1	174	61.9	281
No deliberation	17	35.4	31	64.6	48
Hung	89	61.8	55	38.2	144
Guilty[a]	187	43.6	242	56.4	429
Totals	400		502		902

[a] Includes guilty of a lesser included offense, guilty of some but not all charges, and guilty as charged.

these factors is highly significant (χ^2 = 23.91, 3 df, p < .001). Subsequent 2 × 2 chi-square analyses confirm that this effect is due to those jurors who serve initially on hung juries. They have significantly fewer subsequent services (38%) than either initially acquitting jurors (62%) (χ^2 = 20.63, 1 df, p < .001) or initially convicting juries (56%) (χ^2 = 13.61, 1 df, p < .001). Those who initially convict do not differ from those who acquit. We did not test the miscellaneous category of no jury decision against the other three.

Juror Experience, Foreperson Selection, and Verdicts

Is an experienced juror likely to be selected foreperson at a level higher than chance? With one experienced juror the likelihood is one in 12 that a juror would be selected by chance alone; with each additional experienced juror the chance selection increases by 1/12. When we compared the actual selection ratios (90 experienced jurors; 47 inexperienced) with the chance expectations (78.5 experienced; 58.5 inexperienced), we discovered that seasoned jurors were picked significantly more often than random selection would indicate (χ^2 = 3.95, 1 df, p < .05).

Another factor in foreperson selection is experience as a foreperson. While 82% of forepersons had not previously held that position, when they appeared on a jury, jurors who had previously served as forepersons were picked again at higher than chance levels (χ^2 = 30.65, 1 df, p < .001). Twenty-six of the 146 identifiable forepersons had already served in that capacity.

In addition to their experience, forepersons are more often fore*men* (χ^2 = 64.9, 1 df, p < .001). Eighty-nine percent of the forepersons were male, whereas males comprised only 56% of the jurors who served on trials.

DISCUSSION

The principal findings of this analysis of actual court records are that some indices of juror experience are significantly related to jury verdicts. The primary relationship is that with larger numbers of experienced jurors on a jury, the jury is more likely to convict. A related variable, the total amount of experience represented on the jury, is also positively and significantly related to jury conviction proneness. The selection of a foreperson is significantly predicted by experience, whether as a juror or a previous foreperson, and by sex, with males more often picked. Foreperson experience and sex of the foreperson did not predict jury verdicts.

Our results support Kerr's (1981) conclusions, based on the earlier literature, that the effects of juror experience on verdicts are small but real. Moreover, these prior investigations along with the present study prompt the conclusion that the direction of the effect when it appears is consistently one of experience producing conviction proneness. Questions of the strength and consistency of this effect are being addressed by a replication study covering 18 consecutive months of criminal trials from the Fayette County Circuit. In addition, because jurors in Kentucky sentence as well as determine guilt, we are examining the influence of juror experience on the severity of penalties recommended by jurors.

Some discernible differences in amount of juror experience and methods of quantifying juror experience and jury verdicts in the existing archival investigations may account for their varied results to date. For example, our juries may be distinctive because they had more experienced jurors than either the San Diego sample (Kerr et al., 1982) or the Salt Lake City juries (Werner et al., 1982). Also, examination of the amount of experience in other Kentucky juries suggests the number of experienced jurors was higher than usual in our sample. Indeed this circumstance may have provided a better test of the hypothesis than other studies to date. The effect appeared to emerge in our data (see Figure 1) when the number of experienced jurors on the trial was in the majority. A high percentage of experienced jurors on a jury may be necessary to produce the effect.

The Juror Selection Hypothesis

Quasiexperimentation requires both the use of multiple indicators of important factors and the assessment of the influence of plausible alternative interpretations. Because an apparent effect of juror experience on verdicts could be the result of selection—if jurors who initially acquit or hang are deselected by prosecutors for later service and other jurors are more likely to be dispositionally conviction prone—we examined the selection hypothesis by determining the frequency of service of jurors by kind of initial verdict. There was no evidence that those who convict on their first trial are retained more frequently for subsequent service. There was, however, a surprising result: jurors who initially hang have a lower frequency of subsequent service than either those who acquit or those who convict. How this is achieved is not clear, but jurors who wish to do so can get themselves excused for cause (e.g., by professing they could not be fair), or make an appearance unattractive to one or both sides, generating a peremptory strike. Anecdotal information suggests that the deliberation process culminating in a hung verdict may be unpleasant for many jurors. It may also be that the evidence in such trials creates a decisional conflict more intense than otherwise encountered, prompting subsequent avoidant behavior.

Another more complicated selection process might occur. It might be argued, for example, that prosecutors are able by the use of subtle cues garnered through experience with jurors over a number of trials to improve the prediction of conviction proneness of individual jurors on the venire.[18] This process is unlikely to have produced the effects in our data for two reasons. First, our courtroom

---

[18] An increased ability to predict juror dispositions would permit prosecutors to strike peremptorily acquittal-prone jurors, producing a jury more likely to convict. Now if the experienced jurors are differentially dismissed by the prosecutor, those remaining would be both conviction prone and experienced. And a relationship between juror experience and verdicts would be due to selection and not the effects of service on jurors. This selection process requires the prosecution to employ accurately sophisticated social perception skills in judging jurors during the evidence phase of trials. This alternative possibility was raised by an anonymous reviewer of an earlier draft on this manuscript.

observations of prosecutors in the jurisdiction we studied indicated few peremptory strikes by prosecutors in the variety of trails examined. Second, as noted above, we found no difference between subsequent juror service for those who acquit on their first trial and those who convict. The verdict returned on initial service would surely be one of the cues used by prosecutors in deselecting jurors they consider acquittal prone.

Foreperson Selection

Forepersons are not picked at random. Our findings and those from other archival research (Kerr et al., 1982; Werner et al., 1982) are clear in showing that forepersons are more likely to be experienced jurors and males. Further, our results show that those who have been forepersons previously are chosen again more often than chance would suggest. Questions to be answered about this selection process cannot be addressed from our data, though these questions can be pursued with actual jurors. We need to know about the perceived characteristics of jurors and the influence of observed behavior on attributions. Typically jurors have informal contact with one another and observe other jurors' behaviors, before and after interaction during trials themselves. Except in the infrequent instance of prior acquaintance, those factors in company with general beliefs, schemas, or scripts surely determine who is selected foreperson. Broeder's (1965) post-trial interviews are consistent with these speculations.

The Dynamics of Juror Experience

From research on actual jurors we know that experienced jurors are attitudinally different from first-timers with regard to beliefs about jury service itself (Durand, Bearden, & Gustafson, 1978; Pabst, Munsterman & Mount, 1976; but see Simon, 1975). A parallel quasiexperimental assessment of attitudes, perception, and cognition regarding the trial process and its participants would likely reveal differences between experienced and novice jurors. Moreover, there are other reasons to believe that the consequences of experience appear before deliberation. We know from research on actual trials that the majority at the time of the first ballot determines the final verdict in approximately 90% of the cases (Kalven & Zeisel, 1966). With some equivocation (see Dillehay & Nietzel, 1980) we can interpret the latter finding to show that most jurors make up their minds before they deliberate or early in the deliberation and do not change. Consequently, effects of juror experience on subsequent verdicts likely occur before the conclusion of the evidence phase at trial.

The effects of juror experience should have implications for the acceptance of essential principles of law—the presumption of innocence, the burden of proof, and the standard of reasonable doubt. If this is true, uncovering the processes producing changes will be a most difficult research task. The indicators of changed beliefs in these principles traceable to experience must be sensitive and indirect. Jurors in the courtroom are loathe during voir dire to suggest anything short of absolute endorsement of these cornerstones of justice; as respondents in research they will doubtless be the same. Yet these are the effects of most interest pragmatically and theoretically in a judicial system seeking justice.

ACKNOWLEDGMENT

We wish to thank Glen Rogers for his contribution to an early phase of this research.

REFERENCES

Bailey, F. L., & Rothblatt, H. B. *Successful techniques for criminal trials*. Rochester, New York: The Lawyers Co-operative Publishing Co., 1971.

Belli, M. *Modern Trials* (Vol. 1). Indianapolis: The Bobbs-Merrill Co., 1954.

Broeder, D. W. Previous jury trial service affecting juror behavior. *Insurance Law Journal*, 1965, **506**, 138–143.

Dillehay, R. C., & Nietzel, M. T. Constructing a science of jury behavior. In L. Wheeler, (Ed.), *Review of personality and social psychology*, New York: Sage, 1980.

Durand, R. M., Bearden, W. O., & Gustafson, A. W. Previous jury service as a moderating influence on jurors' beliefs and attitudes. *Psychological Reports*, 1978, **42**, 567–572.

Ginger, A. F. *Jury selection in criminal trials*. Tiburon, California: Law Press Corporation, 1977.

Jurow, G. L. New data on the effect of a "death qualified" jury on the guilt determination process. *Harvard Law Review*, 1970–1971, **84**, 567–611.

Kalven, H., Jr., & Zeisel, H. *The American jury*. Boston: Little, Brown, 1966.

Kerr, N. L. Effects of prior juror experience on juror behavior. *Basic and Applied Social Psychology*, 1981, **2**, 175–193.

Kerr, N. L., Harmon, D. L., & Graves, J. K. Independence of multiple verdicts by jurors and juries. *Journal of Applied Social Psychology*, 1982, **12**, 12–29.

Nietzel, M. T., & Dillehay, R. C. *Psychologists and voir dire: A strategy and its applications*. Paper presented at the meeting of the American Psychological Association, New York City, 1979.

Nietzel, M. T., Dillehay, R. C., & Rogers, G. *Method innovation in jury research: Alternative juries and archival data*. Paper presented at the meeting of the American Psychological Association, Washington, D.C., 1976.

Pabst, W. R., Munsterman, G. T., & Mount, C. H. The myth of the unwilling juror. *Judicature*, 1976, **60**, 164–171.

Reed, J. P. Jury deliberations, voting, and verdict trends. *Southwestern Social Science Quarterly*, 1965, **45**, 361–370.

SAS User's Guide, 1979 Edition. Cary, North Carolina: SAS Institute, 1979.

Simon, C. K. The juror in New York City: Attitudes and experiences. *American Bar Association Journal*, 1975, **61**, 207–211.

Werner, C., Strube, M., Cole, A., & Kagehiro, D. *The impact of case characteristics and prior jury experience on jury verdicts*. Unpublished manuscript (1982).

PSYCHOLOGICAL, COGNITIVE, PERSONALITY AND INTERPERSONAL FACTORS IN JURY VERDICTS

Dr. Jeffery R. Boyll*

In American jurisprudence, the right to a trial by jury has traditionally been symbolic of protection against the arbitrary exercise of state power. Over time, however, jury power has declined considerably while criticism of the competence and fairness of the system has increased. A major criticism aimed at the jury system is that non-evidentiary, extraneous, and emotional factors affect juror decision-making processes.

Ideally, jurors reach verdicts utilizing facts and evidence while putting aside preexisting bias, emotions, feelings, and so on; however, particularly in equivocal cases, this ideal does not coincide with human nature. As one expert has stated, "So overwhelming is the data on behalf of juror bias throughout the trial, that for the most part behavioral scientists do not accept the idea of impartiality and regard it as legal fiction." Considerable evidence supports the assumption that the strength of the evidence presented is the primary influence in juror decision-making.[1] As the strength of the evidence increases, the effects of non-legal or extra-evidentiary factors decrease, and vice versa.

The conclusion reached by certain studies is that if the strength of evidence in the case is clearly superior, the other factors are less meaningful.[2] However, this tends to occur in cases that are settled before trial. Estimates are that less than two percent of cases even go to trial. Consequently, cases that reach trial are often the evidentially close, emotionally charged, high-risk or large-stake ones. In these cases non-evidentiary factors—a critical moment of emotion or an impressive key witness—can be crucial and may be outcome-determinative.

Following an exhaustive review of mock jury research, Gerbasi, Zuckerman and Reis concluded, "It is beyond argument that a multitude of extra-evidentiary factors influence jury decisions.[3]

---

1. See Ford, *The Role of Extralegal Factors in Jury Verdicts*, 11 Jus. Sys. J. 16 (1986).

2. Reskin & Visher, *The Impacts of Evidence and Extralegal Factors in Jurors' Decisions*, 20 Law & Soc'y Rev. 423 (1986).

3. Gerbasi, Zuckerman & Reis, *Justice Needs a New Blindfold: A Review of Mock Jury Research*, 84 Psychological Bull. 323, 323 (1977).

The purpose of this article is to broadly examine the factors that influence jury decision-making processes. The following diagram outlines the primary areas behavioral and social science have found to be influential in affecting jury behavior.

"PSYCHOLOGICAL, COGNITIVE"

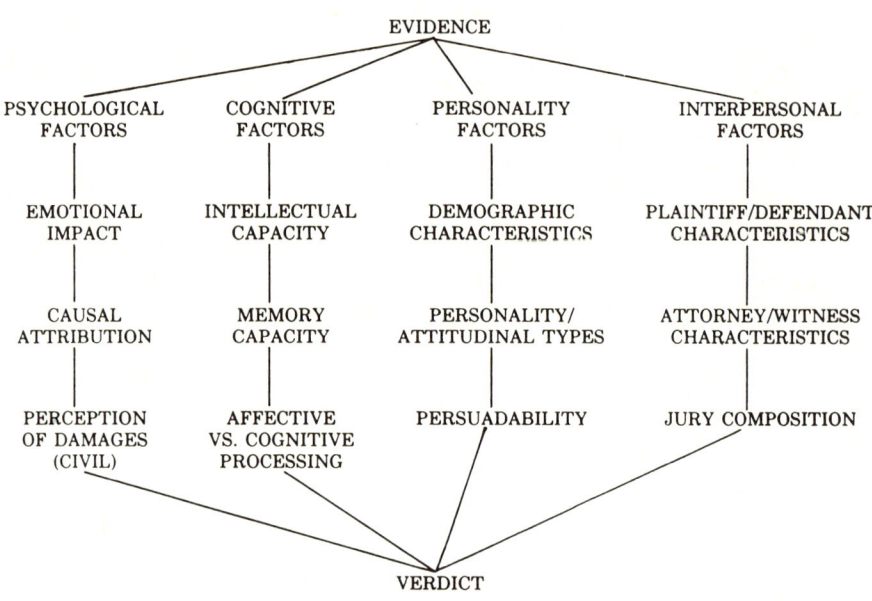

VERDICT

Damage Award/Sentence

VERDICT

Damage Award/Sentence

Evidence is presented at the top of the diagram to represent its ultimate importance. As mentioned earlier, the strength of the evidence plays the most vital role in the trial and thus may counteract the effects of the four other broad categories of extra-evidentiary factors. These categories are psychological, cognitive, personality and interpersonal. Each of these areas will be discussed in turn.

PSYCHOLOGICAL FACTORS

Emotional Impact

Jurors reach verdicts, at least in part, based on emotions and feelings. For example, if a female juror reports that the accused rapist "gave me a creepy feeling," the effectiveness of the accused's testimony, as well as evidence supporting his innocence, is severely compromised.

Most of the information and data derived from research of extra-evidentiary factors were gleaned from review of empirical studies, post-trial interviews with jurors, and pre-trial research utilizing focus groups, mock trials, shadow juries, and so forth.[4] The findings from these studies are reasonably consistent in that 1) many jurors come to decisions very early in the trial, 2) their decisions are frequently based on "gut" or emotional reactions, and 3) these initial impressions are very resistant to change.[5]

The majority of jurors formulate an impression about the verdict very early in the litigation proceedings. This so-called "primacy effect" has been scientifically documented numerous times. For example, in one early study, subjects were asked to describe the personality of a fictitious person using descriptive adjectives, such as intelligent, critical stubborn, etc. The subjects' subsequent descriptions of this imaginary person varied considerably, simply by the order in which the words were presented.[6] Specifically, when the words intelligent and industrious were presented first, the man was described in far more gracious terms than when envious and stubborn were presented first.[7] Researchers have determined that a sizable percentage of jurors have made their decision by the end of the opening statement.[8] Further, this research has shown that jurors are reluctant to modify their initial impressions, and therefore these opinions tend to persist, even in the face of contrary evidence presented later.

---

4. The limitations regarding generalizing such studies to actual trials is outlined. *Id.* at 335.

5. D. VINSON, JURY TRIALS: THE PSYCHOLOGY OF THE WINNING STRATEGY (1986).

6. Lawson, *Experimental Research on the Organization of Persuasive Argument: An Application to Courtroom Communications*, 1970 LAW & SOC. ORD. 579, 597.

7. H. KALVEN & H. ZEISEL, THE AMERICAN JURY (1966).

8. *See id.*

Advertisers typically use brief, emotionally laden, initial impressions to convey their messages. For example, a recent billboard showed a convertible BMW automobile with only the word "SEXY" emblazoned at the top. No facts regarding the engine, cost, or other features were given. This ad was strictly an emotional appeal to consumers. In a typical trial, similar immediate emotional impressions will be formed by jurors regarding the defendant, plaintiff, judge and so forth. For example, if jurors experience sorrow, pity and remorse for the plaintiff while they also experience disgust, rage and contempt for the defendant, much of the effectiveness of evidence and experts may be lost. The damage award is likely to reflect to some degree the strength and direction of these emotions.

Another finding from juror research is that despite the length or complexity of the case, the jury's verdict will generally be based on three to four salient issues, sometimes called psychological hooks or anchors.[9] These issues can be either evidentiary or nonevidentiary and are typically a combination of both. In many cases the salient issues for jurors, whether emotional or evidentiary, are not those that legal counsel predicted or even intended

In sum, most attempts to convince jurors, are at least to effectively change their attitudes, typically rely on information such as relevant facts, issues and legal instructions. Providing pertinent information is the most logical method to influence jurors; however, this assumes that jurors follow the judge's instructions, such as, "Wait until all the facts are presented" or "Disregard that last statement." Unfortunately, the effect of letting the facts speak for themselves is not particularly reliable, especially in emotionally charged cases. Generally, inducing emotions and altering the affective or feeling component of an attitude will affect juror decision-making.

Causal Attribution

How do jurors make decisions about liability or fault in litigation? Social psychologists have been studying this issue for years, generally under the heading of "attribution theory."[10] Such research focuses on how humans attribute causality or blame, as well

---

9. D. Vinson, *supra* note 5, at 173.
10. Kelley, *Attribution Theory in Social Psychology*, Neb. Symp. Motivation, Univ. Neb. 192-238 (1967 D. Levine ed.).

as more general explanations of how humans assess the motivations, judgments, emotions and actions of others. Essentially, when people judge any interpersonal situation, they judge the people involved. Evaluations are made by considering the facts and determining who, if anyone, was at fault. This determination is based on the interaction between external circumstances and perceived personality or internal characteristics of the individual. In other words, did he act that way because of the situation (external attribution) or because of the kind of person he is (internal attribution)? If the latter conclusion is accepted, judgments of guilt and liability will likely be forthcoming.

Consider a hypothetical products liability case. Assume that a man was seriously injured while riding a ten-speed bicycle and the jury has been told that the man was seen careening wildly out of control at a high speed before crashing. The plaintiff claims the brakes were defective and malfunctioned. The defendant manufacturer contends that the plaintiff was reckless and careless. The following is a schematic drawing of juror attribution processes.

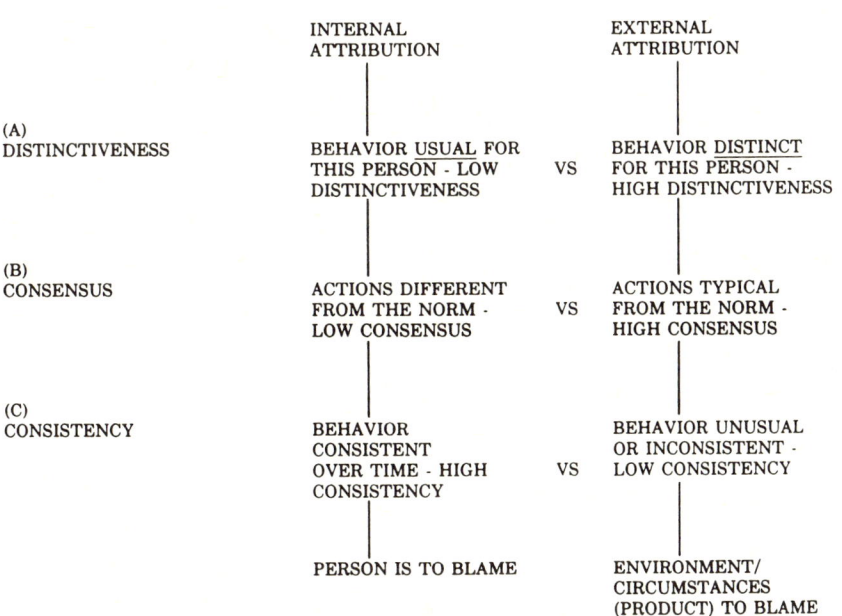

"PSYCHOLOGICAL, COGNITIVE"

	INTERNAL ATTRIBUTION		EXTERNAL ATTRIBUTION
(A) DISTINCTIVENESS	BEHAVIOR <u>USUAL</u> FOR THIS PERSON - LOW DISTINCTIVENESS	VS	BEHAVIOR <u>DISTINCT</u> FOR THIS PERSON - HIGH DISTINCTIVENESS
(B) CONSENSUS	ACTIONS DIFFERENT FROM THE NORM - LOW CONSENSUS	VS	ACTIONS TYPICAL FROM THE NORM - HIGH CONSENSUS
(C) CONSISTENCY	BEHAVIOR CONSISTENT OVER TIME - HIGH CONSISTENCY	VS	BEHAVIOR UNUSUAL OR INCONSISTENT - LOW CONSISTENCY
	PERSON IS TO BLAME		ENVIRONMENT/ CIRCUMSTANCES (PRODUCT) TO BLAME

A. *Distinctiveness*

If the plaintiff's behavior is high in distinctiveness such that it is unusual for this person, the behavior will probably be interpreted as an external attribution. If the circumstances or environment caused the person to act differently or distinctly from his usual behavior, such as the failing of brakes, the interpretation is that it is not the plaintiff's fault.

B. *Consensus*

Would other people act the same way under similar circumstances? If the answer is yes, again the circumstances are to blame. If however, the juror decides that they, and other reasonable people, do not act in such a manner, the actor is to blame on the basis that only he would take such a dangerous road.

C. *Consistency*

Is the person's behavior consistent over time? If so, an internal attribution is suggested, and it may be thought that he has always courted danger. If there is a great deal of inconsistency among the actions under review, an external attribution is more likely.

Causal attribution in a sexual assault case might be as follows: (Statements that produce internal attributions are followed by (I), external by (E).) Prosecution will present evidence that the accused is a corrupt person (I), that he has a prior criminal record showing inability to learn right from wrong (I), and that he has no personal regard for the rules of society (I). The defense may counter this with the argument that he was seduced by the *situation*, i.e. the victim's miniskirt, sexy clothes and seductive demeanor (E).

If jurors are most persuaded by arguments regarding internal attributions, they will likely assume the defendant is a bad person who deserves punishment. Conversely, they will by lenient if the circumstances are perceived to be to blame. This will be particularly true if the defense convincingly presents evidence of internal attributions regarding the alleged victim, such as the victim is a chronic liar (I), is sexually promiscuous (II), and so forth.

Litigators who have considered the above factors are likely to structure arguments so that attributions are made which are favorable to their case. In some cases, however, "defensive attribution" can cause a reverse effect on jury verdicts despite their initial acceptance of an external attribution. This frequently occurs in cases that involve a victim. Research has shown that if a juror perceives the similarities between the victim and himself and realizes that this accident could happen to him, the juror may actually blame the victim.[11] Why? To some degree, people maintain a view of reality that life is safe from catastrophe, especially if they "live right" and follow the rules of society. Faced with the uncomfortable reality that such a horror could happen to them, jurors may react defensively and try to find reasons as to why this event happened to the victim, while it could not possibly happen to them. Thus, this anxiety-provoking situation is neutralized by eliminating outside forces or blind fate (external attribution) and then concluding that the victim suffered injury because of the type of person he or she is (internal attribution). What this undesirable process may mean for plaintiffs' counsel in personal injury cases is that typical methods of producing sorrow or pity for the victim, for example, utilizing "day in the life" videotapes, may sometimes backfire if they are too frightening and if the similarity elements exist to produce a defensive attribution.

Finally, subsequent research has added to basic attribution theory.[12] In recent models, attributions of responsibility are distinguished from attributions of causality. In other words, a person may be determined to have caused something, but also be found not to be morally responsible. Consequently, juries do not always hold litigants responsible for the outcomes of their actions. Many statutes outline a number of additional requirements for an inference of guilt or liability even after an attribution of causality. These requirements might include questions of intent, foreseeability, coercion, capacity, and duty. Additionally, in many civil cases, jurors are asked to decide whether the defendant's *failure to act* implies liability.

Perception of Damages

In recent years, the enormous size of some seemingly unpredictable and possibly inequitable civil damage awards have sparked debate over the effectiveness of the jury system in civil

11. D. Vinson, *supra* note 5, at 56.
12. MacCoun, *Getting Inside the Black Box: Toward a Better Understanding of Civil Jury Behavior*, Rand Note, Rand Inst. Civ. Just. (1987).

litigation. For example, one jury estimated the plaintiff's attorney's fees, and then multiplied that figure by ten to derive a damage award.[13] A recent newspaper report detailed a case in which a woman received $600,000 for injuries sustained after a roll of toilet tissue fell on her head while she was shopping. Even more astonishing is the reported $21 million awarded to Rock Hudson's former lover who *feared* he had AIDS.

How juries calculate damage awards needs much research. Jurors' computational methods have been examined primarily by use of the mock jury. For example, awards are typically larger when the defendant in a wrongful death action is male rather than female. This suggests that jurors tend to assume a greater loss in potential future income for males.[14]

"Evidence from post-trial interviews with civil jurors . . . suggests that the ad damnum—the plaintiff's requested damage award—. . . serves as a reference point for the jury's calculations."[15] In one study, ten "[mock] juries tried a personal injury case in which the ad damnum was systematically varied. Each jury received one of four different damage requests: $10,000, $75,000, $150,000 or an open-ended request for "substantial compensation."[16] The average award in the first three conditions were $18,000, $62,800 and $101,400, respectively; 474,600 was awarded after the request for "substantial compensation."[17] This indicates that a mean increase of over $83,000 was obtained from jurors by simply requesting a larger award.[18] Consequently, "[a]ttorneys are believed to exploit this phenomenon by exaggerating the ad damnum."[19]

Additionally, juries may discriminate against defendants perceived as having "deep pockets."[20] Several studies have found that

---

13. Kalven, *The Dignity of the Civil Jury*, 50 VA. L. REV. 1055, 1069 (1964).

14. MacCoun, *supra* note 12, at 31 (citing Goodman, Loftus & Greene, *Mock Jurors' Damage Awards in Civil Cases*, presented at the annual meeting of the Law and Society Association, Washington, D.C., June 1987).

15. *Id.* at 32 (citing Zuehl, *The Ad Damnum, Jury Instructions, and Personal Injury Damage Awards*, unpublished manuscript, Dept. of Sociology, U. Chicago, Aug. 4, 1982).

16. *Id.*

17. *Id.*

18. *Id.*

19. *Id.* (citing Broeder, *The University of Chicago Jury Project*, 38 NEB. L. REV. 744, 758 (1959)).

20. *Id.* at 34 (citing Hans & Ermann, *Attitudes Toward Corporate Versus*

mock jurors attribute significantly more liability to well endowed litigants.[21] This phenomenon occurs when one alters the description of the defendant to "the Jones Corporation" from "Mr. Jones."[22] Consistent with this, archival analysis also indicates that juror awards are larger when the defendant is a large corporation or government entity.[23]

Summary

There is considerable evidence that psychological factors are influential in juror decision-making. A complex interaction of emotions, causal attribution, the impact of damage requests, and the perception of "deep pocket" defendants have been found to impact jury verdicts and subsequent damage awards.

COGNITIVE FACTORS

Intellectual Capacity

Trial attorneys can unknowingly present arguments and issues that exceed jurors' capacity to understand.[24] It is possible that some attorneys, inherently possessing above average intelligence due to years of education and expertise in the law, sometimes fail to realize that the average juror does not share these attributes.[25] In fact, many jurors may fail to understand the most basic concepts and issues.[26] They most particularly fail to understand legal jargon.[27]

For example, consider the Wechsler Adult Intelligence Scale-Revised (WAIS-R),[28] commonly used to obtain estimates of IQ for legal and educational purposes.[29] "Assuming that all prior ques-

---

Individual Wrong-Doing, presented at the annual meeting of the Law & Soc. Assoc., Chicago, Ill., June 1986).

21. *Id.*

22. *Id.*

23. *Id.* at 32 (citing Chin & Peterson, *Deep Pockets, Empty Pockets: Who Wins in Cooke County Jury Trials*, 1985 RAND CORP. R-3249-1CJ).

24. D. VINSON, *supra* note 5, at 184.

25. Boyll, *Enhancing Juror Comprehension and Memory Retention*, 12 TRIAL DIPL. J. 194, 196 (1989).

26. *Id.*

27. *Id.*

28. Wechsler, D., Manual for the Wechsler Intelligence Scale-Revised, The Psychological Corp., Harcourt Brace Jovanovich, Inc. (1981).

29. Boyll, *supra* note 26, at 196.

tions were answered correctly, a thirty-five- to forty-four-year-old adult of "average" intelligence (IQ = 100, sub-scale score = 10) may be unable to:"

> —define words such as "perimeter, generate, matchless, and fortitude;"
> —"conceptualize how yeast causes dough to rise;"
> —"name three types of blood vessels in the human body;"
> —explain why land in the country costs less than in metropolitan areas;
> —state what similarity a statue and a poem have in common.[30]

"What does this indicate for attorneys asking jurors to evaluate the complexities of antitrust litigation between rival computer technology firms?"[31] The complexities of litigation issues coupled with the average juror's intelligence bring the jury's ability to process the masses of sophisticated and technical information in complex litigation into question. In fact, a "complexity exception" to the Seventh Amendment has been proposed by some, reflecting the idea that the typical jury is not competent to decide complex civil suits.

Thus, a juror's ability to comprehend information presented at trial, as well as how intellectual capacity influences perception of facts and issues, may have a significant impact upon verdict decisions. Other issues related to juror cognitive ability and the effects on their decisions involves the interaction among: 1) the ability of jurors to follow judges' instructions regarding evidence and pretrial publicity; 2) the effects of the number and severity of decision alternatives offered to jurors, and 3) the ability of jurors to understand and apply definitions of guilt and liability. The fourth area, that of the number of arguments presented and the length of the trial, is discussed in the following section.

Memory Capacity

With the increasing complexity of trials comes both an increase in the amount of facts and issues to be presented, as well as the total time duration of the trial. What jurors remember about the trial will affect deliberations and, ultimately, the verdict.

---

30. *Id.*
31. *Id.*

Assuming that the information is presented in a manner that is comprehended by jurors, how much will they retain? We can approach this question by utilizing norms derived from clinical neuropsychological tests. For example, the Wechsler Memory Scale[32] is a standardized and often used device for clinical memory testing.[33] The Logical Memory Section is intended to measure immediate recall of logical material and most closely resembles what is expected of jurors.[34] Subjects are required to remember a passage containing twenty-four bits of information.[35]

The short story used in the study involves a crime whereby a woman is held up and robbed.[36] "The average number of *informational segments* immediately recalled by 'normals' is as follows:

Ages 20-29	Mean = 9.80
Ages 40-49	Mean = 8.65"[37]

As much as two-thirds of what is heard may be *immediately* forgotten.[38] Further, recall that follows time or interference may result in additional forgetting. Thus, "due to limitations in human memory, more than two-thirds of the information given in a single presentation during the trial will be forgotten.[39]

Advertising research has found that "one exposure to a message induced content recall in only 14% of subjects."[40] Reports of similar studies have revealed that "up to seven exposures may be required to activate accurate recall."[41] One of the consequences of poor memory retention during deliberations occurs when a juror associates some facts or witnesses for one side of the case with the wrong party. To avoid the potentially disastrous effects of false associations, litigators may need techniques to enhance juror retention.[42] Repetition to the point of redundancy is often needed to reinforce learning.[43]

---

32. Wechsler, *supra* note 28, discussed in Boyll, *supra* note 30, at 196.
33. *Id.*
34. Boyll, *supra* note 26, at 196.
35. *Id.*
36. *Id.*
37. *Id.*
38. *Id.*
39. *Id.*
40. *Id.* at 197 (quoting D. VINSON, *supra* note 5, at 38).
41. *Id.* (quoting D. VINSON, *supra* note 5, at 38).
42. *Id.*
43. *Id.*

In sum, research on intelligence and memory would suggest that, unless steps are taken by trial attorneys, much of what is presented may be misunderstood, and two-thirds or more may be forgotten.[44]

As a result of problems with juror comprehension and memory retention, legal scholars have recently formulated some noteworthy suggestions. These include litigating complex issues sequentially, providing special training for juries, permitting jurors to ask questions, allowing a day's end summary by counsel and utilizing a panel of experts from the particular technical arena the case involves.

AFFECTIVE VS. COGNITIVE PROCESSING

Thus far, we have focused on how *well* jurors can understand and remember information presented at trial. This section examines how information is *processed* by jurors in order to reach decisions.

There are basically two ways in which people reach decisions: cognitively and affectively. Cognitive thinkers reason inductively; they process bits of information in a relatively logical sequence, mentally weigh and evaluate it, and come to a conclusion. This method is typically how attorneys present the case to jurors, partly because it is generally how attorneys are taught to think. Lawyers engage in the logical reasoning of the A-B-C variety. Many people, and consequently many jurors, however, do not think this way. Most people instinctively utilize deductive reasoning. They first form a conclusion based on how they feel and subsequently fit all other data presented into this framework. This process is just the opposite of inductive reasoning. As mentioned earlier, initial impressions are resistant to change. As a result, deductive thinkers, having made up their mind based on initial impressions, will selectively perceive as salient only information that fits with their beliefs about the case. Thus, these jurors make decisions primarily by emotion and attempt to validate them with logic.

If jurors reach decisions quickly based on emotions and affective thinking and then resist arguments in opposition to these attitudes, of what value is the remainder of the trial? Fortunately attitudes can be changed, although it is sometimes quite difficult.

---

44. *Id.*

Research on cognitive processing suggests that jurors often experience what is termed "cognitive dissonance." Cognitive dissonance, originally proposed by Leon Festinger, can be defined as a state of psychological disequilibrium that occurs when a person's beliefs and behavior are discrepant, or when a person is confronted with facts inconsistent with what he or she "knows" to be true. This mental confusion often happens during the course of a trial as attorneys attempt to persuade or produce attitudinal change.

Behavioral science research suggests that in order to get someone to perform a specific behavior, it must be congruent with his beliefs about that behavior. Take for example the difficulty a firearm salesman will encounter in attempting to persuade a consumer to buy a firearm when the consumer strongly *believes* that individual firearm ownership should be illegal. However, attitudinal change, and subsequent behavioral change, can occur as a result of cognitive dissonance. In the above example, assume this staunch anti-firearm believer inherits a beautiful gun collection. His behavior (as a gun owner) is now incongruent with his beliefs (individuals should not own guns). One of two things must occur in order to reduce cognitive dissonance:

1) The individual sells the guns (no attitude or behavioral change: cognitive dissonance relieved); or

2) The individual keeps the guns and changes his beliefs regarding gun ownership. Again, a reduction in cognitive dissonance. This individual simply cannot continue to own the guns unless attitudinal change occurs. To do so would be consciously hypocritical. He is now much more likely to be supportive of gun ownership (attitudinal change) and vote for liberalized gun laws (behavioral change).

Litigators routinely induce cognitive dissonance on the part of the jury. As noted, this inducement results in temporary feelings of psychological discomfort and even anxiety. To avoid these tensions, jurors will engage in a variety of coping mechanisms, including: 1) minimizing the importance of the information, 2) distorting the information to make it consistent with previously held beliefs, and 3) rejecting the dissonance-inducing information altogether, or 4) changing their original beliefs and attitudes.

An example of cognitive dissonance occurred with many staunch Republicans and Nixon supporters during the Watergate scandal. Nixon's backers first reacted with denial ("It didn't happen"), then with distortion ("The facts are not the way the media presented them"), and lastly by discounting and substitution ("The important thing is his good work with China and foreign relations"). Only in some cases and very late was there a real attitudinal change ("I don't trust him anymore"). Changing strongly held attitudes often involves a journey through these stages.

Summary

A critical aspect of the juror decision-making process involves the capacity to comprehend and retain information presented at trial. Further, how jurors process information—cognitively versus affectively, as well as how they deal with cognitive dissonance—will affect verdict decisions.

PERSONALITY ISSUES

Demographic Characteristics

Every juror evaluates what transpires in the courtrtoom on the basis of his or her life experiences, attitudes and predispositions. Jurors do not come to the trial "tabula rasa," that is, with a blank slate. Their beliefs, attitudes, and morals are well entrenched, and everything that is heard will be filtered and colored by these attitudes. That is precisely the reason for voir dire—to eliminate potential jurors who are too biased to fairly try the case at hand. This goal does not suggest that remaining jurors are always unbiased, but simply that those excused seemingly represent the extremes at the opposite ends of a continuum.

There is a considerable body of literature to support the contention that jury selection is one of the most vital components of the trial proceedings. The case may be one or lost at voir dire. The advent of social science techniques and survey data used to construct "ideal juror profiles," though debated, may be so powerful a technique as to create an unfair advantage.

Nearly everything about a person, from biographical personality to personality features can affect verdict predisposition. These features clearly interact in complex and individual ways, making prediction of juror decision-making extremely difficult, even with the use of large community surveys and complex statistical analysis. The following is a nonexhaustive list of demographic and other variables generally believed to be associated with juror decision-making.

Demographic and Related Variables

Age	Marital Status
Sex	Alcohol Consumption
Race	Crime Victim
Occupation	Place of Residence
Religion (Denomination)	Children
Religion (Frequency/Intensity)	Political Affiliation
Magazines/Subscriptions	Prior Jury Service
Hobbies/Activities	Education
Community Organizations	Income/Economic Status

Obviously, accurate information in each of the categories above will tell a great deal about a prospective juror. It should be reiterated that demographic variables alone are reasonably poor predictors of verdict preference. Because of the extreme variability in individuals, demographics have been found to account for only 15 to 18 percent of the variance in regression models. This finding is not particulary good; however, considering the high stakes in many trials, it still represents an edge unavailable without social science methods.

It is interesting to note that for many years attorneys have relied mostly on hunches, guesswork, stereotypes and folk wisdom in selecting jurors. For example, Clarence Darrow once wrote: "An Irishman . . . is emotional, kindly and sympathetic. If a Presbyterian enters the jury box . . . let him go. He is cold as the grave . . . . Then, too, there are the women. These are now in the jury box . . . I formed a fixed opinion that they are absolutely dependable, but I did not want them.[45]

It is not surprising that attorneys have begun moving towards more scientific and reliable methods of jury selection. One of the most consistent findings from systematic or "scientific jury selection" is that demographics used for prediction are nearly always region-specific and case-specific. In other words, community attitudes vary considerably. To use information gleaned from demographic jury studies in Los Angeles would not adequately represent potential jurors from Boston or Atlanta. Regarding case specificity, the effects of various configurations of demographic characteristics will depend on the specific case. For example, in a liability case

---

45. Darrow, C., *Attorney for the Defense*, ESQUIRE,, 1936, *reprinted in* C. DARROW, VERDICTS OUT OF COURT 315 (1963).

involving an injured child, females, housewives, teachers and those in child-oriented occupations may more likely to be sympathetic to the plaintiff than those not in child-oriented occupations.

Of the few nationwide general findings, the most noteworthy are: 1) females and jurors over the age of thirty tend to award larger punitive damages in civil cases;[46] 2) young jurors (under 25) are more likely to be lenient in verdict and sentencing;[47] and 3) a relationship between gender and criminal verdict exists but is mediated by type of crime (females are more willing to convict in rape cases).[48] The following section examines pre-existing variables that have been somewhat more reliable in predicting verdict preference.

PERSONALITY/ATTITUDINAL TYPES

For many years psychologists have studied personality and attitudinal types as well as the relationship between personality and behavior. Voir dire represents, in part, an attorney's task of determining which of a juror's personality traits, attitudes and beliefs will predispose the juror to be favorable. Many of the conclusions derived form this area of research as applied to litigation are tentative. The following attitudinal "types" have, however, been found to affect verdict decisions.

Authoritarianism: One having this view holds a strong identification with law and order and the rules of society. Authoritarians are predisposed to accept the prosecutor's case in criminal proceedings and are more likely to assume *a priori* guilt. Thus, they tend to make excellent prosecution jurors. In civil proceedings, if jurors identify strongly with big business, the predisposition may be favorable to the defense. However, because of a general punitive tendency towards anyone accused of breaking rules, such as corporate failure to comply with safety standards, authoritarians may side for the plaintiff. Since authoritarianism has been found to be one of the most reliable predictors of bias,

> particularly towards criminal defendants, as such, psychological test instruments have been developed to assess authoritarianism, as well as recommendations that such measures be used

---

46. D. VINSON, *supra* note 5, at 161.
47. Ackerman, MacMahon & Fehr, *Mock Trial Jury Decisions as a Function of Adolescent Juror Guilt and Hostility*, 144 J. GENETIC PSYCHOLOGY, 195 (1984).
48. Ford, *supra* note 1, at 18.

as a screening device in voir dire.[49]

Locus of Control: One having this predisposition views events in life as either caused by external circumstances (e.g., luck, fate), or controlled by internal events (e.g., skill, hard work). Individuals with an internal locus of control are more likely to adopt internal attributions and hold individuals responsible for their actions.

Just World: One having this trait has a general view of life as fair and just, that people get what they deserve and deserve what they get. For this reason, bad things happen only to bad people. Consequently, these types are more likely to adopt defensive attribution in personal injury or products liability cases, resulting in smaller damage awards.

Sense of Entitlement vs. Tort Reformers: While no specific data on this dichotomy exists, there appears to be an attitudinal set predisposed to feel that victims should always be compensated, regardless of fault. This idea is contrasted with that of tort reformers, who strongly hold that damage awards are excessive and must be curtailed. It should be noted that tort reformers often are correlated occupationally, that is, having a personal and financial interest in tort reform, such as business owners, corporate executives, doctors and those in the insurance industry.[50]

Depression/Emotional Stability: Jurors in this category allow mood states, particularly depression, to affect their verdicts. Depressed jurors may be particularly willing to award large damage awards in civil litigation.[51] Apparently, such jurors may tend to identify strongly wit others felt to be victimized. Along the same line, mock jurors scoring high on a measure of guilt were more lenient with alleged criminals. Apparently individuals who tend to find fault with themselves are more sympathetic to the plight of others.

Persuadability

Much of the research on persuadability generally falls under the topic of "conformity," and relates to the type of people who

---

49. Boehm, *Mr. Prejudice, Miss Sympathy, and the Authoritarian Personality: An Application of Psychological Measuring Techniques to the Problem of Jury Bias*, 1968 Wis. L. Rev. 734 (1968).

50. *See* Blue & Boudreaux, *The "Liability Crisis" and Voir Dire*, Trial, 59, 60 (Feb. 1987).

51. D. Vinson, *supra* note 5, at 130.

will conform to the wishes of others and under what circumstances they will do so. For example, if an individual is made to feel like a deviant, conformity is likely, especially if he or she values the group highly. Further, the more cohesive the group is or the more attracted the person is to the group, the greater the conformity. During lengthy trials, what effects these findings have on sequestered juries, members of which have developed strong social bonds, can only be estimated.

Why are some people more resistant to attitudinal change than others? Early social psychology researchers pointed to what was termed "psychological reactance" as an explanation underlying resistance to attitudinal change. This phenomenon occurs most frequently when an individual perceives a threat to his or her independence and, in order to reassert that independence, does the opposite of what he or she is being influenced to do. Other research has suggested that more effective persuaders are resistant to persuasion themselves. Those who are Machiavellian—a term used to describe a personality type that is verbal, manipulative, intelligent, socially astute, and persuasive—are particularly highly resistant to persuasion from others.

Another aspect of persuadability relates to the intellectual capabilities and educational level of the audience. For example, two-sided communications, which present both the pros and cons, are more effective than one-sided communications for better-educated audiences. One-sided communications have been found more effective for less educated and initially sympathetic audiences. Intelligent people "are insulted by a 'one-sided message,' but ignorant people are influenced by it."[52] Further, in lower-educated audiences, persuasive impact is increased if the speaker explicitly draws the conclusion which the audience is supposed to reach.

In general, certain individuals are quite resistant to persuasive arguments, while others are simply gullible. In the trial setting, however, the willingness of a juror to be persuaded by arguments clearly interacts with a multitude of factors, such as preconceived beliefs, intellectual level, self-esteem, and so forth. It is also quite likely that juror types easily persuaded by counsel will be more prone to accept the persuasive arguments of fellow jurors during deliberation.

---

52. D. VINSON, *supra* note 5, at 130.

SUMMARY

The makeup of the jury panel has often been cited as having nearly as much to do with the verdict as the case itself. For this reason, strategic methods of improving voir dire, including "scientific jury selection," have been employed with mixed results. Demographic factors, including place of residence, age, race, sex, and others, have been utilized in attempts to predict "ideal" jurors. More successful, however, are evaluations of critical attitudinal/personality types, such as authoritarians, and emotional features, such as depression. Lastly, intellectual and personality features may dictate how susceptible a juror will be to persuasive arguments.

INTERPERSONAL FACTORS

Plaintiff/Defendant Characteristics:

As human beings, we typically make judgments regarding the character and likability of another person very quickly and with little information. Much has been written about the importance of the first impression in any interpersonal situation. Likewise, plaintiff and defendant will be immediately sized up and evaluated by jurors. Couple this action with the ideas that 1) jurors are consistently harsh towards litigants they dislike, and 2) initial judgments are resistant to change, and one comes to understand that initial impressions are a decisive factor in the case.

Research indicates that some of the primary characteristics jurors evaluate in making their impression of others are as follows:

Attractiveness—This important and essentially uncontrollable variable has consistently been documented to affect interpersonal evaluations. In research simulations, with other variables held constant, more attractive people are more likely to be hired for a job, selected to be on a team, given higher grades, and shown leniency for transgressions. Even as early as kindergarten, children assessed to be more attractive are also rated by their teachers as better behaved and more well adjusted. It is not surprising that criminal mock trial studies have found jurors markedly lenient towards more attractive defendants. An exception to this rule is when the defendant's attractiveness facilitated the crime, as in a swindle.[53]

Similarity—Numerous studies have found a consistent and

---

53. Gerbasi, Zuckerman & Reis, *supra* note 3, at 333.

significant negative relationship between severity of verdict and the fact-finders' perceived similarity to the defendant. Often one of the attorney's goals during voir dire is to obtain jurors similar to her client. In persuasive arguments, attorneys seek to maximize jurors' feelings of similarity towards their client.

Remorse vs. Suffering—Jurors will form impressions regarding the victim's suffering and the defendant's remorse. These impressions can have tremendous impact in the outcome of the case. For example, a recent beating and gang rape incident by a group of youths in New York's Central Park received extensive national publicity and public outrage. Why? Not only was the crime despicable, but the youths arrested reported they were "wilding" and "it was fun." Their apparent lack of remorse over their actions, including leaving the victim permanently brain-damaged, had even the most forgiving types demanding harsh penalties for such behavior.

ATTORNEY/WITNESS CHARACTERISTICS

Much has been written about the persuasive power of attorneys. Given the same case, with identical facts and evidence, there are some attorneys who will be more effective in persuading jurors than others. What characteristics differentiate superb litigators from less superb litigators? Clearly the answer to this question is not a simple one, and there are volumes of instructional manuals designed to teach litigation skills. Much of this talent seems to be inherited, or to come naturally. To some extent this idea is true; however, psychologists and communication scientists have identified several key variables that consistently improve the persuasive impact of a message. Initially and most importantly, the attorney must be perceived as credible. People are more easily influenced by those they consider to be honest and credible. Credibility is generally based on three primary factors:

A. Competence/Expertise (skill and knowledge)

B. Trustworthiness (unbiased and fair)

C. Dynamism (forceful, bold, active)

Second, persuasive techniques used in sales apply to the courtroom. For example, attorneys often attempt to induce reciprocity (people feel obligated to repay others and can be made to feel indebted to the attorney). Additionally, obtaining commitments is extremely helpful. Once a juror has conceded on a small point, the odds of further concessions increase. This effort is sometimes referred to as the "foot-in-the-door" technique.

Furthermore, communication scientists have studied the use of "powerful speech" and "linguistic engineering" to assess the impact of the message.[54] Powerful speech refers to rate, phraseology, tempo and so forth. For example, "powerless" style is characterized by the use of hedges, such as "I think" or "It seems like." Linguistic engineering primarily involves utilizing words and phrases with more effective connotations. For example, referring to "the unborn baby" rather than "the fetus," would affect the listener by suggesting a more human, living being. According to one commentator, "[a] lawyer's linguistic style can mean the difference between winning and losing a case.[55]

In general, how attorneys and witnesses make an impact on jurors from an interpersonal standpoint is affected by many of the variables discussed previously, including appearance, credibility, likability, believability and persuasiveness, and use and style of language.

Jury Composition

Last to be discussed in the area of interpersonal issues deals with how jurors interrelate with each other. A considerable amount of this article has been devoted to the examination of the effects of various extra-evidentiary factors on *individual* juror decision-making. The final verdict in any jury trial, however, results from a *group* decision.

Much information in this area is derived from sociological and psychological studies on group processes. These studies reveal that during deliberations, some jurors will participate far less than others, some will attempt to persuade others, some may acquiesce to others' persuasiveness, while others will hold firm to their beliefs. It has been noted that the failure to strike a few antagonistic jurors can result in disastrous consequences. If a juror has the leadership skills and persuasive ability, the potential to sway the verdict of the others certainly exists. Since the social/psychological composition of the jury as a group affects the ultimate verdict, at-

---

54. Andrews, *Trial by Language*, Oct. 1983 STUDENT LAWYER 11, 12.
55. *Id.*

torneys often attempt to select favorable jurors also perceived as "leaders" or "persuaders."

Additional research in jury composition has examined the effects of six- versus twelve-person juries. Studies of this type do suggest that jury size affects the outcome. For example, several studies have found that when incriminating evidence is strong in criminal cases, it is to the defendant's advantage to have a twelve-member jury. Further, minority members appear to yield more influence then majority members in smaller jury panels. Overall, these studies often disagree with the Supreme Court ruling of 1972, which indicated that six-and twelve-person juries would yield equivalent outcomes.[56]

CONCLUSION

This article was intended to broadly review the critical psychological, cognitive, personality, and interpersonal factors found by research to affect jurors' verdicts. This article is not meant to suggest that the current jury system is incapable of adequately reaching just decisions or that a substantial revision of current procedures is warranted. To the contrary, the jury system performs remarkably well and remains a proud symbol of American democracy. Further, as mentioned at the outset, extralegal factors generally intrude most prominently in cases where the evidence is evenly matched or where emotional issues are involved. Consequently, the extent and degree of influence of any extra-evidentiary factors will be case-specific. However, due to the nature of human beings, particularly in the context of judging the actions and intentions of others, factors other than hard evidence will intervene. As a result, litigators should critically evaluate their case with regard to these factors.

---

56. Gerbasi, Zuckerman & Reis, *supra* note 3, at 342.

ACKNOWLEDGMENTS

Bermant, Gordon, Mary McGuire, William McKinley, and Chris Salo. "The Logic of Simulation in Jury Research." *Criminal Justice and Behavior* 1 (1974): 224–33. Reprinted with the permission of Sage Publications, Inc. Courtesy of Yale University Law Library.

Gerbasi, Kathleen Carrese, Miron Zuckerman, and Harry T. Reis. "Justice Needs a New Blindfold: A Review of Mock Jury Research." *Psychological Bulletin* 84 (1977): 323–45. Copyright 1977 by the American Psychological Association, Inc. Reprinted by permission. Courtesy of Yale University Medical Library.

Roper, Robert T. "A Typology of Jury Research and Discussion of the Structural Correlates of Jury Decisionmaking." *The Justice System Journal* 11 (1986): 5–15. Reprinted with the permission of the Institute for Court Management. Courtesy of *The Justice System Journal* .

Kramer, Geoffrey P. and Norbert L. Kerr. "Laboratory Simulation and Bias in the Study of Juror Behavior: A Methodological Note." *Law and Human Behavior* 13 (1989): 89–99. Reprinted with the permission of Plenum Press. Courtesy of Yale University Law Library.

Penrod, Steven and Reid Hastie. "Models of Jury Decision Making: A Critical Review." *Psychological Bulletin* 86 (1979): 462–92. Copyright 1979 by the American Psychological Association, Inc. Reprinted by permission. Courtesy of Yale University Medical Library.

Bridgeman, Diane L. and David Marlowe. "Jury Decision Making: An Empirical Study Based on Actual Felony Trials." *Journal of Applied Psychology* 64 (1979): 91–98. Reprinted with the permission of the American Psychological Association. Courtesy of Yale University Sterling Memorial Library.

MacCoun, Robert J. "Experimental Research on Jury Decision-Making." *Science* 2 (1989): 1046–50. Reprinted with the permission of the author and *Science*. Copyright 1989 by the AAAS. Courtesy of Yale University Sterling Memorial Library.

Pennington, Nancy and Reid Hastie. "A Cognitive Theory of Juror Decision Making: The Story Model." *Cardozo Law Review* 13 (1991): 519-57. Reprinted with the permission of the *Cardozo Law Review*. Courtesy of Yale University Law Library.

Ostrom, Thomas M., Carol Werner, and Michael J. Saks. "An Integration Theory Analysis of Jurors' Presumptions of Guilt or Innocence." *Journal of Personality and Social Psychology* 36 (1978): 436–50. Copyright 1978 by the American Psychological Association, Inc. Reprinted by permission. Courtesy of Yale University Sterling Memorial Library.

Sealy, A. Philip. "Another Look at Social Psychological Aspects of Juror Bias." *Law and Human Behavior* 5 (1981): 187–200. Reprinted with the permission of Plenum Press. Courtesy of Yale University Law Library.

Sherrod, Drury. "Trial Delay as a Source of Bias in Jury Decision Making." *Law and Human Behavior* 9 (1985): 101–08. Reprinted with the permission of Plenum Press. Courtesy of Yale University Law Library.

Strodtbeck, Fred L. and Richard D. Mann. "Sex Role Differentiation in Jury Deliberations." *Sociometry* 19 (1956): 3–11. Reprinted with the permission of the American Sociological Association. Courtesy of Yale University Sterling Memorial Library.

Snyder, Eloise C. "Sex Role Differential and Juror Decisions." *Sociology & Social Research* 55 (1971): 442–48. Reprinted with the permission of the University of Southern California. Courtesy of Yale University Sterling Memorial Library.

Berg, Kathleen Stirrett and Neil Vidmar. "Authoritarianism and Recall of Evidence about Criminal Behavior." *Journal of Research in Personality* 9 (1975): 147–57. Reprinted with the permission of Academic Press, Inc. Courtesy of Yale University Sterling Memorial Library.

Werner, Carol M., Dorothy K. Kagehiro, and Michael J. Strube. "Conviction Proneness and the Authoritarian Juror: Inability to Disregard Information or Attitudinal Bias?" *Journal of Applied Psychology* 67 (1982): 629–36. Reprinted with the permission of the American Psychological Association. Courtesy of Yale University Sterling Memorial Library.

Mills, Carol J. and Wayne E. Bohannon. "Character Structure and

Jury Behavior: Conceptual and Applied Implications." *Journal of Personality and Social Psychology* 38 (1980): 662–67. Copyright 1980 by the American Psychological Association, Inc. Reprinted by permission. Courtesy of Yale University Sterling Memorial Library.

Catano, Victor M. "Impact on Simulated Jurors of Testimony as a Function of Non-evidential Characteristics of Witness and Defendant." *Psychological Reports* 46 (1980): 343–48. Reproduced with the permission of author and publisher. Courtesy of Yale University Sterling Memorial Library.

Ford, Marilyn Chandler. "The Role of Extralegal Factors in Jury Verdicts." *The Justice System Journal* 11 (1986): 16–39. Reprinted with the permission of the Institute for Court Management. Courtesy of *The Justice System Journal*.

Hepburn, John R. "The Objective Reality of Evidence and the Utility of Systematic Jury Selection." *Law and Human Behavior* 4 (1980): 89–101. Reprinted with the permission of Plenum Press. Courtesy of Yale University Law Library.

Visher, Christy A. "Juror Decision Making: The Importance of Evidence." *Law and Human Behavior* 11 (1987): 1–17. Reprinted with the permission of Plenum Press. Courtesy of Yale University Law Library.

Boehm, Virginia R. "Mr. Prejudice, Miss Sympathy, and the Authoritarian Personality: An Application of Psychological Measuring Techniques to the Problem of Jury Bias." *Wisconsin Law Review* 3 (1968): 734–50. Reprinted with permission of the *Wisconsin Law Review*. Copyright 1968 by the University of Wisconsin. Courtesy of Yale University Law Library.

Saks, Michael J. "The Limits of Scientific Jury Selection: Ethical and Empirical." *Jurimetrics Journal* 17 (1976): 3–22. Reprinted with the permission of the American Bar Association. Courtesy of Yale University Law Library.

Zeisel, Hans and Shari Seidman Diamond. "The Effect of Peremptory Challenges on Jury and Verdict: An Experiment in a Federal District Court." *Stanford Law Review* 30 (1978): 491–531. Reprinted with the permission of the Board of Trustees of the Leland Stanford Junior University. Copyright 1978. Courtesy of Yale University Law Library.

Suggs, David and Bruce Dennis Sales. "Using Communication Cues to Evaluate Prospective Jurors During the Voir Dire." *Arizona Law Review* 20 (1978): 629–42. Reprinted with the permission of the *Arizona Law Review*. Courtesy of Yale University Law Library.

Suggs, David and Bruce D. Sales. "Juror Self-Disclosure in the Voir Dire: A Social Science Analysis." *Indiana Law Journal* 56 (1981): 245–71. Reprinted with the permission of the author and the Trustees of Indiana University. Courtesy of *Indiana Law Journal*.

Hans, Valerie P. "The Conduct of Voir Dire: A Psychological Analysis." *The Justice System Journal* 11 (1986): 40–58. Reprinted with the permission of the Institute for Court Management. Courtesy of *The Justice System Journal*.

Bevan, William, Robert S. Albert, Pierre R. Loiseaux, Peter N. Mayfield, and George Wright. "Jury Behavior as a Function of the Prestige of the Foreman and the Nature of His Leadership." *Journal of Public Law* 7 (1958): 419–49. Reprinted with the permission of the *Emory Law Journal*. Courtesy of Yale University Law Library.

Broeder, Dale W. "The Importance of the Scapegoat in Jury Trial Cases: Some Preliminary Reflections." *Duquesne University Law Review* 4 (1965-66): 513–25. Reprinted with the permission of the *Duquesne University Law Review*. Courtesy of Yale University Law Library.

Adler, Freda. "Socioeconomic Factors Influencing Jury Verdicts." *New York University Review of Law and Social Change* 3 (1973): 1–10. Reprinted with the permission of the New York University School of Law. Courtesy of Yale University Law Library.

Nagao, Dennis H. and James H. Davis. "The Effects of Prior Experience on Mock Juror Case Judgments." *Social Psychology Quarterly* 43 (1980): 190–99. Reprinted with the permission of the American Sociological Association. Courtesy of Yale University Sterling Memorial Library.

Dillehay, Ronald C. and Michael T. Nietzel. "Juror Experience and Jury Verdicts." *Law and Human Behavior* 9 (1985): 179–91. Reprinted with the permission of Plenum Press. Courtesy of Yale University Law Library.

Boyll, Jeffrey R. "Psychological, Cognitive, Personality and Interpersonal Factors in Jury Verdicts." *Law and Psychology Review* 15 (1991): 163–84. Reprinted with the permission of the University of Alabama, School of Law. Courtesy of Yale University Law Library.